RHCE™ Red Hat®
Certified Engineer Linux
Exam Study Guide

(Exam RH302)

THIRD EDITION

Michael Jang

Published by
dreamtech

19-A, Ansari Road, Daryaganj,
New Delhi-110002

©Copyright 2003 by Dreamtech Press, 19-A, Ansari Road, Daryaganj, New Delhi-110002

Original English Language Edition ©Copyright 2003 by **Osborne/McGraw Hill**

This book may not be duplicated in any way without the express written consent of the publisher, except in the form of brief excerpt or quotations for the purposes of review. The information contained herein is for the personal use of the reader and may not be incorporated in any commercial programs, other books, databases, or any kind of software without written consent of the publisher. Making copies of this book or any portion for any purpose other than your own is a violation of copyright laws.

This edition has been published by arrangement with the **Osborne/McGraw Hill 2600, Tenth Street Berkeley, California 94710 USA** and published in India by **Dreamtech Press, 19-A, Ansari Road, Daryaganj, New Delhi-110002.**

LIMITS OF LIABILITY/DISCLAIMER OF WARRANTY : The author and publisher have used their best efforts in preparing this book. The Osborne/McGraw Hill and the author make no representation or warranties with respect to the accuracy or completeness of the contents of this book, and specifically disclaim any implied warranties of merchantability or fitness for any particular purpose. There are no warranties which extend beyond the descriptions contained in this paragraph. No warranty may be created or extended by sales representatives or written sales materials. The accuracy and completeness of the information provided herein and the opinions stated herein are not guaranteed or warranted to produce any particular result, and the advice and strategies contained herein may not be suitable for every individual. Neither The Osborne/McGraw Hill, USA nor author shall be liable for any loss of profit or any other commercial damages, including but not limited to special, incidental, consequential, or other damages.

TRADEMARKS: All brand names and products names used in this book are trademarks, registered trademarks, or trade names of their respective holders. The Osborne is not associated with any product or vendor mentioned in this book.

First Edition : 2003

Printed at : Print Well Offset, New Delhi

ABOUT THE CONTRIBUTORS

Author

Michael Jang (RHCE, LCP, Linux+, MCSE) is currently a full-time writer, specializing in operating systems and networks. His experience with computers goes back to the days of jumbled punch cards. He has written other books on Linux certification, including Linux+ Exam Cram and Sair GNU/Linux Installation and Configuration Exam Cram. His other Linux books include *Mastering Linux, Second Edition* and *Linux Networking Clearly Explained.* He has also written or contributed to books on Microsoft Operating Systems, including *MCSE Guide to Microsoft Windows 98* and *Mastering Windows XP Professional, Second Edition.*

In his previous life as a Boeing engineer, Michael worked a variety of jobs, including project manager for the first FAA type certified In-Seat Video Entertainment systems.

Contributors

David Egan (P. Eng., BASc Engineering U of T 78, MCT, RHCE, RHCX) has lived and worked in several countries and has worked with computers since the early days of the Apple and IBM-type PCs. David's first "hobby-turned-job" was as a Z80 Assembler and C Language programmer for five years. David made the transition into a VMS/Unix/NT/PC Systems Integration Consultant and Technology Instructor— "An Edutainer"—during the past 15 years. David is still consulting and writing the occasional book, but mostly contracting as a Course Director and Course Writer of Unix-, NT-, and Linux-based courses for Global Knowledge, Inc., of Cary, North Carolina (www.globalknowledge.com).

When not on the road—preaching the virtues of Linux and NT from his stage or showing the plan—he resides near Vancouver, B.C., with his lovely wife Deborah, daughter Vanessa, and son Callen.

Larry Karnis (RHCE; HP Certified IT Professional; SCO/Caldera Master Advanced Certified Engineer in UNIXWare 2, UNIXWare 7, and OpenServer 5; Learning Tree UNIX Programming and Systems Professional) is a Senior Consultant for Application Enhancements, a Unix, Linux, and Internet consulting firm located in Toronto. Larry has over 20 years of Unix experience, starting with Unix Version 2.6.

Larry holds a bachelor's degree in Computer Science and Mathematics as well as eight other professional and technical certifications. An avid Linux enthusiast since 1994, he routinely deploys and manages Linux-based desktop, server, firewall, and routing solutions.

Technical Editor

Elizabeth Zinkann is a logical Linux catalyst, a freelance technical editor, and an independent computer consultant. She was a Contributing Editor and Review Columnist for *Sys Admin Magazine* for ten years. (Her most recent reviews have taken refuge at http://www.equillink.com.) Her articles have also appeared in *Performance Computing, Linux Magazine,* and *Network Administrator* magazines. As an independent computer consultant, she has built Linux servers; maintained computers utilizing Linux, Solaris, Macintosh, and Windows environments; programmed databases; and taught Linux, Unix, computer hardware basics, and Internet essentials. In a former life, she also programmed communications features including ISDN at AT&T Network Systems.

About LearnKey

LearnKey provides self-paced learning content and multi-media delivery solutions to enhance personal skills and business productivity. LearnKey claims the largest library of rich streaming media training content that engages learners in dynamic media rich instruction complete with video clips, audio, full motion graphics, and animated illustrations. LearnKey can be found on the Web at www.LearnKey.com.

ACKNOWLEDGMENTS

I personally would like to thank the following people:

- **Nancy E. Cropley, R.N. (d. 2002)** As a political activist, you fought for what you believed in: social justice, peace, and universal health care. You were never afraid to go to jail to support your beliefs. Your example is helping me find a backbone for life.

  As a nurse for the homeless, you helped so many who are less fortunate. You worked tirelessly in the clinics, in the shelters, and on the streets. Your efforts eased the pain of so many people. And you saved lives. Nancy, you are my hero.

  As an Internet entrepreneur, you showed me how to be happy pursuing a life working from home. You made it possible for me to have the freedom to be, instead of getting stuck in the corporate world.

  Nancy, you were my partner, my lover, my soul mate. You helped me find joy in this world. I take your lessons with me. I hold your spirit in my heart. I thank you for the best seven years of my life.

- All the incredibly hard-working folks at McGraw-Hill/Osborne: Brandon Nordin, Scott Rogers, Gareth Hancock, Tim Green, and Patty Mon for their help in producing a great series and being solid team players.

CONTENTS AT A GLANCE

CONTENTS

11   Operational Administration Recovery and Security . . . 625

About the CD **667**

PREFACE

Linux is thriving. Red Hat is at the forefront of the Linux revolution. And Red Hat Certified Engineers are making it happen.

Despite the collapse of the technology boom, Linux is finding its way into business, education, and government. Major corporations from Home Depot to Toyota, and governments such as Germany, the Republic of Korea, and Mexico have made the switch to Linux. When faced with a Microsoft audit for licenses, the Portland Oregon school system switched to Linux. Major movie studios such as Dreamworks use Linux to create the latest motion pictures. Walt Disney has recently announced plans to create new movies using Linux. IBM has invested over a billion dollars in this "free" operating system. Even the U.S. National Security Agency has developed its own version of Linux.

While there are Linux distributions available from a number of companies, Red Hat is far and away the market leader. Most Web servers run Apache on Linux. Many companies run Linux on their servers, even if they have Microsoft desktop computers. Although Microsoft still dominates the desktop market, if you want to work as a systems administrator, chances are good that you need to know Linux.

The RHCE Exam is difficult. About 60 percent of the candidates pass this exam. The pass rate is lower for people taking the exam for the first time. But do not be intimidated. While there are no guarantees, this book can help you prepare for and pass the Red Hat Certified Engineer exam.

To study for this exam, you should have a network of at least two computers. You need to install the latest version of Red Hat Linux on at least one of these computers. That will allow you to configure Linux and test the results. After configuring a service, it's important to be able to check your work from another computer.

In This Book

This book serves as an in-depth review and study guide for all three parts of the Red Hat exam. It fully covers every objective of the RHCE exam. As the actual

RHCE study points change with every release of Red Hat Linux, you should refer to www.redhat.com for the latest information.

This book also includes bonus coverage of the latest available version of Red Hat Linux, which we believe will be Red Hat Linux 8.0. Our information suggests that it will be released by the time this book is published.

This book includes relevant information from Red Hat Linux 8.0, based on the public beta distributions, code name Limbo, for this product. For example, it covers redhat-config-xfree86, which you may use in place of Xconfigurator on the RHCE 8.0 (and later) exam.

As of this writing, the improvements in Red Hat Linux 8.0 include:

- Minor updates to the Linux kernel. While it's based on 2.4.19-pre10-ac2, you'll see it in this book as another version of Linux kernel 2.4.18. Updates include access control list support.

- A new version of the GNU C language compiler, 3.2.x.

- GNOME version 2.0.x.

- Major updates to X configuration; redhat-config-xfree86 replaces Xconfigurator; XFree86 version 3.3.6 is no longer included.

- The Red Hat Linux Setup agent is included to configure several systems not addressed during installation.

- Several new GUI configuration tools are included; most are named redhat-config-*, where the functionality of the tool replaces the asterisk (*).

- Apache 2.0.x is included for the first time.

- RAID clones (Red Hat GUI installer only).

- Logical Volume Management, which allows for flexible partition management after installation.

- A Personal Desktop installation option in the Red Hat Installation program (Anaconda), which includes software packages suitable for home or small business use.

There are many more changes; those that I believe are relevant to the RHCE exam are also included in this book.

In Every Chapter

- Each chapter begins with the **Certification Objectives**—what you need to know in order to pass the section on the exam dealing with the chapter topic. The Certification Objective headings identify the objectives within the chapter, so you'll always know an objective when you see it!

- **Certification Exercises** are interspersed throughout the chapters. These are step-by-step exercises. They help you master skills that are likely to be an area of focus on the exam. Don't just read through the exercises; they are hands-on procedures that you should be comfortable completing. Learning by doing is an effective way to increase your competency with the language and concepts presented.

- **Exam Watch Notes** call attention to information about, and potential pitfalls in, the exam. These helpful hints are written by authors who have taken the exams and received their certification; who better to tell you what to worry about? They know what you're about to go through!

- **Scenario & Solutions** sections lay out specific scenario questions and solutions in a quick and easy-to-read format.

- The **Certification Summary** is a succinct review of the chapter and a restatement of salient points regarding the exam.

- The **Two-Minute Drill** at the end of every chapter is a checklist of the main points of the chapter. It can be used for last-minute review.

Q&A

- The **Self Test** offers questions similar to those found on the certification exam. The answers to these questions, as well as in-depth explanations of the answers, are located at the back of each chapter. By taking the Self Test after completing each chapter, you'll reinforce what you've learned from that chapter, while becoming familiar with the structure of the exam questions.

Some Pointers

Once you've finished reading this book, set aside some time to do a thorough review. You might want to return to the book several times and make use of all the methods it offers for reviewing the material.

1. *Reread all the Two-Minute Drills,* or have someone quiz you. You also can use the drills as a way to do a quick cram before the exam.

2. *Retake the Self Tests.* Taking the tests right after you've read the chapter is a good idea, because it helps reinforce what you've just learned. However, it's an even better idea to go back later and do all the questions in the book in one sitting. As the RHCE is primarily a hands-on exam, focus on the Labs and Certification Exercises.

3. *Complete the exercises.* Did you do the exercises when you read through each chapter? If not, do them! These exercises are designed to cover exam topics, and there's no better way to get to know this material than by practicing.

4. *Take the practice exams.* The two sample exams included on the CD are the closet allowable approximation of the three-part RHCE exam. Take both exams. Study your answers. Learn why each answer is right or wrong. This will help you handle the questions that you actually see when you take the actual RHCE exam.

Red Hat Certified Engineer Certification

We'd like to spend some time covering what you need in order to attain Red Hat Certified Engineer certification status. The details are available on the Red Hat Web site, www.redhat.com. For a summary of the more important information, see the Introduction of this book, "Leaping Ahead of the Competition!"

The CD-ROM

This book comes with a CD-ROM powered by LearnKey that includes test preparation software and provides you with another method for studying. You will find more information on the testing software in the Appendix.

There are two sample exams included with this book, in HTML format on the CD-ROM. Remember, there are three parts to the RHCE exam: Debug, Multiple Choice, and Server Install and Network Services Setup.

Unfortunately, the software associated with the book can only be installed under Microsoft Windows. Even under Microsoft Windows, this provides a test engine only for the Multiple Choice part of the exam.

The RHCE Exam Challenge

This section covers the reasons for pursuing industry-recognized certification, explains the importance of your RHCE certification, and prepares you for taking the actual examination. It gives you a few pointers on how to prepare, what to expect, and what to do on exam day.

Leaping Ahead of the Competition!

The RHCE certification exam is a hands-on exam. As such, it is respected throughout the industry as a sign of genuine practical knowledge. If you pass, you will be head and shoulders above the candidate who has passed only a "standard" multiple-choice certification exam.

There are three parts to the RHCE exam:

- **Part 1** Debug: includes 4 challenges. 100 points. 2.5 hours. No partial credit for any of the 4 challenges. The only possible scores are 0, 25, 50, 75, and 100 points.

- **Part 2** Multiple choice: 50 questions. 100 points. 1 hour.

- **Part 3** Server Install and Network Services Setup: One challenge. Several parts. 2.5 hours. 100 points. Partial credit for each part is possible.

To become a RHCE, you need an overall average of at least 80 percent; you are also required to have a score of at least 50 percent on each of the three exams.

Why a Hands-On Exam?

Most certifications today are based on multiple-choice exams. These types of exams are relatively inexpensive to set up and easy to proctor. Unfortunately, many people are good at taking multiple-choice exams. The skills associated with taking a multiple-choice exam do not correlate to real-world skills. This leads to the complaints of many hiring managers, that people who are certified are really "paper tigers" who do not have any real-world skills.

Red Hat wanted to develop a certification program that matters. For the most part, they have succeeded with the RHCE.

Linux administrators frequently have to debug computers with problems. The four challenges that you will face on the Debug exam are based on real-world problems. As the typical Linux administrator has to work through multiple debug challenges on a daily basis, the RHCE Debug exam provides a credible measure of real-world skills.

Linux administrators have access to reference materials. But to know what they are looking for, they need some grounding in the basics of Linux. For that part of the job, a multiple-choice exam is appropriate, to make sure that you know enough of the basics to look up the answers that you need on the job.

Linux administrators sometimes have to install Linux on a computer. Depending on the configuration, they may need to install Linux from a central source through a network. Installing Linux is not enough to make it useful. Administrators need to know how to configure Linux: add users, install and configure services, create firewalls, and more.

The overall pass rate for RHCE exam candidates has historically hovered around 60 percent. However, this includes candidates who are taking the exam for the first time and the second (and later). In other words, the actual first-time pass rate may be well under 50 percent.

I've taken the RHCE course and exam. Everyone in my class has practical experience administering Linux and/or Unix servers. However, I think the pass rate in my class closely matched the published statistics.

This exam is very Red Hat Linux specific. Knowledge of System V or BSD-based Unix is certainly helpful, as well as experience with file, print, and network services like Apache, Samba, NFS, DNS, iptables, and DHCP. But it is best if you know how to set up, configure, install, and debug these services under Red Hat Linux.

Preparing for the RHCE Exam

Work with the latest version of Red Hat Linux. Install it on a computer that you don't need for any other purpose. Configure the services described in this book.

Find ways to make Linux unbootable, study the characteristics of the problem, and find different ways to fix the problem.

As you go through this book, you'll have the chance to install Red Hat Linux several times. If you have more than one computer, you'll be able to install Red Hat Linux over a network connection. Then you can work with the different network services. Test out each service as you configure it, preferably from another computer on your network. Testing your work becomes especially important when you start working with the security features of Linux.

Red Hat Linux Certification Program

Red Hat offers several courses that can help you prepare for the RHCE. Each of these courses is four or five days long. In some cases, you can take parts of an individual course on an electronic basis.

Table 1 illustrates the available hands-on, instructor-led courses that can also help you prepare for the RHCE Exam.

Should You Take a RHCE Course?

This book is intended as a substitute for the Red Hat "crash course" (RH301). It covers the material described in the RHCE Rapid Track Course Outline, available at www.redhat.com. However, RH300/RH301 is an excellent course. The Red Hat instructors who teach this course are highly skilled. If you feel the need for classroom instruction, read this book, and then take the course.

TABLE I	Red Hat Courses

Course	Description
RH033	Introduction to Linux: basic pre–system administration skills
RH133	Basic System Administration skills for installation and configuration
RH253	Basic Network and Security Administration; requires a basic knowledge of LANs/WANs and TCP/IP
RH300	The Crash Course plus the RHCE exam
RH301	The Crash Course without the RHCE exam
RH302	The RHCE exam

If you're not sure if you're ready for this course or book, read Chapter 1. It is a rapid overview of the prerequisites for RH300/RH301. If you find the material in Chapter 1 to be overwhelming, consider one of the books noted near the start of the chapter, or one of the other RHCE courses. However, if you are just less familiar with a few of the topics covered in Chapter 1, you're probably okay. Even experienced Linux administrators aren't familiar with everything. Just use the references noted at the beginning of Chapter 1 to fill in any gaps in your knowledge.

Alternatively, you may already be familiar with all of the material in this book. You may then have the breadth and depth of knowledge required to pass the RHCE Exam. In that case, you can use this book as a "refresher," to help you focus on the skills and techniques you need to pass the RHCE exam.

Signing Up for the RHCE Course and or Exam

Red Hat provides convenient Web-based registration systems for the courses and test. To sign up for any of the Red Hat courses leading to certification and the RHCE exam, navigate to http://www.redhat.com, click the link for Training and/or the RHCE Program, and select the desired course. Alternatively, you can contact the helpful people at Red Hat Enrollment Central at (866) 626-2994.

Final Preparations

The RHCE exam is grueling. Once you have the skills, the most important thing that you can take to the exam is a clear head. If you're tired or frantic, you may miss the easy solutions that are often available. Get the sleep you need the night before the exam. Eat a good breakfast. Bring snacks with you that can keep your mind in top condition.

Remember, the RHCE exam is six hours long. That is more than twice the length of a world-class marathon!

RED HAT CERTIFIED ENGINEER

1

RHCE Prerequisites

The Red Hat Certified Engineer exam is an advanced challenge. As the RHCE course has a number of prerequisites, this book assumes that you know some basics about Linux. This chapter covers each of these prerequisite topics in a minimum of detail, with references to other books and sources for more information. Unlike in other chapters and other books in this series, the Questions include a number of "zingers" that go beyond this chapter's content. That is the only way to see if you have the prerequisite skills necessary for remaining chapters.

The prerequisites are quite broad; it is okay if you do not feel comfortable with a small number of topics in this chapter. It's in fact quite natural that many experienced Linux administrators don't use every one of the prerequisite topics in their everyday work. Many candidates are successfully able to fill in the "gaps" in their knowledge with some self-study and lots of practice.

Unfortunately, it is not possible to condense all of the prerequisite lessons into one chapter, at least in a way that can be understood by newcomers to Linux and other Unix-based operating systems. If after reading this chapter, you find gaps in your knowledge, please refer to one of the following guides:

■ *Red Hat Linux: The Complete Reference, Second Edition*, by Richard Petersen (McGraw-Hill/Osborne, 2001), provides a detailed step-by-step guide to every part of this operating system. After reading this book, if you want additional exercises in Red Hat Linux, this is the book.

■ *Hacking Linux Exposed: Linux Security Secrets & Solutions* by Hatch, Lee, and Kurtz (McGraw-Hill/Osborne, 2001), gives you a detailed look at how you can secure your Linux system and networks in every possible way.

■ *Linux Programming: A Beginner's Guide*, by Richard Petersen (McGraw-Hill/Osborne, 2001), takes a fundamental look at the scripts you need to administer Linux professionally, and customize tools such as the GNOME and KDE GUIs for your users.

Critical to a Linux administrator is knowledge of one or more text editors to manage the many configuration files on a Linux system. The Linux filesystem hierarchy organizes hardware, drivers, directories, and of course, files. You need to master a number of basic commands to manage Linux. Printer configuration can be a complex topic. Shell scripts enable you to automate many everyday processes. Security is now a huge issue that Linux can handle better than other operating systems; locally, and on larger networks such as the Internet.

As an administrator, you need a good knowledge of basic system administration commands, TCP/IP configuration requirements, and standard network services. The basic hardware knowledge associated with RHCE prerequisites is covered in Chapter 2.

This is not a book for beginners to Linux/Unix-type operating systems. Some of what you read in this chapter may be unfamiliar. Use this chapter to create a list of topics that you may need to study further. In some cases, you'll be able to get up to speed with the material in other chapters. But if you have less experience with Linux or another Unix-type operating system, you may want to refer to the aforementioned books.

CERTIFICATION OBJECTIVE 1.01

Basic Linux Knowledge

Linux and Unix are managed through a series of text files. Linux administrators do not normally use graphical editors to manage these configuration files. Editors such as WordPerfect, StarOffice, and yes, even Microsoft Word normally save files in a binary format that Linux can't read. Popular text editors for Linux configuration files include emacs, pico, joe, and vi.

The VIsual Editor

While emacs may be the most popular text editor in the world of Linux, every administrator needs at least a basic knowledge of vi. While emacs may be more popular and flexible, vi may help you save a broken system. If you ever have to restore a critical configuration file using an emergency boot floppy, vi is probably the only editor that you'll have available.

You need to know how to restore your system from a rescue floppy, which does not have enough room to carry any editor other than vi.

You should know how to use the two basic modes of vi: command and insert. When you use vi to open a file, it opens in command mode. Some of the commands start insert mode. Opening a file is easy; just use the **vi** *filename* command. By default, this starts vi in command mode. An example of vi with the /etc/passwd file is shown in Figure 1-1.

FIGURE 1-1

```
root:x:0:0:root:/root:/bin/bash
bin:x:1:1:bin:/bin:/sbin/nologin
daemon:x:2:2:daemon:/sbin:/sbin/nologin
adm:x:3:4:adm:/var/adm:/sbin/nologin
lp:x:4:7:lp:/var/spool/lpd:/sbin/nologin
sync:x:5:0:sync:/sbin:/bin/sync
shutdown:x:6:0:shutdown:/sbin:/sbin/shutdown
halt:x:7:0:halt:/sbin:/sbin/halt
mail:x:8:12:mail:/var/spool/mail:/sbin/nologin
news:x:9:13:news:/var/spool/news:
uucp:x:10:14:uucp:/var/spool/uucp:/sbin/nologin
operator:x:11:0:operator:/root:/sbin/nologin
games:x:12:100:games:/usr/games:/sbin/nologin
gopher:x:13:30:gopher:/var/gopher:/sbin/nologin
ftp:x:14:50:FTP User:/var/ftp:/sbin/nologin
nobody:x:99:99:Nobody:/:/sbin/nologin
vcsa:x:69:69:virtual console memory owner:/dev:/sbin/nologin
rpm:x:37:37::/var/lib/rpm:/bin/bash
nscd:x:28:28:NSCD Daemon:/:/bin/false
ntp:x:38:38::/etc/ntp:/sbin/nologin
apache:x:48:48:Apache:/var/www:/bin/false
radvd:x:75:75:radvd user:/:/bin/false
mailnull:x:47:47::/var/spool/mqueue:/sbin/nologin
smmsp:x:51:51::/var/spool/mqueue:/sbin/nologin
pcap:x:77:77::/var/arpwatch:/sbin/nologin
sshd:x:74:74:Privilege-separated SSH:/var/empty/sshd:/sbin/nologin
ident:x:98:98:pident user:/:/sbin/nologin
"/etc/passwd" 37L, 1610C                                    5,1        Top
```

The following is only the briefest of introductions to the vi editor. For more information, there are a number of books available, as well as an extensive manual formatted as a HOWTO available from the Linux Documentation Project at www.tldp.org.

vi Command Mode

In command mode, you can do everything you need to a text file except edit it. The options in command mode are broad and varied, and they are the subject of a number of book-length texts. Using vi requires five critical command skills.

- **Search** Start with a backslash, followed by the search term. Remember, Linux is case sensitive, so if you're searching for "Michael" in /etc/passwd, use the **/Michael** (not /michael) command.

- **Write** To save your changes, use the **w** command. You can combine commands; for example, **wq** writes the file and exits vi.

- **Quit** To leave vi, use the **q** command. If you want to abandon any changes that you've made, use the **q!** command.

- **Edit**   You can use a number of commands to edit files through vi, such as **x**, which deletes the currently highlighted character, **dw**, which deletes the currently highlighted word, and **dd**, which deletes the current line. Remember, **p** places text from a buffer, and **u** restores text from a previous change.

- **Insert**   A number of commands allow you to start insert mode, including **i** to start inserting text at the current position of the editor, and **o** to open up a new line immediately below the current position of the cursor.

vi Insert Mode

In modern Linux systems, editing files with vi is easy. Just use the normal navigation keys (arrow keys, PAGE UP, and PAGE DOWN), and then one of the basic commands such as **i** or **o** to start vi's insert mode, and type your changes directly into the file.

When you're finished with insert mode, press the ESC key to return to command mode. You can then save your changes, or abandon them and exit vi.

EXERCISE 1-1

Using vi to Create a New User

In this exercise, you'll create a new user by editing the /etc/passwd file with the vi text editor.

1. Open a Linux command line interface. Go into root or superuser mode, and type the **vi /etc/passwd** command.

2. Navigate to the last line in the file. As you should already know, there are several ways to do this in command mode, including the DOWN ARROW key, the PAGE DOWN key, the **G** command, or even the K key.

3. Make one copy of this line. If you're already comfortable with vi, you should know that you can copy an entire line to the buffer with the **yy** command. You can then restore that line as many times as desired with the **p** command.

4. Change the username, User ID, Group ID, user comment, and home directory for the new user. Based on Figure 1-2, this corresponds to pm, 501, 501, Tony Blair, and /home/pm. Make sure the username corresponds to the home directory.

FIGURE 1-2

Adding a new
user in
/etc/passwd

```
operator:x:11:0:operator:/root:/sbin/nologin
games:x:12:100:games:/usr/games:/sbin/nologin
gopher:x:13:30:gopher:/var/gopher:/sbin/nologin
ftp:x:14:50:FTP User:/var/ftp:/sbin/nologin
nobody:x:99:99:Nobody:/:/sbin/nologin
vcsa:x:69:69:virtual console memory owner:/dev:/sbin/nologin
rpm:x:37:37::/var/lib/rpm:/bin/bash
nscd:x:28:28:NSCD Daemon:/:/bin/false
ntp:x:38:38::/etc/ntp:/sbin/nologin
apache:x:48:48:Apache:/var/www:/bin/false
radvd:x:75:75:radvd user:/:/bin/false
mailnull:x:47:47::/var/spool/mqueue:/sbin/nologin
smmsp:x:51:51::/var/spool/mqueue:/sbin/nologin
pcap:x:77:77::/var/arpwatch:/sbin/nologin
sshd:x:74:74:Privilege-separated SSH:/var/empty/sshd:/sbin/nologin
ident:x:98:98:pident user:/:/sbin/nologin
rpc:x:32:32:Portmapper RPC user:/:/sbin/nologin
rpcuser:x:29:29:RPC Service User:/var/lib/nfs:/sbin/nologin
nfsnobody:x:65534:65534:Anonymous NFS User:/var/lib/nfs:/sbin/nologin
xfs:x:43:43:X Font Server:/etc/X11/fs:/sbin/nologin
gdm:x:42:42::/var/gdm:/sbin/nologin
named:x:25:25:Named:/var/named:/bin/false
postfix:x:89:89::/var/spool/postfix:/bin/true
squid:x:23:23::/var/spool/squid:/dev/null
mj:x:500:500:Michael Jang:/home/mj:/bin/bash
pm:x:501:501:Tony Blair:/home/pm:/bin/bash

                                                    12,25        Bot
```

5. Return to command mode by pressing the ESC key. Save the file with the **wq** command.

6. As the root user, run the **passwd** *newuser* command. Assign the password of your choice to the new user.

CERTIFICATION OBJECTIVE 1.02

Linux/Unix Filesystem Hierarchy and Structure

Everything in Linux can be reduced to a file. Partitions are associated with files such as /dev/hda1. Hardware components are associated with files such as /dev/modem. Detected devices are documented as files in the /proc directory. The Filesystem Hierarchy Standard (FHS) is the official way to organize files in Unix and Linux directories. As with the other sections, this introduction provides only the most basic overview of the FHS. More information is available from the official FHS home page at www.pathname.com/fhs.

Linux/Unix Filesystems and Directories

Several major directories are associated with all modern Unix/Linux operating systems. These directories organize user files, drivers, kernels, logs, programs, utilities, and more into different categories. The standardization of the FHS makes it easier for users of other Unix-based operating systems to understand the basics of Linux.

Every FHS starts with the root directory, also known by its label, the single forward slash (/). All of the other directories shown in Table 1-1 are subdirectories of the root directory. Unless they are mounted separately, you can also find their files on the same partition as the root directory.

on the job

A lot of names in Linux filesystems are used interchangeably. For example, a filesystem can refer to the FHS, an individual partition, or a format such as ext3. Mounted directories are often known as volumes, which can span multiple partitions. However, while the root directory (/) is the top-level directory in the FHS, the root user's home directory (/root) is just a subdirectory.

Media Devices

Several basic types of media are accessible to most PCs, including IDE hard disks, floppy drives, CD/DVD drives, and the various standards of SCSI devices. Other media are accessible through other PC ports, including serial, parallel, USB, and IEEE 1394. To some extent, Linux can manage all of these types of media.

Most media devices are detected automatically. Linux may require a bit of help for some devices described in Chapter 2. But in the context of the Linux FHS, media devices, like all others, are part of the /dev directory. Typical media devices are described in Table 1-2.

Making Reference to Devices in /dev

Take a look at the files in the /dev directory. Use the **ls -l /dev | more** command. Scroll through the long list for a while. Are you confused yet? Well, there's a method to this madness. Some devices are linked to others, and that actually makes it easier to understand what is connected to what. For example, the virtual device files /dev/mouse and /dev/modem are easier to identify than the true device files.

| TABLE 1-1. | Basic Filesystem Hierarchy Standard Directories |

Directory	Description
/	The root directory, the top-level directory in the FHS. All other directories are subdirectories of root, which is always mounted on some partition. All directories that are not mounted on a separate partition are included in the root directory's partition.
/bin	Essential command line utilities. Should not be mounted separately; otherwise, it could be difficult to get to these utilities when using a rescue disk.
/boot	Includes Linux startup files, including the Linux kernel. Can be small; 16MB is usually adequate for a typical modular kernel. If you use multiple kernels, such as for testing a kernel upgrade, increase the size of this partition accordingly.
/dev	Hardware and software device drivers for everything from floppy drives to terminals. Do not mount this directory on a separate partition.
/etc	Most basic configuration files.
/home	Home directories for almost every user.
/lib	Program libraries for the kernel and various command line utilities. Do not mount this directory on a separate partition.
/mnt	The mount point for removable media, including floppy drives, CD-ROMs, and Zip disks.
/opt	Applications such as WordPerfect or StarOffice.
/proc	Currently running kernel-related processes, including device assignments such as IRQ ports, I/O addresses, and DMA channels.
/root	The home directory of the root user.
/sbin	System administration commands. Don't mount this directory separately.
/tmp	Temporary files. By default, Red Hat Linux deletes all files in this directory periodically.
/usr	Small programs accessible to all users. Includes many system administration commands and utilities.
/var	Variable data, including log files and printer spools.

Generally, these devices are automatically linked to the actual device files during Linux installation. For example, the following shows the links between the mouse and modem devices and the actual device files:

```
# ls -l /dev/mouse
lrwxrwxrwx  1 root  root  5 Apr 18 12:17 /dev/mouse -> psaux
```

```
# ls -l /dev/modem
lrwxrwxrwx  1 root  root  5 Apr 18 12:17 /dev/modem -> /dev/ttyS0
```

The first output shows that /dev/mouse is linked directly to the PS/2 device driver port, and that /dev/modem is linked directly to the first serial port, which corresponds to COM1 in the Microsoft world.

Filesystem Formatting and Checking

Three basic tools are available to manage the filesystem on various partitions: fdisk, mkfs, and fsck. They can help you configure partitions as well as create, and then check and repair, different filesystems. As with the rest of this chapter, this section covers only the very basics; for more information, see the man page associated with each respective command tool.

TABLE 1-2   Media Devices

Media Device	Device File
Floppy drive	First floppy (Microsoft A: drive) = /dev/fd0 Second floppy (Microsoft B: drive) = /dev/fd1
IDE hard drive IDE CD/DVD drive	First IDE drive = /dev/ hda Second IDE drive = /dev/hdb Third IDE drive = /dev/hdc Fourth IDE drive = /dev/hdd
SCSI hard drive SCSI CD/DVD drive	First SCSI drive = /dev/sda Second SCSI drive = /dev/sdb ... Twenty-seventh SCSI drive = /dev/sdaa and so on
Parallel port drives	First IDE drive = /dev/pd1 First tape drive: /dev/pt1
USB drives	Varies widely
IEEE 1394 drives	IEEE 1394 (aka FireWire, iLink) is actually a SCSI standard, so these are controlled in Linux as SCSI devices

fdisk

The Linux fdisk utility is a lot more versatile than its Microsoft counterpart. But to open it, you need to know the device file associated with the hard drive that you want to change. Identifying the hard disk device file is covered in Chapter 2. Assuming you want to manage the partitions on the first SCSI hard disk, enter **/sbin/fdisk /dev/sda**. As you can see in Figure 1-3, the fdisk utility is flexible.

Some key fdisk commands are described in Table 1-3.

mkfs

To format a Linux partition, apply the mkfs command. It allows you to format a partition to a number of different filesystems. To format a typical partition such as /dev/hda2 to the current Red Hat standard, the third extended filesystem, run the following command:

```
# mkfs -t ext3 /dev/hda2
```

FIGURE 1-3

Linux fdisk commands; p returns the partition table

```
[root@RedHat80Test mj]# /sbin/fdisk /dev/sda

Command (m for help): m
Command action
   a   toggle a bootable flag
   b   edit bsd disklabel
   c   toggle the dos compatibility flag
   d   delete a partition
   l   list known partition types
   m   print this menu
   n   add a new partition
   o   create a new empty DOS partition table
   p   print the partition table
   q   quit without saving changes
   s   create a new empty Sun disklabel
   t   change a partition's system id
   u   change display/entry units
   v   verify the partition table
   w   write table to disk and exit
   x   extra functionality (experts only)

Command (m for help): p

Disk /dev/sda: 255 heads, 63 sectors, 522 cylinders
Units = cylinders of 16065 * 512 bytes

   Device Boot    Start       End      Blocks   Id  System
/dev/sda1   *         1         6       48163+  83  Linux
/dev/sda2             7       304     2393685   83  Linux
/dev/sda3           305       413      875542+  83  Linux
/dev/sda4           414       522      875542+   5  Extended
/dev/sda5           414       462      393561   83  Linux
/dev/sda6           463       495      265041   83  Linux
/dev/sda7           496       522      216846   82  Linux swap

Command (m for help): []
```

TABLE 1-3	Important fdisk Options

fdisk Command	Description
a	Allows you to specify the bootable Linux partition (with /boot).
l	Lists known partition types; fdisk can create partitions that conform to any of these filesystems.
n	Adds a new partition; works only if there is unpartitioned space on the disk.
q	Quits without saving any changes.
t	Changes the partition filesystem.

The mkfs command also serves as a "front-end," depending on the filesystem format. For example, if you're formatting a Red Hat standard ext3 filesystem, mkfs by itself automatically calls the mkfs.ext3 command. Therefore, if you're reformatting an ext3 filesystem, the following command is sufficient:

```
# mkfs /dev/hda2
```

Be careful with mkfs. First, back up any data on the subject partition and computer. This command erases all data on the specified partition.

fsck

The fsck command is analogous to the Microsoft chkdsk command. It performs an analysis of the specified filesystem and performs repairs as required. Assume you're having problems with files in the /var directory, which happens to be mounted on /dev/hda7. If you want to run fsck, unmount that filesystem first. In some cases, you may need to go into single-user mode with the **init 1** command before you can unmount a filesystem. To unmount, analyze, then remount the filesystem noted in this section, run the following commands:

```
# umount /var
# fsck -t ext3 /dev/hda7
# mount /dev/hda7 /var
```

The fsck command also serves as a "front-end," depending on the filesystem format. For example, if you're formatting an ext2 or ext3 filesystem, fsck by itself automatically calls the e2fsck command (which works for both filesystems). Therefore, if you're checking an ext3 filesystem, the following command is sufficient:

```
# fsck /dev/hda7
```

Multiple Partitions with One Filesystem

The Logical Volume Manager (LVM) enables you to set up one filesystem on multiple partitions. For example, assume you're adding more users and are running out of room in your /home directory. You don't have any unpartitioned space available on your current hard disk.

With the LVM, all you need to do is add another hard disk, configure some partitions, back up /home, and use the LVM tools to combine the new partition and the one used by /home into a volume set. You may need to install the LVM rpm. Once it is installed, the steps are fairly straightforward:

1. Add a new hard disk.

2. Create new partitions. Assign the Linux LVM filesystem to one or more of these partitions. This can be easily done with the Linux **fdisk** utility.

3. Back up /home. Assign the LVM filesystem to that partition.

4. Scan for Linux LVM filesystems with the **/sbin/vgscan** utility, to create a database for other LVM commands.

5. Create volumes for the set with the **/sbin/pvcreate** */dev/partition* command.

6. Add the desired volumes to a specific volume group with the **/sbin/vgcreate** *groupname /dev/partition1 /dev/partition2 ...* command.

7. Finally, you can create a logical volume. Use the **/sbin/lvcreate -L** *xy*M **-n** *volname groupname* command, where xy is the size of the volume in MB, and the groupname is the volume group name from the previous step.

8. Now you can format the logical volume with the **mkfs** command for the desired filesystem (usually ext2 or ext3), using the device name returned by the **lvcreate** command.

on the **job** *As of this writing, the LVM code is new to Red Hat and may not be fully supported. Before using LVM on Red Hat Linux, consult with Red Hat, possibly through one of the Red Hat sponsored mailing lists.*

A detailed discussion of this procedure is available in the LVM-HOWTO, available from the Linux Documentation Project.

Mounting Partitions

The mount command can be used to attach local and network partitions to specified directories. Mount points are not fixed; you can mount a CD drive or even a Samba share to any empty directory where you have appropriate permissions.

There are standard mount points based on the FHS. The following commands mount a floppy with the VFAT filesystem, a CD formatted to the ISO 9660 filesystem, and a Zip drive. The devices may be different on your system; if in doubt, look though the startup messages with **dmesg | less**.

```
# mount -t vfat /dev/fd0 /mnt/floppy
# mount -t iso9660 /dev/cdrom /mnt/cdrom
# mount /dev/sdc
```

CERTIFICATION OBJECTIVE 1.03

Basic Commands

Linux was developed as a clone of Unix, which means that it has the same functionality with different source code. And the essence of both operating systems is at the command line. Basic commands for file manipulation and filters are available to help you do more with a file.

This section covers only the most basic of commands that you can use in Linux. Expect to know considerably more about commands for the RHCE exam. Only a few are addressed in later chapters.

Basic File Operations

Two basic groups of commands are used to manage Linux files. One group helps you get around Linux files and directories. The other group actually does something creative with the files. Remember, in any Linux file operation, you can take advantage of the HISTORY (this is capitalized because it's a standard Environment variable) of previous commands, as well as the characteristics of command completion, which allow you to use the TAB key almost as a wildcard to complete a command or a filename, or give you the options available in terms of the absolute path.

Almost all Linux commands include switches, options that allow you to do more. Few are covered in this chapter. Especially if you're less familiar with any of these commands, use their man pages. Study the switches. Try them out! Only with practice, practice, and more practice can you really understand the power behind some of these commands.

Basic Navigation

Everything in Linux can be reduced to a file. Directories are special types of files that serve as containers for other files. Drivers are files. As discussed earlier, devices are special types of files. The nodes associated with USB hardware are just files. And so on. To navigate around these files, you need some basic commands to tell you where you are, what is there with you, and how to move around.

The Tilde (~) But first, take note of the home base for all users in the bash shell, as represented by the tilde (~). This represents the home directory of the currently logged on user. If your username is tb, your home directory is /home/tb. If you've activated the superuser account, your home directory is /root. Thus, the effect of the **cd ~** command depends on your username; if you're user tb, this command brings you to the /home/tb directory. If you're the root user, this command brings you to the /root directory.

Paths There are two path concepts you need to know when you work with Linux directories: absolute paths and relative paths. An absolute path describes the complete directory structure based on the top level directory, root (/). A relative path is based on the current directory, also known as the present working directory. Relative paths do not include the slash in front.

The difference between an absolute path and a relative one is important. Especially when you're creating a script, absolute paths are essential. Otherwise, scripts executed from other directories may lead to unintended consequences.

pwd In many configurations, you may not know where you are relative to the root (/) directory. The pwd command, which is short for present working directory, can tell you, relative to root (/). Once you know where you are, you can know if you need to move to a different directory.

cd It's easy to change directories in Linux. Just use cd and cite the absolute path of the desired directory. If you use the relative path, just remember that your final destination depends on the present working directory.

ls   The most basic of commands is to list the files in the current directory. But the Linux ls command, with the right switches, can be quite powerful. The right kind of ls can tell you everything about a file, such as creation date, last access date, and size. It can help you organize the listing of files in just about any desired order. Important variations on this command include **ls -a** to reveal hidden files, **ls -l** for long listings, and **ls -i** for inode numbers.

Looking for Files

You have two basic commands for file searches: find and locate.

find   The find command searches through directories and subdirectories for a desired file. For example, if you wanted to find the directory with the XF86Config GUI configuration file, you could use the following command, which would start the search in the root directory:

```
# find / -name XF86Config
```

But this search on my older laptop computer with a 200 MHz CPU took several minutes. Alternatively, if you know that this file is located in the /etc subdirectory tree, you could start in that directory with the following command:

```
# find /etc -name XF86Config
```

locate   If this is all too time consuming, Red Hat Linux includes a default database of all files and directories. Searches with the locate command are almost instantaneous. And locate searches don't require the full filename. The drawback is that the locate command database is normally updated only once each day, as documented in the /etc/cron.daily/slocate.cron script.

The first time I started Red Hat Linux during the RHCE exam, I ran this script; I could then use locate to find the files that I needed—quickly.

Getting into the Files

Now that you see how to find and get around different files, it's time to start reading, copying, and moving the files around. Most Linux configuration files are text files. Linux editors are text editors. Linux commands are designed to read text files. If in doubt, you can check what the file type is by using the file command, since Linux doesn't require a file extension.

cat   The most basic command for reading files is cat. The **cat** *filename* command scrolls the text within the *filename* file. It also works with multiple filenames; it concatenates the file names that you might list - as one continuous output to your screen.

less and more   Larger files demand a command that can help you scroll though the file text at your leisure. Linux has two of these commands: more and less. With the **more** *filename* command, you can scroll through the text of a file, from start to finish, one screen at a time. With the **less** *filename* command, you can scroll in both directions through the same text with the PAGE UP and PAGE DOWN keys. Both commands support vi-style searches.

head and tail   The head and tail commands are separate commands that work in essentially the same way. By default, the **head** *filename* command looks at the first 10 lines of a file; the **tail** *filename* command looks at the last 10 lines of a file. You can specify the number of lines shown with the **-n***xy* switch. Just remember to avoid the space when specifying the number of lines; the **tail -n15 /etc/passwd** command lists the last 15 lines of the /etc/passwd file.

Creating Files

A number of commands are used to create new files. Alternatively, you can let a text editor such as vi create a new file for you.

cp   The copy command allows you to take the contents of one file and place a copy with the same or different name in the directory of your choice. One of the dangers of cp is that it can easily overwrite files in different directories, without prompting you to make sure that's what you really wanted to do.

mv   While you can't rename a file in Linux, you can move it. The mv command essentially puts a different label on a file. Unless you're moving the file to a different partition, everything about the file, including the inode number, remains the same.

ln   You can create a linked file. As discussed earlier, linked files are common with device files such as /dev/modem and /dev/mouse. They're also useful to make sure that multiple users have a copy of the same file in their directories. Hard links include a copy of the file. As long as the hard link is made within the same partition, the inode numbers are identical. You could delete a hard-linked file in one directory, and it would still exist in the other directory.

On the other hand, a soft link serves as a redirect; when you open up a file created with a soft link, you're directed to the original file. If you delete the original file, the file is lost. While the soft link is still there, it has nowhere to go.

File Filters

Linux is rich in commands that can help you filter the contents of a file. There are simple commands to help you search, check, or sort the contents of a file. And there are special files that contain others; these container files are known as tarballs, which are the older alternative to the Red Hat Package Manager.

Tarballs are a common way to distribute Linux packages. They are normally distributed in a compressed format, with a .tar.gz or .tgz file extension, consolidated as a package in a single file. In this respect, they are similar to Microsoft-style compressed zip files.

sort

You can sort the contents of a file in a number of ways. By default, the sort command sorts the contents in alphabetical order depending on the first letter in each line. For example, the **sort /etc/passwd** command would sort all users (including those associated with specific services, etc.) by username.

grep and egrep

The grep command uses a search term to look through a file. It returns the full line that contains the search term. For example, **grep 'Michael Jang' /etc/passwd** looks for the name of this author in the /etc/passwd file.

The egrep command is more forgiving; it allows you to use some unusual characters in your search, including +, ?, |, (, and). While it's possible to set up grep to search for these characters with the help of the backslash, the command can be awkward.

The locate command is essentially a specialized version of grep directed at the database of files on your Linux computer.

wc

The wc command, short for word count, can return the number of lines, words, and characters in a file. The wc options are straightforward; for example, wc -w *filename* returns the number of words in that file.

Administrative Commands

You'll work with a number of administrative commands in this book. But every budding Linux administrator should be familiar with at least two basic administrative commands: ps and who.

ps

It's important to know what's running on your Linux computer. The ps command has a number of critical switches. When trying to diagnose a problem, it's common to get the fullest possible list of running processes, then look for a specific program. For example, if Mozilla were to suddenly crash, you'd want to kill any associated processes. The **ps aux | grep mozilla** command could then help you identify the process(es) that you need to kill.

who and w

If you want to know what users are currently logged into your system, use the who command or the w command. This can help you identify the usernames of those who are logged in, their terminal connections, their times of login, and the processes that they are running.

If you suspect that a username has been compromised, use the w command to check currently logged on users. Look at the terminal. If the user is in the office but the terminal indicates a remote dial-in connection, be suspicious. The w command can also identify the current process being run by that user.

Wildcards

Sometimes you may not know the exact name of the file or the exact search term. That is when a wildcard is handy. The basic wildcards are shown in Table 1-4.

Wildcards are sometimes also known in the Linux world as globbing.

TABLE 1-4	Wildcards in the Shell

Wildcard	Description
*	Any number of alphanumeric characters. For example, the **ls ab*** command would return the following filenames, assuming they exist in the current directory: ab, abc, abcd.
?	One single alphanumeric character: For example, the **ls ?ab** command would return the following filenames, assuming they exist in the current directory: abc, abd, abe.
[]	A range of options. For example, the **ls ab[123]** command would return the following filenames, assuming they exist in the current directory: ab1, ab2, ab3. Alternatively, the **ls ab[X-Z]** command would return the following filenames, assuming they exist in the current directory: abX, abY, abZ.

CERTIFICATION OBJECTIVE 1.04

Printing

As of this writing, printers are not automatically connected or configured during the installation of Red Hat Linux. You'll have to install printers yourself. There are two mutually exclusive print daemons available as of this writing, the older Line Print Daemon, lpd, and the newer daemon based on the Internet Printing Protocol, CUPS.

There are two basic ways: you can edit the /etc/printcap file directly, which can be a difficult process. The language associated with /etc/printcap files seems obscure and difficult to understand, at least on the surface.

A GUI front end is also available for configuring a printer, based on the printconf-gui utility. Once configured, the print commands are fairly straightforward. As printer configuration is also an advanced skill, this process is covered in more detail in Chapter 8.

Red Hat Linux is moving towards the use of CUPS as the default print daemon. Through its support of the Internet Printing Protocol (IPP), CUPS is more suited towards managing printers on a network. CUPS also includes a fairly reliable front-end configuration tool that you can call up in a browser, using TCP/IP port 631. This process is also covered in more detail in Chapter 8.

Adding Printers

The easy way to add a printer is with the Red Hat Printer Configuration Utility, which is also known by the command used to start it from a terminal, printconf-gui. It's fairly easy to configure printers with this tool; just click New as shown in Figure 1-4 and follow the prompts.

As of this writing, the only way to configure printers through CUPS is with the browser-based utility. As you'll see in Chapter 8, once you've enabled the tool in the /etc/xinetd.d/cups configuration file, you can start it up on the local computer by navigating to localhost:631 in your browser.

Print Commands

Three basic commands are associated with printing in Linux, as described in Table 1-5.

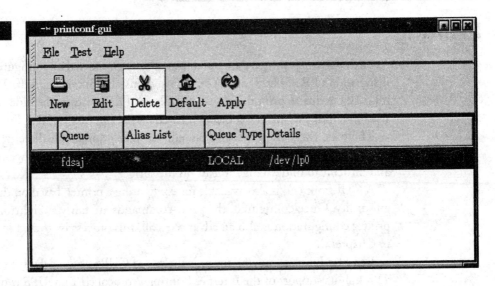

FIGURE 1-4

The Red Hat
Printer
Configuration
Utility

TABLE 1-5	Linux Print Commands

Command	Description
lpr	The basic print command. lpr *filename* prints that file.
lpq	Query the print queue for status. lpr -l lists print job numbers.
lprm	Remove a specific job, usually specified by job number, from the printer queue.

CERTIFICATION OBJECTIVE 1.05

The Linux/Unix Shell

A *shell* is a user interface. The Linux command shell is the prompt that allows you to interact with your computer with various system commands. With the right file permissions, you can set up commands in scripts to run when you want, even in the middle of the night. Linux shells can process commands in various sequences, depending on how you manage the input and output of each command. The way commands are interpreted is in part determined by variables and parameters associated with each shell. Some of these variables make up the environment that is carried over even if you change from one shell to another.

The default shell in Linux is bash, also known as the Bourne Again Shell. A number of other shells are available that are popular with many users. As long as you have installed the appropriate RPMs, users can start any of these shells. As desired, you can change the default shell for individual users in the /etc/passwd file.

Basic Shell Programming

"Real" Linux administrators program their own scripts. They create scripts because they don't want to sit at their computers all of the time. Scripts can allow Linux to automatically back up directories when nobody is in the office. Scripts can help Linux process databases when few people are using the system.

If you're not a programmer, this is not as difficult as it sounds. For example, utilities related to crontab automate the creation of a number of different scripts. The cron system is discussed in more detail in Chapter 6.

Script Execution and Permissions

Any Linux file can be set up as an executable file. Then if the file includes a series of commands that can be interpreted by the shell, the commands in that file are executed. For more information on executable files, read the information under "Basic Security" later in this chapter.

Piping, Input/Output, Error, and Redirection

Linux uses three basic data streams. Data goes in, data comes out, and errors are sent in a different direction. These streams are known as Standard Input (stdin), Standard Output (stdout), and Standard Error (stderr). Normally, input comes from the keyboard and goes out to the screen, while errors are sent to a buffer. In the following example, *filename* is stdin to the lpr command:

```
# lpr filename
```

When you run **cat** *filename*, the contents of that file are sent to the screen as standard output.

You can redirect each of these streams to or from a file. For example, if you have a program named database and a datafile with a lot of data, the contents of that datafile can be sent to the database program with a left redirection arrow. As shown here, datafile is taken as standard input:

```
# database < datafile
```

Standard input can come from the left side of a command as well. For example, if you need to scroll through the boot messages, you can combine the dmesg and less commands with a pipe:

```
# dmesg | less
```

The output from dmesg is redirected as standard input to less, which then allows you to scroll through that output as if it were a separate file.

Standard output is just as easy to redirect. For example, the following command uses the right redirection arrow to send the standard output of the ls command to the file named filelist.

```
# ls > filelist
```

You can add standard output to the end of an existing file with a double redirection arrow with a command such as **ls >> filelist**.

If you believe that a particular program is generating errors, redirect the error stream from it with a command like the following:

```
# program 2> err-list
```

Variables and Parameters

Variables can change. Parameters are set. The bash shell includes a number of standard environment variables. Their default values are shown in the output to the env command. One critical variable is the value of PATH, which you can check at the command line with the **echo $PATH** command. The directories listed in PATH are automatically searched when you try to run a command. You can easily change the PATH variable. For example, if you want to add the /sbin directory to your PATH, just run the following commands:

```
# PATH=$PATH:/sbin
# export PATH
```

The most common parameters are the settings associated with Linux configuration files, which are mostly located in the /etc directory. For example, the /etc/resolv.conf file uses the nameserver parameter to represent the DNS servers for your network. This parameter is normally set to the IP address for that DNS server.

Inherited Environment

It's easy to move from shell to shell. Many experienced Unix users prefer the Korn shell. Once set, with the set command, environment variables stay the same from shell to shell. In contrast, shell variables such as umask may change when you move from shell to shell, or even from user to user. For example, umask is typically different for regular users and the root user.

CERTIFICATION OBJECTIVE 1.06

Basic Security

The basic security of a Linux installation is based on file permissions. Default file permissions are set through the umask shell variable. SUID and SGID permissions can give all users access to specific files. Ownership is based on the default user and group IDs of the person who created a file. Managing permissions and ownership involves commands such as chmod, chown, and chgrp.

Users and groups own files. Users and groups have passwords. Security can be enhanced if you configure users and groups in the Shadow Password Suite.

File Permissions

Linux file permissions are straightforward. Take the following output from **ls -l /sbin/fdisk:**

```
-rwxr-xr-x  1 root  root    73576 Apr  1  18:26    /sbin/fdisk
```

The permissions are shown on the left-hand side of the listing. Ten characters are shown. The first character determines whether it's a regular or a special file. The remaining nine characters are grouped in threes, applicable to the file owner (user), the group owner, and everyone else on that Linux system. The letters are straightforward; r=read, w=write, x=execute. These characters are described in Table 1-6.

Key commands that can help you manage the permissions and ownership of a file are chmod, chown, and chgrp. The chmod command uses the numeric value of permissions associated with the owner, group, and others. In Linux, permissions are assigned the following numeric values: r=4, w=2, and x=1. For example, if you were crazy enough to give read, write, and execute permissions on fdisk for all users, you would run the **chmod 777 /sbin/fdisk** command. The chown and chgrp commands adjust the user and group owners associated with the cited file.

Users, Groups, and umask

Linux, like Unix, is configured with users and groups. Everyone who uses Linux is set up with a username, even if it's just "guest". Take a look at /etc/passwd. One version of this file is shown in Figure 1-5.

TABLE 1-6	Description of File Permissions

Position	Description
1	Type of file; - = regular file, d=directory, b=device, l=linked file
234	Permissions granted to the owner of the file
567	Permissions granted to the group owner of the file
890	Permissions granted to all other users on the Linux system

As you can see, all kinds of usernames are listed in the /etc/passwd file. Even a number of Linux services such as mail, news, nfs, and apache have their own usernames. In any case, the /etc/passwd file follows a specific format, described in more detail in Chapter 4. For now, note that the only users shown in this file are mj and pm, their User IDs (UID) and Group IDs (GID) are 500 and 501, and their home directories match their usernames. The next user gets UID and GID 502, and so on.

umask

The way umask works in Red Hat Linux may surprise you, especially if you're coming from a different Unix style environment. You cannot configure umask to automatically

FIGURE 1-5	

/etc/passwd

```
operator:x:11:0:operator:/root:/sbin/nologin
games:x:12:100:games:/usr/games:/sbin/nologin
gopher:x:13:30:gopher:/var/gopher:/sbin/nologin
ftp:x:14:50:FTP User:/var/ftp:/sbin/nologin
nobody:x:99:99:Nobody:/:/sbin/nologin
vcsa:x:69:69:virtual console memory owner:/dev:/sbin/nologin
rpm:x:37:37::/var/lib/rpm:/bin/bash
nscd:x:28:28:NSCD Daemon:/:/bin/false
ntp:x:38:38::/etc/ntp:/sbin/nologin
apache:x:48:48:Apache:/var/www:/bin/false
radvd:x:75:75:radvd user:/:/bin/false
mailnull:x:47:47::/var/spool/mqueue:/sbin/nologin
smmsp:x:51:51::/var/spool/mqueue:/sbin/nologin
pcap:x:77:77::/var/arpwatch:/sbin/nologin
sshd:x:74:74:Privilege-separated SSH:/var/empty/sshd:/sbin/nologin
ident:x:98:98:pident user:/:/sbin/nologin
rpc:x:32:32:Portmapper RPC user:/:/sbin/nologin
rpcuser:x:29:29:RPC Service User:/var/lib/nfs:/sbin/nologin
nfsnobody:x:65534:65534:Anonymous NFS User:/var/lib/nfs:/sbin/nologin
xfs:x:43:43:X Font Server:/etc/X11/fs:/sbin/nologin
gdm:x:42:42::/var/gdm:/sbin/nologin
named:x:25:25:Named:/var/named:/bin/false
postfix:x:89:89::/var/spool/postfix:/bin/true
squid:x:23:23::/var/spool/squid:/dev/null
mj:x:500:500:Michael Jang:/home/mj:/bin/bash
pm:x:501:501:Tony Blair:/home/pm:/bin/bash
~
                                                        12,23        Bot
```

allow you to create new files with executable permissions. This is a recent change that promotes security; if fewer files have executable permissions, fewer files are available for a cracker to use to run programs to break through your system.

Every time you create a new file, the default permissions are based on the value of umask. In the past, the value of umask cancelled out the value of numeric permissions on a file. For example, if the value of umask is 000, the default permissions for any file created by that user are 777 – 000 = 777, which corresponds to read, write, and execute permissions for all users.

When you type the umask command, you get a four-number output such as 0245. As of this writing, the first number in the umask output is always 0 and is not used. In the future, this first number may be usable to allow for new files that automatically include the SUID or SGID bits.

Also, no matter what the value of umask, new files can no longer be automatically created with executable permissions. In other words, a umask of 0454 leads to identical permissions on new files as a umask of 0545. You need to use commands such as chmod to specifically set executable permissions on a file.

SUID and SGID

Permissions can be a risky business. But you need to give all users access to some programs. To set full read, write, and execute permissions for all users on a Linux system can be dangerous. One alternative is setting the SUID and the SGID permission bits for a file. When active, these bits allow you to configure appropriate permissions on the subject file. For example, one common practice is to set the SUID bit for the KPPP Internet Connection Utility to allow access to all users. You could do this with the **chmod u+s /usr/sbin/kppp** command.

SGID permissions can be useful when you're setting up a special group of users who need to share files on a specific task or project. This process is discussed in more detail in Chapter 11.

Shadow Password Suite

Historically, all that was needed to manage Linux users and groups is the information included in the /etc/passwd and /etc/group files. These files included passwords and are normally set to be readable by all users.

The Shadow Password Suite was created to provide an additional layer of protection. It is used to encrypt user and group passwords in shadow files (/etc/shadow and /etc/gshadow) that are readable only by users with root privileges.

The Shadow Password Suite is now enabled by default in Red Hat Linux. Standard commands for creating new users and groups automatically set up encrypted passwords in the Shadow Password Suite files. These commands are described in more detail in Chapter 4.

But if you're restoring a system, you may not have access to these special commands. The old way of creating new users and groups is by editing the /etc/passwd and /etc/group files directly. Four commands allow you to convert passwords to and from the /etc/shadow and /etc/gshadow files:

- **pwconv**   Converts passwords from /etc/passwd. This command works even if some of the passwords are already encrypted in /etc/shadow.

- **pwunconv**   Opposite of pwconv.

- **grpconv**   Converts passwords from /etc/group. This command works even if some of the passwords are already encrypted in /etc/gshadow.

- **grpunconv**   Opposite of grpconv.

CERTIFICATION OBJECTIVE 1.07

Linux/Unix System Administration

Most system administration tasks require root or superuser privileges.

You should already be familiar with a number of basic Linux system administration commands and files. Standard user files are stored in /etc/skel. Daemons are processes that run in the background and run various Linux services. cron is a special daemon that can run scripts when you want. It's especially useful for setting up backup jobs in the middle of the night. Logging is a key part of monitoring Linux and any services that you choose to run.

Superuser

Generally in Linux, a system administrator does everything possible as a normal user. It's a good practice to use superuser privileges only when absolutely necessary. Good administrators will return to being normal users when they're done with their tasks. Mistakes as the root user can disable your Linux system.

There are two basic ways to make this work:

- **su** The superuser command, su, prompts you for the root password before logging you in with root privileges. A variation, **su -c**, sets up root privileges for one specific command. Many Red Hat GUI utilities are set up to prompt for the root password before they can be started.

- **sudo** The sudo command allows users listed in /etc/sudoers to run administrative commands. You can configure /etc/sudoers to set limits on the root privileges given to a specific user.

However, Red Hat Linux provides some features that make working as root somewhat safer. For example, ftp and telnet logins to remote computers are disabled by default.

/etc/skel

Basic configuration files for individual users are available in the /etc/skel directory. This directory includes a number of hidden files. For a full list, run the **ls -a /etc/skel** command. If you want all future users to get specific files in their home directories, include them here.

Daemons

A *daemon* is a process that runs in the background. It is resident in your computer's RAM and watches for signals before it goes into action. For example, a network daemon such as httpd, the Linux Web server known as Apache, waits for a request from a browser before it actually serves a Web page.

Daemons are often configured to start automatically when you start Linux. This process is documented at various runlevels in the /etc/rc.d directory. Alternatively, you can use a tool such as ntsysv to identify and manage the daemons that are started at various Linux runlevels. This is discussed in more detail in Chapter 4.

Network Service Daemons

Networks don't always work. Sometimes you need to restart a network daemon to implement a configuration change. Red Hat Linux provides easy access to network service daemons in /etc/rc.d/init.d. This directory includes scripts for Linux network services (and more) for everything from the Network File System (NFS) to sendmail.

With these scripts, it's easy to start, stop, status, or restart a network daemon. This is useful to implement or test changes that you make to a specific configuration file. For example, if you make a change to the Apache Web server configuration file in /etc/httpd/conf/httpd.conf, you can implement the change right away with the **/etc/rc.d/init.d/httpd restart** command. Other switches to these scripts allow you to stop, start, or status these services. Network service management is discussed in more detail in Chapter 9.

cron

Perhaps the most important daemon is cron, which can be used to execute a command or a series of commands in a script, on a schedule. Red Hat Linux already includes a series of scripts that are executed by cron on committed schedules in the /etc/cron.hourly, /etc/cron.daily, /etc/cron.weekly, and /etc/cron.monthly directories.

crontab

The easiest way to set up your own cron jobs is through the crontab file, which can be managed through the crontab command. Users can edit their own crontab files with the **crontab -e** command; the superuser can configure the crontab for a specific user with the **crontab -u** *username* **-e** command.

The general format for a crontab file can be found in the /etc/crontab script, which is used to run the scripts in the aforementioned schedule-related directories. A typical crontab entry from that file is:

```
42 4 1 * * root run-parts /etc/cron.monthly
```

Five schedule fields appear on the left-hand side of each crontab entry: minute, hour, day of month, month, and day of week. The preceding line is executed at 4:42 A.M., on the first of every month, no matter what day of the week it is.

Backup and Restore

Hard drives include spinning disks and magnetic media. These are mechanical parts. By definition, all mechanical hard drives will eventually fail. If you're administering a Linux system with multiple users, you do not want to have to hear the complaints of people who know that their data is more important than yours, because you'll know that they are right. Configuring backups involves a number of strategic choices that go beyond Linux.

Using full backups, you can back up the entire drive; using incremental backups, you back up just the data that has changed since the last backup. A wide variety of media are available for backups, including tape drives, writable CD/DVDs, and other hard drives in various RAID configurations. You can back up data locally or over a network. Linux includes a number of quality tools for backups.

It's common to back up through a network to a dedicated backup server. Since you're transferring at least substantial portions of a hard drive during a backup, backups can degrade network performance for other users. So it is best to perform backups when few people are using your Linux system, usually during the middle of the night. For this reason, it's common to automate backups using the previously discussed cron daemon.

Tape Backups

Using magnetic tape in Linux depends on the ftape system, using "tarballs" to group directories into single compressed backup files. Once it is mounted, it's easy to test a tape drive; just use the **mt -f /dev/***tapedevice* command to status, rewind, or eject the tape. If it's a SCSI tape drive, use the st command instead.

Unlike when using regular media, you don't mount a tape; you can actually use switches with the tar command to write or restore directly from the tape device. Just cite the appropriate /dev/*tapedevice* in the command.

CD Backups

Backups to CDs are made in a similar fashion, using iso files instead of tarballs. The **mkisofs -o /tmp/back.cd /home** command can consolidate directories such as /home onto a single file, which can then be recorded onto the CD with a command such as cdrecord.

You can then store the CD and later restore the files from it just by mounting it as you would any regular CD.

Hard Drive (RAID) Backups

Hard drive–based backups are based on the system known as the Redundant Array of Independent Disks, or RAID, which is covered in more detail in Chapter 5. There are several versions of RAID that can automatically restore data once you've replaced a broken hard disk.

System Log File Management

Log files are controlled by the syslog daemon and organized in the /etc/syslog.conf file. It is important to use log files to understand the behavior of your Linux system; deviations may be a sign of problems with recently installed service, or a security breach. Basic log files are organized in the /var/log directory. For more information on system logs, see Chapter 10.

CERTIFICATION OBJECTIVE 1.08

Basic TCP/IP Networking

TCP/IP is a series of protocols organized in layers, known as a protocol suite. It was developed for Unix and eventually adopted as the standard for communication on the Internet. With IP addresses, it can help you organize your network. Then, there are a number of TCP/IP tools and configurations that can help you manage your network.

IP Numbers and Classes

Every computer that communicates on a network needs its own IP address. Some addresses are assigned permanently to a particular computer; these are known as *static* addresses. Others are leased from a DHCP server for a limited amount of time; these are also known as *dynamic* IP addresses.

Two standards for IP addresses are in use today, IP version 4 (IPv4) and IP version 6 (IPv6). IPv4 addresses have 32 bits and are set up in octets in dotted decimal notation. The range of possible IPv4 addresses is between 0.0.0.0 to 255.255.255.255. While over four billion IP addresses are available, that is not nearly enough for the current Internet.

IPv6 addresses have 128 bits and are set up in hexadecimal notation. An IPv6 address is normally organized in eight groups of four hexadecimal numbers each, and it may look like 4abe:03e2:c132:69fa:0000:0000:c0b8:2148. Over 340,000,000,000,000,000,000,000,000,000,000,000,000 IPv6 addresses are available.

To ease the transition, specific IPv6 addresses have been assigned for every one of the four billion IPv4 addresses. There are still over 3.4×10^{38} addresses left over.

While actual routing on the Internet now commonly uses IPv6, network configuration in Linux is still normally based on IPv4 addresses.

IPv4 addresses are organized into five different classes, as shown in Table 1-7.

In addition, there are a number of private IP addresses that are not to be assigned to any computer that is directly connected to the Internet. They are associated with network addresses 10.0.0.0, 172.168.0.0, and 192.168.0.0 through 192.168.255.0.

IP Addresses Define a Network

Three key IP addresses define a network: the network address, the broadcast address, and the subnet mask. The network address is always the first IP address in a range; the broadcast address is always the last address in the same range. The subnet mask defines the difference between the two addresses. You can assign IP addresses between the network and broadcast addresses (not including these addresses) to any computer on the network.

For example, define the range of addresses for a private network. Start with the private network address 192.168.122.0. Use the standard subnet mask for a class C network, 255.255.255.0. Based on these two addresses, the broadcast address is 192.168.122.255, and the range of IP addresses that you can assign on that particular network is 192.168.122.1 through 129.168.122.254.

If this is confusing to you in any way, please refer to the IP Sub-Networking Mini-HOWTO of the Linux Documentation Project at www.tldp.org.

Tools and Commands

You have a substantial number of tools available to manage the TCP/IP protocol suite on your Linux computer. Three of the more important commands are ping, ifconfig, and netstat.

ping

The ping command allows you to test connectivity—locally, within your network, and on the Internet. For the purpose of this section, assume your IP address is 192.168.122.43, and the gateway address on your network is 192.168.122.99. If you're having problems connecting to a network, you should use the ping command in the following order. The first step is to test the integrity of TCP/IP on your computer:

```
# ping 127.0.0.1
```

Normally, ping works continuously on Linux; you'll need to press CTRL-C to stop this command. If you need to see if you're properly connected to your LAN, you should ping your own IP address:

```
# ping 192.168.122.43
```

If that works, ping the address of another computer on your network. Then start tracing the route to the Internet. Ping the address for your gateway, in this case, 192.168.122.99. If possible, ping the address of your network's connection to the Internet. And finally, ping the address of a computer that you know is *active* on the Internet.

You can substitute host names such as www.google.com for an IP address. If the host name doesn't work, there's a problem with the database of host names and IP addresses, more commonly known as a DNS, BIND, or name server.

ifconfig

The ifconfig command can help you check and configure network adapters. Run /sbin/ifconfig, and you can see the adapters that are working on your computer. If you're having trouble configuring something like the first Ethernet adapter, you can assign a specific IRQ with a command such as:

```
# /sbin/ifconfig eth0 irq 10
```

For more information on this command, refer to Chapter 4.

netstat

The netstat command is versatile; it can help you see the channels available for network connections, interface statistics, and more. One important version of this command,

| TABLE 1-7 | IP Address Classes |

Class	Available Address Range	Note
A	1.1.1.1–126.255.255.254	Allows networks of up to 16 million computers
B	128.0.0.1–191.255.255.254	Allows networks of up to 65,000 computers
C	192.0.0.1–223.255.255.254	Allows networks of up to 254 computers
D	224.0.0.1–239.255.255.254	Reserved for multicasts
E	240.0.0.1–255.255.255.254	Reserved for experimental use

netstat -r, displays routing tables that can tell you if your computer knows where to send a message. More information on this command is available in Chapter 4.

Name Resolution

When I used a static IP address on my high-speed Internet connection, I could sometimes memorize those numbers. But how can anyone memorize the IP addresses of every Web site you need on the Internet? Using four configuration files, Linux can help you translate computer host names to IP addresses.

/etc/hosts

The first database of host names and IP addresses was set up in a static text file, /etc/hosts. When there were just a few nodes on the network that eventually turned into the Internet, it was possible to maintain identical /etc/hosts files on each computer. Here's a typical line in /etc/hosts, which lists the IP address, fully qualified domain name, and alias for one computer connection:

```
192.168.132.32    linux1.mommabears.com  laptop
```

/etc/resolv.conf

There are millions of hosts on the Internet. Even if it were possible to collect all domain names and IP addresses into a /etc/hosts file, the file would overwhelm every computer. And it would overwhelm every network administrator who would have to make sure that all the /etc/hosts files on the Internet match—and get updated every time a new Web site appears. That's why the Domain Name System (DNS) was developed, based on the Berkeley Internet Name Domain (BIND). In /etc/resolv.conf, the IP address of each DNS server is listed with a simple line similar to:

```
nameserver 192.168.0.1
```

/etc/host.conf

Many networks configure an /etc/hosts file for the local network and a DNS server for other networks and/or the Internet. When your computer looks for an IP address, this file determines whether it searches though /etc/hosts or DNS first. This is usually a one-line file:

```
order hosts, bind
```

A computer with this line looks through /etc/hosts first. If it can't find the computer name that you want in that file, it next looks to the DNS server (bind) for the computer name.

/etc/nsswitch.conf

This file relates to the configuration on a network of Linux- and Unix-type computers, which are configured to communicate using the Network File System (NFS). When it is used in concert with the Network Information System (NIS), networks can maintain a single database of usernames and passwords for all NFS-enabled computers on that network.

CERTIFICATION OBJECTIVE 1.09

Standard Network Services

Linux is built for networking. The code associated with many standard networking services is integrated into the Linux kernel. A basic understanding of the functionality of standard Linux networking services is essential. Many themes throughout this book assume that you already understand the purpose of network communication protocols, mail services, host name and IP address management, Web services, and more.

In Red Hat Linux, network services may need to be installed separately. Some include different packages for clients and servers. Network services are activated through /etc/xinetd.conf, which reads activation files in the /etc/xinetd.d directory. Some key Red Hat Linux network services are briefly addressed in the following sections.

Network File System

The first network system on Unix and Linux computers is the Network File System (NFS). Ideally, this leads to a seamless Linux interface; for example, you can set up one /home directory for all users on your network on one server. Remember, you need NFS on both server and client computers on your network.

First, make sure NFS support is part of the kernel, as documented in /proc/filesystems. Then NFS should be activated in the /etc/xinetd.d directory, as well as in the appropriate runlevels. Be careful when making NFS part of a computer that's connected to multiple networks, as most firewall configurations block the port used for NFS communication.

Once NFS is configured, directories are shared in /etc/exports and mounted with a command similar to the following:

```
# mount -t nfs nfsserver:/home /mhome
```

For more information on the Network File System, see Chapter 9.

NIS

The Network Information Service was formerly known as the "yellow pages," as it is a centralized database of usernames and passwords on a network with Linux and other Unix-style computers. NIS can be configured as a centralized database for a number of other configuration files in the /etc/ directory. Anything that can standardize the configuration of different computers on a network helps the system administrator. For more information on NIS, see Chapter 10.

Samba

The network system originally developed for networks with Microsoft and IBM computers is based on the Server Message Block (SMB) format. SMB is the basis for Microsoft Windows Workgroup- and Domain-based network communication. When you install Samba on a Linux computer, you can make it part of one of these Microsoft-style networks. It can share files just like any other member of a workgroup network. It can act as a server. Later versions of Samba can even be configured as a Windows NT –style Primary Domain Controller or a Windows 2000/XP–style Domain Controller.

Separate packages are available to set up your Linux computer as a Samba client and as a Samba server. Once shares are configured in /etc/samba/smb.conf, other Samba-enabled Linux clients can mount these directories with a command similar to the following:

```
# mount -t smbfs -o username=user,password=passwd //servername/sharename /mountpoint
```

Samba and the associated configuration tools are discussed extensively in Chapter 8.

File Transfer Protocol (FTP)

Perhaps the most basic file sharing protocol still in common use is the File Transfer Protocol (FTP). It is set up specifically for file transfers; you might already know that file transfers using FTP are generally faster than with any other protocol.

As with NFS and Samba, you need a server and a client. FTP servers can be anonymous, which means they accept all users, or they can be configured to require a specific username and password. Generally, Linux FTP servers share files from the /var/ftp directory.

The original FTP client works from the command line. Most Linux navigational commands work for FTP; just remember that the **get** and **put** commands download and upload specific files. FTP is covered in more detail in Chapter 8.

Web Services

Apache is by far the most popular Web server in use on the Internet. It's a standard part of the Red Hat Linux server installation. The main configuration file is in /etc/httpd/conf/httpd.conf. Configuration is based on an extensive array of modules in the /etc/httpd directory. Basic HTML files, icons, and CGI applets are installed in the /var/www directory. The main Apache log files are part of the /var/logs/httpd directory. Daily log files for the largest Web sites can grow into the GB range. Apache is covered in more detail in Chapter 8.

A substantial number of other Web servers are available for Red Hat Linux, such as Sun's iPlanet and Zeus's Web server.

Dynamic Host Configuration Protocol (DHCP)

IP version 4 addresses are scarce. The Dynamic Host Configuration Protocol (DHCP) was designed to help ration IP addresses. A DHCP server leases a specific IP address to a computer network card for a limited, but renewable, amount of time. DHCP servers can lease IP addresses on different LANs using the BOOTP protocol. More information on setting up DHCP clients and servers is available in Chapter 9.

Sendmail

There are some who suggest that sendmail is the biggest test for Linux system administrators. The sendmail configuration file, sendmail.cf, is complex. But it should not be intimidating. The basic commands define the features you want, the protocols you need, and the way mail is sent and received on your network.

More information on sendmail is available in Chapter 8.

POP, IMAP

The Post Office Protocol (POP) and the Internet Mail Access Protocol (IMAP) are each a set of rules for delivering e-mail from a server such as sendmail to an e-mail client such as Netscape, elm, or pine. While POP3 is the current standard for e-mail that is sent to clients, IMAP4 is more flexible for users such as those who access their mail using different computers. POP3 and IMAP4 configuration is addressed in Chapter 8.

CERTIFICATION OBJECTIVE 1.10

Basic Network Security

Network security in Linux has four basic components. Security by computer can help you manage what computers can send messages into and out of your network. Security by port can help you manage the services that others can use to break into your network. Security by address translation can help you hide the computers inside your network. And finally, security by rule can help you manage the type of data allowed into your network in excruciating detail. Security issues are discussed in more detail in Chapter 10.

Red Hat Linux includes two different tools to help you configure a firewall on your computer, lokkit and redhat-config-securitylevel. As of this writing, work on redhat-config-securitylevel was not complete, and is not yet usable.

Allowing and Denying

The /etc/hosts.allow and /etc/hosts.deny files can help you manage what computers are allowed into your network. You can specify computers by name, IP address, network, or domain name in each file. This can help you limit access to a trusted few computers such as those within your company, or it can protect you from computers that you know may pose a problem.

Port Security

TCP/IP has 65,536 ports, which work like TV channels. If you leave all ports open, you're leaving a lot of options for a cracker who wants to break into your network. With a firewall, you can create a solid barrier and then open only the ports that you need.

Network Address Translation

Most LAN administrators set up Network Address Translation (NAT) as a matter of course on an IPv4 network. Since IPv4 addresses are scarce, it is typical to use private IP addresses inside a LAN, with a regular IP address only on the gateway computer that is directly connected to an outside network such as the Internet.

For example, when a computer inside a LAN wants access to a Web page, NAT sends the IP address of the gateway to the Internet. Nobody outside the LAN need know the real source of the Web page request.

iptables

There are two basic services for filtering information in and out of a network, based on the ipchains and iptables commands. Red Hat Linux has recently implemented iptables as the firewall tool of choice. Once you've configured a firewall and loaded it, the rules are stored in the /etc/sysconfig/iptables file.

The iptables command has three basic ways to look at a data packet: input, output, or forward. Within these and other parameters, you can set up your firewall with instructions to let the packet pass, let it drop, or direct it someplace else.

iptables is covered in more detail in Chapter 10.

CERTIFICATION SUMMARY

The RHCE exam is not for beginners. This chapter covers the elementary skills that you need for the remainder of this book. If the explanations in this chapter are too brief, you may need to refer to other sources.

TWO-MINUTE DRILL

Here are some of the key points from the certification objective in Chapter 1.

Basic Linux Knowledge

❏ Linux is managed through a series of text configuration files.

❏ Even though Red Hat Linux now has a rescue CD with text editors such as emacs, you need to know how to restore a system from a rescue floppy. Rescue floppies normally include just the vi editor. Therefore, you need some basic skills in using vi.

Linux Filesystem Hierarchy and Structure

❏ Linux directories are organized to the Filesystem Hierarchy Standard (FHS).

❏ In the FHS, devices such as media are grouped in the /dev directory. Some /dev files have logical names such as mouse and modem and are linked to the actual device files.

❏ Each FHS partition can be formatted with mkfs to the ext3 standard and more.

❏ The Logical Volume Manager allows you to consolidate multiple partitions in one filesystem, on one directory. Once configured, partitions can be mounted through /etc/fstab or directly with the mount command.

Basic Commands

❏ Managing Linux means that you know how to use the command line interface.

❏ Basic commands allow you to navigate, to find the files that you need, to read file contents, and to create new files.

❏ File filters allow you to search through the files themselves, for specific citations or other file characteristics.

❏ Administrative commands allow you to find what is running and who is logged in.

Printing

❏ There are two mutually exclusive print daemons available, CUPS and lpd. CUPS is based on the Internet Printing Protocol.

❑ CUPS can be configured through a browser based tool on TCP/IP port 631.

❑ If you're using lpd, you can set up a printer directly though /etc/printcap, or with the Red Hat Printer Configuration Utility, printconf-gui.

The Linux/Unix Shells

❑ Command lines are based on a shell.

❑ With the right permissions, you can set up shell programs in executable scripts.

❑ With stdin, stdout, and stderr, you can manage different data streams.

❑ The way a shell works depends on the settings in its variables and parameters. Some variables and parameters are grouped in the inherited environment, which maintains settings from shell to shell.

Basic Security

❑ Basic security within Linux is based on file permissions, users, groups, and umask.

❑ The SUID and SGID bits allow you to share owner-level permissions with different users and groups.

❑ The shadow password suite protects user and group passwords in files that should be accessible only to the root user.

Linux/Unix System Administration

❑ When you administer a system, superuser use should be kept to a minimum.

❑ Standard files for new users are kept in /etc/skel.

❑ Daemons are processes that run in the background.

❑ When you reconfigure a network service, you can stop and restart it through the /etc/rc.d/init.d directory.

❑ The cron daemon helps you schedule different jobs, including backup and restore jobs, which should be done when network use is at a minimum.

❑ When you have problems, system log files, as organized by /etc/syslog.conf, provide important clues to the causes.

Basic TCP/IP Networking

❑ Most of the work in TCP/IP networking is with IP addressing.

❑ There are three different basic classes of IPv4 addresses suitable for setting up TCP/IP on a LAN.

❑ Tools such as ping, ifconfig, and netstat can help you diagnose problems on that LAN.

❑ Name resolution configuration files determine how your computer finds the right IP address.

Standard Network Services

❑ There are a number of standard network services: NFS, NIS, Samba, FTP, DHCP, Apache, sendmail, POP, and IMAP.

❑ Each of these services, when installed, can be configured to start and stop through the activation files in the /etc/xinetd.d directory.

Basic Network Security

❑ Basic network security settings can depend on allowing or denying access to different computers by their IP addresses or by the desired TCP/IP port.

❑ Computers behind a firewall can be protected through Network Address Translation or various iptables commands.

SELF TEST

The following questions will help you measure your understanding of the material presented in this chapter. Read all the choices carefully, as there may be more than one correct answer. Choose all correct answers for each question.

Basic Linux Knowledge

1. One of the administrators has accidentally deleted the /etc/passwd file. Since nobody can log in without that file, you had to use a rescue floppy disk to get into the system. Which of the following editors would you use to edit that file?

A. emacs

B. vi

C. WordPerfect

D. pine

2. Which of the following vi commands would you use to copy the currently highlighted line in the /etc/inittab file?

A. p

B. c

C. yy

D. cw

Linux Filesystem Hierarchy and Structure

3. Which of the following is the top-level directory in Linux?

A. /root

B. /

C. /top

D. /mnt

4. Which of the following directories contains most Linux configuration files?

A. /var

B. ~

C. /etc

D. /tmp

5. Which of the following commands would you use to apply fdisk to the second IDE hard drive?

    A.   /sbin/fdisk /dev/sda

    B.   /sbin/fdisk /dev/hda

    C.   /sbin/fdisk /dev/sdb

    D.   /sbin/fdisk /dev/hdb

6. You're suspecting disk problems with the partition where the /home directory is mounted. Which of the following steps should you take?

    A.   umount /home

    B.   /sbin/fsck /home

    C.   Back up the contents of the /home directory

    D.   Go into single-user mode

7. Which of the following commands would you use to mount a MS-DOS floppy disk?

    A.   mount -t /dev/fd0 /mnt/floppy

    B.   mount -t ext2 /dev/fd0 /mnt/floppy

    C.   mount -t ext3/dev/fd0 /mnt/floppy

    D.   mount -t vfat /dev/fd0 /mnt/floppy

Basic Commands

8. At the command line interface, what would you do to scroll backward through the history of previous commands?

    A.   Run the **history** command.

    B.   Press the PAGE UP key

    C.   Press the PAGE DOWN key

    D.   Press the RIGHT ARROW key

9. You've logged in as user pm. Then you run the **su** command, entered the necessary information when prompted, and then run the **cd ~** command. When you then run **pwd**, what do you see?

    A.   /home/pm

    B.   /home

    C.   /root

    D.   /

10. Which of the following commands returns the actual number of times user mj is logged into your Linux computer?

    A. wc -l

    B. who | grep mj

    C. who | wc -l

    D. who | grep mj | wc -l

Printing

11. You're maintaining a large queue of print jobs on your network, and you need some job numbers to make sure the engineers get highest priority on the printer. Which of the following commands lists print job numbers?

    A. lpr -l

    B. lpq -l

    C. lprm -l

    D. lpd

The Linux/Unix Shells

12. Which of the following commands would you use to add the /usr/sbin directory to your PATH?

    A. $PATH=$PATH:/usr/sbin

    B. $PATH=PATH:/usr/sbin

    C. PATH=$PATH:/sbin

    D. PATH=$PATH:/usr/sbin

Basic Security

13. When you run the umask command, you see the following result: 0000. The next time you create a file, what will be the permissions?

    A. drwxrwxrwx

    B. ----------

    C. -rwxr-xr-x

    D. -rw-rw-rw-

14. You've just added several new users by directly editing the /etc/passwd file. Which of the following things do you need to do to make sure that passwords are properly encrypted per the Shadow Password Suite?

A. pwconv

B. pwunconv

C. grpconv

D. grpunconv

Linux/Unix System Administration

15. You've logged in as a regular user. You've taken advice to heart to keep your use of the superuser account to a minimum. Which of the following commands would run a single program named rooter that requires superuser privileges and then automatically returns to the regular account?

A. su rooter

B. su -c rooter

C. superuser rooter

D. /sbin/su -c rooter

16. In which of the following directories can you find scripts or links to scripts organized by runlevel?

A. /etc/rc.d/init.d

B. /etc/rc.d

C. /rc.d

D. /etc/init.d

17. Based on the following line from one of your users' crontab file, when will the Berkeleylives program be run?

```
0 1 2 3 * Berkeleylives
```

A. At 1:23 A.M. every day

B. At 1:00 A.M. on March 2

C. At 1:00 A.M. on February 3

D. At 2:00 A.M. on March 2

18. Which of the following commands would you use to store the contents of /home in a compressed tarball?

    A. /sbin/tarball czvf /home

    B. tar czvf home.tar.gz /home

    C. tar xzvf home.tar.gz /home

    D. tarball czvf home.tar.gz /home

Basic TCP/IP Networking

19. Which of the following sets of numbers, in order, correspond to an appropriate network address, subnet mask, and broadcast address?

    A. 192.168.14.255, 255.255.255.0 192.168.14.0

    B. 192.168.14.0, 255.255.255.0 192.168.14.255

    C. 255.255.255.0 192.168.14.255, 192.168.14.0

    D. 192.168.14.0, 192.168.14.255, 255.255.255.0

Standard Network Services

20. Which of the following services works to connect Linux to a Microsoft Windows–based network?

    A. NFS

    B. SMB

    C. DNS

    D. Windows for Workgroups

Basic Network Security

21. Which of the following commands are associated with a Red Hat Linux firewall configuration utility?

    A. lokwall

    B. lokkit

    C. firewall-config

    D. firewall-lokkit

LAB QUESTION

You have 18 computers on a LAN behind a firewall. Diagram your computers on a sheet of paper. Connect them together in a "star" configuration. Assign a private IP address to each computer. Take one computer and draw a second connection to the Internet.

SELF TEST ANSWERS

Basic Linux Knowledge

1. ☑ **B.** The vi editor is often the only editor available on a rescue floppy, unlike the Red Hat rescue CD.

☒ **A, C,** and **D** are incorrect because these tools are not available on rescue disks. Furthermore, if you use StarOffice or WordPerfect to edit a configuration file, you may forget to save it in text format, which would make it unreadable to Linux. Pine is just an e-mail manager, not suitable for editing text files.

2. ☑ **C.** The yy command copies the entire line associated with the current location of the cursor. You can then use the p command to insert that line into the file.

☒ **A** is incorrect, since the p command only takes data from the buffer. **B** is incorrect, since there is no c command. **D** is incorrect, since it places only one word into the buffer.

Linux Filesystem Hierarchy and Structure

3. ☑ **B.** The top-level directory, which is also known as the root directory, is represented by a single forward slash, /.

☒ **A** is incorrect, since the /root directory is actually the home directory of the root user. The root directory, / actually stands above /root. **C** and **D** are both incorrect, as they are also subdirectories of root, /.

4. ☑ **C.** The /etc directory contains most Linux configuration files.

☒ **A** is wrong, since /var is dedicated mostly to log files and printer spools. **B** is wrong because the tilde (~) represents the home directory of the current user. **D** is wrong because the /tmp directory is dedicated to temporary storage; the contents of this directory are periodically deleted.

5. ☑ **D.** Linux assigns /dev/hdb to the second IDE hard drive.

☒ **A** is wrong, since /dev/sda represents the first SCSI hard drive. **B** is wrong, since /dev/hda represents the first IDE hard drive. **C** is wrong, since /dev/sdb represents the second SCSI hard drive.

6. ☑ **A, B, C,** and **D.** You need to apply the fsck command to the partition where /home is mounted. But first, since you should not apply this command on a mounted directory, you need to unmount /home. And since fsck can be destructive to your data, you should back up the contents of /home as well. This is often not possible unless you're in single-user mode; it sometimes helps to use a rescue disk (which by default also starts Linux without mounting any directories, in single-user mode).

7. ☑ **D.** Current MS-DOS floppy disks arc usually formatted to VFAT, which supports long filenames.

☒ **A** is not correct, since you need to specify a file type with the -t switch. **B** and **C** are not correct, since ext2 and ext3 are unusable file types for a MS-DOS disk.

Basic Commands

8. ☑ **B.** When you're at the command line interface, the UP ARROW or the PAGE UP key allows you to scroll back through a history of previously executed commands.

☒ **A** is incorrect. This question is a bit tricky, as the history command does put previous commands on your screen. And you could pipe this command to less, which would allow you to scroll back through previous commands at your leisure. But strictly speaking, while the history command does scroll through previous commands, it does not scroll backward. **C** is incorrect, as the PAGE DOWN key scrolls down the history. **D** is incorrect, as it does not do anything in the history of previous commands.

9. ☑ **C.** When you run su and enter the root password, you take the role of the root user. Therefore, when you then run **cd ~**, you're moving to the root user's home directory, /root.

☒ **A** is incorrect, since pm is not the root user. **B** is incorrect, since /home does not correspond to any user's home directory. **D** is not correct, since the top-level root directory, /, is not any user's home directory.

10. ☑ **D.** While this level of piping isn't covered in this chapter, this should be a straightforward question if you're sufficiently familiar with basic command line tools. The who command returns every active login of every user. Piping the result returns just the lines associated with the logins of user mj. Piping that result to **wc -l** returns the actual number of lines.

☒ **A** is not correct, as the wc command needs a file or other input to read first. **B** is not correct, as it returns the lines associated with the logins of user mj. While you could count the number of lines, that does not address the requirements of the question. **C** is not correct, as it would return the number of times all users are logged into this system.

Printing

11. ☑ **B.** The **lpq -l** command checks print queues. If you get an error message from this command, you may need to install a printer first.

☒ **A** is incorrect, as lpr is a print command, and its -l switch tells lpr to expect a binary file. **C** is incorrect, as lprm is for removing print jobs. **D** is incorrect, as lpd is the line print daemon. While this must be running before you can check a print queue, lpd does not itself check print queues.

The Linux/Unix Shells

12. ☑ **D.** The variable is PATH. When you input $PATH, the value of that variable, in this case, the directories in your path, are substituted in this equation.

☒ **A** and **B** are not correct, since $PATH is not itself a variable. **C** is not correct, since /sbin is the wrong directory.

Basic Security

13. ☑ **D.** The effect of umask has changed. Even if you try to set it to allow execute permissions, Red Hat won't let you do this anymore. You'll need to set execute permissions on each file after creation.

☒ **A** is not correct, since the file is not necessarily a directory, and execute permissions are no longer set up by default. **B** is not correct, as this would correspond to a umask value of 0666 or 0777. **C** is not correct, as execute permissions are no longer set up by default.

14. ☑ **A.** The pwconv command converts any passwords in /etc/passwd to /etc/shadow, which is hidden from all but the root user. This is also part of the Shadow Password Suite.

☒ **B** and **D** are incorrect, since they convert user and group passwords from (not to) the Shadow Password Suite. **C** is not correct, since it converts group passwords, and no new group was created in this question.

Linux/Unix System Administration

15. ☑ **B.** The form **su -c** *command* prompts you for the root password. When the command is complete, the shell returns you to the prompt for the original user.

☒ **A** is incorrect because the **su rooter** command tries to log you in as the user named rooter. **C** is incorrect, as there is no superuser command. **D** is not correct, as there is no /sbin/su command.

16. ☑ **B.** There are subdirectories organized by runlevel in the /etc/rc.d directory, including rc0.d, rc1.d, rc2.d, rc3.d, rc4.d, rc5.d, and rc6.d.

☒ **A** is not correct. While the actual scripts are located in the /etc/rc.d/init.d directory, there are no clues here to the actual runlevels. **C** and **D** are incorrect, as there are no /rc.d or /etc/init.d directories, at least in the current version of Red Hat Linux.

17. ☑ **B.** This is based on the convention for the first five entries in a crontab line: minute, hour, day of month, month, and day of week.

☒ **A**, **C**, and **D** are incorrect, as they are readings of the cited crontab line that don't correspond to the convention.

18. ☑ B. While not covered in this chapter, the tar command is quite important to any Linux administrator. The czvf switches collect, compress, and verify the group of files under /home in a specific file. If you're not familiar with how tar switches work, study the references cited at the beginning of this chapter. It's important.

    ☒ A and D are not correct, as there is no tarball command. C is not correct, as this command extracts (x) files.

Basic TCP/IP Networking

19. ☑ B. By convention, a network with a 192.168.14.0 address with a 255.255.255.0 subnet mask uses a 192.168.14.255 broadcast address.

    ☒ A is not correct, as there cannot be a network that starts with a broadcast address. C is not correct, as there cannot be a network that starts with a subnet mask. D is not correct, as 255.255.255.0 is not a qualified broadcast address.

Standard Network Services

20. ☑ B. The Server Message Block (SMB) file system, also known as Samba, is the standard way to connect Linux as a member of a Microsoft Windows- or IBM OS/2-based network.

    ☒ A is not correct. While it is possible to set up "Services for Unix" on some Microsoft Windows computers, that would no longer be a Microsoft Windows-based network. C is not correct, since the Domain Name System has nothing to do with protocols necessary to connect operating systems. D is not correct, since Windows for Workgroups is not an available service in Linux.

Basic Network Security

21. ☑ B and C are both current Red Hat Linux firewall configuration utilities.

    ☒ A and D are not valid Red Hat Linux commands.

LAB ANSWER

There are many ways to configure the IP addresses on a LAN. But it is generally best to do it by setting up a network from one of the private IP address ranges. When you install networking, pay particular attention to the computer that also has a connection to the Internet. The IP address of its connection to your network will be the gateway address for every other computer on your LAN. It's also the logical location for any firewall that you may wish to configure.

2

Planning the Installation

O ne of the strong points of Red Hat Linux is its easy installation. There are several different methods of installation, and each is automated to a considerable degree. In many cases, it's now possible to just pop the first Red Hat installation CD in the drive and install Linux from there.

However, as you become a Linux expert, people are going to rely on you to install Linux in a variety of situations. You need to plan what you're going to do. You need to know the basic hardware available for a personal computer, as well as what hardware is compatible with Red Hat Linux. You'll also want to plan the organization of different Linux directories on individual hard drive partitions.

Remember, one-third of the RHCE exam is based on your ability to install Linux. The exam is based on computers utilizing the Intel-based architecture, which allows for an extensive variety of hardware. Most hardware works well with Linux. In many cases, you can make other hardware work with Linux, even if it was originally built for another operating system such as Microsoft Windows.

CERTIFICATION OBJECTIVE 2.01

Basic Hardware Knowledge

While customized Red Hat Linux distributions are available for such diverse platforms as SPARC, Itanium, and S/390, the focus of the RHCE exam is on computers built to the Intel-based architecture.

The architecture of a personal computer defines the components that it uses as well as the way that they are connected. In other words, the Intel-based architecture describes much more than just the CPU. It includes a number of specific standards for building and connecting other critical hardware components such as the hard drive, the network card, the keyboard, the graphics adapter, and more. All software, including Red Hat Linux, is written for a specific computer architecture.

Even when a manufacturer creates a device for the Intel platform, it may not work with Linux. Therefore, it's important to know some basic architecture of an Intel-based computer. This will be the last section that addresses the basic RHCE exam prerequisites like those covered in Chapter 1.

Intel Communications Channels

Three basic channels are used to communicate in an Intel architecture PC: interrupt request (IRQ) ports, input/output (I/O) addresses, and direct memory address (DMA) channels. An IRQ allows a component such as a keyboard or printer to request service from the CPU. An I/O address is a memory storage location for communication between the CPU and different parts of a computer. A DMA channel is used when a device such as a sound card has an independent processor and can bypass the CPU.

IRQ Settings

An *IRQ* is a signal that is sent by a peripheral device (such as a network card, graphics adapter, mouse, modem, or serial port) to the CPU to request processing time. Each device you attach to a computer may need its own IRQ port. Normally, each device needs a dedicated IRQ (except for USB and some PCI devices). The Intel architecture is currently limited to 16 IRQs (0–15), which is often not enough for a PC with multiple network adapters and hard drives, as well as a sound card, printer, game card, and more.

If you have built your own PC(s), you probably know that there are a number of "bare-bones" PCs available in many computer stores. Even on these bare-bones PCs, basic components such as a keyboard, timer, BIOS clock, and CPU occupy a number of IRQs, leaving perhaps IRQs 5, 7, 9, 10, 11, and 12 free. Then you may add a sound card on IRQ 5 and a printer on IRQ 7. And then each video card, serial mouse, modem (although traditionally, a serial mouse and modem use IRQs 3 and 4) and network card that you install needs its own IRQ—which leaves a total of 1 free. (Maybe!)

If you run out of IRQs, you may still be able to install another PCI device. Several PCI devices can share a single IRQ through the PCI bus, which manages the way each PCI device shares your IRQs. However, this requires BIOS support for PCI sharing, which you can enable through your computer's CMOS settings. Most PCs manufactured after 1994 contain PCI buses.

USB devices can help you conserve IRQs in the same way. The Universal Serial Bus (USB) host controller also regulates attached USB devices, including how they share IRQs. Most PCs manufactured after 2000 contain USB ports.

If you're having a problem with your USB ports, before you check anything in Linux, check your BIOS. Many BIOS menus include an option to turn USB connections on and off.

Planning the IRQ Layout: Standard IRQs

Now you should see that IRQs are a precious commodity on a PC. IRQ conflicts are common when you're connecting a lot of devices. If your printer doesn't work after you've connected a second network card, it can help to know the standard IRQ for printers. You can then assign a different IRQ to that network card. If you don't have any free IRQs to assign to that network card, you may be able to sacrifice a component that uses a standard IRQ. For example, if you always connect to a server remotely, that server PC may not need a keyboard. If you can boot a computer with a CD-ROM, you may not need a floppy drive.

Some IRQs are essential to the operation of a PC and just can't be changed. These are reserved by the motherboard to control devices such as the hard disk controller and the real-time clock. Do not use these interrupts for other devices, or there will be conflicts! Other IRQs are normally assigned to common devices such as a floppy disk and a printer. In Linux, you can check /proc/interrupts to see which interrupts are being used, and which are free for new devices. The reserved and typical IRQ assignments are shown in Table 2-1.

You can find a list of assigned IRQ channels in your /proc/interrupts file.

Input/Output Addresses

Every computer device requires an *input/output (I/O) address*. It's a place where data can wait in line for service from your CPU. I/O addresses are listed in hexadecimal notation (base 16), where the numbers are 0, 1, 2, 3, 4, 5, 6, 7, 8, 9, a, b, c, d, e, and f. Some typical I/O addresses include those for the basic serial ports, known in the Microsoft world as COM1, COM2, COM3, and COM4. These ports normally use the following I/O addresses: 03f8, 02f8, 03e8, and 02e8.

You can find a list of assigned I/O addresses in your /proc/ioports file.

Direct Memory Addresses

A *direct memory address (DMA)* is normally used to transfer information directly between devices, bypassing the CPU. Many components don't need a CPU. For example, many sound cards include their own processor. This allows your PC to set up a DMA channel between a hard drive and a sound card to process and play any music files that you may have stored.

TABLE 2-1	IRQ	Typical Assignments
Standard IRQ Assignments	0	System timer
	1	Keyboard
	2	Cascade for controller 2
	3	Serial ports 2, 4
	4	Serial ports 1, 3
	5	Parallel port 2 or sound card
	6	Floppy disk controller
	7	Parallel port 1
	8	Real-time clock
	9	Redirected to IRQ2
	10	Not assigned (commonly used for a network card)
	11	Not assigned
	12	PS/2 mouse, if installed
	13	Math coprocessor
	14	IDE hard disk controller 1
	15	IDE hard disk controller 2

While DMA channels bypass the CPU, devices that use DMA are still configured with IRQ ports. There are eight standard DMA channels (0–7); DMA 4 is reserved and cannot be used by any device.

You can find a list of assigned DMA addresses in your /proc/dma file.

RAM Requirements

You probably have no idea how much memory you absolutely need. The maximum amount of memory your system will use is the sum of all of the memory requirements of every program that you will ever run at once. That's hard to compute. Therefore, you should buy as much memory as you can afford. Extra RAM is usually cost effective when compared to the time you would spend trying to tune an underpowered system. Linux will comfortably run at the command line for a single user on 32MB of RAM; 64MB is better, while 128MB of RAM and above are magical!

If you're setting up Linux as a server, RAM requirements increase with the number of users who may need to log in simultaneously. The same may be true if you're running a large number of programs or have memory-intensive data such as that required by a database. If possible, install enough RAM to handle some growth in the number of users. Don't hold back because of the cost of RAM. While it's tempting to wait until the price of RAM goes down, the loss of productivity when you install additional RAM can easily exceed any money you might save.

The enterprise version of Linux kernel 2.2 can address up to 4GB of RAM with older Pentium II and equivalent systems. With kernel 2.4, Linux can address up to 64GB of RAM.

The total amount of addressable space for any one program to use is the sum of available RAM and swap space. In general, Linux utilities are usually small, except for something like a database service, which can load huge tables into memory and might possibly use all the available memory while doing so. The same goes for video productions and high-end graphics applications that create cartoons and mapping systems to name a few.

Hard Drive Options (IDE, EIDE, and SCSI)

Before your computer can load Linux, the BIOS has to recognize the active primary partition on the hard drive. This partition should include the Linux boot files. The BIOS can then set up and initialize that hard drive, and then load Linux boot files from that active primary partition.

After Linux has loaded, the settings for the disk subsystems can be modified or dealt with utilities such as fdisk or Disk Druid.

IDE and EIDE

IDE stands for Integrated Drive Electronics. It is built on the IBM PC ISA 16-bit bus standard, and was itself adopted as the Advanced Technology Attachment (ATA) standard in 1990. Unfortunately, the first ATA standard hard drives could access only 504MB of disk space at fairly slow speeds. The Enhanced IDE (EIDE) standard was created in 1994 for larger hard drives and faster access speeds. Support was also added for additional hard disks, direct memory access (DMA), and ATA Packet Interface (ATAPI) devices, such as CD-ROMs and tape drives.

The standard Intel architecture PC is configured to manage up to four IDE drives. If you need more, the typical procedure is to use SCSI devices.

SCSI

The Small Computer System Interface (SCSI), developed by Apple Computer, allows your computer to interface to disk drives, CD-ROMs, tape drives, printers, and scanners. SCSI is faster and more flexible than EIDE, with support for 7, 15, or even 31 devices, depending on the SCSI bus width. Data transfer speeds for SCSI range from 5 to 160 or 320 megabytes per second. SCSI controllers are not common on most modern-day desktop PCs, as SCSI drives are usually more expensive. The major PC vendors, however, will almost always provide SCSI drives and controllers for their high-end server products, as the larger number of hard drives and faster bus speeds make them a better choice.

If you want to use SCSI and IDE drives on the same computer, check your BIOS. Some PC BIOS can be configured to boot an operating system from a SCSI hard drive. Others may defer to the BIOS associated with a SCSI adapter. If that is not possible, you may need to install the Linux boot files on an IDE hard drive partition. Alternatively, you can boot Linux on a SCSI disk from a 1.44MB floppy drive.

CERTIFICATION OBJECTIVE 2.02

Hardware Compatibility

Now it's time to explore in detail the hardware that Red Hat Linux can handle. Unfortunately for Linux, hardware manufacturers are still targeting the Microsoft Windows market. While some manufacturers now include their own Linux hardware drivers, most Linux hardware support come from third parties. Fortunately, there is a vast community of Linux users, many of whom produce drivers for Linux and distribute them freely on the Internet. If a certain piece of hardware is popular, you can be certain that Linux support for that piece of hardware will pop up somewhere on the Internet and will be incorporated into various Linux distributions, including Red Hat Linux.

Be careful when purchasing a new computer to use with Linux. Though Linux has come a long way the last few years, and you should have little problem installing it on most modern PCs, you shouldn't assume Linux will run on *any* PC, especially if the PC in question is a laptop or some new, state-of-the-art machine. The latest and greatest existing technology may not be supported under Linux (not yet, anyway).

The hardware may also be targeted for specific operating systems and configurations. Laptops are often designed with proprietary configurations that work with Linux only after some reverse engineering. Other kinds of hardware, such as "winmodems" and "winprinters," are designed to use Microsoft Windows driver libraries. Integrated hardware (e.g., video chips that share system RAM) and parallel port devices can also be problematic. While there may be ways to make these types of hardware work, the process of actually making them work may cause more frustration than they're worth. Last year's model is an ideal choice; it is less expensive and more likely to be supported. When it comes to laptops, your chances are best with brand names.

Linux runs very well on lower-end computers. This is one of Linux's strong points over other operating systems, such as Microsoft's Windows XP. Linux runs fine on 32MB of RAM, although more is always better, especially if you want to run any graphical applications.

exam
ⓦatch

While it is important to know how to select and configure hardware components to get to a smoothly running Linux computer, the RHCE exam is not a hardware exam.

Linux Hardware Documentation

You are not left without help or resources when choosing the right hardware for Linux. You have many places to turn to for help, including mailing lists and newsgroups. Perhaps the best places to look are the Linux Documentation Project (LDP) or the Red Hat Hardware Compatibility List. The LDP is a global effort to produce reliable documentation for all aspects of the Linux operating system, including hardware compatibility. You can find the Linux Hardware HOWTO at the LDP Web site, www.tldp.org.

Linux Hardware HOWTO

The Linux Hardware HOWTO is a document listing most of the hardware components supported by Linux. It's updated irregularly with added hardware support, so it is a relatively up-to-date source of information. As of this writing, various LDP HOWTOs are supplied on the documentation CD-ROM in text format and in various languages, in the /HOWTOS directory. The official up-to-date list can be found at the LDP Web site.

The Red Hat Hardware List

The Red Hat Hardware List specifies name brand hardware that has been tested with Red Hat Linux. If you purchase an official Red Hat Installation, Red Hat will provide limited installation support for any certified or compatible hardware. Some hardware that has been tested by Red Hat has specifically been found not to work with Red Hat Linux and is therefore not supported. Red Hat hasn't tested all PC hardware; as a courtesy, they also include a list of hardware that others have tested with Red Hat Linux, as "Community Knowledge" hardware. These four categories of hardware are described in Table 2-2.

Like the LDP, the Red Hat Hardware List draws upon the efforts of volunteers. If you want to check if any of the "latest" hardware (such as USB) will run on your Linux system, it's probably best to consult the Red Hat support site first, then maybe LDP's Linux Hardware HOWTO. However, if you want the option of being able to contact Red Hat for support, you should stay within the "supported" list of the Red Hat Hardware List.

Check the documentation for your hardware. Find a component such as a modem or a network card. Cross-check this component against the Red Hat and LDP hardware compatibility lists (HCLs). Find the Red Hat lists by starting at http://www.redhat.com. Find their HCL in their support area. Find the LDP Hardware HOWTO by starting at http://www.tldp.org. Find this list in the LDP section on HOWTOs. Compare the results. While in most cases the results are identical, it's good to know how to search through both sources just in case.

As part of this process, find a component listed on one or both of these HCLs as incompatible with Linux. Do a search on your favorite search engine or the newsgroups based on the name and model of the product. Don't forget to include "linux" in your list of search terms. You might be pleasantly surprised. As of this writing, a searchable newsgroup database is available at groups.google.com.

TABLE 2-2	Status	Description
Red Hat Hardware Compatibility Categories	Certified	Approved by Red Hat, Inc., through the Red Hat Hardware Certification Program.
	Compatible	Reviewed by Red Hat, Inc., and known to be supported.
	Not Supported	Reviewed by Red Hat, Inc., and known not to work with Red Hat Linux.
	Community Knowledge	Untested by Red Hat, Inc.; others have reported some degree of compatibility with Red Hat Linux.

CPU and SMP Support

Red Hat Linux for Intel supports computers with Intel and compatible processors. It is "Itanium-ready," which means that it will be able to support this 64-bit Intel CPU when it is finally released.

Linux is commonly used as a server operating system. Many server applications can take advantage of the flexibility provided by multiple CPUs. This is known as symmetric multiprocessing (SMP) support. With the release of the 2.4 kernel back in 2001, Linux now supports computers with up to eight CPUs.

on the
() o b

Since the release of Linux kernel 2.4, there have been problems with SMP support. Older versions of this kernel don't support SMP with non-Intel processors. As of this writing, current versions may have problems keeping threads limited to one CPU. If you're running Linux on a SMP computer, keep up to date with the latest kernel developments at www.kernel.org.

Plug and Play

Plug and play (PnP) refers to the capability of an operating system to automatically allocate IRQ, I/O, and DMA ports or addresses to specific devices such as hard drives, sound cards, or modems. Linux's capability to work with plug and play devices is somewhat limited. For example, if you have the right network modules installed with the kernel, Linux may be able to automatically detect and install the drivers for a new network card in a PCMCIA slot. However, if you connect a printer to a standard printer port, you'll probably have to use the techniques discussed in Chapter 8 to install the appropriate print driver.

A plug and play system has three parts: the BIOS, the device, and the operating system. Unless all three work perfectly, problems can arise with plug and play. The BIOS has to allow the operating system to find the devices on your computer. Plug and play devices have to accept port and channel assignments from the operating system. And a plug and play operating system is constantly searching each connection for new hardware.

Computer users should not have to tell the computer a plug and play device is there. The operating system should be able to recognize the device and set it up automatically. Plug and play has been available for Macintosh computers for quite some time, and it has been incorporated with varying degrees of success into Microsoft's Windows operating systems. Linux is a little behind on this technology, though it is able to configure most ISA and PCI PnP devices. Red Hat developed the kudzu utility to look for and configure any hardware changes when you boot Linux.

Plug and Play Support in Linux

The unfortunate truth is that Linux doesn't handle plug and play as well as we may want. The main problem lies with plug and play support for devices that run on an ISA bus. ISA is a legacy technology from older IBM PCs, created without plug and play in mind, so support for it is very complicated.

The newer, faster bus technology, PCI, is a different story. As Linux loads, device drivers can easily find PCI devices. This makes plug and play much easier for hardware that runs on a PCI bus. However, conflicts may still arise with ISA devices. Support for PnP devices is improving, so the outlook is hopeful. Just keep in mind that you will probably have more trouble configuring an ISA device than a PCI one. Fortunately, newer PCs include a minimum of ISA devices.

Plug and Play Conflicts

The Linux plug and play subsystem may have problems with the newest computer devices, or some very old ones. If you're having problems with the newest computer equipment, various Web sites are dedicated to offering help. For example, www.linmodems.org can help you configure many so-called "winmodems," and www.linux-usb.org can help you configure the latest USB equipment on Linux.

Many hardware conflicts with relatively old equipment are fairly simple to eliminate. There are three possible areas of conflict:

- A physical hardware jumper is conflicting with another card.
- Your ISA plug and play cards are not properly configured.
- You are out of IRQs or other resources to add to your new device.

Physical hardware jumpers on a card need to be set to available IRQ, I/O, and DMA settings. You can use the /proc files to check the currently used IRQ ports, I/O addresses, and DMA channels. For example, to check the occupied IRQs, issue the following command:

```
# cat /proc/interrupts

          CPU0
   0:    86311180      XT-PIC    timer
   1:       25820      XT-PIC    keyboard
   2:           0      XT-PIC    cascade
   6:         507      XT-PIC    floppy
   7:           0      XT-PIC    soundblaster
```

```
  8:            2      XT-PIC   rtc
  9:       263584      XT-PIC   aic7xxx
 11:      4065120      XT-PIC   eth0
 12:       529582      XT-PIC   PS/2 Mouse
 13:            1      XT-PIC   fpu
 14:       352260      XT-PIC   ide0
NMI:            0
```

This is a list of devices that *are* loaded by the kernel. If there is a conflict, the device is not loaded. You can quickly scan over the left side to see what interrupts are available. In our example, IRQ 5 is not used. To get a list of used I/O addresses and DMA channels, issue the following commands:

```
# cat /proc/ioports

0000-001f : dma1
0020-003f : pic1
0040-005f : timer
0060-006f : keyboard
0070-007f : rtc
0080-008f : dma page reg
00a0-00bf : pic2
00c0-00df : dma2
00f0-00ff : fpu
01f0-01f7 : ide0
0220-022f : soundblaster
02f8-02ff : serial(auto)
0388-038b : Yamaha OPL3
03c0-03df : vga+
03f0-03f5 : floppy
03f6-03f6 : ide0
03f7-03f7 : floppy DIR
03f8-03ff : serial(auto)
f800-f8be : aic7xxx
fc90-fc97 : ide0
fcc0-fcff : eth0
```

For DMA resources:

```
# cat /proc/dma

1: SoundBlaster8
2: floppy
4: cascade
```

The kernel included with Red Hat Linux 8.0 and above should keep plug and play configuration problems to a minimum. When problems arise, two or more devices are probably trying to use the same IRQ, I/O, and/or DMA. In that case, one or both devices may not be loaded. It may take a little detective work to find the device; conflicts may prevent it from being listed in one of the associated /proc directory files. Then select one of the devices, and change its IRQ, I/O, and/or DMA to a free location.

This is usually a two-step process: first, change the settings on the card itself through physical jumpers or a diagnostic disk, as described in the next section. If Linux doesn't detect your changes, use the appropriate configuration utility, such as mouseconfig, sndconfig, modprobe, or ifconfig, to change the settings on your device.

on the **job**

Up to version 7.2, Red Hat Linux included an isapnptools package with utilities such as pnpdump and isapnp to help manually configure devices that did not work well with plug and play. Linux plug and play has advanced to the point where these tools are no longer available with the latest versions of Red Hat Linux. And when problems arise, dedicated configuration tools for a number of devices, including mice, sound cards, network adapters, and printers, can help.

Generally, Linux should not have problems with PCI plug and play cards. Linux should recognize them and set them up with appropriate IRQ ports, I/O addresses, and DMA channels. If you cannot see what your PCI cards are set to, you can type **cat /proc/pci**. If a PCI card that you're concerned about does not show up here, you may be out of IRQs. If you run out of IRQs, you may want to look into alternatives such as combo cards, which have two devices on one card, or Universal Serial Bus (USB) devices.

Manual Configuration

If you have problems with plug and play, you may be able to manually reconfigure one of the conflicting devices. Older devices include physical jumpers that allow you to set a specific IRQ port and/or I/O address. Newer cards have no jumpers; instead, the IRQ port and I/O address are stored in a ROM chip on the card. Many cards include a driver or diagnostic program on a 1.44MB floppy that allows you to change these settings. Alas, it is a Microsoft world, and these utilities usually need DOS to run. If you have a diagnostic disk with DOS files, you'll need a DOS boot disk or partition to be able to configure them.

If you don't have MS-DOS or Windows installed on your Linux computer, you have some possible alternatives. The DOSEMU project is an effort which can allow you to start a DOS style-command line interface. You can download the associated RPM from www.dosemu.org. The emulator known as WINE (www.winehq.com) can run some Windows programs with varying degrees of success. In addition, virtual machine applications such as VMWare and Win4Lin can also run various versions of Microsoft Windows.

APM and ACPI

Closely related to plug and play are the latest computer power management standards, known as Advanced Power Management (APM) and Advanced Configuration and Power Interface (ACPI). Both are efforts to manage PC power consumption. As such, they are important tools to extend the lifetime of battery-operated devices such as laptop computers.

Microsoft has driven developments in both areas toward computers that can be easily suspended and reactivated from a minimum power state. Linux, frankly, has been playing catch-up in both areas. Linux now works well with versions 1.0 and above of the APM standard. On a laptop, this allows you to use the "suspend" button to store the current state of your system, even a GUI, in hard disk memory. Linux support for APM is essentially complete; for example, it works fine on my older laptop computer, which was made in 1998.

As of this writing, Linux support for the ACPI standard is less than complete. If you have an ACPI system that needs full ACPI functionality, check the ACPI4Linux home page, which is currently available at phobos.fachschaften.tu-muenchen.de/acpi. Alternatively, you may be able to adjust a setting in your BIOS from ACPI to APM and still get the power management functionality that you need.

Advanced Power Management (APM) BIOS

The Advanced Power Management (APM) BIOS primarily monitors and controls the system battery. It is an optional service commonly used on older laptop computers. You can also configure it on other computers if you want to implement the BIOS standby and suspend modes that are available on newer PCs.

The daemon that governs APM is apmd. If the apmd daemon is running on your system, it sets up status data in the /proc/apm file:

```
# cat /proc/apm
1.9 1.2 0x07 0x01 0xff 0x80 -1% -1 ?
```

Unfortunately, this format is not very readable. But the **apm** command can help:

```
# apm
AC on-line, battery status high: 100% (2:31)
```

This command reads the information created by apmd in the /proc/apm file and prints it in a much easier-to-read format.

The apmd daemon can be configured to do a variety of different things depending on what BIOS reports back regarding the status of the battery. You can set apmd to log error messages to syslog when the battery life drops below a certain percentage level. You can also have it send a system-wide message to all logged-in users when this warning level is reached. All changes in battery information are logged via syslog. To set up options for apmd, you will need to edit the /etc/sysconfig/ampd file. Open it in your favorite text editor and then check for the following lines:

```
LOGPERCENTCHANGE=10
WARNPERCENT=5
ADDPARAMS="-W"
```

In this example, apmd is instructed to log changes to the syslog file with every 10 percent of battery loss. If the battery drops below 5 percent, apmd will send an alert to syslog. Also, all logged-in users will be notified that the system is about to die (-W).

The apm log is broken down into four parts:

- Percentage of discharge (percentage/minute). This will be a negative amount if the battery is charging.

- Time since total charge, or time since last login, depending on whether the battery is fully charged or not.

- Estimate of battery time left.

- Percentage of battery life left.

When the BIOS tells the apmd daemon about a pending suspend or a standby call, it immediately calls sync (and writes all cached file system information to disk immediately). It will then sleep for two seconds and tell the BIOS to continue.

EXERCISE 2-1

Checking apmd

In this exercise, if you have a common laptop with Linux installed, you can run the apm command with and without AC power. You want to observe the differences in your laptop apm settings in both states, using the apm command. Start with AC power connected to your laptop and a working battery installed. First check the status of your laptop with the following command:

```
$ apm
```

Now halt Linux. You can do this with the **halt** command. Turn off your laptop. Disconnect the power. Restart your computer and boot Linux. (While you could do this by pulling the plug on a laptop with a working charged battery, this procedure is not recommended.) Now check the status of your laptop again:

```
$ apm
```

Now you can halt Linux again, turn off your laptop, reconnect AC power, and restore the original configuration.

Serial, Parallel, USB, and IEEE 1394 Ports

You can install many devices externally to your computer. Generally, they fall into four different categories, depending on their attachment interface. Generally, a device attached to a serial port, such as a mouse or a modem, uses the device associated with that port. Devices attached to parallel, USB, or IEEE 1394 ports normally use their own device files.

In any of these cases, you may need to modify the kernel as discussed in Chapter 6 to enable support for your specific device.

While Linux normally recognizes basic devices attached to serial or USB ports, such as a mouse during installation, configuring other devices may take additional work.

Serial Ports

In many cases, configuring a device for a serial port is as simple as linking to the driver of the associated port. For example, if you have an external modem connected to the only serial port on your computer, the Linux plug and play subsystem may have already linked the device for that port with the device for your modem. Run the **ls -l /dev/modem** command. If it shows something like the following output, you know that Linux has already linked your modem driver with the second serial port:

```
lrwxrwxrwx  1 root   root   10 Apr 4 11:28 /dev/modem -> /dev/ttyS1
```

Otherwise, you can use the **ln** command to create a link to the appropriate port. If you have a serial mouse, you should find the same type of link from /dev/mouse.

Parallel Ports

Configuring devices attached to a parallel port can be more complex. For example, Linux doesn't normally recognize plug and play printers when attached to a parallel port. Further configuration is required with tools such as CUPS or printconf-gui.

If you're connecting an external hard drive to a parallel port, you'll want to install the paride module and the module associated with your device, whether it is a hard drive, a tape drive, or a CD-ROM. Similar steps are required for other parallel port devices. Detailed information on configuring parallel port devices is available from the Linux Parallel Port Web site at www.torque.net/linux-pp.html.

USB

Linux support for USB is growing with the evolution of the latest kernels. While the latest versions of Red Hat Linux supports USB hot-swapping, support for the higher-speed USB 2.0 standard is still in development, as are Linux drivers for many USB devices. For the latest information, see the Linux USB Web site at www.linux-usb.org. You may be able to download your driver and install it using the techniques discussed in Chapter 5.

IEEE 1394

The Institute of Electrical and Electronics Engineers (IEEE) has developed the IEEE 1394 specifications for very high speed data transfer applications, such as digital movies. Equipment designed to these standards is often known by its trade names: FireWire and iLink. The current status is similar to USB; in other words, some IEEE 1394 equipment works with Linux, and development continues. For the latest information, see the Linux IEEE 1394 Web site at linux1394.sourceforge.net/hcl.php.

PC Card (PCMCIA)

Linux has one package called "Card Services" that deals exclusively with PC cards. This package includes all the kernel modules you'll need to manage PCMCIA cards and a set of drivers for specific cards. The package also includes a daemon that handles hot-swapping for most PC cards.

While development of the Card Services package is ongoing, there is often a period where there is no support for the proprietary configurations especially common on laptops. For this reason, the latest laptop is often not a good choice for a Linux installation. However, support for Linux on most name brand laptops is now common even when the laptop is first released. In fact, several companies can configure name brand laptops with some Linux distribution.

Supported PCMCIA Controllers

Linux now supports almost all current PCMCIA controllers. If you have a problem with a specific PCMCIA card, focus on finding a driver for the card itself. A current list of supported PCMCIA controllers can be found on the Hardware HOWTO.

Supported Cards

The Card Services package comes bundled with a file named SUPPORTED.CARDS. Also, you can check the PCMCIA HOWTO or the Red Hat Hardware Compatibility List for supported cards. Alternatively, the Linux PCMCIA Information Page at http://pcmcia-cs.sourceforge.net may also help.

During your career as a computer professional, there will be times you'll be asked to research a specific product or technology. To get an idea of how hard or easy this can be, call a major computer retailer or manufacturer and inquire about their latest laptop. Ask them if it supports Linux. What kind of answer do you get? Ask them if they have any earlier models that will. Do you believe the answers you receive are reliable? Check out the company's Web page, if you can, and find out if they provide any information about the product on the Internet. Doing this kind of research can be very trying, with or without success. Before deciding what kind of hardware you want to install Linux on, you should have a good understanding of what will and will not work. Start early and build a good base of reliable references you can use to find out new computer information. Web sites, such as the Linux Documentation Project, as well as magazines like **Sys Admin Magazine, Linux Magazine,** *and* **Linux Journal,** *will help you stay informed.*

Preinstallation Preparation

Installing Linux on most Intel-based computers is pretty straightforward. In many cases, most installation proceeds without problems. But if you have a problem, you'll save yourself a lot of time and frustration by knowing exactly what hardware you have. You should be familiar with the following components of your system:

- **Drives**   Check to see if you are using SCSI or IDE drives. You should know the manufacturer, model number, and capacity of the drive. In addition, if it's a SCSI drive, make sure you know its SCSI ID number.

- **Hard drive controller**   Know the manufacturer and model number of the drive controller. If this data is hard to find, at least try to find the chipset of the controller. If it's an IDE controller, the documentation is associated with the computer motherboard. If it's a SCSI controller, see the documentation associated with that controller.

- **CD-ROM**   For most standard SCSI or IDE CD-ROMs, the standard drivers should work without problems. However, if you are using a CD-ROM with a proprietary interface (common with older models), you should know the manufacturer, as well as the model number of the drive and controller card. These CD-ROMs are often not plug and play and may require a specific IRQ port and I/O address.

- **Mouse**   You should know the type of mouse that you have—such as PS/2, serial, or USB. If your mouse uses a serial port, it helps if you know which port. For example, if you're converting a computer that's running Microsoft Windows, a serial mouse is associated with a serial port, typically COM1, COM2, COM3, or COM4. The corresponding Linux device files are /dev/ttyS0, /dev/ttyS1, /dev/ttyS2, and /dev/ttyS3. And the number of buttons on a mouse may not be obvious; if you have a two-button mouse with a scrolling wheel that you can click, you actually have a three-button mouse.

- **Graphics card**   If you will be running the Linux graphical user interface (GUI), also known as X or X11, you will need the manufacturer, the model number, the chipset, and the amount of video memory. If it's a fairly common graphics card and you can't find the chipset or memory, you should be able to select a generic or older version of the card from the X installation database.

- **Sound, video, and game adapters** If you want to set up sound on your system, you should know the manufacturer and model number of the sound card. If plug and play doesn't work for your sound card, you'll also need the default IRQ port, I/O address, and DMA channel(s). Especially on laptops, this information may be stored in your BIOS.

- **Network adapters** If you are going to network your Linux system, you should know the manufacturer and model number of the network adapter. If plug and play doesn't work for your network adapter, you should find its default IRQ port and I/O address. Plug and play frequently doesn't work for the second installed network adapter.

- **Monitor** If you will be running X, you will need the manufacturer, model number, available resolutions, and refresh frequencies of the monitor.

on the *job* *Be especially careful with older monitors or laptop displays. Exceeding the frequency refresh capabilities of such monitors could easily overload the display system. Replacing a laptop display is not a pleasant exercise!*

Not all hardware will work with Linux. After you've collected information about your system, you should consult the Red Hat Hardware Compatibility List (HCL) or LDP Hardware HOWTO to determine if your components are compatible with the current version of Red Hat Linux.

CERTIFICATION OBJECTIVE 2.03

Disk Partitions

A disk drive requires a partition table. The *partition* is a logical sequence of cylinders on the disk, while a *cylinder* represents all the sectors that can be read by all heads with one movement of the arm that contains all these heads. You can create up to 15 or 16 partitions on a SCSI, and an IDE hard drive, respectively.

Normally, you should create several partitions when preparing your hard drive to install Linux. This is a good idea for various reasons. First, Red Hat Linux is normally configured with at least two filesystems: a Linux native filesystem, and a Linux swap filesystem. Second, if you want to install Red Hat Linux and another operating system on the same computer, you will have to configure separate partitions for each operating system.

Naming Conventions

Linux has a simple naming standard for disk partitions: three letters followed by a number. The first letter identifies the type of drive (h is for IDE/EIDE, s is for SCSI). The second letter is d for disk, and the third letter represents the relative position of that disk, starting with "a." In other words, the first IDE drive is hda, followed by hdb, hdc, and hdd.

The number that follows is based on the relative position of the partition. There are primary, extended, and logical partitions. Primary partitions can contain the boot files for an operating system. IDE drives can also be configured with one extended partition, which can then contain up to 12 logical partitions.

You are limited to four primary partitions on each hard disk. But four partitions are often not enough. If you need more partitions on an IDE drive, substitute an extended partition for one primary partition. You can then configure logical partitions within that extended partition. IDE disks can have up to 16 total partitions (3 primary and 1 extended, containing up to 12 logical partitions), whereas SCSI disks are limited to 15 partitions. Unfortunately, the partition numbering system is not straightforward. If, for instance, you have one IDE disk and you create a single primary partition, it will be device hda1. If you then create an extended partition, it will be hda2. If you have two primary and one extended partition, the primary partitions will be named hda1 and hda2. The extended partition will be hda3.

You can't install files directly in an extended partition. You must first allocate some extended partition space to at least one logical partition. In all cases, the first logical partition on the first IDE drive is hda5. You can create logical partitions with names between hda5 and hda16 on the first IDE drive, or sda5 and sda15 on a SCSI drive.

In this configuration, if you then created another primary partition from some free space, the IDE drive would renumber the partitions in your BIOS. The numbers wouldn't match the Linux names such as hda2. The boot process would fail.

Each partition is associated with a Linux device file. At least this is straightforward; for example, the device filename associated with the first logical partition on the first IDE drive is /dev/hda5.

exam
ⓦatch

You should know the device name associated with each partition, as well as the starting names and numbers of any logical partitions created on any basic disk drive. Also remember that logical partitions on an IDE hard drive always start with number 5; on the first IDE hard drive on a PC, that is hda5.

EXERCISE 2-2

Partitioning Exercise

You may never have had to plan partitions on a basic Microsoft Windows desktop computer. On a real server, whether you're using Windows or Linux, you should preplan your disk usage and partitions very carefully. This is a preliminary exercise; be prepared to think more deeply about partitions in Chapters 3 and 5.

1. On a piece of paper, draw a rectangle to represent each hard drive on your computer.

2. Label them in order just as Linux would (e.g., Hard Drive 1: /dev/hda, Hard Drive 2: /dev/sda, Hard Drive 3: /dev/sdb).

3. Use this diagram to plan how you are going to partition each drive. While this is a preview of future chapters, you should already know that Linux is set up in multiple directories. Each of these directories can be set up in its own partition. Think about how much space you want to allocate to several major directories, such as /home, /var, /usr, /boot. Don't forget to allocate some area for a swap partition.

Using this method, you can organize your data, keeping system or users' files together, as well as strategically plan where to place your swap partition(s).

Stability and Security

The Linux native filesystem includes a number of directories, which are commonly divided among many hard drive partitions. One recommended configuration for a Linux server includes separate partitions for each of the following directories: /, /boot, /usr, /tmp, /var, and /home. Other partitions may be appropriate for corporate data, database services, and even the Web and FTP sites if they are expected to be large.

Partitioning the hard drive in this manner keeps system, application, and user files isolated from each other. This helps protect the disk space used by the Linux kernel and various applications. Files cannot grow across partitions. Therefore, an application such as a newsgroup server that uses huge amounts of disk space, can't crowd out space needed by the Linux kernel. Another advantage is that if a bad spot develops on the hard drive, the risk to your data is reduced, as is recovery time. Stability is improved.

Security, also, is improved. Multiple partitions give you the ability to set up certain directories as read-only filesystems. For example, if there is no reason for any user (including root) to write to the /usr directory, mounting that partition as read-only will help protect those files from tampering.

While there are many advantages to creating many disk partitions, it isn't always the best solution. When hard drive space is limited, the number of partitions should be kept to a minimum. For example, if you have a 2GB hard drive and want to install 1500MB during Red Hat Linux installation, you may not want to dedicate extra space to the /var directory. You need room for swap space, additional programs, and your own personal files on other directories.

As there is no easy way to resize Linux partitions, it's important to plan how much space you want to dedicate to each partition.

Basic Space Requirements

Linux is a very flexible operating system. While a full installation of Red Hat Linux requires several gigabytes of space, the Red Hat 1.44MB boot disk that you can create during installation is also a complete operating system. Depending on your needs, you can install Red Hat Linux comfortably, without the GUI, on any hard drive larger than 1GB.

In Chapter 3, you'll learn about the different ways you can allocate space on partitions to several different Linux directories.

on the **job**

There is a Linux distribution that fits on a 1.44MB floppy, which you can use to configure an older computer as a router. You don't even need a hard drive on that computer. For more information, read the Web site for the Linux Router Project at www.linuxrouter.org.

You should size your Linux partitions according to your needs and the function of the computer. For example, a mail server will require more space for the /var directory because the mail spool resides in /var/spool/mail. You may even want to create a separate partition just to accommodate /var/spool/mail. Red Hat also configures files associated with Web and FTP servers in the /var directory, which can require significant additional space. Generally, the /boot directory is fairly small, and the rest is split up depending on system use.

Example: File Server

If the Linux system you are installing is to be a file server, then your filesystem could look something like Table 2-3.

The /usr filesystem is large enough to include key services such as Samba and the Linux graphical user interface. Most of the disk space has been allocated to /var, for the log files and for FTP and Web services, to /home for individual user files, and to /home/shared for common files. Of course, this is only an example. The amount of disk space you allocate for file sharing will depend on factors such as the number of users and the type of files they work on.

Linux Swap Space

Linux uses the swap space configured on one or more hard drive partitions to store infrequently used programs and data. Swap space can extend the amount of effective RAM on your system. However, if you don't have enough actual RAM, Linux may use the swap space on your hard drive as virtual memory for currently running programs. Because hard drive access can be 100,000 times slower than RAM, this can cause significant performance problems.

But you can't just buy extra RAM and eliminate swap space. Linux moves infrequently used programs and data to swap space even if you have gigabytes of RAM.

Normally, Linux can use a maximum 4GB of swap space, in partitions no larger than 2GB. This 4GB can be spread over a maximum of eight partitions. The typical rule of thumb suggests that swap space should be two to three times the amount of RAM. However, at larger amounts of RAM, the amount of swap space that you need is debatable.

TABLE 2-3	Filesystem	Size (MB)	Mounted Directory
Example Partition Configuration for a Linux File Server	/dev/sda1	16	/boot
	/dev/sda2	400	/
	/dev/sda5	2000	/var
	/dev/sda6	300	/usr
	/dev/sda7	60	Swap space
	/dev/sda8	1000	/home
	/dev/sda9	3000	/home/shared

The way Red Hat assigns default swap space is based on the amount of RAM on your system, and the space available in your hard drive. For example, if you have 128MB of RAM and at least 6GB of free space on your hard drive, the default Server installation assigns approximately 256MB to a swap partition. If you have less free space on your hard drive, the amount of space assigned to the swap partition goes down.

In any case, you want to make the swap space you create as efficient as possible. Swap partitions near the front of a hard disk, thus on a primary partition, have faster access times. Swap partitions on different hard drives attached to separate disk controllers give Linux flexibility on where to send swap data. Linux can start a program through one hard drive controller, and move files to and from swap space on a separate hard drive controller simultaneously.

BIOS Limits

Some computers built before 1998 may have a BIOS that limits access to hard disks beyond the 1024th cylinder. Some older BIOSes report only 1024 cylinders on a hard drive no matter how many actual cylinders there are. Computers that are subject to this limit can't see partitions beyond this cylinder. In this case, you should configure the Linux /boot directory on its own partition. Make sure that partition is located within the first 1024 cylinders of the hard drive. Otherwise, the BIOS won't be able to find the partition with the Linux kernel.

exam
Watch

Problems due to hardware limitations are common and difficult to troubleshoot if you don't know about them. Familiarize yourself with as many hardware limitations as you can, including the 1024-cylinder limit inherent in some older PC models.

Cylinder/Head/Sector Geometry and Remapping

The size of a hard drive is determined by its geometry. The geometry includes the number of cylinders, heads, and sectors available on the hard disk. Together, these numbers make up an address on the hard disk. Normally, the geometry your BIOS will support is limited to 1024 cylinders, 256 heads, and 63 sectors. All modern-day disk drives use 512 bytes per sector. So the basic capacity of a hard disk is 1024 cylinders times 256 heads times 63 sectors times 512 bytes equals about 8GB (gigabytes) or 8000MB. If your hard disk is larger than 8GB and you have an old BIOS that reports this disk has just 1024 cylinders, your computer will not be able to address the entire hard disk. Most modern-day PCs bypass this problem by using logical block addressing (LBA) for your hard disks.

Since SCSI devices have their own BIOS, this limitation does not affect SCSI hard disks.

Logical Block Addressing (LBA)

Most PCs manufactured after 1998 have a built-in fix called *logical block addressing,* or *LBA*. A system that can report LBA will adjust the cylinder, head, and sector numbers such that the entire disk is available using these logical addresses.

EXERCISE 2-3

Your Computer's CMOS Settings

The menu associated with the start-up sequence on a PC is the BIOS. It is a menu with a number of configurable options. The settings you create through the BIOS are stored in an area of ROM memory known as CMOS. To configure a number of different computers for Linux, it's important to know the BIOS menu and the possible CMOS settings.

1. Reboot your computer.

2. Just after it starts, press the key required to get into the BIQS. This key is commonly the DELETE or F1 or F2 key on your keyboard. If you don't see a message listing which key to press, some trial and error may be required.

3. Browse though your BIOS menus. While BIOS menus vary by manufacturer and computer type, browsing is usually possible with the arrow keys on your keyboard.

4. Locate your hard drive information. This is usually accessible through the first BIOS menu that appears. Take note of the "translation mode" associated with your hard drive, such as CHS, Large, or LBA. If you have an older BIOS, you may not have a translation mode, and you may need to make sure the Linux /boot files are located within the first 504MB of the first hard drive on your system.

5. Locate the IRQ settings that your motherboard assigns to your serial and parallel ports, real-time clock, and hard disk controllers. Can you change any of these settings? (Be careful that you don't save your changes!)

6. Find out if your CMOS supports PCI sharing (for IRQs). If it does, is it turned on or off on your computer?

7. Make sure to select the option that allows you to exit without saving your changes, and then exit from your BIOS.

Multiple Controllers

It is possible and desirable to use more than one disk controller interface card at the same time on the same PC. This is a common method to increase throughput on your system by reducing your read/write bottlenecks to the only disk.

You can use both SCSI and EIDE controllers in the same machine, but you should be aware of a few snags. The BIOS may only have access to the first two EIDE hard drives. Also, SCSI disks may not be accessible if EIDE drives are installed. The BIOS might have a setting to allow you to boot from SCSI hard disks. Make sure you understand which drives the BIOS will be able to access, because if you install /boot on an inaccessible drive, the BIOS won't be able to find your Linux boot files.

Many servers are set up with SCSI and EIDE hard drives. If you have one SCSI and two EIDE hard drives, and your computer is set up to boot Linux from a SCSI disk, the BIOS assigns the number 0x80 to /dev/sda (the SCSI disk) and 0x81 to /dev/hda (the first EIDE drive). Linux, however, assigns 0x80 to /dev/hda, 0x81 to /dev/hdb (the second EIDE disk), and 0x82 to the SCSI disk. There is a disagreement between the BIOS and the boot loader. Your boot loader (GRUB or LILO) will not find the boot sector on /dev/sda and, therefore, will not be able to boot Linux. (See Chapter 4 for more information on configuring GRUB and LILO.)

Partitioning Utilities

Many disk-partitioning utilities are available for Linux—even utilities that do not run under Linux. The basic Linux partitioning utility is fdisk. During installation, Red Hat gives you access to Disk Druid. They all work toward the same end, but Red Hat recommends you use Disk Druid during the installation. It is safer than fdisk, and it has an easier-to-read graphical interface. But Disk Druid is not available after you finish installing Red Hat Linux.

CERTIFICATION SUMMARY

Before you start planning your Linux installation, you need a basic degree of knowledge of PC hardware, specifically the Intel-based architecture. A basic understanding of IRQ ports, I/O addresses, DMA channels, and hard drive systems can help you plan how Linux manages and connects every component in your PC.

But not all hardware is supported by Linux. You should now have enough information to find the hardware that fits your needs. Alternatively, you now know about the resources that help you determine what other hardware you need that also works with Linux. Planning your Linux installation makes it easier to handle a wide variety of hardware. You can imagine how frustrating it would be to begin the installation and then discover something wrong; for example, you have a winmodem or winprinter that isn't supported, or you have more devices than available IRQ ports. Being prepared will help lessen your grief.

There is no easy way to resize a Linux partition. This makes hard drive partition planning quite important. How you assign partitions to directories depends on the size of your hard drives, what you plan to install, and the demands on the system. Appropriately configured partitions can prevent overloads on key systems, allow for appropriate swap space, improve security on key files, and ensure that your BIOS can find the Linux /boot files.

✔ TWO-MINUTE DRILL

Here are some of the key points from the certification objectives in Chapter 2.

Basic Hardware Knowledge

❑ The focus of the RHCE exam is on computers built with an Intel-based architecture.

❑ The architecture of a personal computer describes standards for building and connecting critical components such as the hard drive, network card, keyboard, graphics adapter, and more.

❑ An Intel-architecture PC has three basic communications channels: IRQ ports, I/O addresses, and DMA channels.

❑ An IRQ is a signal sent by a peripheral device. The Intel architecture is limited to 16 IRQs.

❑ PCI and USB devices have internal controllers that allow multiple devices to share IRQs.

❑ Every computer device requires an I/O address for data that's waiting for service from your CPU.

❑ DMA channels bypass the CPU, which accommodates devices such as sound cards that have their own processor.

❑ Extra RAM is often cost effective when compared to the time you would spend trying to tune an underpowered system.

❑ The BIOS has to recognize the active primary partition on your hard drive(s) before your computer can load Linux.

❑ EIDE hard drives overcome the original 504MB disk space limits. Most computers allow up to four EIDE hard drives.

❑ SCSI drives can be faster, and SCSI allows support for 7, 15, or even 31 hard drives.

Hardware Compatibility

❑ Unfortunately for Linux, hardware manufacturers are still targeting the Microsoft Windows market.

❑ Linux has come a long way the last few years, and you should have little problem installing it on most modern PCs.

❑ You should still not assume Linux will run on any PC, especially if it is a laptop or a new, state-of-the-art machine.

❑ Winmodems and winprinters are examples of hardware that can be difficult to adapt for Linux because they are targeted for MS Windows.

❑ The best places to look for compatible hardware are the Hardware HOWTO of the Linux Documentation Project or the Red Hat Hardware Compatibility List.

❑ Linux provides SMP support for up to eight CPUs.

❑ Red Hat Linux has a very capable plug and play service that can configure most current hardware.

❑ Early PnP hardware conflicts are fairly simple to eliminate. Here are three possible areas of conflict:

  1. A physical hardware jumper conflicts with another card.

  2. Your ISA plug and play cards are not properly configured.

  3. You are out of IRQs or other resources.

❑ To resolve a conflict, you need to change the device. If the change isn't detected, you also need to change the configuration within Linux. Changing the device may involve physical jumpers or diagnostic programs. Changing Linux requires the use of specialized utilities such as mouseconfig or sndconfig.

❑ There are four basic categories of external devices: serial, parallel, USB, and IEEE 1394. You may need to modify the kernel to enable support for many external devices.

❑ Serial port devices are usually linked to specific device files. For example, /dev/modem is often linked directly to a specific serial device file.

❑ Parallel port device configuration can be more complex. For example, a separate configuration utility is required to recognize devices such as printers.

❏ While Linux supports USB and IEEE 1394, support for many specific USB and IEEE 1394 devices is still in the works.

❏ Linux supports PCMCIA cards, also known as PC Cards, through the Card Services package, which includes drivers for the PCMCIA adapter and individual cards.

❏ Installing on most Intel-based computers is pretty straightforward, but you'll save yourself much time and frustration by knowing exactly what hardware you have.

❏ You should know the make and model number for each of the following pieces of hardware, if possible: hard drive controllers, network adapters, graphics cards, and sound adapters.

❏ If possible, also find the resolution and horizontal and vertical refresh rates of your monitor.

❏ You might also need other information, such as the base I/O address and interrupt each piece of hardware uses.

❏ If you are using a CD-ROM with a proprietary interface (common with older models), you should know the manufacturer and model number of the drive, as well as those of the controller. Also, for proprietary interfaces, you should know what IRQ it uses.

Disk Partitions

❏ You can create up to 16 total partitions on an IDE drive, of which only 15 are usable. The extended partition is used to contain up to 12 logical partitions.

❏ You can create a total of 15 partitions for SCSI, with all 15 usable.

❏ Linux has a simple naming standard for disk partitions: three letters followed by a number. The first letter reflects the type of drive (h for IDE, s for SCSI). The second letter is d for drive. The third letter represents the relative position of the disk. The number that follows is based on the relative position of the partition on the disk.

❏ The first IDE drive would be hda and the next hdb, then hdc and hdd.

❏ One recommended configuration uses a separate partition for each of these directories: /, /usr, /tmp, /var, and /home.

❑ There should also be separate partitions for corporate data, for database services, and even for larger Web and FTP sites.

❑ Multiple partitions give you the ability to mount some filesystems as read-only. For example, mounting the partition for the /usr directory as read-only will help protect the files in that filesystem from being tampered with, even by root users.

❑ A mail service requires more space for the /var directory because the mail spool resides in /var/spool/mail. You may even want to create a separate partition just to accommodate /var/spool/mail.

❑ Currently, there is no easy way to resize Linux partitions. Therefore, careful consideration should be put into whether you want to partition your disk space and how to do it. This is changing as Red Hat incorporates Logical Volume Management, which is covered in Chapter 5.

❑ Generally, the size requirements of the root partition are relatively modest but grow with kernel development and documentation needs.

❑ Typically, swap space should be two to three times the amount of RAM. However, the amount of swap space you need is debatable when you have larger amounts of RAM.

❑ Linux can use a maximum 4GB of swap space, which can be spread over a maximum of eight partitions. No single swap partition can be larger than 2GB.

❑ You do *not* want your system to be using swap space consistently. You should add more RAM if the swap partition(s) are heavily used.

❑ Some computers built before 1998 may have a BIOS that limits access to hard disks beyond the 1024th cylinder. In this case, you should install /boot on a separate partition contained within these limits.

❑ With LBA addressing, the BIOS on current PCs can see beyond the 1024th cylinder.

❑ It is possible and desirable to use more than one disk controller interface card at the same time on the same PC. This is a common way to increase throughput on your system by reducing the read/write bottlenecks associated with single hard drives.

SELF TEST

The following questions will help you measure your understanding of the material presented in this chapter. Read all the choices carefully, as there may be more than one correct answer. Choose all correct answers for each question.

Basic Hardware Knowledge

1. Which of the following are basic communications channels that you need on a PC based on the Intel architecture?

   A. IRQ

   B. Direct memory access channel

   C. Input/Output address

   D. CPU

2. You've checked your /proc/interrupts file and find that you don't have any leftover IRQ ports. Nevertheless, you want to install another printer and network card. Which of the following actions would let you keep your current devices?

   A. You need to make some hard decisions on what devices you need to remove from your computer before installing anything new.

   B. Use the free PCI slots in your PC for new devices. The PCI system allows all PCI devices to share a single IRQ.

   C. Look through /proc/ioports and /proc/dma. Find free I/O addresses and DMA channels for your new devices. Then IRQ conflicts are not a problem.

   D. Just install the new devices. The Linux plug and play system can make sure that extra devices share the appropriate IRQ ports.

3. How much RAM can be addressed by Linux with kernel 2.4.x installed?

   A. 128MB

   B. 4GB

   C. 64GB

   D. 128GB

4. What problems might you come across when using systems that mix EIDE and SCSI technologies?

    A. You can't mix them together.

    B. IRQ conflicts may arise between the controllers for each device.

    C. The computer's BIOS may not be able to access SCSI devices.

    D. SCSI disks cannot use LBA translations like EIDE devices can.

Hardware Compatibility

5. You get a phone call from a frustrated user who just bought a new modem. The modem is a Lucent 56K winmodem, and the user is having trouble making it work in Linux. Which of the following is most likely the source of his trouble?

    A. An IRQ conflict is preventing Linux from using the modem.

    B. Winmodems are built for Windows operating systems, and in many cases cannot be configured for Linux.

    C. A DMA conflict is preventing Linux from using the modem.

    D. Linux does not support 56K modems.

6. Of the following hardware, which would be the easiest to install Red Hat Linux on?

    A. The latest Dell laptop

    B. An IBM PC XT

    C. A 486DX/100 IBM clone

    D. A PowerMac G4

7. When you look through the Red Hat Hardware Compatibility List, you find that a number of devices in your computer are listed as "community knowledge." What should you do about these devices before installing Linux?

    A. Replace those devices with hardware that you know is compatible.

    B. Examine the LDP Hardware HOWTO.

    C. Check the Web sites of the manufacturers of each community knowledge device.

    D. Look at the documentation for each device, and remove any winmodems from your PC.

8. You're planning a server installation of Red Hat Linux on your computer with eight CPUs from Advanced Micro Devices (AMD). These CPUs are perfectly Intel compatible. What possible problems should you be aware of?

A. Linux kernel 2.4 can handle only up to four CPUs.

B. Red Hat Linux cannot handle symmetric multiprocessing.

C. Older versions of Linux kernel 2.4 may not be able to handle AMD CPUs.

D. Linux kernel 2.4 does not handle SMP perfectly, so you should monitor the Linux kernel Web site for updates.

9. You installed a printer onto a Linux workstation. After changing the IRQ and the I/O address, you find that the sound card no longer works. What is the most likely problem?

A. The sound card was probably a plug and play device, so the printer now conflicts with either the newly assigned IRQ port or the I/O address.

B. There is an IRQ conflict between the printer and the sound card.

C. The sound card and printer are using the same device file in the /dev directory. You need to create a new link to use both devices.

D. None of the above.

10. How would you know if your serial mouse is properly attached to a serial port?

A. Run the **ls -l /dev/mouse** command. You should see a file link to the appropriate serial port.

B. Check the physical connection. If the connection is not solid, Linux may not be receiving signals from your mouse.

C. Run the **ls -l /dev/ttys0** command. You should see a file link to your serial mouse.

D. Run the mouseconfig utility and make sure you have a serial mouse.

11. What must be installed on laptops when peripheral cards are inserted into the PCMCIA/PC card slots?

A. Nothing special is required.

B. PC Card Services should be loaded automatically.

C. PCMCIA.o must be inserted into memory using insmod.

D. PC Card Services should load automatically, but not all devices and buses are probed properly.

12. What kind of information should you collect about your PC's video system if you want to install Linux with a graphical user interface?

A. Model and manufacturer of the graphics card

B. Horizontal and vertical refresh rates of the monitor

C. Video memory

D. Maximum monitor resolution

Disk Partitions

13. What is the maximum number of partitions you can create for EIDE and SCSI disks?

    A. There is no maximum.

    B. 16 for EIDE and 15 for SCSI.

    C. 64 for EIDE and 16 for SCSI.

    D. Linux only supports a total of 64 partitions of all disks together.

14. Which of the following would be the Linux device name for the fourth logical partition on the second IDE drive?

    A. hda4

    B. hda8

    C. hda5

    D. hda9

15. What can you store in an extended partition?

    A. The /boot directory

    B. Any directory

    C. Logical partitions

    D. Nothing

16. What are the advantages of dividing the Linux native filesystem among several partitions?

    A. It keeps system, application, and user files isolated from each other.

    B. It prevents files that may grow from using up disk space needed by other applications including the Linux kernel.

    C. It allows you to mount some key directories as read-only.

    D. It is an efficient way to set up a small hard drive.

17. What downside is there to extensive partitioning? Assume that you have a large hard drive.

    A. Slower disk access.

    B. There is no downside.

    C. Data fragmentation.

    D. The root partition might not be accessible when you boot Linux.

18. You attempt to install Linux on an old 80386 computer. You manage to scavenge an 800MB hard drive to use. However, when you boot the computer, it reports the hard drive to be only 504MB. Why?

    A. The BIOS can access only the first partition, which must be 504MB.

    B. The hard drive must have bad sectors.

    C. The BIOS only supports IDE, not EIDE.

    D. An 80386 CPU can only address 504MB of data.

19. What do you need to do in order to get past the 8GB barrier with an EIDE hard disk controller? Assume your PC was built after 1998.

    A. Add a SCSI controller.

    B. Purchase a hard disk manufactured after 1998.

    C. Set jumpers on the hard disks to support EIDE.

    D. Set the hard drive translation mode to LBA in the BIOS.

LAB QUESTION

Research the Linux compatibility of the major components in your computer. Use the components listed in the Preinstallation Preparation section as a checklist. Start with the Red Hat Hardware Compatibility List. Make a note of those devices that are listed as community knowledge and incompatible. Research these devices through LDP's Hardware HOWTO, as well as the appropriate manufacturer's Web sites.

SELF TEST ANSWERS

Basic Hardware Knowledge

1. ☑ **A, B, and C.** IRQ is short for interrupt request; interrupt request lines allow devices to request service from the CPU. A direct memory address, or DMA, channel lets a device with its own processor, such as a sound card, communicate with another device, such as a hard drive, while bypassing the CPU. All devices need I/O addresses to store information while waiting for access.

   ☒ **D** is incorrect because a CPU is not itself a communications channel in an Intel architecture PC.

2. ☑ **B.** The PCI system really does make sure that installed PCI devices share IRQ ports, as needed.

   ☒ **A** is incorrect because it is possible for PCI devices to share IRQ ports. In fact, USB devices can also share an IRQ port. **C** is incorrect because all devices need CPU service. **D** is incorrect because no plug and play system by itself can compensate for a lack of available IRQs.

3. ☑ **C.** Red Hat Linux, which includes Linux kernel 2.4, can address up to 64GB of RAM.

   ☒ **A, B,** and **D** are all incorrect.

4. ☑ **C.** Some computer BIOS can't access SCSI disks or SCSI BIOSes, which can cause problems when trying to boot Linux. Your BIOS might even assign different names to your hard disks, which means that it won't be able to find the disk with your Linux boot files.

   ☒ **B** might be true, but only if you installed incorrect hardware settings. **A** and **D** are incorrect because you *can* mix these technologies in the same machine, and SCSI disks *do* use LBA when needed.

Hardware Compatibility

5. ☑ **B.** Winmodems are generally not supported under Linux. They are hardware devices that are incomplete when it comes to hardware design. This is made up for by using Microsoft Windows driver libraries.

   ☒ **A** and **C** may be correct too, but those are issues separate from winmodems. And the Linux plug and play system is good enough that IRQ and DMA conflicts should not be that common. **D** is incorrect, as Linux does support 56K modems.

6. ☑ **A.** It is very likely the laptop will not have problems with the current version of Linux. While the latest hardware sometimes has problems, Dell is a brand name manufacturer that in fact has paid careful attention to using components that are compatible with Linux.

☒ **B** and **C** are both incorrect. You might be able to get the 486DX/100 and the XT to install, but it would not be worth it. Get a small floppy disk version of Linux instead (and you can make the computer a firewall or router!). Special versions of Linux configured for a 1.44MB floppy are available from www.linuxrouter.org. **D** is also incorrect (but debatable). While there were previous versions of Red Hat Linux that you could install on PowerPC-based computers such as the Macintosh, Red Hat has discontinued these efforts. Apple has designed its own Unix-style operating system for its latest models.

7. ☑ **B** and **C**. Red Hat Linux community knowledge hardware lists devices that have not been tested by Red Hat. But others in the Linux community have tested such hardware, and the results are often documented in the LDP's Hardware HOWTO. Many device manufacturers now include any special installation instructions that you may need to install their devices on Linux.
☒ **A** and **D** are both incorrect. Most devices are compatible with Linux. It would be a waste to remove hardware from your PC that Red Hat Linux would recognize without any problems. While winmodems are a special case, some winmodems can be made to work with Red Hat Linux.

8. ☑ **C** and **D**. Older versions of the Linux 2.4 kernel had some trouble with non-Intel CPUs. This condition does not apply to later versions of the Linux 2.4 kernel included with Red Hat Linux 8.0 and above.
☒ **A** and **B** are both incorrect. The Linux kernel 2.4 can handle up to eight CPUs through a process known as symmetrical multiprocessing (SMP).

9. ☑ **A** and **B**. The default IRQ for a parallel port (what the printer is using) is 5 or 7. You probably configured the printer to use the same settings as the sound card. Try running **cat /proc/interrupts** to see what IRQs are being used, then choose a free one to assign to the sound card.
☒ **D** and **C** are incorrect, as this is a hardware problem, not a filename problem in Linux.

10. ☑ **A**. As with modems, the /dev/mouse file is linked to the port used by your mouse.
☒ **B**, **C**, and **D** are incorrect. **B** is incorrect, since the question addresses device filenames in Linux; not any hardware issue. **C** is incorrect, since you don't know which serial port is attached to your mouse. **D** is incorrect, since you shouldn't have to reconfigure your mouse just to find the serial port to which it is attached.

11. ☑ **D**. With each release, the laptop PC Card Services both improve and degrade. More cards are supported, but many laptops use new proprietary PC Card technology that may not work.
☒ **A** and **B** may be correct if all goes well as with most brand name laptops. **C** is incorrect, as this is not a required file.

12. ☑ **A**, **B**, **C**, and **D**. Most Linux installation programs allow you specify the model and manufacturer of the graphics card. This information is correlated as part of the Linux installation database to provide information on other needed settings, including chipset and video memory.

You do want to make sure Linux does not exceed the horizontal or vertical refresh capabilities of the monitor, to minimize the risk of damage. The video memory allows you to verify what the Red Hat Linux installation program reads from your system. If you exceed the resolution capabilities of the monitor, the graphics may degrade.

   ☒   There are no incorrect answer choices.

Disk Partitions

13. ☑ **B**. 16 for EIDE and 15 for SCSI. Of course, you need to use extended (on EIDE) and logical partitions to reach these limits.

   ☒   No devices support 64 partitions, as suggested in **C**, and Linux has no partition limits for all disks, as proposed in **A** and **D**.

14. ☑ **B**. By definition, the first logical partition on the first IDE drive on a computer is hda5. Since logical partitions are then numbered in sequence, the fourth logical partition on this drive is hda8.

   ☒   The other answers do not match the defined partition naming criteria for the fourth logical partition.

15. ☑ **C**. While you can't store files or directories in an extended partition, it does serve as a container for logical partitions.

   ☒   Since you can't store files or directories in an extended partition, answers **A** and **B** are not correct. Since an extended partition is subdivided into logical partitions, data is stored in an extended partition. Thus, answer **D** is incorrect.

16. ☑ **A**, **B**, and **C**. Isolating key directories can prevent rapidly growing files from crowding out the space needed by essential programs and processes. In fact, this allows you to set up some key directories with files that rarely change as read-only, even to a root user.

   ☒   **D** is incorrect because if you divide Linux into many partitions on a small hard drive, you may end up with a lot of wasted space on one or more partitions. For example, it would not be helpful to have a /home directory partition that is so small that users can't store the files that they need in their home directories.

17. ☑ **B**. As long as your hard drive is fairly large, there is no downside. In fact, it is recommended that you separate specific file systems that are user-writable for security reasons and for ease of management.

   ☒   **C** is only partially correct, as less active partitions remain defragmented while the data partitions get heavily fragmented with time. **A**, too, is somewhat true, but with the many advancements in drive technology, disk access is probably not a major issue. **D** is incorrect as the root partition is found and mounted after the kernel has initialized.

18. ☑ **C.** The original IDE standard does not support hard disks larger than 504MB. The 80386 computer was most likely manufactured before support for large drives was added with EIDE.

☒ This is not a partition issue as indicated in **A**, nor does it involve bad sectors, as proposed by **B**, since the computer can see some of the drive. **D** is incorrect because the CPU does not by itself affect the maximum size of the hard drive.

19. ☑ **D.** EIDE controllers support hard disks larger than 504MB, but your computer's BIOS may not be able to access the entire drive unless LBA translation is used.

☒ A SCSI controller would not help with an EIDE drive (**A**), even the newest hard drives do not by themselves enable LBA translation (**B**), and changing the jumpers on the hard drive won't enable LBA translation either (**C**).

LAB ANSWER

1. Create a matrix based on the list shown in the Preinstallation Preparation section.

2. Include columns for the manufacturer, model number, and other key data that depends on the device.

3. Make a note of those devices that community knowledge suggests may be compatible, as well as those listed as incompatible.

4. Navigate to the LDP Web site at www.tldp.org. Find the Hardware HOWTO. Search this document for each of the devices noted in step 3.

5. For those devices not listed in the Hardware HOWTO, or are still listed as being incompatible, note the manufacturer, and find any Linux-related information on each manufacturer's Web site.

3

Installation

Installation is one of the three parts of the RHCE exam. To pass this part of the exam, you'll need to know a lot more than just the basic GUI installation process for a single computer! Once you've studied the installation chapters (2, 3, and 5), you'll be able to install Red Hat Linux in a number of ways: directly from the CD, using boot disks, managing special situations on laptop computers, accessing from networks, and using automated Kickstart-based tools.

While this chapter covers the "basics," the basics are important. You'll learn the nuances of different installation classes. Both fdisk and Disk Druid are useful tools for configuring your hard drives. Both GRUB and LILO are popular and flexible options as boot loaders. And if you're managing a LAN and don't want to spend all night inserting CDs and typing in commands at every computer, you need to learn how to install Red Hat Linux in various network configurations.

Many users download their version of Red Hat Linux directly from one of many FTP sites on the Internet. That is a common practice in a software world governed by the Linux General Public License. There are four basic installation routes that you can take—but they all use the same packages, and customization is possible in each case.

All you need to get started is sufficient unformatted free disk space. The easiest way to get this is by adding a new disk drive to your system. The mechanics of adding a drive and changing your CMOS settings (so your CD-ROM is a bootable device) are beyond the scope of this book, but neither operation is complicated. Once the new drive is installed and your system is configured to boot from the CD-ROM drive, just stick the first Red Hat Installation CD-ROM into the CD drive and reboot! Take the defaults for a Workstation installation and see what happens; it will probably just install, dual-boot automatically, and voilà! You are ready to play!

exam
⟨ⁿ⟩atch

As you prepare for the RHCE exam, remember to think in terms of what is practical. While it is important to know how to download and set up a Red Hat Installation CD, it wouldn't be practical for a group of students to all be downloading the Red Hat installation CDs during an actual exam.

CERTIFICATION OBJECTIVE 3.01

Selecting an Installation Option

Red Hat Linux includes its own installation program. The graphical version of this program is known as Anaconda. There are five basic directions you can take during the installation process: Personal Desktop, Workstation, Server, Custom, and Upgrade. This section will help you understand the implications of each of these choices, as illustrated in Figure 3-1.

exam
Watch

Time is usually of the essence on the RHCE exam. As text mode installation is the fastest way to install Red Hat Linux, all of the Figures in this chapter are based on that installation method.

The two most important options are Workstation and Server. Almost by definition, a Workstation installation is much simpler than a Server installation. Furthermore, Workstation installs are optimized for local user applications associated with the X Window system. While many Linux administrators don't even bother installing the X Window on a Linux server, expect to install the X Window for regular users.

FIGURE 3-1	

Red Hat installation options

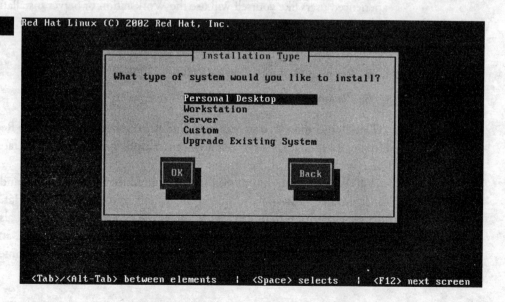

It's important for administrators to know how to configure the X Window on a Linux computer.

The server installation includes more network servers and management features. The default Red Hat Linux server includes several distinct partitions that make up the filesystem, including separate /usr, /home, and /var directories. By splitting out the /home directories to one partition, disk quotas can be maintained on just that filesystem, and backups and restores are more specific. With smaller filesystems, it is easier to recover from a disaster. In addition, it is easier to expand a smaller filesystem.

Depending on your needs, you can set up a system with anywhere from 500MB to 4.7GB of files. Of course, you have to have additional room for user files, log files, and any additional applications that you may want to install in the future.

The essence of each installation is in the installed packages. As you examine each of the options, focus on the installed packages.

Several partitions are associated with specific sizes. For example, the current default size for /boot is 100 MB. The actual size that you see in your installation will vary depending on the size and number of cylinders on your hard drive(s).

Personal Desktop

The Personal Desktop option includes packages for basic Linux users. Generally, more experienced users like yourself will use the Workstation or Server installation options. The following lists the minimum disk space requirements for a basic US Personal Desktop installation.

- Personal Desktop with GNOME or KDE: 1.8GB
- Personal Desktop with GNOME and KDE: 1.9GB

Please note, these figures may vary slightly from those shown in the Red Hat Linux documentation. They were taken from a sample installation of the latest Red Hat Linux beta available at the time of this writing.

This is just the minimum disk space required for Linux packages and other files. You'll also need a swap partition. In the default configuration, Red Hat Linux sets up a swap partition that is twice the size of the detected RAM. You'll also require more for actual data files such as documents, downloads, source files, and more. If you've set up additional partitions for separate directories such as /home, /usr, and /tmp, the space requirements will also increase.

If you are testing Linux for the first time, add at least several hundred megabytes of additional space; more if you plan to reconfigure your kernel. With other applications available during Red Hat Linux installation, you may need 4GB or more of disk space.

Behind the Scenes: The Partition Layout for Personal Desktop

The Personal Desktop installation option first deletes all Linux partitions. Other partitions, such as those created for Microsoft Windows filesystems such as VFAT and NTFS, are untouched. The deleted Linux partitions are added to the free space on your hard drive. Then the default Workstation installation configures the following three partitions in that free space:

- A swap partition twice the size of your RAM. (This may change if the amount of RAM is large or the size of your hard drive is small.)
- A 100MB /boot partition.
- A variable-sized partition for the root directory, configured to consume all remaining free space.

As of Red Hat 8.0, there is no longer a separate installation option for laptop computers.

Dual-Boot with Previous OS

Any previous operating system that existed on the machine is left intact. This provides several advantages. It is appropriate on a test or development computer where you need both operating systems. Alternatively, if you're making the transition to Linux, you may still need the old operating system for a few files and applications.

Please note, the figures for required hard disk space may vary from those shown in the Red Hat Linux documentation. They were taken from a sample installation of the latest Red Hat Linux beta available at the time of this writing.

Workstation

The following lists the minimum recommended disk space requirements for a basic workstation installation.

- Workstation with GNOME or KDE: 2.1GB
- Workstation with GNOME and KDE: 2.3GB

This is just the minimum disk space required for Linux packages and other files. You'll also need a swap partition. In the default configuration, Red Hat Linux sets up a swap partition that is twice the size of the detected RAM. You'll also require more for actual data files such as documents, downloads, source files, and more. If you are testing Linux for the first time, add at least several hundred megabytes of additional space; more if you plan to reconfigure your kernel.

Behind the Scenes: The Partition Layout for Workstation

The Workstation installation option first deletes all Linux partitions. Other partitions, such as those created for Microsoft Windows filesystems such as VFAT and NTFS, are untouched. The deleted Linux partitions are added to the free space on your hard drive. Then the default Workstation installation configures the following three partitions in that free space:

- A swap partition twice the size of your RAM. (This may change if the amount of RAM is large or the size of your hard drive is small.)
- A 100MB /boot partition
- A variable-sized partition for the root directory, configured to consume all remaining free space

*The Apache Web Server package is **not installed** with a Workstation installation. You can add the required packages at any time using the rpm utility.*

Dual-Boot with Previous OS

Any previous operating system that existed on the machine is left intact. This provides several advantages. It is appropriate on a test or development computer where you need both operating systems. Alternatively, if you're making the transition to Linux, you may still need the old operating system for a few files and applications.

Workstation Option Packages Installed

The list of file packages installed by a default Workstation installation is listed on the CD-ROM in /RedHat/base/comps.xml. This list contains references, either directly or indirectly through the use of group names, to the hundreds of packages installed. Each package contains at least one file, and sometimes dozens or more.

```
<group>
  <id>workstation-common</id>
  <uservisible>false</uservisible>
  <name>Workstation Common</name>
  <grouplist>
    <groupreq>base</groupreq>
    <groupreq>base-x</groupreq>
    <groupreq>admin-tools</groupreq>
    <groupreq>editors</groupreq>
    <groupreq>sound-and-video</groupreq>
    <groupreq>dialup</groupreq>
    <groupreq>office</groupreq>
    <groupreq>graphical-internet</groupreq>
    <groupreq>text-internet</groupreq>
    <groupreq>authoring-and-publishing</groupreq>
    <groupreq>printing</groupreq>
    <groupreq>graphics</groupreq>
    <groupreq>games</groupreq>
  </grouplist>
</group>
```

Notice that the workstation contains 13 groups (referenced by the <groupreq> container preceding the group name) of software packages. You can use this syntax to customize the installation process, if you use the automated Kickstart system discussed in Chapter 5.

Server

The server option includes a default group of packages that allow you to manage this computer as a Linux Server. Before starting a server installation, move any data that you might need from this computer. The server installation removes all partitions on all disks.

This installation option removes all partitions on all disks.

Server Partitions

The default Red Hat Linux 8.0 server installation includes packages that require at least 735MB of total disk space. However, since these packages are installed in different partitions, considerable additional hard disk space is required. The default installation sets up seven different partitions: three primary, one extended, and three logical partitions, as shown in Table 3-1.

TABLE 3-1	Partition	Default Size
Default Red Hat Server Installation Partitions	/	500MB
	/boot	100MB
	/home	Depends on available hard disk space
	/usr	Depends on available hard disk space
	/var	Depends on available hard disk space
	Swap	Twice available RAM
	Extended	Depends on available hard disk space

The Custom Installation Option

The Custom Installation option provides the most flexibility for an experienced Linux or Unix administrator. This option allows you to select all of the package groups that you need. If you know exactly what you want, you can even select from a list of individual RPM packages.

Selecting Package Groups

The custom installation process allows you to select as many of the package groups as you need. Each group encompasses a list of RPM packages. As explained in Chapter 4,

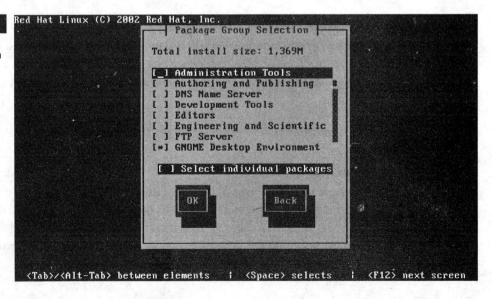

FIGURE 3-2

Red Hat Custom Installation Packages, first screen

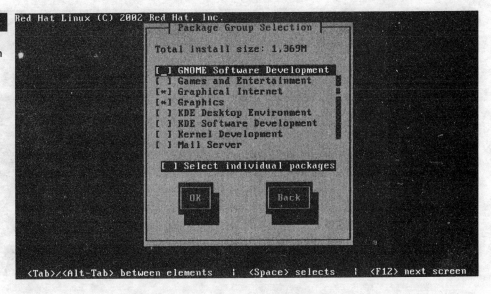

FIGURE 3-3

Red Hat Custom
Installation
Packages,
second screen

some RPMs such as certain kernel libraries won't work unless the appropriate C language
compiler is installed. These are known as dependencies. The Red Hat installation
program includes routines to make sure that all dependencies are satisfied.

Figures 3-2 through 3-5 show the various package groups available, based on the
Custom installation option. It is straightforward. Selected packages include a checkmark
in the box to the left of the package group name.

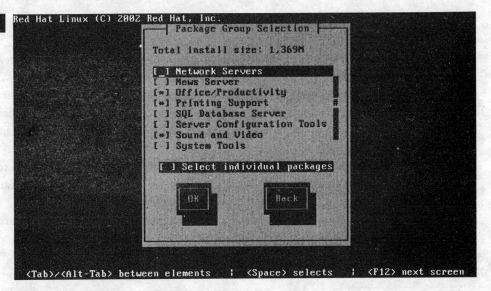

FIGURE 3-4

Red Hat Custom
Installation
Packages,
third screen

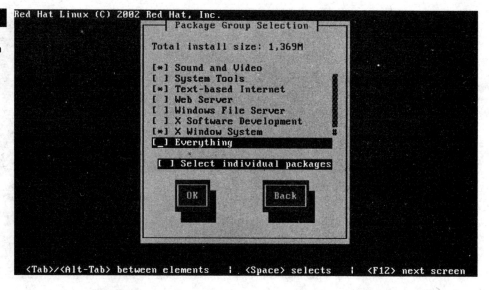

FIGURE 3-5

Red Hat Custom
Installation
Packages,
fourth screen

It's important to pick only the package groups you need. Fewer installed packages means more room for personal files for you and your users, as well as the log files you need to monitor your system and actually get some use from your applications. See the next section for more information on each package.

on the
j o b

Understanding how these package groups work is important in a kickstart installation, which is described in more detail in Chapter 5.

Packages

This section includes the briefest possible overview of each of the packages you can select when you use the Custom installation option in Red Hat Linux. While the details will vary as Red Hat Linux evolves, the spirit of what is installed by these packages is relatively constant. Remember, some of these packages depend on others; for example, if you want to install Dialup Support, Red Hat will make sure that you install Network Support as well.

For complete details of the RPMs associated with each package, go to the first Red Hat Linux installation CD, and read the comps.xml file in the /RedHat/base directory in the text editor or Web browser of your choice.

These packages are based on the latest beta version of Red Hat Linux 8.0 available as of this writing, and are therefore subject to change.

You can modify the comps.xml file to group packages in any way you desire. Since the Red Hat installer, Anaconda, reads from the /RedHat/base/comps.xml file on the installation directory, it will read any package group that you choose to add to this file. You'll see the result on one of the screens shown in Figures 3-2, 3-3, 3-4, or 3-5.

Administration Tools

Red Hat is developing a series of graphical administration tools for Linux, such as redhat-config-date and redhat-config-users. There are other Red Hat graphical administration tools available as part of the Server Configuration Tools package group.

Authoring and Publishing

The Authoring and Publishing group includes support for several documentation systems, such as DocBook and TeX.

DNS Name Server

The DNS Name Server group includes the tools you need to configure and maintain a Domain Name System server on the local Linux computer. In the Linux world, a DNS server is also known as a nameserver, based on the Berkeley Internet Name Domain (bind).

Development Tools

This group includes a large number of development tools. Additional development tools are included when you install other packages such as GNOME Development, Graphics, Web Server, News Server, and more.

Editors

These include the basic text editors associated with Linux, including vi, emacs, and joe. While it's essential that you know vi to use the Linux rescue mode, the emacs text editor may be the most popular text editor in the world of Linux and Unix. It also requires an extensive series of packages, which makes it impossible to include emacs on a rescue floppy that is limited to 1.44MB.

Engineering and Scientific

Red Hat Linux includes a group of packages for mathematical and scientific purposes, such as gnuplot, pvm and units.

FTP Server

This includes two of the more important FTP servers: anonftp and vsftpd.

GNOME Desktop Environment

The GNOME group includes the basic packages required to install the GNOME Network Object Model Environment. While GNOME is the default GUI for Red Hat Linux, the desktop manager that you configure does not matter for the exam.

GNOME Software Development

The GNOME group includes the basic packages required to develop additional GTK+ and GNOME GUI applications.

Games and Entertainment

Be careful with this package group. Do you really want to install games on a business computing system? Some believe that computer games are useful to help newer users to become comfortable with Linux.

Graphical Internet

Linux now includes a number of different GUI clients for Internet access, from the mozilla Web browser, the xchat and gaim instant message utilities, and the evolution and kmail e-mail readers. Closely related to the Text-based Internet package group.

Graphics

This package group automatically incorporates the X Window package, and a number of graphical applications. This includes the most prominent Linux graphics application, The GIMP. Depending on whether you also install GNOME and/or KDE, this also installs graphical packages associated with each of these GUIs.

KDE

The KDE group includes the basic packages required to install the K Desktop Environment, which is the main alternative GUI for Red Hat Linux. It is the default GUI for a number of other Linux distributions.

KDE Software Development

The GNOME group includes the basic packages required to develop additional QT and KDE GUI applications.

Kernel Development

This group includes the very large Kernel source packages, which currently require around 400MB of disk space. It also requires the installation of the Software Development package.

Mail Server

This group includes the packages required to configure a sendmail based IMAP or a postfix mail server.

Network Servers

This package group includes a number of smaller servers that are useful for running a network, including DHCP, telnet, and rsh. It does not include larger network daemons such as Apache, news, FTP, or DNS.

News Server

This is a simple group, incorporating the inn (Internet Network News) server.

Office/Productivity

This group includes two of the major Linux office suites, KOffice and openoffice, as well as related packages such as pdf viewers. It is very large at around 300MB. If you don't need these tools on your Linux computer, you should consider leaving this out of the installation.

Time is of the essence on the RHCE exam. If you choose not to install large package groups such as the Office/Productivity package group, you may save some time on the Server Installation and Network Services Setup exam.

Printing Support

Red Hat Linux currently includes support for two different print systems. The LPRng system, short for Line PRinter, next generation, is based on the original lpr daemon developed for Unix. Red Hat manages lpr-based printers well. Red Hat includes a printer configuration utility, printconf-gui, which can automate the configuration of the otherwise difficult /etc/printcap configuration file.

While Red Hat Linux also includes support for CUPS, this system is not included in the Red Hat Linux 8.0 Printing Support package group. As of this writing, you'll need to install CUPS packages separately. CUPS is the Common Unix Printing System which supports the next-generation printing protocol, known as IPP. Once installed, it can help detect network printers, with a Web-based interface.

As of this writing, LPRng is the default for Red Hat Linux 8.0; it is reasonable to expect the RHCE 8.0 exam to focus on this print system. However, Red Hat is in the process of moving to CUPS. Expect later RHCE exams to cover this other print system. For the latest information, see the latest Red Hat exam prep guide at www.redhat.com.

SQL Database Server

The structured query language (SQL) is one of the basic database languages. This group includes support for the PostgreSQL and mysql database systems.

Server Configuration Tools

Red Hat is developing a series of server configuration tools for Linux, such as redhat-config-bind and redhat-config-samba. There are other Red Hat graphical administration tools available as part of the Administration Tools package group.

Sound and Video

Not surprisingly, the Sound and Video group installs the packages required to allow you to use sound cards and interconnect the basic components of your sound and video system: sound card, speakers, microphone, and CD/DVD drive.

System Tools

This package group includes a varied array of tools, from the Samba client to the ethereal network traffic reader and the gnome-lokkit front end to the lokkit firewall configurator.

Text-based Internet

Linux includes a number of different text-based clients for Internet access, from the lynx Web browser, the ncftp FTP client, and the pine and mutt e-mail readers. These are closely related to the Graphical Internet package group.

Web Server

The Web Server group installs Apache, Squid, and the extensive array of supporting modules and configuration files.

Windows File Server

This is not a very complex group; it includes the Samba packages required to set up Linux as a client and as a server on a Windows-based network.

X Software Development

The X Software Development group includes the basic packages such as XFree86-devel required to develop additional GUI applications.

X Window System

This package group includes a number of basic Linux GUI fonts, libraries, and critical tools such as redhat-config-xfree86.

Xconfigurator has been replaced by redhat-config-xfree86.

Upgrade Installation

The final option for installing the latest version of Red Hat Linux is to upgrade, which allows you to upgrade packages from a previous version of Red Hat Linux. It does not change any current partition. It does allow you to change the boot loader from LILO to GRUB or vice-versa. And once your current packages are identified, you can choose to upgrade those packages or more.

When you're planning an upgrade of any version of Red Hat Linux on several computers, try the upgrade on a test computer first. If you have a working service that you don't want to change yet, such as Apache, you can exclude those packages from the upgrade. If you're ready to upgrade, remember to back up your system first, or at least the configuration files that you used, so that you can go back if something goes wrong.

Baseline Packages

Every installation of Red Hat Linux gets a series of packages, organized into the Core and Base package groups. You can find a list of these on the first Red Hat Installation CD-ROM in /RedHat/base/comps.xml, at the top of this text file. Figure 3-6 shows the first few base packages from this file.

FIGURE 3-6

Red Hat Linux
base packages

```xml
<group>
  <id>core</id>
  <name>Core</name>
  <default>true</default>
  <description>Smallest possible installation</description>
  <uservisible>false</uservisible>
  <packagelist>
    <packagereq type="mandatory">ash</packagereq>
    <packagereq type="mandatory">basesystem</packagereq>
    <packagereq type="mandatory">bash</packagereq>
    <packagereq type="mandatory">bdflush</packagereq>
    <packagereq type="mandatory">cpio</packagereq>
    <packagereq type="mandatory">e2fsprogs</packagereq>
    <packagereq type="mandatory">ed</packagereq>
    <packagereq type="mandatory">file</packagereq>
    <packagereq type="mandatory">filesystem</packagereq>
    <packagereq type="mandatory">glibc</packagereq>
    <packagereq type="mandatory">grub</packagereq>
    <packagereq type="mandatory">hdparm</packagereq>
    <packagereq type="mandatory">hotplug</packagereq>
    <packagereq type="mandatory">initscripts</packagereq>
    <packagereq type="mandatory">iproute</packagereq>
    <packagereq type="mandatory">iputils</packagereq>
    <packagereq type="mandatory">kbd</packagereq>
    <packagereq type="mandatory">kernel</packagereq>
    <packagereq type="mandatory">ksymoops</packagereq>
    <packagereq type="mandatory">libtermcap</packagereq>
    <packagereq type="mandatory">losetup</packagereq>
    <packagereq type="mandatory">passwd</packagereq>
```

CERTIFICATION OBJECTIVE 3.02

Required Disk Space

Most new computers come with very large disks, easily supporting even the nearly 5GB of files associated with a full installation of Red Hat Linux. If you do not have this much space available, you should carefully consider the space requirements associated with each type of installation. When considering the following options, remember to leave adequate room for swap space, personal files, log files, and any applications that you may want to install after Red Hat Linux installation is complete.

It's common to install Linux on older computers with limited hard disk space. Linux functions quite well on older computers. It's common to configure such computers as servers for DNS, DHCP, NIS, and more.

Workstation- and Personal Desktop Space Requirements

A Workstation-class installation, with GNOME or KDE (and swap space), normally takes over 2GB free space, before you add other files. You can add additional packages during the Red Hat workstation-class installation process. Personal Desktop-class installation requirements are nearly identical.

Server-Class Space Requirements

The space requirements of a server-class installation can vary. By default, Red Hat Linux installs less than 1GB of files in this type of installation. But the default Red Hat server partition scheme sets up seven different partitions in this type of installation, which requires nearly 4GB of disk space. Obviously, you can't install everything, which requires enough space for 4.7GB of files.

You can add additional packages during the Red Hat server-class installation process, installing up to 4.7GB of files within the default partition setup.

Custom-Class Space Requirements

A custom-class installation requires around 500MB for a minimal installation and over 4.7GB of free space if every package is selected.

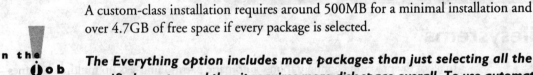

The Everything option includes more packages than just selecting all the specified groups, and thus it requires more disk space overall. To use automatic partitioning, you must have enough free disk space available. If you do not have enough free disk space, the automatic partitioning option will not work, and you will be required to partition the disk.

How Much More Space Is Needed?

The question of disk space needed over and above operating system needs is always relevant. You will require as much as it takes, and probably more. The absolute minimum for a Red Hat Linux OS is around 500MB of disk space, if you install Linux with few server services and without X. With 800MB, you could probably sneak in X, but you still wouldn't have enough room for a few server services and games. You still should have at least 100MB or more to work with. And if you want GNOME or KDE, you'll need another 200MB or so.

For a Workstation installation, 2GB+ of disk space is merely a starting point; you'll likely need lots of additional space for user data. Fortunately, it is relatively easy to add additional physical hard disks to Linux. You can then use tools like fdisk and LVM as discussed here and Chapter 5 to expand your filesystem.

Then, if you are new to Linux, select either Workstation for a single dedicated user or the Server option for Web, FTP, File and Print, DNS, and NFS services. If you have some Linux or Unix experience, you will probably want to use the Custom installation option for additional flexibility.

You'll also need to remember swap space requirements. By default, Red Hat usually configures a swap partition that is about twice the amount of RAM on your computer. The actual amount of swap space that you may need is a highly debatable issue. Some suggest that Linux computers can use a swap partition that is up to three or even four times the amount of available RAM. Others suggest that at higher levels of RAM, 100MB of swap space is more than sufficient.

on the **Job**

Remember, the true cost of disk space is the cost of the disk space itself plus the cost of the backup media and associated backup hardware!

CERTIFICATION OBJECTIVE 3.03

Filesystems

In all of the preceding configurations, automatic partitioning sets up multiple volumes— separate volumes on each directory. The advantage of separate partitions for certain directories is that it limits the risks to your system. For example, many Webmasters configure their Web sites to write daily log files with data relating to all users who visit their sites. These files can become quite large, especially for large online merchants.

Before you decide how to set up partitions, you need to know about each of the major Linux directories. Linux directories are organized according to something known as the Filesystem Hierarchy Standard (FHS).

Filesystem Hierarchy Standard

The FHS is a standard for organizing directories for Linux- and Unix-based systems. Every FHS-compliant operating system starts with a top directory, root, symbolized by the forward slash. All other directories are subdirectories of root. The major FHS directories are shown in Table 3-2.

TABLE 3-2	Directory	Description
Filesystem Hierarchy Standard Directories	/	The root directory. Other directories are below root in the FHS hierarchy. Unless mounted separately, the contents of other directories are in the root directory partition.
	/bin	Essential command line commands. Do not mount this directory on a separate volume, or else you may not be able to find these commands when you use a rescue disk.
	/boot	Linux startup programs. Normally includes the Linux kernel. Separate /boot partitions are common; the default size is currently 100MB.
	/dev	Linux device drivers. Do not mount this directory on a separate partition.
	/etc	Basic configuration files.
	/home	User home directories (except the root user).
	/lib	Program libraries. Do not mount this directory on a separate partition.
	/mnt	Mount point for removable media (floppy disks, CD drives).
	/opt	For applications, such as StarOffice or VMWare.
	/proc	Running kernel processes.
	/root	Home directory for the root user. Do not mount this directory separately.
	/sbin	System administration commands. Do not mount this directory separately.
	/tmp	Temporary file default directory.
	/usr	Small programs.
	/var	Log files, print spools, other variable-sized data.

Why Separate Filesystems?

Unix was developed when disk space was scarce. As Unix was an operating system for larger companies and universities, administrators could get multiple disks for each Unix computer. They took advantage of the space by splitting up the filesystem into smaller, more manageable pieces. Different directories were mounted on different physical drives.

This has a number of advantages. Small partitions are easier to maintain. Smaller partitions are easier to back up and restore. The size of a partition can limit the space taken by any specific directory. You can set up specific partitions as "read-only" for additional security.

There is at least one case where you should not mount different Linux directories on different partitions. If you're limited to a smaller hard drive, you need all of the spare room that you can get. This may apply to an older laptop computer, or an older computer that you're using for a dedicated purpose, such as a DNS server or a gateway router.

Configuring Linux Filesystems on Different Partitions

When you set up a Red Hat Server filesystem, you can let Red Hat configure the partitions for you. The following is the default server filesystem breakdown.

Partition	Description
/boot	Used for larger hard drives on older computers, which can see only the first 1024 cylinders on a disk.
/home	If you're limiting the disk space for each user, you should also mount /home on a separate partition to make sure you don't let user requests get out of control.
/var	The variable area gets written to by memory; often used for mail and spooling; system memory data becomes very fragmented.
/usr	Programs that you may want to protect. If you mount /usr separately, consider making it read-only in /etc/fstab.
/	The root directory for all other files.

Any additional filesystems that you create can also be mounted on separate partitions to meet additional or specific needs of related groups of users. Some examples include: /development, /dbms, /financials, /inventory. The /tmp directory is often also mounted on a separate partition, to limit the space allocated to what should be temporary storage.

Other Possible Separate Filesystems

Dedicated services are also good candidates for separate filesystems. For example, specific applications such as Web and FTP services can take up gigabytes of data. You want to protect the rest of your computer if problems arise with a specific service. File and print sharing services such as NFS and Samba present security risks because they expose shared directories to other users.

If you don't mount these services on separate partitions, anyone who uploads a large number of files could conceivably fill your hard disk.

If the number of files and users are large, you may even want to spread shared files over several partitions on different physical drives. In this situation, not every user will want data from the same drive all of the time. The load is shared by the different drives. Performance is improved.

CERTIFICATION OBJECTIVE 3.04

The Installation Process

You have many interrelated questions to answer during installation, just as you have many ways to access installation files, and many options on how to install the operating system. The following installation outline is designed to get you through the process in as simple a fashion as possible, with just enough detail to keep you going. While other sections and chapters address the special situations that you're more likely to encounter on the RHCE exam, you need to know how to install Red Hat Linux before you can work though the other installation scenarios.

Booting the First CD-ROM

Most current Intel-based PC hardware systems allow you to boot directly from the CD-ROM drive. The latest official copy of Red Hat Linux, as well as Red Hat Linux installation CDs that you might download from alternate sources, is also designed to boot directly into the installation program.

Figure 3-7 shows the Red Hat 8.0 startup screen. You should be able to access this screen by booting from the CD-ROM, or with the help of one of the following floppy disk images: boot.img, bootnet.img, or pcmcia.img.

If You Need an Installation Floppy

If your hardware does not boot from the CD-ROM, you will need to create one or more DOS-based boot disks, from the image files supplied with the first Red Hat installation CD-ROM.

FIGURE 3-7

The Startup
installation screen
for Red Hat
Linux 8.0

```
  - To install or upgrade Red Hat Linux in graphical mode,
    press the <ENTER> key.

  - To install or upgrade Red Hat Linux in text mode, type:
    linux text <ENTER>.

  - Use the function keys listed below for more information.

[F1-Main] [F2-Options] [F3-General] [F4-Kernel] [F5-Rescue]
boot: _
```

Installation floppies are easy to create. Depending on your hardware and location of the Red Hat installation files, select one of the following disk images:

- **boot.img**   Local installation from a hard disk or CD-ROM
- **bootnet.img**   Network installation through HTTP, FTP, or NFS
- **pcmcia.img**   Laptop computer–based installation. Supports installation from local or network sources.

Depending on your hardware, you may also need one of the following images on a floppy disk:

- **pcmciadd.img**   Additional support for PCMCIA adapters
- **drvblock.img**   Additional drivers for special hardware
- **drvnet.img**   Additional network card drivers

Creating Boot Floppies

There are two easy ways to project the boot images from the first Red Hat Installation CD-ROM onto a floppy disk.

In a Microsoft Windows–based operating system, open an MS-DOS window. Navigate to the drive associated with your CD-ROM. For example, if your CD-ROM is drive E: on your Microsoft-based system, just enter: **E:\> \dosutils\rawrite**.

The rawrite program prompts you for the filename to write to the diskette. Next, it prompts you for the target drive, normally the A: drive.

At the first prompt, enter the full path to the desired filename as follows:

```
E:\images\filename.img
```

You can view the files on any of the floppies that you create with MS-DOS commands. You also must repeat this entire rawrite process for each image file you wish to create, as illustrated in Figure 3-8.

Once the boot image is transferred to disk, it's easy to read, as shown in Figure 3-9.

Creating Diskette Images with Any Unix/Linux System

You can also create diskette images with the dd command from any running Unix or Linux computer, along with the desired image files on the CD-ROM. For example, the following commands mount the appropriate CD and "disk dumps" the image into a disk on a floppy drive.

```
# mount /mnt/cdrom
# dd  if=/mnt/cdrom/images/bootnet.img  of=/dev/fd0
```

FIGURE 3-8

Using the rawrite utility

```
H:\>\dosutils\rawrite
Enter disk image source file name: H:\images\pcmcia.img
Enter target diskette drive: A:
Please insert a formatted diskette into drive A: and press -ENTER- :

H:\>\dosutils\rawrite
Enter disk image source file name: H:\images\bootnet.img
Enter target diskette drive: A
Please insert a formatted diskette into drive A: and press -ENTER- :

H:\>_
```

FIGURE 3-9

Files extracted
from bootnet.img

```
Command Prompt                                                    _ □ X
H:\>dir a:
Volume in drive A has no label.
Volume Serial Number is 3CC0-6449

Directory of A:\

04/19/2002  01:39p             6,192 LDLINUX.SYS
04/19/2002  01:39p               715 SYSLINUX.CFG
04/19/2002  01:39p           556,336 INITRD.IMG
04/19/2002  01:39p           802,662 UMLINUZ
04/19/2002  01:39p               877 BOOT.MSG
04/19/2002  01:39p             1,145 GENERAL.MSG
04/19/2002  01:39p               853 PARAM.MSG
04/19/2002  01:39p               494 RESCUE.MSG
04/19/2002  01:39p               545 SNAKE.MSG
               9 File(s)      1,369,819 bytes
               0 Dir(s)          92,160 bytes free

H:\>
```

Alternatively, you can just "cat" the disk image of your choice directly to a floppy drive
device. For example, the following command reads the laptop boot disk directly to
the first floppy drive:

```
# cat /mnt/cdrom/images/pcmcia.img  > /dev/fd0
```

*Know how to create the right boot disk for your system. If you have a problem,
the installation boot disk can also serve as a rescue disk. At the boot prompt,
the linux rescue command will eventually bring you to a rescue mode that
can help you mount your partitions or recover specific files or directories.*

Almost Ready to Install

Now you have your Red Hat Installation CD-ROMs. If necessary, you also have boot
floppies to get to the Red Hat installation files. Your system is now configured to boot
either from the CD-ROM directly or from one of the boot floppies created from one
of the previously mentioned boot images (boot.img, bootnet.img, pcmcia.img). Now
install your first Red Hat Linux Installation CD-ROM, and reboot your computer.

Bootable CD-ROM

Most newer computers can be set to boot directly from the CD-ROM. Just after your
computer reboots, go into the BIOS menu, as discussed in Chapter 2. You should
be able to change the boot order to look to the CD-ROM drive first. If this option
is not available, you're just going to have to use an installation boot floppy.

CD-ROM or Boot Diskette Starts Installation

Now your PC should boot from the CD-ROM or the installation boot floppy. After a few files are opened and decompressed, a Welcome To Red Hat Linux screen should appear, as shown in Figure 3-10.

You are finally at the first stage of installing Red Hat Linux. Press the F2 button. As you can see in Figure 3-11, a number of options are available to you when you start. Especially if you're working from installation CDs that you downloaded from the Internet, your first step should be to check the media. While Red Hat provides checksums that you can use for this purpose, the easiest way to check your CDs is with the **linux mediacheck** option. Type in that command at the boot: prompt, and you'll see an option to test the media as shown in Figure 3-12.

on the *job*

If you have a problem with your graphics hardware press F3 from the first screen. You can try to force a resolution with a command such as linux resolution=800x600.

FIGURE 3-10

The First Red Hat installation screen

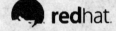

```
-  To install or upgrade Red Hat Linux in graphical mode,
   press the <ENTER> key.

-  To install or upgrade Red Hat Linux in text mode, type:
   linux text <ENTER>.

-  Use the function keys listed below for more information.

[F1-Main] [F2-Options] [F3-General] [F4-Kernel] [F5-Rescue]
boot: _
```

FIGURE 3-11

Other Red Hat
Linux Installation
Options

```
                        Installer Boot Options
       -  To disable hardware probing, type: linux noprobe <ENTER>.

       -  To test the install media you are using, type: linux mediacheck <ENTER>.

       -  To enable rescue mode, type: linux rescue <ENTER>.
          Press <F4> for more information about rescue mode.

       -  If you have a driver disk, type: linux dd <ENTER>.

       -  To prompt for the install method being used on a CD-ROM install,
          type linux askmethod <ENTER>.

       -  If you have an installer update disk, type: linux updates <ENTER>.

       [F1-Main] [F2-Options] [F3-General] [F4-Kernel] [F5-Rescue]
       boot: _
```

Click OK. Here you can test the CD currently in the drive, or eject it and place a
different Red Hat installation CD into the drive. Depending on the speed of your
system, the test may take several minutes. If successful, you'll see a screen like
Figure 3-13.

FIGURE 3-12

Checking
installation
CD integrity

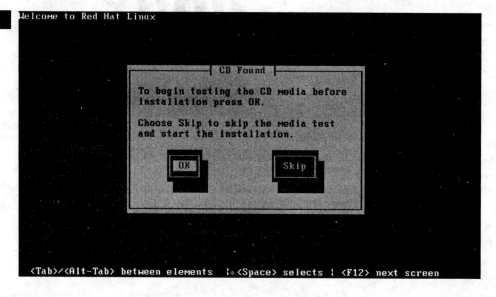

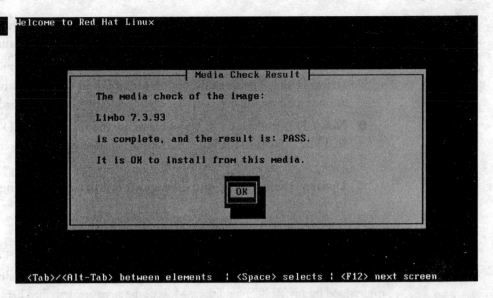

FIGURE·3-13

The CD is OK.

Click OK and the CD should be automatically ejected. You can then insert the next Red Hat installation CD for checks. Once this process is complete, you can reinsert the first Red Hat installation CD and then proceed with the standard Graphical Mode installation.

If you want to install Red Hat Linux in another way, restart your computer again with the first Red Hat Linux installation CD in the drive. The standard Red Hat Linux installation options are based on Figure 3-10 and 3-11:

- **Graphical Mode**   The default is a graphically based Red Hat installation using the program known as Anaconda.

- **Text Mode**   The **linux text** option starts a low-intensity graphical installation known as text mode that all but the most graphically challenged computers can handle. If your computer can't even handle text mode, consider upgrading for Red Hat Linux.

- **Disable Hardware Probing**   The **linux noprobe** option allows you to enter your own drivers, starting with the hard drive. Options are available to set IRQ ports, I/O channels, and DMA addresses during this process. Text-mode installation is also possible using the **text noprobe** option. While this mode can help you get around special hardware detection problems, be ready with driver disks as well as the settings that you desire for each hardware component.

- **Rescue**   The **linux rescue** option allows you to use the Red Hat Installation CD as a rescue disk. The Red Hat rescue disk includes a bare minimum of tools including the vi text editor. It does not include emacs. It does include an option where it tries to detect and mount the appropriate directories on the appropriate partitions, so linux rescue may be all you need.

- **Driver Disk** The **linux dd** option prompts you to enter a driver disk, such as one based on the drivers.img or pcmciadd.img files described earlier.

- **Non-CD Installation** It's possible to use the Installation CD to access the Red Hat Linux installation files from other sources such as over a network, with the **linux askmethod** option.

- **Updates** Red Hat hopes to have update disks available for groups of packages in the future.

Basic Installation Overview

The basic Red Hat Linux installation is straightforward and should already be well understood by any RHCE candidate. Most of the steps are described here for reference; it's useful to remember this process as you work on advanced configuration situations such as Kickstart files, which are described in Chapter 5.

The first screen, as shown in Figure 3-14, welcomes you to the installation of Red Hat Linux. If you selected the standard installation option, a graphical screen with similar content is shown. In most cases, you can click OK or Next or press the F12 key to continue to the next screen.

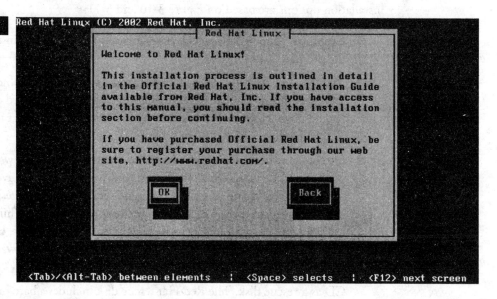

FIGURE 3-14

Welcome to Red Hat Linux Installation

Red Hat Linux tries to detect some of your hardware automatically. If successful, it may skip the associated configuration step. So do not be surprised if your installation varies somewhat from what you see here.

The next screen, as shown in Figure 3-15, allows you to select a language during the installation process.

The Keyboard Configuration screen shown in Figure 3-16 allows you to select from a variety of different keyboards in different language configurations. After Linux is installed, you can use the **redhat-config-keyboard** utility to enable special characters such as an *é* with "dead keys."

You can always reconfigure your keyboard after Linux is installed with the redhat-config-keyboard utility.

The Mouse Configuration screen shown in Figure 3-17 allows you to select from several different types of pointing devices. As you can see in the figure, the Red Hat installation program can also help you set up many different types of USB mice.

If your mouse has only two buttons, you may wish to select the Emulate 3 Buttons option. With this option, if you click both left and right mouse buttons simultaneously, Linux interprets the action as a middle mouse button entry. If you have a scrolling wheel, try pressing it down. If it clicks, Linux may recognize it as a middle mouse button.

You can always reconfigure your mouse after installation with the **redhat-config-mouse** utility.

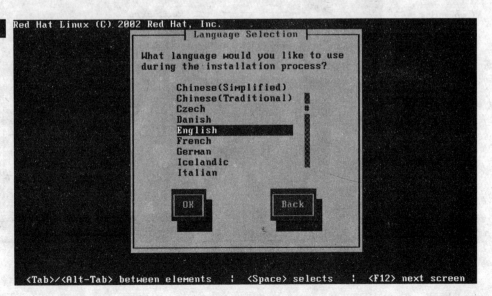

FIGURE 3-15

Selecting
a language

FIGURE 3-16

Configuring
a keyboard

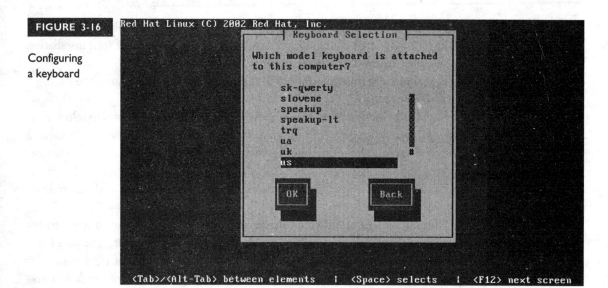

The Install Options screen shown in Figure 3-18 should already be familiar. Since you are supposed to be an expert in Red Hat Linux, we'll proceed with the most difficult of the options, that of Custom installation.

FIGURE 3-17

Configuring
a mouse

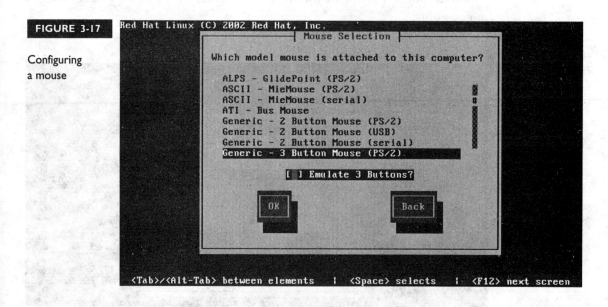

The Installation Process **125**

FIGURE 3-18

Installation
options

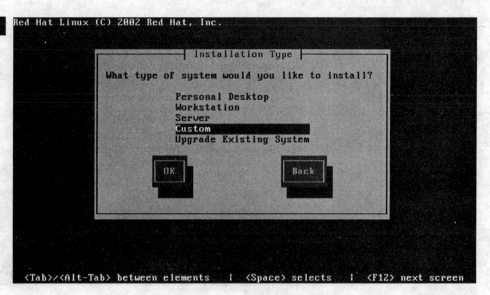

Red Hat Linux (C) 2002 Red Hat, Inc.

┌─ Installation Type ─┐

What type of system would you like to install?

Personal Desktop
Workstation
Server
Custom
Upgrade Existing System

OK   Back

\<Tab\>/\<Alt-Tab\> between elements | \<Space\> selects | \<F12\> next screen

on the job

Server or Custom installations by default delete all data on all detected drives, including those that might contain another operating system such as Microsoft Windows. Workstation or Personal Desktop installations delete all data on all detected Linux partitions. While the Upgrade option isn't supposed to delete any critical data, the effects of upgrades on specific packages can be difficult to predict. Before you continue, make sure you've backed up any critical data on your system.

Three options are shown in Figure 3-19 for setting up your hard disks. Red Hat includes a default partition setup for each of the installation options. Alternatively, you can set up partitions manually with fdisk or Disk Druid. The fdisk option is described in more detail later in this chapter. For now, select automatic partitioning; you can change the partitions in the following step.

The installation screens are evolving. I anticipate that there will be a review option available in Figure 3-20 as soon as the final release of Red Hat Linux 8.0. If available, select it for the purpose of this section. This allows the Red Hat installation program to create default partitions and then allow you to change them as needed.

Disk Druid makes it easy to specify all you need about each partition. Select a specific partition and click Edit. As shown in Figure 3-21, one screen allows you to edit

FIGURE 3-19

Disk Partitioning
Setup

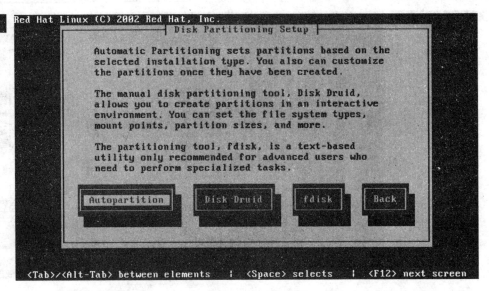

the directory to be mounted (Mount Point), the filesystem format (ext3), the drives
used (Allowable Drives), the default size of the partition, and Additional Size Options
for any leftover hard disk space. If this partition includes the /boot directory, you should
force it to be a primary partition. Make sure it's installed below cylinder 1024. And
at least the first time you set up Linux, you should make the installation program check
for bad blocks on all partitions.

FIGURE 3-20

Automatic
Partitioning

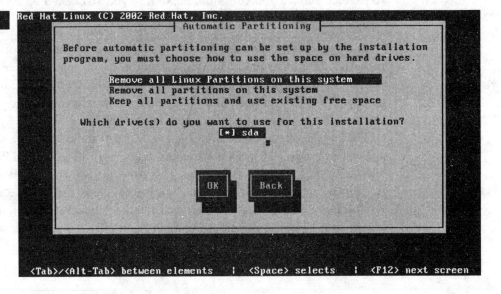

FIGURE 3-21

Add Partition screen

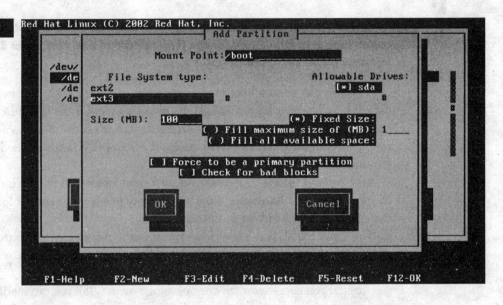

If you use Disk Druid to create your partitions, the last partition can be tricky. If you try to configure the last partition with the exact amount of free space in MB, Disk Druid might add a cylinder and think you're trying to use more space than is available. The Fill to Maximum Allowable Size option shown in Figure 3-21 can help you get around this issue.

FROM THE CLASSROOM

RAID from Disk Druid

Disk Druid can help you configure RAID partitions. Depending on the type, RAID requires two or more partitions. Create the RAID partitions that you need. Make sure the "File System type" shown in Figure 3-21 is "Software RAID." Once you have individual RAID partitions, click the Make RAID button. Disk Druid brings up a menu that allows you to format your RAID system to the ext2, ext3,

Linux swap, or VFAT filesystems. It also allows you to configure your partitions to RAID 0, RAID 1, or RAID 5.

The Red Hat Linux Installation program provides a number of user-friendly tools for configuration. The more that you can configure during the installation process, the easier your tasks are after installation is complete.

on the **!** job

As of this writing, I anticipate that Red Hat will incorporate LVM configuration capabilities into Disk Druid for the final release of Red Hat Linux 8.0. For more information on LVM, see Chapter 5.

Now you can select a boot loader, as shown in Figure 3-22. The new Red Hat default boot loader is known as GRUB, which is short for the GRand Unified Boot Loader. The old standard is LILO, short for the Linux Loader. Both boot loaders can easily be configured to boot both Linux and Microsoft Windows–based operating systems, as discussed in Chapter 5.

As shown in Figure 3-23, you can set up Kernel Parameters to help Linux recognize memory or specific hardware. What you enter depends on your boot loader; some examples are described later in this chapter.

If you select GRUB as a boot loader, you can set up a password so that individual users aren't able to pass options to the kernel that might compromise security. This is shown in Figure 3-24.

Finally, if you have more than one operating system (OS), you can specify the default, as well as the label associated with each OS. This is shown in Figure 3-25.

Figure 3-26 illustrates your choices on where to install GRUB or LILO. If you're going to use GRUB or LILO to boot Linux and possibly other operating systems, install it on the Master Boot Record of the hard disk. If you're using another boot loader

FIGURE 3-22	
Boot Loader Configuration basic options	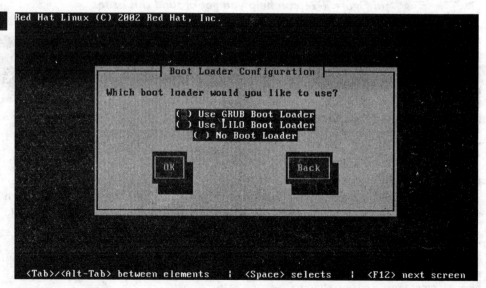

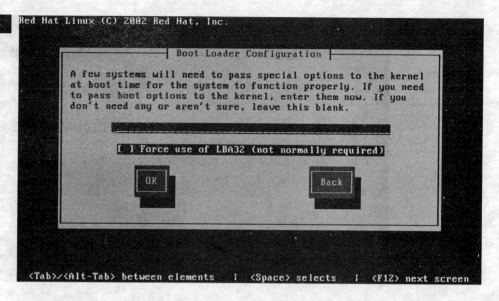

FIGURE 3-23

Boot Loader
Configuration
kernel
parameters

```
Red Hat Linux (C) 2002 Red Hat, Inc.
```

┌─────────────────────── Boot Loader Configuration ───────────────────────┐

A few systems will need to pass special options to the kernel
at boot time for the system to function properly. If you need
to pass boot options to the kernel, enter them now. If you
don't need any or aren't sure, leave this blank.

```
_____
```

[ ] Force use of LBA32 (not normally required)

```
       OK                                Back
```

```
<Tab>/<Alt-Tab> between elements  |  <Space> selects  |  <F12> next screen
```

such as Windows' NTLDR or a third-party manager such as System Commander, install it on the first sector of the partition with the /boot directory.

Next, you can set up the Network Configuration for your computer as shown in Figure 3-27. If you have a DHCP server on your LAN (or access to DHCP on another

FIGURE 3-24

Boot Loader
Configuration
for a GRUB
Password

```
Red Hat Linux (C) 2002 Red Hat, Inc.
```

┌─────────────────────── Boot Loader Configuration ───────────────────────┐

A boot loader password prevents users from passing
arbitrary options to the kernel. For highest
security, we recommend setting a password, but this
is not necessary for more casual users.

[*] Use a GRUB Password

Boot Loader Password: _____
Confirm: _____

```
       OK                                Back
```

```
<Tab>/<Alt-Tab> between elements  |  <Space> selects  |  <F12> next screen
```

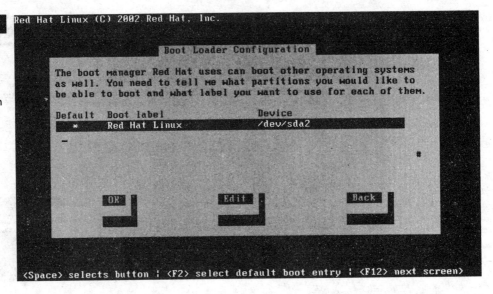

FIGURE 3-25

Boot Loader
Configuration
for the default
operating system

LAN via the bootp protocol), your Red Hat Linux installation can automatically get the necessary TCP/IP configuration information. Alternatively, if you have a static IP address, you can enter that information here as well.

It's easy to change the network configuration after Red Hat Linux is installed. Just use a tool such as /sbin/ifconfig or redhat-config-network as described in Chapter 4.

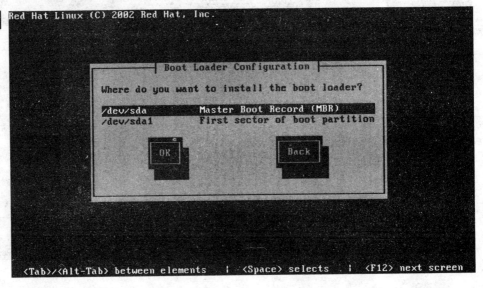

FIGURE 3-26

Boot Loader
Configuration for
the installation
location

FIGURE 3-27

Network
Configuration

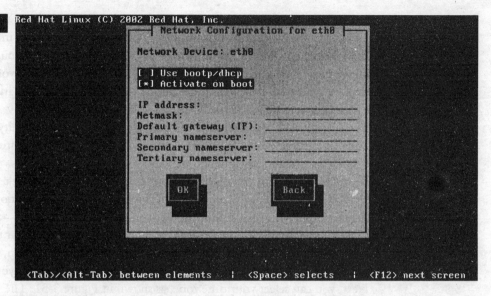

Now you can set up a firewall on this computer. It's a good idea especially if this computer is going to be connected to an outside network such as the Internet. There are three basic firewall configurations available: High, Medium, or None, as shown in Figure 3-28.

FIGURE 3-28

Firewall
Configuration

For the purpose of this exercise, select High or Medium, then click Customize. This brings you to the Firewall Configuration - Customize screen shown in Figure 3-29. If Red Hat Linux has detected more than one network adapter on your computer, you'll see more than one entry in the trusted devices list. Normally, you'd set up a firewall on a network device that's connected to the Internet, and mark the adapter that's connected to your internal LAN as a "Trusted Device."

The firewall tool you see here is based on the /usr/sbin/lokkit utility, which you can call up to revise your firewall at any time. At the time of this writing, lokkit has just been converted to use iptables to secure your network.

If you're planning to use a DHCP server from an external network, you'll need to select DHCP in the Allow Incoming list. This lets in DHCP configuration information for your computers from outside your network.

Once you've completed the firewall configuration, you're ready for the next step. Select the language or languages you want to install on your system, as shown in Figure 3-30. You'll still need to activate the language in the GUI of your choice.

Next, you can select your time zone, as shown in Figure 3-31. The list is long and extensive. If Linux is the only operating system on your computer, select "Hardware clock set to GMT". This allows the Linux time configuration tools to change your clocks for Daylight Saving Time. However, if you're dual-booting with another operating system such as Microsoft Windows, this option would affect the other operating system's clock settings.

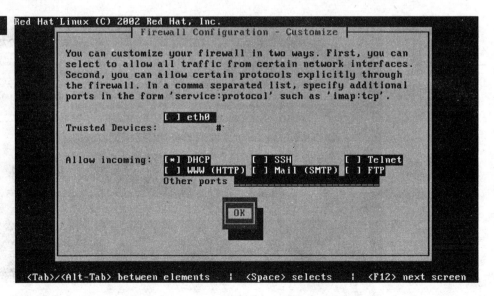

FIGURE 3-29

Firewall Configuration - Customize

FIGURE 3-30

Language Support

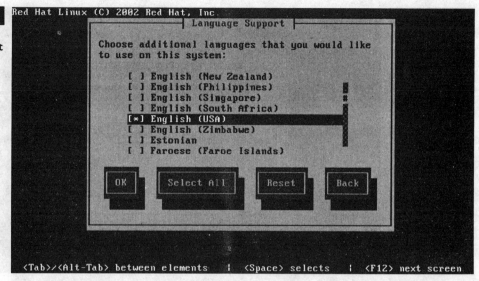

In the Root Password screen shown in Figure 3-32, you're required to pick a root password. You need to type the password twice to make sure you get the root password correct. However, if you forget the root password, there are ways to reset it, as discussed in later chapters. The Red Hat Linux installation program does not allow you to proceed until you select a root password.

FIGURE 3-31

Time Zone
Selection

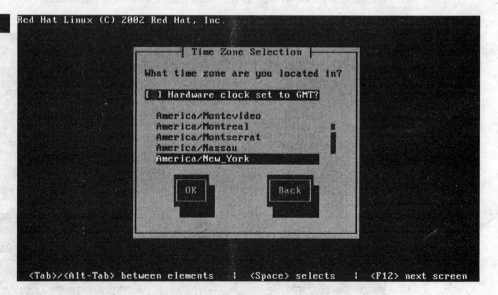

FIGURE 3-32

Choosing a Root
Password

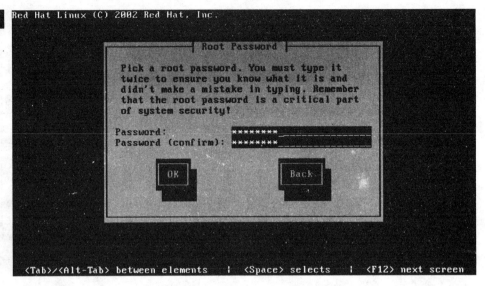

In the Add User screen shown in Figure 3-33, you can add other user accounts. The User Name and Password is what the user would type in to log into the account. The Full Name can be any name of your choice. If you add a user, you're taken to a screen where you can add more users. However, you're not required to add any users. If you prefer, just press F12 or click OK to continue. Refer to Chapter 4 for other tools to create new users, as well as the importance of strong passwords.

FIGURE 3-33

Adding more
users

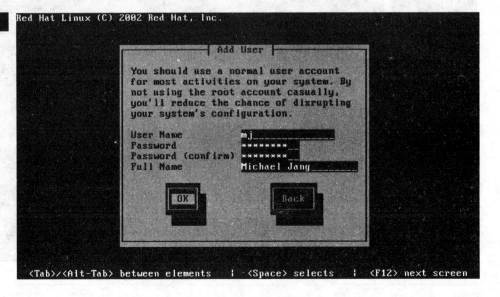

In the Authentication Configuration screen shown in Figure 3-34, you can set up four categories of account management. Enabling MD5 allows passwords of up to 256 characters, and enabling shadow passwords allows encryption in /etc/shadow and /etc/gshadow as discussed in Chapter 4.

It's easy to make changes to your Authentication Configuration after Linux is installed. For now, just use the authconfig utility. The utility name may change in later versions of Red Hat Linux.

There are a number of other things you can configure in the Authentication Configuration screen. NIS, the Network Information System, sets up a common database of usernames, passwords, and possibly other configuration files on a network with other Linux and Unix computers. This requires the installation of the Network File System (NFS) package.

LDAP, the Lightweight Directory Assistance Protocol, is used in certain types of databases such as directories.

Kerberos 5 is a secure authentication system developed at MIT.

In future releases of Red Hat Linux, you may also be able to set up Authentication Configuration on a Microsoft network via Samba. This is based on the Linux/Unix implementation of the Server Message Block protocol, developed by Microsoft and IBM for networks with their computers.

In the next step, you identify the package groups you want installed with Red Hat Linux. You've already seen the package groups earlier in this chapter. For the purpose of this section, activate the "Select individual packages" option.

FIGURE 3-34
Authentication Configuration

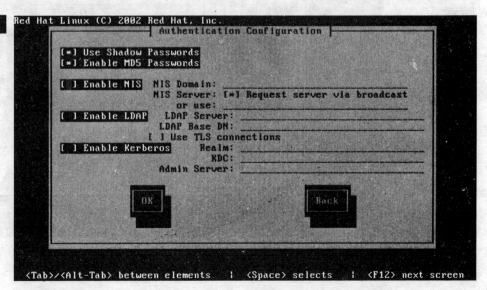

In the Individual Package Selection screen shown in Figure 3-35, you can add individual packages that you need. Alternatively, you can add packages after Red Hat Linux is installed with the rpm utility. But the concept of individual packages can be important when you're customizing a special installation for a number of computers through the Kickstart system discussed in Chapter 5.

The Red Hat Linux installation program checks for dependencies. If they exist, they are listed as shown in Figure 3-36. You have three choices on what to do about these packages:

- **Install packages to satisfy dependencies** takes all prerequisite packages and installs them along with the individual packages that you've selected.

- **Do not install packages that have dependencies** deselects any packages that require other software.

- **Ignore package dependencies** installs packages without installing other software that may be required. This is akin to the --nodeps switch for the rpm command. Use this option at your peril.

At this point, the installer is ready to begin installing Red Hat Linux on your computer. After all packages are installed, you are given a chance to create a boot

FIGURE 3-35

Individual Package Selection

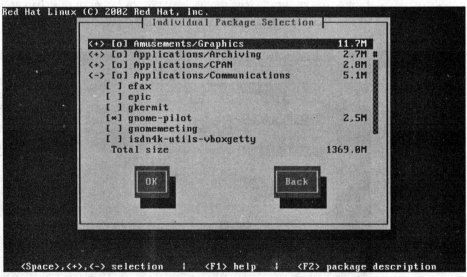

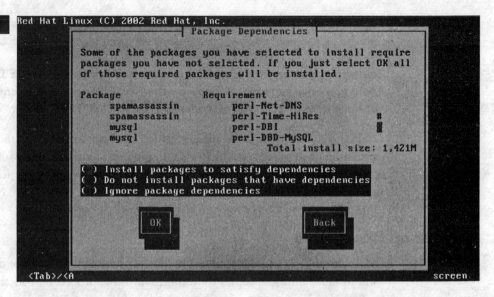

FIGURE 3-36

Package
Dependencies

Red Hat Linux (C) 2002 Red Hat, Inc.

┌─────────────┤ Package Dependencies ├─────────────┐

Some of the packages you have selected to install require
packages you have not selected. If you just select OK all
of those required packages will be installed.

Package   Requirement
    spamassassin   perl-Net-DNS
    spamassassin   perl-Time-HiRes   #
    mysql   perl-DBI   ▒
    mysql   perl-DBD-MySQL
                              Total install size: 1,421M

( ) Install packages to satisfy dependencies
( ) Do not install packages that have dependencies
( ) Ignore package dependencies

        OK   Back

<Tab>/<A   screen

disk. If you ever have a problem with the boot loader (LILO or GRUB) on your
hard drive, you'll be able to use the boot disk to start your Linux system.

If your system allows it, you can configure your graphics card and monitor in later
screens. If you know the make and model of your card, enter it here, along with the
amount of installed Video RAM. Otherwise, it's easy enough to use the redhat-config-
xfree86 utility to configure the Linux GUI after Red Hat Linux is installed.

on the job

*If you don't configure X Window during Linux installation, make sure that you
don't set up booting into a GUI. If you do, you'll need to use the linux rescue
mode discussed in Chapter 11 to boot into your system. Then you can edit
/etc/inittab to make sure that you boot into text mode in the future.*

Caveat Emptor on Installation

Do not worry if you make a mistake the first time on a test machine. Just redo the
installation; it will be significantly faster and easier than trying to correct a problem.
There are so many options and possibilities in the overview just presented that it is
not possible to name them all or take them all into account. In most cases, the default
is sufficient if you do not understand the question posed. Move on and get it installed;
then read the FAQs, HOWTOs, and other related docs once you are up and running.

You can always reinstall; the second and third installs are actually a very good thing considering you need to know this process very well for the RHCE Exam.

Remember, you are not allowed to reinstall Linux on the RHCE Debug exam. And if you have to reinstall Linux on the RHCE Installation exam, you may not have time to configure services as required.

Although you have finished the installation and have worked with the concepts of partitioning (and possibly multiple operating system boots), there are still a few more details to note, such as GRUB configuration, LILO errors, BIOS issues, and others, all described in the following sections.

A Note on Boot Disks

One major danger with a floppy is the chance of damaging that boot disk. You may want to make multiple copies to minimize possible problems. You can use the dd command to make multiple copies of the disk. Here is an example of the commands needed to create a copy of the original diskette to a local file and how to create duplicates from this local file:

```
$ dd if=/dev/fd0 of=diskettebootup.img # stores a copy of diskette
$ dd if=/diskettebootup.img of=/dev/fd0  # makes the copy
```

There is a utility supplied with Linux called mkbootdisk that will create a boot diskette from your running system with the required root and /boot partitions. You need to know the name of the running kernel, but you can have the shell generate that for you and substitute it into the command line as follows:

```
$ # to create a boot disk for the 'current kernel number'
$ mkbootdisk  /dev/fd0  `uname -r`
```

Remember the effects of double, single, and back quotes in the shell. Regular double quotes interpret only variables within before processing the result as standard input. Single quotes do not interpret the enclosed commands or variables. Back quotes process the enclosed command even if it's further contained within double quotes.

Boot Loaders: GRUB and LILO

The original Intel motherboard design provided a mechanism to start any operating system. It would load a boot program from the Master Boot Record of the first available disk. In the Microsoft world, this was the A: drive followed by the C: drive. This program then loads the actual operating system's boot control program(s), which, in turn, starts the operating system.

One problem is that this process does not work unless the MBR is located within the first 1024 cylinders of the hard disk. Older BIOSes cannot see any number larger than 2^{10}, or 1024. Newer BIOSes overcome this problem with Logical Block Addressing, which is also known as LBA mode. LBA mode reads "logical" values for the cylinder, head, and sector, which allows the BIOS to "see" a larger disk drive.

If you have multiple hard drives, there is one more caveat. If your drives are IDE hard drives, the /boot directory must be on a hard drive attached to the primary IDE controller. If your drives are all SCSI hard drives, the /boot directory must be located on a hard drive with SCSI ID 0 or ID 1. If you have a mix of hard drives, the /boot directory must be located on either the first IDE drive or a SCSI drive with ID 0.

GRUB, the GRand Unified Bootloader

Red Hat Linux has adopted a new set of files to boot Linux. These files are known as GRUB, which is short for the GRand Unified Bootloader. When you start your computer and get to GRUB, you'll see a menu similar to Figure 3-37. If you've configured multiple operating systems, you'll be able to select between them here.

If you need to do something special with GRUB, you can edit the commands. If GRUB is password protected, you'll need to start with the **p** command. Use the **e** command to open up the file. You'll see the basic commands for booting Red Hat Linux as shown under the window in Figure 3-38. The commands you see here are somewhat different from those in any current Linux text editor.

The commands that you can use to edit a GRUB file are shown in Table 3-3.

Unlike when using LILO, you don't have to write any GRUB changes to the MBR.

FIGURE 3-37

The GRand
Unified
Bootloader
(GRUB)

FIGURE 3-38

GRUB commands

TABLE 3-3	Command	Description
	b	Boot the currently listed operating system
GRUB Editing	d	Delete the current line
Commands	e	Edit the current line
	o	Create an empty line underneath the current line
	O	Create an empty line above the current line

You can also use GRUB to boot other operating systems, including various versions of Microsoft Windows. See Chapter 5 for more information, including a detailed line-by-line analysis of a dual-boot /etc/grub.conf file.

If you've previously installed LILO and now want to install GRUB, edit the /etc/grub.conf file and then run the /sbin/grub-install /dev/*xdy* where *xdy* represents the hard disk with your /boot directory.

The LILO Alternative

The more traditional boot loader is LILO, the Linux Loader. Its configuration file is /etc/lilo.conf. If you edit this file, you need to implement these changes with the /sbin/lilo command. The following is a typical /etc/lilo.conf file:

```
=========================================================
boot=/dev/hda
map=/boot/map
install=/boot/boot.b
prompt
timeout=50
default=linux
image=/boot/vmlinuz-2.4.18-3
        label=linux
        root=/dev/hda8
        initrd=/boot/initrd-2.4.18-3.img
        read-only
other=/dev/hda1
        label=Win98
        table=/dev/hda
```

Now here's the line-by-line interpretation of this file:

```
boot=/dev/hda
map=/boot/map
```

The system looks for boot and map information on the first IDE hard disk.

```
install=/boot/boot.b
```

This is the secondary boot loader.

```
prompt
```

This forces the lilo boot: prompt to appear on the console.

```
timeout=50
default=linux
```

This forces LILO to wait five seconds (50 tenths of a second) before moving to the default operating system, labeled linux.

```
image=/boot/vmlinuz-2.4.18-3
```

This is the actual virtual memory compressed kernel (version 2.4.18, with the -3 representing the Red Hat revision number) of Linux.

```
label=linux
```

This identifies the "boot option" label that appears if you press TAB at the LILO prompt.

```
root=/dev/hda8
```

This shows the location of the root, /, directory filesystem partition.

```
initrd=/boot/initrd-2.4.18-3.img
```

This reveals the location of the second stage loader, the RAM disk.

```
read-only
```

During installation, the RAM disk filesystem is started in read-only mode. After the second stage is finished with a few tests, the RAM disk is unloaded from memory, and the real root partition is mounted from the filesystem, normally in read/write mode.

The next section is another boot option—in this case, to boot Windows 98 on the first partition, /dev/hda1.

```
other=/dev/hda1
        label=Win98
        table=/dev/hda
```

The table is the location of the partition table to be used—in this case, the first physical IDE hard disk.

If you edit this file, you need to run the /sbin/lilo command to write the result to the appropriate boot record, usually the MBR.

GRUB and LILO Parameters

To pass a parameter to GRUB, type the **a** command in the first GRUB menu. This allows you to append the command sent to the kernel. After typing the **a** command, you might see something like the following:

```
grub append> ro root=LABEL=/
```

You can add the command of your choice to the end of this command. For example, if you add "single" after the end, Linux starts in single-user mode. If you're having trouble getting Linux to recognize all of the RAM on your computer, add **mem=xyzM** to the end of the line.

LILO works in a similar way; at the LILO boot: prompt, type the parameter after the label name. For example, if you wanted to start your system in rescue mode, you would type **linux rescue**. If you wanted to start your system in single-user mode, type the following command at the prompt:

```
Lilo boot: linux single
```

A wide variety of boot parameters are available; run the **man bootparam** command for more information.

Single-User Mode

Single-user mode is the most commonly used option. This is the system maintenance mode for experienced Linux administrators. You are then able to do clean backups and restores to any partitions in this mode. You also have the ability to run administration commands, recover or repair password and shadow password files, run filesystem checks, and so forth.

In some cases, to get out of single-user mode you just have to type **exit** and your system will go into multiuser mode. If you have made changes or repairs to any partitions, you should reboot the computer. Type the reboot command to reboot from within single-user mode.

LILO Errors

The LILO first stage will also indicate some common and not-so-common problems:

```
(nothing)    did not get to lilo at all
L            first stage loaded and started
LI           second stage loaded from /boot
LILO         all of lilo is loaded correctly
```

Occasionally, there may be an error due to partition table changes, bad blocks, and so forth. On these rare occurrences, you will only get partial LILO prompts:

```
LIL          second stage boot loader is started
LIL?         Second stage loaded at an incorrect address
LIL-         the descriptor table is corrupt
```

CERTIFICATION OBJECTIVE 3.06

Creating Partitions: Details

Now that you have the partition layout for your system, you need to actually create them. For this, you will probably use the fdisk utility, either from a boot diskette or from the running system. The next section details exactly how to use fdisk to create your system partitions.

In the following code, the first command, df, displays the total, used, and available free space on all currently mounted filesystems. The second command, mount, shows the type of filesystem. In this case, the device /dev/hda1 is mounted using VFAT as /DosC and represents direct access to what would be the C: drive of the Windows operating system on this first partition. Linux can directly access many other native filesystems.

```
===================================================================
[root@linux8 /root]# df
Filesystem          1k-blocks      Used Available Use% Mounted on
/dev/hda8            932833      502478    382162  57% /
/dev/hda7             23300        2588     19509  12% /boot
/dev/hda1           1052064      914784    137280  87% /dosC
/dev/hda6           1052064      111648    940416  11% /dosE
/dev/hdb             556054      556054         0 100% /mnt/cdrom
```

```
[root@linux8 /root]# mount
/dev/hda8 on /          type ext3 (rw)
none      on /proc      type proc (rw)
/dev/hda7 on /boot      type ext3 (rw)
/dev/hda1 on /dosC      type vfat (rw)
/dev/hda6 on /dosE      type vfat (rw)
none      on /dev/pts   type devpts (rw,mode=0622)
/dev/hdb  on /mnt/cdrom type iso9660 (ro)
[root@linux8 /root]# ls /dosC
CDsetup.bat     boot.ini      detlog.old    io.sys         sbide.sys
Exchange        bootlog.prv   detlog.txt    mscdex.exe     scandisk.log
My Documents    bootlog.txt   digipix       msdos.--       setuplog.old
Program Files   bootsect.dos  drvspace.bin  msdos.bak      setuplog.txt
RescuedDoc1.txt ca_appsw      dswin         msdos.dos      suhdlog.--
RescuedDoc.txt  command.com   ffastun.ffa   msdos.sys      suhdlog.dat
acess           command.dos   ffastun.ffl   mskids         system.1st
autoexec.bat    config.dos    ffastun.ffo   netlog.txt     temp
autoexec.dos    config.sys    ffastun0.ffx  ntdetect.com   w98undo.dat
autoexec.old    config.win    himem.sys     ntldr          w98undo.ini
boot.--         dblspace.bin  io.dos        recycled       win98
[root@linux8 /root]#
=================================================================
```

This listing shows a typical Workstation installation with two additional mount points for the C: and E: drives used by the Win9x and NT operating systems also installed on this computer. As of this writing, Linux can reliably recognize NTFS partitions only in read-only mode.

One of the benefits is that you can move and copy files between the Linux and the DOS partitions using standard Linux commands. You cannot, however, run any Windows applications within Linux unless you run a DOS or Windows Emulation package.

The fdisk Utility

The fdisk utility is universally available and should be one of the first tools you get acquainted with. There are many commands, even an expert mode, but you only need to know a few as discussed here.

Though you can modify the physical disk partition layout using many programs, we will be discussing the Linux implementation of fdisk. FDISK.EXE from DOS has the same name and is also used for creating partitions, but it doesn't incorporate any Linux-compatible features. It also includes a different interface.

Using fdisk: Starting, Getting Help, and Quitting

The following screen output lists commands that show how to start the fdisk program, how to get help, and how to quit the program.

```
======================================================
#  /sbin/fdisk /dev/hda
Command (m for help): m
Command action
   a    toggle a bootable flag
   b    edit bsd disklabel
   c    toggle the dos compatibility flag
   d    delete a partition
   l    list known partition types
   m    print this menu
   n    add a new partition
   o    create a new empty DOS partition table
   p    print the partition table
   q    quit without saving changes
   s    create a new empty Sun disklabel
   t    change a partition's system id
   u    change display/entry units
   v    verify the partition table
   w    write table to disk and exit
   x    extra functionality (experts only)

Command (m for help): q
======================================================
```

Using fdisk: In a Nutshell

Start with the print the partition table command (p) to review the current entries in the partition table. You then create a new (n) partition, either primary (p) or logical (l). Remember that there are four primary partitions; which correspond to numbers 1 through 4. One of these partitions can be redesignated as an extended partition. The remaining partitions are logical partitions, numbered between 5 and 16.

When you assign space to a partition, you're assigning a block of cylinders on that hard disk. If you have free space, the default is to start the new partition at the first available cylinder. The actual size of the partition depends on disk geometry; do not worry about exact size here. Normally, fdisk defaults to creating a Linux Native type (83) partition. For the swap partition, the partition type has to be toggled (t) to type 82, swap. Repeat these general steps for each required partition. You have a chance to cancel your changes with the quit (q) command. The fdisk utility doesn't actually write the changes to your hard disk until you run the write (w) command.

Using fdisk: Deleting and Creating Partitions

In the following screen output sample, you will remove the only partition. The sample output screen first starts fdisk. Then you print (p) the current partition table, delete (d) the partition by number (1 in this case), write (w) the changes to the disk, and quit (q) from the program.

This is the last chance to change your mind before deleting the current partition. If you want to change your mind, exit from fdisk with the q command.

```
=====================================================
#/sbin/fdisk /dev/hdb
Command (m for help): p
Disk /dev/hdb: 255 heads, 63 sectors, 525 cylinders
Units = cylinders of 16065 * 512 bytes

Device    Boot    Start      End    Blocks    Id  System
/dev/hdb1   *         1      525   4217031     6  FAT16
Command (m for help): d
Partition number (1-1): 1

Command (m for help): w
=====================================================
```

You did it! Now you can create the partitions you need.

Using fdisk: A New PC with No Partitions

After installing Linux on a new PC, you'll want to use fdisk to configure additional physical disks attached to the system. For example, if it's the first disk attached to the secondary IDE controller, run the **/sbin/fdisk /dev/hdc** command.

Remember the limitations on partitions. If you need more than four partitions on the new physical disk, configure type **Primary** for the first three partitions, and then **Extended** for the rest of the disk as partition 4. You can then creating logical partitions 5–16 within the extended partition.

Using fdisk: Creating Partitions

The following screen output sample shows the steps used to create (n) the first (/boot) partition, make it bootable (a), and then finally write (w) the partition information to the disk. (Note: Although you may ask for a 50MB partition, the geometry of the disk may not allow that precise size, as shown in the example.)

```
========================================================
# /sbin/fdisk /dev/hdb

Command (m for help): n
Command action
   l   logical (5 or over)
   p   primary partition (1-4)
p
First cylinder (1-256, default 1): 1
Last cylinder or +size or +sizeM or +sizeK (2-256,def 256): +50M

Command (m for help): p
Disk /dev/hdb: 255 heads, 63 sectors, 256 cylinders
Units = cylinders of 16065 * 512 bytes
   Device Boot    Start       End     Blocks   Id  System
/dev/hdb1             1         6      48163   83  Linux
========================================================
```

Repeat the commands to create the rest of the partitions. After all are created, you should end up with the final design as illustrated in the following output screen sample:

```
========================================================
Command (m for help): p

Disk /dev/hdb: 255 heads, 63 sectors, 256 cylinders
Units = cylinders of 16065 * 512 bytes
   Device Boot    Start       End     Blocks   Id  System
/dev/hdb1             1         2      16044   83  Linux
/dev/hdb2             3        18      64176   82  swap
/dev/hdb3            19       169    1203300   83  Linux
/dev/hdb4           170       250     649782    5  Extended
/dev/hdb5           170       201     248682   83  Linux
/dev/hdb6           202       257     449232   83  Linux

Command (m for help): w
========================================================
```

Disk Druid

One of the excellent additional programs supplied with the Red Hat Linux installation is the graphical Disk Druid program, which provides a more intuitive interface. The actions are similar, but the interface hides the need to know about the partition ID (it just uses a text name ID) and has an option called Growable. This option allows the system to determine how much disk space a partition will take based on available free space. However, Disk Druid is available only when you are installing Red Hat Linux.

This Growable option is very beneficial in the kickstart scripts (automated installation scripts), where the target hardware may have varying sized disks. All partition space can be allocated by allowing it to "Grow" to fill the disk during installation. This is something fdisk cannot do.

CERTIFICATION OBJECTIVE 3.07

Other Installation Sources

The default is to install Red Hat Linux from a CD-ROM directly onto the local computer. There are a number of other ways to install Red Hat Linux. You can install Linux from ISO images located on the local hard disk. You can set up Red Hat Linux files in the /RedHat directory tree on a remote server; the connection can be made through several different network protocols. When you use an installation source other than a local Red Hat CD, you generally can only use text mode for installation. While the look and feel of text mode is different from the graphical Anaconda screen, the steps you take to configure and install Red Hat Linux in text mode are virtually identical.

As of this writing, you can install Linux from a CD-ROM, from an ISO image of a CD on a hard drive, or from files configured on an NFS, HTTP, or FTP server.

Linux on Laptops

Unless you're just installing Red Hat Linux from a local CD, you'll need to start the Red Hat Linux installation program using an installation boot floppy. If you are installing Linux on a laptop computer with PCMCIA (PC Card) slot, use a boot floppy created from the pcmcia.img disk image file on the first Red Hat Linux installation CD. You may also need the PCMCIA driver disk, created from the pcmciadd.img disk image file. After your laptop loads the Linux PCMCIA driver files, you'll be able to install Linux from files on a hard disk or any of the network servers discussed in this section.

Hard Disk Installation

Rather than install from a CD-ROM, you can choose to copy the CD-ROM image to a hard drive and install from the hard drive. To accomplish this, you must obtain the ISO (CD-ROM) images for the distribution CDs. Rather than burn those images onto CDs, you'd simply place the ISO files into a directory of your choice and provide that directory name when prompted.

It's easy to create an ISO file from the Red Hat Linux installation CD. If you've already mounted a CD-ROM on /mnt/cdrom, you can create an ISO with the following command:

```
# mkisofs -J -r -T -o /tmp/firstcd.iso /mnt/cdrom
```

You'll also need to create a boot installation floppy from the boot.img file in the /images directory on the first Red Hat Installation CD. Use it to boot your computer, then follow the prompts until you see the screen shown in Figure 3-39.

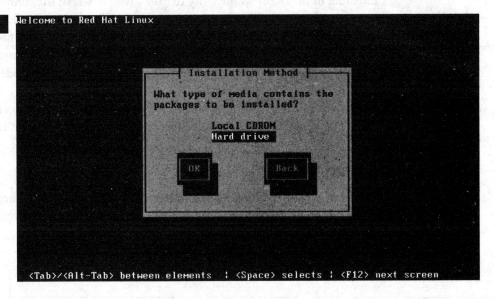

FIGURE 3-39

Installing from a hard drive

Now you'll need to select the partition and the directory with the ISO images from the Red Hat installation CDs. In the scenario shown in Figure 3-40, the Red Hat ISO images are in the /home/mj/RedHat directory. The /home directory filesystem is mounted on /dev/sda3.

The installation program assumes a *relative* path. Since /home is normally mounted on /dev/sda3, you need to enter the relative path to the ISO images from /home, which in this case is mj/RedHat.

Source Files from Network Installations

Before you can get to any network source files, you need to configure your network card to be a part of the network. If there's a DHCP server for your network, this is easy.

Otherwise, you'll need to configure your computer manually. In this case, you'll need a valid, unused IP address, the local network mask, the default gateway IP address (if network resource is on another network segment), and optionally, the primary DNS IP address, a domain name such as example.com, and the host name to use for this machine.

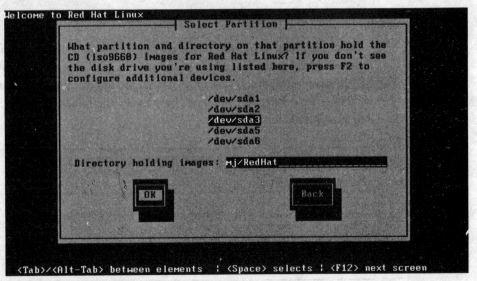

FIGURE 3-40

The relative path to the ISO images

You are presented with three options during installation for configuring networking on your computer:

Static IP Address	You fill it in; you know the numbers.
BOOTP	Dynamically sent to you from a BOOTP server.
DHCP	Dynamically sent to you from a DHCP server.

The last two options are the easiest. Your computer sends out a BOOTP or DHCP request and these network-type services send back all the IP information your computer needs to get on the network. Of course, this requires an existing DHCP server on the current or a connected network.

The first option allows you to enter IP address information directly. If you are on a local network, an IP address and the associated Network Mask are enough information to get you on to your local network with access to a local server. For example, if your network IP address is 206.195.1.0, and your host address is 222, you could enter the following:

IP Address	206.195.1.222
Network Mask	255.255.255.0

You may also need or want to use advanced host name resolution so that you don't have to remember the IP address of the servers. This is possible if you already have a DNS server on your network. DNS is what the Internet uses for host name resolution. If DNS is not configured, you'll just have to cite the IP address of the server with the Red Hat installation files.

IP Address	206.195.1.222
Network Mask	255.255.255.0
Default Gateway	206.195.1.254
Primary Name Server	192.168.15.1
Domain Name	example.com
Host Name	linux56.example.com

The Default Gateway IP is the portal to the rest of the network. In the preceding scenario, the DNS server is on another network somewhere and you will need the Gateway IP address to access it.

If you're installing Red Hat Linux from files on a network server, check your firewall. The Red Hat Linux firewall may cut off network communication to whatever FTP, HTTP, or NFS server you might be using to store the /RedHat directory tree. If the server is inside your network, already behind a firewall, with no other connection to an outside network such as the Internet, you might consider temporarily disabling the firewall on that computer.

Source Files from FTP and HTTP

An FTP or HTTP server can be a convenient source of installation files. To access an FTP or HTTP server, you need to start the Red Hat Linux installation program from a boot floppy, created from the bootnet.img or pcmcia.img disk image files.

To use either an FTP or HTTP server, you need to know the IP address and the pathname to the directory with the /RedHat directory tree. Here is an example:

- Server IP Address: 192.168.0.121

- Full Directory Path: /*serverroot*/RedHat

- Home Directory of the FTP or HTTP server: /*serverroot*

IP Address	192.168.0.121	Or use the full domain name
Directory	/	Directory under *serverroot* which contains RedHat/

You can review an example of this process in Figures 3-41 and 3-42. Since this is set up to use nonanonymous FTP, a username and password is required on the FTP server computer.

Source Files from NFS

This installation option allows an NFS server on the network configured as an export server to provide the /RedHat directory files via a network connection. To access an

FIGURE 3-41

Connecting to an FTP server with installation files

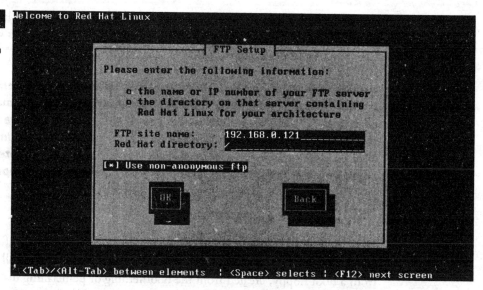

NFS server, you need to start the Red Hat Linux installation program from a boot floppy, created from the bootnet.img or pcmcia.img disk image files.

FIGURE 3-42

Logging into an FTP server

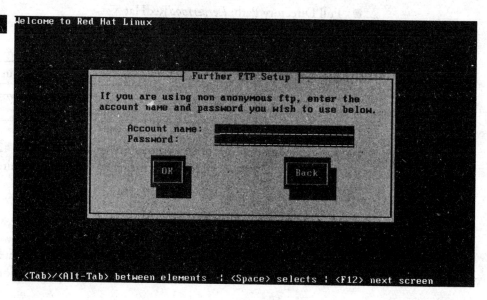

This assumes you have NFS running on another host accessible via a network connection on the target machine and that you have the installation files exported from that host. You will be asked for the NFS server IP address and the name of the exported directory. Based on the following information:

- Server IP Address: 192.168.0.129
- Full Directory Path: /nfs/exports

you'll enter the following information when prompted:

| NFS Address | 192.168.0.129 | Or use the full domain name |
| NFS export | /nfs/exports | Directory containing /RedHat/ |

This configuration is illustrated in Figure 3-43.

Creating an NFS Export Service

To create an NFS install server, you should copy the Red Hat directory installation tree from the CD-ROM to a hard drive on the NFS server.

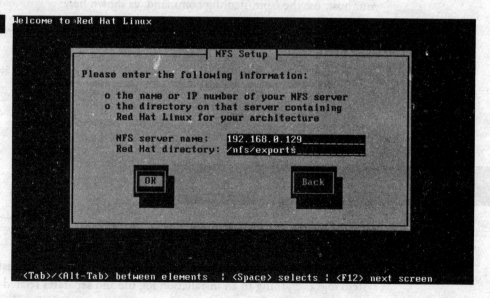

| FIGURE 3-43 |

Connecting
to Red Hat
installation files
via NFS

The following output sample shows how to make a directory to hold the /RedHat files and directories from the installation CD.

```
===============================================================
# mkdir -p /nfs/exports
#
# mount /mnt/cdrom
#          # copy to a local file system
# cp -a /mnt/cdrom/RedHat    /nfs/exports
#          # add the export request
# echo '/nfs/exports *(ro,sync)' >> /etc/exports
#          # export the directory
# exportfs -a
#          # stop and start the nfs service
# /etc/rc.d/init.d/nfs   stop
# /etc/rc.d/init.d/nfs   start
===============================================================
```

At the Server   You need to know the IP address of your NFS server as well as the name of the NFS export service and enter these when prompted. At an NT server, you can use the IPCONFIG /ALL command to find IP address information at the local computer. At the Unix or Linux NFS server, to display the IP information for your host, use the /sbin/ifconfig command, as shown here:

```
===============================================================
 [mj@RH80 mj]# /sbin/ifconfig
eth0 Link encap:Ethernet  HWaddr 00:00:C0:A8:16:BA
     inet addr:192.168.0.222  Bcast:192.168.0.255  Mask:255.255.255.0
     UP BROADCAST RUNNING MULTICAST  MTU:1500  Metric:1
...
 [mj@RH80 mj]#
===============================================================
```

CERTIFICATION OBJECTIVE 3.08

Viewing Boot Time Information

There are actually many processes running and many parts to the installation. The system logs everything to an installation log file and separates related information between four of the five virtual console screens supported during the installation.

The Console Installation Output Screens

When you start the installation, you are on the first virtual console, which can be accessed using ALT-F1. A bash shell is on the second, the installation message log is on the third, kernel messages are on the fourth, and the output of mke2fs on each filesystem is displayed. If you want to see the other screens, you can press the following key sequences in any order at any time:

ALT-F1	Installation display
ALT-F2	Bash shell gives you access to limited system information
ALT-F3	The Installation message log is displayed
ALT-F4	Displays all kernel messages
ALT-F5	Installation displays partition formatting

The partition formatting display includes the alternate superblocks. In an emergency situation in which a filesystem disk is corrupt and cannot be repaired by /sbin/fsck, you may want to try an alternate superblock. These are usually a multiple of some block size, like 8K. Block 8192 ends the first 8K, so 8193 is the next block and is a duplicate copy of the primary superblock. This ALT-F5 virtual terminal will provide the list of alternate superblock numbers. Superblocks contain the inode information and used bit block map, among other things. You can also get a listing of the internal filesystem information using the dumpefs program, as illustrated in the following sample screen output. The first command line lists the filesystem characteristics of the hda5 partition:

```
============================================================
[mj@RH80 mj]# dumpe2fs /dev/hda5 | head -5
dumpe2fs 1.27, (8-Mar-2002)
Filesystem volume name:    /
Last mounted on:           <not available>
Filesystem UUID:           96a1b50a-6f62-11d3-9656-c2da53691d05
Filesystem magic number:   0xEF53
Filesystem revision #      1 (dynamic)
[mj@RH80 mj]#
============================================================
```

CERTIFICATION OBJECTIVE 3.09

Postinstallation Validation

Red Hat Linux creates a number of files when installation is complete. These files essentially document what happened. There is the basic installation log file, /tmp/install.log, the /var/log/dmesg file with boot information, and the /root/anaconda-ks.cfg file with the kickstart information. Kickstart is discussed in more detail in Chapter 5.

During the installation process, you selected a graphical or a text-based logon as well.

The Installation Log File

During every installation, a copy of the installation options and the related files is written to an installation log file called /tmp/install.log. This information is duplicated to the various console displays during the installation. Be sure to copy this file to a backup before you, or the system, inadvertently delete the file. You can view most of the information about your installation on one of the other virtual terminals maintained during the installation.

dmesg Boot Messages

The /var/log/dmesg file contains boot messages duplicated from the console output as seen each time Linux boots. These messages contain hardware information, process initialization, and sequencing information among other things, as shown in Figure 3-44.

Graphical or Text Login Screen

After the installation is done, the installation script shuts down and reboots the machine. If you configured a graphical login, Linux starts in runlevel 5, the X Window login screen. Alternatively, if you configured a text login, Linux starts in runlevel 3.

If your X Window server is not configured properly, you can press CTRL-ALT-F2 to go back to a text-based login screen.

It's easy to change between runlevels. The **/sbin/init** x command, where x represents the runlevel, modifies the Linux system accordingly.

FIGURE 3-44	``` Linux version 2.4.18-3 (bhcompile@daffy.perf.redhat.com) (gcc version 2.96 2000073 1 (Red Hat Linux 7.3 2.96-110)) #1 Thu Apr 18 07:37:53 EDT 2002 ```

```
Linux version 2.4.18-3 (bhcompile@daffy.perf.redhat.com) (gcc version 2.96 2000073
1 (Red Hat Linux 7.3 2.96-110)) #1 Thu Apr 18 07:37:53 EDT 2002
BIOS-provided physical RAM map:
 BIOS-e820: 0000000000000000 - 000000000009f800 (usable)
 BIOS-e820: 000000000009f800 - 00000000000a0000 (reserved)
 BIOS-e820: 00000000000e7800 - 0000000000100000 (reserved)
 BIOS-e820: 0000000000100000 - 000000000c000000 (usable)
 BIOS-e820: 000000000fffe0000 - 0000000100000000 (reserved)
On node 0 totalpages: 49152
zone(0): 4096 pages.
zone(1): 45056 pages.
zone(2): 0 pages.
Kernel command line: ro root=/dev/sda5
Initializing CPU#0
Detected 1193.452 MHz processor.
Console: colour VGA+ 80x25
Calibrating delay loop... 2352.74 BogoMIPS
Memory: 190768k/196608k available (1119k kernel code, 5452k reserved, 775k data, 2
80k init, 0k highmem)
Dentry cache hash table entries: 32768 (order: 6, 262144 bytes)
Inode cache hash table entries: 16384 (order: 5, 131072 bytes)
Mount-cache hash table entries: 4096 (order: 3, 32768 bytes)
Buffer cache hash table entries: 16384 (order: 4, 65536 bytes)
Page-cache hash table entries: 65536 (order: 6, 262144 bytes)
CPU: Before vendor init, caps: 0383f9ff 00000000 00000000, vendor = 0
CPU: L1 I cache: 16K, L1 D cache: 16K
CPU: L2 cache: 512K
                                                            5,1        Top
```

Boot messages

CERTIFICATION OBJECTIVE 3.10

Sample Installation Exercises

The following exercises are meant to provide you with a step-by-step set of progressively more complex installation exercises that cover everything from basic workstations to very specific and advanced server installations.

You should do these exercises on test machines only. One possible option is a virtual machine that can simulate a computer inside your operating system. An example of this is VMWare, available from www.vmware.com.

Introduction to Installation Exercises

All these exercises assume you have a basic PC available at your disposal to work with as a learning station. You do not need a network connection, nor do you need to know how to configure X for these exercises—you can simply select the default answers in most cases.

These exercises are designed to provide progressive development to help further your knowledge about installing Linux. Both Workstation and Server installations will do all the disk partitioning for you. In these exercises, you will be asked to configure the installation for a specific usage and customize the disk partition table to meet the needs of the intended usage. This will require that you do a Custom installation in all but one of the exercises.

These exercises also assume your machine boots from the floppy during a normal reboot, that there is no pertinent information on these test machines, and that you realize all data will be overwritten on these machines.

EXERCISE 3-1

Advanced Workstation Installation

In this exercise, you will distribute your filesystem over more than just one partition. You will need to create the partitions on a 20GB or larger hard disk (see Table 3-4).

1. Create a Linux installation floppy from the boot.img image file; then reboot the system.

2. Choose Custom Installation.

3. Use Disk Druid to reconfigure the partition table.

4. Delete all partitions.

5. Create the first partition with 100MB of disk space, ext3, and assign to /boot.

6. Create the next primary partition, hda2, as Linux Swap, and assign to ID 83.

TABLE 3-4	Partition	Size	Use	Comment
Custom Installation as a Workstation (No Other OS), 1.2 GHz Pentium, 20GB Single Disk, 256MB of Memory	hda1	100MB	/boot	Maintains boot files
	hda2	512MB	swap	Plenty of space
	hda3	5.5GB	/	The root directory
	hda4	14GB	Extended partition	Solely a container for logical partitions
	hda5	4GB	/var	For print spool files
	hda6	5GB	/home	Web server—RAID 1
	hda7	5GB	/home	Web server—RAID 1

7. Create a third partition with about 5500MB of disk space, ext3, and assign it to the root directory, /.

8. Create an extended partition containing all the rest of the disk space. Make it growable.

9. Create the first logical partition, fifth in number, with about 4GB, and assign it to /var.

10. Create two more logical partitions, hda6 and hda7. Split the remaining space between these two partitions (about 5GB each). Set it up with a software RAID filesystem.

11. Make a RAID 1 device from the two new software RAID partitions, formatted to ext3, and assign it to /home.

12. When asked to select packages, leave the default choices in place.

13. Enter a root password.

14. Finish the Workstation installation normally; do not configure the network or X.

15. Reboot the machine and log in as root.

EXERCISE 3-2

Disk Partitioning a Server Installation

In this exercise, you will use a Custom installation option to create a basic server. You will need to create the partitions on a 10GB or larger hard disk (see Table 3-5).

1. Create a Linux installation floppy from the boot.img image file; then reboot the system.

2. Choose Custom installation.

3. When prompted, select Disk Druid to edit partitions.

4. Delete all partitions.

5. Create the first partition with 100MB of disk space, formatted to ext3, and assign it to /boot.

TABLE 3-5	Partition	Size	Use	Comment
	hda1	100MB	/boot	Maintains boot files
Custom	hda2	500MB	swap	Probably plenty of space
Installation	hda3	5GB	/	The root directory
as a Server,	hda4	4500MB	Extended partition	Solely a container for logical partitions
2 GHz Pentium,	hda5	500MB	/var	For print spool files
10GB single disk,	hda6	1000MB	/var/www	Web services
256MB memory	hda7	2000MB	/home	No interactive users
	hda8	1000MB	/usr	Additional network services...

6. Create the next primary partition, hda2, with about 500MB of disk space, as Linux Swap.

7. Create third partition with about 5GB disk space, Linux Native, and assign to the root directory, /.

8. Create an extended partition containing all the rest of the disk space, 4500MB.

9. Create the first logical partition, hda5, with about 500MB, formatted to ext3, and assign to /var.

10. Create the next logical partition, hda6, with about 1000MB, formatted to ext3, and assign it to /var/www.

11. Create the next logical partition, hda7, with about 2000MB, formatted to ext3, and assign it to /home.

12. Create the next logical partition, hda8, with about 1000MB, formatted to ext3, and assign to /usr.

13. When asked to select packages, include Apache Web service, Novell service, DHCP service, and DNS service.

14. Enter a root password.

15. Finish the installation normally.

16. Reboot when prompted and log in as root.

EXERCISE 3-3

Disk Partitioning Strategy for Database Server Installation

In this exercise, you will use a Custom installation option and configure the partitions for an imaginary database server. You will need to create the partitions on a 25GB or larger hard disk (see Table 3-6). The main use for such a system is as a database, file, and print server, with few interactive users.

1. Create a Linux installation floppy from the boot.img image file; then reboot the system.

2. Choose Custom installation.

3. When prompted, select Disk Druid to edit partitions.

4. Delete all partitions.

5. Create the first partition with 100MB of disk space, formatted to ext3, and assign it to /boot.

6. Create the next primary partition, hda2, with about 1000MB of disk space, as Linux Swap.

7. Create third partition with about 10GB disk space, Linux Native, and assign to / (root).

TABLE 3-6	Partition	Size	Use	Comment
Custom Installation as a Server (No Other OS), 2.4 GHz Pentium II, 25GB Single Disk, 512MB Memory	hda1	100MB	/boot	Maintains boot files
	hda2	1000MB	swap	Probably plenty of space
	hda3	10GB	/	The root directory
	hda4	14GB	Extended partition	Solely a container for logical partitions
	hda5	3GB	/var	For print spool files
	hda6	3.5GB	/opt	Database system using RAID 1
	hda7	3.5GB	/opt	Database system using RAID 1
	hda8	2GB	/usr	File services using RAID 0
	hda9	2GB	/usr	File services using RAID 0

8. Create an extended partition containing all the rest of the disk space, about 14GB.

9. Create the first logical partition, hda5, with about 3GB, formatted to ext3, and assign it to /var.

10. Create the next two logical partitions, hda6 and hda7 with about 3.5GB each. Format each to the software RAID filesystem.

11. Use the Make RAID option to set up a RAID 1 array from these two partitions. Format it to ext3 and assign it to /opt.

12. Create the next two logical partitions, hda8 and hda9, with about 2GB each. Format each to the software RAID filesystem.

13. Use the Make RAID option to set up a RAID 0 array from these two partitions. Format it to ext3 and assign it to /usr.

14. When asked to select packages, include the SQL Database Server.

15. Enter a root password.

16. Finish the installation normally.

17. Reboot and log in as root.

With all this new-found knowledge and practice in regard to installing Linux, here are some questions about a few real-world scenarios, along with their answers.

CERTIFICATION SUMMARY

One of the three parts of the RHCE certification is an exam that tests your ability to install Linux in different situations. In this chapter, you learned to install Red Hat Linux locally, and over a network. You've also worked with the major configuration tools that are part of the installation process.

You can purchase the latest distribution of Red Hat Linux, or you can download it through the Internet. ISO files help make CD-sized downloads easier to manage.

There are five basic installation options: Personal Desktop, Workstation, Server, Custom, and Upgrade. While the Upgrade option retains your current partitions, the others delete all data on at least the Linux partitions of your system, while providing a set of default partitions and packages. You can revise the default partitions during the installation process with Disk Druid or fdisk. And you can choose to set up individual packages. If there are unmet dependencies, the Red Hat Linux installation program can install any additional packages that may be required.

The Workstation installation creates three partitions from all scavenged Linux partition space, plus any unused disk space such as /boot, swap, and the root directory, /. It installs a preconfigured set of mostly user application–type packages. If you already have another operating system such as Microsoft Windows, it then sets up your machine to dual-boot between the old OS and Linux.

The Server installation option deletes all old partitions on all of your hard drives, creates six partitions dedicated to specific directories, installs all the network services software packages, and configures the boot loader of your choice, GRUB or LILO, to load this installation only.

The Custom installation option provides the most flexibility but also requires the most knowledge concerning the details of installations.

With the right network connections, you can also install Red Hat Linux over an FTP, HTTP, or NFS network. You can even install from files placed on a local hard drive. These alternative installation methods require the use of an installation boot floppy, which you can create from the boot.img, bootnet.img, or pcmcia.img disk image files.

Understanding the installation process is one of the keys to success on the RHCE exam. Find a spare computer. Practice every installation scenario that you can think of. Repeat this process as you work through the advanced installation scenarios in Chapter 5.

TWO-MINUTE DRILL

The following are some of the key points from the certification objectives in Chapter 3.

Selecting an Installation Option

❑ The Personal Desktop installation deletes all Linux partitions and then installs a default set of packages that can help newer Linux users make the transition from Microsoft Windows.

❑ The Workstation installation deletes all Linux partitions and then installs a default set of packages that include support for networking, graphics, Windows interoperability, and more.

❑ The Server installation deletes all partitions on your hard disks and then installs a default set of packages that include support for a number of different network servers.

❑ The Custom option can actually be used to create either a Server or Workstation installation; you can make more changes to the default package sets.

❑ If you want to change the default partition layout or preserve an already installed operating system of a certain type, use the Custom installation option.

❑ An Upgrade installation upgrades packages from a previous version of Red Hat Linux. If desired, you can choose not to upgrade all of the packages on your system.

Required Disk Space

❑ A Personal Desktop installation, with either GNOME or KDE, requires nearly 2GB of files. The default partition scheme requires additional free space.

❑ A Workstation installation, with either GNOME or KDE, requires over 2GB of files. The default partition scheme requires additional free space.

❑ A Server installation installs about 800MB of files. The default partition scheme actually requires more than 3GB of disk space.

❑ A Custom installation allows you to install anywhere from 500MB to 4.7GB of files when you install Red Hat Linux.

❑ When you plan space for any Red Hat Linux installation, remember to leave room for user data, additional applications, services, and a swap partition.

Filesystems

❑ To know how you want to set up partitions, you need to understand the Filesystem Hierarchy Standard (FHS).

❑ The FHS is a standard for organizing directories for Linux and Unix based systems.

❑ You can organize different directories within the FHS on different partitions. Such a configuration is easier to maintain, and easier to secure.

❑ There are several filesystems that you should consider mounting on separate partitions: /tmp, /boot, /usr/local, /var, and /home.

❑ Depending on installed services such as Web, FTP, NFS, or Samba, it may be appropriate to configure other filesystems on separate partitions.

The Installation Process

❑ You can usually install Red Hat Linux directly from a bootable CD-ROM.

❑ In some configurations, it is helpful to have an installation floppy, which is easy to create with the DOS rewrite command or the Linux dd command.

❑ The installation process is fairly straightforward and self-explanatory.

❑ When you practice installing Red Hat Linux, don't worry if you make a mistake during the process. It is usually easiest to restart the process from the beginning.

❑ Boot disks are important but fragile; with the dd command, boot disks are easy to copy.

Boot Loaders: GRUB and LILO

❑ The original Intel motherboard design provided a mechanism to start any operating system. It would load a boot program from the Master Boot Record of the first available disk.

❑ This process does not work unless the MBR is found in the first 1024 cylinders of any disk.

❑ Newer motherboards use a mechanism called Logical Block Addressing, or LBA mode, which can overcome this issue.

❑ The new default Red Hat bootloader is GRUB, the GRand Unified Bootloader.

❑ You can edit GRUB directly during the boot process, or pass commands to the kernel. For example, at the GRUB screen, if you add the word **single** to the end of the kernel argument, Linux starts in single-user mode.

❑ LILO, the Linux Loader, is the traditional alternative to GRUB.

❑ To pass a parameter to LILO, type the parameter after the label name; for example, **linux single** starts Linux in single-user mode.

❑ Single-user mode is the most commonly used option. This is the system maintenance mode for experienced Linux administrators.

Other Installation Details

❑ With either fdisk or the Disk Druid utility, you must understand basic partitioning concepts.

❑ You can only use 15 of the partitions on IDE drives, and all 15 partitions on SCSI drives.

❑ It is recommended to spread the load out across as many disks and controllers as available to improve performance.

Creating Partitions: Details

❑ The fdisk utility is universally available and should be one of the first tools you should learn as a Linux administrator.

❑ Linux natively supports many other filesystems, such as DOS, HPFS, FAT, and VFAT. This allows you to access files on the same computer created by other operating systems such as OS/2 or Windows 9x. Linux also has read-only access to NTFS partitions, which allows you to work with data on a Windows NT/2000/XP partition.

❑ Disk Druid is the alternative to fdisk that is available only during the Red Hat installation process.

Other Installation Sources

❑ Installing Red Hat Linux from a CD-ROM is the default. But there are many other ways to access Red Hat Linux installation files, such as from a local hard drive or through a network.

❑ You can install Linux on a laptop over a network. All you need is help from PCMCIA boot and driver disks, which you can create from the pcmcia.img and pcmciadd.img disk image files. These disks can enable your laptop to access installation files locally or over a network.

❑ If you're installing Red Hat Linux from a local hard disk partition, you need to set up ISO files in a subdirectory named RedHat.

❑ Before installing Red Hat Linux over a network, you need basic IP configuration information for your computer. If there is no DHCP server available, you'll need to do it manually.

❑ On the server with the Red Hat installation files, watch your firewall. Even a standard "medium" strength firewall would prevent access over an NFS network.

❑ From a nonlaptop computer, you'll need an installation floppy created from the bootnet.img disk image file to connect to an FTP, HTTP, or NFS source.

❑ To set up Red Hat installation files on an FTP or HTTP server, you need to set up the /RedHat directory tree under the base root directory for that server. If the server is on a Linux or Unix computer, don't forget to restart the service.

❑ To set up Red Hat installation files on an NFS server, you need to set up the /RedHat directory tree under an exported NFS directory. Once you've added the directory to /etc/exports, don't forget to stop and start NFS.

Viewing Boot Time Information

❑ When you start the installation, you are on the first virtual console. This console is accessed with ALT-F1. A bash shell is on the second virtual console, an installation message log is on the third, kernel messages are on the fourth, and the output of format commands on each filesystem is displayed. If you want to see other screens, press the following key sequences at any time:

❑ **ALT-F1** Installation display (this is what you normally see, all others are FYI)

❑ **ALT-F2** The bash shell gives you access to limited system information

❑ **ALT-F3** The Installation message log is displayed

❑ **ALT-F4** Displays all kernel messages

❑ **ALT-F5** The installation displays partition formatting

Postinstallation Validation

❑ The file /var/log/dmesg contains boot messages duplicated from the console output, as seen during each time you boot Linux.

❑ The /tmp/install.log contains a copy of the installation options. If you want to keep this file, copy it to another directory, as /tmp is regularly purged.

❑ The installation program reboots your computer when it's done. If you configured a graphical login, Linux starts in runlevel 5. Alternatively, if you configured a text login, Linux starts in runlevel 3.

Logging In as root

❑ This account should only be used for system administration. You should create regular accounts for all users including yourself.

❑ This is the only privileged account on the system after installation and has full privileges on your system.

Sample Installation Exercises

❑ One of the key decisions when you plan a Linux installation is partitioning. This section sets up a number of partitioning exercises for installing Red Hat Linux in different scenarios.

SELF TEST

The following questions will help you measure your understanding of the material presented in this chapter. Read all the choices carefully, as there may be more than one correct answer. Choose all correct answers for each question.

Selecting an Installation Option

1. If you already have a PC with a previous version of Linux on it that you don't want to keep, which installation option will automatically delete only the Linux partitions and install a basic network and X Window–ready Linux system?

   A. Workstation

   B. Server

   C. Custom

   D. Personal Desktop

2. What program(s) can be used to manage a dual boot between Linux and Win98?

   A. LILO

   B. Disk Druid

   C. fdisk

   D. GRUB

3. By default, there is a minimum amount of files that you need to install Red Hat Linux. How would you create a minimum installation?

   A. Select the Workstation installation, and then deselect all package options.

   B. Select the Server installation, and then deselect all package options.

   C. Select the Upgrade installation, and then deselect all package options.

   D. Select the Custom installation, and then deselect all package options.

4. A Windows administrator is puzzled by the amount of swap space configured and wants to know what is recommended for Linux.

   A. The same as RAM memory.

   B. 40–90MB.

   C. The same as the server uses.

   D. Two to three times the RAM.

   E. There is no recommended amount of swap space.

Filesystems

5. Why would you organize different filesystems on different partitions?

    A. Because you barely have enough space to install Linux on your current hard drive

    B. To make it easier to back up and restore your data

    C. To limit the space taken by a specific directory

    D. For a dedicated single-use computer such as a DNS server or a gateway router

6. What other situations might be a good candidate for a separate filesystem?

    A. A Web server

    B. The /bin directory

    C. A group of shared files

    D. Users' home directories

The Installation Process

7. You have installed different versions of Linux before. During the installation, you are given a second option to create disk partitions, but you are only familiar with the text-based disk partition management utility. Hint: you can use it during the installation of Red Hat Linux. What is the name of this utility?

    A. fixdisk

    B. rdisk

    C. fdisk

    D. druidisk

8. Which of the following steps can you take to test the integrity of your Installation CDs?

    A. Start the installation process with the **linux mediacheck** command.

    B. Start the installation process with the **linux md5** command.

    C. Nothing. You just have to run the installation CDs and hope there is no problem.

    D. Get an official boxed set of Red Hat Installation CDs.

9. You've specified a Server installation of Red Hat Linux but want to change the default partition configuration. What can you do?

    A. At the appropriate time, select Automatic Partitioning and make sure the review option is checked.

    B. At the appropriate time, select Manually Partition with Disk Druid.

    C. At the appropriate time, select Manually Partition with fdisk.

    D. Nothing. The Server installation partition configuration cannot be changed during the installation process.

10. During the installation, the authentication screen provides several options. One of them is NIS. What does NIS do?

    A. Network Inode Slave—provides shared disk resources on a Linux/Unix network.

    B. Network Information Service—provides centralized authentication on a Linux/Unix network.

    C. New Internet Standard—provides centralized authentication of shared access on a Linux/ Unix network.

    D. Newton Interrupt Sequence—file sharing protocol on a Linux/Unix network.

11. You did not create a boot disk during the installation process. Now that you realize that you can have boot disk that is customized for your installation, you want one now. What can you do?

    A. Use the dd command to create a boot disk from the boot.img disk image file on the first Red Hat installation CD.

    B. Use the rawrite command to create a boot disk from the boot.img disk image file on the first Red Hat installation CD.

    C. Use the **mkboot /dev/fd0 'uname -r'** command.

    D. Use the **mkbootdisk /dev/fd0 'uname -r'** command.

Boot Loaders: GRUB and LILO

12. In the GRand Unified Bootloader, what should you do if you wanted to start Linux in single-user mode for a quick repair?

    A. Enter **linux single** at the boot prompt.

    B. Run the **a** command and then add **single** at the end of the line that appears.

    C. Get a LILO boot disk and then run **linux sum** at the boot prompt.

    D. Boot Linux and then edit the /etc/grub.conf file to automatically start Linux in single-user mode, then reboot.

13. When you see the **root=/dev/sda7** command in either GRUB or LILO, what does it mean?

    A. The root directory, /, is located on the third logical partition of the first SCSI hard disk.

    B. The /root directory is located on the third logical partition of the first SCSI hard disk.

    C. If it's GRUB, this represents the root directory, /. If it's LILO, this represents the /root directory. In either case, it is located on the third logical partition of the first SCSI hard disk.

    D. It is an error in either boot loader.

Creating Partitions: Details

14. You are told to check the Web server drive table after installation. There are eight partitions. Your MIS manager asks how that can be. Her DOS OS machine can only create one primary and one extended partition. How many (E)IDE primary partitions can any one disk drive contain?

    A. 4 primary, 1 of which is an extended partition, making for 16 total partitions

    B. 3 primary, 2 of which are extended, making for a total of 12 partitions

    C. 12 primary, with 1 an extended partition

    D. 16 extended partitions

15. Once you're in the fdisk utility, which command gives you the current partition table?

    A. m

    B. p

    C. x

    D. w

Other Installation Sources

16. During the installation, you are asked to configure your network card to access the installation source files from an NFS server. Assuming you have already input the IP address and netmask for this host, you need to have what?

    A. DNS Server IP, BOOTP Server IP, NFS export name

    B. DNS export name, BOOTP Server IP, NFS Server IP

    C. DHCP Server IP, DHCP name, NFS export name

    D. NFS export name, NFS Server IP

17. You're installing Linux on a new hard disk from ISO files on the local computer. The files are located in the /tmp/RedHat directory, which itself is mounted on /dev/hda6. When prompted by the Red Hat Linux installation program, what do you enter in the Directory holding images text box?

    A. /tmp/RedHat

    B. /tmp

    C. /RedHat

    D. RedHat

Viewing Boot Time Information

18. While the installation is in progress, which of the following key combinations display kernel messages?

    A. ALT-F1

    B. ALT-F2

    C. ALT-F3

    D. ALT-F4

Postinstallation Validation

19. Which of the following commands display the messages that scrolled on your screen when you last booted Linux?

    A. cat /var/messages

    B. cat /var/log/dmesg

    C. cat /var/log/messages

    D. /sbin/messages

LAB QUESTION

Part 1

You need to test Red Hat 8.0 as a replacement for your current RH 6.2 installed Web Server. *But,* you do not want to lose the current 6.2 Web setup just yet. You just want to test 8.0 using the Web pages and CGI scripts to see if they will work. What can you do?

Part 2

You want to test the **linux rescue** option from a boot disk or Installation CD. To make this work, you'll need access to installation media locally (from a CD-ROM or hard disk) or over a network (from an NFS, FTP, or HTTP server). If required, create one of the boot disks from the images described earlier in this chapter (boot.img, bootnet.img, pcmcia.img).

1. Insert the appropriate installation media (boot disk or CD) into the drive.

2. Reboot your computer. If necessary, adjust the boot order in your computer's BIOS menu to boot from the appropriate media.

3. When you see the first Red Hat Linux installation screen, type **linux rescue** and then press ENTER.

4. Go through the text mode prompts for language and keyboard.

5. The next screen is entitled Rescue Method. Select the system (CD, hard disk, NFS, FTP, HTTP) with your installation media.

6. Enter the data required to point the Red Hat Linux installation program at your installation media. The details vary with the method. For more information, refer to the appropriate sections earlier in this chapter.

7. You should now see a text mode Rescue screen. Select Continue and press ENTER to continue.

8. If successful, you'll see a message that "Your system has been mounted under /mnt/sysimage." Click OK to continue.

9. Run several commands to see what the rescue disk has done to your system: **df, ls -l /, ls -l /mnt/sysimage**. Observe the results.

10. Run the **man mount** command. Observe the results. Why do you think the **man** command isn't working?

11. Run the **chroot /mnt/sysimage** command. Run the commands shown in steps 9 and 10. What happened?

12. If you're feeling adventurous, repeat this process. At step 7, select Skip instead of Continue. What is the difference? Could you mount the partition with the root directory on the /mnt/sysimage directory?

SELF TEST ANSWERS

Selecting an Installation Option

1. ☑ **A and D.** This is the main benefit of the Workstation and Personal Desktop options: little user interaction. The system creates the partitions from unused or previous Linux type partitions, and everything installs for a basic network-ready system.

   ☒ The server option (**B**) would wipe out all other OS versions, and a Custom installation (**C**) requires you answer a plethora of questions.

2. ☑ **A and D.** Both LILO, the Linux Loader, and GRUB, the GRand Unified Bootloader, can be set up to manage a dual boot.

   ☒ **B** and **C** are incorrect. Disk Druid and fdisk are both partition managers.

3. ☑ **D.** The Custom installation option provides this kind of flexibility.

   ☒ **A**, **B**, and **C** are incorrect. The Workstation and Server installations require additional packages. The Upgrade installation would serve this purpose only for a Linux installation that already had a minimum number of packages.

4. ☑ **D.** It is recommended you have two to three times the amount of RAM, but there is no absolute here. The total amount of memory available to all programs is the sum of RAM and swap. Get as much RAM as you can. If you need more RAM but cannot afford it, your system will use swap space. However, this comes with a major hit on performance due to the slow speed of disks. If you do use swap space regularly, then you need more RAM for the system.

   ☒ Technically speaking, all the other answers may be right, but **D** is the rule of thumb most commonly used.

Filesystems

5. ☑ **B and C.** Filesystems on different partitions allow you to back up and restore data, one partition at a time. The amount of space taken by a specific directory is limited by the size of the partition.

   ☒ **A** and **D** are incorrect. Extra partitions waste space. If you barely have enough space on the current hard drive, you may not be able to install Linux. If you have a dedicated single-use computer, the amount of data is small, so there is no reason for different partitions.

6. ☑ **A, C, and D.** Web servers take up lots of space, and the associated log files can grow quickly. Shared files on a separate partition reduce the security risk. A separate filesystem ensures that it won't crowd out other partitions.

   ☒ **B** is incorrect. If the /bin directory is mounted on a separate filesystem, you may not be able to get to the associated commands if you have to use a rescue disk.

The Installation Process

7. ☑ C. During an installation, there is Disk Druid from Red Hat and the universal fdisk utility (*not* the DOS-based utility).

   ☒ Although names can be almost anything in Linux and Unix, druidisk, rdisk, and fixdisk are not known utilities, hence **A**, **B**, and **D** are all wrong.

8. ☑ A. The **linux mediacheck** command adds a step where you can check the integrity of each of the Red Hat Linux installation CDs.

   ☒ **B**, **C**, and **D** are all wrong. There is no linux md5 command. There is something you can do to check before you find a problem. And while official boxed sets are probably more reliable, getting such CDs does not by itself check their integrity.

9. ☑ A, B, and C. All of these options are available at some point during the Red Hat Linux installation process.

   ☒ **D** is not correct, since you can use the other options to change partitions during the installation process.

10. ☑ B. NIS, the Network Information System, is a standard centralized master copy of the authentication files distributed to all other hosts in a trusted network.

   ☒ **A**, **C**, and **D** are bogus.

11. ☑ D. Among the available choices, only the mkbootdisk command can create a boot disk customized to your installation.

   ☒ **A**, **B**, and **C** are not correct. The dd and rawrite commands, when applied to the standard boot.img file, create a standard installation boot disk. The mkboot command is a little trickier, since that works in Debian Linux.

Boot Loaders: GRUB and LILO

12. ☑ B. The a command in GRUB accesses the information passed to the kernel. The **single** command makes the kernel access single-user mode.

   ☒ **A**, **C**, and **D** are not correct. There is no boot prompt in GRUB. The **linux sum** command has no meaning at the LILO boot: prompt. While answer **D** could work, it is at best inefficient.

13. ☑ A. In both LILO and GRUB, the **root=/dev/sda7** command indicates that the root directory, /, is located on the third logical partition of the first SCSI hard disk.

   ☒ **B**, **C**, and **D** are not correct. In either boot loader, root represents the top-level / directory, not the home directory of the root user (/root). It is not an error in either boot loader.

Creating Partitions: Details

14. ☑ **A.** 4 total, 3 that are called primary and one that is a primary partition that is configured as an extended partition. Extended partitions can contain up to 12 logical partitions. 12 + 4 = 16.
☒ **B, C, and D** are all incorrect configurations.

15. ☑ **B.** The **p** command "prints" the current partition table to the screen.
☒ **A, C, and D** are all incorrect. The **m** command lists other available commands within fdisk. The **x** command exits from fdisk. The **w** command writes your changes to the partition table.

Other Installation Sources

16. ☑ **D.** The IP address of the NFS server and the export directory name. You must already have an IP address and netmask (as well as an optional gateway IP if the services are on another network), or be using DHCP or BOOTP to obtain it, for the install host.
☒ A BOOTP server provides a special Unix diskless workstation bootup service (DNS is not used during installations). Hence **A, B, and C** are all incorrect configurations.

17. ☑ **D.** Since /tmp is mounted on /dev/hda6, all you need is the relative path from that directory to the ISO installation files.
☒ **A, B, and C** are all incorrect. Because of the way the Red Hat Linux installation program mounts these filesystems on a temporary directory (not /tmp), none of these other options would work.

Viewing Boot Time Information

18. ☑ **D.** The ALT-F4 key combination accesses the screen with kernel messages during the Red Hat Linux installation process.
☒ **A, B, and C** are all incorrect, as they access the default installation display, the bash shell, and the installation message log, respectively.

Postinstallation Validation

19. ☑ **B.** The /var/log/dmesg file contains boot messages.
☒ **A, C, and D** are all incorrect. The /var/log/messages file is significant as the location for service startup and shutdown messages.

LAB ANSWER

Part 1

Scenario 1: Buy a new disk and add it to the system. Then do a custom install to create a new installation of RH 8.0 to partitions on the new disk, adding an entry to /etc/grub.conf or /etc/lilo.conf to provide a boot option to both versions of Linux.

Scenario 2: If you can find about 500MB of free space on any current disk, you can do a custom installation and prune the packages down to just the minimum needed for the OS and Apache. You could use FIPS to repartition the 500MB (assuming you had not already created 16 partitions on IDE or 15 on SCSI) and use that as your sole root (/) partition, reusing the current swap partition. You could then update GRUB or LILO accordingly.

Scenario 3: No space on server. Hmm…you've got to get creative and either find a test machine you can do the test install on *or* back up everything on the main server after taking it off line. Do a quick 8.0 upgrade to the current 6.2 and see how it works. If it fails, you restore everything back to the way it was. Note: Test your backups first before proceeding!!!!

Part 2

This is a useful exercise in using the Linux rescue system. If the problem is relatively minor, the steps shown will create a RAM disk with some essential tools on the root (/) filesystem. You can use these tools to repair damaged filesystems or partitions on your hard disk. The **man** pages don't work right away, because what is normally your root (/) directory is actually mounted on /mnt/sysimage.

The **chroot /mnt/sysimage** command makes the /mnt/sysimage directory into your root (/) directory. Everything such as **man** pages should work normally now.

The other option, to Skip the mount process during **linux rescue** setup, does not mount any of your partitions. You can now mount them individually. If you create a /mnt/sysimage directory, you can even mount them in the same way as you saw during the first part of this exercise. Since your partitions are not mounted, you can fix damaged filesystems with commands such as **fsck**.

4

Basic Configuration and Administration

A fter installation is complete on your Red Hat Linux system, you still have some work to do to customize the system to meet your needs. User accounts need to be set up, filesystems must be configured, and additional packages may need to be added or removed.

This chapter will get you started with the basics that every Red Hat Linux administrator should know. At the end of this chapter, you should know how to manage user accounts and environments; configure and mount filesystems; use RPM to manage packages; manage system daemons; and configure virtual consoles, keyboards, and mice.

CERTIFICATION OBJECTIVE 4.01

Adding, Deleting, and Modifying User Accounts

The default Red Hat installation gives you just a single login account: root. You should set up more accounts. Even if you're going to be the only user on the system, it's a good idea to create at least one nonadministrative account to do your day-to-day work. Then you can use the root account only when it's necessary to administer the system. Accounts can be added to Red Hat Linux systems using various utilities, including the vi text editor (the manual method), the useradd command (the command line method), and the Red Hat User Manager utility (the graphical method).

User Account Categories

Linux user accounts are of three basic types: administrative (root), regular, and service. The account that you have to create when you install Linux is the root user account, with administrative privileges to all services on your Linux computer. Crackers would love a chance to take control of this account, for it would help them take full control of your system.

Nevertheless, there are times when it is appropriate to log in as an administrator (i.e., as the root user). Red Hat Linux builds in safeguards for root users. Run the **alias** command. You'll see entries such as:

```
alias rm='rm -i'
```

which prompt for confirmation before the rm command deletes a file. Unfortunately, a command such as **rm -rf directoryname** would supersede this safety setting.

In the world of Linux, hackers are good people who just want to improve software. Crackers are people who are interested in breaking into computer systems for malicious purposes.

Regular users have the necessary privileges to perform standard tasks on a Linux computer. They can access programs such as word processors, databases, Web browsers. They can store files in their own home directories. Since regular users do not normally have administrative privileges, they cannot accidentally delete configuration files. You can assign a regular account to most users, safe in the knowledge that they can't disrupt your system with the privileges that they have on that account.

Services such as Apache, Samba, mail, games, and printing have their own individual service accounts. These accounts exist to allow each of these services to interact with your computer. Normally, you won't need to change any service account; but if you see that someone has logged in through one of these accounts, be wary. Someone may have broken into your system.

To review recent logins, run the utmpdump /var/log/wtmp | less command. If the login is from a remote location, it will be associated with a specific IP address.

Basic Command Line Tools

You have two basic ways of adding users through the command line interface. You can do it directly by editing the /etc/passwd file in your favorite text editor. As discussed in Chapter 1, the text editor of choice for most Linux administrators is vi. Open it up, and then scroll to the bottom of /etc/passwd. You should see lines like the following:

```
mj:x:500:500:Michael Jang:/home/mj:/bin/bash
```

Each entry in /etc/passwd is delineated by a colon. The seven types of entries are described in Table 4-1, using the example of the preceding line of code. When you edit /etc/passwd, you can substitute the information of your choice. Just make sure not to duplicate the username. There's a standard series of files in the /etc/skel directory that you can copy to the new user's home directory to help set up a default environment. The /etc/skel directory is covered in more detail later in this chapter.

Now that you've created a new user, you need to create a home directory for that user. For example, if you've just created user mj, you need to create directory /home/mj. You'll also need to make sure that mj has ownership permissions on that directory and all of the files that you're going to put in that directory. Normally, every Linux user needs configuration files. The files in the /etc/skel directory contain default configuration files.

Alternatively, you can automate this process with the useradd command. If you wanted to add a new user named pm, you could just type **useradd pm** to add this user to the /etc/passwd file. By default, it creates a home directory, /home/pm, adds standard files from the /etc/skel directory, and assigns the default shell, /bin/bash. But useradd is versatile. It includes a number of command options, shown in Table 4-2.

You can now use the **passwd** *username* command to assign a new password to that user. For example, the **passwd pm** command lets you assign a new password

TABLE 4-1	Field	Purpose
/etc/passwd Categories	mj	The user logs in with this name. The login name should contain only alphanumeric characters. It can also include hyphens (-) or underscores (_). In almost all cases, the login name should not contain uppercase letters. Although a login name can be up to 256 characters, you typically want to keep it to 10 or less, for ease of account maintenance.
	x	The password. Don't enter anything here. You can set this password from the command line interface with the **passwd** *username* command. If the entry in this field is "x," the actual password is encrypted in /etc/shadow. Otherwise, the encrypted password is shown here, with a group of seemingly random letters and numbers.
	500	The unique numeric user ID (UID) for that user. By default, Red Hat Linux starts user IDs at 500.
	500	The numeric group ID (GID) the user will belong to. By default, Red Hat Linux creates a new group for every new user. If you want all your users to be in the Users group (GID=100), enter 100 here.
	Michael Jang	You can enter the information of your choice in this field. While it's helpful to enter the full name of the user here, you can also enter other identifying information such as the user's telephone number, e-mail address, or physical location. No entry is required.
	/home/mj	By default, Red Hat Linux places new home directories in /home/*username*.
	/bin/bash	By default, Red Hat Linux assigns the bash shell as the login shell for each new user.

	Option	Purpose
TABLE 4-2 useradd Command Options	-u *UID*	Overrides the default assigned UID, which is normally the number in sequence after the one assigned to the newest user.
	-g *GID*	Overrides the default assigned GID, which normally corresponds to the UID.
	-c *info*	Enters the comment of your choice about the user, such as his or her name.
	-d *dir*	Overrides the default home directory for the user, /home/*username*.
	-s *shell*	Overrides the default shell for the user, /bin/bash.

to user pm. You're prompted to enter a password twice. While passwords based on dictionary words or shorter than six characters are discouraged for security reasons, they are legal, and such a password is accepted by the passwd command when you type it in a second time.

If passwords are encrypted in /etc/shadow, as discussed in Table 4-1, then you'll also need to run the pwconv command to secure any passwords that you create for new users.

Good passwords are important. Any cracker who may have tapped into the communications channels on your network can try to match the password of any of your users. If it's a dictionary word or based on a simple pattern, a password cracking program may be able to find that password in a matter of minutes. In contrast, a more complex password such as Ila451MS (which could stand for "I live at 451 Main Street") may take hours for that same program to crack.

The Red Hat User Manager

The Red Hat User Manager can be run only from the Linux graphical user interface (GUI), also known as X or X11. If you have already configured X and are running a graphical desktop, enter **redhat-config-users** from a command line interface. If your username does not have root privileges, you'll be prompted for a root password. Figure 4-1 shows the Red Hat User Manager window.

FIGURE 4-1

The Red Hat
User Manager

EXERCISE 4-1

Adding a User with the Red Hat User Manager

To add a user with the Red Hat User Manager:

1. Run **redhat-config-users** from a command line terminal such as Konsole or
gnome-terminal in a GUI.

2. Click the New User button, or click Action | New Users. (This notation
indicates you should click the Action button on the toolbar, then click New
Users in the pop-up menu that appears.) This will open the Create New User
window, as shown here:

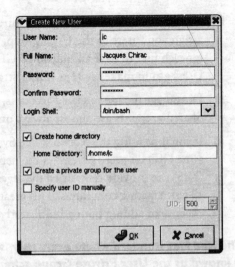

3. Complete the form. All entries are required, except Full Name. The entries are fairly self-explanatory; see the previous sections for more information on each field. The password should be at least six characters (you'll get an error message if it's less than six characters) and should contain a mix of upper- and lowercase letters, numbers, and symbols to keep it from being easily found by one of the standard password cracking programs. Enter the identical password in the Confirm Password field. Click OK when you are done.

4. When you have finished adding users, select Cancel to return to the Red Hat User Manager.

User Account Management Tips

Although creating user accounts may seem to be a straightforward process, you have a few things to watch out for:

■ Red Hat Linux by default configures individual private group IDs (GID) for each user. As this provides additional security, this is also known as the Red Hat User Private Group scheme. In the default Red Hat scenario, everyone has a unique private GID, and nobody has access to other users' home directories. These users can still share access to special directories; see Chapter 11 for more information.

- If your configuration doesn't require each user to have his or her own GID, assign your users to the Users group, which is GID 100. There's rarely a need for each user to have an individual GID, and having most users assigned to the Users group makes system administration easier.

- Discourage the use of shared accounts, where several people use a single account. Shared accounts are almost always unnecessary and are easily compromised.

- If you'll be using the Network File System (NFS), make sure all users have the same UID on every system on the network. The Network Information System (NIS) can provide centralized management of all user accounts for NFS across all participating computers. This greatly simplifies account maintenance at the expense of adding both administrative and network overhead.

The Red Hat standard where every user is a member of its own exclusive group is known as the User Private Group scheme.

Deleting a User Account

Removing user accounts is as straightforward as adding them, with a few exceptions. The simplest method is with the userdel command. By default, this command retains files in the user's home directory. Alternatively, the **userdel -r** *username* command would remove all of these files.

Modifying a User Account

You may want to add some limitations to an individual user account. The easiest way to illustrate these features is through the Red Hat User Manager. Start **redhat-config-users** from a GUI text console, select a currently configured user, and then click Action | Properties to open the User Properties dialog box. Click the Account Info tab for the account expiration information shown in Figure 4-2.

As shown in Figure 4-3, you can set up temporary accounts that expire on a specific date, or you can disable an account by locking it. Click the Password Info tab.

As shown in Figure 4-3, you can set several characteristics related to an individual user's password. Even when you set good passwords, frequent password changes can help provide additional security. The categories shown in Figure 4-3 are self-explanatory. Click the Groups tab.

Users can belong to more than one group in Linux. Under the Group properties tab shown in Figure 4-4, you can assign the subject user to other groups. For example,

FIGURE 4-2

User Properties, Account Info

User Properties

| User Data | Account Info | Password Info | Groups |

☑ Enable account expiration

Account expires on date: _____ / _____ / _____

☐ User account is locked

OK   Cancel

if you want to collect the files for a specific project together in a directory, you can give access to these files to the group named project. You can then assign members of that project team to the project group through the Groups tab.

exam
Watch

You may not have access to a GUI during part of the RHCE exam. Therefore, you need to know how to manage users independent of any tool such as redhat-config-users.

Regular User Management Commands

While the redhat-config-users GUI utility is convenient, you still need to know how to perform the associated administrative functions at the command line interface. The other key commands that have not yet been addressed are usermod and chage.

FIGURE 4-3

User Properties, Password Info

User Properties

| User Data | Account Info | Password Info | Groups |

User last changed password on: Tue Jul 30 2002

☑ Enable password expiration

Days before change allowed: 0

Days before change required: 0

Days warning before change: 0

Days before account inactive: 0

OK   Cancel

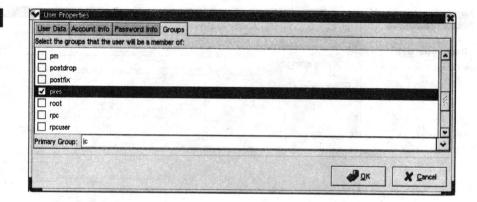

FIGURE 4-4

User Properties, Groups

usermod

The usermod command modifies various settings in /etc/passwd. In addition, you can use it to set an expiration date for an account or an additional group. For example, the following command sets the account associated with user test1 to expire on June 8, 2003:

```
# /usr/sbin/usermod -e 2003-06-08 test1
```

The following command makes user test1 a member of the *special* group:

```
# /usr/sbin/usermod -G special test1
```

chage

You can use the chage command to manage the expiration date of a password. This is all related to the /etc/shadow file; password age characteristics are part of each user entry in this file. In order, the columns in /etc/shadow are shown in Table 4-3. The associated switch is shown with the description. For example, if you wanted to make user test1 keep a password for at least two days, use the **chage test1 -m 2** command.

TABLE 4-3

Entries in /etc/shadow

Column	Description
1	User name
2	Encrypted password
3	Number of days of the last password change after 1/1/1970.
4	Minimum number of days which you must keep a password (-m)

TABLE 4-3	Column	Description
Entries in /etc/shadow (continued)	5	Maximum number of days after which a password has to be changed (-M)
	6	Number of days before password expiration - when a warning is given (-W)
	7	Number of days after password expiration when an account is made inactive (-I)
	8	Number of days after password expiration when an account is disabled (-E)

CERTIFICATION OBJECTIVE 4.02

The Basic User Environment

Each user on your Red Hat Linux system has an *environment* when logged on to the system. The environment defines where the system looks for programs to be executed, what the login prompt looks like, what terminal type is being used, and more. This section explains how default environments are configured.

Home Directories and /etc/skel

Red Hat Linux provides a set of standard templates for new users' home directories in /etc/skel.

Home Directories

The home directory is where users start when they first log on to a Red Hat Linux system. For most normal users, this will be /home/*username,* where *username* is the user's login name. Users typically have write permission in their own home directory, so they're free to read and write their own files there. In Chapter 5, you'll learn how to configure disk quotas, so users don't take more than their fair share of disk space.

/etc/skel

The /etc/skel directory contains default environment files for new accounts. The useradd command and the Red Hat User Manager copy these files to the home directory when a new account is created. Depending on the software installed, the files included in /etc/skel and their purposes are listed in Table 4-4.

TABLE 4-4	Files	Purpose
Default User Configuration Files in /etc/skel	.bashrc	The basic bash configuration file. May contain a reference to the general /etc/bashrc configuration file.
	.bash_logout	A file executed when you exit a bash shell.
	.bash_profile	Configures the bash startup environment, including the PATH.
	.kde	A directory that includes autostart settings for the K Desktop Environment.
	.screenrc	Customizes terminal settings such as messages and bells. Also configures xterm.

As the system administrator, you can edit these files, or place your own customized files in /etc/skel. When new users are created, these files are propagated to the new users' home directories. Additional entries are placed there by various programs during installation, such as emacs and secure shell (ssh).

Window Manager Configuration File Locations

Red Hat Linux comes with several window managers. You will at some point want to configure one or more of them for use on your system. Window manager configuration files are stored in the /etc/X11/*windowmanager* directory, where *windowmanager* is the name of the specific window manager. While this includes other window managers such as twm and xdm, KDE configuration files are included in /etc/skel.

CERTIFICATION OBJECTIVE 4.03

Filesystem Configuration

There are as many, if not more, filesystem types as there are operating systems. Red Hat Linux can understand many of these formats.

Filesystem Types

At the heart of every Red Hat Linux installation are the filesystems on which it relies. Linux supports a rich variety of filesystem types. A sampling of these types is shown in Table 4-5.

TABLE 4-5	Filesystem Type	Description
Linux Filesystem Types	MS-DOS, VFAT, and UMSDOS	These filesystems allow you to read MS-DOS-formatted filesystems. MS-DOS lets you read pre–Windows 95 partitions, or regular Windows partitions within the limits of short filenames. VFAT lets you read Windows 95 and later partitions that are formatted to this filesystem. UMSDOS allows you to run Linux from a DOS partition (not currently supported by Red Hat).
	ISO 9660 CDROM	The standard filesystem for CD-ROMs. It is also known as the High Sierra File System, or HSFS on other Unix systems.
	Minix	The standard filesystem for the Minix operating system. This is the original default Linux filesystem. The current Linux standard is ext3.
	NTFS	NTFS is the Microsoft Windows NT/2000/XP filesystem designed for username / password security. Currently supported as a read-only system.
	OS/2 HPFS	The standard for IBM's OS/2 operating system.
	/proc	The /proc filesystem is a Linux *virtual* filesystem. *Virtual* means that it doesn't occupy real disk space. Instead, files are created as needed. /proc is used to provide information on kernel configuration and device status.
	/dev/pts	The /dev/pts filesystem is the Linux implementation of the Open Group's Unix98 PTY support.
	ROM	The ROM filesystem is a read-only filesystem, intended primarily for initial RAM disks such as an installation boot floppy.
	Second Extended (ext2)	The basis for ext3, the standard Linux filesystem. The ext3 filesystem is essentially ext2 with journaling.
	Third Extended (ext3)	The standard Linux filesystem.
	NFS	The Network File System. This is the system most commonly used to share files and printers between Linux and Unix computers.
	SMB	Server Message Block (SMB) is based on Microsoft and IBM network protocols. Linux can use SMB to share files and printers with Microsoft Windows operating systems.
	NCP	Netware Core Protocol (NCP) is the network filesystem used by Novell, using the IPX/SPX protocol stack. NCP allows Linux to use NCP as a client.

on the job

If you have the kernel source RPMs loaded on your system, you can see which filesystems any version or distribution of Linux currently supports. Navigate to the /usr/src/linux-2.x.y directory (where x and y represent the actual version number of your kernel. Run the make menuconfig command and use your arrow keys to navigate to the filesystems section.

The Filesystem Table

Information about your local and remotely mounted filesystems is stored in /etc/fstab. Each filesystem is described on a separate line. Each line is composed of multiple fields, each separated by spaces or tabs. When your system boots, it processes each filesystem in the order listed.

A sample /etc/fstab might look like the following:

```
LABEL=/          /            ext3       defaults                    1   1
LABEL=/boot      /boot        ext3       defaults                    1   2
/dev/hda2        swap         swap       defaults                    0   0
LABEL=/usr       /usr         ext3       defaults                    1   2
LABEL=/tmp       /tmp         ext3       defaults                    1   2
LABEL=/var       /var         ext3       defaults                    1   2
LABEL=/home      /home        ext3       defaults                    1   2
/dev/cdrom       /mnt/cdrom   iso9660    noauto,owner,kudzu,ro 0   0
none             /proc        proc       defaults                    0   0
```

Table 4-6 provides a description of each field, from left to right.

TABLE 4-6	Field Name	Description
/etc/fstab Column Descriptions from Left to Right	Label	Lists the device to be mounted.
	Mount point	Notes the directory where the filesystem will be mounted.
	Filesystem Format	Describes the filesystem type. Valid filesystem types include minix, ext, ext2, ext3, msdos, vfat, iso9660, nfs, and swap. If you have an unused partition, you can set this field to "ignore."
	Mount Options	Covered in the following section.
	Dump Value	Either 0 or 1. A value of 1 means that the filesystem is automatically saved to disk by the dump(8) command when you exit Linux.
	Filesystem Check Order	Determines the order that filesystems are checked during the boot process by fsck(8). The root directory (/) filesystem should be set to 1, and other local filesystems should be set to 2. Remote filesystems should be set to 0, which means that they are not checked on boot.

Mount Options

Although "defaults" is the right mount option for most /etc/fstab filesystems, there are other options, as listed in Table 4-7. If you want to use multiple options, separate them by commas. Don't use spaces between options.

The list in Table 4-7 is not comprehensive. Consult the mount(8) man page for more information.

TABLE 4-7 Linux /etc/fstab Mount Options	Mount Option	Description
	async	Data is read and written asynchronously.
	atime	Part of the defaults option. The inode associated with each file is updated each time the file is accessed.
	auto	The **mount -a** command mounts all of the filesystems with this option.
	defaults	Uses default mount options: rw, suid, dev, exec, auto, nouser, and async.
	dev	Permits access to character devices such as terminals or consoles and block devices such as drives.
	exec	Allows binaries (compiled programs) to be run on this filesystem.
	noatime	The inode associated with each file is not updated when accessed.
	noauto	Requires explicit mounting. Common option for CD and floppy drives.
	nodev	Devices on this filesystem are not read or interpreted.
	noexec	Binaries (compiled programs) cannot be run on this filesystem so mounted.
	nosuid	Disallows setuid or setgid permissions on this filesystem.
	nouser	Only root users are allowed to mount the specified filesystem.
	remount	Remounts a currently mounted filesystem. Also an option for the mount command.
	ro	Mounts the filesystem as read-only.
	rw	Mounts the filesystem as read/write.
	suid	Allows setuid or setgid permissions on programs on this filesystem.
	sync	Reads and writes are done at the same speed (synchronously) on this filesystem.
	user	Allows nonroot users to mount this filesystem. By default, this also sets the noexec, nosuid, and nodev options.

Using the Red Hat Package Manager

One of the major duties of a system administrator is software management. Applications are upgraded. Kernels are patched. Without the right tools, it can be difficult to figure out what software is on a system, what is the latest update, and what applications depend on other software. Space is wasted on outdated files, because nobody knows if they are important. Worse, you may install a new software package only to find it has overwritten a crucial file from a currently installed package. The Red Hat Package Manager (RPM) was designed to eliminate these problems. With RPM, software is managed in discrete "packages," where a *package* is a collection of the files required for the software, along with instructions for adding, removing, and upgrading those files. The RPM system also makes sure you never lose configuration files; key files are backed up before being overwritten. This system also makes it easy to find the currently installed version of any RPM-based application.

Another advantage of RPM is that a package can be specified just like an Internet address, in Uniform Resource Locator (URL) format. For example, if the foo.rpm package is on the /pub directory of the ftp.rpmdownloads.com FTP server, you can download this file by specifying the ftp://ftp.rpmdownloads.com/pub/foo.rpm file. Assuming you're connected to the Internet, the rpm command logs onto the FTP server anonymously and downloads the file.

If the FTP server requires a username and password, you can use the following format: ftp://*username*:*password*@*hostname*:*port*/*path*/*to*/*remote*/*package*/*file*.rpm, where *username* and *password* are the username and password you need to log on to this system, and *port*, if required, specifies a nonstandard port used on the remote FTP server. Based on the preceding example, you could install the foo.rpm package with a username of mjang and a password of Ila451MS with the following command:

```
rpm -i ftp://mjang:Ila451MS@ftp.rpmdownloads.com/pub/foo.rpm
```

What Is a Package?

In the generic sense, a package is a container. It includes the group of files needed to install a specific program or application, which normally includes binaries, configuration, and documentation files. It also includes instructions on how and where these files should be installed and uninstalled. An RPM package name usually includes the version, the release, and the architecture for which it was built. For example, the fictional penguin-3.4.5-26.i386.rpm package is version 3.4.5, release 26. The "i386" indicates that it is suitable for computers built to the Intel architecture.

Normally, you should be able to use the information in the /proc/cpuinfo file to find the type of CPU on your system, such as i386, i586, and i686. Many RPM packages are CPU specific. If in doubt, use packages with the i386 or noarch labels, as they are most generic.

What Is RPM?

At the heart of this system is the RPM database. Among other things, this database tracks the version and location of each file in each RPM. The RPM database also maintains an MD5 checksum of each file. With the checksum, you can use the **rpm -V** *package* command to see if any file from that RPM package has changed. The RPM database makes adding, removing, and upgrading packages easy, because RPM knows which files to handle, and where to put them.

RPM also manages conflicts between packages. For example, assume you have two different packages that use configuration files with the same name. Call the original configuration file /etc/someconfig. You've already installed package X. If you then try to install package Y, RPM backs up the original /etc/someconfig before installing package Y.

The key to this system is the rpm command. We'll cover the four most common modes associated with this command: query, install, upgrade, and remove. But first, in this age of insecure downloads, you should know how to validate the signature associated with an RPM, as well as verifying the files in a specific package.

Validating a Package Signature

RPM uses two methods of checking the integrity of a package: MD5 checksum and GPG signature. MD5 alone is adequate for verifying that the file is intact (no data was lost or corrupted while copying or downloading the file). GPG is used to establish the authenticity of the file; it can be used to confirm, for example, that an RPM file is indeed an official Red Hat RPM. Red Hat provides a GPG public key for its RPM files; the key is located in the RPM-GPG-KEY file on your distribution CD or can be downloaded from www.redhat.com/about/contact.html.

To authenticate your RPMs using the GPG system, import the key file using the command (assuming it's a CD-based keyfile, mounted on the /mnt/cdrom directory):

```
# rpm --import /mnt/cdrom/RPM_GPG_KEY
```

You can then verify both the integrity and the authenticity of an RPM with a command like this (assuming you're checking the integrity of an RPM on the standard directory on a Red Hat installation CD):

```
# rpm --checksig /mnt/cdrom/RedHat/RPMS/pkg-0.0.0-0.rpm
```

Verifying One or More Packages

Verifying an installed package compares information about that package with information from the RPM database on your system, or the original package. Verify does a check against the size, MD5 checksum, permissions, type, owner, and group of each file in the package. Here are a few verify examples:

■ Verify all packages

```
# rpm --verify -a
```

■ Verify all files within a package against an RPM file on a mounted CD-ROM

```
# rpm --verify -p /mnt/cdrom/RedHat/RPMS/fileutils-4.0-1.i386.rpm
```

■ Verify a file associated with a particular package

```
# rpm --verify --file /bin/ls
```

If the files or packages you were verifying checked out okay, you will see no output; otherwise, you'll see what checks failed. The output will be a string of eight characters, possibly with a "c" denoting configuration file, followed by the filename that failed. Each character in the eight-character field contains the result of a particular test. A "." (period) indicates that test passed. The following example shows /bin/vi with an incorrect group ID assignment:

```
# rpm --verify --file /bin/vi
......G.    /bin/vi
```

Table 4-8 lists the failure codes and their meanings.

TABLE 4-8	Failure Code	Meaning
RPM --verify Error Codes	5	MD5 checksum
	S	File size
	L	Symbolic link
	T	File modification time
	D	Device
	U	User
	G	Group
	M	Mode

Looking for the Right RPM

Sometimes you need a file or a command, and just don't know what is the correct package to install. Red Hat provides a database that can associate the right RPM package with a specific file. Naturally, this database can be installed from the rpmdb-redhat-* RPM. Once you install this RPM, you can find the RPM associated with any available file from the Red Hat installation CDs. For example, if you're looking for the package associated with /etc/passwd, run the following command:

```
# rpm --redhatprovides /etc/passwd
```

The --redhatprovides feature is a recent update to the rpm command, version 4.1, included with Red Hat Linux 8.0 and above.

Adding and Removing RPM Packages

RPM makes it easy to add and remove software packages to your system. It maintains a database regarding the proper way to add, upgrade, and remove packages. This makes it relatively simple to add and remove software with a single command.

Install Mode

The Install mode, as its name suggests, is used to install RPM packages on your system. Installing a package is accomplished with the -i option.

```
# rpm -i penguin-3.4.5-26.i386.rpm
```

If the package is available on a remote FTP server, you could install it directly from that server with a command like the following:

```
# rpm -i ftp://ftp.rpmdownloads.com/pub/penguin-3.4.5-26.i386.rpm
```

Before installing the package, RPM performs several checks. First, it makes sure the package you're trying to install isn't already installed—normally, RPM won't let you install a package on top of itself. It also checks to make sure you aren't installing an older version of the package. Next, RPM does a dependency check. Some programs won't work unless others are already installed. In this example, you've just downloaded the latest RPM version of the Penguin utilities, and you now want to install it.

```
# rpm -i penguin-3.4.5-26.i386.rpm
failed dependencies:
iceberg >>= 7.1 is needed by penguin-3.26.i386.rpm
```

This error tells you that rpm did not install the Penguin package because it requires the iceberg package, version 7.1 or later. You'll have to find and install the iceberg package, and any packages iceberg may require.

Finally, RPM checks to see if it would overwrite any configuration files when it installs a package. RPM tries to make intelligent decisions about what to do in this situation. If RPM chooses to replace an existing configuration file, it gives you a warning like:

```
# rpm -i penguin-3.26.i386.rpm
warning: /etc/someconfig saved as /etc/someconfig.rpmsave
```

It's up to you to look at both files and determine what, if any, modifications need to be made.

on the job

If you've already customized a package and upgrade it with rpm, go to the saved configuration file. Use it as a guide to change the settings in the new configuration file. Since you may need to make different changes to the new configuration file, you should test the result in every way that package may be used in a production environment.

Upgrade Mode

The -U switch is used to upgrade existing packages. For example, if Penguin utilities, version 3-4.5-25, is already installed, the following command:

```
# rpm -U penguin-3.26.i386.rpm
```

will upgrade the old version of the package with the new one. In fact, if you've never installed this package before, the -U switch works just like -i. The package is simply installed for the first time.

Remove Mode

The **rpm -e** command removes a package from your system. But before removing a package, RPM checks a few things first. It does a dependency check to make sure no other packages need what you're trying to remove. If it finds dependent packages, **rpm -e** fails with an error message identifying these packages.

If you have modified any of the configuration files, RPM makes a copy of the file, adds .rpmsave to the end of the filename, and then erases the original. Finally, after removing all files from your system and the RPM database, it removes the package name from the database.

Be very careful about which packages you remove from your system. Like most Linux utilities, RPM may silently let you shoot yourself in the foot. For example, if you were to remove the packages for /etc/passwd or the kernel, that would devastate your system.

Adding Updates, Security Fixes, and Other Items

Red Hat Linux is constantly being updated. As bugs or security problems are found, they are collected on Red Hat's Errata Web page, currently located at www.redhat.com/support/docs/errata.html. You should check this page regularly to ensure your system is up to date.

EXERCISE 4-2

Updating from the Red Hat Errata Page

Here's a good checklist to follow whenever you review the errata page:

1. Go to http://www.redhat.com/support/docs/errata.html. Find the General Red Hat Linux Errata link for your distribution.

2. For the latest version of Red Hat Linux, the page includes links for security alerts, bug fixes, and enhancements. The security alerts are especially important if your system is on a network. Click the security alerts link.

3. You may not have installed some of the affected packages. Use the **rpm -qi** *packagename* command to check. If you have installed an affected package on your system, consider the recommended upgrade.

4. Before replacing an affected package, consider the ramifications. You may need to bring the system down to single-user or perform a reboot, which can affect other users who are connected to your system. If a production computer is affected, you may want to test the changes on another computer first.

5. If you choose to make an upgrade, back up at least the relevant files on your current system. Upgrades do fail on occasion.

6. When performing the upgrade, watch for configuration file warnings. If your local configuration files are replaced with new files, you may need to change the new configuration files to reflect your current settings.

7. Thoroughly test the new package. Make sure you have it configured correctly.

8. If a package is listed in the errata but not installed on your system, chances are there's no reason to put it on your system now. Read the detailed errata entry for that package carefully, and only install it if needed.

Red Hat has now included an RH Network Software Manager service that you can configure to check for revised packages, new packages, errata, and other information. As of this writing, there are three levels of support: Demo (free), Basic, and Enterprise. Needless to say, Red Hat provides additional services with paid subscriptions. You may subscribe to any of these services by registering through www.redhat.com/network.

Seeing What Packages Are Installed

Without RPM, you'd need to search around your filesystems to figure out whether a particular software package is installed. RPM makes it easy for you to figure out what RPM packages are installed and get information about those packages.

Query Mode

One of the strengths of RPM is that it can account for every package or application file that was installed using an RPM file. With RPM's query mode, you can learn if a specific package is installed or identify the files associated with a particular package. If you use query mode to list the files in an RPM before installation, you can see if any of these files might cause problems, such as by overwriting configuration files.

The -q switch is used to query packages. The **rpm -q** *packagename* command will return the installed version of a specified package. For example, to find the version number of an installed lynx text browser, run the following command:

```
# rpm -q lynx
lynx-2.8.5-6
```

If you want to see which installed package owns a file, use the -f modifier. Here we want to identify the package that owns /etc/passwd:

```
# rpm -qf /etc/passwd
setup-2.5.16-1
```

Likewise, if you want to generate a list of files belonging to a certain package, use the -l modifier.

```
# rpm -ql setup
/etc/bashrc
/etc/csh.cshrc
/etc/csh.login
/etc/exports
/etc/filesystems
/etc/group
/etc/gshadow
/etc/host.conf
/etc/hosts.allow
/etc/hosts.deny
/etc/inputrc
/etc/motd
/etc/passwd
/etc/printcap
/etc/profile
/etc/profile.d
/etc/protocols
/etc/securetty
/etc/services
/etc/shadow
/etc/shells
/usr/share/doc/setup-2.5.16
/usr/share/doc/setup-2.5.16/uidgid
/var/log/lastlog
```

One of the most common modifiers to -q is -a, a query for all installed packages on your system. A default Workstation system has over 350 packages installed. Here's a truncated output:

```
# rpm -qa
ghostscript-fonts-5.50-6
libmng-1.0.4-1
libtiff-3.5.7-6
ncurses-5.2-28
arts-1.0.2-3
...
rpm404-python4.0.4-8x.26
sendmail-devel-8.12.5-5
```

on the job

It's common to use the rpm -qa command as a searchable database. All you need to do is pipe the output with a search term through grep. For example, the rpm -qa | grep kde command makes it easy to identify all packages related to the K Desktop Environment.

For even more information about a specific package, use the -i (information) modifier. Table 4-9 lists some of the most important entries from the package output.

```
# rpm -qi passwd
Name        : passwd              Relocations: (not relocateable)
Version     : 0.67               Vendor: Red Hat, Inc.
Release     : 3                  Build Date: Tue 28 May 2002 01:53:00 PM EST
Install date: Thu 30 Jul 2002 04:06:15: AM EDT      Build Host:
daffy.perf.redhat.com
Group       : System Environment/Base    Source RPM: passwd-0.67-3.src.rpm
Size        : 19016              License: BSD
Packager    : Red Hat, Inc. <http://bugzilla.redhat.com/bugzilla>
Summary     : The passwd utility for setting/changing passwords using PAM.
Description :
The passwd package contains a system utility (passwd) which sets
and/or changes passwords, using PAM (Pluggable Authentication
Modules).

To use passwd, you should have PAM installed on your system.
```

TABLE 4-9	Tag	Description
	Name	The name of the package.
RPM -qi Key Information Categories	Version	The version of the package.
	Release	The number of times this package has been released using the same version of the software.
	Install Date	When this package was installed on your system.
	Group	Your RPM database is divided into groups, which describe the functionality of the software. Every time you install a package, it will be grouped accordingly.
	Size	The total size in bytes of all the files in the package.
	License	The license under which the original software was released.

Creating and Using Custom RPMs

A source RPM is, as the name indicates, a package of source code used to build architecture-specific packages. Properly labeled source RPMs include the "src" identifier as part of the filename, such as:

```
polarbear-2.07-2.src.rpm
```

Binary RPMs are built from source RPMs. The source RPM contains the source code and specifications necessary to create the binary RPM.

For building RPMs from source, you can also install the rpm-build- package and then use the rpmbuild command. The same switches described in this section will also work with that command. In fact, in future releases of Red Hat Linux, the rpmbuild command may become the only way to build an RPM from source code or a tarball.*

Installing Source RPMs

Like normal RPMs, a source RPM (SRPM) is installed with the -i option. This installs the contents of the SRPM within the /usr/src/redhat directory structure.

The /usr/src/redhat/ Directory Structure

Five subdirectories appear within the /usr/src/redhat directory structure, as described in Table 4-10.

When you build an SRPM, you will build it within this structure. If you install an SRPM, it will be extracted into this structure.

TABLE 4-10	Directory	Purpose
Build Directories for RPM Source Files	/usr/src/redhat/SOURCES	Contains the original program source code.
	/usr/src/redhat/SPECS	Contains spec files, which control the RPM build process.
	/usr/src/redhat/BUILD	Source code is unpacked and built here.
	/usr/src/redhat/RPMS	Contains the output binary RPM.
	/usr/src/redhat/SRPMS	Contains the SRPM created by the build process.

Changing Compile Options for a Source RPM

While most precompiled RPMs will serve your needs, at times you will want to modify the source code or compile options in the corresponding SRPMs.

The Spec File   To change the compile options in an SRPM, you must understand spec files. The spec file is stored in /usr/src/redhat/SPECS/*packagename*.spec. The spec file controls the way a package is built, and what actions are performed when it is installed or removed from a system. A spec file has eight different sections, as described in Table 4-11. Several of the sections include commands that can be run as individual shell scripts.

You would change the compile-time options for a package in the build section of the spec file. Here's a sample build section in a spec file:

```
%build
rm -rf $RPM_BUILD_ROOT
mkdir -p $RPM_BUILD_ROOT/usr/bin $RPM_BUILD_ROOT/etc
./configure --prefix=/usr --exec-prefix=/
make CFLAGS="$RPM_OPT_FLAGS" LDFLAGS=-s
```

This section, a shell script, begins with some housekeeping, removing any files that may be left over from a previous build. A directory structure is created for the source files. Then the package is configured and compiled with a "make."

For a different package, you might modify the make command line to compile other components after LDFLAGS. The compile options from $RPM_OPT_FLAGS are defaults, set by RPM. Alternatively, you could use this variable to set other compile time options such as a different CPU.

TABLE 4-11	Section	Description
Build Directories for RPM Source Files	Preamble	Describes what information a user sees when requesting information about this package, such as with an rpm -qi command. This normally includes a package description, as well as applied sources and patches. It may also include an icon for use with a graphical RPM manager such as redhat-config-packages or kpackage.
	Prep	If work needs to be done to the source code before actually building it, it's set up here. At a minimum, this usually means unpacking the source code.
	Build	Commands to actually compile the spec file and build sources.
	Install	Commands to install the software on a system.
	Install and uninstall scripts	This section contains scripts that will be run on the end user's system to install or remove the software. RPM can execute a script before the package is installed, after the package is installed, before the package is removed, and after the package is removed.
	Verify	Although RPM takes care of most verification tasks, a script can be inserted here for any desired extra checks.
	Clean	A script can be specified here to perform any necessary cleanup tasks.
	Files	A list of files in the package.

Perhaps the essential reference guide to the RPM system is a book called Maximum RPM. It's normally included on the Red Hat Documents CD in HTML format. The start page for this book is located on that CD in the /RH-DOCS/maximum-rpm-1.0/html/index.html file.

Building Custom Source and Binary RPMs

By now, you should understand where you should modify an SRPM spec file to change compiletime options in the Build section. However, there's much more to building customized RPMs. Once you have modified the spec file, you need to tell RPM to build a new RPM and SRPM.

Starting a Build

You can build an RPM with the rpm build switch, -b. By itself, **rpm -b** calls the scripts specified in the Prep, Build, and Install parts of the spec file. Normally, you'll modify the -b with an "a," which makes RPM go through the build process, step by step. The RPM build operation is directed at a spec file. For example, the command

```
# rpm -ba foo-2.2.spec
```

directs RPM to create binary and source RPMs from this spec file. Alternatively, if you just want the binary RPM, the following command will do the job:

```
# rpm -bb foo-2.2.spec
```

Building an RPM from a Tar Archive

Now that you understand the basics of building an RPM from an SRPM, it's relatively easy to build an SRPM and an RPM from a tar archive, sometimes also known as a "tarball."

Obtain the Source Files

You'll need to obtain the source code for the package you want to create. You'll need to locate the FTP or Web site for the software you want, obtain the version of your choice, download it, and then put it in the SOURCES directory.

Create the Spec File

Here's where you get to brew a spec file from scratch. While spec files can be complex, this section just covers the basics you'll need to get a spec file running.

The Preamble   Open up a spec file in your favorite text editor. Start with the preamble. Here's the preamble (abridged) from version 4.1 of the fileutils.spec configuration file:

```
Summary: The GNU versions of common file management utilities.
Name: fileutils
Version: 4.1
Release: 10
License: GPL
Group: Applications/File
Source0: ftp://alpha.gnu.org/gnu/fetish/%{name}-%{version}.tar.bz2
Source1: DIR_COLORS
```

```
Source2: colorls.sh
Source3: colorls.csh
Patch1: fileutils-4.0-spacedir.patch
Patch2: fileutils-4.0s-sparc.patch
...
Patch15: fileutils-4.1-chown-optparse.patch
Buildroot: %{_tmppath}/%{name}-%{version}-root
Prereq: /sbin/install-info
BuildRequires: libtermcap-devel glibc-devel gcc make binutils fileutils
%description
The fileutils package includes a number of GNU versions of common and
popular file management utilities. Fileutils includes the following...
```

Preamble entries consist of a tag, followed by a colon, followed by information. Some entries are language-specific; these are denoted by a two-letter country code in parentheses just before the colon. The order of the lines is unimportant. Table 4-12 lists entries that may be part of the preamble.

TABLE 4-12	Tag	Description
Preamble Entries in a Spec File	Name	The name of the package.
	Version	The version of the software being packaged.
	Release	The number of times this software has been packaged.
	Buildroot	The directory this package was built in.
	Copyright	Contains the software's copyright information.
	Group	The software category associated with this package.
	Patch	Patches applied to the software.
	Source	Two entries are associated with this tag. The first indicates where the packaged software's source may be found. The second gives the name of the source file in the SOURCES subdirectory.
	Summary	A short, one-line description of the software being packaged.
	URL	If present, this lists the Web page that contains documentation for this package.
	Distribution	The company this package was created for, such as Red Hat. Usually includes a version number such as 8.0.
	Vendor	The group or organization that distributes the package.
	Packager	The group or organization that packaged this software.
	Description	A detailed description of the packaged software.

The Prep Section   The prep section prepares the source files for packaging. Usually it starts by deleting leftover files from previous builds with a command such as **rm -rf**. Then it unarchives the source files and applies any required patches. A sample prep section might look like this:

```
%prep
/bin/rm -rf $RPM_BUILD_DIR/foo-2.2
/bin/tar xzf $RPM_SOURCE_DIR/foo-2.2.tar.gz
```

Note that the prep section is nothing more than a shell script. The environment variables RPM_BUILD_DIR and RPM_SOURCE_DIR are preset by RPM. They expand to /usr/src/redhat/BUILD and /usr/src/redhat/SOURCE, respectively. This prep script extracts the contents of foo-2.2.tar.gz into the SOURCE directory. Any patches to the source would be applied here.

There is a predefined macro that will handle both steps from the previous example. The %setup macro removes any files left over from a previous build and then extracts the contents of the source file. Now, we can simplify the prep script:

```
%prep
%setup
```

The Build Section   Like the prep section, the build section is also a shell script. This script will handle building binary programs out of the source code. Depending on the software, this step may be very easy, or quite involved. A sample build script might be:

```
%build
make clean
./configure -prefix=/usr -exec-prefix=/
make
```

The "make clean" command removes old objects and configuration files. Then the configure script is run with some options which sets up the installation on a computer such as one based on the Intel architecture. The make command then can compile the software.

The Install Section   Yet another shell script, the install section, allows you to build a set of installation files within the source distribution. If the application is straightforward, the install commands may be as simple as:

```
%install
make install
```

The Files Section   This is a list of files that will become part of the package. Any files you want to distribute in the package must be listed here.

You may specify a %doc directive on a line, which indicates that the file listed on this line is documentation. That file will be placed in the /usr/doc/*package* subdirectory when the end user installs this package on the system. Here's an example of a files section from our fictional package foo-2.2:

```
%files
%doc README
%doc FAQ
/usr/bin/foo
/usr/man/man1/foo.1
```

This example installs the README and FAQ files in the /usr/doc/foo-2.2 subdirectory.

Building the RPM and the SRPM

Now that you've prepared your spec file, you're ready to build the RPM and the SRPM with the following command:

```
# rpm -ba foo-2.2.spec
```

You can build your packages in slightly different ways, as described in the command switches shown in Table 4-13.

Testing Your RPM

It's important you test your RPM thoroughly before releasing it for general distribution. Install it, uninstall it, run the program through its paces. Make sure the documentation and man pages were installed correctly and that configuration files are present and have sane defaults.

TABLE 4-13	Option	Description
rpm Switches for Building RPMs and SRPMs	-bp	Execute only the prep section.
	-bl	Check the files section to make sure all the files exist.
	-bc	Execute only the build section.
	-bi	Execute only the install section.
	-bs	Build only the SRPM.
	--test	Do not execute any build stages. (Useful for testing the syntax of your spec file.)

Like many other Linux commands, rpm has short and long versions of the same switch. For example, -i is the same as --install (note the double dash before the long version). You can learn which options have "long" equivalents by checking the man page for that command.

CERTIFICATION OBJECTIVE 4.05

Basic Networking

The network is where the power of Red Hat Linux really comes alive; however, getting there may not be trivial. As in all other things Linux, it's a learning experience.

Learn the scripts in the /etc/sysconfig and /etc/sysconfig/network directories. These are crucial to the configuration of Red Hat Linux. If you have a configuration to change or repair, it probably involves files in one of these directories. Red Hat appears to be consolidating a number of its key configuration files in its directories, so expect them to become even more important in the future.

The /etc/sysconfig/network scripts

We'll start our tour in the /etc/sysconfig directory. This is where Red Hat Linux stores and retrieves its networking information. With the various Red Hat configuration tools, you'll almost never have to touch these files, but it's good to know they're there. A few representative scripts are shown in Table 4-14.

/etc/sysconfig Files for Clock, Mouse, Static Routes, Keyboard, and PCMCIA

While we're in /etc/sysconfig, let's take a little detour and discuss some of the other things in here that make your system run. Configuration files for the system clock, mouse, keyboard, and PCMCIA adapter are shown in Table 4-15. Some of these files can be configured with other Red Hat tools discussed later in this chapter.

TABLE 4-14   Some Network Scripts in /etc/sysconfig

Filename	Description
/etc/sysconfig/network	This file stores your system's host name, IP forwarding information, NIS domain, gateway address, gateway device, and whether networking is active on your system.
/etc/sysconfig/network-scripts/	This directory stores the networking scripts necessary for your system to get itself up on the network.
/etc/sysconfig/network-scripts/ifcfg-lo	The loopback device configuration script. The loopback device is a virtual device that makes sure that TCP/IP is properly installed.
/etc/sysconfig/network-scripts/ifcfg-*	Each installed network adapter, such as eth0, is associated with an ifcfg-* script, such as ifcfg-eth0. This file includes the IP address information required to identify this network adapter on a network. It also notes whether this adapter should be activated when you boot Linux. The script associated with other adapters such as PPP modems may be more complex.
/sbin/ifup /sbin/ifdown	These scripts take a network interface device such as eth0 as an argument. For example, **ifup eth0** activates eth0; **ifdown eth0** deactivates this device.
/etc/sysconfig/network-scripts/network-functions	This script contains functions used by other network scripts to bring network interfaces up and down. This script should never be called directly.
/etc/sysconfig/network-scripts/ifup-post	This script is called whenever a network device (except SLIP) is activated. It sets up static routes with the ifup-routes script for static routes, configures aliases, sets the host name and IP address as required, and notifies programs that monitor network events.
/sbin/dhclient	dhclient is a command daemon that helps a network interface lease an IP address from a DHCP server. If your network adapter is configured to use DHCP or BOOTP in /etc/sysconfig/network, the /sbin/ifup script should start it. Supersedes previous scripts including /sbin/pump and /sbin/dhcpcd in previous versions of Red Hat Linux.
/etc/sysconfig/network-scripts/ifup-* and /etc/sysconfig/network-scripts/ifdown-*	These scripts activate and deactivate their assigned protocols. For example, ifup-ipx brings up the IPX protocol.
/sbin/ifconfig	The main network interface configuration utility. Can return or set the network parameters on a network device.

TABLE 4-15	File	Description
Some Nonnetwork /etc/sysconfig Files	/etc/sysconfig/clock	Contains defaults for the system clock, including time zone, UTC settings, and ARC (Alpha CPU-based) settings. If UTC=true, the BIOS is set to Greenwich Mean Time.
	/etc/sysconfig/mouse	Contains mouse configuration data: FULLNAME is a generic text description of the type of mouse. MOUSETYPE=*type*, where *type* is a generic model such as ps/2, msbm, or Microsoft. Closely related to the GUI XMOUSETYPE variable. If XEMU3=yes, a two-button mouse is set to emulate a third button. If WHEEL=yes, the mouse is set up with a scroll wheel.
	/etc/sysconfig/keyboard	Contains keyboard configuration data: KEYBOARDTYPE, usually "pc" and KEYTABLE, usually "us".
	/etc/sysconfig/pcmcia	Contains PCMCIA configuration data. If PCMCIA=yes, Linux loads PCMCIA modules on boot.

Setting Up a Network Interface

Using the redhat-config-network utility, you can modify your system name, as well as add, remove, and edit network interfaces. The redhat-config tools work only in a GUI.

EXERCISE 4-3

Changing Your System Name with redhat-config-network

1. From a GUI terminal, run **redhat-config-network**. This opens the Network Configuration dialog box.

2. Click the Hosts tab. You will see a display similar to the following illustration. The host name depends on what you assigned during the installation of Red Hat Linux. The default alias is "localhost.localdomain."

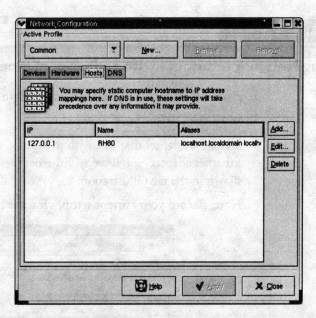

3. Replace your host name with a new host name (for example, RedHat80Test), followed by the domain name assigned to your network. Highlight the entry for your computer, and then click Edit. You can make the change in the Add/Edit Host entry dialog box that appears. Click OK when you're done. (For example, if you are in the *example.com* domain, use RedHat80Test.example.com.)

4. Back in redhat-config-network, select the Apply button for your new host name to take effect.

5. At the command line, enter the command **hostname**. You should see your new name.

6. Check your /etc/hosts file. You should see the new hostname here as well. Think about it: would it be easier just to edit the /etc/hosts file from the command line?

7. Reboot the computer; you should see the new host name at the login prompt.

EXERCISE 4-4

Modifying Network Interfaces with redhat-config-network

1. From a GUI terminal, start **redhat-config-network**.

2. Select the Devices tab if required.

3. Select the adapter that you wish to modify, and then select Edit. If it is an Ethernet adapter, you'll see an Ethernet Device dialog box similar to the one shown in the next illustration.

   Note: Record your current settings for this interface before proceeding.

III 4-3

4. Change the IP value to 192.168.1.11 and the network mask to 255.255.255.0.

   Note: If your computer is on the 192.168.1.0 private network, use a different private IP address. It should isolate you from all other hosts on the local network. Test this after step 5 by pinging other hosts on your network.

5. Select the OK button and wait for the process to complete.

6. At the command prompt, enter **/sbin/ifconfig** and check your new IP settings.

7. Repeat steps 1–3 and then reset the values to your previous settings. Run **/sbin/ifconfig** again to make sure you've restored your original network configuration.

Many values are associated with each network interface. At minimum, each network adapter requires a valid, unique IP address, as well as an appropriate network mask. redhat-config-network provides four convenient tabs which you can use to customize each network adapter:

■ The Devices tab allows you to add a new network adapter, or edit a configured adapter. You can revise the name of the adapter, IP address assignments, static routing, and hardware device information.

■ The Hardware tab lets you modify the IRQ port, Memory location, I/O address(es), and DMA channel(s) associated with the adapter.

Linux sometimes has trouble recognizing second network adapters, unless you specify at least the IRQ port.

■ The Hosts tab allows you to modify the name, alias, and IP address assigned to the specified adapter.

■ The DNS tab lets you add the addresses of DNS servers available to network adapters on the given network.

In addition, the Active Profile option allows you to create different network configurations, which can be useful for flexible configurations. For example, if you have a laptop computer and a docking port, your configuration may change depending on whether the laptop is connected to the docking port.

ifup/ifdown

For each installed network adapter, there is a corresponding ifcfg-* file in /etc/sysconfig/network-scripts. You can activate or deactivate that adapter with the ifup and ifdown commands. Either one of the following commands will activate the eth0 network adapter:

```
ifup ifcfg-eth0
ifup eth0
```

ifconfig

The ifconfig command is used to configure and display network devices. Here is some sample output of an ifconfig command:

```
# /sbin/ifconfig eth0
eth0      Link encap:Ethernet  HWaddr 00:50:56:40:1E:6A
          inet addr:192.168.199.131  Bcast:192.168.199.255  Mask:255.255.255.0
```

```
UP BROADCAST NOTRAILERS RUNNING MULTICAST  MTU:1500  Metric:1
RX packets:11253 errors:0 dropped:0 overruns:0 frame:0
TX packets:1304 errors:0 dropped:0 overruns:0 carrier:0
collisions:0 txqueuelen:100
RX bytes:2092656 (1.9 Mb)  TX bytes:161329 (157.5 Kb)
Interrupt:10 Base address:0x10a0
```

The preceding command requests configuration data for the first Ethernet device on the system, eth0. If you just specify eth0 (or another device), ifconfig displays information about only the specified interface. If you don't specify a device, ifconfig shows all network adapters, including the loopback adapter. Table 4-16 describes the significant fields in the output from the /sbin/ifconfig command.

The ifconfig command can also be used to configure network interfaces. For example, you can assign a new IP address for eth0 with the following command:

```
# /sbin/ifconfig eth0 207.174.142.142
```

The first parameter, eth0, tells us which interface is being configured. The next argument, 207.174.142.142, indicates the new IP address being assigned to this interface. If we want to make sure our change worked, we issue the ifconfig command again to view its current settings.

```
# /sbin/ifconfig eth0
eth0      Link encap:Ethernet  HWaddr 00:50:56:40:1E:6A
          inet addr: 207.174.142.142  Bcast:192.168.199.255  Mask:255.255.255.0
          UP BROADCAST NOTRAILERS RUNNING MULTICAST  MTU:1500  Metric:1
          RX packets:11253 errors:0 dropped:0 overruns:0 frame:0
          TX packets:1304 errors:0 dropped:0 overruns:0 carrier:0
          collisions:0 txqueuelen:100
          RX bytes:2092656 (1.9 Mb)  TX bytes:161329 (157.5 Kb)
          Interrupt:10 Base address:0x10a0
```

TABLE 4-16	Field	Description
Key Fields in ifconfig Output	RX and TX	Indicates the number of received and transmitted error-free packets, along with the number of errors, dropped packets, and buffer overruns.
	inet addr	The IP address assigned to this interface.
	Bcast	The network broadcast address.
	Mask	The netmask used by this subnet.
	Interrupt	The IRQ port assigned to this device.
	Base address	The I/O address assigned to this device.

Looking at the output of our command, we successfully changed the IP address on the eth0 interface to 207.174.142.142. With the right switch, the ifconfig command can modify a number of other settings for your network adapter. Some of these switches are shown in Table 4-17.

netstat -r

The netstat command is used to display a plethora of network connectivity information. The most commonly used option, **netstat -r**, is used to display local routing tables. Here's a sample **netstat -r** output:

```
# netstat -nr
Kernel routing table
Destination        Gateway           Genmask          Flags MSS Window  irtt Iface
127.0.0.0          *                 255.0.0.0        UH    40  0          0 lo
191.72.1.0         *                 255.255.255.0    U     40  0          0 eth0
0.0.0.0            191.72.1.1        255.255.255.0    UG    40  0          0 eth0
```

Did you notice we used a -n flag? -n tells netstat to display addresses as IP addresses, instead of as host names. This makes it a little easier for us to see what's going on.

TABLE 4-17	Parameter	Description
ifconfig Switches That Modify Network Adapter Settings	Up	Activates the specified adapter.
	Down	Deactivates the specified adapter.
	netmask *address*	Assigns the *address* subnet mask.
	broadcast *address*	Assigns the *address* as the broadcast address. Rarely required, since the default broadcast address is standard for most current networks.
	Metric *N*	Allows you to set a metric value of *N* for the routing table associated with the network adapter.
	mtu *N*	Sets the maximum transmission unit as *N*, in bytes.
	-arp	Deactivates the address resolution protocol, which collects network adapter hardware addresses.
	promisc	Activates promiscuous mode. This allows the network adapter to read all packets to all hosts on the LAN. Can be used to analyze the network for problems, or to try to crack messages between other users.
	-promisc	Deactivates promiscuous mode.
	irq *port*	Assigns a specific IRQ port.
	io_addr *address*	Assigns a specific I/O address.

The Destination column lists networks by their IP addresses. The Gateway column indicates gateway addresses. If the destination is on the LAN, no gateway is required, so an asterisk is shown in this column. The Genmask column lists the network mask. Networks look for a route appropriate to the destination IP address. The IP address is compared against the destination networks, in order. When the IP address is found to be part of one of these networks, it's sent in that direction. If there is a gateway address, it's sent to the computer with that gateway. The Flags column describes how this is done. Flag values are listed in Table 4-18.

arp as a Diagnostic Tool

The Address Resolution Protocol associates the hardware address of a network adapter with an IP address. The arp command displays a table of hardware and IP addresses on the local computer. With arp, you can detect problems such as duplicate addresses on the network, or you can manually add arp entries as required. Here's a sample arp command, showing all arp entries in the local database:

```
# /sbin/arp
Address            HWtype   HWaddress           Flags Mask          Iface
192.168.0.121      ether    52:A5:CB:54:52:A2   C                   eth0
192.168.0.113      ether    00:A0:C5:E2:49:02   C                   eth0
```

The address column lists known IP addresses, usually on the LAN. The HW Type column shows the hardware type of the adapter, while the HW Address column shows the hardware address of the adapter.

You can use the -H option to limit arp's output to a specific hardware type, such as ax25, ether, or pronet. The default is ether, which is short for Ethernet.

The arp command can help you with duplicate IP addresses, which can stop a network completely. To remove the offending machine's arp entry from your arp table, use the -d option:

```
# arp -d bugsy
```

TABLE 4-18	Flag	Description
The netstat Flag Column Indicates the Route	G	The route uses a gateway.
	U	The network adapter (Iface) is up.
	H	Only a single host can be reached via this route.
	D	This entry was created by an ICMP redirect message.
	M	This entry was modified by an ICMP redirect message.

This removes all arp information for the host "bugsy." To add an arp entry, use the -s option:

```
# arp -s bugsy 00:00:c0:cf:a1:33
```

This entry will add the host bugsy with the given hardware address to the arp table. IP addresses won't work in this case.

CERTIFICATION OBJECTIVE 4.06

The Basic Boot Process

Understanding how your system boots and shuts down will help you immensely as a Red Hat system administrator. Red Hat Linux uses a boot process called System V init, which means that after the kernel is loaded, it starts a program called init, which then starts everything else. To understand the process better, let's go through the steps Red Hat Linux takes to boot itself up to a usable system.

Once you understand the basic boot process, Red Hat Linux provides two utilities that assist the system's administrator in configuring and maintaining the commands that make up that startup and shutdown process. The ntsysv utility provides a screen-oriented interface, while chkconfig provides a command line interface.

Runlevels

Six basic runlevels are used in Red Hat Linux, as shown in /etc/inittab. Each runlevel is associated with a level of functionality in Linux. For example, in single-user mode, only one user is allowed to connect to that Linux system. X11 mode starts Linux into a GUI login screen. The Red Hat definitions for System V init runlevels are shown in Table 4-19.

Making each runlevel work is the province of a substantial number of scripts. Each script can start or stop fundamental Linux processes such as printing (cups), scheduling (crond), Apache (httpd), Samba (smbd), and more. The starting and stopping of the right scripts becomes part of the boot process.

It should go without saying that if you set your initdefault to 0, your system will shut down when Linux tries to boot. Likewise, if you set the initdefault to 6, Linux will enter a continuous reboot cycle.

TABLE 4-19	Runlevel	Description
Red Hat Linux Runlevels	0	Halt
	1	Single-user mode, for maintenance (backups/restores) and repairs
	2	Multiuser, without networking
	3	Multiuser, with networking
	4	Unused
	5	X11, defaults to a GUI login screen. Logins bring the user to a GUI desktop.
	6	Reboot (never set initdefault in /etc/inittab to this value!)

The Boot Process

The init process is the first program called by the kernel. This process in turn runs /etc/rc.d/rc.sysinit, which performs a number of tasks, including network configuration, keymaps, mounting partitions, and setting the host name. The init process then determines which runlevel it should be in by looking at the initdefault entry in /etc/inittab. A runlevel is defined as a group of activities. For example, the entry:

```
id:5:initdefault:
```

shows a default starting point in runlevel 5. Next, init starts the appropriate scripts associated with runlevel 5, from the /etc/rc.d directory. That directory includes the following subdirectories:

```
init.d
rc0.d
rc1.d
rc2.d
rc3.d
rc4.d
rc5.d
rc6.d
```

If the default runlevel is 5, init will look in /etc/rc.d/rc5.d and run each "kill" and "start" script it finds in that directory. A kill script is any file or symbolically linked file with a name that begins with a "K." Likewise, start scripts start with "S." If you run an **ls -l** command in this directory, you'll see only symbolic links to the actual scripts in /etc/rc.d/init.d. Observe current examples of Kill and Start scripts at runlevel 5 in Figures 4-5 and 4-6.

FIGURE 4-5

Kill scripts
at runlevel 5

```
[root@RH80 rc5.d]# ls -l K* | more
lrwxrwxrwx   1 root     root          19 Aug  1 01:38 K05saslauthd -> ../init.d/saslauthd
lrwxrwxrwx   1 root     root          15 Aug  1 02:04 K15httpd -> ../init.d/httpd
lrwxrwxrwx   1 root     root          13 Aug  1 01:43 K20nfs -> ../init.d/nfs
lrwxrwxrwx   1 root     root          14 Aug  1 01:40 K24irda -> ../init.d/irda
lrwxrwxrwx   1 root     root          15 Aug  1 02:06 K25squid -> ../init.d/squid
lrwxrwxrwx   1 root     root          19 Aug  1 02:01 K34yppasswdd -> ../init.d/yppasswdd
lrwxrwxrwx   1 root     root          13 Aug  1 02:05 K35smb -> ../init.d/smb
lrwxrwxrwx   1 root     root          17 Aug  1 02:05 K35winbind -> ../init.d/winbind
lrwxrwxrwx   1 root     root          15 Aug  1 01:39 K45named -> ../init.d/named
lrwxrwxrwx   1 root     root          15 Aug  1 01:41 K50snmpd -> ../init.d/snmpd
lrwxrwxrwx   1 root     root          19 Aug  1 01:41 K50snmptrapd -> ../init.d/snmptrapd
lrwxrwxrwx   1 root     root          13 Aug  1 02:06 K50tux -> ../init.d/tux
lrwxrwxrwx   1 root     root          13 Aug  1 02:01 K54pxe -> ../init.d/pxe
lrwxrwxrwx   1 root     root          17 Aug  1 02:04 K70aep1000 -> ../init.d/aep1000
lrwxrwxrwx   1 root     root          17 Aug  1 02:04 K70bcm5820 -> ../init.d/bcm5820
lrwxrwxrwx   1 root     root          14 Aug  1 01:38 K74ntpd -> ../init.d/ntpd
lrwxrwxrwx   1 root     root          16 Aug  1 02:01 K74ypserv -> ../init.d/ypserv
lrwxrwxrwx   1 root     root          16 Aug  1 02:01 K74ypxfrd -> ../init.d/ypxfrd
[root@RH80 rc5.d]#
```

FIGURE 4-6

Start scripts
at runlevel 5

```
[root@RH80 rc5.d]# ls -l S* | more
lrwxrwxrwx   1 root     root          15 Aug  1 01:40 S05kudzu -> ../init.d/kudzu
lrwxrwxrwx   1 root     root          18 Aug  1 01:42 S08iptables -> ../init.d/iptables
lrwxrwxrwx   1 root     root          14 Aug  1 01:40 S09isdn -> ../init.d/isdn
lrwxrwxrwx   1 root     root          20 Aug  1 06:14 S10dualconf -> /etc/init.d/dualconf
lrwxrwxrwx   1 root     root          17 Aug  1 01:38 S10network -> ../init.d/network
lrwxrwxrwx   1 root     root          16 Aug  1 01:38 S12syslog -> ../init.d/syslog
lrwxrwxrwx   1 root     root          17 Aug  1 01:39 S13portmap -> ../init.d/portmap
lrwxrwxrwx   1 root     root          17 Aug  1 01:43 S14nfslock -> ../init.d/nfslock
lrwxrwxrwx   1 root     root          18 Aug  1 01:40 S17keytable -> ../init.d/keytable
lrwxrwxrwx   1 root     root          16 Aug  1 01:38 S20random -> ../init.d/random
lrwxrwxrwx   1 root     root          16 Aug  1 01:43 S24pcmcia -> ../init.d/pcmcia
lrwxrwxrwx   1 root     root          15 Aug  1 01:38 S25netfs -> ../init.d/netfs
lrwxrwxrwx   1 root     root          14 Aug  1 01:39 S26apmd -> ../init.d/apmd
lrwxrwxrwx   1 root     root          16 Aug  1 01:42 S28autofs -> ../init.d/autofs
lrwxrwxrwx   1 root     root          14 Aug  1 01:41 S55sshd -> ../init.d/sshd
lrwxrwxrwx   1 root     root          20 Aug  1 01:38 S56rawdevices -> ../init.d/rawdevices
lrwxrwxrwx   1 root     root          16 Aug  1 01:38 S56xinetd -> ../init.d/xinetd
lrwxrwxrwx   1 root     root          13 Aug  1 01:47 S60lpd -> ../init.d/lpd
lrwxrwxrwx   1 root     root          18 Aug  1 01:42 S80sendmail -> ../init.d/sendmail
lrwxrwxrwx   1 root     root          13 Aug  1 01:40 S85gpm -> ../init.d/gpm
lrwxrwxrwx   1 root     root          15 Aug  1 01:43 S90crond -> ../init.d/crond
lrwxrwxrwx   1 root     root          13 Aug  1 01:44 S90xfs -> ../init.d/xfs
lrwxrwxrwx   1 root     root          17 Aug  1 01:43 S95anacron -> ../init.d/anacron
lrwxrwxrwx   1 root     root          13 Aug  1 01:39 S95atd -> ../init.d/atd
lrwxrwxrwx   1 root     root          19 Aug  1 01:49 S95firstboot -> ../init.d/firstboot
lrwxrwxrwx   1 root     root          15 Aug  1 01:43 S97rhnsd -> ../init.d/rhnsd
lrwxrwxrwx   1 root     root          11 Aug  1 01:38 S99local -> ../rc.local
[root@RH80 rc5.d]#
```

What's going on here? System V init knows to go to the directory associated with a particular runlevel. Once there, init runs the scripts in that directory that start with a K and then the scripts starting with an S. The K scripts stop processes that aren't supposed to operate in that runlevel. The S scripts start the processes associated with that runlevel. Within each category, scripts are run in numeric order; for example, K50tux is run before K74ntpd, which is run before S10network.

Red Hat Linux uses six different runlevels: 0, 1, 2, 3, 5, and 6. (runlevel 4 is unused as of this writing.) Symbolic links allows the collection of all init scripts in one directory, /etc/init.d. Any changes to a start or stop script can be made in that directory.

You can run a startup script yourself, with some key switches. For example, you can run the smb (Samba) and sshd (secure shell daemon) scripts with the following options:

```
# /etc/rc.d/init.d/smb
Usage: /etc/rc.d/init.d/smb {start|stop|restart|reload|status|condrestart}
# service smb    # service is a shortcut to the management scripts
Usage: /etc/rc.d/init.d/smb {start|stop|restart|reload|status|condrestart}
# service sshd
Usage: sshd {start|stop|restart|reload|condrestart|status}
#
```

For example, the /etc/rc.d/init.d/smb restart command stops and starts Samba.

This is used by the scripts at each runlevel. In other words, if there is a K script for the smb daemon, init runs /etc/rc.d/init.d/smb stop. And naturally, an S script for the ssh daemon runs /etc/rc.d/init.d/sshd start.

exam
ⓦatch *Make sure you go through the /etc/rc.d hierarchy as well as the /etc/inittab, and /etc/rc.d/rc.sysinit files, and understand what's happening along the way. This is the key to understanding what's happening during the boot process.*

The chkconfig Utility

The chkconfig command gives you a simple way to maintain different runlevels within the /etc/rc.d directory structure. With chkconfig, you can add, remove, and change services; list startup information; and check the state of a particular service. For example, you can check the runlevels where the sendmail service is set to run with the following command:

```
# /sbin/chkconfig --list sendmail
sendmail 0:off 1:off 2:on 3:on 4:on 5:on 6:off
```

which indicates that sendmail is configured to run in runlevels 2, 3, 4, and 5. If you want to turn the Sendmail service off for runlevel 4, execute the following command:

```
# /sbin/chkconfig --level 4 sendmail off
```

Now sendmail is configured to run only on runlevels 2, 3, and 5. To turn it back on, you run the same command, substituting **on** for **off**. With chkconfig, you can also add or delete services with the --add and --del switches. Adding a service sets up the appropriate links within the /etc/rc.d/ hierarchy. Deleting a service removes the associated links in the /etc/rc.d hierarchy.

When you configure or repair a service, use /sbin/chkconfig (or a related utility such as ntsysv) to make sure that the service is activated at the appropriate runlevels. The work that you do on the RHCE exam to configure or repair a service will not do you much good if the service isn't active after someone reboots your Linux computer.

The ntsysv Utility

The ntsysv command takes the functionality of chkconfig and wraps it into an easy-to-use screen interface. By default, ntsysv configures the current runlevel, which you can find with the /sbin/runlevel command. You can specify a different runlevel for ntsysv with the --level flag.

The ntsysv interface is extremely easy to use. Open up this utility with the /usr/sbin/ntsysv command, to get an interface similar to Figure 4-7. Select the service you want to modify using the arrow keys. Toggle the service on or off with the SPACEBAR. Selecting OK will commit the changes, while selecting Cancel will cancel any changes you made.

The Service Configuration Utility

Red Hat's Service Configuration utility provides another "front end" to managing services at different runlevels on your Linux computer. In a GUI such as GNOME or KDE, open a text console, and start the Service Configuration utility with the serviceconf command. You should see a Service Configuration window similar to Figure 4-8.

The Editing Runlevel line tells you which runlevel is currently being configured. For example, for the scenario shown in Figure 4-8, you could set up Linux to load the AEP coprocessor driver in runlevel 5 by selecting the highlighted check box.

FIGURE 4-7

The ntsysv Utility

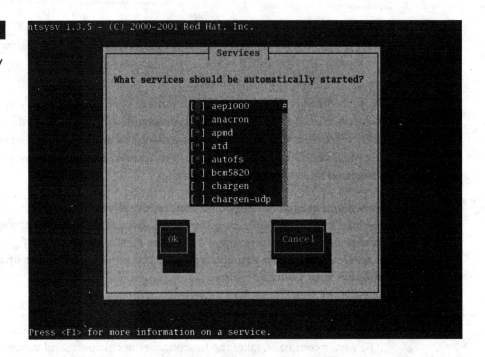

The Edit Runlevel menu on the toolbar allows you to switch this tool between runlevels 3, 4, and 5.

FIGURE 4-8

The Service
Configuration
utility

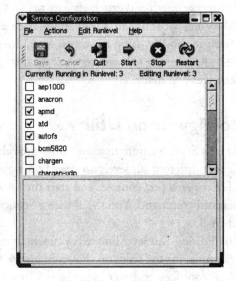

Virtual Consoles

Because Red Hat Linux is a multiterminal operating system, you can log into Linux, even with the same user ID, several times. This is made possible through the use of virtual consoles.

It's easy to open up a new virtual console. Just use the appropriate ALT-function key combination. For example, pressing the ALT key and F2 at the same time brings you to the second virtual console. You can switch between adjacent virtual consoles by pressing ALT-RIGHT ARROW or ALT-LEFT ARROW. For example, to move from virtual console 2 to virtual console 3, press ALT-RIGHT ARROW.

/etc/inittab

Virtual consoles are configured in the init configuration file, /etc/inittab. By default, Red Hat Linux is configured with six virtual consoles. You can add up to six more virtual consoles in /etc/inittab. Here are the default /etc/inittab entries for the first six virtual consoles:

```
1:2345:respawn:/sbin/mingetty tty1
2:2345:respawn:/sbin/mingetty tty2
3:2345:respawn:/sbin/mingetty tty3
4:2345:respawn:/sbin/mingetty tty4
5:2345:respawn:/sbin/mingetty tty5
6:2345:respawn:/sbin/mingetty tty6
```

Virtual consoles really bring the multiuser capabilities of Linux to life. You can be viewing a man page on one console, compiling a program in another, and editing a document in yet a third virtual console. Other users who are connected through a network can do the same thing at the same time.

The Graphical Console

The GUI is, in one way, just another console. By default, six virtual consoles are configured with Linux, so the GUI is next in line, at console 7. To switch from the GUI to a regular virtual console, press CTRL-ALT-Fx, where x represents one of the other virtual consoles.

CERTIFICATION OBJECTIVE 4.08

Other Configuration Tools

A number of other tools can help you configure and manage your Linux computer. Four screen-oriented programs included with Red Hat Linux can help you configure your keyboard, system time, mouse, and printer. You can access these tools and more through the /usr/sbin/setup command. This serves as a front end for other tools as shown in Figure 4-9.

kbdconfig

The kbdconfig utility allows you to set the type of keyboard you have. Figure 4-10 shows the main kbdconfig menu. Navigating through this utility to highlight the proper keyboard is easy with arrow and PGUP and PGDN keys. Then use the TAB key to highlight OK to save your changes to the /etc/sysconfig/keyboard file.

FIGURE 4-9

The setup utility

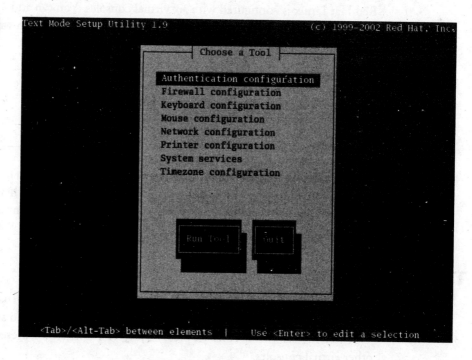

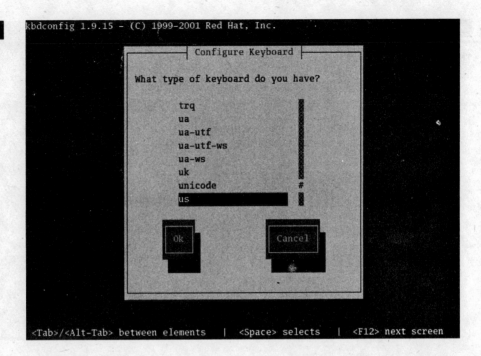

FIGURE 4-10

The kbdconfig
utility

```
kbdconfig 1.9.15 - (C) 1999-2001 Red Hat, Inc.

                        ┌─────────────┤ Configure Keyboard ├─────────────┐

                         What type of keyboard do you have?

                                   trq
                                   ua
                                   ua-utf
                                   ua-utf-ws
                                   ua-ws
                                   uk
                                   unicode                         #
                                   us


                              ┌──────┐              ┌────────┐
                              │  Ok  │              │ Cancel │
                              └──────┘              └────────┘



  <Tab>/<Alt-Tab> between elements   |   <Space> selects   |   <F12> next screen
```

timeconfig

The timeconfig utility allows you to set your time zone. Figure 4-11 shows the
timeconfig screen. If your system clock is set to Greenwich Mean Time (GMT), select
the Hardware Clock Set To GMT entry. This allows Linux to change your clock for
daylight saving time. You can navigate through this menu as with the kbdconfig utility.
Changes are saved to the /etc/sysconfig/clock file.

mouseconfig

The mouseconfig utility allows you to set your mouse setting to the correct type.
Figure 4-12 shows the mouseconfig screen. If you are using a two-button mouse
and wish to emulate three buttons, select the Emulate 3 Buttons option. In this
way, you can emulate the functionality of a middle mouse button by clicking both
buttons simultaneously. This utility can also help you configure a USB mouse. You
can navigate through this menu as with the kbdconfig utility. Changes are saved to
/etc/sysconfig/mouse.

FIGURE 4-11

The timeconfig
utility

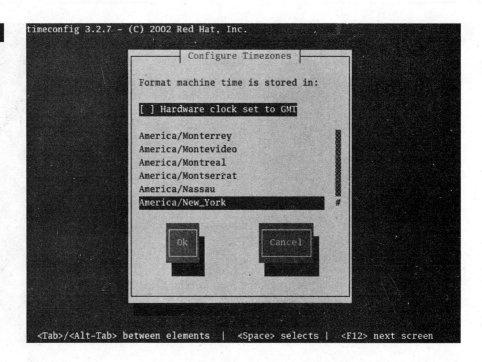

```
timeconfig 3.2.7 - (C) 2002 Red Hat, Inc.
```

```
┌──────────────┤ Configure Timezones ├──────────────┐


    Format machine time is stored in:

    [ ] Hardware clock set to GMT


    America/Monterrey
    America/Montevideo
    America/Montreal
    America/Montserrat
    America/Nassau
    America/New_York                           #


          Ok                  Cancel


<Tab>/<Alt-Tab> between elements  |  <Space> selects  |  <F12> next screen
```

on the
job *Some mice have two buttons and a center wheel between the buttons. This wheel is designed to scroll through a long list, such as a Web page. Some wheels can be depressed like a mouse button. This may work as a middle button in the GUI.*

CERTIFICATION OBJECTIVE 4.09

Mounting Floppy Disks and Removable Media

To read floppy disks and other removable media with Red Hat Linux, you need to mount the device, just as you would with any other network share or hard drive partition. Default mount points are available in the /mnt directory for at least CDs and floppy drives. Depending on the hardware that Linux detects, other mount points may also appear under /mnt. Naturally, /mnt/floppy is for mounting a single floppy disk, while

FIGURE 4-12

The mouseconfig
utility

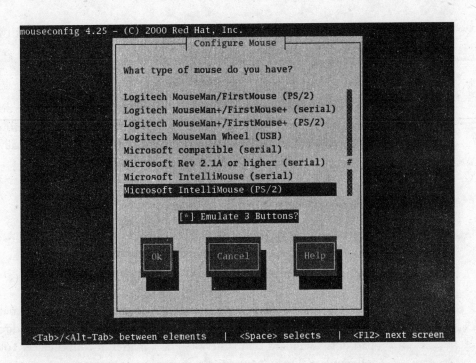

/mnt/cdrom is used to mount a single CD-ROM. To mount an MS-DOS-formatted
floppy, run:

```
# mount -t vfat /dev/fd0 /mnt/floppy
```

The -t switch specifies the type of filesystem (vfat). The device file /dev/fd0 represents
the first floppy drive; /mnt/floppy is the directory though which you can access the
files on the floppy after mounting.

But the command that you actually need may be simpler. Take a look at your
/etc/fstab configuration file. You'll probably see something like the following:

```
/dev/fd0          /mnt/floppy          auto      noauto,owner,kudzu    0 0
```

This /etc/fstab line sets the default configuration for the first floppy drive (/dev/fd0).
Normally, it's mounted on the /mnt/floppy directory. The format is *auto*, which
means that the mount command searches through the /etc/filesystems configuration
file. As long as vfat is part of this file, you do not need to specify the filesystem type.
The mount command reads the filesystem on the floppy and mounts it with the

correct filesystem automatically. So all you really need to mount the floppy is the following command:

```
# mount /dev/fd0 /mnt/floppy
```

But wait; if you know something about /etc/fstab, you know that the device and mount points are effectively linked. If you specify either, mount looks through /etc/fstab for the appropriate device, label, or mount point. Therefore, all you actually need to mount the floppy is either one of the following two commands:

```
# mount /dev/fd0
# mount /mnt/floppy
```

Similarly, the device for your CD-ROM is normally /dev/cdrom. To mount an ISO 9660 CD-ROM, run the following command:

```
# mount -rt iso9660 /dev/cdrom /mnt/cdrom
```

Now you can read the contents of /mnt/cdrom as if it were a normal file system on your system. You don't have to use the /mnt/floppy or /mnt/cdrom directories. They're part of the standard Linux filesystem as a matter of convenience. You can mount a floppy or CD on an empty directory of your choice.

But wait, the actual command that you need is simpler. Take a look at the relevant default line from /etc/fstab:

```
/dev/cdrom       /mnt/cdrom       iso9660    noauto,owner,kudzu,ro    0 0
```

As you can see, iso9660 is already specified as the default CD filesystem, and CDs are mounted as read-only (ro) by default. Therefore, all you actually need to mount the CD is either one of the following two commands:

```
# mount /dev/cdrom
# mount /mnt/cdrom
```

To unmount a floppy or CD-ROM, use the umount command with the mount point as an argument. The following commands unmount both our floppy and our CD-ROM:

(*Remember, the command is umount, not unmount.*)

```
# umount /mnt/floppy
# umount /mnt/cdrom
```

It is important you unmount floppy disks before removing them. Otherwise, the data that you thought you wrote to the disk might still be in the cache. In that case, you would lose that data.

One system has a Zip drive of 100MB. The device is /dev/hdd and was formatted as a Linux Native (ext3) Filesystem on partition /dev/hdd1. The directory /mnt/zip was created, and a permanent entry in /etc/fstab was added to mount the device at every reboot. You can now manually mount, unmount, and eject the Zip drive with the following commands:

```
# mount /dev/hdd1 /mnt/zip
The command to manually unmount the Zip drive:
# umount /dev/hdd1
The command to eject the Zip drive (which automatically unmounts it):
# eject /dev/hdd1
```

CERTIFICATION SUMMARY

This chapter covered basic configuration and administration of a Red Hat Linux system. We learned the steps necessary to create a basic user, how to populate a user's home directory with the templates in /etc/skel, and where window manager configuration files are located. We also covered the different types of filesystems Linux uses, discussed how to mount them, and described what mount options to use with them.

This chapter covered the management of RPM packages. We learned the steps necessary to validate a package signature; how to add, remove, and upgrade packages; and how to add updates. We also talked about verifying packages and how to see what package a file belongs to. We finished the topic with a discussion on installing SRPMs and building RPMs from SRPMs and tar archives.

In the "Basic Networking" section, we covered the configuration files in the /etc/sysconfig hierarchy, including files for the clock, mouse, static routes, keyboard, network, and PCMCIA. We also discussed the ifup, ifdown, ifconfig, netstat, and arp commands.

We concluded the chapter by talking about virtual consoles; the kbdconfig, timeconfig, mouseconfig, and sndconfig screen utilities; and how to mount floppy disks and removable media.

TWO-MINUTE DRILL

Here are some of the key points from the certification objectives in Chapter 4.

Adding, Deleting, and Modifying User Accounts

❑ After installation, your system may have only a single login account: the root account. For most installations, you'll want to create more accounts. Even if you're going to be the only user on the system, it's a good idea to create a single, nonprivileged account to do your day-to-day work and use the root account only for administering the system.

❑ Accounts can be added directly by editing /etc/passwd, or though useradd. The advantage of useradd is that it automatically sets up configuration files from /etc/skel, as well as the new home directory.

❑ Accounts can be added to Red Hat Linux systems using the Red Hat User Manager utility. You can also use this utility to further configure the account with parameters such as a password lifetime or a time limit on the account.

❑ A password cracking program may be able to find a dictionary-based password in a matter of minutes. In contrast, a more complex password such as Ila451MS (which could stand for "I live at 451 Main Street") may take hours for that same program to crack.

❑ If your installation doesn't require each user having his or her own unique group ID (GID), assign users to the Users group. There's rarely a need for each user to have an individual GID, and having most users assigned to the Users group makes system administration easier.

❑ Discourage the use of shared accounts, where several people use a single account. Shared accounts are almost always unnecessary, and they are easily compromised.

❑ If you'll be using the Network File System (NFS), make user accounts with the same UID across systems. The Network Information System (NIS) can serve this purpose.

The Basic User Environment

❑ Each user on your Red Hat Linux system has an *environment* when logged on to the system.

❑ The home directory for each login account is the initial directory in which users are placed when they first log on to a Red Hat Linux system.

❑ Window manager configuration files are often stored in /etc/X11/*windowmanager*, where *windowmanager* is the name of the window manager. KDE window manager files are stored in each user's home directory.

Filesystem Configuration

❑ If you have the kernel source RPMs loaded on your system, you can see which filesystems any version or distribution of Linux currently supports. Look at the file /usr/src/linux-2.x.y/fs/filesystems.c.

❑ A number of mount options are available for /etc/fstab. The defaults mount option sets up a partition as rw (read/write), suid (superuser ID files allowed), dev (device files read), exec (binaries can be run), auto (automatic mounting), nouser (mountable only by root), async (data is read asynchronously).

Using the Red Hat Package Manager

❑ The RPM database tracks where each file in a package is located, its version, and much more.

❑ Verifying an installed package compares information about that package with information from the RPM database on your system or the original package.

❑ The Install mode of RPM, as its name suggests, is used to install RPM packages on your system.

❑ The Upgrade mode of RPM will replace the old version of the package with the new one.

❑ The rpm -e command (erase) removes a package from your system.

❑ Using RPM's query mode, you can determine which packages are installed on your system or what file belongs to a particular package.

❑ Source RPMs are, as the name indicates, the source codes used to build architecture-specific packages.

❑ The spec file is stored in /usr/src/redhat/SPECS/*packagename*.spec. It controls the way a package is built, and what actions are performed when it is installed or removed from a system.

❑ Run **rpm -ba** *packagename* **spec** to build your RPM and SRPM. If you have the rpm-build-* package installed, you can use the **rpmbuild -ba** *packagename* **spec** command instead.

❑ Like many Linux tools, RPM has short options that have long option equivalents. For example, the -i option (a "short" option) can also be specified using the --install option (a "long" option). Learn which options have "long" equivalents by checking the man pages for that command.

Basic Networking

❑ To change your system name, run **redhat-config-network**.

❑ To manage network settings on each interface, use **dhclient** (dhcp/bootp client management), **ifup**, and **ifdown**.

❑ The **ifconfig** command is used to configure and display network devices.

❑ Use **ifup eth0** and **ifdown eth0** to activate and deactivate the eth0 interface.

❑ The **netstat** command is used to display a plethora of network connectivity information.

❑ Network communication doesn't start until network adapters know each other's hardware address. The Address Resolution Protocol (ARP) documents network adapter addresses. The **arp** command is used to view or modify the local ARP database.

The Basic Boot Process

❑ Red Hat Linux uses a boot process called System V init, which means that after the kernel is loaded, it starts a program called init, which then starts /etc/rc.sysinit.

❑ Make sure you go through the /etc/rc.d hierarchy and the /etc/inittab and /etc/rc.d/rc.sysinit files, and understand what's happening along the way. This is the key to understanding what's happening during the boot process.

❑ The chkconfig command gives you a simple way to maintain the /etc/rc.d directory structure.

❑ The ntsysv command takes the functionality of chkconfig and wraps it into an easy-to-use screen interface. By default, ntsysv allows you to configure the services at the current runlevel.

❑ The Service Configuration utility performs a similar function to ntsysv in a graphical user interface.

Virtual Consoles

❑ Because Red Hat Linux is a multiterminal operating system, it allows you to have more than one login session on the system console at a time using virtual consoles.

❑ By default, six virtual consoles are started at boot time.

❑ You can switch between virtual consoles by pressing ALT-F1 to ALT-F6. By default, you start on the first virtual (ALT-F1) console screen.

❑ You can get to console mode from your X Window session with CTRL-ALT-(F1 to F6). Return to X Window with ALT-F7.

Other Configuration Tools

❑ The kbdconfig utility enables you to change your keyboard settings.

❑ The timeconfig utility enables you to set your time zone.

❑ The mouseconfig utility enables you to set your mouse to the correct type.

Mounting Floppy Disks and Removable Media

❑ To read floppy disks and other removable media with Red Hat Linux, you need to mount the device, just as you would any other filesystem.

❑ Red Hat has created mount points in the /mnt directory for just this purpose.

❑ If your /etc/fstab is configured with the *auto* switch for your floppy drive, you should be able to mount it with the mount /dev/fd0 /mnt/floppy command.

SELF TEST

The following questions will help you measure your understanding of the material presented in this chapter. Read all the choices carefully, as there may be more than one correct answer. Choose all correct answers for each question.

Adding, Deleting, and Modifying User Accounts

1. When adding a user using the Red Hat User Manager, what information is not required?

    A. Full name

    B. User name

    C. Default shell

    D. Home directory

2. When deleting a user account using userdel, which command switch deletes that user's home directory?

    A. -d

    B. -r

    C. -h

    D. -a

The Basic User Environment

3. Where are individual users' configuration files for the KDE window manager stored?

    A. /usr/lib/X11/.kde

    B. ~/.kde

    C. /etc/X11/.kde

    D. /etc/skel/.kde

Filesystem Configuration

4. To change the mount options for a local filesystem, which of the following files would you edit?

    A. /etc/filesystems

    B. /etc/fstab

    C. /etc/group

    D. /etc/mnttab

5. When mounting a filesystem, which option would you use so that binaries cannot be run on that filesystem?

   A. nouser

   B. nosuid

   C. noauto

   D. noexec

Using the Red Hat Package Manager

6. Which of the following commands correctly installs the package penguin-3.26.i386.rpm?

   A. rpm -I penguin-3.26.i386.rpm

   B. rpm -i penguin

   C. rpm -i penguin-3.26.i386.rpm

   D. rpm --install penguin.rpm

7. When you check Red Hat's Errata Web page, you find a package that is currently installed on your system. What should you do about it?

   A. Determine if upgrades affect current users.

   B. Check the backups that may be made if and when configuration files are replaced.

   C. Test the new package to ensure it's been configured correctly.

   D. All of the above.

8. Source RPMs are, by default, installed in which directory?

   A. /usr/lib/rpm

   B. /usr/src/rpm

   C. /usr/src/redhat

   D. /usr/src/redhat/rpm

9. What subdirectories are used for source RPM files in the /usr/src/redhat directory?

   A. SOURCES, SPECS, BUILD, RPMS, SRPMS

   B. SOURCES, SPECS, LIBS, RPMS, DESC

   C. SOURCES, SPECS, BINS, RPMS, DESC

   D. SOURCES, SPECS, ETC, RPMS, SRPMS

10. Which section of an RPM spec file is used to compile the source code?

    A. Clean

    B. Prep

    C. Build

    D. Install

11. The prep section of an RPM spec file serves what purpose?

    A. Describes what information users see when they request information about this package

    B. Contains commands to compile and build the binaries from source code

    C. Takes care of extra tasks to be performed when a verify command is issued

    D. Unpacks the source code and configures it for building

12. When building an RPM from a tar archive, where should you put the tar file?

    A. /usr/src/redhat

    B. /usr/src/redhat/SOURCES

    C. /usr/src/redhat/TAR

    D. /usr/src/redhat/SRPMS

13. What happens when you run **rpm -bc foo-2.2.spec**? Assume foo-2.2 is a real package.

    A. Binary and source RPMs are created on the basis of the spec file.

    B. Only the SRPM is built.

    C. Only the install section of the spec file is run.

    D. Only the build section of the spec file is run.

Basic Networking

14. What information can you find in the /etc/sysconfig/network file?

    A. Your computer's host name

    B. The devices used for your network connections

    C. Chat scripts for PPP and SLIP connections

    D. The status of the network

15. What command is used to configure and display network devices?

    A. netstat

    B. arp

    C. ifconfig

    D. ifup

16. What does the **netstat -r** command do?

    A. Display kernel routing tables

    B. Display gateway metrics

    C. Configure kernel routing tables

    D. Configure gateway metrics

17. What does the **arp -d rhino** command do? Assume rhino is the host name of a remote computer on the network.

    A. It removes all ARP tables from the computer named rhino.

    B. It removes all ARP information about the computer named rhino.

    C. It displays all ARP tables on the computer named rhino.

    D. All ARP information pertaining to the host rhino is displayed.

The Basic Boot Process

18. Upon boot, the kernel starts init. What does init start next?

    A. /etc/rc.d/init.d

    B. /etc/inittab

    C. /etc/rc.d/initdefault

    D. /etc/rc.d/rc.sysinit

19. If you want to find the runlevels where crond is supposed to start, which command would you use?

    A. chkconfig --list --crond

    B. chkconfig -l crond

    C. chkconfig --list crond

    D. chkconfig crond

Virtual Consoles

20. To switch to the fourth virtual console, which keys would you press?

    A. ALT-4

    B. ALT-F4

    C. CTRL-4

    D. CTRL-F4

21. To switch from a text-based current virtual console to the X Window display, which keys would you press?

    A. ALT-1

    B. ALT-F1

    C. ALT-7

    D. ALT-F7

LAB QUESTION

Part 1

In this exercise, you are going to experiment with a few other neat utilities for system management, KDE's SysV-Init Editor and GNOME's Service Configuration utility.

1. From a text console window such as Konsole or gnome-terminal, run **ksysv** or **serviceconf**. These are the KDE and GNOME graphical equivalents to chkconfig and ntsysv. Run the applicable graphical tool in the background so that you can still use this terminal window with one of the following commands:

   ```
   [root]# ksysv &
   [root]# serviceconf &
   ```

2. This will present a graphical tool for controlling the services that are started and stopped at each runlevel.

3. These next steps assume that the autofs service is already running and installed; if not, pick another service to add and remove (it does not matter which as long as you put it back exactly as it was before).

4. From within the graphical tool, edit the autofs record and record the current order number. If you're running the Service Configuration utility, you'll need to run an **ls /etc/rc.d/rc3.d** command to find this number.

5. Remove the autofs service from level 3.

6. Switch back to the console window and run the **/sbin/chkconfig --list autofs** command to see if it has been removed.

7. Add the autofs service back in with order number 29.

8. Switch back to the console window and run the **/sbin/chkconfig --list autofs** command to verify that it is back.

9. Although KDE's SysV-Init Editor and GNOME's Service Configuration utility both provide nice graphical interfaces, the chkconfig utility is probably faster and easier to remember, especially since X is not always available in an emergency or through remote login.

Part 2

While the Red Hat User Manager provides a convenient interface to add new users, it's important for the exam to know the basic command line tools. Specifically, you can use the useradd, usermod, and userdel commands to add, modify, and delete user accounts.

1. Use the man pages for useradd (or just type **useradd** with no arguments for a simple help summary) to find the switches you need to add the following account with each of these attributes:

   ```
   login: brianr
   name: brian rite
   UID: 5010
   GID: nobody
   shell: /bin/bash
   ```

2. Change the passwd for brianr to RvRg49().

3. Telnet into localhost and log in as brianr. What files are present in this new account? Exit from this login.

4. Remove the brianr account using the userdel command. Is the brianr home directory gone? What option would have done this for you?

Part 3

In this lab, you'll observe what happens when you avoid mounting the /boot filesystem. This of course assumes that you have a computer configured with /boot mounted on a separate partition.

1. Back up your /etc/fstab configuration file to something you can easily remember, such as /etc/bak.fstab.

2. Run the df command and make a note of the mounted filesystems, especially the partition associated with /boot.

3. Open /etc/fstab in the text editor of your choice. You should have a line associated with the /boot directory. If you do not, **stop, as you cannot continue with this lab. Trying to continue with this lab under these circumstances will probably render your system unbootable.**

4. Comment out the line with the /boot directory. Add a "#" in front of that line. For example, your /etc/fstab /boot directory line might read something like:

   ```
   # LABEL=/boot        /boot           ext3          defaults  1 2
   ```

5. Save /etc/fstab and reboot Linux.

6. Observe the results? Does Linux start normally?

7. Look at your boot directory. Are there any files missing? How did Linux boot without benefit of a vmlinuz kernel or a mkinird RAM disk file?

8. Run the df command and make a note of the mounted filesystems.

9. Open /etc/fstab again. Remove the comment field, the "#", in front of the /boot directory line. Save /etc/fstab. This should restore your /etc/fstab to the original configuration.

10. Mount the /boot directory with the **mount /boot** command.

11. Open your GRUB configuration file, /boot/grub/grub.conf in your text editor.

12. Observe the line associated with the **root** variable. This should correspond to the default partition for the /boot directory. Note that GRUB does not require that a partition is mounted to access a file.

13. Reboot your system. Run the df command and compare the list of mounted filesystems to step 2. If they are the same, stop here. Otherwise, restore your /etc/fstab from the backup file, /etc/bak.fstab.

SELF TEST ANSWERS

Adding, Deleting, and Modifying User Accounts

1. ☑ A. While it's helpful to include the name of the new user, it isn't required.
   ☒ B, C, and D are incorrect. To create a user with any tool, including the Red Hat User Manager, you need a username (B), default shell (C), and home directory (D).

2. ☑ B. The **userdel -r** *username* command deletes the user as well as all of the files in the /home/*username* directory.
   ☒ A, C, and D are not real switches for the userdel command.

The Basic User Environment

3. ☑ B. The tilde (~) is the generic term for each user's home directory. When users are created, these files are transferred from /etc/skel to the right home directory.
   ☒ A and C are not valid locations for KDE configuration files. While the generic KDE configuration files are stored in /etc/skel, they do not belong to any particular user (D).

Filesystem Configuration

4. ☑ B. Information regarding filesystems, including mount options, is stored in /etc/fstab.
   ☒ A, C, and D are incorrect. The /etc/filesystems file lists currently supported filesystem formats (A). Group information and passwords are documented in /etc/group (C). /etc/mnttab (D) is an invalid filename.

5. ☑ D. The noexec option prevents binaries from being run on a filesystem.
   ☒ A, B, and C are incorrect. The noauto option (C) stops automounting; nosuid (B) stops any program where the SUID bit is set; the nouser option (A) stops nonroot users from mounting this filesystem.

Using the Red Hat Package Manager

6. ☑ C, rpm -i penguin-3.26.i386.rpm. When installing a package, the -i option is used, followed by the name of the RPM file.
   ☒ D is almost correct. It has the wrong filename for the RPM, but it would work otherwise. B also does not use the full filename. An asterisk at the end would make it work (as in penguin*), but this would install every package starting with the name penguin, so it may install more than you want. The -I option is invalid with rpm (A).

7. ☑ D. All of the above. A, B, and C are all good strategies when updating an RPM on your system.
   ☒ There are no incorrect answer choices.

8. ☑ C. When installing SRPMs, they are, by default, extracted into the /usr/src/redhat directory structure.
   ☒ A, B, and D are nonexistent files and directories.

9. ☑ A. SOURCES, SPECS, BUILD, RPMS, SRPMS are the subdirectories within the /usr/src/redhat directory structure.
   ☒ B, C, and D all include a subdirectory that's not part of the standard /usr/src/redhat directory structure.

10. ☑ C. Build. The build section of the spec file is used to compile the source code.
    ☒ A, B, and D are incorrect. The clean option removes old files (A), the prep section unpacks the source code and runs configuration commands (B), while the build section compiles the source code (D).

11. ☑ D. The prep section is executed just before the build section and usually is used to unpack the source code and run any configuration commands.
    ☒ A refers to the Preamble section of the spec file, B refers to the Build section of the spec file, and C refers to the Verify section of the spec file.

12. ☑ B. To build an RPM from a Tar archive, the tar files should first be copied to the /usr/src/redhat/SOURCES directory.
    ☒ The directories listed in answers A, C, and D are not used.

13. ☑ D. Only the build section of the spec file is executed.
    ☒ You would use **rpm -bs** for B, **rpm -bi** for C, and **rpm -ba** for A.

Basic Networking

14. ☑ A. If networking is enabled, the file will contain your host name, and possibly configuration information for NIS and packet forwarding.
    ☒ It will not identify the network device, nor will it contain status information, or any chat scripts (B, C, and D).

15. ☑ C. The ifconfig command is used to configure and display network devices.
    ☒ The ifup command (D) can be used to start|stop|status an interface, arp (B) manages the arp table in memory, and netstat (A) displays network statistics.

16. ☑ A. **netstat -r** is used to display the kernel's network routing tables.
    ☒ A Gateway metric measures the number of networks that a message can traverse, and is not

a function of netstat (**B**). This command can't configure the routing table, nor can it configure any gateway metrics (**C** and **D**).

17. ☑ **B**. The **arp -d** *hostname* command tells the kernel to remove all arp info regarding a specified host.

 ☒ The previous statement also means **D** is incorrect. **A** and **C** are incorrect because arp can't remove or display the hardware address table from a remote host.

The Basic Boot Process

18. ☑ **D**. init runs /etc/rc.d/rc.sysinit, which performs a number of tasks, including configuring the network and setting up keymapping, swapping, and the host name.

 ☒ **A** is a directory. **B**, /etc/inittab, is the init configuration file, which sets the runlevel at startup. However, /etc/inittab is not a script. While **C**, /etc/rc.d/initdefault is not a real filename, initdefault is a variable within /etc/inittab that determines the default runlevel of your system.

19. ☑ **C**. **chkconfig --list crond**. The output of this command is: crond 0:off 1:off 2:on 3:on 4:on 5:on 6:off.

 ☒ The -l option is not valid, nor is the --crond option (**A** and **B**). Since a switch is required for chkconfig, answer **D** is incorrect.

Virtual Consoles

20. ☑ **B**. Press ALT-F4. Each virtual console has an ALT-function key associated with it to move to that virtual console.

 ☒ **A**, **C**, and **D** normally do not do anything when you are at a regular virtual console.

21. ☑ **D**. Press ALT-F7 to switch from a virtual console to the default X Window display.

 ☒ **A**, **B**, and **C** normally do not do anything when you are at a regular virtual console.

LAB ANSWER

Part I

1. From a text console window such as Konsole or gnome-terminal, run **ksysv** or **serviceconf**. These start the KDE and GNOME graphical equivalents to chkconfig and ntsysv. Run the applicable graphical tool in the background so you can still use this terminal window with one of the following commands:

```
[root]# ksysv &
[root]# serviceconf &
```

2. From within the graphical tool, or by inspection via **ls /etc/rc.d/rc3.d**, edit the autofs record and record the current order number, 28.

3. Remove the autofs service from level 3.

4. Switch back to the console window and run chkconfig to see if it has been removed.

```
root] # chkconfig --list autofs
```

5. Add the autofs service back in with order number 29.

6. Switch back to the console window and run chkconfig to verify that it is back.

```
root] # chkconfig --list autofs
```

This should show that the autofs is started in runlevel 3.

Part 2

1. To add the account, enter:

```
[root]# useradd brianr -u 5010 -g nobody -c 'brian rite' -s /bin/bash
```

2. Change the password:

```
[root]# passwd brianr
```

3. Log into the new account:

```
[root]# telnet localhost
```

4. What files are there? Include all the hidden files to see the skeleton files copied over from the /etc/skel directory.

```
[brianr]$ ls -a
```

5. Remove the brianr account using the userdel command. Is the brianr home directory gone? What option would have done this for you?

```
[root]# userdel brianr       # leaves the home directory
[root]# userdel -r brianr    # also removes home directory
```

Part 3

Remember, you should not try this exercise if you don't have a separate line for the /boot filesystem in /etc/fstab. And this assumes that GRUB is your default bootloader.

This should be a self-explanatory exercise. Essentially, you're just making a minor modification to the /etc/fstab file. If you do it correctly, Linux should boot normally, even if it does not mount the /boot filesystem. The key is within the GRUB configuration file, as the **root** variable in /boot/grub/grub.conf doesn't require a mounted filesystem to read your vmlinuz kernel or your mkinird initial RAM disk files.

5

Advanced Installation

I n this chapter, you will learn how to manage Linux in advanced installation and configuration scenarios. The installation topics cover creating automated installation scripts and managing kernel modules. You will learn how to implement a Redundant Array of Inexpensive Disks (RAID), as well as an array of disks for the Logical Volume Manager (LVM), and master the intricate details of the automated Kickstart installation process. Finally, you'll get a basic sense of how you can modularize the kernel to your advantage.

Remember, one of the three RHCE exams is based on how well you know the installation process. By the time you finish this chapter, you should be ready to install Linux in an automated fashion from a local boot disk or over a network from an NFS or HTTP server. And as you work with kernel modules near the end of the chapter, you'll examine some of the techniques you can use on the RHCE troubleshooting exam to ensure that the kernel is properly set up to work with your hardware.

CERTIFICATION OBJECTIVE 5.01

RAID Configuration

A Redundant Array of Independent Disks (RAID) is a series of disks that can save your data even if there is a catastrophic failure on one of the disks. While some versions of RAID make complete copies of your data, others use the so-called parity bit to allow your computer to rebuild the data on lost disks.

Linux RAID has come a long way. A substantial number of hardware RAID products support Linux, especially from name brand PC manufacturers. Dedicated RAID hardware can ensure the integrity of your data even if there is a catastrophic *physical* failure on one of the disks. Alternatively, you can configure software-based RAID on multiple partitions on the same physical disk. While this can protect you from a failure on a specific hard drive sector, it does not protect your data if there is a failure of the entire physical hard drive.

Depending on your definitions, RAID has nine or ten different levels, which can accommodate different levels of data redundancy. Only three levels of RAID are supported directly by current versions of Red Hat Linux: levels 0, 1, and 5. Hardware RAID uses a RAID controller connected to an array of several hard disks. A driver must be installed to be able to use the controller. Linux, meanwhile, offers a software solution to RAID with the md kernel module. Once RAID is configured on your system, Linux can use it just as it would any other block device.

The RAID md device is a meta device. In other words, it is a composite of two or more other devices such as /dev/hda1 and /dev/hdb1 that might be components of a RAID array.

The following are the basic RAID levels supported by Red Hat Linux. In addition, Red Hat Linux is starting to incorporate the Logical Volume Management (LVM) system. Theoretically, it will allow you to resize or reallocate partitions as your needs evolve. In practice, LVM is new to Red Hat, and support for this system is not complete as of this writing.

RAID 0

This level of RAID makes it faster to read and write to the hard drives. However, RAID 0 provides no data redundancy. It requires at least two hard disks.

Reads and writes to the hard disks are done in parallel, in other words, to two or more hard disks simultaneously. All hard drives in a RAID 0 array are filled equally. But since RAID 0 does not provide data redundancy, a failure of any one of the drives will result in total data loss. RAID 0 is also known as "striping without parity."

RAID 1

This level of RAID mirrors information to two or more other disks. In other words, the same set of information is written to two different hard disks. If one disk is damaged or removed, you still have all of the data on the other hard disk. The disadvantage of RAID 1 is that data has to be written twice, which can reduce performance. You can come close to maintaining the same level of performance if you also use separate hard disk controllers. That prevents the hard disk controller from becoming a bottleneck.

And it is expensive. To support RAID 1, you need an additional hard disk for every hard disk worth of data. RAID 1 is also known as disk mirroring.

RAID 4

While this level of RAID is not directly supported by current versions of Red Hat Linux, it is still supported by the current Linux kernel. RAID 4 requires three or more disks. As with RAID 0, data reads and writes are done in parallel to all disks. One of the disks maintains the parity information, which can be used to reconstruct the data. Reliability is improved, but since parity information is updated with every write operation, the parity disk can be a bottleneck on the system. RAID 4 is known as disk striping with parity.

RAID 5

Like RAID 4, RAID 5 requires three or more disks. Unlike RAID 4, RAID 5 distributes, or "stripes," parity information evenly across all the disks. If one disk fails, the data can be reconstructed from the parity data on the remaining disks. RAID does not stop; all data is still available even after a single disk failure. RAID level 5 is the preferred choice in most cases: the performance is good, data integrity is ensured, and only one disk's worth of space is lost to parity data. RAID 5 is also known as disk striping with parity.

on the
job

Hardware RAID systems should be "hot-swappable." In other words, if one disk fails, the administrator can replace the failed disk while the server is still running. The system will then automatically rebuild the data onto the new disk. Since you can configure different partitions from the same physical disk for a software RAID system, the resulting configuration can easily fail if you use two or more partitions on the same physical disk.

exam
Watch

The exam may use examples from any level of RAID.

RAID in Practice

RAID is associated with a substantial amount of data on a server. It's not uncommon to have a couple dozen hard disks working together in a RAID array. That much data can be rather valuable.

If continued performance through a hardware failure is important, you can assign additional disks for "failover," which sets up spare disks for the RAID array. When one disk fails, it is marked as bad. The data is almost immediately reconstructed on the first spare disk, resulting in little or no downtime. The next example demonstrates this practice in both RAID 1 and RAID 5 arrays. Assuming your server has four drives, with the OS loaded on the first, it should look something like this:

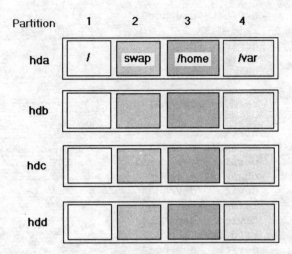

All four drives (hda, hdb, hdc, hdd) should be approximately the same size.

This first example shows how to mirror both the /home and the /var directories (RAID 1) on Drive 2 and Drive 3, leaving Drive 4 as a spare.

You need to create nearly identically sized partitions on Drives 2 and 3. In this example, four disks are configured with four partitions of the same size. Mark the last two partitions on all drives as type 0xFD (for autodetection) using the Linux fdisk program. You can use the "t" option to toggle the drive ID type.

In the partition table of the first drive is /dev/hda3 (currently mounted as /home) and /dev/hda4 (currently mounted as /var). The second drive includes /dev/hdb3 and /dev/hdb4. The third drive is set up with /dev/hdc3 and /dev/hdc4, while the last drive has /dev/hdd3 and /dev/hdd4. All of these partitions have been marked with partition IDs of type 0xFD.

Next, update the configuration file /etc/raidtab as follows:

```
raiddev /dev/md0
raid-level 1

nr-raid-disks 3
nr-spare-disks 1
persistent-superblock 1
chunk-size 4
device   /dev/hda3
raid-disk 0
device   /dev/hdb3
raid-disk 1
```

```
device  /dev/hdc3
raid-disk 2
device  /dev/hdd3
spare-disk 0


raiddev /dev/md1
raid-level 1
nr-raid-disks 3
nr-spare-disks 1
persistent-superblock 1
chunk-size 4
device  /dev/hda4
raid-disk 0
device  /dev/hdb4
raid-disk 1
device  /dev/hdc4
raid-disk 2
device  /dev/hdd4
spare-disk 0
```

Table 5-1 shows what some of the commands are, along with a brief description of what they do.

exam
ⓦatch

Take special note that raid-disks and spare-disks start counting at 0; nr-raid-disks and nr-spare-disks are the correct number of drives. For example: If nr-raid-disks = 3, then the raid-disks are 0, 1, and 2.

If necessary, now is the time to convert these partitions to the default ext3 filesystem. You can do this by adding journaling to each partition. Based on the previous example, the commands would be:

```
tune2fs -j /dev/hda4
tune2fs -j /dev/hdb4
tune2fs -j /dev/hdc4
tune2fs -j /dev/hdd4
```

Alternatively, you could have set up an ext3 filesystem when you configured a specific partition; such as with the **mkfs -j /dev/hda4** command. The -j switch sets up a journal. When a journal is added to the ext2 filesystem, it creates an ext3 filesystem.

Now to start RAID 1, initialize the md0 and md1 devices with the following commands:

```
mkraid /dev/md0; mkraid /dev/md1
```

TABLE 5-1	Command	Description
RAID Commands	nr-raid-disks	Number of RAID disks to use
	nr-spare-disks	Number of spare disks to use
	persistent-superblock	Required for autodetection
	chunk-size	Amount of data to read/write
	parity-algorithm	How RAID 5 should use parity

The /proc/mdstat file will show you the status on your RAID configurations. You can now mount the device, format it, and continue with your project.

For a RAID 5 array on the /var partition (in order to preserve mail, print spools, and log files), the /etc/raidtab file should be modified as follows:

```
raiddev /dev/md0
raid-level 5
nr-raid-disks 3
nr-spare-disks 1
persistent-superblock 1
chunksize 32
parity-algorithm right-symmetric
device  /dev/hda4
raid-disk 0
device  /dev/hdb4
raid-disk 1
device  /dev/hdc4
raid-disk 2
device  /dev/hdd4
spare-disk 0
```

Again, run **mkraid /dev/md0** to initialize RAID 5.

Formatting the RAID Partition

Before you run mke2fs to format each partition, you should understand how to use the special mke2fs stripe option. For instance, if you have a chunk-size of 32KB, use 64 blocks per chunk. If you format using 4K block sizes, then use 8 blocks per chunk. If you specify the chunk size (stride) when you format a RAID 5 device, you will see a considerable increase in performance. For example, the following command sets up a format with a 4K block size and 8 blocks per chunk on RAID device /dev/md0.

```
mke2fs -b 4096 -R stride=8 /dev/md0
```

on the job

The mkfs command is a "front-end" to mke2fs for most standard Linux partitions. In other words, both commands work the same for most Linux partitions.

For autodetection to work properly, you need to have the partitions set to type 0xFD, as described earlier. You also must have autodetection turned on in the kernel, and use the persistent-superblock option. If all is well, when the kernel boots, it will automatically detect RAID and fix any errors from crashes during the boot process.

Setting up a RAID level root device is a bit trickier. Because of the importance of this data, manually copy the contents of the root partition to a different drive. Set up and write /etc/lilo.conf or /etc/grub.conf to the other drive as well.

Then if there's a problem creating the root RAID array, you can still boot Linux from the other drive. Fortunately, this is an advanced skill beyond the scope of the RHCE exam. For more information on this process, go to the Linux Documentation Project Web site and read the Root-RAID-HOWTO.

EXERCISE 5-1

Mirror the /home Partition Using Software RAID

Don't do this exercise on a production computer. If you have a computer with Red Hat Linux already installed that you can use for testing, that is best. One alternative is to use virtual machine technology such as VMWare, which can allow you to set up these exercises with minimal risk to a production system. When you're ready, use the Linux fdisk techniques discussed in Chapter 3 to configure the following two-drive partition scheme:

```
Drive 1:
hda1     256      /
hda2      64      swap
hda3     500      /home
hda4     256      /var

Drive 2:
hdb1    1200      /usr
hdb2      64      swap
hdb3     100      /tmp
hdb4     500      (not allocated)
```

Now create a mirror of hda3 to hdb4 partition. (The partition sizes do not have to be identical.)

If you're making fdisk changes on a production computer, *back up* the /home partition first. Otherwise, all data on the current /dev/hda3 will be *lost*.

1. Mark the two partition IDs as type 0xFD using the Linux fdisk utility.

```
[root]# fdisk /dev/hda
Command (m for help) : t
Partition number (1-4)
3
Partition ID (L to list options): FD
Command (m for help) : w
Command (m for help) : q
# fdisk /dev/hdb
Command (m for help) : t
Partition number (1-4)
4
Partition ID (L to list options): FD
Command (m for help) : w
Command (m for help) :q
```

2. Update the configuration file /etc/raidtab with these lines of code:

```
[root]# vi /etc/raidtab
raiddev /dev/md0
raid-level 1

nr-raid-disks 2
nr-spare-disks 0
persistent-superblock 1
chunk-size 4
device  /dev/hda3
raid-disk 0
device  /dev/hdb4
raid-disk 1
```

3. Now make the RAID device file md0 and format it this way:

```
[root]# mkraid /dev/md0
[root]# mke2fs -b 4096 -R stride=8 /dev/md0
```

4. Update each device to the ext3 filesystem by adding journaling. (Alternatively, you could have just added the -j switch when using mke2fs to format the /dev/md0 device.):

```
tune2fs -j /dev/hda3
tune2fs -j /dev/hdb4
```

5. All that's left is to restore the files to the device, mount it, and you are done!

Logical Volume Management

Logical Volume Management (LVM) should allow you to manage active partitions. For example, if you find that you have extra space on the /home directory partition and need more space on your /var directory partition for log files, LVM will let you reallocate the space. Alternatively, if you are managing a server on a growing network, new users will be common. You may come to the point where you need more room on your /home directory partition. With LVM, you can add a new physical disk, and allocate its storage capacity to an existing /home directory partition.

As LVM is new to Red Hat Linux 8.0, it seems unlikely that Red Hat will make this part of the RHCE 8.0 exam. Nevertheless, LVM is potentially too good of a tool for any Linux administrator. Other Linux distributions such as S.u.S.E. have incorporated LVM in their distributions for some time now. I would expect Red Hat to incorporate LVM requirements in later versions of the RHCE exam. In either case, check the RHCE exam guide for the latest information.

While LVM can be an important tool to manage partitions, it does not by itself provide redundancy. Do not use it as a substitute for RAID. However, you can use LVM in addition to a properly configured RAID array.

LVM Concepts

The LVM system organizes hard disks into Logical Volume (LV) groups. Essentially, physical hard disk partitions (or possibly RAID arrays) are set up in a bunch of equal-sized chunks known as Physical Extents. As there are several other concepts associated with the LVM system, start with some basic definitions:

- **Physical Volume (PV)** is the standard partition that you add to the LVM mix. Normally, a physical volume is a standard primary or logical partition. It can also be a RAID array.

- **Physical Extent (PE)** is a chunk of disk space. Every PV is divided into a number of equal sized PEs. Every PE in a LV group is the same size. Different LV groups can have different sized PEs.

- **Logical Extent (LE)** is also a chunk of disk space. Every LE is mapped to a specific PE.

- **Logical Volume (LV)** is composed of a group of LEs. You can mount a filesystem such as /home and /var on a LV.

- **Volume Group (VG)** is composed of a group of LVs. It is the organizational group for LVM. Most of the commands that you'll use apply to a specific VG.

Creating a LVM

As of this writing, there are two basic ways to create a LVM Volume Group in Red Hat Linux. You can set up a LVM through Disk Druid, starting with Red Hat Linux 8.0. In addition, you can use the basic LVM commands to create and manage Volume Groups after Red Hat Linux is installed. As LVM is not much good unless you can add and delete specific LVs, you should know the basic LVM commands.

The first step to create a LVM is to initialize a physical disk. To create a new PV on a freshly installed hard disk such as /dev/hdc, run the following command:

```
# pvcreate /dev/hdc
```

This command won't work if you already have set up a partition table on this drive. Alternatively, you can set up a new PV on a properly formatted partition. For example, assume that you've added a new partition, /dev/hdc1. You could then use fdisk or a similar tool to set it to the Linux LVM partition type. In fdisk, this corresponds to partition type 8e. Once your partition is ready, you can run a command such as the following to create a new PV:

```
# pvcreate /dev/hdc1
```

Once you have two or more PVs, you can create a Volume Group (VG). You can substitute the name of your choice for *volumegroup*.

```
# vgcreate volumegroup /dev/hdc1 /dev/hdd1
```

When you create a new partition that you want to add to the VG, just extend it with the following command:

```
# vgextend volumegroup /dev/sda1
```

But a new VG doesn't help you unless you can mount a filesystem on it. So you need to create a logical volume (LV), for this purpose. The following command creates a LV. You can add as many chunks of disk space (aka Physical Extents - PE) as you need.

```
# lvcreate -l number_of_PEs volumegroup -n logvol
```

This creates a device named /dev/*volumegroup/logvol*. You can then format this device like any regular disk partition, and then mount the filesystem of your choice on your new logical volume.

CERTIFICATION OBJECTIVE 5.02

Using Kickstart to Automate Installation

Kickstart is Red Hat's solution for an automated installation of Red Hat. All of the questions asked during setup can be automatically supplied with one text file. You can easily set up nearly identical systems very quickly. Kickstart files are very useful for quick deployment and distribution of Linux systems.

There are three methods for creating the required kickstart configuration file:

- Copy and edit the sample.ks file from the RH-DOCS directory of the Red Hat Documentation CD.

- Use the anaconda-ks.cfg file from the root user's home directory, /root.

- Use the graphical Kickstart Configurator, accessible through the /usr/sbin/ksconfig command.

The first option requires you to copy and modify the kickstart sample file from the CD. The second option lets you use the kickstart template file created for your computer by Anaconda, the Red Hat Linux installation program. The final option, the Kickstart Configurator, is discussed in detail later in this chapter.

Copy this kickstart template file and make the appropriate changes suitable for each generic host (same disk partition scheme, same size of disk or bigger, same video card and monitor, same mouse, etc.). Place this file where the Anaconda can read it; either locally from the boot disk or remotely from the DHCP/BOOTP server.

If you want to put the file on a DHCP/BOOTP server, open the /etc/dhcpd.conf configuration file on that server. Specify the kickstart file. For example, if the kickstart file is on the DHCP server in the /usr/kickstart directory, add the **filename "/usr/kickstart/"** command to dhcpd.conf, where *filename* is the name of the kickstart file that you want to use. Then the setup program will look in the DHCP server's directory for a *client_ip*-kickstart file. Alternatively, if the kickstart file isn't stored on the DHCP server, add the **next-server** *servername* option to the dhcpd.conf configuration file.

No matter where you choose to put the kickstart file, you will typically boot with a floppy. You can even put the kickstart file on the Red Hat boot floppy. Just mount the floppy and copy it as the **ks.cfg** file from wherever you've saved your kickstart configuration file.

At the time of this writing, boot disks still bring up the LILO prompt. Use LILO's boot options to initiate the kickstart file. To boot, and then perform the kickstart installation from a floppy, type

```
boot: linux ks=floppy
```

Installing Red Hat Linux using a kickstart file on a boot floppy is perhaps the easiest method. As long as you have a DHCP server on your network, you may be able to use the same Red Hat Linux installation boot floppy. Just boot each new Linux computer from that floppy, type in the `linux ks=floppy` command at the boot prompt, give the computer a moment to read the ks.cfg file, and insert the same floppy in the next new Linux computer.

If you're booting from the Red Hat installation CD-ROM, you can still refer to a kickstart configuration file on a floppy or hard disk with the following commands:

```
boot: linux ks=hd:fd0/ks.cfg
boot: linux ks=hd:hda2/home/mj/ks.cfg
```

This assumes the kickstart configuration file is called ks.cfg and is located on the first floppy or the second partition of the first IDE drive in the /home/mj directory.

You don't need to get a kickstart file from a DHCP server. To boot from a specific NFS or HTTP server on the network, say with an IP address of 192.168.17.18, from the /kicks/ks.cfg file, type one of the following commands:

```
boot: linux ks=nfs:192.168.17.18:/kicks/ks.cfg
boot: linux ks=http:192.168.17.18:/kicks/ks.cfg
```

Most of the options in the sample kickstart file are self-explanatory. Every option is in the sample file and is well commented. Follow these ground rules and guidelines to use when setting up a kickstart file:

- Do *not* change the order of the options.
- You do not need to use all the options.
- If you leave out a required option, the user will be prompted for the answer.
- For upgrades, you *must* have the following options defined:
  - Language
  - Installation method

- Device specification
- Keyboard setup
- The upgrade keyword
- Bootloader (GRUB or LILO) configuration

If you leave out an option, you will be prompted to complete it. This is an easy way to see if your kickstart is configured correctly. But as some kickstart options change the partitions on your hard drive, even testing this file can delete all of the data on your computer. So make sure to have a test computer available to test your kickstart configuration file.

To understand Kickstart, it may be helpful to look through the sample kickstart file from the Red Hat Documentation CD, as shown in Figures 5-1 through 5-4. While

---

FIGURE 5-1

Sample Kickstart
Installation File,
Part 1

```
### Installation Language
lang en_US
### Installed Languages
langsupport --default en_US fr_FR

### Network Configuration
network --bootproto dhcp
#network --bootproto static --ip 192.168.0.1 --netmask 255.255.254.0 --gateway 192
.168.0.1 --nameserver 192.168.0.254

### Source File Location
cdrom
#nfs --server porkchop.redhat.com --dir /mnt/test/qa0301.0/i386

### Ethernet Device Configuration
#device ethernet wd --opts "io=0x280, irq=3"

### Keyboard Configuration
### Will get set to 'us' by default
### if nothing specified in /etc/sysconfig/keyboard
keyboard us

### Partitioning Information
### Whether to clear out the Master Boot Record (yes/no)
### Which partitions to format (--linux/--all)
###       --linux - only format existing linux partitions
###       --all   - format all existing partitions
### Which partitions to set up on new system as well
### as size of those partitions
### Specify software RAID partitions (optional)
zerombr yes
clearpart --linux
part /boot --size 35
part swap --size 128
#part swap --recommended
                                                    34,1              Top
```

FIGURE 5-2

Sample Kickstart
Installation File,
Part 2

```
part swap --size 128
#part swap --recommended
part / --size 1000 --grow --maxsize 1400
#part raid.0 --size 80 --ondisk sda
#part raid.1 --size 80 --ondisk sdb
#raid swap raid.0 raid.1 --level 1 --device md0
install

### Perform kickstart installation in text mode
#text

### Stop at each screen during the kickstart
### installation
#interactive

### Mouse Configuration
### Will only setup 3 types of mice
###     generic        - 2-button serial
###     genericps/2    - 2-button ps/2
###     msintellips/2  - MS Intellimouse
### All three can be setup with or without 3-button
### emulation
### Run 'mouseconfig --help' in order to see other
### supported mouse type and make appropriate change
### NOTE: You will need to run 'mouseconfig' manually
### after installation if you have a non-ps/2 mouse
### and are installing X, as a ps/2 mouse is setup
### by default
#mouse generic --device ttyS0
mouse generic3ps/2

### Firewall Configuration
### options are high, medium, and disabled
# firewall --high --trust eth0 --ssh --port 1234:udp
firewall --high
```
                                                        33,1   35%

this sample file is pretty self-explanatory, a couple of key options need further
explanation.

Network

Most options are obvious, but static network configuration options (which require
manually configuring the IP settings) need special attention. Here is an example of
a static network configuration:

```
network --bootproto static --ip 172.16.16.5 --netmask 255.255.255.0
--gateway 172.16.15.254 --nameserver 172.16.16.1
```

Please note that all options *must* be on *one* line. Line wrapping, if the options exceed
the space in your editor, is acceptable.

FIGURE 5-3

Sample Kickstart
Installation File,
Part 3

```
# firewall --high --trust eth0 --ssh --port 1234:udp
firewall --high


### Time Zone Configuration
### Will get set to 'US/Eastern' if ZONE is missing
### from /etc/sysconfig/clock or if file is missing entirely
timezone --utc America/New_York

### X Configuration
### Will skip X configuration
### You may wish to run Xconfigurator manually after system installation
skipx
### You can uncomment and modify this line if you know the X configuration for you
r system
#xconfig --server "SVGA" --monitor "viewsonic g773" --depth 16 --resolution 800x60
0 --defaultdesktop=GNOME  --startxonboot --card "Matrox Millennium" --videoram 102
4

### Root Password Designation
### e.g. 'rootpw ThisIsThePassword' will get root's password to
### "ThisIsThePassword"
rootpw paSSword
#rootpw --iscrypted g.UJ.RQeOV3Bg

### Reboot system after installation complete
#reboot

### Authorization Configuration
auth --useshadow --enablemd5

### Boot Loader Configuration
### GRUB is default bootloader
### lilo command has been replaced with bootloader
bootloader --location=mbr
                                                            66,1          69%
```

If the client has SCSI, Ethernet, or non-ATAPI CD-ROM devices, don't forget to specify them. For example:

```
device scsi aha154x
```

If you have modules that require a specific IRQ port and I/O address, you can also specify those. For example:

```
device ethernet 3c509 --opts "io=0x330, irq=7"
```

Add the --continue option if you have more than one device, such as two different SCSI adapters or Ethernet cards.

You have full control of the partitioning options, too. You can clear all partitions with **clearpart --all**, or just clear any Linux-type partitions **clearpart --linux**, or just add to the end of the current partitions. You can create partitions on more than one drive, but you need to identify each device specifically.

FIGURE 5-4

Sample Kickstart
Installation File,
Part 4

```
### lilo command has been replaced with bootloader
bootloader --location=mbr
#bootloader --location=mbr --append hdd=ide-scsi --password=GRUBpasswd

### Package Designation
### The package names, as well as the groups they are a part of can be
### found in the /RedHat/base/comps file; individual packages can be
### specified by entering their names one per line;
### groups (e.g. 'X Window System') can be specified
### by appending a "@" in front of the group name;
### e.g. '@ X Window System'
%packages
### Automatically resolve dependences
#%packages --resolvedeps
### Ignore unresolved dependencies
#%packages --ignoredeps
python
@ X Window System

### Include the contents of another file in the kickstart
### file
#%include /path/to/file

### Commands to be run immediately after this file has been parsed
%pre
echo "Kickstart-installed Red Hat Linux `/bin/date`"

### Commands to be run post-installation
%post
echo "Kickstart installation" > /tmp/message
~
~
~
~
~
                                                      96,1        Bot
```

To add Linux partitions, use the "part" command with the following syntax:

```
part mount dir --size size [--grow] [--maxsize size]
```

The *size* is in megabytes. You can use the --grow option to allow the partition to expand and fill all remaining disk space (or share it with any other partitions marked "grow" on the same disk). This will not expand on the fly; but rather, when all fixed-size partitions are added, these "growable" partitions will use the rest of the space. If you specify multiple partitions with the --grow option, their space will be divided evenly. You can also specify a --maxsize, which will allow the partition to grow only to the size specified in megabytes.

There is one more important issue in a kickstart file: when you specify the root password, encrypt it as follows:

```
rootpw --iscrypted Your_encrypted_password
```

Then copy the actual encrypted root password from /etc/shadow or /etc/passwd and paste it into this file.

Kickstart is an essential concept to understand, since installation is such an important part of the RHCE exam.

EXERCISE 5-2

Creating a Sample Kickstart File from a Running System for a Second Similar System Installation

In this exercise, you will use the anaconda-ks.cfg file to duplicate the installation from one computer to another with identical hardware. This exercise simply installs all the exact same packages with the same partition configuration on the second computer. Assume that both computers use DHCP to set up their IP addresses. Add one root partition of 1300MB with a 64MB swap file. (This means you must have at least 1364MB of space available. If you have more space, let it remain unused for now.) You want to install all the same packages as your current installation, so you do not need to make any package changes to the default anaconda kickstart file in the /root directory.

If you do not have multiple computers for this exercise, one alternative as discussed earlier is VMWare.

1. Review the /root/anaconda-ks.cfg file. Copy it to ks.cfg.

2. Create the boot disk and add this ks.cfg file to it:

```
dd if=/mnt/cdrom/images/bootnet.img of=/dev/fd0
mount /dev/fd0 /mnt/floppy
cp ks.cfg /mnt/floppy
```

3. Prepare the second computer so that it has the same disk configuration, the same C: drive size if it was present, and same amount of unused and unpartitioned space as the first computer. Reboot the second computer with the Linux boot file with the kickstart file in the floppy drive and the first binary CD in the CD-ROM.

4. At the Red Hat Installation menu boot prompt, enter the following startup command:

```
boot: linux ks=floppy
```

You should now see the system installation creating the same setup as the first system. You may be asked to put the second binary CD into the CD-ROM drive, if required.

OPTIONAL EXERCISE 5-2

Modify the Packages to Be Installed

Edit the ks.cfg file on the floppy and remove all the game packages you can find. Alternatively, set up an interactive installation so that you can test and observe the result on another computer.

The Kickstart Configurator

Now that you understand the basics of what goes into a kickstart file, it's time to solidify your understanding through the graphical Kickstart Configurator. Go into the Linux GUI. Open a command line interface shell. Start the Kickstart Configurator with the **/usr/sbin/ksconfig** command. The following sections should look familiar, as they are based on the choices you made when you installed Red Hat Linux.

The first section is Basic Configuration, as shown in Figure 5-5. As you can see, this allows you to set up the Language, Keyboard, Mouse, Time Zone, and the language of the kernel modules associated with this installation. By default, the system is to be rebooted after Linux is installed, which should lead to a Linux login screen. Installation in text mode installation may be faster, especially if the subject computers have limited graphics capabilities. Interactive mode is appropriate if you need to edit the ks.cfg file before applying it to several other computers. And remember to enter a root password. Installation cannot proceed automatically without it.

The next section lists Boot Loader Options, as shown in Figure 5-6. The two boot loaders available to Linux are GRUB and LILO. Linux boot loaders are normally installed on the MBR. If you're dual-booting with Windows NT/2000/XP with LILO, you need to set up the Windows boot loader to point to LILO on the first sector of the Linux partition with the files in the /boot directory. Kernel parameters allow you to pass commands to LILO as described in Chapter 3. If you're using LILO, linear mode is also known as Large Disk mode in many BIOS menus, and lba32 mode often allows Linux to look beyond the 1024th cylinder for Linux /boot files. And if you're upgrading Red Hat Linux, the Upgrade boot loader option allows you to upgrade the package associated with your currently installed boot loader.

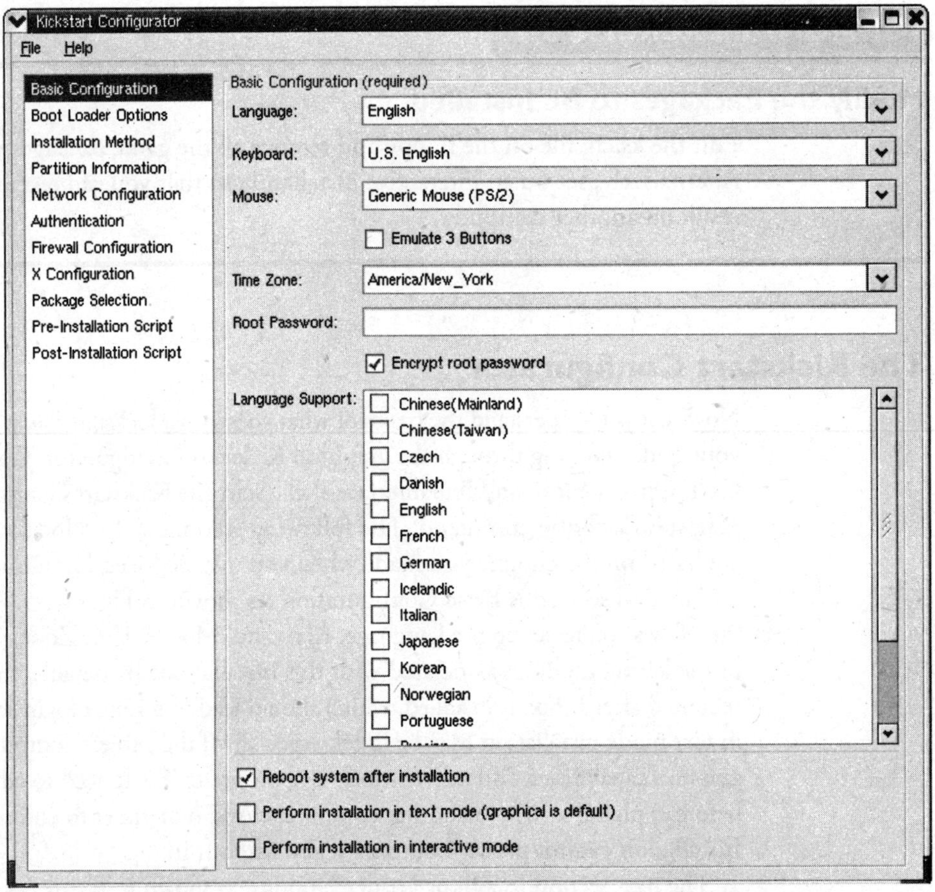

FIGURE 5-5

Kickstart
Configurator,
Basic
Configuration
Options

The Installation Method options shown in Figure 5-7 are more straightforward than what is shown in the Red Hat installation program. You're either installing Linux for the first time or upgrading a previous installation. Since you'll be selecting your own packages, the preselected package sets associated with Workstation, Server, or Laptop installations are not relevant. The installation method is based on the location of the installation files.

The Partition Information options shown in Figure 5-8 determine how this installation configures the hard disks on the affected computers. The Clear Master Boot Record option allows you to wipe the MBR from an older hard disk that might have a problem there; it sets up the **zerombr yes** command in the kickstart file.

Don't use the zerombr yes option if you want to keep an alternate such as the NT Boot Loader.

You can remove partitions depending on whether they've been created to a Linux filesystem. If you're using a new hard drive, you'll want to Initialize the Disk Label as well. As of this writing, the Make RAID Device and Make LVM Partition options are not functional.

In the Partition Information section, select Add. The Partition Options dialog box shown in Figure 5-9 allows you to add the partitions that you need. The Additional Size Options let you specify whether the partition should be allowed to grow into the available space on the drive, or some other limit. You want the partition with /boot

FIGURE 5-7

Kickstart
Configurator,
Installation
Method

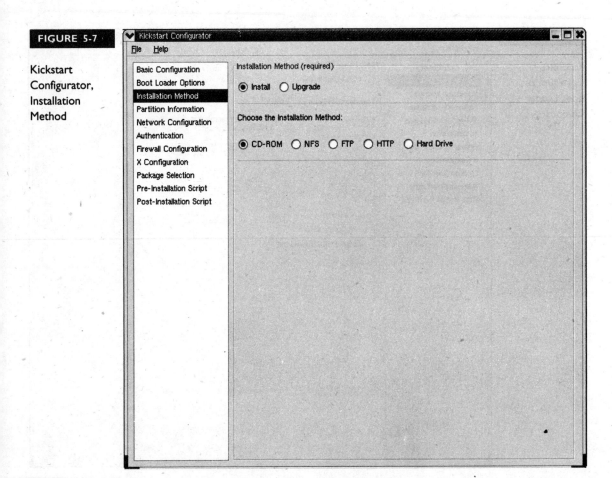

files to be a primary partition. If you have multiple hard drives or partitions, you may want to specify the drive or partition for the Mount Point. And unless you're upgrading, you should format each partition.

The Network Configuration section shown in Figure 5-10 enables you to set up the IP configuration for this specific computer. Since kickstart files are generally used to install Linux on multiple computers, you don't want to have to specify different IP address information for each computer. DHCP servers can serve this purpose. Support for different network configuration options is not complete; if the DHCP server is on a remote network, you'll have to go into the ks.cfg file afterward and change "dhcp" in the `network --bootproto dhcp` line to `bootp`.

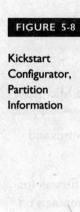

FIGURE 5-8

Kickstart
Configurator,
Partition
Information

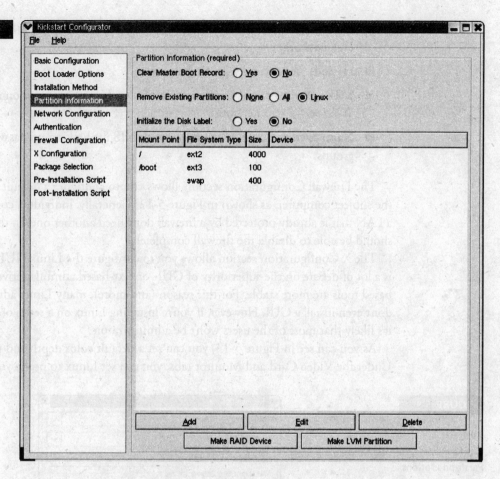

The Authentication section, as shown in Figure 5-11, lets you set up two forms of security for user passwords: Shadow Passwords, which encrypts user passwords in the /etc/shadow file, and MD5 encryption. This section also allows you to set up authentication information for various protocols:

- **NIS**   Network Information Service for one login database on a network with Unix and Linux computers on a network.

- **LDAP**   The Lightweight Directory Assistance Protocol is used for certain types of databases such as directories.

- **Kerberos 5** The MIT system for strong cryptography to authenticate users on a network.

- **Hesiod** Associated with Kerberos 5.

- **SMB** Samba allows configuration of your Linux computer on a Microsoft Windows–based network.

- **Name Switch Cache** Associated with NIS for looking up passwords and groups.

The Firewall Configuration section allows you to configure a default firewall for the subject computer, as shown in Figure 5-12. Generally, individual computers on a LAN that is already protected by a firewall don't need another one. In that case, you should be able to disable the firewall completely.

The X Configuration section allows you to configure the Linux GUI. While there is a lot of debate on the superiority of GUI- or text-based administrative tools, text-based tools are more stable. For this reason (and more), many Linux administrators don't even install a GUI. However, if you're installing Linux on a series of computers, it's likely that most of the users won't be administrators.

As you can see in Figure 5-13, you can set a default color depth and resolution. Under the Video Card and Monitor tabs, you can set Linux to probe your hardware,

FIGURE 5-9

Kickstart
Configurator,
Partition Options

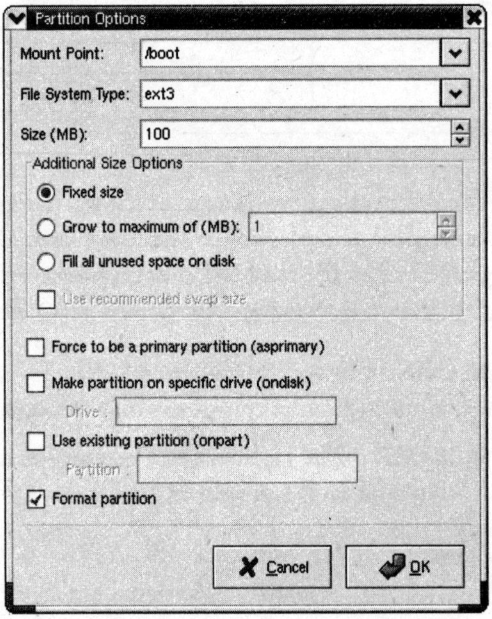

FIGURE 5-10

Kickstart
Configurator,
Network
Configuration

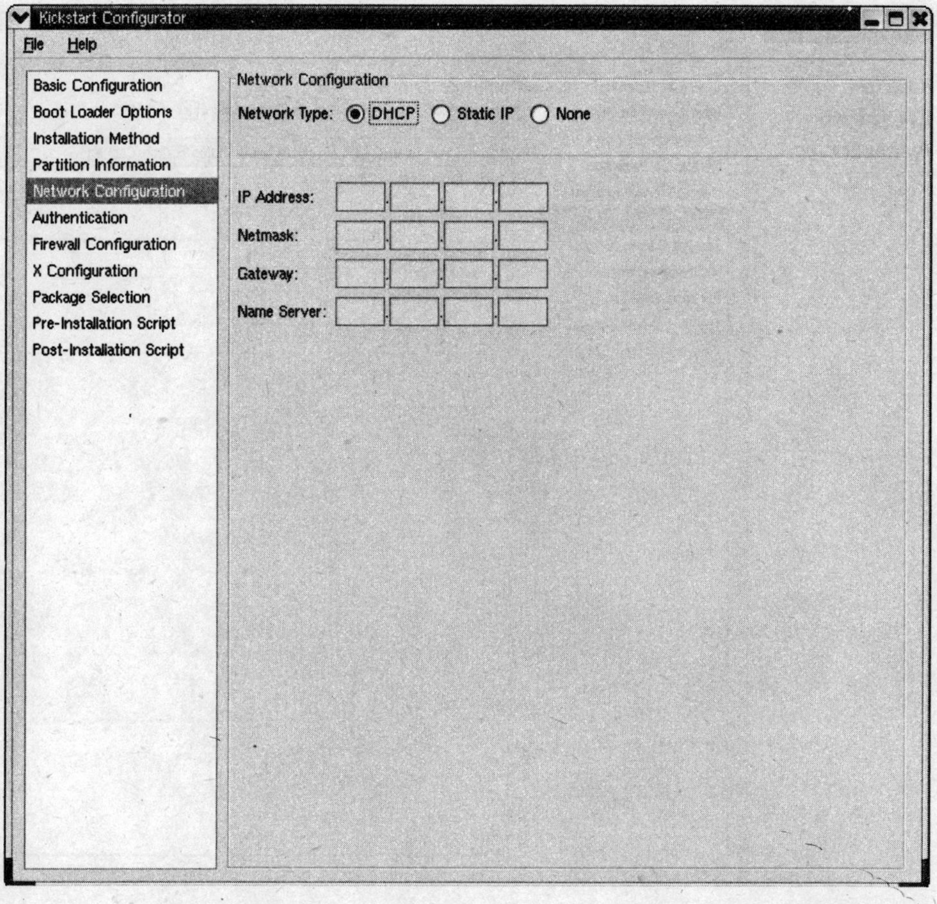

or specify the hardware from a list. If you want to do something fancy such as specifying multiple resolutions, you'll need to modify the ks.cfg file directly.

The Package Selection section, as shown in Figure 5-14, allows you to select packages by groups. If you want to select individual packages, you'll need to modify the ks.cfg file directly. And it's a good idea to check the Automatically Resolve Dependencies option; if you miss a package or a package group, Anaconda can find the critical package and install it with your list.

You can add PreInstallation and PostInstallation scripts to the kickstart file. Postinstallation scripts are more common, and they can help you configure other parts of a Linux operating system in a common way. For example, if you wanted to install a directory with employee benefits information, you could add the appropriate cp commands to a postinstallation script.

FIGURE 5-11

Kickstart
Configurator,
Authentication

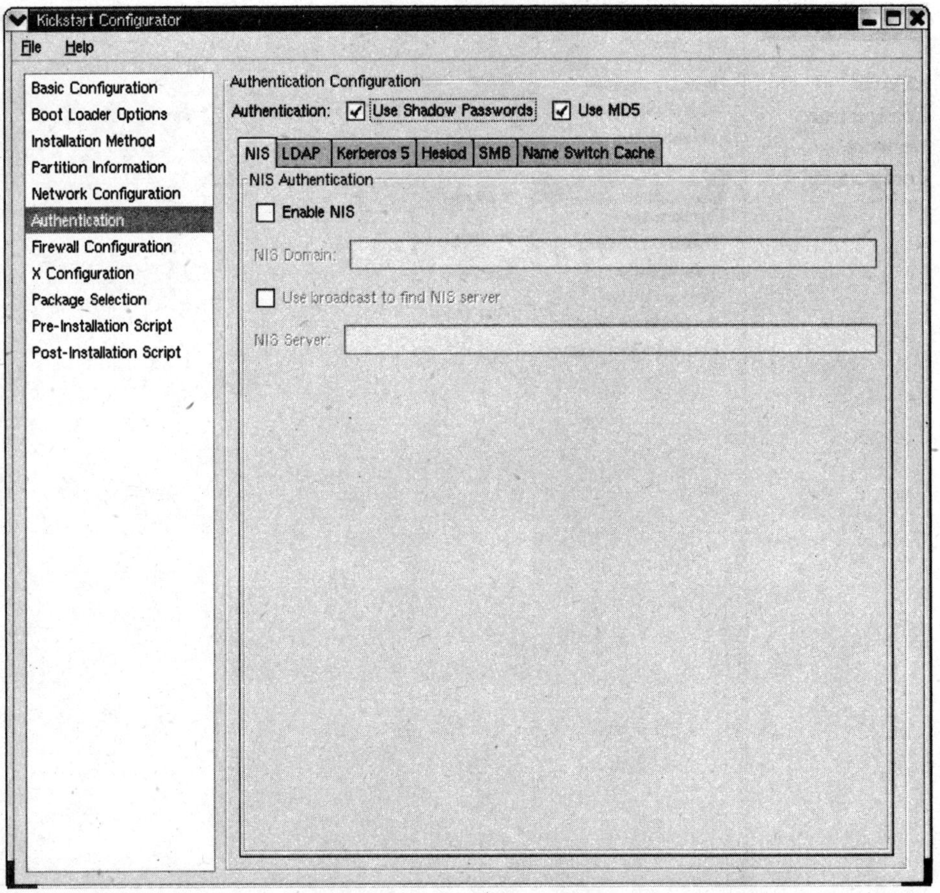

on the
job *Starting with Red Hat 8.0, the Kickstart Configurator automatically includes the reboot command. If you don't see it in your ks.cfg file, you can include it as a Post-Installation script. This makes sure that Anaconda finishes the presumably automated installation process. If you are installing Linux during the night, this should reboot each computer so that all users see the login prompt of your choice.*

Once you've completed what you wanted to customize through the graphical Kickstart Configurator, select File | Preview. A Kickstart Configuration Preview Options window opens that reviews the kickstart file that will be saved. When you click Save File, you have a chance to save this configuration with the filename of your choice.

FIGURE 5-12

Kickstart
Configurator,
Firewall
Configuration

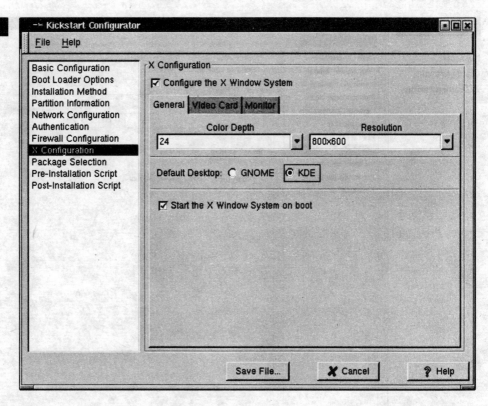

You can then edit that file for any options that are beyond the configuration capabilities of the current graphical Kickstart Configurator, such as acquiring network information through the BOOTP protocol, or installing individual packages.

CERTIFICATION OBJECTIVE 5.03

Understanding Kernel Modules

When you compile your kernel, you can set up a monolithic kernel with every driver that you might ever need. Unfortunately, such kernels are large, are unwieldy, and take a lot of time to load. Generally, most Linux administrators use kernel modules. A *kernel module* is not compiled directly into the kernel but instead operates as a pluggable driver that can be loaded and unloaded into the kernel as needed.

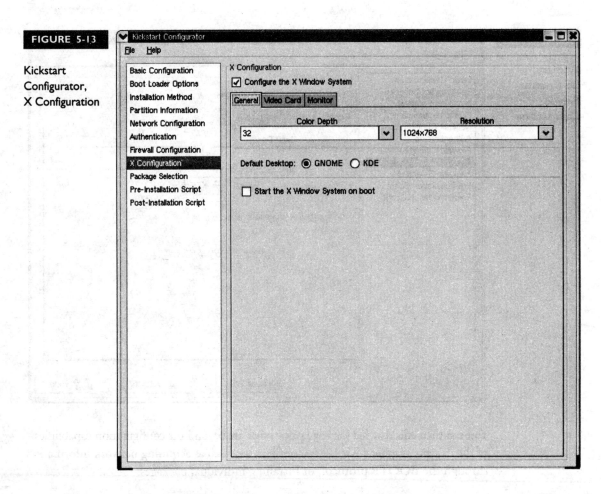

FIGURE 5-13

Kickstart
Configurator,
X Configuration

The kernel modules approach has three basic advantages:

- It reduces the size of the kernel.
- Smaller kernels are faster.
- When a module isn't required, it can be dynamically unloaded to take up less memory.

To have the kernel dynamically load and unload kernel modules as needed, a special kernel thread, kmod, is called upon to control the loading and unloading of modules. For special parameters and options, edit the /etc/modules.conf file.

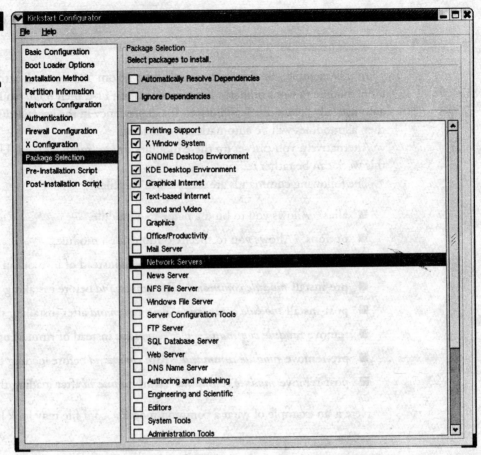

FIGURE 5-14

**Kickstart
Configurator,
Package Selection**

To load modules on the command line, you should first issue the following command:

```
/sbin/depmod -a
```

This will scan through your modules, find out what the different dependencies for all your modules are, and map them out to a file (modules.dep). This command also creates a number of other files in the /lib/modules/*x.y.z*/ directory, where *x.y.z* is your kernel version. This command is usually run during execution of the boot scripts, normally /etc/rc.d/rc.sysinit. Once the depmod module scan is complete, you can load additional kernel modules. If that module has dependencies, then all the needed modules will automatically load first.

To load a module, use the modprobe command with the name of a specific driver:

```
# modprobe 3c503
```

In this example, the Ethernet module for a 3Com 503 network card requires the 8390 module to work properly. If depmod was run first, then 8390 would have loaded automatically before the 3c503 driver. If a dependency in the list fails during loading, then all modules will be automatically unloaded.

Alternatively, you can set up these modules in /etc/modules.conf. Unfortunately, this work can be rather tedious.

The following commands are accepted in this file:

- **alias**   Allows you to bind a name to a module.

- **options**   Allows you to specify options for a module.

- **install** *module command*   Use *command* instead of insmod on this module.

- **pre-install** *module command*   Run *command* before installing this module.

- **post-install** *module command*   Run *command* after installing this module.

- **remove** *module command*   Use *command* instead of rmmod on this module.

- **pre-remove** *module command*   Run *command* before loading this module.

- **post-remove** *module command*   Run *command* after loading this module.

Here is an example of what a common modules.conf file may look like:

```
alias eth0 3c59x
options sb irq=5 io=0x220 dma=1
alias midi awe_wave
alias parport_lowlevel parport_pc
```

Here the eth0 name is bound to the 3c59x module. To load the network card, you can simply type **modprobe eth0** without knowing what card is in the machine. The next two lines show the configuration of a Soundblaster (sb) module. This information includes a specific IRQ port, I/O address, and DMA channel. The options line specifies these options and binds them to the sb alias. The sound card happens to be a Sound Blaster AWE 32 model card; therefore, the midi alias is bound to the awe_wave module. Finally, a parallel port module is bound to the parport_lowlevel alias.

The rc.sysinit script recognizes certain aliases and will load them if it finds them in this file. You need to specifically place the sound modules in modules.conf to have them automatically loaded. To have the sound modules automatically loaded during bootup without having to edit the /etc/rc.d/rc.sysinit file, you can simply create an alias to sound and or midi in the modules.conf file.

To see what modules are loaded, you can type either

```
# cat /proc/modules
```

or

```
# lsmod
```

Both commands return output that looks something like this:

```
Module                Size  Used by     Not tainted
nls_iso8859-1         2816  1 (autoclean)
smbfs                35232  1 (autoclean)
autofs               10244  0 (autoclean) (unused)
ide-cd               27264  1 (autoclean)
cdrom                27872  0 (autoclean) [ide-cd]
ipchains             36904  16
usb-uhci             21636  0 (unused)
usbcore              59072  1 [usb-uhci]
pcnet32              13600  1
mii                   1408  0 [pcnet32]
ext3                 62048  5
jbd                  40376  5 [ext3]
BusLogic             88384  6
sd_mod               11552  12
scsi_mod             96524  2 [BusLogic sd_mod]
```

The module name is listed on the left, and its size is in the second column. The "Used by" column shows more detail on how the module is being handled. An (autoclean) message means that the kernel (using the kmod thread) is taking care of the module and will handle removing it. If a module name, such as ext3, is listed in brackets, then the module depends on the module in brackets. In our example, jbd depends on the ext3 module.

The /lib/modules/*kernel_version*/ Directory Structure

All kernel modules are stored in the /lib/modules/*kernel_version*/ directory, where *kernel_version* is your kernel version. If you have recently compiled a kernel and your modules are not loading properly, then you have probably forgotten to compile and install the modules. In the /usr/src/linux source directory, run the following commands:

```
make modules
make modules_install
```

The first line compiles the modules, while the second places them under the proper directory tree. In this directory tree, different subdirectories represent different groupings. The following is a sample of a module directory:

```
# ls -l /lib/modules/2.4-19-2/kernel/drivers
total 96
drwxr-xr-x    8 root     root         4096 Aug  1 20:22 addon
drwxr-xr-x    2 root     root         4096 Aug  1 20:22 atm
drwxr-xr-x    3 root     root         4096 Aug  1 20:22 block
drwxr-xr-x    2 root     root         4096 Aug  1 20:22 bluetooth
drwxr-xr-x    2 root     root         4096 Aug  1 20:22 cdrom
drwxr-xr-x    8 root     root         4096 Aug  1 20:22 char
drwxr-xr-x    3 root     root         4096 Aug  1 20:22 crypto
drwxr-xr-x    2 root     root         4096 Aug  1 20:22 i2c
drwxr-xr-x    2 root     root         4096 Aug  1 20:22 ide
drwxr-xr-x    2 root     root         4096 Aug  1 20:22 ieee1394
drwxr-xr-x    2 root     root         4096 Aug  1 20:22 input
drwxr-xr-x   10 root     root         4096 Aug  1 20:22 isdn
drwxr-xr-x    2 root     root         4096 Aug  1 20:22 md
drwxr-xr-x    4 root     root         4096 Aug  1 20:22 media
drwxr-xr-x    4 root     root         4096 Aug  1 20:22 message
drwxr-xr-x   17 root     root         2048 Aug  1 20:22 net
drwxr-xr-x    2 root     root         4096 Aug  1 20:22 parport
drwxr-xr-x    2 root     root         4096 Aug  1 20:22 pcmcia
drwxr-xr-x    7 root     root         2048 Aug  1 20:22 scsi
drwxr-xr-x    2 root     root         4096 Aug  1 20:22 sensors
drwxr-xr-x    4 root     root         4096 Aug  1 20:22 sound
drwxr-xr-x    2 root     root         4096 Aug  1 20:22 telephony
drwxr-xr-x    5 root     root         4096 Aug  1 20:22 usb
drwxr-xr-x    6 root     root         4096 Aug  1 20:22 video
```

Remember that each /lib/modules/*kernel_version* directory contains a modules.dep file that lists all the dependencies for all the modules within the directories. Each of these module directories includes a group of kernel modules for a common type of hardware. You might want to become familiar with where to find certain modules when needed. Here are some module types you can find under each directory:

- **addon**   High-end cards such as for server racks
- **atm**   ATM network adapters
- **block**   Block devices: parallel port ide drives, network block devices, XT disks, hardware raid devices
- **bluetooth**   Specification for wireless adapters
- **cdrom**   Non-ATAPI CD-ROM drivers: Mitsumi, Sony
- **char**   Miscellaneous input and serial devices
- **crypto**   Integrated security chips
- **i2c**   Integrated circuit controllers
- **ide**   Hard disk drivers
- **ieee1394**   FireWire / iLink drivers
- **input**   Input devices (keyboards, mice)
- **isdn**   ISDN adapters
- **md**   RAID devices
- **media**   Specialty multimedia video and audio
- **message**   Specialized I/O adapters
- **net**   Network modules: basic network cards, generic ppp, slip
- **parport**   Parallel port devices (not printers)
- **pcmcia**   Drivers used by the pcmcia cardmgr daemon (the actual cards use separate drivers)
- **scsi**   SCSI tape, RAID, and hard drive modules, video (special video modules for Linux)
- **sensors**   Specialized monitors
- **sound**   Sound adapters

- **telephony** Network telephone devices
- **usb** Universal Serial Bus hubs and devices
- **video** Graphics adapters

All modules have .o for an extension (e.g., pcnet32.o). You do not need to specify the full name, just the first part of the module file (pcnet32). Once you know the directory structure, you can have modprobe load all modules for a certain category. For instance, if you are on a PC and you don't know the network card, you can simply type

```
modprobe -t net
```

This will attempt to load all modules in /lib/modules/*kernel_version*/net, stopping when a match is found. To remove a module and all its dependencies, you can type either

```
modprobe -r 3c503
```

or

```
rmmod -r 3c503
```

Both these commands will remove the modules and all their dependencies, provided they are not in use by another module. If you want to remove only the module and leave the other dependent drivers, run the rmmod command without the -r switch.

EXERCISE 5-3

Load Any Dependent Modules

In this exercise, you will use modprobe to attempt to load any currently uninstalled modules for the various groups (unless some module is missing, nothing should happen. Use rmmod "modulename" at the risk of rebooting):

```
/sbin/modprobe -t net
modprobe: Nothing to load ???
Specify at least a module or a wildcard like \*
```

If you don't have any missing modules in the specified category, you'll get the same message.

```
/sbin/modprobe -t fs
/sbin/modprobe -t pcmcia
/sbin/modprobe -t cdrom
/sbin/modprobe -t scsi
```

Remember, you can allow the kernel thread to maintain this area. Except with a few troublesome (usually older) drivers, you probably won't ever need to manage these modules manually.

CERTIFICATION SUMMARY

The Linux installation is extremely flexible.

You can set up RAID level devices to mirror and stripe your drives. RAID levels 1 and 0 require that you have two or more drives, while RAID 4 and 5 requires three or more. You can also set up linear mode to combine multiple physical hard disks into a single volume.

You can automate your entire installation of Red Hat Linux with the kickstart system. You have three ways to set up the kickstart configuration file: from the anaconda-ks.cfg file based on your local installation, from the sample ks.cfg file, and through the GUI Kickstart Configurator. In this way, you can automate the installation of Linux from a local source such as a CD-ROM, or through an NFS or HTTP network connection.

One more difficult part of the Linux installation process is proper management of the kernel. By default, the installed kernel is modular. Normally, kernel module drivers for each hardware component are automatically detected and installed. If you have problems, you can load additional modules with the depmod and modprobe commands. Alternatively, you can set them up in /etc/modules.conf. If you can't find the module you need, available modules are stored in the /lib/modules/*kernel_version* directory. You can use modprobe to have Linux run through the modules for each category and load additional modules that can help configure your system.

TWO-MINUTE DRILL

The following are some of the key points from the certification objectives in Chapter 5.

RAID Configuration

❑ Software-based RAID can be set up on any number of physical partitions. Hardware-based RAID requires separate physical drives for each partition.

❑ There is strong hardware-based RAID support for Linux, especially from the big name brand PC manufacturers. Dedicated RAID hardware is definitely the most robust solution. You can set up software or hardware based RAID through the Red Hat Linux installation program.

❑ RAID has several different levels. Only three are currently supported by Red Hat Linux: levels 0, 1, and 5. Only RAID levels 1 and 5 offer true data protection against the failure of a single hard drive.

❑ RAID 0 and 1 require two or more drives, while RAID 5 requires three or more drives.

❑ The numbering system for RAID in kickstart is a bit different. The first raid-disks and spare-disks variables are number 0. The nr-raid-disks and nr-spare-disks variables represent the correct number of drives. For example, if nr-raid-disks = 3, then the last raid-disk will be 2.

Using Kickstart to Automate Installation

❑ Kickstart is Red Hat's solution for an automated simultaneous installation of Red Hat Linux on several computers.

❑ Kickstart installations can be configured to take installation files from a CD-ROM, an NFS server, or an HTTP server. As of this writing, FTP and SMB servers are not supported.

❑ There are three ways to create a kickstart file: from the standard file in the Red Hat Linux Documents CD, from the configuration from when you installed Linux as documented in the /root/anaconda-ks.cfg file, or from what you can configure with the GUI Kickstart Configurator.

Understanding Kernel Modules

❑ When you compile your kernel, you have the option to compile components as modules. Kernel modules are not compiled directly into the kernel but are pluggable drivers that can be loaded and unloaded as needed.

❑ To have the kernel dynamically load and unload kernel modules as needed, a special kernel thread, kmod, is called upon to control the loading and unloading of modules. For special parameters and options, you should edit the /etc/modules.conf file.

❑ You can use lsmod to list the modules in memory and **modprobe -t** *group* to see all the modules for any of the following groups: net, pcmcia, usb, cdrom, media, and scsi.

❑ Kernel modules are stored in the /lib/modules/2.4.X.*yy*/ directory, where 2.4.X.*yy* represents the version number of your kernel.

SELF TEST

The following questions will help you measure your understanding of the material presented in this chapter. Read all the choices carefully, as there may be more than one correct answer. Choose all correct answers for each question.

RAID Configuration

1. You have a mirrored RAID system with three drives. The first two are mirrored and the third is supposed to be a spare. When you look at the /etc/raidtab file, you see that it says spare-disks 0. What does this entry tell you?

   A. The raidtab entry is set up correctly.

   B. Spare-disks support is turned off. To turn it on, change spare-disks to 1.

   C. Currently no spare disks are loaded.

   D. The mirror failed and had to use the spare disk.

2. Which of the following versions of RAID does not provide data redundancy?

   A. RAID 0

   B. RAID 1

   C. RAID 4

   D. RAID 5

3. Which of the following device categories is associated with RAID?

   A. /dev/raid

   B. /dev/parity

   C. /dev/md

   D. /dev/mirror

4. Assume you're trying to configure RAID on a computer with several relatively small hard disks. You're trying to set up that computer to handle the large data files associated with an e-commerce Web site. Each of the hard disks, individually, is too small to handle the data you expect in the /var directory. Redundancy is not a concern. Which version of RAID would most efficiently help you address this issue?

   A. RAID 1

   B. RAID 4

C. RAID 5

D. RAID 0

Using Kickstart to Automate Installation

5. You need to set up multiple Red Hat Linux systems over the network and decide to have a bootdisk connect to your DHCP/BOOTP server to load a kickstart file. The kickstart file resides on the DHCP/BOOTP server with the following syntax: *client_ip-kickstart*. You plan to have the kickstart install Linux from an FTP server that does not reside on the DHCP/BOOTP server. What is the problem with this plan?

A. You cannot have the FTP server on a different server than your DHCP/BOOTP servers.

B. The kickstart filename is incorrect.

C. A BOOTP server can be used only to load kernels and will not load a kickstart file.

D. There is no problem.

6. You need to install Linux on several similar computers at your site. You decide the best way to do this is to have all the installation answers preconfigured in a kickstart file, use a local DHCP server to obtain the required network configuration, and install using NFS. You are concerned that anyone sniffing on the network might possibly see the root password in the kickstart configuration. What can you do?

A. Encrypt the kickstart file that resides on the DHCP/BOOTP server.

B. Boot the disk by typing **linux ks=encrypted**.

C. Use rootpw --iscrypted in the kickstart file.

D. There is nothing you can do.

7. You're using the Kickstart Configurator and want to set up a workstation installation on a number of computers in your office. But on the Installation Method page, you can't find an option for a workstation installation. What can you do?

A. Install Red Hat Linux from CD-ROM on one of the workstations, and use the /root/anaconda-ks.cfg file as your kickstart file.

B. Select Upgrade. By default, this sets up a workstation installation of Red Hat Linux.

C. Select NFS. By default, this sets up a workstation installation of Red Hat Linux.

D. Select Install. By default, this sets up a workstation installation of Red Hat Linux.

8. You're using the Kickstart Configurator to create a ks.cfg file for several computers. Which of the following lines allows for a growable /var partition with no limit on growth save the capacity of the hard disk?

    A. part /var --size 1000 --grow yes --maxsize no

    B. part /var --size 1000 --maxsize 0

    C. part /var --size 1000 --grow --maxsize 100000

    D. part /var --size 1000 --grow

Understanding Kernel Modules

9. Which of the following does *not* describe why kernel modules are used?

    A. They may make the kernel size smaller.

    B. They may increase the kernel speed.

    C. You can dynamically unload modules from a running kernel.

    D. Modules have .dll extensions.

The /lib/ modules /kernel_version/ Directory Structure

10. You have a network card that needs to have options specified at the command line when loading the module. You need this network card only occasionally, so you want to leave it as a module. What can you do to simplify loading of the module?

    A. Add a bind command to the modules.conf file.

    B. Add an options command to the modules.conf file.

    C. Add options to the end of the alias command in the modules.conf.file.

    D. None of the above.

11. When you type **lsmod** and see a list of running modules, you notice that some of them say (autoclean). What does this mean?

    A. The module will "automatically" remove its own files in the /tmp directory.

    B. The module is not in use and should be removed.

    C. The kernel will automatically take care of removing it from memory.

    D. The modprobe command has set the module to autoclean.

12. You are on a foreign computer and are not sure what network card is inside it. You have checked dmesg, but no network cards are listed, and even though you have a bunch of compiled network modules, none are currently loaded. What could you do to load the unknown network device most quickly?

    A. Try loading each module manually.

    B. modprobe *

    C. Nothing. The kernel will load the module when you try to connect to the network.

    D. modprobe -t net

13. You want to conserve as much memory as possible. While doing some checking, you notice some modules that are loaded but unused. What command could you employ to remove these modules? (Choose all that apply.)

    A. rmmod

    B. rmmod -r

    C. modprobe -r

    D. modprobe -d

14. You notice that a module you want to load will not load because its dependencies fail. When you examine the /lib/modules/*kernel_version*/ directory more closely, you notice that the modules.dep file does not exist. What would be the easiest way to recreate this file?

    A. Add the dependencies by hand.

    B. In the /usr/src/linux directory, type **make modules_install**

    C. depmod -a

    D. None of the above.

15. You can't find any modules in the /lib/modules/*kernel_version*/kernel/drivers (or similar) directories. Which of the following actions would set up these modules?

    A. Go into the /lib/modules/*kernel_version* directory and run the **make modules** command.

    B. Go into the /lib/modules/*kernel_version* directory and run the **make modules** and **make modules_install** commands.

    C. Go into the /usr/src/linux directory and run the **make modules** command.

    D. Go into the /usr/src/linux directory and run the **make modules** and **make modules_install** commands.

LAB QUESTION

1. You just got hold of ten new PCs for the Human Resources department from a name brand PC manufacturer and you want to install Red Hat Linux from the CD-ROM set that was included with each computer. You want to install Linux on all of them with an optimized set of packages, and you want to do it quickly.

   Each of these machines has a standard 3Com network card that you know Linux has support for because you ordered the machines that way. They also each have one big 10GB disk that already contains Windows 98, and they each have a CD-ROM. You do not have time to install each machine manually. What should you do?

2. What would you do differently, assuming that you have configured a DHCP server for your network?

SELF TEST ANSWERS

RAID Configuration

1. ☑   **A.** The first spare-disks variable is number 0. Since we have one spare disk, the raidtab entry is set up correctly.

   ☒   **B, C,** and **D** are incorrect. There is no way to know from this file the status of the raid disks, nor the current loading, as this is a configuration file, not a log of the running service.

2. ☑   **A** and **B.** RAID 0 does not include any parity data or any other way to recover data from a failed disk. RAID 1 includes an identical copy of data on two different disks. No parity data is required in this version of RAID.

   ☒   **C** and **D** are incorrect. Both RAID 4 and RAID 5 use parity bits. If one drive on either of these systems is lost, the data from that drive can be rebuilt from the parity bits.

3. ☑   **C.** The md device category is associated with RAID. For confirmation, list the drivers in this category, which as of this writing is located in the /lib/modules/*kernel_version*/kernel/drivers/md directory.

   ☒   **A, B,** and **D** are incorrect. There is no raid, parity, or mirror device.

4. ☑   **D.** Linear mode with RAID 0 allows you to most efficiently combine two different physical disks in one filesystem directory such as /var.

   ☒   **A, B,** and **C** are incorrect. It is possible to configure a combination of disks set up in linear mode in any of these versions of RAID. However, these versions of RAID all use additional space for parity or mirroring and are therefore less efficient.

Using Kickstart to Automate Installation

5. ☑   **D** is correct because answers **A, B,** and **C** are not correct.

   ☒   **A, B,** and **C** are incorrect. While you can use kickstart to load from an NFS or HTTP server, the file has to be in a certain location, so **A** is most likely incorrect. The name is correct assuming you used the actual client IP address in the name, as in 192.168.0.1-kickstart (so **B** is incorrect) and kernels are loaded by LILO, not kickstart (which makes **C** incorrect).

6. ☑   **C.** Use rootpw --iscrypted in the kickstart file. If you paste an encrypted password after this line, then the encrypted version of the password will be sent. Incidentally, one of the risks of using a networked kickstart file, as opposed to one on a boot floppy, is that a network protocol analyzer might have access to the encrypted version of the password. In combination with a high-

strength password cracking program, that might put your system at risk. But if your network is secure, the risk should be small.

☒ **A, B, and D** are incorrect. **A** would not work, since Anaconda currently cannot read an encrypted kickstart file. **B** is not a legal option for LILO. Since there *is* something that can be done, **D** is incorrect.

7. ☑ **A.** Since there is no option for a Workstation installation in the Kickstart Configurator, the only way to make this work is based on the kickstart template created through a regular Red Hat Linux Workstation installation.

☒ **B, C, and D** are incorrect. None of these options would result in a default workstation installation of Red Hat Linux. In any of these cases, you'll still need to select the packages or package groups to install.

8. ☑ **D.** The --grow switch alone is enough to accommodate a growable partition. If there is no --maxsize switch, that implies that you do not want to limit the size of this partition.

☒ **A, B, and C** are incorrect. Neither the --grow nor the --maxsize switch is associated with a yes or a no, so **A** is incorrect. A --maxsize switch alone without --grow is not meaningful, so **B** is incorrect. Answer **C** includes a limit on the size of the /var partition.

Understanding Kernel Modules

9. ☑ **D.** Module files do *not* have .dll extensions (Microsoft Windows Dynamic Link Libraries); they have .o (object libraries in Linux) extensions.

☒ **A, B, and C** are incorrect because they do describe reasons why kernel modules are used.

The /lib/ modules /*kernel_version*/ Directory Structure

10. ☑ **B.** Add an options command to the modules.conf file. Once you have done this, simply type **modprobe** *module* and the module will be added with the specified options.

☒ **A, C, and D** are incorrect. There is no such thing as the bind command for modules (which makes **A** incorrect), nor is an option part of the alias command in modules.conf (which makes **C** incorrect). **D** is incorrect because there *is* a correct answer.

11. ☑ **C.** The kernel will automatically take care of removing it from memory.

☒ **A, B, and D** are incorrect. This has nothing to do with the modprobe command (which makes **D** incorrect), since it is controlled by the kernel thread managing modules. Since the kernel thread handles modules automatically, you should not need to remove an "autoclean" module; hence **B** is incorrect. Modules are stored in memory, not the /tmp directory as a file, and therefore **A** is incorrect.

12. ☑ D. The **modprobe -t net** command will run through your /lib/modules/*kernel_version*/ kernel/drivers/net directory and try each module. It will stop when a module successfully loads. ☒ A, B, and C are incorrect. The card module must be loaded before the computer can connect to the network, so C is incorrect. You might try loading all modules manually, but that is not efficient, so A is incorrect. While the **modprobe *** would test all options, it is less efficient, so B is also incorrect.

13. ☑ A, B, and C. The commands **rmmod**, **rmmod -r**, and **modprobe -r** will remove modules. (You need to specify modules for **rmmod**.) Only **rmmod -r** and **modprobe -r** will remove the module and all of its dependencies. rmmod will remove only the module specified. ☒ D is incorrect because modprobe has no -d switch, at least as of this writing.

14. ☑ C, Run the **depmod -a** command. This command will go through all your modules and find all dependencies. It then creates the modules.dep file for you. ☒ A, B, and D are incorrect. Writing this file by hand is not as easy as **depmod -a**, so A is incorrect. The **make modules_install** command can configure modules in the /lib/modules/*kernel_version* directory tree, but it does not configure a modules.dep file, so B is incorrect.

15. ☑ D. These commands together compile your modules and then place them in the appropriate directory trees. Because these are kernel-related commands, they have to be run from /usr/src/linux. ☒ A, B, and C are incorrect. The **make modules** command just compiles the modules, so A and C are not correct. The /lib/modules/*kernel_version* directory is the wrong place to apply these commands, so B is incorrect.

LAB ANSWER

1. The solution is simple. Install Linux on one computer, and then edit the /root/anaconda-ks.cfg file to remove the packages that you don't want. Modify this file with the **clearpart --all** command to wipe out all the old partitions, including the Windows 98 partitions. (This assumes you've backed up any needed data files first.) Use this as a configuration file for installing Linux on each of your computers. Since you have a copy of the Red Hat Linux installation CDs for each computer, you can just duplicate the floppy disk nine times and run each machine installation independently and quickly. No sweat!

2. Alternatively, if the ten computers are connected to a network with a DHCP server, set up a Red Hat Linux boot disk from the bootnet.img file described in Chapter 3. Make sure the Network Configuration section includes a command to get network information from that server. Then you can include the protocol, server name, and directory with the Red Hat installation files in the Source File Location section of the kickstart configuration file.

6

Advanced User Administration

I n this chapter, you will learn how to create and implement policies for managing disk usage—by user or by group. Next, you will learn how to upgrade, configure, compile, and install your own custom kernels. You will learn about the advantages and disadvantages of monolithic and modular kernels. You have three different ways to customize and optimize your kernel configuration for size and functionality. You will also learn the recommended techniques for configuring and installing the kernel.

Finally, you will learn how to set up the Linux startup shell configuration scripts so that users' sessions are configured according to your (and their) requirements, and how to schedule the periodic execution of jobs.

For the RHCE exam, the skills you learn in this chapter are important for the Installation and Network Services Exam. As described in the Red Hat Exam Prep guide, the configuration elements of this exam require that you know how to manage accounts and set up the user environment. Managing kernels, writing initialization scripts, and scheduling jobs are all key skills for any Linux administrator.

CERTIFICATION OBJECTIVE 6.01

Setting Up and Managing Disk Quotas

Quotas are used to limit a user's or a group of users' ability to consume disk space. This prevents a small group of users from monopolizing disk capacity and potentially interfering with other users or the entire system. Disk quotas are commonly used by ISPs, by Web hosting companies, on FTP sites, or on corporate file servers to ensure continued availability of their systems.

Without quotas, one or more users can upload files on an FTP server to the point of filling a filesystem. Once the affected partition is full, other users are effectively denied upload access to the disk. This is also a reason to mount different filesystem directories on different partitions. For example, if you only had partitions for your root (/) directory and swap space, someone uploading to your computer could fill up all of the space in your root directory (/). Without some free space in root (/), your system could become unstable or even crash.

You have two ways to set quotas for users. You can limit users by inodes or by kilobyte-sized disk blocks. Every Linux file requires an inode, so you can set limits by the number of files or by absolute space.

Limits on disk blocks restrict the amount of disk space available to a user on your system. Older versions of Red Hat Linux included LinuxConf, which included a graphical tool to configure quotas. As of this writing, Red Hat Linux no longer has a graphical quota configuration tool. Today, the quota system may be configured only through the command line interface.

Learn to focus on command line tools. Red Hat used to make LinuxConf available as a graphical tool for a number of system administration functions, including quotas. While Red Hat may create another GUI quota manager, don't count on it. And GUI tools have been known to crash. On the job, as well as on the exam, command line tools are the only sure way to address just about any Linux configuration issue. Besides, command line tools are faster, and time is often of the essence on the RHCE exam.

Kernel Configuration

Resource consumption is managed by the kernel. Thus, before you can set up quotas, you should make sure this feature is active in your kernel. Fortunately, the standard Red Hat Linux kernel enables quota support by default. However, if you download a new kernel, you may not be so fortunate. This chapter includes instructions on installing kernel sources to enable features such as quotas.

To verify quota support in any custom-built kernels you may have, issue the following command:

```
# grep CONFIG_QUOTA /usr/src/linux-2.4/.config
```

There are three possible results. If you see the following, quota support is enabled:

```
CONFIG_QUOTA=y
```

Alternatively, if you see the following, quota support is not enabled:

```
CONFIG_QUOTA=n
```

If you don't see any output, then you haven't installed the kernel source files.

If you have a custom or upgraded kernel, use either the **make menuconfig** or **make xconfig** command to enable quota support. The quota support option is located in the filesystem section. Simply turn on quota support and rebuild and install your new kernel. (There will be more on building and installing kernels later in this chapter.)

To complete the job, you will need to reboot to your new kernel and then install the quota RPMs.

The Quota Package

First, check to see if you have the quota RPM installed on your system. You can check with the following command:

```
[root@notebook /]# rpm -q quota
quota-3.07-3
```

You have several ways to get the quota RPM file and install it. The most direct would be to install this RPM directly from your Red Hat installation CD-ROM:

```
mount /mnt/cdrom
```

Load the quota RPM with the following command:

```
rpm -Uvh /mnt/cdrom/RedHat/RPMS/quota-*
```

This command allows rpm to update (or install if a previous version of the quota RPM is not present, -U), to install verbosely (-v), and to use a series of hashes (-h) to indicate the current progress while installing the software. The asterisk is especially useful if you're installing the package from an FTP or HTTP server, since the version number may be different from what you expect.

on the **Job**

It can be time consuming to find the right Red Hat Installation CD. One tip used by many administrators is to install all RPMs from the Red Hat Installation CDs on a /RedHat/RPMs directory on a networked server. This can be the same directory that you use to install Red Hat Linux over a network, as discussed in Chapter 5. As the actual location of an RPM can change from version to version of Red Hat Linux, this book does not specify the CD that you need to use.

The quota package includes the following commands:

- **/sbin/quotaon** */fs* Enables quotas for the */fs* filesystem.
- **/sbin/quotaoff** */fs* Disables quota tracking.
- **/usr/sbin/edquota** *name* Edits the quota settings for user *name*. Can also be used to set defaults, or to copy quota settings from one user to another.

- **quota**   Allows users to see their current resource consumption and limits.

- **repquota**   Generates a report of disk consumption by all users for a quota-enabled filesystem.

- **quotacheck**   Scans a filesystem for quota usage. Initializes the quota databases.

The next step is to ensure the quotas are turned on and checked when Linux boots on your system.

sysinit Quota Handling

The /etc/rc.d/rc.sysinit script as described in Chapter 4 is used to provide system initialization services for Linux during the boot process. Included in the script are commands to enable quota services. Specifically, this script runs both /sbin/quotacheck (to ensure that disk consumption usage records are accurate) and /sbin/quotaon (to enable quotas on all filesystems indicated in /etc/fstab).

While you can run /sbin/quotaon and /sbn/quotaoff manually, there is usually little need. Red Hat's /etc/rc.d/rc.sysinit ensures quotas are enabled during the boot process. When your computer shuts down, Red Hat runs the umount command on all filesystems. When each quota-enabled filesystem is unmounted, the kernel's latest information on resource consumption by users, groups, files, and inodes for that filesystem is written back to the partition.

Quota Activation in /etc/fstab

The file /etc/fstab tells Linux which filesystems you wish to mount at boot time. The options column of this file is used to configure the way a directory is mounted. As Linux continues the boot process, these options are passed to the mount command. To get Linux to enable quotas when you boot, you need to add the appropriate entries to /etc/fstab for users, groups, or both.

on the **Job**

Whenever you edit a key configuration file such as /etc/fstab, it's a good idea to back it up and save it to any boot or rescue disks that you may have. If your changes lead to a catastrophic failure, you can boot your system from a rescue disk and then restore the original configuration file.

Here is a sample /etc/fstab before editing:

Device	Mount point	Filesys	Options	dump	Fsck
LABEL=/	/	ext3	defaults	1	1
/dev/cdrom	/mnt/cdrom	iso9660	noauto,owner,kudzu,ro	0	0
/dev/fd0	/mnt/floppy	auto	noauto,owner,kudzu	0	0
none	/proc	proc	defaults	0	0
none	/dev/pts	devpts	gid=5,mode=620	0	0
none	/dev/shm	tmpfs	defaults	0	0
/dev/hda5	swap	swap	defaults	0	0
LABEL=/win	/win	vfat	uid=500,gid=500,owner,rw	0	0
LABEL=/home	/home	ext3	defaults	0	0

In this configuration, we can enable quotas only on the root filesystem (LABEL=/) and the /home filesystem (/dev/hda6). To enable user quota tracking on a filesystem, add the keyword *usrquota* to the values listed in the options column. Similarly, you enable group quota tracking with the *grpquota* option. Use vi or your favorite text editor to update /etc/fstab.

In our example, we will add both user and group quotas to the root filesystem:

Device	Mount point	Filesys	Options	dump	Fsck
LABEL=/	/	ext3	exec,dev,suid,rw,usrquota,grpquota	1	1
/dev/cdrom	/mnt/cdrom	iso9660	noauto,owner,kudzu,ro	0	0
/dev/fd0	/mnt/floppy	auto	noauto,owner,kudzu	0	0
none	/proc	proc	defaults	0	0
none	/dev/pts	devpts	gid=5,mode=620	0	0
none	/dev/shm	tmpfs	defaults	0	0
/dev/hda5	swap	swap	defaults	0	0
/dev/hda1	/win	vfat	uid=500,gid=500,owner,rw	0	0
/dev/hda6	/home	ext3	defaults	0	0

If you edit the /etc/fstab file by hand, you'll need to ensure that the line you are editing does not wrap to the next line. If it does, the format for your /etc/fstab will be invalid and you may not be able to successfully boot Linux.

on the job

You can test changes to /etc/fstab by remounting a filesystem. For example, if you've just added an usrquota entry to the /home directory filesystem, you can test it with the mount -o remount /home *command.*

Quota Management Commands

You need quota files before you can activate actual quotas. First, you need to create the /aquota.user and /aquota.group files. To do it by hand, create the empty files in the root of the object partition and set the security so that only root has read and write permissions. For example:

```
# touch /aquota.user /aquota.group
# chmod 600 /aquota.user /aquota.group
```

If the directory where you're configuring quotas is different, revise these commands accordingly.

 If you're more familiar with a Linux distribution with kernel 2.2.x, these files were quota.user and quota.group.

Once you create these files, run **/sbin/quotacheck -avugm**. It automatically scans /etc/mtab, which is based on the mounted directories from /etc/fstab. The options for quotacheck are:

- **-a** Scans all filesystems with quotas enabled by checking /etc/mtab.
- **-v** Performs a verbose scan.
- **-u** Scans for user quotas.
- **-g** Scans for group quotas.
- **-m** Remounts the scanned filesystem.

This will check the current quota information for all users, groups, and partitions. It stores this information in the appropriate quota partitions. If you did not create these files by hand, they will be created now and should have the appropriate security already set, but you should double-check just to be safe:

```
# ls -l /aquota.user /aquota.group
```

No matter how you create the files, you need to run quotacheck to collect initial information on your users. This can be accomplished either by rebooting or by issuing quotacheck if you haven't already. For example, to initialize your quota files on the root directory, use

```
/sbin/quotacheck -m /
```

Using edquota to Set Up Disk Quotas

To specify disk quotas, you need to run edquota. This command will edit the aquota.user or aquota.group file with the vi editor. You can change the editor by specifying a different one with the $EDITOR (i.e., EDITOR=/path/to/new/editor; export EDITOR) variable. In our example, we will pretend we have a user named mj, and we want to restrict how much disk space he is allowed to use. We type the following command to edit his quota record:

```
# /usr/sbin/edquota -u mj
```

Unless you've changed the default editor, this launches vi and opens the quota information for user mj as shown in Figure 6-1.

In this example, our soft and hard limits are set to 0 for both inodes and files. This is per the default and means we currently may consume as many inodes or as many disk blocks as we wish. We can see that this user is currently using 3224 blocks and has 425 files (inodes) on this partition. Each block takes up 1KB of space; thus user mj is using 3.2MB. We want to set a limit so that user mj does not take more than 20MB of space with his files.

First, we need to elaborate on the meaning of soft and hard limits.

- **Soft limit** This is the maximum amount of space a user can have on that partition. If you have set a grace period, then this will act as an alarm. The user will then be notified he is in quota violation. If you have set a grace period, you will also need to set a hard limit. A grace period is the number of days a user is allowed to be above the given quota. After the grace period is over, the user must get under the soft limit to continue.

- **Hard limit** Hard limits are necessary only when you are using grace periods. If grace periods are enabled, this will be the absolute limit a person can use. Any attempt to consume resources beyond this limit will be denied. If you are not using grace periods, the soft limit is the maximum amount of available to each user.

FIGURE 6-1	
Quota information	

```
Disk quotas for user mj (uid 500):
  Filesystem              blocks       soft       hard     inodes       soft
  hard
  /dev/sda3                 3224          0          0        425          0
      0
~
~
```

FIGURE 6-2	
Quota information with soft and hard space limits	

```
Disk quotas for user mj (uid 500):
 Filesystem                blocks        soft        hard      inodes        soft
 hard
   /dev/sda3                 3224       18000       20000         425           0
      0
~
~
~
"/tmp//EdP.agLz0uw" 3L, 213C
```

In our example, we will set our user an 18MB soft limit and a 20MB hard limit. As shown in Figure 6-2, this is written as a number of 1KB blocks in the quota file.

Note that we have not limited user mj's use of inodes. He is still able to use as many inodes (thus as many files) as he likes. Now we must save this file. Assuming you're still using the default vi editor, the **wq** command does this job nicely.

We will also give user mj a seven-day grace period to get his stuff cleaned up. To set the grace period, we use the edquota command, but provide -t as an argument:

```
# /usr/sbin/edquota -t
```

Next, vi will load, and you will see something similar to what you see in Figure 6-3.

Here, Linux has provided us with the default of seven days for both inodes and block usage. That is, a user may exceed his soft limit on either resource for up to seven days. After that, further requests to use inodes or disk blocks will be denied. Our user mj would have to delete files to get his total disk block consumption under 18MB before he could create new files or grow existing files.

To activate the new grace period, just save the file.

There is a quirk to quotas that you should be aware of. When you use edquota and specify the grace period, you cannot have a space between the number and the

FIGURE 6-3	
Default quota grace period	

```
Grace period before enforcing soft limits for users:
Time units may be: days, hours, minutes, or seconds
 Filesystem              Block grace period      Inode grace period
   /dev/sda3                   7days                   7days
~
~
~
~
"/tmp//EdP.aUmMixp" 4L, 233C
```

unit. That is, the entry "7 days" will not work, but "7days" will. If you get an error message similar to:

```
Can't parse grace period time 7
```

you'll know you forgot to remove the blank.

The edquota command allows you to use an already configured user's quota as a template for new users. To use this feature, you need to add the following switch and options: -p *configured_user* arguments:

```
# /usr/sbin/edquota -up mj bob sue
```

This command will not provide any output, but it will take the quota configuration settings of user mj and apply them to both bob and sue. You can list as many users as you want to edit or apply templates to.

You can also set up quotas on a per-group basis. To do this, simply run edquota with the -g *group_name* argument. Here, *group_name* would need to be a valid group as specified in the /etc/group file.

```
# /usr/sbin/edquota -g mj
```

This opens the block and inode quota for group mj, as shown in Figure 6-4.

Automating Quota Settings

Methods are available to apply these quotas to all users. First, for quota maintenance, it's useful to run the aforementioned quotacheck command on a regular basis. As you'll see later in this chapter, that is easy to do through the cron system. A simple command in the right cron file like the following automatically runs the quotacheck command at 4:00 A.M. every Saturday:

```
0 4 * * 6 /sbin/quotacheck -avug
```

FIGURE 6-4	Disk quotas for group mj (gid 500):					
	▯ Filesystem	blocks	soft	hard	inodes	soft
	hard					
Group quota	/dev/sda3	3216	0	0	422	0
	0					
	～					
	～					
	～					

You can also use the edquota command to apply quotas to all users on your system. For example, the following command applies the quotas that you've already set on user mj to all other real users on the system:

```
edquota -p mj `awk -F: '$3 > 499 {print $1}' /etc/passwd`
```

Note that this command lists the first column ($1) of /etc/passwd, which is the user name. And in keeping with the UIDs for regular Red Hat users, this is limited to users with UIDs of 500 or higher. You can add this type of command to the appropriate cron file as well, which makes sure that the quotas are applied to all existing and new users.

Quota Reports

It is always nice to see reports on who is using the most disk space. You can generate reports on users, groups, or everybody on every partition. To view a report showing all the quota information, run the **/usr/sbin/repquota -a** command. You'll get a result similar to what is shown in Figure 6-5.

If you have multiple filesystems with quotas, you can use repquota to isolate a specific filesystem with a command such as:

```
# /usr/sbin/repquota -u /home
```

To see specific information on just one user, the following quota command can be used:

```
# quota -uv mj
Disk quotas for user mj(uid 500):
Filesystem  blocks  quota  limit  grace  files  quota  limit  grace
/dev/sda3    4096   18000  20000          431      0      0
```

An individual user can check his or her own usage with the quota command, but only root can use the -u option to examine the quotas for other users.

<table>
<tr><td>**FIGURE 6-5**</td><td></td></tr>
<tr><td></td><td></td></tr>
<tr><td>Quota report</td><td></td></tr>
</table>

```
[root@RH80 mj]# /usr/sbin/repquota -a
*** Report for user quotas on device /dev/sda3
Block grace time: 7days; Inode grace time: 7days
                       Block limits              File limits
User            used   soft   hard  grace   used  soft  hard  grace
--------------------------------------------------------------------
root      --  669956      0      0              9     0     0
mj        --    3768  18000  20000            429     0     0

[root@RH80 mj]# []
```

Quotas on NFS Directories

The Network File System (NFS) allows users to share files and directories on a network with Linux and Unix computers. Users across the network mount a shared NFS directory from a specific computer. Users are normally in a single database in an NFS setup. Disk quotas can be applied to these users in virtually the same way as on a regular Linux computer. For example, if you create a local user called nfsuser, and you translate all remote requests to this user, then you need to set up quota restrictions for nfsuser on the mounted partition. This will limit the disk consumption of all incoming NFS users. See Chapter 7 for more about NFS.

EXERCISE 6-1

Configure Quotas

In this exercise, we will set up user quotas for one user on your system. These quotas will allow a soft limit of 80MB and a hard limit of 100MB for each user. No limits are to be placed on the number of inodes. Assume the /home directory is mounted on a separate partition. (If you don't have a /usr/src/linux-2.4/.config file, you may want to come back to this exercise after the end of the next section.) To do this, use the following steps:

1. Check your kernel configuration for the CONFIG_QUOTA variable, using the /usr/src/linux-2.4/.config file. It should be set to "Y." If not, proceed to the Lab at the end of this chapter for instructions on how to revise your kernel. If the .config file is not there, you're probably using the stock Red Hat Linux kernel, which is set to allow quotas by default.

2. Make sure to install the quota package. Mount the appropriate Red Hat Installation CD and use the **rpm -Uvh** command.

3. Add quotas to /etc/fstab. Add the usrquota variable to the Options column for /home. Make sure this line is in /etc/fstab.

4. Activate the quotas. You can unmount and remount the /home directory, or you can reboot Linux.

5. Use the **/sbin/quotacheck -avug** command to activate the quota files in the /home directory.

6. Make sure this command worked. Look for the aquota.user file in the /home directory.

7. Now you're ready to set up quotas for a specific user. If necessary, look up user names in /etc/passwd. Use the **/usr/sbin/edquota -u** *username* command to edit the quotas for the user of your choice.

8. Under the soft and hard columns, change the 0 to 80000 and 100000, respectively. Remember, these files are set up for 1KB blocks. Save the file.

CERTIFICATION OBJECTIVE 6.02

Kernel Sources

One of Linux's strong features is the ease with which you can rebuild your kernel to exactly meet your needs. The kernel is the heart of the whole operating system; it manages the hardware, decides which processes to run, and provides each process with an isolated, virtual address space in which to run.

The Kernel Source Tree and Documentation

Once installed, the source code for the kernel can be easily accessed through the /usr/src/linux-2.4 directory. Installation procedures are addressed in following sections. Once the source code is installed, the /usr/src directory should look similar to the following:

```
# ls -l /usr/src/
total 12
lrwxrwxrwx   1 root     root          17 Jul 30 13:29 linux-2.4 -> linux-2.4.19-7
drwxr-xr-x  16 root     root        4096 Jul 30 13:35 linux-2.4.19-7
```

In this case, the physical directory is linux-2.4.19-7, and there is a soft link called linux-2.4 that points to this directory. (Your configuration may differ.) Using this method, you can create a directory for a new kernel, change the link to point to the new directory, and still keep your old source for reference.

Periodically, you may wish to upgrade your kernel. When installing a new set of kernel sources, you should recreate a symbolic link from linux-2.4 to the real name of the new kernel (e.g., sym-link it to linux-2.4.24). You could do this with

```
# ln -s linux-2.4.24 linux-2.4
```

The /usr/src/linux-2.4 directory is laid out as follows:

```
abi       COPYING        drivers   init     lib           mm       REPORTING-BUGS
arch      CREDITS        fs        ipc      MAINTAINERS   net      Rules.make
configs   Documentation  include   kernel   Makefile      README   scripts
```

Begin your study of the current kernel with the README file. While the instructions in this chapter work with the current configuration of Red Hat Linux 8.0 on my computer, things can change from kernel to kernel. Also, examine the Documentation directory. It contains everything you need, from information on setting up symmetrical multiprocessors to serial consoles. The other directories mainly contain source, and you probably won't need to spend time examining those files (unless you *really* want to see how TCP/IP works). There is also a hidden file named .config that may be present in this directory. It will be described in more detail later in this chapter.

The Kernel RPMs and the Linux Kernel Tar File

If you don't see the directories mentioned in the preceding section, then you haven't installed the kernel's source code. To install the source provided with your Red Hat installation, access the Red Hat RPMs from CD or another source and install the kernel RPM. The following example is based on an installation from the appropriate Red Hat Installation CD:

```
# mount /mnt/cdrom
# rpm -Uvh /mnt/cdrom/RedHat/RPMS/kernel-source-*
```

Depending on the packages you've specified when you installed Red Hat Linux, this may be all you need. However, this command may bring up some error messages similar to the following:

```
error: cannot open Packages index using db3 - No such file or directory (2)
error: Failed dependencies:
        gcc >= 3.2-0.1 is needed by kernel-source-2.4.22
```

which suggests that you need to install some other RPM packages, as described in the next section.

Alternatively, you can download the newest kernel from http://www.kernel.org. The version numbers are discussed in the next section. Once you have downloaded the kernel source, you will need to properly install it. For our example, we will assume you downloaded linux-2.4.20.tar.gz into the /usr/src/ directory.

```
# cd /usr/src
# mkdir linux-2.4.20
# rm linux-2.4
# tar xzvf linux-2.4.20.tar.gz
# ln -s linux-2.4.20 linux-2.4
```

Here we manually created a new directory for the kernel. Then we removed the old link, and then uncompress the tar.gz file. Then you can link linux-2.4 to the new directory created when you uncompress the tar.gz file.

Compressed tar files are shown in tar.gz format; they are also known as "tarballs."

Required RPMs

In order to build a kernel from sources, you need to ensure you have all the RPMs necessary, not only for the kernel, but also for the tools needed to build the kernel. Check your system to ensure you have the RPM packages described in Table 6-1. If not, mount the appropriate Red Hat installation CDs and install the needed

TABLE 6-1

Required Kernel Packages

Package	Description
kernel-source-*	Kernel source files
glibc-kernheaders-*	Kernel header files
glibc-devel-*	Required for C libraries
cpp-*	C language preprocessor
ncurses4-*	Required for menuconfig screen
ncurses-devel-*	Development libraries for ncurses
binutils-*	Required binary utilities
gcc-*	C language compiler
tcl-*	TCL scripting language—required for xconfig screen
tk-*	TK X Window widgets—required for xconfig screen

packages with the **rpm -Uvh** *packagename* command. If the revision associated with your package and architecture are different, revise the package names accordingly.

The packages in Table 6-1 end with a *, because version numbers change frequently. In any case, the objective is to install these packages; for example, to install the tk package, an **rpm -Uvh /mnt/cdrom/RedHat/RPMS/tk-*** command is all you need. Normally, you should not have to specify the complete name of the RPM package file.

on the Job *Wildcards such as an * are often also known as globbing.*

Understanding Kernel Version Numbers

The version number may look a little confusing, but it is actually very useful. For our example, we will use kernel version 2.4.33, in a *majorversion.majorrevision.patch* format.

The first number (2) is the major version number. These are drastic changes to the kernel. Typically, older version stuff will *not* work in the newer version when this number changes. Kernel major version numbers are reserved for completely new kernel designs.

The second number (4) actually has two meanings. First, it indicates this is the fourth major revision of major version 2 of the kernel. Second, since it is an even number, it indicates that the kernel release is a stable release. If it were an odd number, it would be a developmental kernel, not suitable for production computers.

The third number (33) is the patch version number for the kernel. These changes are typically small changes, bug fixes, security fixes, and enhancements. Generally, you can use the zcat command to increment one patch at a time. For example, if your current kernel is version 2.4.33, you can use the patch-2.4.34.gz file to upgrade your kernel to version 2.4.34.

Usually, software that has kernel version requirements will refer only to the first two major numbers. For example, you may install software that will work only with version 2.2 and later kernels. This would mean that all 2.2.*x* and later kernels would be required for this software. Older 2.0.x kernels would not likely be able to run this software. For example, 2.0.x kernels cannot run ipchains, and 2.2.x kernels (generally) cannot run iptables.

Finally, it is common practice for Red Hat to tag an extra number onto all packages, including the kernel. This is the Red Hat revision level. For example, a 2.4.22-5 kernel released by Red Hat is the fifth revision of the 2.4.22 kernel.

Kernel Patches

Sometimes, all you need is a simple patch to a kernel. Patches usually work fairly well if you're upgrading from one patch version to the next higher version, such as from 2.4.22 to 2.4.23.

Kernel patches are easily available from Internet sites such as ftp.kernel.org. For example, if you want to upgrade from kernel version 2.4.19 to kernel version 2.4.20, download the patch-2.4.20.gz file from the Internet. Copy the patch to the /usr/src directory. Move to that directory, and run a command similar to the following to make the upgrade:

```
zcat patch-2.4.20.gz | patch -p0
```

If it doesn't work, you'll see files with a .rej extension somewhere in your kernel source tree. Use a command such as **find** to check for such files. If you don't find any of these files, you can proceed with the **make clean**, **make menuconfig**, and **make dep** commands as described in the next section.

CERTIFICATION OBJECTIVE 6.03

Kernel Recompilation and Installation

The kernel is what GRUB or LILO loads into memory. And it is the kernel that decides what device driver modules are required, as well as how hardware resources are allocated (i.e., IRQ ports, I/O addresses, and DMA channels).

When you recompile your kernel, you can

■ Greatly improve the speed at which kernel services run by building in direct support for often-used drivers and dynamically loading less frequently needed drivers as modules.

■ Lower the memory consumption of your kernel by removing unneeded components.

■ Configure support for high-end hardware, such as memory above 4GB, hardware array controllers, symmetric multiprocessing (multiple CPU) support, and more.

In essence, you can customize the Linux kernel any way you want. The best way to do it is to make it fit every detail of your hardware.

Best Practices

You should compile your kernel with only the things you need. The more you can leave out, the faster your whole system will run. For example, if you don't have a sound card, you can remove sound card support from your kernel. By removing unneeded devices, you will

- Decrease the size of the kernel.
- Provide a modest increase in speed for the devices that are present.
- Make more hardware resources (I/O addresses, IRQ ports, and so on) available for other hardware such as network cards, disk controllers, and more.
- Reduce the chance of hardware limits, such as those that may be based on the size of the compressed kernel.

Generally, it is a good idea to have device drivers compiled as modules for any equipment that you may add in the near future. For example, if you may use your Linux computer as a router, you'll need a second network card, and you can add support for that card to your kernel. For example, if you have a 3Com 3c595 network card installed but you also have some 3Com 3c905 cards in storage, then it may be a good idea to include the 3c905 module. That way, you will just have to swap in the new card and let the module load, causing minimum downtime.

Modules are kernel extensions. They are not compiled directly into the kernel but can be plugged in and removed as needed. So any hardware failure such as that of a network card would not cause the whole system to fail.

Kernel Concepts

You will need to understand some basic kernel concepts before you can compile your own kernel. Kernels can be organized as one big unit, or as a lot of interconnected pieces. Kernels are called up by boot loaders when you boot your computer.

Monolithic Versus Modular

A *monolithic* kernel is a kernel where all the device modules are built directly into the kernel. *Modular* kernels have many of their devices built as separate loadable modules. Monolithic kernels can communicate with devices faster, since modular kernels can talk to the hardware only indirectly through a module table.

Unfortunately, monolithic Linux kernels are huge. Bigger kernels reduce available RAM. In addition, some systems just can't boot a kernel that's too large.

There used to be advantages to   monolithic kernel. Linux has problems loading modular kernels for some hardware. With a monolithic kernel, the drivers would already be there. But now modular kernels load new drivers a lot more reliably.

A modular kernel has greater flexibility. You can compile almost all your drivers as modules, and then each module can be inserted into the kernel whenever you need it. Modules keep the initial kernel size low, which decreases the boot time and improves overall performance. If Linux has trouble loading a kernel module, you can use the /sbin/modprobe or /sbin/insmod commands to load modules as needed.

Updating the Kernel

Updating the kernel is not as difficult as it looks. You should always keep a copy of your old kernel around in case you make a mistake. New kernels are handled by installing the newly built kernel in /boot and then adding another boot option to LILO or GRUB for the new kernel. LILO or GRUB treats the new kernel as if it were an entirely new operating system.

If you do make a drastic mistake and the kernel doesn't boot, then you can simply reboot the server and select your old kernel at the GRUB or LILO prompt. You should also save your kernel configuration files so that you can easily copy to the newer kernels and use them as a guideline. This will be discussed in more detail later in this chapter.

The /boot Partition

The Linux kernel is stored in the partition with the /boot directory. New kernels must also be transferred to this directory. By default, Red Hat Linux sets up a partition of about 100MB for the /boot directory. This provides enough room for your current kernel plus some additional upgraded kernels.

The /proc Filesystem

The /proc directory is based on a virtual filesystem; in other words, it does not include any files that are stored on the hard drive. But it is a window into what the kernel sees of your computer. It's a good idea to study the files and directories in /proc, as it can help you diagnose a wide range of problems. Figure 6-6 shows the /proc from a typical Red Hat Linux 8.0 computer.

The numbered items are based on process IDs. For example, the process ID of init is 1. The files in this directory include the memory segments that make up the active process. The contents of each of these files include the active memory for that process.

The other items in the listing are files and directories that correspond to configuration information for components such as DMA channels or whole subsystems such as memory information.

Take a look at some of these files. For example, the /proc/meminfo file provides excellent information as to the state of memory on the local computer, as shown in Figure 6-7.

FIGURE 6-6

A typical /proc directory

```
[root@RH80 root]# ls /proc/
1     1119  1223  1243  5    848    devices      ioports  modules     stat
1016  1130  1227  1274  6    871    dma          irq                  swaps
1052  1131  1229  1275  620  895    driver       kcore    mtrr        sys
1061  1134  1230  1277  625  924    execdomains  kmsg     net         sysvipc
1062  1148  1232  17    651  948    fb           ksyms    partitions  tty
1063  1200  1234  179   679  966    filesystems  loadavg  pci         uptime
1064  1203  1235  2     7    apm    fs           locks    scsi        version
1065  1206  1237  3     794  bus    ide          mdstat
1066  1208  1239  382   8    cmdline interrupts  meminfo  slabinfo
1069  1218  1241  4     84   cpuinfo iomem       misc     speakup
[root@RH80 root]# []
```

FIGURE 6-7

Memory information from /proc/meminfo

```
           total:     used:      free: shared: buffers:  cached:
Mem:    195862528 189284352   6578176       0 35258368 113381376
Swap:   320745472  20631552 300113920
MemTotal:        191272 kB
MemFree:           6424 kB
MemShared:            0 kB
Buffers:          34432 kB
Cached:          109276 kB
SwapCached:        1448 kB
Active:           97516 kB
Inact_dirty:      56916 kB
Inact_clean:       8820 kB
Inact_target:     32648 kB
HighTotal:            0 kB
HighFree:             0 kB
LowTotal:        191272 kB
LowFree:           6424 kB
SwapTotal:       313228 kB
SwapFree:        293080 kB
Committed_AS:     51220 kB
~
~
~
~
~
~
~
~
"/proc/meminfo" [readonly] 20L, 600C                    5,9        All
```

Now you can examine how Linux looks at your CPU in the /proc/cpuinfo file, as shown in Figure 6-8. In this particular case, the *cpu family* information is important; the number 6 in this figure corresponds to a 686 CPU.

We can even see what hardware resources are used by examining files like /proc/ioports, /proc/iomem, and /proc/dma. The /proc/ioports file is shown in Figure 6-9.

Many programs are available that simply look at the information stored in /proc and interpret it in a more readable format. The top utility is a perfect example. It reads the process table, queries RAM and swap usage and the level of CPU use, and presents it all on one screen. An example of output from top is shown in Figure 6-10.

More importantly, there are kernel variables you can alter to change the way the kernel behaves while it's running. If your computer has two or more network cards, the following command activates *IP forwarding*, which effectively sets up your computer as a router.

```
# cat /proc/sys/net/ipv4/ip_forward
0
# echo 1 >> /proc/sys/net/ipv4/ip_forward
# cat /proc/sys/net/ipv4/ip_forward
1
```

FIGURE 6-8

CPU information from /proc/cpuinfo

```
processor        : 0
vendor_id        : GenuineIntel
cpu family       : 6
model            : 11
model name       : Intel(R) Pentium(R) III Mobile CPU       1200MHz
stepping         : 1
cpu MHz          : 1193.582
cache size       : 512 KB
fdiv_bug         : no
hlt_bug          : no
f00f_bug         : no
coma_bug         : no
fpu              : yes
fpu_exception    : yes
cpuid level      : 2
wp               : yes
flags            : fpu vme de pse tsc msr pae mce cx8 sep mtrr pge mca cmov pat pse
36 mmx fxsr sse
bogomips         : 2365.84
[]
~
~
~
~
~
~
~
~
"/proc/cpuinfo" [readonly] 19L, 402C                          19,0-1        All
```

FIGURE 6-9

I/O address information from /proc/ioports

```
0000-001f : dma1
0020-003f : pic1
0040-005f : timer
0060-006f : keyboard
0070-007f : rtc
0080-008f : dma page reg
00a0-00bf : pic2
00c0-00df : dma2
00f0-00ff : fpu
0170-0177 : ide1
02e8-02ef : serial(auto)
02f8-02ff : serial(auto)
0376-0376 : ide1
03bc-03be : parport0
03c0-03df : vga+
03e8-03ef : serial(auto)
03f8-03ff : serial(auto)
0cf8-0cff : PCI conf1
1000-103f : Intel Corp. 82371AB PIIX4 ACPI
1040-105f : Intel Corp. 82371AB PIIX4 ACPI
1060-107f : Intel Corp. 82371AB PIIX4 USB
  1060-107f : usb-uhci
1080-109f : BusLogic BT-946C (BA80C30) [MultiMaster 10]
  1080-1083 : BusLogic BT-958
10a0-10bf : Advanced Micro Devices [AMD] 79c970 [PCnet LANCE]
  10a0-10bf : PCnet/PCI II 79C970A
10c0-10cf : PCI device 15ad:0405 (VMware Inc)
10d0-10df : Intel Corp. 82371AB PIIX4 IDE
[] 10d8-10df : ide1
~
                                                             29,1          All
```

FIGURE 6-10

Output from the
top command
comes from /proc

```
 4:25pm  up 22:54,  3 users,  load average: 0.00, 0.02, 0.00
64 processes: 61 sleeping, 3 running, 0 zombie, 0 stopped
CPU states:  6.7% user,  5.5% system,  0.0% nice, 87.6% idle
Mem:   191272K av,  182952K used,    8320K free,         OK shrd,    34784K buff
Swap:  313228K av,   20148K used,  293080K free                    107432K cached

  PID USER      PRI  NI  SIZE  RSS SHARE STAT %CPU %MEM   TIME COMMAND
 1334 root       16   0 17700 8000  2268 R     7.5  4.1  1:20 X
 3806 mj         16   0  2708 2708  2264 S     1.5  1.4  0:00 screenshot
 1413 mj         15   0 10184 9492  8744 S     0.9  4.9  0:09 kdeinit
 1418 mj         15   0 11376  10M  9404 S     0.7  5.5  0:15 kdeinit
 1414 mj         15   0  8988 6188  3752 S     0.3  3.2  0:05 gimp
 3805 mj         15   0  1032 1032   832 R     0.3  0.5  0:00 top
  192 root       15   0     0    0     0 SW    0.1  0.0  0:00 kjournald
 1391 mj         15   0  8852 8092  7804 S     0.1  4.2  0:06 kdeinit
 3750 mj         15   0 11500  10M  9828 R     0.1  5.8  0:01 kdeinit
    1 root       15   0   472  432   416 S     0.0  0.2  0:04 init
    2 root       15   0     0    0     0 SW    0.0  0.0  0:00 keventd
    3 root       15   0     0    0     0 SW    0.0  0.0  0:00 kapmd
    4 root       34  19     0    0     0 SWN   0.0  0.0  0:00 ksoftirqd_CPU0
    5 root       15   0     0    0     0 SW    0.0  0.0  0:01 kswapd
    6 root       15   0     0    0     0 SW    0.0  0.0  0:00 bdflush
    7 root       15   0     0    0     0 SW    0.0  0.0  0:00 kupdated
    8 root       25   0     0    0     0 SW    0.0  0.0  0:00 mdrecoveryd
   16 root       15   0     0    0     0 SW    0.0  0.0  0:00 khubd
   95 root       15   0     0    0     0 SW    0.0  0.0  0:00 kjournald
  189 root       15   0     0    0     0 SW    0.0  0.0  0:00 kjournald
  190 root       15   0     0    0     0 SW    0.0  0.0  0:00 kjournald
```

The following is another useful change to a proc kernel variable, which enables the use of TCP SYN packet cookies. These cookies prevent SYN flood attacks on your system, including the so-called "ping of death."

```
# echo 1 >> /proc/sys/net/ipv4/tcp_syncookies
```

The Kernel Configuration Scripts

Once you've configured a kernel once, the configuration information is stored in a hidden file, /usr/src/linux-2.4/.config. It is structured as a listing of variables. Here are some entries from the .config file:

```
CONFIG_NETDEVICES=y
CONFIG_DUMMY=m
# CONFIG_HAPPYMEAL is not set
```

Here are the three main types of variables you'll see in this file. The first will compile in direct support (because of the "y"), the second entry will compile in support as a module (the "m"), and the third is commented out, so this feature will be left out of the kernel we are building. You should never have to edit this file directly, as there are easier ways to configure your kernel.

Move to the directory with your kernel source files. If you've installed the Red Hat 8.0 kernel-source RPM, you can use the /usr/src/linux-2.4 directory. If you've installed the latest kernel from www.kernel.org, it may be in the /usr/src/linux directory. Three tools can help you configure the kernel configuration file: **make config**, **make menuconfig**, and **make xconfig**.

Back Up Your Configuration

If you've reconfigured your kernel before, the configuration will be saved in the /usr/src/linux-2.4/.config file. Remember, files with a period in front are hidden. Back up this file on another location such as a rescue floppy so that you can restore your current kernel configuration if all else fails. If you don't have a .config file, that usually means that the kernel on this computer has not yet been reconfigured. There are a number of standard configuration files in the /usr/src/linux-2.4/configs directory. Use the one that corresponds most closely to your hardware. Set this as the starting point for your configuration by copying it to the /usr/src/linux-2.4/.config file.

on the job

There is a default kernel configuration file in the /usr/src/linux-2.4/configs directory. It's associated with your CPU hardware; for example, if you have an Athlon CPU, you'll find it in a file named kernel-versionnumber-athlon.config.

make config

Once you're in the directory with the kernel source files, you can call a simple script to configure a new kernel with the following command:

```
# make config
```

This script will prompt you through your different options. Figure 6-11 shows an excerpt from the output for this script.

Here the kernel variables are listed in parentheses and the possible answers are in brackets. The default answer is in capital letters. If you type in a ?, then you will see a help page explaining this option. Since several hundred questions are associated with this script, most administrators use one of the other two scripts to manage their Linux kernels.

make menuconfig

A nicer way to create the .config file is to use the **make menuconfig** command. This requires the ncurses4 and ncurses-devel packages. This opens a text-based menu-

FIGURE 6-11

make config
options

```
*
* Code maturity level options
*
Prompt for development and/or incomplete code/drivers (CONFIG_EXPERIMENTAL) [Y/n/?
]
*
* Loadable module support
*
Enable loadable module support (CONFIG_MODULES) [Y/n/?]
  Set version information on all module symbols (CONFIG_MODVERSIONS) [Y/n/?]
  Kernel module loader (CONFIG_KMOD) [Y/n/?]
*
* Processor type and features
*
Low latency scheduling (CONFIG_LOLAT) [Y/n/?]
Control low latency with sysctl (CONFIG_LOLAT_SYSCTL) [N/y/?]
Processor family (386, 486, 586/K5/5x86/6x86/6x86MX, Pentium-Classic, Pentium-MMX,
 Pentium-Pro/Celeron/Pentium-II, Pentium-III/Celeron(Coppermine), Pentium-4, K6/K6
-II/K6-III, Athlon/Duron/K7, Elan, Crusoe, Winchip-C6, Winchip-2, Winchip-2A/Winch
ip-3, CyrixIII/VIA-C3/VIA-C5) [Pentium-Pro/Celeron/Pentium-II]
  defined CONFIG_M686
PGE extensions (not for Cyrix/Transmeta) (CONFIG_X86_PGE) [N/y/?]
Machine Check Exception (CONFIG_X86_MCE) [Y/n/?]
CPU Frequency scaling (CONFIG_CPU_FREQ) [Y/n/?]
 AMD K6-2/K6-3 PowerNow! (CONFIG_X86_POWERNOW_K6) [M/n/y/?]
 VIA C3/C5/Cyrix III Longhaul (CONFIG_X86_LONGHAUL) [M/n/y/?]
  Scale voltage according to speed (CONFIG_X86_LONGHAUL_SCALE_VOLTAGE) [N/y/?]
 Intel Speedstep (CONFIG_X86_SPEEDSTEP) [M/n/y/?] []
```

driven system that classifies and organizes the changes that you can make to a kernel. Figure 6-12 illustrates the main menuconfig menu.

The nice thing about menuconfig is that it works very nicely over a Telnet connection from other Linux computers (or perhaps that is dangerous!). Also, options appear at the bottom of the menu to load or save the configuration file from a different location.

make xconfig

The last way to make changes to the kernel is to use X Window. You can generate a graphical menu system to configure your kernel by running the **make xconfig** command. Figure 6-13 shows the xconfig main menu.

You can also use xconfig to load or save the configuration from a different file. While this menu may look slightly different from version to version of Red Hat Linux, the principles and basic options remain fairly constant. Each of the Kernel Configuration Options discussed on the following pages are presented for completeness; it is important for a Linux administrator to have a detailed understanding of the hows and whys about reconfiguring and recompiling the kernel.

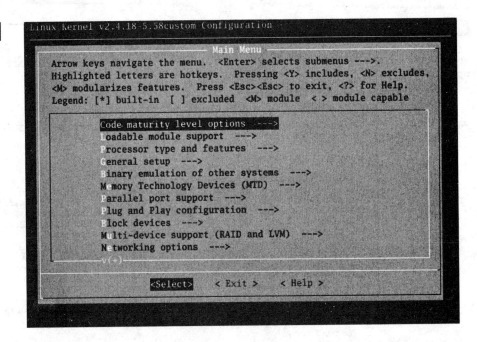

FIGURE 6-12

The make menuconfig Configuration menu

Understanding Kernel Configuration Options

To configure a kernel, you need to understand some of the main kernel configuration options. Each of the aforementioned kernel configuration tools includes help menus for just about every available option.

FIGURE 6-13

The xconfig Main menu

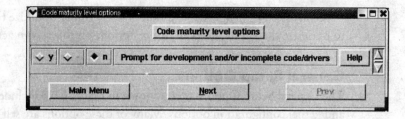

FIGURE 6-14

Code Maturity
Level submenu

The Standard Red Hat Kernel Configuration

The standard distribution kernel supports just about everything. Almost every module that could be made is made. This is a big kernel, and numerous modules can be used for it with the standard installation. This is not a problem when you install Red Hat Linux, but it is highly recommended you streamline the standard kernel and remove unwanted modules. All xconfig images displayed in this chapter are from the Red Hat Linux 8.0 beta configuration.

Code Maturity Level Options

The Code Maturity Level options, shown in Figure 6-14, allow you to incorporate experimental code in the kernel. Common examples include drivers for new hardware, esoteric filesystems, and network protocols. Experimental code is often also known as alpha level software. If you have obsolete code that you want to incorporate into your kernel, it also falls in this category, as newer kernels often omit support for older features.

Generally, you shouldn't enable this option unless you're a developer or otherwise need to test such experimental software.

Loadable Modules Support Options

The Loadable Module Support screen is shown in Figure 6-15. This screen allows you to enable loadable modules. The kernel module loader will automatically load modules for most new hardware, when detected.

FIGURE 6-15

Loadable Module
Support menu

◆ y	◇ -	◇ n	Enable loadable module support	Help
◆ y	◇ -	◇ n	Set version information on all module symbols	Help
◆ y	◇ -	◇ n	Kernel module loader	Help

Loadable module support

Main Menu   Next   Prev

As discussed earlier, loadable modules allow you to optimize the kernel. If you want to optimize the kernel, keep all of the options on this screen active.

General Setup Options

The General Setup Options menu shown in Figure 6-16 includes some basic hardware and kernel configuration options. Many of these options are self explanatory, and the defaults are generally acceptable. If you need more information, click the Help button associated with a specific kernel option.

On a network, you want networking support. Most computers have PCI cards, and the defaults give you full PCI support, using BIOS detection, documenting the detected cards in the /proc directory. ISA and EISA cards are still common; IBM-style Microchannel (MCA) cards are not.

Various types of hot-pluggable devices are now popular, including PCMCIA cards for laptops and PCI hotplug support for removable drives.

FIGURE 6-16

General Setup Options

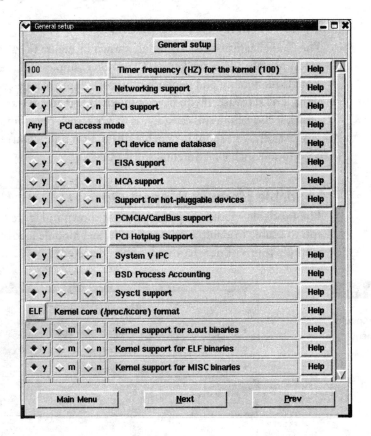

The System V IPC, BSD Process Accounting, and Sysctrl support parameters are all standard for current kernels. While Linux kernels are normally associated with ELF binaries, the other binaries may help with certain programs.

General Setup also allows you to configure ACPI and APM support, as shown in the bottom half of this menu (scroll down to see these settings). Remember, ACPI support is currently experimental and should generally not be configured on a production computer. Even if you do everything "right," you may have problems with ACPI support that are beyond normal "hacking" efforts.

Binary Emulation of Other Systems

The options shown in Figure 6-17 allow you to configure Linux to run binary programs from other Unix- or Linux-related operating systems. Unless you're planning to run binary programs based on one of the other operating systems listed under this menu, disable all of the options here.

Memory Technology Devices

The options shown in Figure 6-18 allow you to set up Linux for basic "Flash" memory cards, including those that might be installed through a PCMCIA adapter. Unless you're planning to use some of these devices in the future, keep this option disabled.

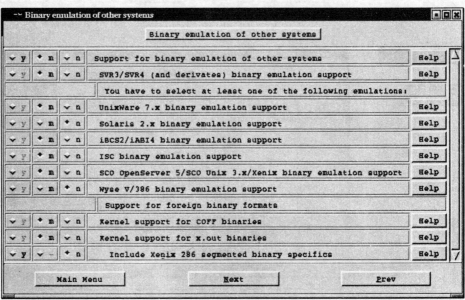

FIGURE 6-17

Binary Emulation of Other Systems menu

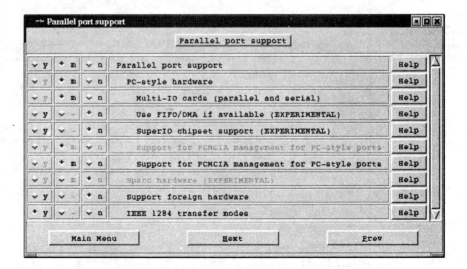

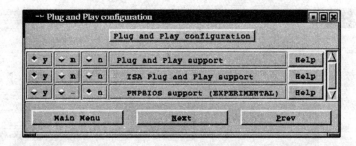

FIGURE 6-20

Plug and Play
Configuration
menu

Parallel Port Support

The options shown in Figure 6-19 are based on hardware that may be connected to your computer through a parallel port. This includes everything from printers through parallel port hard drives. Remember that it is normally best to avoid the Experimental options unless you are a developer who is working on supporting the associated drivers.

Plug and Play Configuration

The options shown in Figure 6-20 activate basic plug and play support on your Linux computer. Generally you should keep the defaults. While Linux plug and play does not handle all ISA and PCI devices, it does help you configure your computer for Linux.

Block Device Options

Here you specify your floppy devices and nonstandard hard disks, as shown in Figure 6-21. You can specify support for ATAPI CD-ROMs, tape drives, and even ATAPI floppy drives. You can also enable loopback support and network block support (which lets you use a physical disk on the network as if it were a local disk). If you have any parallel port devices such as external CD-ROMs or hard drives, you could enable support for those here. You can also set up support for RAM disks here as well.

Multidevice Support for RAID and LVM

If you're ever going to set up a RAID array of disks to help protect your data, you can enable that option in the Linux kernel here. If you ever want to put together a volume set, where a directory can span more than one partition on more than one physical hard disk, you can enable that option here as well. Figure 6-22 illustrates the default options on this menu.

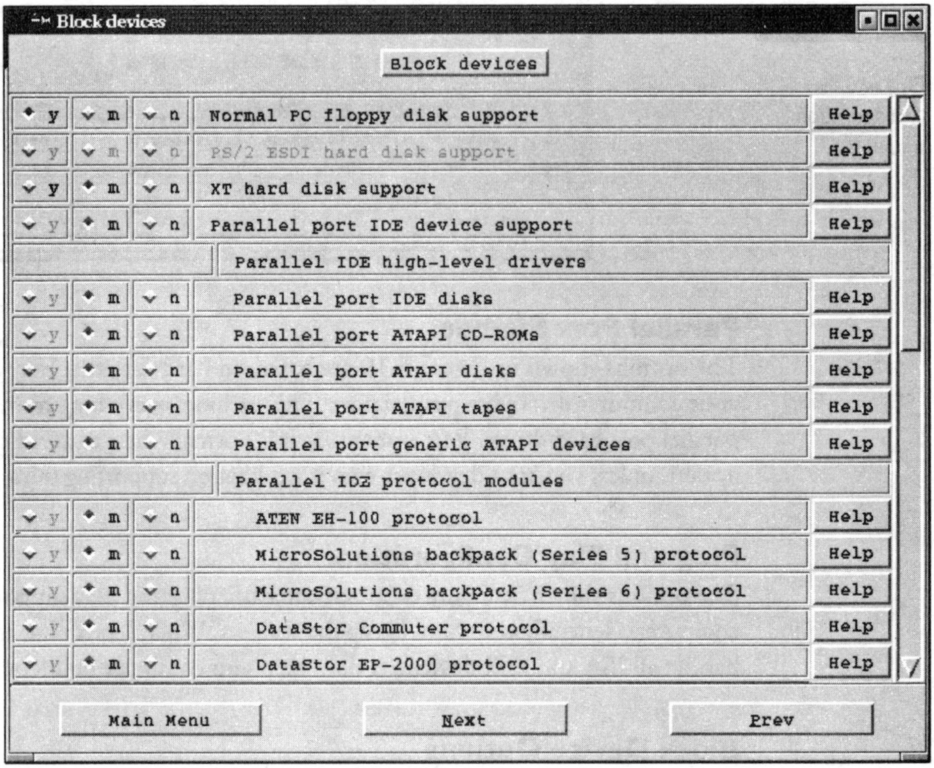

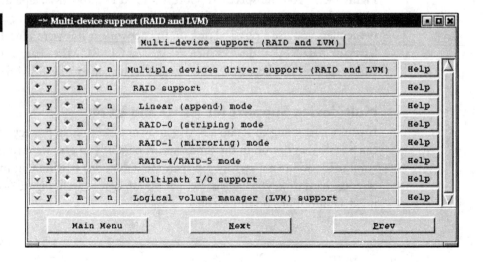

FIGURE 6-21

Block Devices menu

FIGURE 6-22

Multi-Device Support (RAID and LVM) menu

FIGURE 6-23

Networking
Options menu

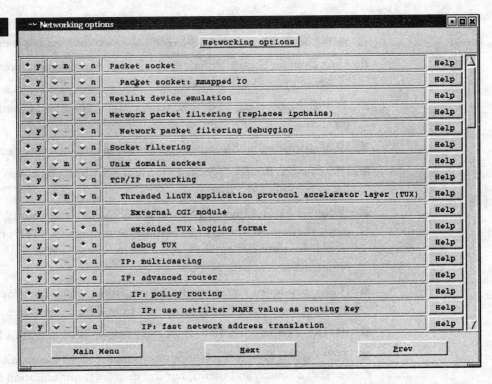

While there is support for RAID-4 in the Linux kernel, it is not directly supported by the version of Red Hat Linux available as of this writing.

Networking and Network Device Options

There are many options for networking in the Linux kernel, which we will now discuss in more detail. A few of these options are shown in Figure 6-23.

- **Packet Socket** can be enabled to use low-level network programs. These programs typically do not use a network protocol and are usually protocol analyzer (a.k.a. "sniffer") applications, such as tcpdump and Ethereal.

- **Netlink Device Emulation** allows devices to use special nodes such as /dev/route.

- **Network Packet Filtering** enables you to set up a packet-level firewall, using iptables. You also need Netfilter (Firewalling) Support to use packet filtering. The IP Masquerading option also requires Netfilter Support.

- **Socket Filtering** allows user programs to attach to a socket and filter their specific socket. This is based on the BSD-styled socket filtering but is much simpler.

- **Unix Domain Sockets** include the basic channels for network communication. Generally, you should keep this active.

- **TCP/IP Networking** needs to be active if you're going to use the default TCP/IP protocol.

- **IP Multicasting** enables you to participate in a multicast transmission.

- **IP Advanced Router** activates IP forwarding, which allows you to set up your Linux computer as a router.

- **IP Kernel-Level Autoconfiguration** allows you to set up your IP address from either the command line when booting, or through BOOTP or DHCP. You would also want this option if you want to boot a diskless workstation to a remote filesystem with NFS.

- **IP Tunneling** lets you configure encapsulation, which can allow you to let users connect with portable computers from different locations.

- **IP GRE Tunnels over IP** enables you to set up IPv6 over IPv4 hardware.

- **TCP Explicit Congestion Notification Support** allows communication between congested routers and clients; but this disables communication through some firewalls.

- **IP TCP Syncookie Support** will protect you from SYN flooding attacks. These attacks are denial-of-service attacks that can severely slow down your server's network performance. Enabling syncookies will help make your computer resistant to this type of attack. After compiling this option, you will also need to issue the following command:

```
echo 1 >>/proc/sys/net/ipv4/tcp_syncookies
```

- **IP Netfilter Configuration** includes a series of options for configuring iptables.

- **IP Virtual Server Configuration** is an experimental service to enable you to manage and balance network loads on "server farms."

- **Asynchronous Transfer Mode (ATM)** is a network commonly used in very high speed applications. Linux support for ATM is still "experimental."

- **802.1Q VLAN Support** enables you to group certain computers in a "virtual" LAN that is different from a physical LAN.

- **IPX, DECnet, Acorn Econet** are alternatives to TCP/IP for different networks.

- **Appletalk** sets up netatalk for communication on Apple Macintosh–based networks.

- **802.1d Ethernet Bridging** sets up network segments based on the "Spanning Tree" protocol.

- **CCITT X.25 Packet Layer** is an experimental interface to support the old X.25 protocol that was popular with telephone networks.

- **LAPB Data Link Driver** is another experimental interface related to X.25.

- **ANSI/IEEE 802.2 Data Link Layer Protocol** supports X.25 over Ethernet.

- **Frame Diverter** is an experimental interface for managing network traffic.

- **WAN Router** will cut the cost of a typically high-priced WAN router in half. All you'll need is a WAN interface card, the WAN-tools package, and to enable this option to build a WAN router.

- **Fast Switching** is an option that allows you to connect two computers directly together with a network cable. This is an extremely fast way for two computers to communicate. This option is not compatible with IP FIREWALL, but it will work with the IP ADVANCED ROUTER options.

- **QoS and/or Fair Queuing** allow you to set up decision rules for which packet to route. Enabling this option can give you many different ways of determining which packets you'll route and which you will queue or drop. This can allow for priority IPs to always get certain bandwidths, while at the same time forcing other IPs to use bandwidth consumption limits. QoS stands for Quality of Service and is currently being used, so people who pay more, get more. In the network device section, you can enable traffic shaping to limit outbound bandwidth.

Telephony Support

Telephony support on a computer network uses special network cards to convert voice into the type of data that can be sent over a network. Linux offers some limited telephony support as shown in Figure 6-24.

FIGURE 6-24

Telephony
Support menu

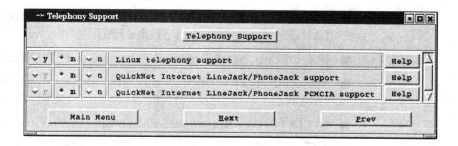

ATA/IDE/MFM/RLL Support

These acronyms all relate to various types of regular PC hard disk and CD drive interfaces. Normally, you shouldn't disable this kernel option unless all hard disk storage on your system is based on a SCSI interface. Even then, the flexibility of being able to install IDE devices is usually worth the extra code this adds to the kernel. The basic option is simple and is shown in Figure 6-25.

SCSI Support Options and Low-Level Drivers

You can enable SCSI hard disks, tape drivers, and CD-ROM support in this section, as shown in Figure 6-26. If you have a SCSI CD-ROM jukebox, or any other device that requires more than one SCSI Logical Unit Number (LUN), you may have to enable probing of all LUNs.

There is a section for verbose SCSI error reporting. This option adds about 12K to the kernel, but it makes debugging SCSI errors easier. You may want to enable specific low-level SCSI support for your controller and disable all others, as shown in Figure 6-27. This will save a lot of room and improve your loading. Generally, if you have an ADAPTEC controller, you should disable all other SCSI controllers.

Note that Red Hat Linux includes support for high-end hardware RAID-enabled SCSI host adapters, including 64-bit PCI adapters. Scroll down this menu for a full list of SCSI adapters that Linux can support.

FIGURE 6-25

ATA/IDE/MFM/
RLL Support
options

> -- ATA/IDE/MFM/RLL support
>
> ATA/IDE/MFM/RLL support
>
> ● y ▾ m ▾ n   ATA/IDE/MFM/RLL support   Help
>
> IDE, ATA and ATAPI Block devices
>
> Main Menu   Next   Prev

FIGURE 6-26

SCSI Support
menu

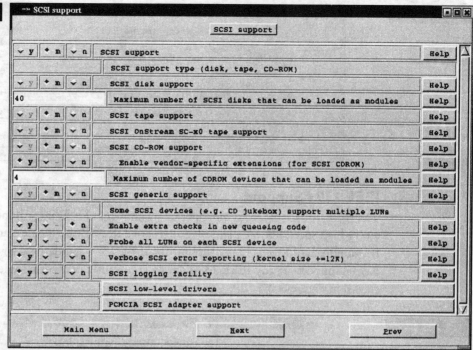

Fusion MPT Device Support

This provides very high speed support for SCSI adapters, associated with hardware developed by LSI logic. The menu is shown in Figure 6-28.

FIGURE 6-27

SCSI Low-Level
Drivers menu

FIGURE 6-28

Fusion MPT
Device Support
menu

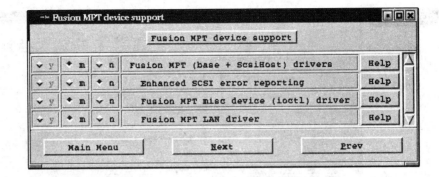

IEEE 1394 Support

The IEEE 1394 standard is more popularly known as FireWire or iLink. It's basically a very high speed hot plug and play alternative to USB, with data transfer speeds in the hundreds of Mbps. Linux support for IEEE 1394 standards is far from complete. Kernel support for any IEEE 1394 device is currently in the experimental stage, as shown in Figure 6-29.

FIGURE 6-29

IEEE 1394
Support menu

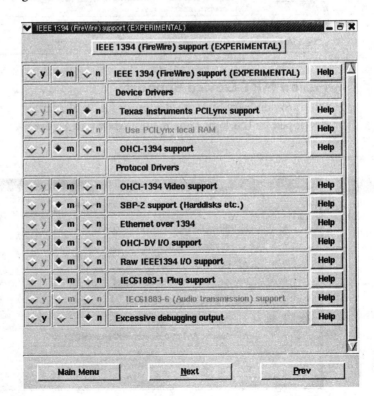

I2O Device Support

The I2O specification, also known as Intelligent I/O, supports split drivers which can optimize communication performance between a device and the rest of your computer. The I2O menu is shown in Figure 6-30. Don't enable I2O haphazardly; it requires hardware that supports it.

Network Device Support

Linux supports a wide range of network cards. The Network Device Support menu shown in Figure 6-31 allows you to enable support for the adapters you may need. Generally, you should enable support for only network devices that you're using now or may use in the future.

Amateur Radio Support

Linux supports connections to various amateur radios, as shown in Figure 6-32. Unless you plan to connect your computer to an amateur radio station in the future, there is no need to enable support for any of these devices.

IrDA Support

Linux supports Infrared connections, mostly for network support. The IrLAN protocol supports wireless access points. The IrNET protocol requires PPP. The IrCOMM protocol sets up port emulation, useful for setting up terminals and printers. For a list of supported infrared-port device drivers, click that button and activate the devices that you need. The IrDA support menu is shown in Figure 6-33.

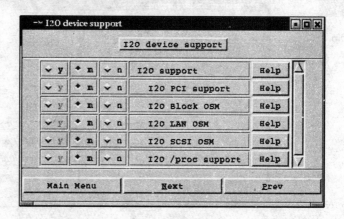

FIGURE 6-30

I2O Device
Support menu

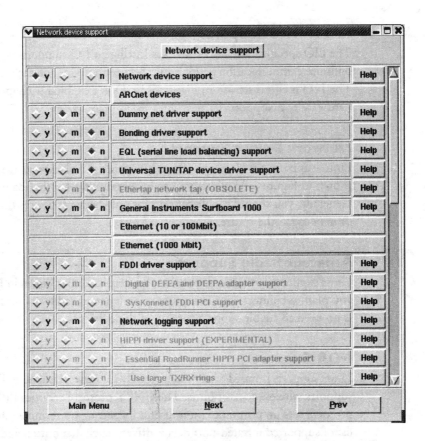

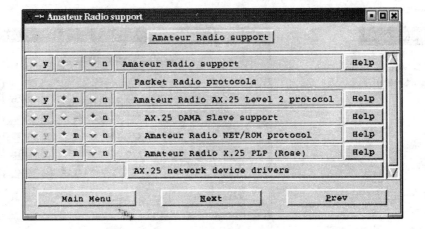

FIGURE 6-33

IrDA (infrared) support

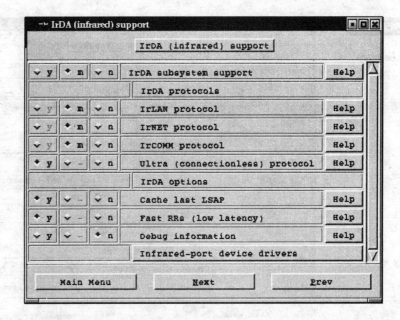

ISDN Options

Integrated Services Digital Networks (ISDN) lines are a fairly popular high-speed digital option, especially outside of North America. Adding ISDN support allows you to use an ISDN card for inbound or outbound dialing connections. The ISDN device has a built-in AT-compatible modem emulator, autodial, channel-bundling, callback, and caller authentication without the need for an external daemon to be running.

As shown in Figure 6-34, you can enable synchronous Point-to-Point Protocol (PPP) connections. (You need to download the ipppd daemon to take advantage of this feature.) With synchronous PPP and support for generic MP, you can bundle multiple ISDN lines together to increase your bandwidth. The Passive and Active ISDN Cards buttons allow you to activate the ISDN drivers that you need for your system.

Older CD-ROM Support Options

If you have an older CD-ROM that is not an IDE or SCSI CD-ROM, then you need to enable special support for it, as shown in Figure 6-35. This section has many drivers for Mitsumi, Goldstar, Philips, Sony, SoundBlaster, and other old CD-ROM and disk types. All of these drivers can be loaded as modules. Note that this hardware was popular in the early and mid 1990s and was found typically on 486 class systems as well as early Pentium machines. These systems (because of their age) are not suitable for production work and should be configured only for experimental use.

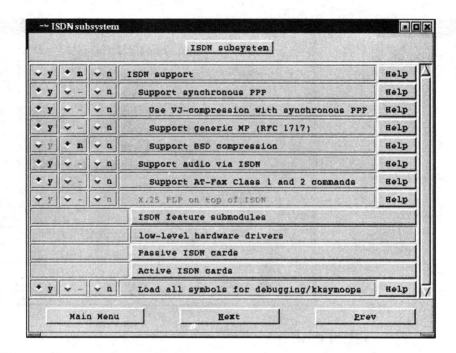

FIGURE 6-34

ISDN Subsystem
menu

Input Core Support

The Input Core Support section configures support for various basic input devices:
keyboards, mice, and joysticks. These devices are modular by default, which allows
Linux to recognize these basic devices using plug and play. This menu is shown in
Figure 6-36.

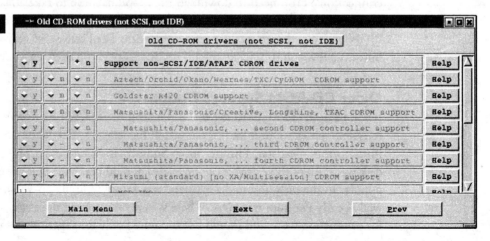

FIGURE 6-35

Old CD-ROM
Drivers menu

FIGURE 6-36

Input Core
Support menu

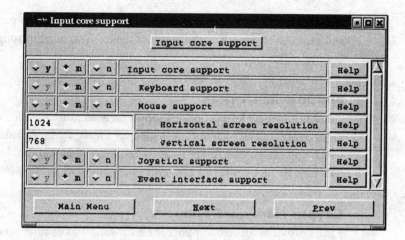

Character Device Options

Character devices send their data in byte streams. Typical character devices range from serial ports to virtual consoles. The Character Devices submenu, shown in Figure 6-37, allows you to specify support for a wide variety of devices, including virtual terminals, serial ports, newer AGP video cards, mice, joysticks, non-SCSI tape drives, and more.

Many different types of standard or smart serial boards are supported. If you are using Linux on an embedded device, you probably don't have any virtual terminals and need to connect via a serial board. You can reconfigure your computer to send all system messages through that serial board. Just disable the virtual terminal part of the kernel.

FIGURE 6-37

Character
Devices menu

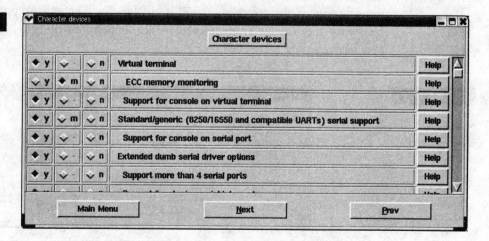

Other major character devices include Watchdog timers, parallel port printers, and tape drives, as well as the graphics devices you need to support different types of terminals.

Multimedia Devices

The Multimedia Devices options support a wide range of video capture and AM/FM radio devices. Click each option (Video for Linux, Radio Adapters) for a list of drivers which you can enable. As always, it is best keep what you enable to a minimum. The Multimedia Devices menu is shown in Figure 6-38.

Crypto Hardware Support

Linux provides limited support for hardware that enables secure connections. For example, the Broadcom 5820 device allows for a large number of simultaneous connections on secure Web pages. The Crypto Hardware support menu is shown in Figure 6-39.

Filesystem Options

The File Systems subsection is a list of all the different types of filesystems Linux supports. Select the Quota option if you need to support quotas. You can also compile in the kernel automounter to support remote filesystems here. The menu for selecting supported filesystems is presented in Figure 6-40.

Because Linux supports so many different hardware platforms, it includes support for a large number of filesystem types. However, because of the proprietary nature of some filesystems, the degree of support is variable. You'll note that support for a lot of filesystems in this menu is experimental; in fact, support for writing to NTFS filesystems may be dangerous!

FIGURE 6-38

Multimedia
Devices menu

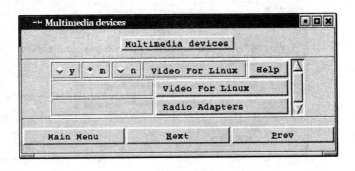

FIGURE 6-39

Crypto Hardware
Support menu

FIGURE 6-39

Crypto Hardware
Support menu

Console Driver Options

Linux supports console drivers, which can set up text on most graphics systems, even when Linux doesn't detect the right cards or monitors. The Frame Buffer Support option shown in Figure 6-41 supports video adapters that store images in frame buffers.

Sound System Support Options

Most popular sound cards are supported by Linux. These include:

- Ensoniq AudioPCI
- S3 SonicVibes
- Turtle Beach MultiSound Classic and Pinnacle

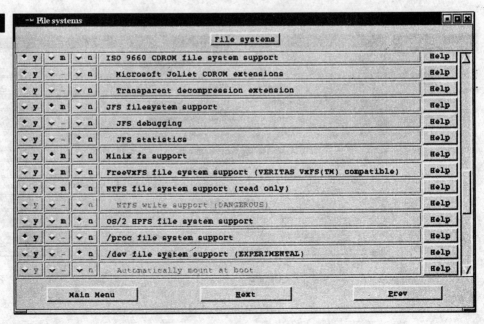

FIGURE 6-40

File Systems
menu

- ProAudioSpectrum 16
- SoundBlaster and 100 percent compatible cards
- Yamaha OPL2/OPL3 FM synthesizer
- Gravis Ultrasound
- PSS
- Microsoft Sound System
- Ensoniq SoundScape
- MediaTrix AudioTrix Pro
- OPTi MAD16 (Mozart)
- Crystal CS4232-based PnP cards
- Aztech Sound Galaxy (non-PnP)
- Loopback MIDI
- 6850 UART
- ACI mixer
- AWE32 synch
- And many others

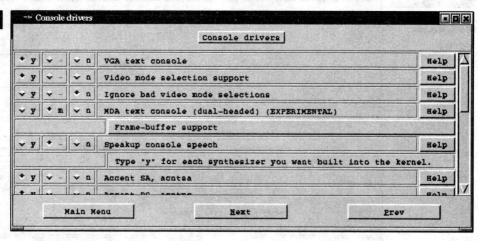

FIGURE 6-41

Console Drivers menu

You can also use these drivers for cards that emulate the appropriate hardware. Check the Sound submenu for the latest list of supported hardware for your kernel. If you have a card not named in the previous list, try to see if it emulates any card on the list. Many proprietary cards do emulate products from SoundBlaster or offer OPL/2 or OPL/3 compatibility. However, if your card was made for Windows and needs to load a Microsoft driver to emulate a generic sound card, there is a strong possibility that it won't work with Linux. Figure 6-42 shows the configuration screen for the Sound submenu.

USB Support

Linux support for USB is improving, though some USB drivers that you'll see in the USB support menu in Figure 6-43 are still considered to be experimental. Unfortunately, Linux support for the faster USB 2.0 standard still falls into this category.

FIGURE 6-42

Sound menu

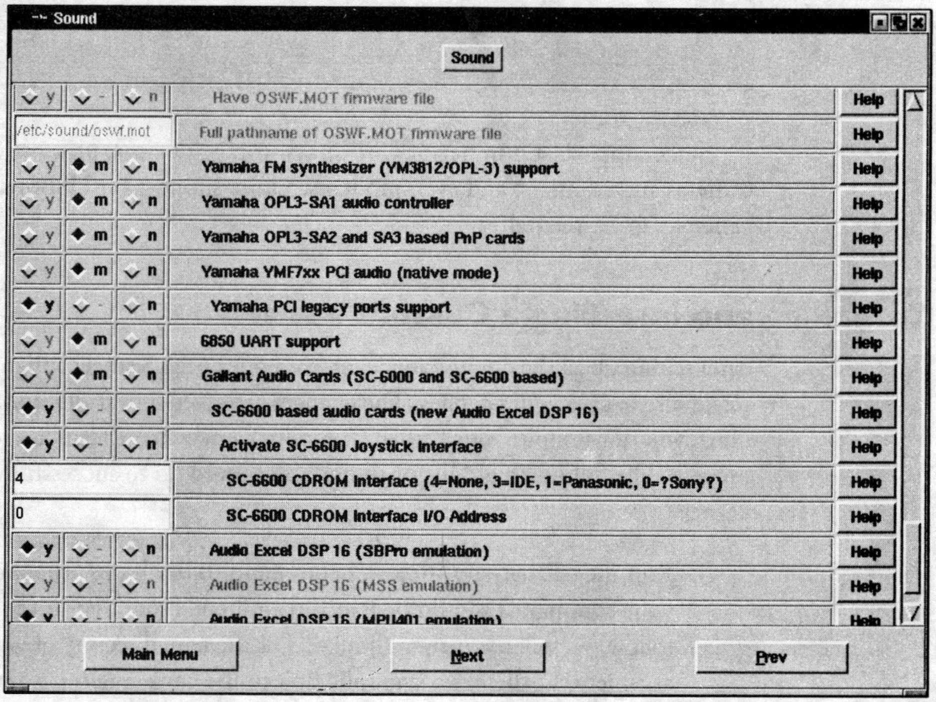

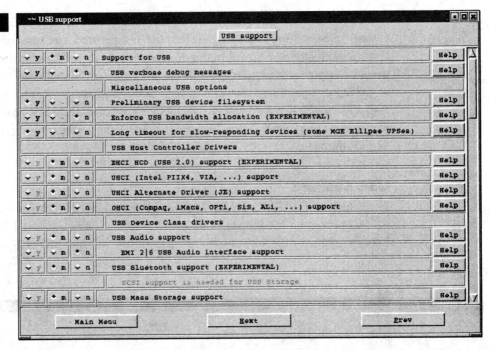

FIGURE 6-43

USB Support
menu

Linux supports a number of USB mass storage devices, printers, input devices, cameras and scanners, and even modems. Linux support for USB networking is still generally experimental.

Compiling and Installing a Custom Kernel

After setting up all the options you want from one of the Kernel configuration programs, make sure to save your changes. The changes are saved in the appropriate .config file. Next, you can compile your kernel. Compiling a new kernel can be a long and detailed process. The following is a list of things you should do to successfully compile your kernel:

1. Run the **cd /usr/src/linux-2.4** command to reach the proper directory. All of your commands should be issued from here. Note that in the procedures that follow, we will use /usr/src/linux-2.4 as the base directory of your kernel. This assumes that there is a symbolic link to the correct kernel source tree.

2. Edit the EXTRAVERSION line of /usr/src/linux-2.4/Makefile. Change the definition for EXTRAVERSION=*versionnumber* to something that uniquely identifies your kernel. We'll use EXTRAVERSION=-RHcustom as an example. Use your initials, the month/day of your build, anything to uniquely define this kernel. Later on, we'll build a map of the kernel so that modules can load, using the name you select here. Be sure to remember what you entered!

3. Run the **make mrproper** command to ensure your source files are in a consistent and clean state.

4. Save your old configuration file. Rebuilding the kernel involves making a new /usr/src/linux-2.4/.config. If you change your mind and choose to abandon your changes, it is nice to have a copy that is known to work. Red Hat ships with a standard config file located in the /usr/src/linux-2.4/configs/ directory. Copy the default configuration file for your architecture to an alternate location such as a rescue floppy. If you're unsure about your architecture (e.g. i386, i586, i686), consult the /proc/cpuinfo file.

5. If you want to start from the standard configuration, copy the appropriate file from the /usr/src/linux-2.4/configs/ directory to /usr/src/linux-2.4/.config. Use **make oldconfig**.

6. Customize your /usr/src/linux/.config file. Use the **make config** command, which will run the text-based configuration script. You can also issue **make menuconfig** for an ncurses menu configuration script, or run **make xconfig** to use the X Window configuration tool. Assuming you enable modules, disable as many individual modules as you can. Otherwise, you may not be able to install the new kernel on a boot or rescue floppy.

7. The **make dep** command will set up all your dependencies correctly. This takes the settings present in /usr/src/linux-2.4/.config and pushes them down into the correct source code subdirectory.

8. The **make bzImage** command creates a gzip compressed kernel image file. You can use a few other options besides bzImage here; they are discussed next. Note that on earlier kernels, the less space-efficient **make zImage** command was used.

9. This is when the kernel is actually compiled. Compilation can be a fairly time-consuming process. On a 386 or 486, you will probably have to let it compile

all night. If you have one of the latest multi-GHz CPU computers, it will probably take around 10–15 minutes to compile your new kernel. Be patient, your system must recompile hundreds of megabytes of program code! At the end of the process, watch for the following message, within a couple of lines from the new command prompt. If you see this, you may not be able to set up your new kernel as part of a boot or rescue floppy disk.

```
warning: kernel is too big for standalone boot from floppy
```

10. Now you need to build your modules (you did include kernel module support, didn't you?). Use **make modules** to build all your modules. If you did not disable enough modules when you edited the kernel configuration, this process could take quite a bit longer than compiling the kernel itself. This can also be a time-consuming process; for example, this command took over 45 minutes when I ran it on a computer with a 600 MHz CPU.

11. With our kernel now built, we need to move it to /boot before we can boot from it. Use **cp /usr/src/linux-2.4/arch/i386/boot/bzImage/boot/vmlinuz-2.4.19-RHcustom**.

12. Now you need to install your newly made modules, which will install all your loadable modules into /lib/modules/2.4.19-RHcustom to correspond with the release and EXTRAVERSION setting of your kernel. If this name already exists, the new modules will overwrite your existing modules. This could render both your old kernel and your new kernel unbootable. Always be sure to set a unique EXTRAVERSION value for each kernel. Use **make modules_install** to install your modules.

If you already have a kernel up and running, and you want to add support for another device but you didn't create the module for it, you can simply rerun the kernel configurator. Start it (using make menuconfig or make xconfig), select your new module, and choose M for module support for the device. Next, run **make modules** and then **make modules_install**. After that, you can immediately load the modules with /sbin/modprobe or /sbin/insmod. This will save a lot of time by just compiling the missing module. If the module fails, try **/sbin/modprobe *** to load all modules with dependency checking.

Building a kernel is an involved process, but it follows a standard pattern. It is very important that you become familiar with kernel construction procedures and troubleshooting. Refer to the following Scenario and Solution for some common problems encountered and their recommended solutions.

SCENARIO & SOLUTION

You looked under /usr/src/ but did not see the Linux kernel source code. What did you do wrong?	You did not install the kernel source code. Install the kernel-source RPM or download a new kernel from www.kernel.org, or from ftp.redhat.com.
You configured the kernel as a monolithic kernel, but when you run make bzImage, it fails, saying the kernel is too big. What should you do?	You must reconfigure your kernel to use modules. There are limits on the size of a compressed kernel, so you should always build a modular kernel.
You can't find your new kernel.	Were you sure to use the kernel's extra version initials at every step of the process? If not, then you may not be able to correctly locate the kernel or its modules.

Post-Build Procedures

You still have some more steps to complete before you can use your new kernel. These include:

- Building support for an initial RAM disk (to be used when you boot your computer)
- Copying the remaining files to the /boot directory

The mkinitrd command creates an initial RAM disk (initrd) image. This image is loaded when the kernel first boots. The initrd normally loads essential block devices such as SCSI disk driver modules that are not incorporated in the main body of the kernel.

For example, if you use a high-end, hardware RAID controller, the driver isn't included in the main body of the kernel. While we can load the driver as a module, only the features associated with the main kernel are available during the boot process.

If you booted just from a regular kernel on a floppy, you wouldn't have access to the RAID controller. You wouldn't be able to get to the disks that are connected to this controller. That is where a RAM disk can help. When you boot, a RAM disk loads the kernel image, a mini-root filesystem, and the loadable drivers that you need. You then have access to the RAID disks, and the boot process can continue.

This command automatically loads all SCSI devices found in the /etc/conf.modules, as well as all other modules specified by /etc/conf.modules.

To make your initial RAM disk, use the command

```
# mkinitrd /boot/initrd-2.4.19-RHcustom.img 2.4.19-RHcustom.img
```

This installs your initial RAM disk on the /boot filesystem. Remember, -RHcustom is based on the EXTRAVERSION variable in the Makefile. If your variable is different, adjust your command accordingly.

Next, we need to copy the new kernel's symbol table to the /boot partition. Use

```
# cp /usr/src/linux-2.4/System.map /boot/System.map-2.4.19-RHcustom
```

And finally, it is a good idea to keep a copy of your /usr/src/linux/.config file on the /boot partition as well (as new runs of menuconfig or xconfig could change your configuration significantly). Copy your config file with

```
# cp /usr/src/linux-2.4/.config /boot/config-2.4.19-RHcustom
```

Updating Your Boot Manager

Now you can modify your boot manager to include this new kernel as an option. Whether you're using GRUB or LILO, it is advisable to keep your old kernel in case something goes wrong. So you'll be adding a stanza to either /etc/grub.conf or /etc/lilo.conf. In either case, the changes that you'll make will be as if you're setting up two different operating systems.

/etc/grub.conf is actually a link to the actual GRUB configuration file in /boot/grub/grub.conf.

Updating GRUB

Look at your /etc/grub.conf file. If you have Linux on your system and use GRUB, you should already have a stanza that points to the appropriate locations for the Kernel and Initial RAM disk. For example, here is an excerpt from my /etc/grub.conf file:

```
Title Red Hat Linux (2.4.19-6)
    root (hd0,0)
    kernel /vmlinuz-2.4.19-6 ro root=LABEL=/
    initrd /initrd-2.4.19-6.img
```

In Red Hat Linux, the vmlinuz and initrd files are already in the /boot directory. Since you've copied the revised kernels to the same directory, all you need is a second stanza that points to your revised files. When I revised a kernel for this chapter, my EXTRAVERSION variable in /usr/src/linux-2.4/Makefile was -RHcustom. So part of my revised /etc/grub.conf file looked like the following:

```
Title Red Hat Linux (2.4.19-6)
    root (hd0,0)
    kernel /vmlinuz-2.4.19-6 ro root=LABEL=/
    initrd /initrd-2.4.19-6.img
Title Red Hat Linux (2.4.19-RHcustom)
    root (hd0,0)
    kernel /vmlinuz-2.4.19-RHcustom ro root=LABEL=/
    initrd /initrd-2.4.19-RHcustom.img
```

Since you don't need to load /etc/grub.conf into the MBR, no further action is required. The resulting GRUB menu looks like Figure 6-44.

FIGURE 6-44

GRUB menu with two kernels

```
GRUB  version 0.92  (638K lower / 130048K upper memory)

┌─────────────────────────────────────────────────────────────┐
│ Red Hat Linux (2.4.19-6)                                      │
│ Red Hat Linux (2.4.19-RHcustom)                               │
│                                                               │
│                                                               │
│                                                               │
│                                                               │
│                                                               │
└─────────────────────────────────────────────────────────────┘

     Use the ↑ and ↓ keys to select which entry is highlighted.
     Press enter to boot the selected OS, 'e' to edit the
     commands before booting, 'a' to modify the kernel arguments
     before booting, or 'c' for a command-line.


                          redhat.
```

Updating LILO

Alternatively, if you're using LILO as a boot manager, you'll need to revise /etc/lilo.conf. Add a stanza that points to the new kernel. Take a look at the following excerpt from /etc/lilo.conf:

```
image=/boot/vmlinuz-2.4.19-6
      label=linux
      read-only
      root=/dev/hda2
```

From this information, you can see that the original kernel is called vmlinuz-2.4.19-6 and resides on the second partition (hda2) of our primary IDE hard disk (hda). Assume LILO resides on the MBR of the first disk and controls the boot process.

Now add another stanza for the new kernel. The changes are in bold:

```
image=/boot/vmlinuz-2.4.19-6
      label=linux
      read-only
      root=/dev/hda2

image=/boot/vmlinuz-2.4.19-RHcustom
      label=newLinux
      read-only
      root=/dev/hda2
```

Save this file, then run **/sbin/lilo -v**. The output should resemble the following:

```
LILO version 21.4-4, Copyright (C) 1992-1998 Werner Almesberger
'lba32' extensions Copyright (C) 1999,2000 John Coffman

Reading boot sector from /dev/hda
Merging with /boot/boot.b
Mapping message file /boot/message
Boot image: /boot/vmlinuz-2.4.19-3
Mapping RAM disk /boot/initrd-2.4.19-3
Added linux *
Boot image: /boot/vmlinuz-2.4.19-3rh
Added newLinux
Backup copy of boot sector in /boot/boot.0300
Writing boot sector.
```

When you reboot, LILO will wait for you to enter a label, in this case, either linux or newLinux.

While you can use the boot loader of your choice, Red Hat is focusing on GRUB. Therefore, you can expect to work with GRUB on the RHCE exam.

Kernel Upgrade by RPM

In contrast, upgrading a kernel from a Red Hat RPM is fairly easy. Basically, all you need to do is install the new kernel with the appropriate rpm command. When properly configured, the RPM automatically upgrades your default boot loader as well. For example, say you've just downloaded the newest 2.4.22 kernel RPM from one of the FTP servers with Red Hat RPMs to the /tmp directory. When you install the new kernel with a command such as

```
rpm -i /tmp/kernel-2.4.22-3.i386.rpm
```

the kernel, initial RAM disk, System.map, module-info, and config files are automatically installed in the /boot directory. In addition, a new stanza is added to /boot/grub/grub.conf.

Be careful. Install (-i), don't upgrade (-U) your new kernel. Otherwise, if you have a problem, you won't be able to go back to the old working kernel.

To change the default boot stanza in GRUB, change the default variable. For example, if default=0, the default kernel loaded is the first stanza in /boot/grub/grub.conf. Similarly, if default=1, the default kernel loaded is the second stanza in /boot/grub/grub.conf.

mkbootdisk

The mkbootdisk utility creates a bootdisk customized for your configuration. This is basically a rescue disk. After creating this disk, you can use it to simply boot your system, or you can type **rescue** at the boot prompt. It's a simple command; in most cases, all you need to do is specify the version number associated with the desired kernel as follows:

```
# /sbin/mkbootdisk 2.4.19-RHcustom
```

This command automatically takes the kernel with the specified version number from the /boot directory and writes it with appropriate configuration information to the first floppy drive, /dev/fd0. Table 6-2 lists a few other options that may come in handy when using mkbootdisk.

Here is another example of the mkbootdisk command:

```
# mkbootdisk --device /dev/fd1 --verbose --noprompt 2.4.19-3rh
```

TABLE 6-2	Command	Description
Options for the mkbootdisk Command	--device *device file*	Specifies where to put the image.
	--mkinitrdargs *args*	Passes arguments to mkinitrd.
	--noprompt	Won't prompt to insert a disk.
	--verbose	Normally, mkbootdisk has no output. This option turns the output on.

This command creates a bootdisk on the second floppy drive. It does not suppress output, nor does it prompt for a disk to be inserted. It uses kernel version 2.4.19-3rh. When you boot Linux with this disk, you can use it as a rescue disk. Just type **linux rescue** at the boot prompt.

A significant portion of the practical exam tests your ability to recover a system that has failed in some way. While I am prohibited by the Red Hat Non-disclosure agreement from giving you the exact nature of the problems, I can say that being able to use rescue disks is a very important Linux administration skill.

CERTIFICATION OBJECTIVE 6.04

The cron System

The cron system is essentially a smart alarm clock. When the alarm sounds, Linux runs the commands of your choice automatically. You can set the alarm clock to run at all sorts of regular intervals.

The cron daemon, crond, checks a series of directories for jobs to run, every minute of every hour of every day. The crond checks the /var/spool/cron directory for jobs by user. It also checks for general scheduled jobs under /etc/crontab and in the /etc/cron.d/ directory.

The behavior of the Linux cron is different from under Unix, where the cron daemon wakes up only when it needs to launch a program.

Because cron always checks for changes, you do not have to restart cron every time you make a change.

The System crontab and Components

The crontab command is used to edit the cron files. You can use four switches with crontab:

- ■ **-u** *user* Allows the root user to edit the crontab of another specific user.
- ■ **-l** Lists the current entries in the crontab file.
- ■ **-r** Removes cron entries.
- ■ **-e** Edits an existing crontab entry. By default, crontab uses vi.

The crontab file is set up in a specific format. Each line can be blank, a comment (which begins with "#"), a variable, or a command. Blank lines and comments are ignored.

When you run a regular command, the actions of the shell are based on environmental variables. To see your environmental variables, run the **env** command. Some of the standard variables in Red Hat Linux include: HOME as your home directory, SHELL as the default shell, and LOGNAME as the username.

You can set different variables within the crontab file, or you can set environmental variables with the following syntax:

```
Variable=Value
```

Some variables are already set for you: HOME is your home directory, SHELL is the user's default shell, and PATH is where the shell looks for commands. You can set these variables to different values in your crontab file. For example, the default /etc/crontab file includes the following variables:

```
SHELL=/bin/bash
PATH=/sbin:/bin:/usr/sbin:/usr/bin
MAILTO=root
HOME=/
```

Note that the values of PATH, MAILTO, and HOME are different from those for the standard environment variables.

on the **job** *The MAILTO variable can help you administer several Linux systems. The cron daemon sends output by e-mail. Just add a line like the following: MAILTO=me@somewhere.com to route all cron messages associated with that file to that e-mail address.*

exam
ⓦatch

Note how the PATH variable in a crontab may be different from the PATH variable associated with your shell. In fact, the two variables are independent. Therefore, you'll want to know the exact path of every command in your crontab. Specify the absolute path with the command if it isn't in the crontab PATH.

Here is the format of a line in crontab. Each of these columns is explained in more detail in Table 6-3.

```
#minute, hour, day of month, month, day of week, command
*       *     *             *      *                command
```

If you see an asterisk in any column, cron runs that command for all possible values of that column. For example, a * in the minute field means that the command is run every minute during the specified hour(s). Take another example, as shown here:

```
1  5  3  4  *  ls
```

This line runs the **ls** command every April 3, at 5:01 A.M. The asterisk in the day of week column simply means that it does not matter what day of the week it is; crontab still runs the **ls** command at the specified time.

The crontab file is flexible. For example, a 7-10 entry in the hour field would run the specified command at 7:00 A.M., 8:00 A.M., 9:00 A.M., and 10:00 A.M. A list of entries in the minute field such as: 0,5,10,15,20,25,30,35,40,45,50,55 would run the specified command every five minutes. The cron daemon also recognizes abbreviations for months and the day of the week.

TABLE 6-3	Field	Value
Entries in a crontab Line	Minute	0-59
	Hour	Based on a 24-hour clock; for example, 23 = 11 P.M.
	Day of month	1-31
	Month	1-12, or Jan, Feb, Mar, etc.
	Day of week	0-7; where 0 and 7 are both Sunday; or Sun, Mon, Tue, etc.
	Command	The command you want to run

The actual command is the sixth field. You can set up new lines with a percent (%) symbol. This is useful for formatting standard input. The example that follows formats input for an e-mail message. Here is an example cron file:

```
# crontab -l
# Sample crontab file
#
# Force /bin/sh to be my shell for all of my scripts.
SHELL=/bin/sh
# Run 15 minutes past Midnight every Saturday
15 0 * * sat   $HOME/scripts/scary.script
# Do routine cleanup on the first of every Month at 4:30 AM
30 4 1 * *     /usr/scripts/removecores >> /tmp/core.tmp 2>>&1
# Mail a message at 10:45 AM every Friday
45 10 * * fri  mail -s "Project Update employees%Can I have a status
update on your project?%%Your Boss.%
# Every other hour check for alert messages
0 */2 * * * /usr/scripts/check.alerts
```

Securing cron

You may not want everyone to be able to run a job in the middle of the night. If there is a security flaw in your system, someone may download important data or worse, and it could be days before you discover the security breach.

As with network firewalls, you can allow or deny users the privilege of using cron. You can set up users in /etc/cron.allow and /etc/cron.deny files. If these files don't exist, cron usage is not restricted. If users are named in /etc/cron.allow file, all other users won't be able to use cron. Any users named in /etc/cron.deny can't use cron either.

EXERCISE 6-2

Create a cron Job

In this exercise, we will create a cron job that will update the locate database at 4:00 A.M. every night and mail a disk usage report every Friday. To do this, use the following steps:

1. Log in as root.

2. Run crontab -e.

3. Type in the following line to update the locate database:

```
00 4 * * * updatedb &2>>/dev/null
```

4. Add the following line to mail a disk usage report to your account. The remote admin account is admin@remote.site.com.

```
00 9 * * 5 df | mail admin@remote.site.com -s DiskFree &2>>/dev/null
```

5. Save and exit.

CERTIFICATION OBJECTIVE 6.05

System-Wide Shell Configuration Files for Bourne and Bash Shells

All system-wide shell configuration files are kept in the /etc directory. These files are bashrc, profile, and the scripts in the /etc/profile.d directory. These files and scripts are supplemented by hidden files in each user's home directory.

/etc/bashrc

The /etc/bashrc file is used for system-wide aliases and functions. Open and analyze the file on your own. The current /etc/bashrc file does set the following parameters for each user who calls the bash shell:

- It sets umask, which creates the default permissions for newly created files.
- It assigns a prompt, which is what you see just before the cursor at the command prompt.

The settings here are called by the .bashrc file in each user's home directory. The settings are supplemented by the .bash_history and .bash_logout files in each user's home directory.

/etc/profile

The /etc/profile file is used for system-wide environments and startup files. The following is the profile script from the Red Hat 8.0 beta available at the time of this writing. The first part of the file sets the PATH for searching for commands. Then it sets the PATH, USER, LOGNAME, MAIL, HOSTNAME, HISTSIZE, and INPUTRC variables, and finally it runs the scripts in /etc/profile.d/. You can check the current value of any of these variables with the **echo $***variable* command.

```
# /etc/profile

# System wide environment and startup programs, for login setup
# Functions and aliases go in /etc/bashrc

pathmunge () {
  if ! echo $PATH | /bin/egrep -q "(^|:)$1($|:)" ; then
    if [ "$2" = "after" ] ; then
      PATH=$PATH:$1
    else
      PATH=$1:$PATH
    fi
  fi
}

# Path manipulation
if [ `id -u` = 0 ]; then
  pathmunge /sbin
  pathmunge /usr/sbin
  pathmunge /usr/local/sbin
fi

pathmunge /usr/X11R6/bin after

unset pathmunge

# No core files by default
ulimit -S -c 0 > /dev/null 2>&1

USER="`id -un`"
LOGNAME=$USER
MAIL="/var/spool/mail/$USER"

HOSTNAME=`/bin/hostname`
HISTSIZE=1000
```

```
if [ -z "$INPUTRC" -a ! -f "$HOME/.inputrc" ]; then
    INPUTRC=/etc/inputrc
fi

export PATH USER LOGNAME MAIL HOSTNAME HISTSIZE INPUTRC

for i in /etc/profile.d/*.sh ; do
    if [ -r "$i" ]; then
      . $i
    fi
done

unset i
```

/etc/profile.d/

Actually, /etc/profile.d is not a script, but a directory of little scripts. You may have noticed that the /etc/profile script is actually the script in charge of handling this directory. Here is a partial directory listing:

```
-rwxr-xr-x    1 root      root            693 Jul 15 20:23  colorls.sh
-rwxr-xr-x    1 root      root             70 Jun 27 22:27  gnome-ssh-askpass.sh
-rwxr-xr-x    1 root      root           2362 Jul 22 12:35  lang.sh
-rwxr-xr-x    1 root      root            267 Jun 20 16:10  less.sh
-rwxr-xr-x    1 root      root            170 Jun 28 18:12  which-2.sh
```

By looking at the /etc/profile script, you can see that any script in this directory that ends with an "sh" and is set as an executable will be run when /etc/profile is executed.

EXERCISE 6-3

Securing Our System

We want to keep our system as secure as possible. To do this, we must change the default permissions users have for new files and directories they make. We'll set all new files and directories to No Access to group or other members.

1. Edit the /etc/bashrc file. Two lines in the file set the umask. One of the two lines is selected depending on the if statement above them. See if you can determine which line gets executed for an average user.

2. The if statement tests to see if the user ID (uid) and group ID (gid) are the same, and that the uid is greater than 99. If this is true, then the first umask

is executed; otherwise, the second is executed. The second umask is for root and other key system accounts. The first is for users.

3. Change the first umask statement to exclude all permissions for groups and others. Use umask 077 to do the job.

4. Save and exit the file.

5. Log in as a nonprivileged user. Use the touch command to make a new empty file. Use ls -l to verify the permissions.

6. Log in as root. Again, use the touch command to make a new empty file and use ls -l to verify their permissions.

You have just changed the default umask for all shell users.

CERTIFICATION SUMMARY

You can have great control over how your Linux installation is set up and configured. You can control almost all aspects of user security, as well as the details of your kernel. You can set up quotas to limit the user's disk usage. You can set up one quota per partition, and set soft and hard limits for users. With grace periods, you can set up a soft limit to give users an appropriate warning.

The kernel can be optimized for your particular installation and hardware, and you have detailed control over its configuration. To make a modular kernel, you need to run six commands: **make mrproper**, **make config**, **make dep**, **make clean**, **make modules**, and **make modules_install**. If you are compiling a monolithic kernel, you will *not* need to run the last two module-related commands.

The cron daemon allows you to schedule jobs to run at any given time. Any variables or system-wide functions you may need to run can be kept in the /etc/bashrc or /etc/profile script.

TWO-MINUTE DRILL

Here are some of the key points from the certification objectives in Chapter 6.

Setting Up and Managing Disk Quotas

❑ Quotas are used to limit a user's or a group of users' ability to consume disk space.

❑ Quotas are set on specific filesystems mounted to standard Linux formats.

❑ Quota support must be enabled in the kernel. By default, quotas are enabled in Red Hat kernels.

❑ Quotas have soft limits and hard limits. If both soft and hard limits are set, then a user can exceed his or her soft limit for a modest period of time.

❑ Users and Groups may never exceed their hard limits.

Kernel Sources

❑ The kernel source tree is accessible through /usr/src/linux-2.4, which is normally linked to the actual directory with kernel source files.

❑ Kernel sources can be loaded from the kernel-source RPM or from a Linux kernel tarball downloaded from a site such as ftp.kernel.org.

❑ Kernel version numbers are organized in a majorversion.majorrevision.patch format.

Kernel Recompilation and Installation

❑ A *monolithic* kernel is one where all the device modules are built directly into it.

❑ A monolithic kernel uses the most memory and will probably waste space with unused drivers. However, it communicates more quickly with drivers than a modular kernel.

❑ The /proc directory is a virtual directory. It includes files that format and display values actually present in the kernel.

❑ Changing the values of variables in the /proc directory can change the behavior of your running kernel. For example, setting ip_forward = 1 enables routing.

❑ The Code Maturity Level option is used to enable prompting for kernel source code drivers not yet fully developed.

❑ The Loadable Module Support screen is where you enable the use of modules with your kernel.

❑ mkbootdisk is a utility that can create a bootdisk. This may be needed to perform a system rescue after a crash. System rescues can also be done via your install CD (CD #1).

The cron System

❑ The cron system allows any user to schedule jobs so they run at given intervals.

❑ The crontab command is used to work with cron files. Use **crontab -e** to edit, **crontab -l** to list, or **crontab -d** to delete cron files.

❑ The /etc/cron.allow and /etc/cron.deny files are used to control access to the cron job scheduler.

System-Wide Shell Configuration Files for the Bourne and Bash Shells

❑ All system-wide shell configuration files are kept in the /etc directory.

❑ /etc/profile is the system-wide startup shell script for bash users.

SELF TEST

The following questions will help you measure your understanding of the material presented in this chapter. Read all the choices carefully, as there may be more than one correct answer. Choose all correct answers for each question.

Setting Up and Managing Disk Quotas

1. You have several users on your system. You want to restrict their disk space in their home directories, but because of the complexity of some of their programs, they need large temporary space. How could you restrict their disk usage in their home directories, but allow them unlimited access to the /tmp directory? Assume that quotas are properly configured in /etc/fstab.

   A. Use edquota /home to edit the users' quotas for their home directories.

   B. Use edquota and specify only the home directories in the text file.

   C. Mount the /tmp directory to a separate partition and use edquota on the partition that contains the /home directory.

   D. None of these options will work.

2. You are running an ISP service and provide space for users' Web pages. You want them to use no more than 40MB of space, but you will allow up to 50MB until they can clean up their stuff. How could you use quotas to enforce this policy?

   A. Enable grace periods; set the hard limit to 40MB and the soft limit to 50MB.

   B. Enable grace periods; set the soft limit to 50MB and the hard limit to 40MB.

   C. Enable grace periods; set the soft limit to 40MB, and the hard limit to 50MB.

   D. None of the above.

3. The CIO of your company wants to see a full report on how much disk space each user on the system is utilizing. What command would you use to display this information?

   A. repquota -a

   B. quotareport -a

   C. quotareport -all

   D. quotashow -a

4. If you wanted to configure quotas on the /home directory, what would you add to the options in /etc/fstab?

   A. quota

   B. usrquota

C. grpquota

D. userquota

5. Which of the following commands applies the same quota rules for user mj to user pm?

   A. /usr/sbin/edquota -u mj pm

   B. /usr/sbin/edquota -up mj pm

   C. /usr/sbin/appquota -p mj pm

   D. /usr/sbin/appquota -up mj pm

Kernel Sources

6. You're not sure which kernel source tree is active for your Linux computer. Which of the following directories should be linked to that source tree?

   A. /usr/src/linux

   B. /usr/src/linux-2.4

   C. /usr/src/linux-2.4rh

   D. /usr/src

7. You're trying to upgrade your kernel and have downloaded the linux-2.4.24.tar.gz kernel from ftp.kernel.org. What commands would you use to unpack this tarball?

   A. cd /usr/src; tar czvf linux-2.4.24.tar.gz

   B. cd /usr/src/linux; tar xzvf linux-2.4.24.tar.gz

   C. cd /usr/src; tar xzvf linux-2.4.24.tar.gz

   D. cd /usr/src/linux-2.4; tar xzvf linux-2.4.24.tar.gz

Kernel Recompilation and Installation

8. Which commands would you *not* execute when building a monolithic kernel?

   A. make bzImage

   B. make lilo

   C. make modules

   D. make modules_install

9. You are almost finished building a new router for your company. You have both network cards properly set up to two different networks. Each side can successfully ping its network card, but neither side can ping the other network. After checking your firewall and forwarding rules, you feel they are set up correctly. All the kernel configuration settings such as IP Firewalling are enabled. What is most likely the cause of this problem?

A. You didn't load the router module.

B. You need to enable the environmental variable, ENABLE_ROUTING=1.

C. You need to add a "1" to the kernel variables file /proc/sys/net/ipv4/ip_forward.

D. None of the above.

10. Which one of these kernels is a development kernel?

A. 2.0.0

B. 1.2.25

C. 2.3.4

D. 3.0.13

11. When compiling a kernel, what are the valid configuration options used by make?

A. config

B. menuconfig

C. windowconfig

D. xconfig

12. After specifying all the options for your kernel, you type in your final command: make bzImage. The kernel goes through its final stages of compiling, but at the end complains the kernel is too large. What steps could you use to fix this problem?

A. Edit your kernel configurations to configure as many modules as you can.

B. Set up a monolithic kernel.

C. Remove some of the kernel source code.

D. Use **make zImage -compress.**

13. What does the command mkinitrd /boot/initrd-2.4.19 do?

A. It creates a list of kernel modules for kernel 2.4.19.

B. It appends the system's /boot/initrd to kernel 2.4.19.

C. Nothing. The /boot directory is referenced by the kernel only during boot time.

D. It creates an initial RAM disk to load necessary modules during boot time.

14. You have just compiled a new kernel. You compiled the kernel with the command make bzImage. You need to copy the kernel to the /boot directory. Where is the kernel currently located?

    A. /usr/src/linux/

    B. /boot/

    C. /usr/src/linux/kernel/bzImage/

    D. /usr/src/linux/arch/i386/boot/bzImage

15. You have just compiled a new kernel, vmlinuz-2.4.24, and want to set up GRUB to boot your new kernel by default yet still giving you the option to boot the old kernel, if necessary. You have already copied your kernel to the /boot directory. How would you specify the location of the kernel in the /etc/grub.conf file?

    A. kernel /boot/vmlinuz-2.4.24

    B. kernel /vmlinuz-2.4.24

    C. kernel vmlinux-2.4.24

    D. kernel /boot/vmlinux-2.4.24.img

16. Where would you find the default configuration file for the kernel installed with your distribution of Red Hat Linux?

    A. /usr/src/linux-*versionnumber*

    B. /usr/src/linux-*versionnumber* /.config

    C. /usr/src/linux-*versionnumber* /config

    D. /usr/src/linux-*versionnumber* /configs

17. What command could you use to easily create a bootable recovery disk for your system?

    A. fdrescue

    B. mkrescuedisk

    C. mkbootdisk

    D. None of the above

18. When you install an updated kernel from a Red Hat RPM, which of the following steps do you need to take?

    A. Add information on the new kernel in a GRUB stanza.

    B. Add a new Initial RAM disk to the /boot directory.

    C. Reconfigure the /usr/src/.config file.

    D. None of the above.

The cron System

19. You want to schedule a maintenance job to run on the first of every month at 4:00 A.M. Which of the following cron entries are correct?

    A. 0   4   1   *   *   ~/maintenance.pl

    B. 4   1   *   *   ~/maintenance.pl

    C. 0   4   31   *   *   ~/maintenance.pl

    D. 1   4   0   0   ~/maintenance.pl

20. You want to restrict the usage of crontab on your system to user mj. Which of the following actions do you need to take?

    A. Add user mj to the /var/cron.allow file.

    B. Add user mj to the /etc/cron.allow file.

    C. Add "All" to the /etc/cron.deny file.

    D. Add "All -mj" to the /etc/cron.deny file.

System-Wide Shell Configuration Files for the Bourne and Bash Shells

21. The system-wide shell startup file is:

    A. /etc/shells.conf

    B. /etc/startup.sh

    C. /etc/profile

    D. There is no system-wide shell startup file.

LAB QUESTION

Part I

Rather than offer a lab, I want to take the reader through a detailed kernel-building exercise. The exercise will include concise steps on how to configure, install, and test a new kernel. Note that this is not only a good thing to know from the perspective of earning your RHCE certificate, it is also something you will need to do at some point in time as a Linux system administrator. See the Lab Answer section at the end of this chapter for the exercise.

Part 2

In this second lab, you'll be updating your kernel from another source. One proviso—this lab will work only if there is a Red Hat RPM kernel file that is a later version from what is already installed on your computer.

1. Check ftp.redhat.com or another source such as www.rpmfind.net for an updated kernel.

2. Download the new kernel to the /tmp directory.

3. Back up your current /boot/grub/grub.conf configuration file, as well as the current files in your boot directory, in case something goes wrong.

4. Use the **rpm -i** *kernelfile* command to install the new kernel.

5. Observe the results. Check the files in /boot. Which files look like they're duplicated but with a different version number?

6. Check your boot loader file. Assuming it's GRUB, edit the /boot/grub/grub.conf file. Change the *default* variable in this file to point to the new kernel. If it's LILO, remember to run /sbin/lilo to record the change in the MBR.

7. Reboot your computer to test the new kernel.

SELF TEST ANSWERS

Setting Up and Managing Disk Quotas

1. ☑ **C. Mount the /tmp directory to a separate partition and use edquota on the partition that contains the /home directory. You can specify only one quota per user per partition. If you move /tmp to its own partition, you can control it separately.**
   ☒ **A** is partially correct, but doesn't address the problem of unlimited file size and inode access for files in /tmp. **B** is incorrect because quotas are set on a filesystem-by-filesystem basis. Since there is an answer, **D** is incorrect.

2. ☑ **C. Enable grace periods; set the soft limit to 40MB, and the hard limit to 50MB. This will warn users they are over their limit after the grace period, but will make sure they do not exceed the 50MB true maximum barrier.**
   ☒ **A** is incorrect because the soft limit must be less than the hard limit. **B** is incorrect because it is actually the same as **A**. **D** is incorrect because **C** does the job.

3. ☑ **A. The repquota command will display a report of all users on your system. It shows the used space, as well as their soft and hard limits.**
   ☒ **B, C,** and **D** refer to programs that don't exist on Red Hat Linux.

4. ☑ **B and C. The usrquota and grpquota options allow the configuration of quotas on the given filesystem on user and group bases.**
   ☒ **A** and **D** are not valid options for /etc/fstab.

5. ☑ **B. The edquota command edits user quotas. The -u switch applies quota editing to users. The -p switch duplicates quotas.**
   ☒ **A** is incorrect because there is nothing to duplicate the quota for user mj on user pm. **C** and **D** use the invalid appquota command.

Kernel Sources

6. ☑ **B. The /usr/src/linux-2.4 directory is normally soft-linked to the actual directory with the active kernel source files.**
   ☒ **A, C,** and **D** all specify directories that aren't normally linked to the Linux kernel source tree, at least for kernel version 2.4.x.

7. ☑ **C. You need to be in the /usr/src directory; then unpacking the tarball, the file with the tar.gz extension, copies the file into the appropriate directory. The next step would be to create**

a soft link between the /usr/src/linux-2.4 directory and whatever directory is unpacked from linux-2.4.24.tar.gz.

☒ **A** is wrong because tar's c switch compresses and does not extract. **B** and **D** are wrong because they would extract the source files in the wrong directory. Though the directories would actually be usable with the appropriate link, a substantial number of programs depend on having the kernel source directories in the right place; some developers may need it for their drivers. It is therefore best to stay with the convention for kernel source locations.

Kernel Recompilation and Installation

8. ☑ **C** and **D**, **make modules** and **make modules_install**. These two commands are necessary only when building a modular kernel. A monolithic kernel contains all the drivers directly in the main kernel itself.

☒ **A** is done regardless of the type of kernel you are building. **B** is incorrect because there is no such argument to make.

9. ☑ **C**. You need to add a "1" to the kernel variables file /proc/sys/net/ipv4/ip_forward. By default, routing is not enabled by the kernel. To enable it, you can simply add a "1" to this file with the following command: **echo 1 >> /proc/sys/net/ipv4/ip_forward**. Note that, to make the system a router permanently, you should edit the /etc/sysctl.conf file and set this variable in the file.

☒ **A** is incorrect because there is no such module. **B** is incorrect because there is no such variable. **D** is incorrect because performing the action in **C** will enable routing in your kernel.

10. ☑ **C**. The second number determines if it is a stable release or a development kernel. If the second number is an odd number, it is a development kernel, not suitable for a production computer. If it is an even number, it is a stable kernel release.

☒ **A**, **B**, and **D** all refer to "stable" kernel versions (in fact, **D** refers to a kernel architecture that doesn't even exist!).

11. ☑ **A**, **B**, and **D**; config, menuconfig, and xconfig. config is a basic text-based utility. menuconfig is a text-based menu utility, and xconfig is a graphical X Window utility.

☒ **C** is incorrect because there is no such option.

12. ☑ **A**. Creating modules will greatly decrease the size of your kernel.

☒ **B** is incorrect because monolithic kernels are generally larger than modular kernels. **C** is incorrect because if you remove some of the source code you need, your kernel won't compile, and if you try to remove source code you don't need, you'll find it isn't in the kernel to begin with. **D** is incorrect because the older zImage kernel is less compressed and is therefore actually bigger than the bzImage kernel.

13. ☑ **D.** It creates an initial RAM disk. An initial RAM disk is a RAM-based filesystem that contains the kernel and all required kernel modules. It is used to load a kernel and initialize any special hardware drivers needed to access the disk-based kernel and its modules. In essence, it loads the necessary modules for our 2.4.19 kernel during the boot process.

☒ **A** is incorrect because it doesn't describe the creation of a RAM disk image from the available modules. **B** is incorrect because there is no /boot/initrd file. **C** is just plain wrong!

14. ☑ **D.** /usr/src/linux/arch/i386/boot/bzImage. The kernels are always compiled to this directory and will have a name of bzImage.

☒ **A, B,** and **C** are all incorrect locations.

15. ☑ **B.** In GRUB, the root directory is actually /boot. Therefore, the kernel location is /vmlinuz-2.4.24.

☒ **A** is incorrect because the root directory in GRUB is actually /boot. **C** and **D** are incorrect because they specify incorrect kernel files.

16. ☑ **D.** The default Red Hat configuration file is located in the /usr/src/linux-2.4.19-3/configs directory, in a filename associated with the architecture for your computer.

☒ **A** is incorrect because there is no .config file in the stated directory. **B** is incorrect since the /usr/src/linux-*versionnumber*/.config file is the configuration file for the current kernel, which may vary from the default configuration. **C** is incorrect because it is the wrong directory.

17. ☑ **C,** mkbootdisk. This command will allow you to make a boot disk for your system that has the option of typing **rescue** at the LILO prompt.

☒ **A** and **B** are incorrect because there are no such commands. **D** is incorrect because we can make boot floppy diskettes with mkbootdisk.

18. ☑ **D,** None of the above. GRUB is automatically updated when you install a new Red Hat kernel from RPM; however, you may want to change the default parameter in /boot/grub/grub.conf. A new Initial RAM disk initrd-*versionnumber* is automatically added to /boot. And you don't need to change /usr/src/.config unless you want to recompile this new kernel.

☒ **A, B,** and **C** are all not required and are therefore incorrect.

The cron System

19. ☑ **A.** The syntax for cron is minute, hour, day of month, month of year, week day, and then the command.

☒ **B** executes at 4 minutes after 1 in the morning for every day. However, there are only four time fields, not five, so the entire line would be considered invalid. **C** is incorrect because it runs the job at 4 A.M. on the 31st of the month, and then only if the month has 31 days. **D** is incorrect because it executes the program at one minute after 4 A.M. But there are only four time values, and the day-of-month and month-of-year values start with a 1, not a 0.

20. ☑ **B.** All you need to do is add user mj to the /etc/cron.allow file. There is no need for a /etc/cron.deny file; it is assumed that no other users (other than root) are allowed to use the cron daemon.

☒ **A** is incorrect because the /var directory does not contain configuration files. **C** is incorrect because that would simply deny access to all users. **D** is incorrect because the syntax is not consistent with what you can put in either /etc/cron.allow or /etc/cron.deny.

System-Wide Shell Configuration Files for the Bourne and Bash Shells

21. ☑ **C.** This is the system-wide shell script executed whenever a user logs in.

☒ **A** and **B** are incorrect because there are no such files. **D** is incorrect because answer **C** is correct.

LAB ANSWER

Part 1

Before we can build a new kernel, we have to ensure we have all the correct RPMs.

1. Make sure that the following RPMs are properly installed. It's easy to check with the **rpm -q** *packagename* command. If some are not installed, the **rpm -Uvh** *packagename**command can help:

```
kernel-source-*glibc-kernelheaders-*
glibc-devel-*
cpp-*
ncurses4-*
ncurses-devel-*
binutils-*
gcc-*
```

If you set up Red Hat Linux 8.0 in a server configuration, most of these packages are already installed. Alternatively, if you set up Red Hat Linux in a different configuration, there is a slight issue with the glibc-devel-* package; as of this writing, it cites a dependency on a kernel-headers* package. The kernel-headers* package from previous versions of Red Hat is now part of the glibc-kernheaders* package.

You may have to install these packages in a certain order to overcome "dependencies." Alternatively, if you're confident that this package list is complete, use the --nodeps option to force package installation despite any dependencies. (This package list is complete, but it is a good idea in principle to always check dependencies, to make sure you don't forget a critical package.)

It's necessary to make a new kernel configuration before we build our kernel. To do this, we need to give our new kernel a unique name, as well as identify what components will (and will not) be in the kernel.

2. Run the cd command to /usr/src and do a long listing. Write down the name of the item that the linux-2.4 directory is pointing to. If you were to install a newer kernel, you would need to make the linux-2.4 directory symbolically link to the base directory of the new source tree. To do this, you would run something like the following:

```
# rm linux-2.4
# ln -s linux-2.4.19-3 linux-2.4
```

3. Run the cd command to the linux-2.4 directory, and edit Makefile. Look for the line that starts with EXTRAVERSION. This is a suffix that Red Hat adds to the kernel included with Linux. Change the entry to add your initials after the existing suffix. Save and exit.

4. Jot down your EXTRAVERSION value here: _____

5. Determine the correct CPU on your hardware. Use the command

```
# cat /proc/cpuinfo
```

6. Jot down the CPU Model Name here: _____

(Our classroom equipment uses Pentium IIIs, which are considered i686s.)

7. Take the default configuration that Red Hat used for this kernel and save it as the default configuration. Use the command

```
# cp -p /usr/src/linux-2.4/configs/kernel-*i686.config
/usr/src/linux-2.4/arch/i386/defconfig
```

8. Clean up from previous configurations by using

```
# make mrproper
```

9. Install the existing "old" configuration so that we are ready to modify it to our requirements:

```
# make oldconfig
```

10. Wait until the messages are complete. Problems are rare at this stage.

11. Next, it is time to configure your kernel. You need to define the features and other customizations you need for your kernel, using one of the three major tools:

■ **make config**   A line-by-line tool that gives you a choice with all kernel options

■ **make menuconfig**   A text-based menu that allows you to select just the changes you want

■ **make xconfig**   A GUI interface that works only in the X Window

12. Set the processor type to match your hardware (e.g., Pentium, Pentium II, Pentium III, Pentium IV).

13. When you save the new configuration, the result is sent to a hidden file called .config. Copy it to your /boot directory for safekeeping.

```
# cp .config /boot/config.2.4.19-3Initials
```

14. Return to the kernel configuration tool of your choice. Turn off all unneeded devices. Some possible unneeded devices include:

■ ISDN subsystem

■ I2O

■ Old CD-ROMs

■ Amateur Radio

■ Telephony Support

■ Symmetric multiprocessing support

■ MTR Memory support

15. Be sure to turn on kernel loadable modules support.

16. Save your changes and exit.

17. Resolve all kernel dependencies (between sources). This will produce a lot of output and may take several minutes. Run

```
# make dep
```

18. Once your dependencies are resolved, it's time to build a new compressed kernel image. The command to use is

```
# make bzImage
```

19. This is the actual kernel build, which will take some time. You may want to run top from another terminal or console screen to watch the load on the system as the kernel builds.

20. The easiest way to see if the kernel build worked is to run the following command immediately after the messages from make bzImage stop:

```
# echo $?
0
```

21. If you got a 0, everything worked (success). Anything else indicates a failure. Go back and reconfigure your kernel to make a configuration that works.

22. Check for the existence of two new files. Run this command:

```
# ls -l System.map arch/i386/boot/bzImage
```

23. It should show you two files, a relatively small System.map and a much larger bzImage.

24. Make the loadable modules that will be used by this kernel.

```
# make modules
```

25. Install the new custom kernel files into their correct locations and update LILO so that it knows about your new kernel.

26. Copy your new kernel onto the /boot filesystem. If the version number of the kernel and the EXTRAVERSION number in the Makefile are different, change the command accordingly:

```
# cp -p arch/i386/boot/bzImage /boot/vmlinuz-2.4.19-3mj
# cp -p System.map /boot/System.map-2.4.19-3mj
# make modules_install
```

27. If your kernel includes any modules needed at boot time, you will need to make an initial RAM disk (initrd). To do this, use the command

```
# mkinitrd /boot/initrd-2.4.19-3mj.img 2.4.19-3mj
```

28. Your kernel has just been properly installed.

29. The last step is to configure your boot loader, GRUB or LILO, to make your new kernel available. In either case, you should to set up a new stanza, treating the new kernel as though it were a separate operating system.

Here is an excerpt from a /etc/grub.conf file with a new Title section for your new kernel. The new Title section is in bold. Note that we took the previous Title section, copied it, and changed the image filename to match the kernel image we installed into /boot. Since GRUB is not loaded directly into the MBR, that's it, you're ready to test-drive your new kernel!

```
Title Red Hat Linux (2.4.19-3)
            root (hd0,0)
            kernel /vmlinuz-2.4.19-3 ro root=LABEL=/
            initrd /initrd-2.4.19-3.img
Title Red Hat Linux (2.4.19-3mj)
            root (hd0,0)
            kernel /vmlinuz-2.4.19-3mj ro root=LABEL=/
            initrd /initrd-2.4.19-3mj.img
```

Here is an excerpt from a /etc/lilo.conf file with a new image= section for your new kernel. The new image= section is in bold. Note that we took the previous image= section, copied it, and changed the image filename to match the kernel image we installed into /boot.

```
image=/boot/vmlinuz-2.4.19-3mj
    label=newlinux
    read-only
    root=/dev/hda2

image=/boot/vmlinuz-2.4.19-3
    label=linux
    read-only
    root=/dev/hda2
```

30. Install your new LILO updates, using the command

    ```
    # lilo -v -v
    ```

31. This produces extra verbose output. Read over the output and look for any error messages. To test your new kernel, reboot your system. At the Red Hat splash screen, you should see your new kernel name on the list of images that can be booted. Select your kernel and press ENTER.

    Congratulations, you have just installed a custom kernel on your new system.

Part 2

Assuming everything works with the updated Red Hat RPM kernel package, you should not have to update anything, especially if your boot loader is GRUB. The steps described in the lab should help you confirm this.

7

X Window System

O ne of the most important aspects of getting a Red Hat Linux system up and running is configuring the user interface. For most nonadministrative users, this means configuring the *X Window* interface. The *X Window System* is the Linux graphical user interface (GUI). While the GUI plays an integral part of other operating systems such as Microsoft Windows, the X Window System on Linux is essentially just another application. Many administrators don't even bother with the GUI; the command line interface is enough for most administrative purposes.

However, regular users on a Linux workstation become more productive with the GUI and the multitude of X Window–based applications. If you are helping users migrate from Microsoft Windows to Linux, the X Window System allows you to provide a less intimidating environment.

Some Linux systems simply don't need the X Window System. For example, computers that are used as dedicated DHCP, DNS, or NFS servers generally don't serve as workstations for anyone and therefore don't need any sort of GUI. Many Linux gurus have a negative bias toward the GUI. While Red Hat and others have developed some helpful GUI tools, they are almost always "front ends," or programs that customize one or more commands at the command line interface.

But if you're administering a network of Red Hat Linux computers, you'll need to know how to administer the X Window System, a skill that requires a basic understanding of the available desktops and window managers.

exam
ⓦatch

You need to know how to configure X Window, and how to configure your Linux computer for a specific graphical logon manager.

CERTIFICATION OBJECTIVE 7.01

X Server

The X Window System is designed as a flexible and powerful client/server-based system. In order to configure and troubleshoot the X Window interface, it is important you understand the client/server nature of the X Window System.

As you might have guessed from the terms *client* and *server,* the X Window System is designed to work in a networked environment. This does not mean your Linux system must be connected to a network in order to use X Window applications; the X Window System will work on a *stand-alone* system as well as a networked system. If your system is part of a network, not only can you run X applications on your system, you can employ the powerful network capabilities of the X Window System to run X applications on other computers on your network; graphical displays from those applications are sent to your monitor. In fact, X Window applications handle this task so well that, providing the network is fast enough, you really can't tell from a performance point of view which applications are running *locally* and which applications are running *remotely.*

Different Meanings for Client and Server

X Window clients and servers use a different paradigm from the usual client/server relation. The *X server* controls the graphics on the local computer. The X server draws images on your screen and takes input from your keyboard and mouse. In contrast, X clients are local or remote applications such as xclock that you can run on an X server.

X clients can run *locally* or *remotely. Local* X clients run on your workstation; *remote* X clients run on the local X server. When you run a remote X Window client application, you start the program on a different computer and send its output to use the X server on your local computer. Figure 7-1 shows a local X server with one local X client and one remote one.

Before we can talk about running X client applications, we need to look first at getting an X server running on our system.

Supported Hardware

Getting the X Window System configured and working can be one of the most difficult tasks in setting up a Linux system. Fortunately, Red Hat Linux comes with tools and drivers that make this job relatively painless and easy.

One of the most important steps you can take to ensure that you wind up with a working X Window configuration is selecting the proper hardware. Ironically, the latest and greatest video card or monitor is not always the best option. Many video cards and monitors include proprietary software; it may take some time before Linux developers are able to "reverse-engineer" a video card or a monitor. For the latest official information, check the Red Hat hardware compatibility list.

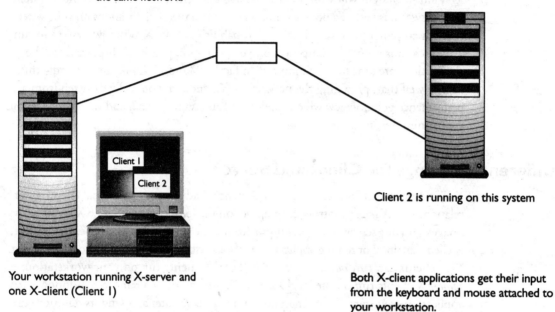

FIGURE 7-1 You can run X Window clients from the local computer and/or remote computers on the same network.

Client 2 is running on this system

Your workstation running X-server and one X-client (Client 1)

Both X-client applications get their input from the keyboard and mouse attached to your workstation.

on the job

Despite these limitations, Linux provides world-class support for graphics. Movie studios such as Dreamworks create the latest animated movies and special effects using Linux workstations. Even Disney has declared its intent to make movies using Linux. If you need more intensive graphics support, you may want to consider some commercial alternatives to XFree86. Two are Metro-X from Metro Link (www.metrolink.com) and Accelerated-X from X-Inside (www.xinside.com).

Hardware: X Server Selection

The X Window server program shipped with Red Hat Linux is an open-source X server program called XFree86. The XFree86 Server included with Red Hat Linux has support for hundreds of video cards and monitors. The best place to check to see whether your video card and monitor are supported is the Red Hat Hardware Compatibility List, currently available from http://www.redhat.com/support/hardware/index.html. Alternatively, use the **rpm -q XFree86** command to check your version of the XFree86 server. Navigate to the XFree86 Web site at www.xfree86.org to find the latest support information.

As of this writing, the latest version of Red Hat Linux will include only the XFree86 (4.2.x) server. There may be a few video cards that require the older XFree86 server, version 3.3.x. Hopefully these cases are now rare. If you find that you are unlucky in this way and cannot upgrade your video card, first try a standard VGA or VESA configuration. As a last resort, download the older XFree86 Server from www.xfree86.org.

Servers and XFree86

The latest version of XFree86 includes modules for different video servers. Unlike the XFree86 3.x series, this one doesn't require you to install different packages for each video server. Hardware support for most video servers is already there. If you learn of updates, changes are easy. Just add the module, and then point to it in the /etc/X11/XF86Config configuration file.

If you are using an unsupported video card, support is also included for generic VGA devices. Most video cards and monitors will work with these X servers.

Several recent versions of Red Hat Linux included an /etc/X11/XF86Config-4 file for the XFree86 version 4 server. As of this writing, Red Hat is removing support for XFree86 version 3.x servers; starting with Red Hat Linux 8.0, the Red Hat Linux X configuration file should be /etc/X11/XF86Config.

Tools for X Configuration

The preferred Red Hat configuration tool for XFree86 is redhat-config-xfree86. The configuration tool that ships with XFree86 is xf86config. Either tool can be used to configure your graphics environment, but you really need to practice using redhat-config-xfree86.

You can install the X Window System during or after the Linux installation process. You can use redhat-config-xfree86 to reconfigure X Window at any time.

The default Red Hat installation program runs in graphics mode if it detects a graphics driver. As discussed in Chapter 2, when configuring your graphics display, get the best information that you can on the make, model, chipset (clockchip), version, and video memory of your graphics card. You'll also need the manufacturer, model, frequency range, and allowable resolutions for your monitor.

redhat-config-xfree86

The redhat-config-xfree86 program is a stand-alone program that you can run at any time from the command line. The basic routines within redhat-config-xfree86 are also used by the Red Hat installation program if you choose to install and configure the X Window System at that time.

The redhat-config-xfree86 program is a character-based menu-driven interface that helps you to configure your video hardware. It automatically probes your video card and tries to select the appropriate X server image for it. If redhat-config-xfree86 cannot determine the make and model of your graphics card, it allows you to select them from the list of supported video cards.

on the
()ob
If for some reason, redhat-config-xfree86 does not work, the surest alternative is the text-based xf86config utility.

Running redhat-config-xfree86

Starting redhat-config-xfree86 is easy. Just type **redhat-config-xfree86** at a command line interface. It provides a simple GUI, even if you start it from a regular text console. When you start redhat-config-xfree86, you'll see the Display Settings window similar to that shown in Figure 7-2. You can use the arrow or PAGE DOWN keys to scroll through the welcome message.

If redhat-config-xfree86 is successful at identifying your hardware, you'll see it listed under the Display tab. In the case shown in Figure 7-2, nothing was detected; it's an "Unknown monitor with Unknown video card."

You can now set the default resolution and color depth under the Display tab.

on the
()ob
redhat-config-xfree86 replaces Xconfigurator. It should theoretically work fine even from a text console screen. However, as of this writing, there are still problems associated with redhat-config-xfree86 and a few video systems. Using xf86config is still a viable alternative. Just remember to save the settings you create to /etc/X11/XF86Config.

Next, you can configure the video hardware from a list. Click the Advanced tab, as shown in Figure 7-3.

You'll see options to configure your monitor and video card. Click the Configure button in the Video Card section. This should bring up the Video Card Settings dialog box shown in Figure 7-4. If the Probe Videocard option is active, redhat-config-

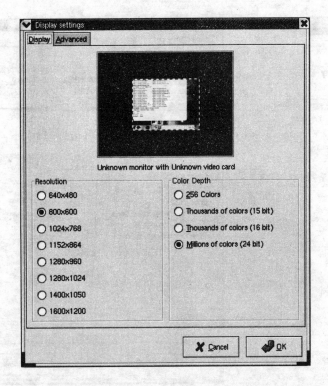

FIGURE 7-2

redhat-config-
xfree86 Display
Settings,
Display tab

xfree86 may be able to configure your card for you. Otherwise, search through the list of video cards. If you do not see your graphics card here, it may not be supported. In this case, you have several options:

- Select a video card similar to your model. Alternatively, you may find a generic server such as VESA that is compatible with your video card. Test, and if necessary edit the /etc/X11/XF86Config file to complete your changes.

- Check the Web for others who are running the X Window System with the same type of hardware. A useful database is available by searching through newsgroup messages at groups.google.com.

- Use the Unsupported VGA-compatible X Window server.

- Select one of the more generic cards. When you click the Custom Memory Size option, you can select the amount of memory associated with your card.

FIGURE 7-3

redhat-config-
xfree86 Display
Settings,
Advanced tab

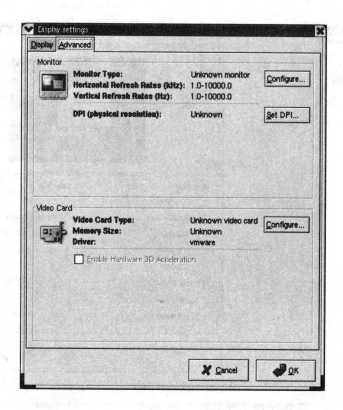

You can also add one of the many configuration options associated with /etc/
X11/XF86Config. For examples, see www.xfree86.org.

■ Go to http://www.xfree86.org and download the latest drivers.

Once your selections are complete, click OK. This returns you to the Advanced
tab. If your video card is so capable, you'll be able to check the Enable Hardware 3D
Acceleration option. Next, configure the Monitor. Click the Configure button in the
Monitor section of the Advanced tab. You should see something like the dialog box
shown in Figure 7-5.

Move on to the monitor selection screen. If the Probe Monitor button is active,
redhat-config-xfree86 may be able to probe your hardware. Otherwise, select the
option that most closely matches your monitor. If you don't see the make and model
for your monitor, select one of the Generic monitors. You can then customize the
Horizontal and Vertical settings per your monitor's documentation.

FIGURE 7-4

redhat-config-
xfree86 allows
you to choose
a card.

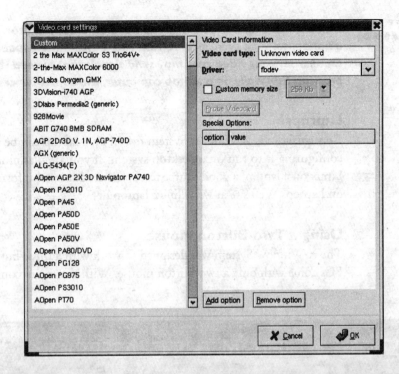

FIGURE 7-5

redhat-config-
xfree86 allows
you to choose
a monitor.

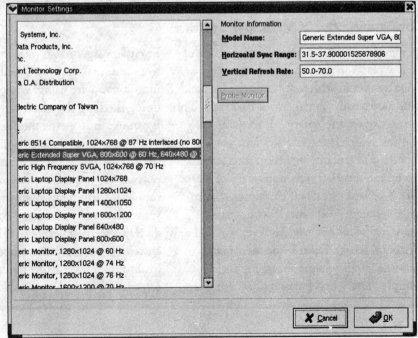

Don't select Probe Monitor if you have an older monitor. And don't configure a horizontal sync or vertical refresh rate beyond the capability of your monitor. Otherwise, your video card may send signals that exceed the capability of your monitor. Especially on a laptop computer, the consequences can be rather costly.

Laptops

Configuring the X Window System to run on a laptop can be more challenging than configuring it to run on a desktop system. If you are planning to install Red Hat Linux on a laptop, a good source for tips and additional information is the Linux on Laptops Web site at www.linux-laptop.net.

Using a Two-Button Mouse

The X Window System was designed to work with a three-button mouse. Many PCs come with only a two-button mouse. With the mouseconfig utility, you can

FROM THE CLASSROOM

Configuring the X Window System

Configuring the X Window System is one of the few places in the process of setting up a Linux system in which the choices you make could potentially damage your hardware. This fact pertains to the *refresh rate* for your monitor, which is the rate at which your graphics card redraws images on your screen. The refresh rate is expressed in terms of Hertz (Hz). A refresh rate of 60 Hz means that an image is redrawn 60 times in one second. Computer monitors have both vertical and a horizontal refresh rates. Some monitors, known as multisync monitors, support multiple vertical and horizontal refresh rates.

In either case, refresh rates vary from monitor to monitor. When you specify the type of monitor you are using, what you are really doing is telling the video card what frequencies it can use to *drive* the monitor.

If the monitor you configure does not match the type of hardware you actually have, it is possible for your video card to overtax your monitor, resulting in a blown monitor. This is a special concern with laptop computers. Laptop display screens are expensive; it is often more cost-effective to replace a laptop computer instead of replacing just the laptop display screen.

set up Linux to emulate the middle button when you press both buttons simultaneously.

Alternatively, you may have a mouse with a scrolling wheel. If you have one of these mice, try pressing the scroll wheel. If it clicks, it probably will work as a middle mouse button.

As of this writing, if you want to configure scrolling, you'll need to edit the /etc/X11/XF86Config file directly. The following is an example of how a mouse with a scroll wheel might be configured:

```
Section "Input Device"
      Identifier "Mouse1"
      Driver       "mouse"
      Option "Protocol" "IMPS/2"
      Option "Device"   "/dev/mouse"
      Option "ZAxisMapping"   Y
EndSection
```

"Mouse1" helps identify the mouse in other parts of this configuration file. The driver is mouse; the device is /dev/mouse. The protocol, IMPS/2, is associated with a standard PS/2 mouse. And the ZAxisMapping variable translates motion from the wheel to "Y," which corresponds to up and down motion in the active window.

exam
watch

The Red Hat Certified Engineer exam is primarily a performance-based exam. It is very important, therefore, that you try out the concepts presented in this chapter and experiment with them. Don't just read about them.

X Configuration Files

Information about your X Window configuration is stored in the /etc/X11 directory, as shown in Figure 7-6.

The primary X Window configuration file is XF86Config. It's instructive to read the associated man page carefully. It is well documented. It includes a number of commented sample commands that can help you configure your system in a number of special ways. For example, it includes tips on how you can:

- Disable the key sequence that automatically exits the GUI (CTRL-ALT-BACKSPACE)

- Configure different keyboards

- Set up multiple monitors, in what is known as a "multi-head" configuration

FIGURE 7-6	total 88							
	drwxr-xr-x	5 root	root	4096	Jul	30	07:06	applnk
X Window	drwxr-xr-x	2 root	root	4096	Jul	30	06:37	desktop-menus
configuration files	drwxr-xr-x	2 root	root	4096	Jul	30	06:46	fs
	drwxr-xr-x	6 root	root	4096	Jul	30	07:03	gdm
	drwxr-xr-x	2 root	root	4096	Jul	30	07:02	lbxproxy
	-rwxr-xr-x	1 root	root	1316	Jul	24	17:32	prefdm
	drwxr-xr-x	2 root	root	4096	Jul	30	07:02	proxymngr
	drwxr-xr-x	4 root	root	4096	Jul	30	07:02	rstart
	drwxr-xr-x	2 root	root	4096	Jul	30	07:02	serverconfig
	drwxr-xr-x	2 root	root	4096	Jul	30	07:02	starthere
	drwxr-xr-x	2 root	root	4096	Jul	30	07:16	sysconfig
	drwxr-xr-x	2 root	root	4096	Jul	30	07:03	twm
	lrwxrwxrwx	1 root	root	27	Jul	30	07:23	X -> ../../usr/X11R6/bin/XFree86
	drwxr-xr-x	3 root	root	4096	Jul	30	07:10	xdm
	-rw-r--r--	1 root	root	3011	Jul	31	05:50	XF86Config
	lrwxrwxrwx	1 root	root	24	Jul	31	05:08	XF86Config-4.deprecated -> /etc/X11
	/XF86Config-4.vm							
	-rw-r--r--	1 root	root	0	Jul	30	12:28	XF86Config-4.org
	-rw-r--r--	1 root	root	0	Jul	30	11:29	XF86Config-4.org.old.1
	-rw-r--r--	1 root	root	3201	Jul	30	12:28	XF86Config-4.vm
	-rw-r--r--	1 root	root	3201	Jul	30	11:29	XF86Config-4.vm.old.1
	-rw-r--r--	1 root	root	531	Jul	26	09:13	XftConfig.README-OBSOLETE
	drwxr-xr-x	3 root	root	4096	Jul	30	07:03	xinit
	lrwxrwxrwx	1 root	root	27	Jul	30	07:02	xkb -> ../../usr/X11R6/lib/X11/xkb
	-rw-r--r--	1 root	root	613	Jul	20	09:38	Xmodmap
	-rw-r--r--	1 root	root	338	Jul	20	09:38	Xresources
	drwxr-xr-x	2 root	root	4096	Jul	30	07:02	xserver
	drwxr-xr-x	2 root	root	4096	Jul	30	07:02	xsm
	[root@RH80 X11]#							

The default server is linked to the X command. X is called up by the **startx** command. Both of these commands are located in the /usr/X11R6/bin directory. Examine the long listing for the X command. You'll see that it's linked to the version 4 all-in-one server package, XFree86:

```
# ls -l /usr/X11R6/bin/X
lrwxrwxrwx   1 root    root          7 Jul 30 07:33 /usr/X11R6/bin/X ->>
 XFree86
```

redhat-config-xfree86 normally writes its changes to /etc/X11/XF86Config. When the XFree86 X server starts, it reads this file.

EXERCISE 7-1

X Server

In this exercise, you will start your X server without a window manager. You'll then start an xterm X client application. Some of the commands used in this exercise are covered later in the chapter. If the X Window System is not running, you can skip steps 1 and 3.

1. If the X Window System is running, change to a text console by pressing CTRL-ALT-F1.

2. If you see a login prompt, log in at the text console as root. Otherwise, press CTRL-C to stop X Window.

3. If you logged in at the text console, stop the current X Window server by typing this:

```
/sbin/init 3
```

4. Start the XFree86 X server by typing the command:

```
# X &
```

Your X server will start, but all you will see is a blank gray screen, with an "x" that represents your mouse cursor.

5. Switch back to your text console session by pressing CTRL-ALT-F1.

6. Type the following command:

```
xterm -display localhost:0.0  &
```

(Note: xterm starts with a lowercase x, and there is only one dash before the display switch.)

7. Switch back to your X Window display by pressing ALT-F7.

You should now have an xterm terminal window. Select the window and try to enter commands from the xterm command line. Check out the contents of /usr/X11R6/bin. Try starting other X client applications such as xcalc and xclock from the xterm command line. Reboot your system to return things to normal.

One last keystroke hint for X: pressing the CTRL-ALT-BACKSPACE keys sends a termination signal to the X server. In some situations, the Linux GUI crashes and it's not possible to start a text console session by pressing CTRL-ALT-F1. In this case, the CTRL-ALT-BACKSPACE key combination can keep you from having to reboot your computer.

EXERCISE 7-2

Multiple X Servers

In this exercise, you will start two different X servers. If the X Window System is not running, you can skip steps 1 and 3.

1. If the X Window System is running, change to a text console by pressing CTRL-ALT-F1.

2. If you see a login prompt, log in at the text console as root. Otherwise, press CTRL-C to stop X Window.

3. If you logged in at the text console, stop the current X Window server by typing this:

   ```
   init 3
   ```

4. Start the XFree86 X server by typing the command:

   ```
   # startx &
   ```

   Your normal GUI will start.

5. Switch back to your text console session by pressing CTRL-ALT-F1. Return to your GUI by pressing ALT-F7. Switch back again to your text console session.

6. Type the following command:

   ```
   # startx -- :1 &
   ```

7. You should now have two different GUIs. Switch to the first GUI by pressing CTRL-ALT-F7. Return to the second GUI by pressing CTRL-ALT-F8.

8. Exit from both GUIs.

CERTIFICATION OBJECTIVE 7.02

X Clients

Once you have your X server working, you are (almost) ready to start connecting to various X Window client applications. An X Window client is an application program. This client uses your X server's graphical services to display output. While one X server process controls the display, you can run as many X clients as your hardware resources, primarily RAM, will support. If your Linux system is part of a network, you may also start X clients on other systems on the network and have those clients send their displays to your X server.

X clients exist for almost any every basic application. There are X clients for word processing, spreadsheets, games, and more. Most command line utilities, including many system administration utilities, are available as X clients. There are even X client versions of popular utilities such as the emacs editor.

Starting X Clients and Command Line Options

Starting an X client is very easy. When you start the X Window System for the first time on Red Hat Linux, several X clients such as icons or other windows will already be started for you. You can start additional X clients by selecting a program from a menu, or you can start an X client from a command line terminal screen.

But before you start running X clients on remote servers, you need to give permission. As discussed later in this chapter, the **xhost +** *client* command on your Linux computer allows a remote computer named *client* to run X clients on your server.

X client applications are standard Linux applications. If you choose to start an X client from a command line, you can follow the command name with any number of options. Most X clients understand a common set of options. These options are used to control such things as the size and location of the X client's window, the font the application uses to display the text, and even the display on which the application should display its output. Table 7-1 lists some of the more useful options you can supply when you start an X client from the command line.

The behavior of most of the command line options in Table 7-1 is self-descriptive, but we need to take a more detailed look at how some of the options work. We will examine at the --display option in more detail when we look at running remote X clients.

The -geometry option is used to specify both the size of the window that the X client starts up in and the location of the window. Notice that the first two numbers, the *XSIZE* and the *YSIZE,* are separated by a lowercase "x." These two numbers specify the size of the client window in either pixels or characters, depending on the application. If you are starting an xterm window, for example, the size represents a terminal screen with *XSIZE* columns and *YSIZE* lines. If you are starting an xclock, the size represents a window *XSIZE*x *YSIZE* in pixels.

The next two numbers specify where you want the client window to appear on your display. The numbers are relative to the upper-left and lower-right corners of

TABLE 7-1	Common X Client Command Line Options	
Option	**Example**	**Result**
-display *server*:0.0	-display frodo:0.0	Send output to the X server running on the computer named frodo.
-geometry *XSIZE×YSIZE* +*XOFF* +*YOFF*	-geometry 100×100 +10 +20	Specify the size and location of the window. In this case, we want a window 100×100 pixels in size, offset from the upper-left corner by 10 pixels horizontally and 20 pixels vertically.
-font *fontname*	-font lucidasans-14	Display text for this client using a specific font.
-background *color*	-background blue	Set the window background to blue.
-foreground *color*	-foreground white	Set the window foreground to white.
-title *string*	-title "My Window"	Place a title on the client window's title bar.
-bordercolor *color*	-bordercolor green	Make the window border green.
-borderwidth *pixels*	-borderwidth 5	Make the window border 5 pixels wide.

the desktop. While +0+0 represents the upper-left corner, -0-0 represents the lower-right corner. These specs are shown in Table 7-2.

Therefore, for *XOFF* + *YOFF*, if you specify + 10 + 10, the client is positioned 10 pixels from the left edge of the screen and 10 pixels from the top of the screen. Alternatively, -10-10 positions the client 10 pixels from the right edge of the screen and 10 pixels up from the bottom of the screen.

The -font option specifies the font that the X client should use to display text. The X Window System comes with a wide variety of both fixed and proportionally spaced fonts. The default list is located in the /usr/X11R6/lib/X11/fonts directory.

TABLE 7-2	**XSIZExYSIZE**	**Description**
X Client Geometrical Positioning	-0-0	Lower-right corner
	-0+0	Upper-right corner
	+0-0	Lower-left corner
	+0+0	Upper-left corner

This directory contains a number of subdirectories, each of which contains font files for the various types of fonts installed on your system.

Many of the X client command line options enable you to specify colors for different parts of the client window. You can specify a simple color such as red, green, white, and black. Alternatively, you can specify a color by indicating the red, green, and blue components of the color:

```
xclock -background RGB:FF/00/FF
```

xterm

One of the most useful X clients is a program called xterm. As its name implies, xterm is an X client application that creates a terminal window on your X display. So, after all the hard work you've gone through to get a nice windowing display, you're right back where you started, with a command line interface.

The difference is that now you can start up as many of these command line interfaces as you like, and you can switch between them with the click of a mouse. Since xterm is an X client, you can even open terminal windows on other computers on your network and have them display to your desktop. You can start xterm either from a menu or from a command line prompt.

The two major desktops include their own versions of xterm. The KDE desktop includes konsole, and the GNOME desktop includes gnome-terminal. You'll learn about these terminals in following sections.

X Font Server

The X Window System needs fonts. Linux manages fonts through the X Font Server. Red Hat Linux manages the X Font Server with the xfs service script. In most configurations, X Window needs the X Font Server before it can start. Many different fonts are normally available in the /usr/X1R6/lib/X11/fonts directory.

The X Font Server can be an Achilles' heel for X Window. A number of things can go wrong with xfs:

- The xfs service could be stopped or dead. In this case, you may need to try restarting xfs.

- The filesystems with /tmp or /home could be full. The xfs service can't start if either of these filesystems is full. There may also be problems if /tmp is on a different physical hard disk from other X Window files.

- Fonts could be misconfigured in /etc/X11/XF86Config.

- Fonts could be missing from the default /usr/X1R6/lib/X11/fonts directory. For example, missing 100 dpi or 75 dpi fonts could cause applications in a Linux GUI to look strange.

Any of these problems could make it impossible for you to start a Linux X Window. In addition, if you've set up a default X Window login, these problems could keep you from getting to the graphical login manager.

on the **Job**

Do not confuse the X Font Server service script, xfs, with the filesystem with the same initials, which was developed by Silicon Graphics.

CERTIFICATION OBJECTIVE 7.03

Window Managers

Once you have your X server running, you're almost ready to start running X-applications. Before you get to that point, however, we need to look at a special type of X client known as a *window manager*.

When you start the XFree86 X server, it turns your display into a blank electronic canvas. You may even glimpse this canvas as your system goes through the process of starting the X Window System. What you are seeing is the default desktop display for XFree86, which is an uninteresting textured gray background. The default mouse pointer for the X Window display is a graphic representation of an "X."

Once XFree86 starts and you have this canvas on your screen, the X server is ready to start serving X clients. In fact, you can start X clients up at this point, and your X server will open up windows to display their output. You will notice, however, that the windows seem to be missing something. You could use the methods in the preceding section to set up various X clients; for example, the **xclock -display localhost:0.0** command would lead to the screen shown in Figure 7-7.

Still, you don't have any of the useful features such as borders, title bars, menu bars, and minimize-maximize buttons that you've come to expect from a graphical user interface. For this purpose, you need a *window manager*. A window manager is a special type of X client that cannot run on its own. Instead, it needs the services of an X server to do its job. The window manager controls how other X clients appear

FIGURE 7-7

A single X client
on an X server

on your display. This includes everything from placing title bars and drawing borders around the window for each X client application you start, to determining the size of your desktop. In a nutshell, the window manager controls the look and feel of your GUI.

As is usually the case with all things Linux, you have multiple ways to accomplish the same task. Red Hat Linux comes with several different window managers and desktops. Your choice of window manager and desktop will determine how the X Window System appears, and to some extent how it functions.

The GNOME and KDE Desktops

Two powerful virtual desktop environments that come with Red Hat Linux are the GNOME (GNU Network Object Model Environment) desktop environment and KDE (the K Desktop Environment). The GNOME desktop, shown in Figure 7-8, is the default desktop for Red Hat Linux and is the desktop you first see after installing the X Window System. The KDE desktop, shown in Figure 7-9, is the main alternate desktop system. KDE is the default for several other Linux distributions.

FIGURE 7-8

The GNOME
desktop

GNOME Features

The GNOME desktop includes support for the Common Object Request Broker Architecture (CORBA), which allows GNOME software components written in any language and running on different systems to work together. In addition, the GNOME developer community is also working on an architecture similar to Microsoft's Object Linking and Embedding (OLE) architecture that will allow one GNOME application to call and control another GNOME application. One very nice feature of GNOME-compliant applications is that they are *session aware*; that is, when you quit an application, the application "remembers" the location in the document where you were last working and will reposition your cursor to that point when you restart the application.

Sawfish Window Manager

Even though you may be using GNOME as your desktop environment, you still need the services of a window manager. The best way to think of the relationship between the window manager and GNOME is that they work together to control

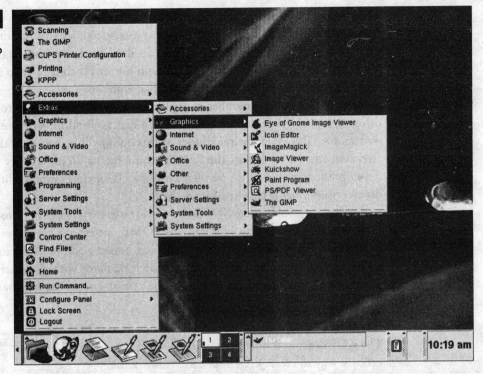

FIGURE 7-9

The KDE desktop

what you see on your display. The GNOME desktop will work with any window manager, but it works best with a GNOME-compliant window manager. Under Red Hat Linux, the default GNOME window manager is the Sawfish. Popular alternative window managers include Enlightenment and IceWM. You can find more information about GNOME at http://www.gnome.org.

Using GNOME

Many of the features of the GNOME interface will be familiar to you from other desktop environments. On the left side of the screen are icons representing files and applications that can be opened by double-clicking them with the mouse. The GNOME desktop environment also provides you with a virtual desktop. Next to the application buttons on the right side of the panel is a pager you can use to move from one area of the desktop to another.

One of the key features of GNOME is the *panel*, which you can see at the bottom of the screen in Figure 7-8. The panel is the control center for most of your activities while you use GNOME. The button at the far left of the panel with the imprint of a red hat is the Main Menu button. Use your mouse to click this button, and you will see a list of applications you can run. You can also launch applications from the panel by clicking the appropriate icon. The default buttons include a Help menu (the life-saver icon) and the gnome-terminal terminal emulator.

GNOME includes a number of applications, including graphics tools and an office suite, GNOME Office. As most Red Hat GUI administrative utilities are written for GNOME, the remainder of this book will be based on this desktop environment. Nevertheless, the RHCE requirements do not specify a preferred desktop; there should be no problems using KDE or the command line console to do everything that is required for the exam.

As you'll be configuring GNOME for your users, you may want to configure GNOME in a special way. Normally, GNOME opens with a number of icons and possibly default applications such as nautilus. You can add more default applications such as a new terminal window or the xcalc calculator with the Startup Programs utility, which you can access via the gnome-session-properties command.

KDE Features

The KDE desktop is built on the Qt C++ cross-platform GUI toolkit. This is another versatile way to create GUI applications for Linux.

Many of the features of KDE should also be familiar to you from other desktop environments. In fact, you can configure KDE to a look and feel that is quite similar to Windows 9x. As shown in Figure 7-9, it includes a Main Menu button, represented by the red hat and folder in the lower-left corner of the desktop. Like GNOME, it includes pagers and buttons representing the open programs on the desktop.

Default Desktop

Once you've configured X Window, it's easy to start a Linux GUI. Just run the startx command. This command, in the /usr/X11R6/bin directory, calls up various other configuration files in your home directory. If the configuration files don't exist in your home directory, they are taken from the default directory for GUI configuration, /etc/X11.

To manage the default desktop, use the switchdesk utility. For example, the following commands set the default desktop to KDE and GNOME, respectively:

```
# switchdesk KDE
# switchdesk GNOME
```

The switchdesk program creates two hidden files in your home directory, ~/.Xclients and ~/.Xclients-default, that are used to start your alternate desktop. You don't need to use **switchdesk**; once you have an ~/.Xclients-default file, you can edit it directly. It is a simple file; if your default desktop is KDE, this file has one line:

```
exec startkde
```

If your default desktop is GNOME, this file has a different line:

```
exec gnome-session
```

Alternatively, you can use switchdesk to set up twm, known as Tom's Window Manager. The version of twm in the latest version of Red Hat Linux includes just the same textured gray screen that you get with the X command. The ~/.Xclients-default file would include the following line:

```
exec /usr/X11R6/bin/twm
```

If you have other desktops or window managers installed, you can use those instead. When run at the command line, the switchdesk command can also let you set FVWM, Enlightenment, or WindowMaker as the default window manager. You'll see the new default the next time you run the **startx** command from a console command line interface.

EXERCISE 7-3

Desktops

Let's use switchdesk to explore the various window managers available to us with Linux.

1. Open a terminal window in a GUI and run the command **switchdesk**.

2. Your current desktop (probably GNOME) is selected. Try one of the other desktops (such as KDE, the other popular desktop for Linux).

3. Log out of your current session. (GNOME Main Menu | Log Out)

4. Log back in again. This time you should see KDE.

5. Try switching to twm. You should see that twm is a much more basic window manager. You'll need to log out again for your changes to take effect. Remember, to exit from twm, which doesn't have a menu button, press CTRL-ALT-BACKSPACE.

6. Run switchdesk one last time. Select your favorite window manager. Log out and back in again to activate your favorite window manager.

Alternatively, you can run switchdesk from a regular console at the command line interface. Just include the name of the window manager or desktop that you want as your new default. Try at least KDE, GNOME, and twm. If you have the FVWM, Enlightenment, or WindowMaker window managers installed, you can try these as well.

Commercial Unix vendors like Sun Microsystems and Hewlett-Packard have officially endorsed GNOME and are working to make their proprietary versions of Unix (Solaris and HP-UX) fully GNOME-compliant. If you get comfortable with GNOME, you will find moving to Solaris or HP-UX much easier. Alternatively, several Linux distributions, including S.u.S.E. and Caldera, use KDE as their default desktop.

Startup

You can configure the X Window interface to start automatically when your system boots, or you can choose to start the X Window System manually. Recall that this is the last decision you make when running redhat-config-xfree86.

For regular users, if the X Window configuration appears to be working correctly, you will probably want to go ahead and tell redhat-config-xfree86 to make the changes necessary to boot that computer directly into the Linux GUI. Otherwise, Red Hat will boot with a text-based console screen, and you can start the X Window System manually by using the startx command.

startx

You use the startx command to start the X Window interface manually from a command line prompt. Simply type

```
startx
```

at the Linux command prompt. This starts XFree86 and switches your display into graphics mode. If you run startx and the X Window System is already started, you will receive an error message telling you that an X server is already running on your display.

When you exit an X Window session that was started through startx, your display returns to the command line interface.

The startx command is actually a customizable shell script that serves as a front end to the xinit command. The default location for both the startx and xinit is /usr/X11R6/bin.

You can still use the virtual console feature of Red Hat Linux when you're running the X Window System. You can switch between six text consoles and one GUI console. You can use several key combinations to control your X Window session (Table 7-3).

You can use a number of configuration files to customize the behavior of your X Window session. These files are hidden files that reside in your home directory. Typically they are shell scripts, read and executed by the X Window startup routines. If the X Window startup program doesn't find a particular configuration file in your home directory, it will use a system-wide default version of the same file.

Look at two of the starting lines in the startx script, located in /usr/X11R6/bin/startx:

```
userclientrc=$HOME/.xinitrc
sysclientrc=/etc/X11/xinit/xinitrc
```

When you start the X Window System with the startx command, the xinit program looks for a file to run named .xinitrc in your home directory. If the startx command cannot find $HOME/.xinitrc, it will run the file /etc/X11/xinit/xinitrc. This file, in turn, will run either the file $HOME /.Xclients or, if that file doesn't exist, /etc/X11/xinit/Xclients.

The ~/.xinitrc file usually contains a series of commands that start various X clients. (Remember, the tilde (~) represents the home directory.) Figure 7-10 shows an example of a simple ~/.xinitrc file. The first line tells Linux which shell program

TABLE 7-3	Key Combinations for the X Window System

Key Combinations	Description
CTRL-ALT-F1 through CTRL-ALT-F6	Switch from X Window GUI to virtual console 1, 2, etc.
ALT-F7	Switches from text console to X Window GUI.
CTRL-ALT-+(plus sign on the numeric keypad) CTRL-ALT--(minus sign on the numeric keypad)	Toggle forward or backward between X Window video modes.
CTRL-ALT-BACKSPACE	Terminates the X Window session.

FIGURE 7-10

A simple.
~/.xinitrc file can
customize startx.

```
#!/bin/bash
xterm &
xclock -geometry 200x200-20+20 &
xcalc -geometry 300x300-20-20 &
exec twm
~
~
~
~
~
~
~
```

to use to run the ~/.xinitrc script. The next line starts up an xterm terminal client. The following line starts up the xclock application to display a clock on your screen. The line after that brings up an X Window calculator. Notice that the first two command lines end with an ampersand (&). This is important; it tells the shell to run each command line and return control to the calling program (~/.xinitrc) without waiting for the program started on the command line to finish running. The final line in the ~/.xinitrc file uses the exec command to start the twm window manager. This tells Linux to run the twm program and specifies that twm should take control of the process that is running the .xinitrc shell script so that when the twm process exits—that is, when you choose to exit the X Window System—the other programs started by the ~/.xinitrc process will be terminated.

You can create an ~/.xinitrc file with any text editor. After you have saved the file and exited the editor, you should make sure the file is executable by issuing this command:

```
chmod a+x ~/.xinitrc
```

Remember, the a switch applies this command to all users. Now take a look at what this does to the GUI. The next time you use startx to start the Linux GUI, you'll see the components that you configured in the ~/.xinitrc file in the twm window manager, as shown in Figure 7-11.

Text and Graphical Login Modes

In order to gain access to a Linux system, you need to log in. In other words, you identify yourself to the system with a username and a password. But this requires a login program. When you log into Linux at a regular command line interface,

FIGURE 7-11

Simplified GUI
configuration

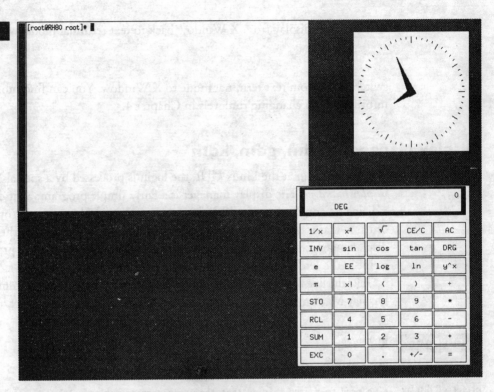

mingetty calls up a login program that prompts you for your username and password.
Six mingetty terminals are configured through /etc/inittab.

It's easy to change the default boot mode from the command line to X Window.
Just edit the /etc/inittab file. Go to the line with initdefault. To make the X Window
System your default runlevel when Linux starts, use your favorite text editor and
change the line in /etc/inittab that reads

```
id:3:initdefault:
```

to

```
id:5:initdefault:
```

Of course, you can reverse this process. Note that this change will not take effect
until you reboot. If you are running as the root user, you can also use the init
command to switch between runlevel 5 and runlevel 3. Running this command

```
/sbin/init 3
```

switches your display from X Window back to text terminal mode, whereas

```
/sbin/init 5
```

switches you from text terminal mode to X Window. You can find more information on changing runlevels in Chapter 4.

Display Managers: xdm, gdm, kdm

When you log in at the Linux GUI, the login is processed by a special X client, the *display manager.* The display manager is a fairly simple program; all it does is display a dialog box on the screen asking for your username and password. You can use any of three major display managers. The default display manager is the GNOME display manager, or gdm. To change your display manager, edit the prefdm shell script in the /etc/X11 directory, as shown in Figure 7-12.

Take the line that contains preferred= and add either kdm, gdm, or xdm for the KDE Display Manager, GNOME Display Manager, or X Display Manager, respectively.

FIGURE 7-12

Set your preferred display manager in /etc/X11/prefdm.

```
#!/bin/sh

PATH=/sbin:/usr/sbin:/bin:/usr/bin:/usr/X11R6/bin

# We need to source this so that the login screens get translated
[ -f /etc/profile.d/lang.sh ] && . /etc/profile.d/lang.sh

# Run preferred X display manager

 Try autologin first, if wanted...
 if [ -f /etc/sysconfig/autologin -a -x /usr/sbin/autologin ]; then
        if /usr/sbin/autologin; then
                exit 0
        fi
        # If autologin fails (bad permissions, etc.), we get here -
        # time to start a real display manager.
 fi

preferred=xdm
if [ -f /etc/sysconfig/desktop ]; then
        . /etc/sysconfig/desktop
        [ -n "$DISPLAYMANAGER" ] && DESKTOP=$DISPLAYMANAGER
        if [ "$DESKTOP" = GNOME ]; then
                preferred=gdm
        elif [ "$DESKTOP" = KDE -o "$DESKTOP" = KDE1 -o "$DESKTOP" = KDE2 ]; then
                preferred=kdm
        fi
fi
```

How you start the X Window System affects how it behaves. Assume you start X Window through one of the graphical display managers. When you exit an X Window session, you're returned to the same display manager. To continue, you would need to login again.

The default behavior for the gdm window manager is to launch a GNOME session for you. The kdm window manager launches a KDE session. As an alternative to using the switchdesk utility, both the gdm window manager and the kdm window manager have option buttons to allow you to log in under a different desktop environment than the default. You can even set up the generic xdm window manager, which gives you the login screen shown in Figure 7-13.

If you log in using a display manager, X Window starts somewhat differently when compared to using startx. When you run startx, the X Window session runs as a child process of your text-based login shell. You can verify this with the runlevel command. Even though the X Window System is running, Linux is still at runlevel 3. After you exit the X Window System, you still have to log out of this shell to terminate your login session.

FIGURE 7-13

An xdm login
screen

When you log in from a display manager, Linux does not start an interactive shell. Instead, the display manager launches a program called the session manager, which is the controlling process for your X Window login session. If you are running the GNOME desktop, this program is /usr/bin/gnome-session; if you are running KDE, it is /usr/bin/kwin.

All X clients that you run from your X Window session are child processes of the session manager process. When you exit the session manager, all child processes of the session manager are terminated also. When you log in via a display manager, the session manager does not use the ~/.xinitrc configuration file.

Through the use of option buttons, both the GNOME and KDE display managers allow you to choose the desktop environment you wish to start. From the GNOME display manager, click the Sessions menu, then select the session manager you want to use. This is shown in Figure 7-14. From the KDE display manager, click the drop-down text box adjacent to session type. This is shown in Figure 7-15. Both GNOME and the KDE environment use their own startup files.

FIGURE 7-14

The GNOME
display manager

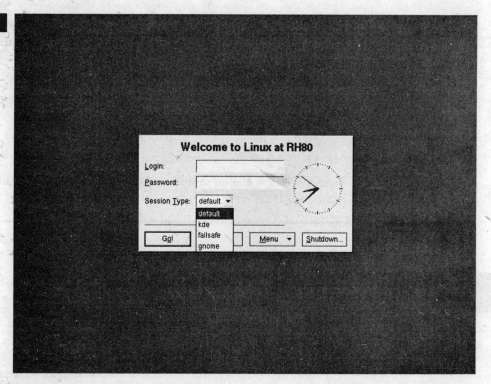

FIGURE 7-15

The KDE display manager

EXERCISE 7-4

startx

In this exercise, we will start the X Window System using startx with a customized .xinitrc file.

1. If the X Window System is running, change to a text console by pressing CTRL-ALT-F1.

2. If you see a login prompt, log in at the text console as root. Otherwise, press CTRL-C to stop X Window.

3. If you logged in at the text console, stop the current X Window server by typing this:

```
/sbin/init 3
```

4. Make sure you're in your home directory. Use your favorite text editor to create a .xinitrc file. If you're not sure what to do, use the sample file shown in Figure 7-10.

5. Make sure the .xinitrc file is executable by typing this:

```
chmod a+x .xinitrc
```

6. Start the X Window System by typing this:

```
startx
```

Your X Window session should automatically start the applications in your .xinitrc file.

CERTIFICATION OBJECTIVE 7.04

Remote Display of X Apps

One of the most powerful features of the X Window System is the strength of its networking support. The X Window System was designed from the beginning to run in a networked environment. If you are a system manager with a number of Red Hat Linux systems under your care, there's no need to leave your office and make a journey to the server room every time you want to run a GUI administration tool. With the X Window System, you can connect to any number of systems and redirect the output from X clients running on those systems back to the X server running on your desktop.

Security

Before you can run remote clients and have them redirect their output back to your X server, take a look at some of the basics of X Window security. When working with remote X applications, all other Linux security features are still in effect. You will still need a user account and password in order to connect to the remote system to start an X client. You need to make sure that a firewall isn't blocking access.

Authentication problems or network problems at layers below the X Window System can prevent your X Window client applications from running.

Part of the job of the X server running on your local computer is to listen for requests from X clients that want to send their output to your display. Those requests can come from applications that are running on your local computer, or they can come from applications running on another computer on your network.

Without some form of access control, any X client application on any system on your network can send its output to the display controlled by your X server. This includes client applications started up by other users on other systems. Although on a small network you might want to allow indiscriminate network access to your display, in a larger network environment or a production network environment, you will want to limit who can send client output to your X server.

The simplest way to control access to your display is with the xhost command. The xhost command controls access to your X server display on a computer-by-computer basis. Table 7-4 shows how you use the xhost command to secure your X server. Note that you can substitute IP addresses for specific computer host names, when appropriate.

The xhost command allows you to control X Server security on your computer. One more sophisticated alternative is the xauth command, which can use encryption to verify not just remote computers, but the permissions that you may grant to remote users. Access information for these other validation methods is stored in the hidden binary file ~/.Xauthority.

If the DISPLAY variable has not been set, xhost may not work. You can set a local DISPLAY variable with a simple equation such as DISPLAY=localhost:0.0. Then you can export that variable with the export DISPLAY command.

TABLE 7-4	Command	Description
Using xhost to Secure Your X Server	xhost	Show current security settings.
	xhost +	Disable security; allow connections from any system.
	xhost -	Enable security.
	xhost +apps.xyz.com	Allow connection from apps.xyz.com.
	xhost -apps.xyz.com	Disable connections from apps.xyz.com.

Remote X Clients

Running a remote X client requires that you have access to the remote system on which the client will run. In turn, the remote system, and possibly the account you are using on the remote system, must have permission to connect to the X server display that the X client you start will use for its console. In the following example, we will take a step-by-step look at running an X client on a remote system, apps.xyz.com, and sending the output back to our local desktop computer, desk.xyz.com.

The first step in the process is to make sure we allow apps access to the display on our local system. You need to run this from a command line in the Linux GUI:

```
xhost +apps.xyz.com
```

If we have already granted apps access to our display, we can skip this step.

The next step in the process is to log in to apps. Here, we will use the telnet command, but this could be done using any program, such as rsh, ssh, or rlogin, that allows us to establish a remote login session on server1:

```
[root@desk]$ telnet apps.xyz.com
Trying 192.168.1.2...
Connected to apps.xyz.com.
Escape character is '^]'.
Red Hat Linux release 8.0
Kernel 2.4.18-10 on an i586
login: mj
password:
[mj@apps]$
```

on the **job**

Telnet is not a secure form of communication on a network, and it may be blocked by a firewall. However, firewalls aren't necessary between computers on an internal network. In addition, Telnet is disabled by default in Red Hat Linux. Enabling Telnet requires several steps: make sure the Telnet port (23) is not blocked in your firewall, and then make sure telnet is enabled in the /etc/xinetd.d/telnet configuration file.

Since we are going to be running X Window client applications, we will probably want to make sure the X Window binary directory is in our search path. Check with the **echo $PATH** command; if it isn't there, you can add it with the following command:

```
[mj@apps]$ PATH=$PATH:/usr/X11R6/bin
```

The final step in the process is to start our remote X client, or X clients if we plan to start up more than one remote program. At this point, we can choose to start our X client in one of two ways. For this example, we will start the same X client application using each method. The X client program we will run is xclock.

Since X Window clients behave like Linux applications, all we need to do to run the xclock program is type the program name on the command line. Since this program is an X Window client application, however, we need to provide it with one crucial piece of information: the name of the X server it is going to use. We can provide this information on the command line when we start the application by specifying the -display option:

```
[root@apps]$ xclock -display desk.xyz.com:0.0 &
```

This starts the xclock application on the computer named apps, but the output from the program is displayed on the computer named desk. At this point, your telnet session on desk appears to be locked up. This is because the xclock application is running as your foreground process. Unless you received an error message when you started the application, you can't tell if anything is happening on server1. The output from xclock is being sent to the X server on desk. To regain control of your telnet session, you can either terminate xclock by pressing CTRL-C, or you can suspend it by pressing CTRL-Z. If you are going to be starting multiple X client applications, you should end each command line with an ampersand (&) to tell Linux to run the X client as a background process.

The second part of the DISPLAY line (0.0) requires further explanation. A single X server can control multiple GUI displays attached to a single system. Each GUI display has its own set of input and output devices (monitor, keyboard, and mouse). In addition, each GUI display can have multiple screens or monitors. When you are redirecting the output for an X client, you must tell it not only which system to connect to but also which GUI display and which screen on that display to use. On most systems this will be servername, display 0, console 0 (written as *host*:0.0). The server portion of this entry can be a hostname, a fully qualified domain name, or an IP address. The following are all valid specifications for remote displays:

- desk:0.0
- desk.xyz.com:0.0
- 192.168.1.5:0.0

The other method for starting an X client from the command prompt uses a shell environment variable to pass the display information to the X client. When you start an X client without the -display option, the X client looks for the DISPLAY environment variable in your current process. In fact, this is how X clients you run on your local system determine where to send their output. When you log in to your workstation from the display manager, the DISPLAY variable is automatically set to point to the X server running on your workstation. If you are connecting to a remote host and will be starting multiple X clients, you should set this variable so that you don't have to specify the -display option for every X client you run. Having pressed CTRL-C to regain control of our telnet session, we can set the DISPLAY variable and rerun xclock:

```
[root@apps]$ export DISPLAY=desk.xyz.com:0.0      # works on sh,ksh,bash
[root@apps]$ xclock
```

Troubleshooting

The X Window System is very robust and stable, but occasionally problems can arise. You can try several things when you troubleshoot X Window problems:

- Session managers create log files in your home directory such as ~/ .xsession-errors. Check these log files as well as /var/log/messages and /var/log/ XFree86.0.log for error messages from your X server.

- Problems with the .xinitrc or .Xclients shell scripts may cause problems. Try deleting or renaming these files.

- Check the DISPLAY environment variable to make sure it is set correctly. If you are running X clients locally, they still use this variable. You can set it with this command:

   ```
   export DISPLAY=localhost:0.0
   ```

   or

   ```
   export DISPLAY=:0.0
   ```

- Make sure /usr/X11R6/bin is in your $PATH.

- Check for underlying system problems or network problems that could be causing problems with the X Window System.

- Check the X Font Server for problems described earlier in this chapter.
- Even if your X server is not responding or you can't read the display, don't forget that you can switch to a text console to gain access to the system.
- If you are troubleshooting X server problems on a remote system, try starting an X client from your workstation using the remote X server's display. Note that you will need appropriate X security access to do this:

```
xclock -display remotesys:0.0
```

EXERCISE 7-5

Troubleshooting DISPLAY Problems

In this exercise, we will see what happens if you unset the DISPLAY variable.

1. Log in to an X Window session.
2. Bring up a terminal window from the panel or a menu.
3. Start the xclock application using this command:

```
xclock &
```

4. Unset your DISPLAY variable:

```
unset DISPLAY
```

5. Start another xclock:

```
xclock &
```

6. You should get an error message saying that the X client can't find your display. Reset the DISPLAY variable with the command:

```
export DISPLAY=localhost:0.0
```

7. Try starting the xclock application again.

Now that you have seen how X Window clients and the X Window server work together, refer to the following Scenario & Solution for some common situations you may encounter, along with their solutions.

SCENARIO & SOLUTION

I'm having problems getting XFree86 to run on my hardware.	Check the Red Hat hardware support site. Run redhat-config-xfree86. If that doesn't work, try xf86config.
I want to use a different desktop environment.	Use the switchdesk utility to change your desktop environment.
I want to stop the X Window System without halting Linux.	Use the /sbin/init command to change the system runlevel to runlevel 3.
I'm having problems starting an X client.	Check that the DISPLAY variable is set and exported. For example: # export DISPLAY=localhost:0.0 Check for underlying network problems. Check X security problems.
My X Window display is acting strangely and I can't log in.	Switch to a virtual console and log in. Check the error logs. See if your X Font Server (xfs) is running. If it isn't, check for errors in ~/.xsession-errors and /var/log/messages. A full /tmp or /home directory can also keep xfs from starting. As a last resort, rerun redhat-config-xfree86.

CERTIFICATION SUMMARY

The X Window System provides a state-of-the-art graphical user interface and offers features not found in other GUI environments. Although the X Window System can be complicated, the redhat-config-xfree86 program simplifies the process of setting it up. One of the most important steps you can take in setting up the X Window System on Red Hat Linux is to select graphics cards and monitors that are supported by the XFree86 X server.

The look and feel of the X Window interface is determined by your choice of window manager. Red Hat Linux comes with several desktop environments, including GNOME, KDE, twm, AfterStep, WindowMaker, and fvwm. The GNOME desktop interface is the default for Red Hat Linux.

The X Window System is designed to run on networked systems. You run client applications, both locally and remotely, that use the X server on your workstation for their console.

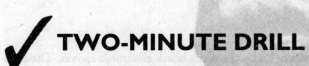

✓ TWO-MINUTE DRILL

Here are some of the key points from the certification objectives in Chapter 7.

X Server

❑ The X server is the software that manages the graphics display on the local computer, which includes your monitor/graphics adapter, keyboard, and mouse.

❑ X servers work with local and remote X clients to keep your display up-to-date. X servers send inputs from the keyboard and mouse to X clients. Then X clients send instructions to the X server to update the graphics on the monitor.

❑ The latest X server included with Red Hat Linux is XFree86 version 4. But some graphics cards are only supported under the older version of XFree86, 3.36.

❑ The preferred Red Hat Linux configuration tool for XFree86 is redhat-config-xfree86. It provides an easy way to edit the /etc/X11/XF86Config file.

X Clients

❑ Red Hat Linux provides a great number of X client programs for your use. Popular programs include terminal emulators, desktop accessories (such as the File Manager), games, and more.

❑ The list of supplied X clients includes graphics manipulation tools (GIMP, the GNU Image Manipulation Tool), CD players, and more.

❑ You can send the display of an X client program to a remote system by using the -display option followed by the remote system and display (-display my.machine.com:0.0).

❑ The X Window System cannot start unless you have a functioning X Font Server. If you ever have a problem starting X Window, the xfs service may not be running, possibly due to a full /tmp filesystem.

Window Managers

❑ The X Window System just gives you a blank electronic canvas. The look and feel of a GUI is provided by the window manager and desktop.

❑ The two main desktop environments are GNOME and KDE.

❑ You can use switchdesk from a terminal window or the command line interface console to select your default desktop.

Startup

❑ You can configure the X Window interface to start automatically, or you can start it manually from the command line console with the startx command.

❑ The startx command uses settings in the ~/.xinitrc or /etc/X11/xinit/xinitrc file to load the desktop and X clients that you configure.

❑ You can set up graphical logins with the X display manager, the KDE display manager, or the GNOME display manager.

Remote Display of X Apps

❑ By default, X clients send display outputs to the local computer.

❑ You can send display output to other computers with the -display command line option.

❑ The remote system must be willing to accept your remote request. On the remote system, use the xhosts + command to accept display information from the remote computer.

❑ You can set the DISPLAY environment variable on the X client computer to direct all display output to a remote X server.

SELF TEST

The following questions will help you measure your understanding of the material presented in this chapter. Read all the choices carefully, as there may be more than one correct answer. Choose all correct answers for each question.

X Server

1. Which of the following is true about the X Window System?

   A. The X server runs on your workstation; X clients run on your workstation or on other computers on the network.

   B. If an X server is running on your workstation, then X client applications running on your computer cannot send their output to an X server running on another system on the network.

   C. An X client application gets its input from the keyboard and mouse attached to the same X server where the client is sending its output.

   D. Aside from the steps necessary to start the remote application, there is no difference between running an X client locally and running one remotely.

2. Your supervisor comes to you and says he is thinking of purchasing some new workstations for the graphics department and that he has decided they will run Red Hat Linux. However, they must be purchased and installed as quickly as possible. He has found what appears to be a good deal on some brand-name systems and would like you to determine whether they will be suitable for the planned task. You follow up on his suggestion and discover that the video card for the systems is built around a completely new video chip design, not yet supported by Red Hat. What recommendation do you make regarding the purchase?

   A. Go ahead and purchase the systems as they are.

   B. Since the graphics department will use these systems, make sure they have plenty of disk space to store graphics files.

   C. Purchase the systems, but have the vendor replace the new video cards with a model that is listed on the Red Hat Linux support site.

   D. Make sure the systems have 100 Mbps Ethernet cards so that graphics files can be transferred across the network as quickly as possible.

3. You performed a new install of Red Hat Linux and ran into problems when you tried to install the X Window System. Your system is now active, and you can log in to a command prompt. How do you go about reconfiguring the X Window System?

    A. Use the vi editor and modify the /etc/X11/XF86Config file.

    B. Run the redhat-config-xfree86 utility from the command line.

    C. Run the xf86config utility from the command line.

    D. Reinstall Red Hat Linux.

4. A user who is new to the X Window System calls you with a question about his mouse. He has been reading some documentation, and it keeps referring to his middle mouse button, but he only has a two-button mouse. What do you tell him?

    A. Hold down the CTRL key and click the left mouse button.

    B. He will have to purchase a three-button mouse to use the X Window interface.

    C. Click the left and right mouse buttons simultaneously.

    D. He will have to run redhat-config-xfree86 and configure the X Window System to use a two-button mouse.

5. Your X Window configuration appears to be working, and you have an gnome-terminal window open on your desktop. Whenever you try to start other X clients from the command line, however, you keep getting the error message "command not found." What is the likely cause of the problem?

    A. You have too many X clients running, and Linux is unable to start any additional applications.

    B. The /usr/X11R6/bin directory is missing from your PATH.

    C. The /etc/X11/XF86Config directory is missing from your PATH.

    D. You need to use the xhost command to allow X clients to access your server.

X Clients

6. You want to start an xterm X client that is 80 columns wide by 30 lines high from the command line and position it in the upper-right corner of your display when it starts. What command would you use?

    A. xterm -geometry +0-0 -font 80×30

    B. xterm -geometry 80×30-0+0

C. xterm -geometry 80~~-30-0-0~~

D. xterm -display 80×30-0+0

7. Which of the following are valid X client command line options?

A. -display

B. -windowsize

C. -background

D. -forecolor

E. -bordercolor

Window Managers

8. When you migrate a Windows 98 user to a Linux workstation, what steps can you take to minimize the learning curve for this person?

A. Install the full set of online documentation.

B. Configure the GNOME desktop environment.

C. Use the switchdesk utility and set the user's desktop environment to KDE.

D. Set Linux to boot to runlevel 3.

9. You are using the GNOME desktop environment. You know that you just started up the GNOME spreadsheet application, but now it seems to have disappeared from your screen. How can you get it back?

A. Look at the task bar at the bottom of the screen and see if you have accidentally switched virtual desktops.

B. Log out and log back in. GNOME will restart the application.

C. Use the Main Menu button to restart the application.

D. Run the switchdesk utility.

10. You are troubleshooting a system that appears not to have been set to boot into the X Window System, but you know that the system has been configured to run an X server. What is the first step you should try?

A. Type X to start the X server.

B. Run the startx command to start the X Window System.

C. Edit /etc/X11/XF86Config and set the X Window System to start on system boot.

D. Run the file .xinitrc in your home directory.

11. When you installed Red Hat Linux, you configured the X Window System but chose not to have Linux boot up with the X Window System running. You have been starting the X Window System with the startx command and everything is working without any problems. You would now like to make the X Window GUI the default runlevel for your system. How would you do this?

   A. Edit /etc/inittab and look for the line that reads "id:3:initdefault," replace it with a line that reads "id:5:initdefault," and reboot.

   B. Run redhat-config-xfree86.

   C. Change the /etc/X11/prefdm link.

   D. Execute the runlevel 5 command.

12. You are troubleshooting a Linux server that boots into runlevel 5 and need to temporarily shut down the X Window System. How would you do this?

   A. Use the ps command to obtain the process of the XFree86 server and use the kill command to stop it.

   B. Edit /etc/inittab and look for the line that reads "id:3:initdefault," then replace it with a line that reads "id:5:initdefault" and reboot.

   C. Use the /sbin/init 3 command.

   D. Use the stopx command.

13. Your system is using the xdm display manager. You want to use the GNOME display manager (gdm). How can you do this?

   A. Change the /etc/X11/prefdm shell script and define the preferred= variable.

   B. Run redhat-config-xfree86.

   C. Edit /etc/X11/XF86Config.

   D. Use the GNOME Control Panel to change the display manager.

Startup

14. You would like to automatically start up the xclock application whenever you start up an X Window session with startx. How would you do this?

   A. Create or edit the file .Xdefault and add this command:

   ```
   xclock &
   ```

B. Create or edit the file xinitrc in the /etc/X11/xinit directory with this command:

```
xclock -geometry 200x200-0+0 &
```

C. Edit /etc/X11/XF86Config and add this command:

```
xclock -geometry 200x200-0+0 &
```

D. Create or edit the file .xinitrc in your home directory and add this command:

```
xclock &
```

15. How could you start a KDE session from a system running the gdm display manager?

A. Relink /etc/X11/prefdm.

B. Click the Sessions menu on the gdm login message box and select KDE.

C. Log in normally and use switchdesk to change your default desktop.

D. You can't log in to the KDE environment from the gdm display manager.

16. What command would you issue to allow X clients running on the system with an IP address of 172.16.200.99 to access your X server?

A. xauth +172.16.200.99

B. xhost -172.16.200.99

C. xhost +

D. xhost +172.16.200.99

Remote Display of X Apps

17. You log in to a remote system via telnet with the intention of starting up several remote X clients that will send their output to your local display (admin1.xyz.com). What can you do to make this easier?

A. Use the -display admin1.xyz.com option.

B. Create a DISPLAY variable with this command:

```
DISPLAY=admin1.xyz.com:0.0
```

C. Create a DISPLAY variable with this command:

```
export DISPLAY=admin1.xyz.com
```

D. Create a DISPLAY variable with this command:

```
export DISPLAY=admin1.xyz.com:0.0
```

18. A user calls up to report that she is having problems getting a remote molecular modeling application to display on her screen. Assuming she has disabled all security on her X server, how could you use the display option to help troubleshoot the situation? Your workstation is admin1.xyz.com; her workstation is ws97.xyz.com.

    A. Tell her to run the redhat-config-xfree86 utility with the -display option so that you know what kind of monitor she is using.

    B. Have her try to start an X client and direct its display to her X server with this command:

```
xclock -display localhost:0.0
```

    C. Have her try to start an X client and direct its display to your X server with this command:

```
xclock -display admin1.xyz.com:0.0
```

    D. You start an X client from the command line and direct its display to her X server with this command:

```
xclock -display ws97.xyz.com:0.0
```

19. The X server on your company's Web server appears to be locked up. How might you gain access to the console?

    A. Press CTRL-ALT- +

    B. Press CTRL-ALT-F1.

    C. Press ALT-F1.

    D. Press CTRL-ALT-DEL to reboot the system.

20. You're trying to gain Telnet access to another computer on your LAN, so you can run X clients from the remote system. That computer is refusing access. Neither computer has a firewall. What do you need to do on that remote computer before it will accept your Telnet inputs?

    A. Restart telnet with the **/etc/rc.d/init.d/telnet restart** command.

    B. Enable telnet in the /etc/xinted.d/telnet configuration file

    C. Disable firewalls on the network.

    D. Restart xinetd with the **/etc/rc.d/inet.d/xinetd restart** command.

LAB QUESTION

Part 1

We want to upgrade the video card in our Linux system. Our old video card is slow and doesn't have enough display memory to provide us with the resolution and color depth we require. We have obtained a new ATI 32MB Radeon card (I'm using this product for example purposes only). What steps might we follow to replace our old card with our new card?

Part 2

We want to see what happens when there are problems starting the Linux GUI. This lab assumes that your computer is configured with XFree86 Version 4.x; in this case, you'll have an /etc/X11/XF86Config configuration file. Before X Window starts, it reads this file.

1. Back up your XFree86 configuration file.

2. Delete /etc/X11/XF86Config.

3. If Linux starts in console mode when you start your computer, edit the /etc/inittab file. Change the starting runlevel to 5.

4. Reboot your computer

5. What happens?

SELF TEST ANSWERS

X Server

1. ☑ **A, C, and D. A** is correct because the X server runs on the system that has the graphics hardware, while X clients may run locally or remotely. **C** is correct because the X server sends keyboard and mouse inputs to local or remote X clients. **D** is also correct because remote X clients interact with the X server in the same way as a local X client.

   ☒ **B** is incorrect because there simply is no such restriction.

2. ☑ **C.** Since the workstations are going to be used by the graphics department, they are going to be running the X Window System. Although you might be able to get the new video cards working given ample time for experimentation, the requirement to have the new workstations up as quickly as possible precludes this. To be sure you don't have any problems configuring the X Window System, it is best to replace the newer video card with a supported video card.

   ☒ **A** would require you to find drivers for the new video hardware. Since they may not even exist, you might be forced to write the drivers yourself. This would add unnecessary costs and delays to your workstation rollout. **B** and **D** are incorrect because the size of the graphics files used is irrelevant to the project if you don't have the capability to manipulate them.

3. ☑ **B and C.** You should use the redhat-config-xfree86 program any time you need to make changes to your X Window configuration. The xf86config utility is a command line alternative to redhat-config-xfree86.

   ☒ **A** is possibly correct assuming we understand enough about the XF86Config file to make the necessary changes. From experience, I would suggest you only edit this file if you have an (almost) working configuration you only wish to fine-tune. **D** is extreme. The only justification for this might be if we performed a custom install and perhaps neglected to include all the components of the X Window System. Even if this is the case, you can still install the needed RPMs from the command line.

4. ☑ **C.** Assuming you've configured the mouse properly, you can emulate the missing middle button by clicking the left and right mouse buttons at the same time.

   ☒ **A** won't provide the effect of clicking the middle mouse button. **B** will work but is unnecessary. Also, if the user does replace the mouse with a three-button mouse, that user would have to run mouseconfig (as root) to update their mouse settings. **D** is incorrect. While you can use redhat-config-xfree86 to use a two-button mouse, it does not help the user get the functionality of the middle mouse button.

5. ☑ **B.** Any time you receive the message "command not found," it suggests that your PATH variable is set incorrectly. In order to run X client applications without having to specify an

absolute pathname, make sure the /usr/X11R6/bin directory is in your search path.

☒ **A** is incorrect because Linux should let you start as many applications as you desire. Even if you run up against an X client limit, you won't get a "command not found" message. **C** is incorrect because this is a configuration file. Only directories belong in the PATH variable. **D** is also incorrect because X clients are supposed to have access to the local X server. Besides, if this were truly the case, the X client would complain that it "cannot open display," rather than the shell saying the command was not found.

X Clients

6. ☑ **B.** The correct option is -geometry 80×30-0+0. Since you are creating a terminal window, the size specification 80×30 refers to the number of columns and lines. The offset specification -0+0 specifies that the right border of the xterm window should be offset 0 pixels from the right edge of the display and that the top border of the xterm window should be offset 0 pixels from the top of the display.

☒ **A** is incorrect because the -font option is used to specify the default font for the window, not the window location. **C** is incorrect because the window size is specified by 80×30, not 80+30. **D** is incorrect because -display is the wrong switch for sizing and positioning the xterm window.

7. ☑ **A, C,** and **E** are valid command line options for X clients. The -display option identifies the system that receives the display for this command. -background sets the background color, and -bordercolor sets the border color for the window.

☒ **B** is incorrect because the -windowsize option does not exist. The window size is set by the first two values of the -display option. **D** is incorrect because the -forecolor option does not exist. The foreground color is set with the -foreground option.

Window Managers

8. ☑ **C.** The KDE desktop (available as an option box) from switchdesk can be configured to closely resemble the look and feel of Windows 9x. This interface would be a good choice for someone migrating from that operating system.

☒ **A** is likely incorrect because, while the Linux online documentation is (usually) useful, it is presented in a manner different from Windows 9x. **B** is incorrect because the GNOME environment is quite different from Windows 9x. **D** is incorrect because at runlevel 3, the user would only see the command line. If they were only comfortable working with a GUI, the Linux command line would be very uncomfortable to them!

9. ☑ **A.** GNOME sets up four virtual desktops that you can switch between just by clicking the desired desktop. It is possible (if you aren't used to virtual desktops) that you could have

accidentally switched to another virtual desktop. All you would need to do to find your application would be to click your other virtual desktops until you found your application.

☒ **B** is incorrect because if you log out of GNOME, all your applications will be terminated. While GNOME is "session-aware," that only applies after an application is restarted. **C** is incorrect because restarting your application would give you a new instance of that application, but wouldn't necessarily provide you with the same information/updates you had in the application you misplaced. **D** is incorrect because the switchdesk utility determines the default GUI desktop, which does not address the missing application.

10. ☑ **B.** The startx command is used to start the X Window System if it is not already started.

☒ **A** is incorrect because, by running X, you would get an X server with no window managers and no client programs. The session would be unusable. **C** is incorrect because the file you edit to start X automatically on the next boot is /etc/inittab. **D** is incorrect because the .xinitrc command is used to launch X clients automatically when the server starts. It is incapable of starting the server itself.

11. ☑ **A.** The easiest way to change the default runlevel for your Linux system is to edit the /etc/inittab file and change the initdefault setting to runlevel 5. You could then enter the command **/sbin/init 5** to change to runlevel 5.

☒ **B** is incorrect because redhat-config-xfree86 does not provide any facility for changing /etc/inittab. **C** is incorrect because this just configures the preferred display manager. **D** is incorrect because the runlevel command is used to report on the previous and current runlevels, not to set the new default runlevel.

12. ☑ **C.** You use the init command to change from the X Window runlevel to runlevel 3. This will shut down the X server. You can restart the X Window System by issuing an **/sbin/init 5** command.

☒ **A** is incorrect because, even if you did shut down the X server this way, the init process would just detect the termination of the X server and launch a new one. **B** is incorrect because the change recommended would permanently change the system to turn off graphics mode, and the question asked for a temporary change only. **D** is incorrect because there is no such command.

13. ☑ **A.** The file /etc/X11/prefdm is a script that starts your preferred display manager. By default, the preferred= variable is not set, so Red Hat launches gdm (the GNOME display manager). To force a different display manager, set the preferred= variable to either kdm (for the KDE display manager) or xdm (for the X display manager).

☒ **B** is incorrect because redhat-config-xfree86 does not set the preferred display manager. **C** is incorrect because the preferred display manager is not set in XF86Config. **D** is incorrect because there is no such option in the GNOME Control Panel.

Startup

14. ☑ **D.** The startx command can be run by any user, not just the root account. You should put any customization commands in the .xinitrc hidden file in your home directory.

☒ **A** is incorrect because .Xdefault is not used to launch applications when your X server is started. **B** is incorrect because it says we need to make an .xinitrc file in the /etc/X11/xinit directory. We actually need to make it in our account's home directory. **C** is incorrect because the XF86Config file is used to configure the X server to the correct hardware settings, not launch a user's favorite applications.

15. ☑ **B** and **C** are both correct. The advantage to B, however, is that you do not have to log out and log back in.

☒ **A** is incorrect because the prefdm file is used to select the preferred display manager on startup. The question specifically states that we need to select a KDE session while running gdm. Clearly, **D** is incorrect.

16. ☑ **D.** The xhost command is used to grant other systems access to your X server. The command xhost +172.16.200.99 enables access only from this remote system.

☒ **A** is incorrect because xauth is the incorrect tool. **B** is incorrect because xhost -172.16.200.99 would disable access for that particular computer. **C** would do the job because it enables access to all remote hosts. While this includes our client system (with an IP of 172.16.200.99), it also includes every other system on the network and consequently does much more than the question asks.

Remote Display of X Apps

17. ☑ **D.** X client applications use the DISPLAY environment variable to determine where to send their output. It must be an environment variable, so you must use the export command to create it.

☒ **A** suggests using the -display option to every remote X client we wish to start. While this is not the easiest way to do it, it could work. To make the option effective, though, we would have to write it as -display admin1.xyz.com:0.0. **B** is incorrect because it makes a variable called DISPLAY with the correct value, but it neglects to export the variable. With the bash shell, (as with the original Bourne shell [sh] and the Korn shell [ksh]), all shell variables are private (unshared) unless they are explicitly exported. **C** is not quite correct. While we do export DISPLAY, we have neglected to identify the X graphics display and the screen (0.0).

18. ☑ **B** and **D.** I would first try B to see if the problem lies with the user's X server configuration, or with the program they are attempting to run. If xclock will run locally but the modeling application won't, then the fault probably lies with the modeling program. Next, I'd see if I could send a simple X client from my workstation to my users. By trying D, I'd be able to determine if the users' X server is correctly responding to remote X client requests. A failure here could be indicative of a network configuration error on the user's computer.

☒ A is incorrect because, while useful, redhat-config-xfree86 won't help determine why an X server that is correctly configured for the local hardware is refusing to allow X clients to use the display. C won't help because having the user send an X client window to my workstation won't help determine the cause of a problem with the user's workstation.

19. ☑ **B.** Since your company Web server is running on the system, you want to try to avoid rebooting. If your X Window display doesn't appear to be working, you can switch to a standard text console with CTRL-ALT-F1. An alternative would be to press the CTRL-ALT-BACKSPACE keys. This sends a termination signal to the local X server.

☒ A is incorrect because CTRL-ALT-+ is used to change between configured resolutions. C is incorrect because ALT-F1 is used within the X server and won't help us gain control of our system. D isn't correct for a number of reasons. While this may work if your initdefault is set to 3 in /etc/inittab, it is a poor idea. Many Linux systems are configured to ignore the CTRL-ALT-DEL key combination. Anyone who is using your server gets cut off and could very well lose their work.

20. ☑ **B, D.** The telnet utility is disabled by default in Red Hat Linux. You need to enable it in /etc/xinetd.d/telnet (answer B) and then restart the xinetd daemon (answer D) to implement the change.

☒ A is incorrect because there is no telnet script in the /etc/rc.d/init.d directory. C is incorrect because there are no firewalls blocking access between the two computers.

LAB ANSWER

Part I

1. Before we bring down our computer, we should configure it so it no longer attempts to start the X server when Linux boots. This is controlled by the initdefault line in the /etc/inittab file. Edit this file and change field two to the value of 3 (Multi-User With No X Support) from the value 5 (Multi-User With X Support). We could use vi, pico, or any other suitable text editor to do this job.

2. Perform an orderly shutdown on our system at a safe time. Use the command **shutdown -h now**.

3. Swap our video card.

4. Power up our Linux system and let it come up in multi-user mode. During the boot process, the Red Hat kudzu tool automatically probes for new hardware. If this probe finds our new video card, we can configure it when prompted.

5. If kudzu (the new hardware probe tool) fails to find our new hardware, we should log in as root and run redhat-config-xfree86.

6. The redhat-config-xfree86 program should correctly identify our new hardware. We should select the correct amount of display memory (32MB) and the graphics resolutions and color depths we desire. Next, redhat-config-xfree86 will request to test our new configuration. Allow it to do so.

7. Finally, redhat-config-xfree86 will ask whether it should arrange to start the X Window System automatically. If you answer yes, Linux will boot to runlevel 5 in the future.

8. Change to runlevel 5 to start using our new, high-performance card. Use the command **/sbin/init 5**.

9. You have just replaced your video card on Red Hat Linux.

Part 2

1. Back up /etc/X11/XF86Config to a safe location such as your home directory.

2. As the root user, delete or rename the /etc/X11/XF86Config file.

3. Open /etc/inittab in your favorite text editor. Look at the line with initdefault. Change the number right before this variable from a 3 to a 5 if required.

4. When you reboot your computer, observe what happens when Linux tries to find the default login display manager.

5. Restore your original settings.

If you are interested in more experiments, try deactivating the X Font Server. Run the **/sbin/chkconfig xfs off** command. Change your initdefault in /etc/inittab from 3 to 5 again. Restart your computer and observe what happens.

8

Network
Client Services

U

nix was developed by AT&T in the late 1960s and early 1970s, and was freely distributed among a number of major universities during this time. Concurrently, these universities were developing the network that evolved into the Internet.

When AT&T started charging for Unix, a number of developers tried to create clones of this operating system. In one of these efforts, Linux was developed in the early 1990s.

With current refinements, this makes Linux perhaps the most Internet-friendly network operating system available. The extensive network services available with Linux are not only the tops in their field, they create one of the most powerful and useful Internet-ready platforms available today at any price.

Red Hat Linux includes the Apache Web Server. According to the Netcraft (www.netcraft.com) survey, which tracks the Web server associated with virtually every site on the Internet, Apache is currently used by more Internet Web sites than all the other Web servers combined.

The anonymous FTP and WU_FTP (Washington University FTP) packages provide both basic and secure FTP server services. With WU-FTP, you can secure users, directories, subdirectories, and files with various levels of access control.

Other standard services in the Linux/Unix world are e-mail services using the sendmail SMTP server and the POP and IMAP e-mail client services. These are the de facto standards for e-mail on the Internet.

Along with the traditional network services already mentioned, Red Hat Linux also provides interoperability packages for all of the most popular operating systems, including Windows (SMB/Samba) and Macintosh (Netatalk) networking.

Windows-based operating systems use the SMB file and print sharing protocol on top of TCP/IP. Samba services provide a stable, reliable, fast, and highly compatible file and print sharing service that allows your computer to act as a client, a server, or even a Domain Controller on Microsoft-based networks.

In fact, Samba is so transparent that Microsoft clients cannot tell your Linux server from a genuine Windows NT/2000/XP server, and with Samba there are no server, client, or client access licenses to purchase.

Additionally, you can install Novell and/or Macintosh client utilities, as well as Novell and/or Macintosh "look-alike" server services. These services are beyond the scope of this book.

Printing is a fundamental service for all operating systems. You now have two options for configuring printers. The default is the line print daemon, lpd, based on the BSD utilities and services for local and remote Unix-style print services. The alternative is CUPS, the Common UNIX Printing System, which supports autoconfiguration of shared network printers and includes a Web interface configuration tool. Linux also provides connectivity to several other network print services via their native protocols.

exam Watch

The line print daemon has been officially deprecated. As of this writing, however, it will be the default for Red Hat 8.0. At some point, you may need to know CUPS for the RHCE exam. Watch the official RHCE exam prep guide at www.redhat.com/training/rhce/examprep.html for the latest information.

This chapter deals with the basic concepts surrounding the use of these services, and a basic level of configuration. In all cases, the assumption is that your network settings are correct and functioning properly. If you're having problems with your network configuration, read Chapter 4.

As for the RHCE exam, you may have to configure or troubleshoot any of the services discussed in this chapter. So as you read this chapter and look through the configuration files and exercises, be willing to experiment. And practice, practice, practice what you learn.

CERTIFICATION OBJECTIVE 8.01

Apache

Apache is by far the most popular Web server today. Based on the HTTP daemon (httpd), Apache provides simple and secure access to all types of content, based on the regular HTTP protocol, as well as its secure cousin, HTTPS.

Apache is based on the server code developed by the National Center for Supercomputing Applications (NCSA). It included so many "patches" it was known as "a patchy" server. The Apache Web Server continues to advance the art of the Web and provides one of the most stable, secure, robust, and reliable Web servers available. This server is under constant development by the Apache Software Foundation (www.apache.org).

You can install numerous other Web servers on Linux, including (but not limited to) iPlanet, Stronghold, Zeus, and Tux. Of the alternative Web servers available, only Tux is included in current Red Hat installation CDs. Therefore, it is possible that the RHCE exam will cover Tux in the future. As always, watch the latest RHCE exam prep criteria for the latest information.

Apache 2.0

Red Hat Linux has recently incorporated the latest major release of Apache. While there are major differences if you're a Web administrator or developer, the differences if you are focused on the RHCE exam are fairly straightforward.

- **New packages**   If you're installing Apache from the Red Hat Installation RPMs, all the package names have changed. As you'll see in the following section, most start with httpd. Strangely enough, the username associated with Apache services is now apache.

- **Different directives**   Basic directives, such as those based on Perl or php, are now configured separately, in the /etc/httpd/conf.d directory.

- **Revised variables**   Some variables have changed. For example, Apache listens for computers that are looking for Web pages on port 80. You can now change that port with the *Listen* variable.

- **Virtual hosts**   Apache is more focused on virtual hosts, which allows you to host multiple Web sites on the same Apache server, using a single IP address.

Installation

If you selected a Server or Custom installation and selected the Web Server package group, you already have the Apache Web Server installed. Otherwise, Apache is relatively easy to install from the RPMs available on the Installation CD or from the network. Figure 8-1 shows how to install the various packages required by the Apache Web Server from a mounted directory of Red Hat Installation RPMs. This could easily be from a Red Hat Installation CD-ROM. Each package is described in Table 8-1.

Once Apache is installed, use the chkconfig utility to set it to start with runlevels 3 and 5. The chkconfig utility ensures that Apache runs the next time your system boots (or you run the **/sbin/init 3** or **/sbin/init 5** command), but it will not start

FIGURE 8-1

Installing Apache
from Red Hat
installation RPMs

```
[root@RH80 root]# rpm -Uvh /mnt/source/RPMS/autoconf-2.53-7.noarch.rpm
Preparing...                ########################################### [100%]
   1:autoconf               ########################################### [100%]
[root@RH80 root]# rpm -Uvh /mnt/source/RPMS/automake-1.6.2-2.noarch.rpm
Preparing...                ########################################### [100%]
   1:automake               ########################################### [100%]
[root@RH80 root]# rpm -Uvh /mnt/source/RPMS/libtool-1.4.2-10.i386.rpm
Preparing...                ########################################### [100%]
   1:libtool                ########################################### [100%]
[root@RH80 root]# rpm -Uvh /mnt/source/RPMS/httpd-*
Preparing...                ########################################### [100%]
   1:httpd                  ########################################### [ 33%]
   2:httpd-devel            ########################################### [ 66%]
   3:httpd-manual           ########################################### [100%]
[root@RH80 root]# rpm -Uvh /mnt/source/RPMS/redhat-config-httpd-1.0.1-4.noarch.rpm
Preparing...                ########################################### [100%]
   1:redhat-config-httpd    ########################################### [100%]
[root@RH80 root]# rpm -Uvh /mnt/source/RPMS/mod_perl-1.99_04-2.i386.rpm
Preparing...                ########################################### [100%]
   1:mod_perl               ########################################### [100%]
[root@RH80 root]# rpm -Uvh /mnt/source/RPMS/mod_ssl-2.0.36-7.i386.rpm
Preparing...                ########################################### [100%]
   1:mod_ssl                ########################################### [100%]
[root@RH80 root]# rpm -Uvh /mnt/source/RPMS/mod_python-3.0.0-6.i386.rpm
Preparing...                ########################################### [100%]
   1:mod_python             ########################################### [100%]
[root@RH80 root]#
```

TABLE 8-1   Apache Packages

Package	Description
httpd	The Web server
httpd-devel	Allows you to compile additional modules
redhat-config-httpd	The Apache GUI configuration tool
httpd-manual	Installation of the Apache Documentation files is optional; these are installed in the /var/www/html/manual directory
autoconf	For creating scripts
automake	Includes makefile
libtool	For generic shared libraries
mod_perl	Perl language interpreter for Apache
mod_ssl	Supports encryption using protocols like secure HTTP
mod_python	Python language interpreter for Apache

Apache right now. Here is how to run chkconfig to let Apache start when you boot into runlevels 3 or 5.

```
[root@redhattest mj] /sbin/chkconfig --level 35 httpd on
```

To see if the chkconfig command worked, use the --list switch:

```
[root@redhattest mj] /sbin/chkconfig --list httpd
```

To start Apache, use the Apache service script in /etc/rc.d/init.d directory, as follows:

```
[root@redhattest mj] /etc/rc.d/init.d/httpd start
```

Once you've got Apache running, start a Web browser and enter a URL of http://localhost. If Apache installation is successful, you should see the screen in Figure 8-2.

FIGURE 8-2	

The default Apache Web page in Red Hat Linux

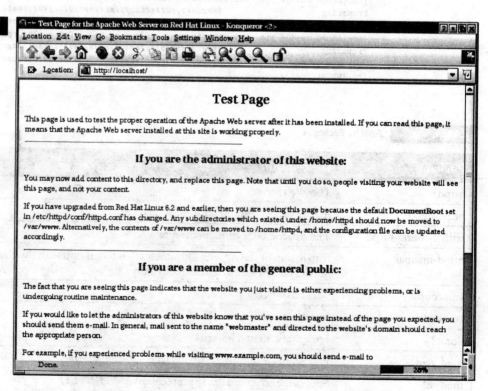

While Netscape Communicator is still available for Linux, it is no longer included with the Red Hat Installation CDs. In fact, the default Web browsers have changed. If you're using GNOME, open up the Mozilla browser, which you can start with the mozilla command from a console. Alternatively, if you're using KDE, the default Web browser is Konqueror, which you can start with the konqueror command from a console.

When you read the screen, you will see that Red Hat is advising us that the directories used by Apache have changed since Red Hat 6.2. In Red Hat 6.2 and earlier, the DocumentRoot (your Web content) was stored in /home/httpd. The new default DocumentRoot directory is /var/www. The configuration files can be found in the /etc/httpd/conf directory.

EXERCISE 8-1

Installing the Apache Server

In this exercise, you'll be installing all of the packages generally associated with the Apache server. Then you'll test and activate the result so that the Apache daemon, httpd, is active the next time you reboot Linux.

1. Mount the Red Hat RPM source files for Apache. They may be located on CD, or you may have copied them in a previous chapter to a network source.

2. Locate the Apache RPM packages: httpd, httpd-devel, redhat-config-httpd, mod_python, autoconf, automake, libtool, mod_perl, and mod_ssl. If you can't find some of these packages, you may have to repeat steps 1–3 with a different Red Hat Installation CD.

3. Load the Apache RPM packages.

4. Use chkconfig to verify that Apache is not configured to start.

5. Now, use chkconfig to start Apache for runlevels 3 and 5.

6. Start Apache by hand by invoking the Apache management script (httpd) in /etc/rc.d/init.d.

7. Start a Web browser such as Mozilla or Konqueror. Point it at http://localhost. You should see the default Apache Web page for Red Hat Linux.

8. Close your Web browser.

Basic Apache Configuration for a Simple Web Server

You have three main configuration files for your Web server. The installation creates a generic Web server service you can further customize and optimize, as desired. You can fine-tune your Web server by making changes to the main Apache configuration file, /etc/httpd/conf/httpd.conf.

Previous versions of Apache, 1.3.x and below, required two other Apache configuration files in the same directory, access.conf and srm.conf. Even though these files were essentially blank in later versions of Apache 1.3.x, they were still required. These files are no longer required in any way in Apache 2.x.

The config files listed in Figure 8-3 are located under the directory /etc/httpd/conf. The main configuration for Apache is httpd.conf. Browse through this file in your favorite text editor or with a command such as less.

There are a couple of basic constructs in this configuration file. First, when directories, files, and modules are configured, they are configured in containers. Containers start with the name of the directory, file, or module to be configured, contained in directional brackets (< >). Examples of this include:

```
<Directory "/var/www/icons">
<Files ~ "^\.ht">
<IfModule mod_mime_magic.c>
```

The end of the container starts with a forward slash. The container end for these examples would be:

```
</Directory>
</Files>
</IfModule>
```

FIGURE 8-3	

Apache configuration file directory

```
[root@RH80 root]# ls -l /etc/httpd/conf
total 72
-rw-r--r--    1 root     root       34565 06-26 11:00 httpd.conf
-rw-r--r--    1 root     root       12959 06-26 11:00 magic
drwxr-xr-x    2 root     root        4096 06-26 11:00 ssl.crl
drwxr-xr-x    2 root     root        4096 06-26 11:00 ssl.crt
drwxr-xr-x    2 root     root        4096 06-26 11:00 ssl.csr
drwxr-xr-x    2 root     root        4096 06-26 11:00 ssl.key
drwxr-xr-x    2 root     root        4096 06-26 11:00 ssl.prm
[root@RH80 root]# []
```

Next, Apache includes a substantial number of directives, which are commands that Apache can understand that have some resemblance to English. For example, the ExecCGI directive allows executable CGI scripts in the given container.

Access Restrictions

The httpd.conf configuration file can define which types of services are allowed on a directory-by-directory basis. These controls are for directories directly accessed by the server, and possibly by anyone who connects through the server. The settings in this file probably do not apply to regular users who log into Linux normally.

These restrictions are recursive from the parent directory. The first directory to configure is the root directory for your Web server. As you can see in Figure 8-4, that is the root directory (/). You should configure the default to be a very restrictive set of permissions. You can then adjust these permissions on other selected directory subtrees such as the DocumentRoot, and the cgi-bin directory if you plan to use cgi scripts. Figure 8-4 displays an excerpt from httpd.conf that sets default directory access permissions.

The next limited access directory is normally /var/www/html, which contains the HTML files for your Web pages. Figure 8-5 displays an excerpt from the default httpd.conf file that sets access controls on the /var/www/html directory.

FIGURE 8-4

Default access settings are controlled by <Directory path>. Lower-level directories inherit these settings.

```
#
# Each directory to which Apache has access can be configured with respect
# to which services and features are allowed and/or disabled in that
# directory (and its subdirectories).
#
# First, we configure the "default" to be a very restrictive set of
# features.
#
<Directory />
    Options FollowSymLinks
    AllowOverride None
</Directory>

#
# Note that from this point forward you must specifically allow
# particular features to be enabled - so if something's not working as
# you might expect, make sure that you have specifically enabled it
# below.
#
□
#
# This should be changed to whatever you set DocumentRoot to.
#
                                                      299,0-1        27%
```

FIGURE 8-5

Access control settings on the default Web page directory

```
#
# This should be changed to whatever you set DocumentRoot to.
#
<Directory "/var/www/html">
□
#
# Possible values for the Options directive are "None", "All",
# or any combination of:
#    Indexes Includes FollowSymLinks SymLinksifOwnerMatch ExecCGI Multiviews
#
# Note that "MultiViews" must be named *explicitly* --- "Options All"
# doesn't give it to you.
#
# The Options directive is both complicated and important.  Please see
# http://httpd.apache.org/docs-2.0/mod/core.html#options
# for more information.
#
    Options Indexes FollowSymLinks


#
# AllowOverride controls what directives may be placed in .htaccess files.
# It can be "All", "None", or any combination of the keywords:
#   Options FileInfo AuthConfig Limit
#
    AllowOverride None


#
# Controls who can get stuff from this server.
#
    Order allow,deny
    Allow from all

</Directory>
                                                    304,0-1        30%
```

Control by Directory through .htaccess   There is a way to override these inherited permissions in any subdirectory. Create a hidden file called .htaccess in the target directory. Directives in it can override the permission settings unless the "AllowOverride Options" is not set in httpd.conf. You can put an .htaccess control file in every directory that may be accessed by your Web server and customize access differently from the primary DocumentRoot access.

The Options directive can have many choices, in many combinations. Two examples include:

None	For no custom options in force
All	To allow all options except MultiViews

You can also use a specific keyword. Some examples include:

ExecCGI	Permits Web pages to run CGI scripts
FollowSymLinks	Permits symbolic links to directories outside of DocumentRoot
Includes	Allows server-side includes
Indexes	To permit FTP-style directory indexing

The Indexes directive controls directory indexing, which is the name for file lists that are generated automatically by Apache.

You have many different ways to set up Apache resources; some might be available in different languages, different media types, or more. When you set up multiple resources, Apache can choose depending on the browser-supplied preferences for media type, languages, character set, and encoding.

You can use the ScriptAlias variable for directories with executable CGI files. An Alias variable essentially links one file or directory to another. The ScriptAlias variable links the default cgi-bin directory to /var/www/cgi-bin. You can set up CGI scripts in a different directory and change the reference accordingly.

```
<Directory /var/www/cgi-bin>
    AllowOverride None       # .htaccess files ignored
    Options ExecCGI          # allow execution of any CGI scripts
    Order allow,deny
    Allow from all
</Directory>
```

In this sample excerpt from /etc/httpd/conf/httpd.conf, we identify the directory for our CGI programs (/var/www/cgi-bin). The AllowOverride None line keeps regular users from changing permissions/settings in the CGI directory. Otherwise, smarter users could read the CGI files in your directory, potentially compromising the security of your Web server. The Options ExecCGI line allows you to execute CGI scripts in the given directory. The Order allow,deny line sets up authorization checks; Allow from all lets all users run scripts in this directory.

The Server installation includes access to documentation, but through an alias name. The actual directory with the documentation has restricted access options. This is useful if you wish to map a directory out of a server's DocumentRoot directory into DocumentRoot. The default httpd.conf script does this to reference the /var/www/icons directory as the /icons directory inside the DocumentRoot directory

(/var/www/html). See Figure 8-6 to see how an Alias directive is used to map the /var/www/icons directory to the /var/www/html/icons (DocumentRoot + /icons/) directory.

Finally, you can add access control for any other directories available via your Web interface. Just wrap the directory you wish to control in a <Directory /path/to/dir>. . . </Directory> container and set the access restrictions you need.

```
========================================================================
<Directory /path/to/your/directory/goes/here/>
    Options Indexes FollowSymLinks
    order deny,allow                     # Access restrictions
    deny from .evil.crackers.net         # This test is applied first
    allow from .yourdomain.net           # Access is limited to .yourdomain.net
</Directory>
========================================================================
```

For more information on any of these core features, you can review the Apache Web page. But if you've installed the apache-manual RPM, you can also find this information in /var/www/html/manual/mod/core.html.

FIGURE 8-6

Using aliases for directories relative to DocumentRoot

```
#
# Aliases: Add here as many aliases as you need (with no limit). The format is
# Alias fakename realname
#
# Note that if you include a trailing / on fakename then the server will
# require it to be present in the URL.  So "/icons" isn't aliased in this
# example, only "/icons/".  If the fakename is slash-terminated, then the
# realname must also be slash terminated, and if the fakename omits the
# trailing slash, the realname must also omit it.
#
# We include the /icons/ alias for FancyIndexed directory listings.  If you
# do not use FancyIndexing, you may comment this out.
#
Alias /icons/ "/var/www/icons/"

<Directory "/var/www/icons">
    Options Indexes MultiViews
    AllowOverride None
    Order allow,deny
    Allow from all
</Directory>

#
# This should be changed to the ServerRoot/manual/.  The alias provides
# the manual, even if you choose to move your DocumentRoot.  You may comment
# this out if you do not care for the documentation.
                                                       532,1          50%
```

Virtual Hosts

Another useful feature of Apache is the ability to create virtual Web sites. A virtual Web site allows the Apache server to respond to more than one domain name that is linked to a single IP address. Take a look at Section 3 of httpd.conf, which is used to define virtual hosts. A sample of this is shown in Figure 8-7. You can use a number of lines currently in comments to configure a Web site as a virtual host.

You can do this by setting up an IP-address-based or a name-based virtual host. In either case, uncomment the NameVirtualHost directive. If you're using a name-based host, leave the asterisk after this directive. Otherwise, set the IP address for your interface.

The next step is to make a <VirtualHost> container. Add the e-mail address of the administrator for the site (ServerAdmin) and the DocumentRoot for the site's content; then set the ServerName by supplying the fully qualified domain name for your site. If you like, customize the ErrorLog and CustomLog paths. Then restart Apache (/etc/rc.d/init.d/httpd restart), and as long as the right files are available in the DocumentRoot, your new virtual site should be operational.

FIGURE 8-7	

Creating a
virtual host

```
### Section 3: Virtual Hosts
#
# VirtualHost: If you want to maintain multiple domains/hostnames on your
# machine you can setup VirtualHost containers for them. Most configurations
# use only name-based virtual hosts so the server doesn't need to worry about
# IP addresses. This is indicated by the asterisks in the directives below.
#
# Please see the documentation at
# <URL:http://httpd.apache.org/docs-2.0/vhosts/>
# for further details before you try to setup virtual hosts.
#
# You may use the command line option '-S' to verify your virtual host
# configuration.


#
# Use name-based virtual hosting.
#
#NameVirtualHost *


#
# VirtualHost example:
# Almost any Apache directive may go into a VirtualHost container.
# The first VirtualHost section is used for requests without a known
# server name.
#
#<VirtualHost *>
#    ServerAdmin webmaster@dummy-host.example.com
#    DocumentRoot /www/docs/dummy-host.example.com
#    ServerName dummy-host.example.com
#    ErrorLog logs/dummy-host.example.com-error_log
#    CustomLog logs/dummy-host.example.com-access_log common
#</VirtualHost>
                                                          997,1        Bot
```

on the job

There's another way to access the scripts in the /etc/rc.d/init.d directory. Use the /sbin/service script. For example, the /sbin/service httpd restart command is functionally identical to /etc/rc.d/init.d/httpd restart.

The beauty of VirtualHost containers is that you can repeat the process. With name-based virtual hosting, you can set up as many Web sites on your Apache server as your computer can handle. All you require is one IP address. When you set up your new VirtualHost container, make sure to revise the ServerName, the locations of the log files, and the DocumentRoot.

Web Server Log Files

The log files are shown in two locations; they're listed in /etc/httpd/logs, which is a directory that is linked to /var/logs/httpd. You can change both the number and the format of each log file. By default, there is only one log file for all access events (access_log) and one log file for all errors (error_log). If you want more detail about your Web site for tuning or statistical reasons, you can have the Web server generate more information; generate separate log files for each virtual Web site; and create new log files periodically, such as daily, weekly, or monthly.

There are standard log file formats. For more information, take a look at the LogFormat directive as shown in Figure 8-8. Four different formats are shown: combined, common, the referer (the Web page with the link used to get to our site), and the agent (the users' Web browser).

The first two LogFormat lines include a number of percent signs followed by lowercase letters. These variables determine what goes into the log.

We then use the CustomLog format to select where to put our log files and which log file format we wish to use.

on the job

Some Web hit log analyzers have specific requirements for log file formats. For example, the popular Open Source tool awstats (advanced Web Stats) requires the combined log format. It will fail to run if you leave the default common format. Awstats is a great tool for graphically displaying site activity. You can download it from a site such as www.sourceforge.net.

Log Configuration Options The log files have a very specific format for the information stored in them, per the HTTP RFC. You probably do not need to change these. Figure 8-9 is an excerpt from the mod_log_config.html help file in the /var/www/html/manual/mod/ directory.

FIGURE 8-8

Customizing
Apache logs in
httpd.conf

```
# ErrorLog: The location of the error log file.
# If you do not specify an ErrorLog directive within a <VirtualHost>
# container, error messages relating to that virtual host will be
# logged here.  If you *do* define an error logfile for a <VirtualHost>
# container, that host's errors will be logged there and not here.
#
ErrorLog logs/error_log

#
# LogLevel: Control the number of messages logged to the error_log.
# Possible values include: debug, info, notice, warn, error, crit,
# alert, emerg.
#
LogLevel warn

#
# The following directives define some format nicknames for use with
# a CustomLog directive (see below).
#
LogFormat "%h %l %u %t \"%r\" %>s %b \"%{Referer}i\" \"%{User-Agent}i\"" combined
LogFormat "%h %l %u %t \"%r\" %>s %b" common
LogFormat "%{Referer}i -> %U" referer
LogFormat "%{User-agent}i" agent

#
# The location and format of the access logfile (Common Logfile Format).
# If you do not define any access logfiles within a <VirtualHost>
# container, they will be logged here.  Contrariwise, if you *do*
# define per-<VirtualHost> access logfiles, transactions will be
# logged therein and *not* in this file.
#
# CustomLog logs/access_log common
CustomLog logs/access_log combined

#
# If you would like to have agent and referer logfiles, uncomment the
# following directives.
#
#CustomLog logs/referer_log referer
#CustomLog logs/agent_log agent
                                                    450,1        45%
```

Note that the common log format is defined by the string "%h %l %u %t \"%r\" %s %b", which can be used as the basis for extending the format, if desired (e.g., to add extra fields at the end). NCSA's extended/combined log format would be

```
"%h %l %u %t \"%r\" %s %b \"%{Referer}i\" \"%{User-agent}i\"".
```

The log format is consistent with the standard NCSA format and generally does not need to be changed. (The backslashes negate the normal meaning of a character, in this case, the double quotes.)

FIGURE 8-9

Log format
options

%...a:	Remote IP-address
%...A:	Local IP-address
%...B:	Bytes sent, excluding HTTP headers.
%...b:	Bytes sent, excluding HTTP headers. In CLF format i.e. a '-' rather than a 0 when no bytes are sent.
%...{Foobar}C:	The contents of cookie "Foobar" in the request sent to the server.
%...D:	The time taken to serve the request, in microseconds.
%...{FOOBAR}e:	The contents of the environment variable FOOBAR
%...f:	Filename
%...h:	Remote host
%...H	The request protocol
%...{Foobar}i:	The contents of Foobar: header line(s) in the request sent to the server.
%...l:	Remote logname (from identd, if supplied)
%...m:	The request method
%...{Foobar}n:	The contents of note "Foobar" from another module.
%...{Foobar}o:	The contents of Foobar: header line(s) in the reply.
%...p:	The canonical Port of the server serving the request
%...P:	The process ID of the child that serviced the request.
%...q:	The query string (prepended with a ? if a query string exists, otherwise an empty string)
%...r:	First line of request
%...s:	Status. For requests that got internally redirected, this is the status of the "original" request --- %...>s for the last.
%...t:	Time, in common log format time format (standard english format)
%...{format}t:	The time, in the form given by format, which should be in strftime(3) format. (potentially localized)
%...T:	The time taken to serve the request, in seconds.
%...u:	Remote user (from auth; may be bogus if return status (%s) is 401)
%...U:	The URL path requested, not including any query string.
%...v:	The canonical ServerName of the server serving the request.

Done.

Starting the Apache Web Server

The actual binary file for Apache is /usr/sbin/httpd. You can also start Apache using the httpd system initialization script in the /etc/rc.d/init.d directory.

By default, when you start Apache, you're actually starting Apache a number of times. If you run the **ps aux | grep httpd** command, you'll probably see several instances of Apache, which allow multiple users to connect to your Web server simultaneously.

Testing Your Configuration   After you edit httpd.conf, there's an easy way to test the syntax. Just use the following command:

```
# httpd -t
```

and Apache will verify your configuration or identify specific problems. When you run this command on the default configuration, you'll get the following message:

```
[Fri May 24 18:00:42 2002] [alert] httpd: Could not determine the server's fully
 qualified domain name, using 127.0.0.1 for ServerName
Syntax OK
```

This message is nothing to worry about during initial testing; it just notes that you haven't set a fully qualified domain name for your Web site through the ServerName directive.

Assuming there were no problems, you should be able to start your Web server and connect to your local service with a browser request. Open your Web browser and try the following URLs.

```
http://localhost/            # Just requires default /etc/hosts
http://206.195.1.222/        # Substitute your IP address
http://www.yourweb.org/      # Substitute the value of ServerName
```

Server Management   Four variables from the httpd.conf file, shown next, govern the capacity of your Apache server. This does not address other limitations such as RAM, hard drive space, and network speed that may affect the capacity of Apache on your computer.

```
StartServers 8             # initial servers
MinSpareServers 5          # Minimum available servers
MaxSpareServers 20         # kill off extras as necessary
MaxClients 150             # all processes are renewed regularly
```

When Apache starts, it begins with a number of StartServers, ready to send Web pages from your Apache server to the Web browsers on any connected computer. Each of these servers is a process.

While some Apache processes may end, a minimum number of spare servers are available, MinSpareServers. If a lot of computers are connecting simultaneously, Apache adds extra servers, up to the limit shown by MaxSpareServers.

And there is a limit on the number of simultaneous requests for Web pages, as defined by MaxClients.

Potential Problems and Solutions   When you install the right Apache packages, the default configuration normally creates a running system. But if you're setting up a real Web site, you probably want more than just the test page. Before you start changing the configuration, back up the httpd.conf Apache configuration file. If something goes wrong and the following suggestions don't work, you can then always start over.

- Error message about an inability to "bind" to an address: Another network process may already be using the default http port (80). Alternatively, your computer is running httpd as a normal user (not the user apache) with a port below 1024.

- Network addressing or routing errors: Double-check your network settings. For more information on configuring your computer for networking, see Chapter 4.

- Apache isn't running: Check the error message when you start or restart httpd. Check the error_log; by default, you'll find it in the /etc/httpd/logs directory.

- Apache isn't running after a reboot: Run **chkconfig --list httpd**. Make sure Apache (httpd) is started at runlevels 3 and 5 during the boot process with the following command:

```
# chkconfig --level 35 httpd on
```

- You need to stop Apache: Send the parent process a TERM signal, based on its PID. By default, this is located in /var/run/httpd.pid. You kill Apache with a command such as:

```
#kill -TERM `cat /var/run/httpd.pid`
```

Alternatively, you can use the **/etc/rc.d/init.d/httpd stop** command.

- Check the logs associated with your Apache configuration. As discussed earlier, they are located in the /var/log/httpd directory.

Web Site Content

The content of any Web site consists of HTML pages, pictures, CGI scripts, and more. For Apache, these files are included in the /var/www/html directory.

By default, Linux Web page files have .html (not .htm) extensions. Linux is case sensitive; thus, a file named Index.html is different from index.html.

These top directory files are supplied with the installation:

```
index.html       the default page returned by server
poweredby.gif    picture logo of Red Hat (in index.html)
manual/          manual pages and gifs
mrtg/            Multi Router Traffic Grapher
usage/           Webalyzer pictures
```

Default Web Page File

In many cases, the full name of a Web site includes a filename such as index.html. But most people don't add the filename to the end of a URL. So Apache goes looking for a file, based on the DirectoryIndex directive. An example of this directive is shown in Figure 8-10, which shows an index file with a variety of possible extensions. Apache looks for the names of these files, in the order shown in the httpd.conf configuration file.

Basics of HTML Coding   Apache has a default Web page. You can change this or any other Web page with a text- or HTML-specific editor. If you use a text editor, you need to know something about the basic tags used by a browser.

A basic Web page can be a simple text file. Tags such as <HTML> and <HEAD> are commands to the client browser to display something a special way. An example of a simple Web page is shown in the following section.

If you are not familiar with HTML tags, don't worry. There are a number of good graphical applications that can automate the process for you. If you need to go into a text file for a simple edit, the HTML format is relatively straightforward. HTML tags are similar to Apache containers. For example, the title is placed between a start-of-format tag such as <HEAD> and an end-of-format tag such as </HEAD>.

FIGURE 8-10

DirectoryIndex directive lists default home page files.

```
# DirectoryIndex: sets the file that Apache will serve if a directory
# is requested.
#
# The index.html.var file (a type-map) is used to deliver content-
# negotiated documents.  The MultiViews Option can be used for the
# same purpose, but it is much slower.
#
DirectoryIndex index.html index.html.var


#
# AccessFileName: The name of the file to look for in each directory
# for access control information.  See also the AllowOverride directive.
#
AccessFileName .htaccess


#
# The following lines prevent .htaccess and .htpasswd files from being
# viewed by Web clients.
#
<Files ~ "^\.ht">
    Order allow,deny
    Deny from all </Files>

                                                     411,0-1        38%
```

The first part of the HTML code for the default Apache Web page is shown in Figure 8-11.

Browsing Your Home Page

As long as your computer and network are properly configured or connected, you can use any browser from any computer on the network. Alternatively, you can use a browser on the local computer, using the http://localhost address to connect to your server's home page.

You don't even need a GUI. There is a text-based alternative browser that you can install from one of the Red Hat installation CDs.

Text-Based Browser: lynx   You can connect to any text-capable Web site with the lynx browser. This browser simply ignores all font and font size requests, as well as any directives to display graphics. lynx displays the HTML strings as single lines. Tags and links are shown in a different color. You can move your cursor to links or tags with the UP- and DOWN-ARROW keys. To connect to the desired link or tag, press the RIGHT-ARROW key; to go back, press the LEFT-ARROW key. To exit lynx, press Q. A sample from a real Web site is shown in Figure 8-12.

FIGURE 8-11

The default
Apache Server
Web page in
HTML

```
!DOCTYPE HTML PUBLIC "-//W3C//DTD HTML 3.2 Final//EN">
<HTML>
 <HEAD>
  <TITLE>Test Page for the Apache Web Server on Red Hat Linux</TITLE>
 </HEAD>
<!-- Background white, links blue (unvisited), navy (visited), red (active) -->
<BODY BGCOLOR="#FFFFFF">

  <H1 ALIGN="CENTER">Test Page</H1>
  This page is used to test the proper operation of the Apache Web server after
  it has been installed.  If you can read this page, it means that the Apache
  Web server installed at this site is working properly.

  <HR WIDTH="50%">

  <H2 ALIGN="CENTER">If you are the administrator of this website:</H2>
  <P>
  You may now add content to this directory, and replace this page.  Note that
  until you do so, people visiting your website will see this page, and not your
  content.
  </P>

  <P>If you have upgraded from Red Hat Linux 6.2 and earlier, then you are
  seeing this page because the default <A
  href="manual/mod/core.html#documentroot"><STRONG>DocumentRoot</STRONG></A>
  set in <TT>/etc/httpd/conf/httpd.conf</TT> has changed.  Any subdirectories
  which existed under <TT>/home/httpd</TT> should now be moved to
  <TT>/var/www</TT>.  Alternatively, the contents of <TT>/var/www</TT> can be
  moved to <TT>/home/httpd</TT>, and the configuration file can be updated
  accordingly.
  </P>

  <HR WIDTH="50%">
  <H2 ALIGN="CENTER">If you are a member of the general public:</H2>
"/var/www/error/noindex.html" 86L, 2898C                       1,1           Top
```

FIGURE 8-12	Momma Bears' Bears! Your source for Grateful Dead Bears and Gift (p1 of 5)

Using Lynx to
browse the
Internet

```
             Welcome to Momma Bears' Bears,
          your source for collectible Grateful Dead Bears!

                   Momma Bears' Bears logo

  We specialize in Grateful Dead Bears, gifts and T-shirts and Celebrity
                              Bears.

                        [sumhorsa.gif]

                       Current specials:

                 20% off all orders over $25!
  The shopping cart will automatically apply your discount. Applies only
  to in-stock items. Does not apply to the new limited edition Grateful
  Dead Bear (Cold Rain), pre-sales, special orders or previous orders.

     50% off clearance on all but our newest Celebrity Bears~
              See each Celebrity Bear page
              50% off gift items

     JUST IN!   COLD RAIN limited edition Grateful Dead Bear.


                        [sumhorsa.gif]

            We ship almost anywhere in the world!
                 We do not ship to Indonesia.

                     Credit card logos
-- press space for next page --
   Arrow keys: Up and Down to move.  Right to follow a link; Left to go back.
 H)elp O)ptions P)rint G)o M)ain screen Q)uit /=search [delete]=history list
```

EXERCISE 8-2

Updating a Home Page

In this exercise, you'll update the home page associated with your Web site on the
Apache server. You can use these techniques to copy the actual HTML formatted
pages that you'll need for your Web site.

1. Start the Apache Web server with the default configuration.

2. Copy an html file such as /var/www/error/noindex.html to
   /var/www/html/index.html.

3. Edit the file /var/www/html/index.html.

4. Change the title of the page to reflect your personal or corporate name.

5. Use the lynx text-based browser to connect to localhost (or 127.0.0.1).

Hosting a Virtual Web Site

You can add virtual hosts to /etc/httpd/conf/httpd.conf by adding a set of entries for each virtual host, including the local host itself:

Here is a relevant excerpt from the end of the original configuration file:

```
#NameVirtualHost *
#<VirtualHost host.some_domain.com>
#       ServerAdmin webmaster@host.some_domain.com
#       DocumentRoot /www/docs/host.some_domain.com
#       ServerName host.some_domain.com
#       ErrorLog logs/host.some_domain.com-error_log
#       TransferLog logs/host.some_domain.com-access_log
#</VirtualHost>
```

These directives are easy to change. If all of your virtual hosts are to be associated with one IP address, you can assign it to the NameVirtualHost directive. An example for a specific Web site is shown here:

```
<VirtualHost www.pfr.nnn>
    ServerAdmin    guru@pfr.nnn        # admin email
    DocumentRoot   /pfr/html           # must include home page file
    ServerName   www.pfr.nnn           # fully qualified domain name
    ErrorLog  /pfr/logs/error_log      # configure as desired
    TransferLog  /pfr/logs/access_log  # transaction logs
    ScriptAlias  /cgi/  /pfr/cgi-bin    # associates virtual with real dir.
<Directory /pfr/html>                   # document root
    Options  ExecCGI  Indexes  Includes # described above
</Directory>
</VirtualHost>
```

To test your new virtual host setup, you can restart the Apache Web Server as follows:

```
[root@redhattest root]#  /etc/rc.d/init.d/httpd    restart
```

Assuming your Web pages are written properly, you should now be able to check the Web content page of all your virtual Web sites with any browser.

Apache administration is a necessary skill for any Linux system administrator. You should develop the ability to install, configure, and troubleshoot Apache quickly. You should also be able to set up and customize virtual Web sites, which will make you a more effective Webmaster. You can test your skills using the exercise that follows.

EXERCISE 8-3

Set up a Virtual Web Server

In this exercise, you'll set up a Virtual Web Server. You can use this technique with different directories to set up additional Virtual Web Servers on the same Apache server.

1. Back up your httpd.conf file.

2. Add a virtual Web site for the fictional company SnoBard, called www.snobard.net.

3. Create a DocumentRoot directory called /snobard. (Don't forget to create this directory on your system as well.)

4. Copy the file /var/www/html/index.html to /snobard/index.html.

5. Edit the file /snobard/index.html.

6. Change the title of the page to reflect the SnoBard corporate name.

7. Open the browser of your choice. Test access the virtual Web site (www.snobard.com) and the local Web site (localhost).

The Red Hat httpd Configuration Tool

Red Hat has recently introduced its own graphical configuration tool for Apache, redhat-config-httpd, which you can install from the RPM of the same name. Before using this tool, back up your current /etc/httpd/conf/httpd.conf configuration file. Any changes that you make with this tool overwrite this file.

You will find that redhat-config-httpd is a straightforward tool, with four different tabs that can help you configure the following:

- **Basic Configuration** The Main tab allows you to set basic parameters for your Apache server, including the ServerName, the Webmaster e-mail address, and the Listen variable.

- **Virtual Hosts** The Virtual Hosts tab permits you to set the properties for different Web sites that you host on your Apache server. This includes the DocumentRoot, basic html filenames and locations, SSL support, basic log file configuration, CGI script variables, and default directories.

- **Server** The Server tab enables you to set the basic lock and PID files, as well as the user and group associated with the httpd service. In most cases, you should not have to change these settings.

- **Performance Tuning** The Performance Tuning tab allows you to set basic connection parameters.

As this tool is fairly new, reliability is less than certain. No Red Hat documentation was available as of this writing. In any case, it is still faster to reconfigure the Apache configuration file, /etc/httpd/conf/httpd.conf, directly in a text editor. And remember, time may be of the essence when you take the RHCE exam.

CERTIFICATION OBJECTIVE 8.02

FTP

FTP, the File Transfer Protocol, is one of the original network applications developed with the TCP/IP protocol suite. It follows the standard model for network services, as FTP requires a client and a server. The FTP client is installed by default on most operating systems, including Red Hat Linux. The FTP server often needs to be installed separately.

Unlike other network services, FTP servers are controlled through the xinetd superserver. If you have installed an FTP server such as wu-ftpd, you'll find it controlled through the /etc/xinetd.d directory. By default, these types of servers are disabled.

FTP Client

The original FTP client software was a basic command line, text-oriented client application that offered a simple but efficient interface. Most Web browsers offer a graphical interface and can also be used as an FTP client.

Any FTP client allows you to view the directory tree and files. Using ftp as a client is easy. Take a look at ftp.redhat.com with the commands shown in Figure 8-13. The RedHat FTP site requires anonymous logins.

FIGURE 8-13

Using the FTP
text client

```
[mj@RH80 mj]$ ftp ftp.redhat.com
Trying 66.77.185.38...
Connected to ftp.redhat.com (66.77.185.38).
220 Red Hat FTP server ready. All transfers are logged.
Name (ftp.redhat.com:root): anonymous
331 Please specify the password.
Password:
230 Login successful. Have fun.
Remote system type is UNIX.
Using binary mode to transfer files.
ftp> ls
227 Entering Passive Mode (66,77,185,38,41,118)
150 Here comes the directory listing.
d--x--x--x    2 0        0            4096 Jun 05 01:59 bin
d--x--x--x    2 0        0            4096 Jun 05 01:59 etc
drwxr-xr-x    2 0        0            4096 Jun 05 01:59 lib
drwxr-xr-x    5 0        0            4096 Jun 09 04:20 pub
226 Directory send OK.
ftp> █
```

Almost all commands in FTP mode are run at the remote host, similar to a Telnet
session. You can also run commands locally from the FTP prompt. When you start
the command with an *!*, you can run regular shell commands. Basic FTP client
commands are shown in Figure 8-14.

FIGURE 8-14

Basic FTP client
commands

```
==================================================================
Remote Commands (Process on remote host)
cd      to change the current working directory at the remote host
ls      commands to list files at the remote host
get     to retrieve one file from the remote host
mget    to retrieve many files using wildcards or full filenames.
     (if logged in with a local login account, not anonymous)
put     to upload one file from your machine to the target host
mput    to upload many files to the target remote host
pwd     print working directory on remote host
quit    end the FTP session
     Local Commands (Process on your host)
!ls     list files on your host machine, current directory
lcd     change local host directory for upload/download
!pwd    print working directory on local host
==================================================================
```

This is only a subset of the commands available from the FTP client. Typing the **help** command will give you a full list of the available commands. The command **help** *cmd* yields a brief description of the command itself.

For a more functional command line–driven FTP client, check out the ncftp package, which is currently available on one of the Red Hat Installation CDs. This FTP client adds these features:

- Recursive directory downloads
- Command line recall and edit (in the style of bash)
- Command line history
- Automatic anonymous logins
- Much easier command line FTP use

One graphical FTP client for Linux is GNOME FTP (GFTP). GNOME FTP provides an easy-to-use GUI interface to FTP. It also offers these features:

- Restartable transfers
- Multiple independent transfers
- Download file queuing
- Transferring whole directory trees (recursive transfers)
- Drag-and-drop transfer activation
- Session names and settings

all without requiring you to know a single FTP command. See Figure 8-15 for a view of GNOME FTP.

You can start the GFTP client from the command line with the gftp command from a GUI terminal window.

FTP Installation

Two of the ways you can set up an FTP server are with the following packages: anonftp and wu-ftpd. As always, you can check whether or not they're installed with the **rpm -q** *packagename* command.

FIGURE 8-15

The GNOME
FTP client

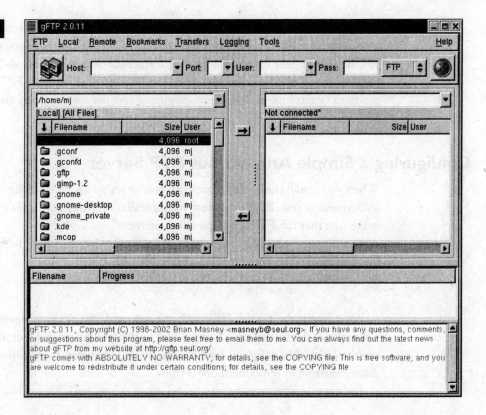

anonftp

The anonftp package allows you to set up an FTP server without having to go through the trouble of setting up user accounts for those who need access. The installation creates a /var/ftp directory tree. Add files that you want to make available through the anonftp server to the /var/ftp/pub directory.

For security, users won't be able to cd above the /var/ftp directory. This limitation is made possible through anonftp's use of the chroot system call. This means that users who connect to your anonymous FTP server see /var/ftp as the root (/) directory.

WU-FTP

The FTP server for authenticated (known) users is known as wu-ftpd. This package lets you set up usernames, passwords, and more for all users who connect to this server. Additional features include control of transfer and command logs, on-the-fly compression and archiving (using gzip), user type and location classification, limits on a per-class (local, remote) basis, directory upload permissions, restricted guest accounts, messages per directory and system, and virtual name support.

One of the other excellent advanced features of WU-FTP is its ability to provide full user and group-specific authorization of FTP services. WU-FTP adds a third group of "guest" users. You can configure access for various users and groups in /etc/ftpaccess.

Configuring a Simple Anonymous FTP Server

When you install the anonftp package, you've set up an FTP service that allows anonymous access. Before you test your installation from any host on the network, make sure that the FTP server service is active.

As strange as it sounds, you can activate anonftp by changing the following line in /etc/xinetd.d/wu-ftpd from yes to no:

```
disable      = yes
```

Then restart the xinetd script with the **/etc/rc.d/init.d/xinetd restart** command. This rereads the settings in all of the files in the /etc/xinetd.d directory. Alternatively, use the **/sbin/chkconfig wu-ftpd on** command. That also changes the value of the *disable* variable in /etc/xinetd.d/wu-ftpd.

For more information on the xinetd super-server, see Chapter 10.

Testing Your FTP Service   Now you can test the anonymous login features of your new FTP server. From any command line, use the FTP client to connect to any FTP server. Like any network connection, the FTP client needs a valid network address. If you use a host name, the system needs to be able to resolve the computer name such as redhattest to an IP address, using a file such as /etc/hosts, or a DNS server.

on the
Job

Never believe the e-mail address provided as a password by anonymous FTP users. There is little that can be done to check the validity of the e-mail address provided through anonymous FTP. If the e-mail address is so unreliable, you might wonder why it is even requested. The answer is that in the early days of the Internet (before evil crackers, viruses, and so on), everyone was expected to be polite and considerate.

By default, anonymous FTP sessions are logged to /var/log/messages. This includes the date and time of the session, as well as the e-mail name offered as the password. The log line looks like the following:

```
May 25 12:02:09 RH80 ftpd[3380]: ANONYMOUS FTP LOGIN FROM othercomp
[10.21.34.12], cracker@example.com.
```

Working from a home-based office and traveling the world can sometimes cause you to miss some important files. If your computer is always on, you can still have access. Just install an anonymous FTP service or wu-ftpd on your Red Hat Linux server. Put any files that you might need under the anonymous public access directory (/home/ftp/pub). Use WU-FTP to manage access by privileged users to specific directories. Just remember to check with your ISP first; some ISPs may not allow this type of access.

Configuring wu-ftpd

The anonymous FTP service allows downloads only from /var/ftp. If you have users who want remote access to their home directory files or any generally accessible files on your system, the wu-ftpd service provides secure control over the users and groups that can access your system.

A few files control security on wu-ftpd. They can be used to restrict or control basic service access, allow additional groups, and permit guest users to access the site—all with different access privileges. These files can be seen with the **ls /etc/ftp*** command. The most important of these files is /etc/ftpaccess.

The /etc/ftpaccess file controls the behavior of the FTP server. You can use it to restrict how a user uses the server (for example, disallow system accounts), you can identify programs for uncompressing files on demand during download, set login failure policies, and direct error and log messages to the appropriate place. Review the contents of the /etc/ftpaccess file.

The /etc/ftpconversions file is a special file that the FTP service uses to automatically compress and/or decompress files for transfer. The correct tool is selected according to the applicable file extension. By default, FTP decompresses files that are being downloaded. This feature allows FTP administrators to store files on the server in compressed format (so they take up less space). When an FTP client requests a file, the FTP server automatically decompresses the file and transfers it. That way, the users get the files they were expecting.

The commands in /etc/ftpconversions can be found in the /var/ftp/bin directory.

EXERCISE 8-4

Configuring GFTPD

In this exercise, you'll configure the GFTPD utility to connect to ftp.redhat.com, which can help you download the latest RPM packages for your system.

1. Insert and mount the appropriate Red Hat Installation CD, or access these files over the network.

2. Identify packages that provide FTP services with the **ls /mnt/cdrom/RedHat/RPMs/*ftp*** command. (This assumes the Installation CD is mounted on /mnt/cdrom.)

3. Use **rpm -Uvh** *packagename* to install the appropriate packages.

4. Test anonymous FTP access. Use anonymous as the username, and your e-mail address as the password. Check /etc/log/messages for the e-mail address.

5. Run the **ls** command while connected. What directories can you see?

6. Quit anonymous FTP.

7. Try GNOME FTP (gftp). Log in as a "real" user. What limitations does GFTP place on you?

8. If you have an Internet connection, try pointing GFTP at ftp.redhat.com. Look under the appropriate binaries directory such as i386 or i686 for your release of Red Hat. Are there any updates available for your FTP packages? If so, download and install them now.

9. Close your GFTP session.

CERTIFICATION OBJECTIVE 8.03

Samba

Microsoft computers can share files and printers on a network through a facility called SMB, Server Message Block. This type of network communication over a Microsoft-based network is also known as NetBIOS over TCP/IP. Through the collective works of Andrew Tridgell and many others (in the Samba group), Linux systems provide transparent and reliable SMB support over TCP/IP via a package known as Samba.

You can do four basic things with Samba:

- Share a Linux directory tree with Windows computers.
- Share a Windows directory with Linux computers.
- Share a Linux printer with Windows computers.
- Share a Windows printer with Linux computers.

Samba emulates many of the advanced network features and functions associated with the Win9x and NT/2000/XP operating systems through the SMB protocol. Complete information can be found at the official Samba Web site at http://www.samba.org.

It is easy to configure Samba to do a number of things on a Microsoft-based network:

- Participate in a Microsoft Windows 9x–style Workgroup or an NT/2000/XP Domain as a client or a server.
- Act as a Primary or Backup Domain Controller.
- Share user home directories.
- Act as a WINS client or server.
- Link to or manage a workgroup browse service.
- Act as a Master Browser.
- Provide user/password and share security databases locally, from another Samba server, or from a Microsoft Domain Controller.
- Configure local directories as shared SMB filesystems.
- Synchronize passwords between Windows and Linux systems.
- Download print drivers to Microsoft clients.

While Samba can do more, you get the idea. Samba features are configured throu one very big file called smb.conf. While this file may be intimidating, the Samba We Administration Tool (SWAT) can help. This is a Web-based interface with CGI scri￼ that can help you configure all of these features through smb.conf.

e x a m
ⓦa t c h

SWAT is developing a reputation as a reliable GUI front end configuration tool for Samba. But remember, time is of the essence on the RHCE exam. If you know how to edit the /etc/samba/smb.conf configuration file in a text editor, you're more likely to have time to configure the other elements you need to pass the exam.

Installing Samba Services

If you selected the Windows File Server package when you installed Red Hat Linux, then the Samba package is already installed. As of this writing, you'll just want to install the Samba-swat RPM package after installation. These are the four Samba RPM packages that you need:

- The Samba package includes the basic SMB server software for sharing files and printers.

- The Samba-common package contains common Samba configuration files.

- The Samba-client package provides the utilities needed to connect to shares from Microsoft computers.

- The Samba-swat package includes the aforementioned SWAT configuration tool.

Finally, be sure to enable SWAT as a service. Like the FTP servers from earlier in this chapter, SWAT is a service controlled by the xinetd superserver. That means you'll need to activate SWAT through the /etc/xinetd.d/swat configuration file and then restart the xinetd daemon. First, open the /etc/xinetd.d/swat configuration file in a text editor, and change the following line from Yes to No:

```
disable    = yes
```

Save your changes, and now restart the xinetd daemon with the **/etc/rc.d/inet.d/xinetd restart** command. Next, make sure SWAT is activated whenever you boot Linux. Run the chkconfig command shown here, to activate it for runlevels 3 and 5:

```
[root@redhattest mj] /sbin/chkconfig swat --list 35 on
```

Finally, verify that SWAT is running.

```
[root]# chkconfig --list | grep swat
        swat: on
```

Now, let's try launching SWAT. Samba runs on your localhost and listens on TCP/IP port 901. Let's start a Web browser to take a look at SWAT. Use the URL http://localhost:901. SWAT should prompt you for the Samba administrator name and password, which is **root** and the root user's password. This should open the SWAT main configuration screen, as shown in Figure 8-16.

SWAT runs with root level privileges and can be used to completely reconfigure your Samba service. Because username and password information to a browser travels across the network in clear text, don't access SWAT from another computer on the network unless you're confident in the security of that network.

If you get an xinetd error about the connection being refused, let xinetd reload its configuration file. Run the xinetd management script with the reload option, with the following command:

```
[root@redhattest mj] # /etc/rc.d/init.d/xinetd reload
```

SWAT should now be recognized as a valid service. Try the preceding URL again.

FIGURE 8-16

The Main SWAT configuration screen

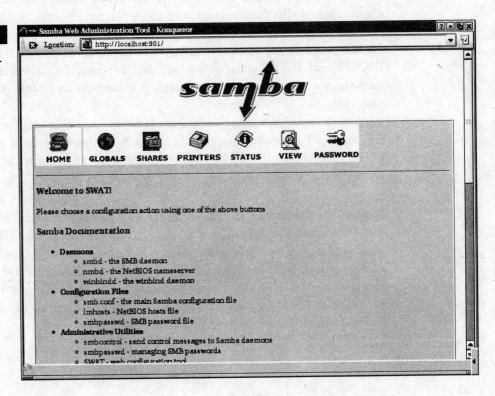

Basics of Samba Services

Samba services provide interoperability between the Microsoft Windows and Linux/Unix computers. Before you begin configuring Samba, you need a basic understanding of how Microsoft Windows networking works with TCP/IP.

The original Microsoft Windows networks were configured with computer host names, known as NetBIOS names, which are limited to 15 characters. These unique host names provided a simple, flat host name system for the computers on a LAN. All computer identification requests were made through broadcasts. This overall network transport system is known as NetBEUI, which is not "routable." In other words, it does not allow communication between two different LANs. As a result, the original Microsoft-based PC networks were limited in size to 255 nodes.

While Windows networks could use the Novell IPX/SPX protocol stack to route messages between networks, that was not enough. As the Internet grew, so did the dominance of TCP/IP. Microsoft adapted its NetBIOS system to TCP/IP with the Server Message Block (SMB). Since Microsoft published SMB as an industry-wide standard, anyone could set up their own service to work with SMB.

One of the nice features of Windows networks is the browser service. All computers register their NetBIOS names with one "elected" master browser, the keeper of the database of network-wide services. In fact, a browse database is maintained by some "elected" host for every protocol running on the network. For instance, if the NetBEUI, IPX/SPX, and TCP/IP protocols were installed on a host, then three duplicate browse databases were required—one per protocol, as the services available may differ between protocols.

As the Internet grew, there was a demand for a system that could maintain a database of all connected computers. This led to the development of the Berkeley Internet Name Domain (BIND), which is commonly implemented as the Domain Name Service (DNS).

Name Resolution: DNS DNS contains a distributed database of host names and IP addresses. On the Internet, no one DNS server contains the URLs and IP addresses for all computers on the Internet. But a properly configured DNS server knows where to look for names that are not in its local database. A DNS record is simply a host name and the related IP address. For example, Table 8-2 shows two records from a DNS configuration file. Each record associates an IP address with a fully qualified domain name of a specific computer.

TABLE 8-2	Sample from a DNS Database: A = Address Record

DNS Name	Type	IP Address
www.foo.bar	A	10.1.1.1
ftp.foo.bar	A	10.1.1.2

In this case, when a computer asks DNS for the IP address of www.foo.bar, DNS returns the IP address 10.1.1.1. Each DNS server has a Zone of Authority, which may include one or more LANs. That DNS is responsible for keeping track of the host names and IP addresses for all computers in that Zone. While some DNS servers are still manually maintained, more are configured as so-called "Dynamic DNS" servers that are updated automatically.

Dynamic DNS is replacing the still popular Windows Internet Naming Service (WINS). WINS is a database of IP addresses and the related NetBIOS names.

Automated IP Addressing: DHCP   For almost all network clients, there is an automatic IP configuration service, called the Dynamic Host Configuration Protocol (DHCP). When a DHCP client boots, it asks a DHCP server for a free IP address and related configuration information. The DHCP server can supply all the IP addressing information that a computer could need, including key Windows IP parameters, such as the IP address of the WINS server.

Name Resolution: WINS   WINS was designed as a dynamic, centralized, and robust service. It was supposed to become a viable alternative to DNS. Each WINS server maintained a central database with multiple records for all machines. On a large network, this was a big data file.

WINS needs about three to ten data records for each computer. Naturally, this is cumbersome for larger networks. This is another reason why Microsoft is phasing out WINS.

What About Samba?   This is where Samba fits in. Samba on Linux provides all the Windows networking services available on any Windows TCP/IP client or server.

To configure Samba, you simply need to know the name of your NT/2000/XP Domain or Windows 9x–style Workgroup, and configure the parameters accordingly for your Linux workstation or server to match the settings on the local Microsoft network.

Fortunately, Samba comes with extensive online documentation (with examples) available in the smb.conf configuration file and through the SWAT menus. This chapter addresses two basic configurations: a basic workstation participating in a workgroup, and a server acting as part of a domain.

The following code lists some of the key components of Samba:

```
================================================================
/usr/sbin/smbd          - main SMB service daemon
/usr/sbin/nmbd          - NetBIOS name service daemon
/etc/samba/smb.conf     - SAMBA's primary configuration file
/usr/bin/smbclient      - connects to SMB shares, ftp-like syntax
/usr/bin/testparm       - tests validity of /etc/smb.conf file
/etc/rc.d/init.d/smb    - daemon start and stop control script
smbfs                   - file system extension to mount SMB shares on
                          directories; use with the mount -t command.
/usr/bin/smbprint       - a script to print to a printer on an SMB host
/usr/bin/smbstatus      - lists current SMB connections for the local host
================================================================
```

Samba Has Two Daemons

You need two daemons to run Samba: smbd and nmbd, both located in /usr/sbin. Both are configured through the /etc/samba/smb.conf configuration file. It's easy to check the syntax of this large configuration file with **testparm**. If problems arise, this program produces error messages to help you correct them.

Main Configuration File of Samba: /etc/samba/smb.conf

The main configuration file is long and includes many sections that require a good understanding of Microsoft Windows networking. The SWAT home page includes links to some very helpful documents, even the full text of the O'Reilly book on Samba. The default smb.conf file also includes helpful documentation with suggestions and example configurations that you can use.

SWAT's job is to manage the creation of the /etc/samba/smb.conf file and update it for you. In the past, Samba administrators had to create and edit this file by hand. Considering the range of functionality and the number of options and settings available, this was no small task. With SWAT, Samba administrators can define server settings, manage file and print shares, manage users and user authentication, and set up access restrictions on shared directories.

It's useful to study the original /etc/samba/smb.conf file. Once we see how the file is structured, back it up, and then use SWAT to help us configure this file. The following code is essentially a complete view of this file, with a few options and a few example sections removed for brevity. Some of the comments have been shortened, and additional comments are shown in bold. You might want to browse your own /etc/samba/smb.conf file as well.

The smb.conf file includes two types of comments. The hash symbol (#) is used for a general text comment. This is typically verbiage that describes a feature. The second comment symbol is the semicolon (;), used to comment out Samba directives (that we may later wish to uncomment in order to enable the disabled feature).

on the **Job** *The default /etc/samba/smb.conf file contains a wealth of hints to help guide you through Samba configuration. However, when you update your configuration with SWAT, all comments are removed! It is a good idea to back up a copy of this file before you reconfigure it with SWAT.*

```
================================================================
# This is the main Samba configuration file. You should read the
# smb.conf(5) manual page in order to understand the options listed
# here. Samba has a huge number of configurable options (perhaps too
# many!) most of which are not shown in this example
#
# Any line which starts with a ; (semi-colon) or a # (hash)
# is a comment and is ignored. In this example we will use a #
# for commentry and a ; for parts of the config file that you
# may wish to enable
#
# NOTE: Whenever you modify this file you should run the command "testparm"
# to check that you have not made any basic syntactic errors.
#
#======================= Global Settings =====================================
[global]
# workgroup = NT-Domain-Name or Workgroup-Name
   workgroup = MYGROUP

# server string is the equivalent of the NT/2000/XP Description field
   server string = Samba Server
```

```
# This option is important for security. It allows you to restrict
# connections to machines which are on your local network. The
# following example restricts access to two C class networks and
# the "loopback" interface. For more examples of the syntax see
# the smb.conf man page
;    hosts allow = 192.168.1. 192.168.2. 127.

# if you want to automatically load your printer list rather
# than setting them up individually then you'll need this
   printcap name = /etc/printcap
   load printers = yes

# It should not be necessary to spell out the print system type unless
# yours is non-standard. Currently supported print systems include:
# bsd, sysv, plp, lprng, aix, hpux, qnx
   printing = lprng

# Uncomment this if you want a guest account, you must add this to /etc/passwd
# otherwise the user "nobody" is used
;  guest account = pcguest

# this tells Samba to use a separate log file for each machine
# that connects
   log file = /var/log/samba/%m.log

# Put a capping on the size of the log files (in Kb).
   max log size = 0

# Security mode. Most people will want user level security. See
# security_level.txt for details.
   security = user

# Use password server option only with security = server
# The argument list may include:
#    password server = My_PDC_Name [My_BDC_Name] [My_Next_BDC_Name]
# or to auto-locate the domain controller/s
#    password server = *
;    password server = <NT-Server-Name>

# Password Level allows matching of _n_ characters of the password for
# all combinations of upper and lower case.
;  password level = 8
;  username level = 8
```

```
# You may wish to use password encryption. Please read
# ENCRYPTION.txt, Win95.txt and WinNT.txt in the Samba documentation.
# Do not enable this option unless you have read those documents
   encrypt passwords = yes
   smb passwd file = /etc/samba/smbpasswd

# The following is needed to keep smbclient from spouting spurious errors
# when Samba is built with support for SSL.
;   ssl CA certFile = /usr/share/ssl/certs/ca-bundle.crt

# The following are needed to allow password changing from Windows to
# update the Linux system password also.
# NOTE: Use these with 'encrypt passwords' and 'smb passwd file' above.
# NOTE2: You do NOT need these to allow workstations to change only
#        the encrypted SMB passwords. They allow the Unix password
#        to be kept in sync with the SMB password.
   unix password sync = Yes
   passwd program = /usr/bin/passwd %u
   passwd chat = *New*password* %n\n *Retype*new*password* %n\n
*passwd:*all*authentication*tokens*updated*successfully*

# You can use PAM's password change control flag for Samba. If
# enabled, then PAM will be used for password changes when requested
# by an SMB client instead of the program listed in passwd program.
# It should be possible to enable this without changing your passwd
# chat parameter for most setups.

   pam password change = yes

# Unix users can map to different SMB User names
;   username map = /etc/samba/smbusers

# Using the following line enables you to customise your configuration
# on a per machine basis. The %m gets replaced with the netbios name
# of the machine that is connecting
;   include = /etc/samba/smb.conf.%m

# This parameter will control whether or not Samba should obey PAM's
# account and session management directives. The default behavior is
# to use PAM for clear text authentication only and to ignore any
# account or session management. Note that Samba always ignores PAM
# for authentication in the case of encrypt passwords = yes

   obey pam restrictions = yes
```

```
# Most people will find that this option gives better performance.
# See speed.txt and the manual pages for details
    socket options = TCP_NODELAY SO_RCVBUF=8192 SO_SNDBUF=8192


# Configure Samba to use multiple interfaces
# If you have multiple network interfaces then you must list them
# here. See the man page for details.
;   interfaces = 192.168.12.2/24 192.168.13.2/24


# Configure remote browse list synchronisation here
#  request announcement to, or browse list sync from:
#     a specific host or from / to a whole subnet (see below)
;   remote browse sync = 192.168.3.25 192.168.5.255
# Cause this host to announce itself to local subnets here
;   remote announce = 192.168.1.255 192.168.2.44


# Browser Control Options:
# set local master to no if you don't want Samba to become a master
# browser on your network. Otherwise the normal election rules apply
;   local master = no


# OS Level determines the precedence of this server in master browser
# elections. The default value should be reasonable
;   os level = 33


# Domain Master specifies Samba to be the Domain Master Browser. This
# allows Samba to collate browse lists between subnets. Don't use this
# if you already have a Windows NT domain controller doing this job
;   domain master = yes


# Preferred Master causes Samba to force a local browser election on startup
# and gives it a slightly higher chance of winning the election
;   preferred master = yes


# Enable this if you want Samba to be a domain logon server for
# Windows95 workstations.
;   domain logons = yes


# if you enable domain logons then you may want a per-machine or
# per user logon script
# run a specific logon batch file per workstation (machine)
;   logon script = %m.bat
# run a specific logon batch file per username
;   logon script = %U.bat
```

```
# Where to store roving profiles (only for Win95 and WinNT)
#        %L substitutes for this servers netbios name, %U is username
#        You must uncomment the [Profiles] share below
;    logon path = \\%L\Profiles\%U


# Windows Internet Name Serving Support Section:
# WINS Support - Tells the NMBD component of Samba to enable it's WINS Server
;    wins support = yes


# WINS Server - Tells the NMBD components of Samba to be a WINS Client
#    Note: Samba can be either a WINS Server, or a WINS Client, but NOT both
;    wins server = w.x.y.z


# WINS Proxy - Tells Samba to answer name resolution queries on
# behalf of a non WINS capable client, for this to work there must be
# at least one    WINS Server on the network. The default is NO.
;    wins proxy = yes


# DNS Proxy - tells Samba whether or not to try to resolve NetBIOS names
# via DNS nslookups. The built-in default for versions 1.9.17 is yes,
# this has been changed in version 1.9.18 to no.
   dns proxy = no
# Case Preservation can be handy - system default is _no_
# NOTE: These can be set on a per share basis
;  preserve case = no
;  short preserve case = no
# Default case is normally upper case for all DOS files
;  default case = lower
# Be very careful with case sensitivity - it can break things!
;  case sensitive = no
#============================= Share Definitions ================================
[homes]
   comment = Home Directories
   browseable = no
   writable = yes
   valid users = %S
   create mode = 0664
   directory mode = 0775
# If you want users samba doesn't recognize to be mapped to a guest user
; map to guest = bad user


# Un-comment the following and create the netlogon directory for Domain Logons
; [netlogon]
;    comment = Network Logon Service
```

```
;    path = /usr/local/samba/lib/netlogon
;    guest ok = yes
;    writable = no
;    share modes = no

# Un-comment the following to provide a specific roving profile share
# the default is to use the user's home directory
;[Profiles]
;     path = /usr/local/samba/profiles
;     browseable = no
;     guest ok = yes

# NOTE: If you have a BSD-style print system there is no need to
# specifically define each individual printer
[printers]
    comment = All Printers
    path = /var/spool/samba
    browseable = no
# Set public = yes to allow user 'guest account' to print
    guest ok = no
    writable = no
    printable = yes


# This one is useful for people to share files
;[tmp]
;    comment = Temporary file space
;    path = /tmp
;    read only = no
;    public = yes


# A publicly accessible directory, but read only, except for people in
# the "staff" group
;[public]
;    comment = Public Stuff
;    path = /home/samba
;    public = yes
;    writable = yes
;    printable = no
;    write list = @staff

# Other examples.
#
# A private printer, usable only by fred. Spool data will be placed in fred's
# home directory. Note that fred must have write access to the spool directory,
# wherever it is.
```

```
;[fredsprn]
;    comment = Fred's Printer
;    valid users = fred
;    path = /home/fred
;    printer = freds_printer
;    public = no
;    writable = no
;    printable = yes


# A private directory, usable only by fred. Note that fred requires write
# access to the directory.
;[fredsdir]
;    comment = Fred's Service
;    path = /usr/somewhere/private
;    valid users = fred
;    public = no
;    writable = yes
;    printable = no


# a service which has a different directory for each machine that connects
# this allows you to tailor configurations to incoming machines. You could
# also use the %U option to tailor it by user name.
# The %m gets replaced with the machine name that is connecting.
;[pchome]
;    comment = PC Directories
;    path = /usr/local/pc/%m
;    public = no
;    writable = yes


# A publicly accessible directory, read/write to all users. Note that all files
# created in the directory by users will be owned by the default user, so
# any user with access can delete any other user's files. Obviously this
# directory must be writable by the default user. Another user could of course
# be specified, in which case all files would be owned by that user instead.
;[public]
;    path = /usr/somewhere/else/public
;    public = yes
;    only guest = yes
;    writable = yes
;    printable = no


# The following two entries demonstrate how to share a directory so that two
# users can place files there that will be owned by the specific users. In this
# setup, the directory should be writable by both users and should have the
# sticky bit set on it to prevent abuse. Obviously this could be extended to
```

```
# as many users as required.
;[myshare]
;    comment = Mary's and Fred's stuff
;    path = /usr/somewhere/shared
;    valid users = mary fred
;    public = no
;    writable = yes
;    printable = no
;    create mask = 0765
=================================================================
```

Global Settings   The first major section of smb.conf includes global settings, which define the overall attributes of your server. These attributes include:

- Your server's Microsoft Workgroup name, NetBIOS name, and identification string

- User password management policies, at share, user, and domain levels

- Mobile logon scripts on a domain

- Access limits by domain names and IP address groups

- Master browser election settings for a Domain, LAN, or Workgroup

- WINS and DNS support options

- Case sensitivity settings

SWAT simplifies Samba configuration by:

- Offering help for every option, with text explanations just a click away

- Allowing you to select a reasonable default by using the Set Default button

- Making choices available via a drop-down box (wherever possible), rather than forcing the user to enter a setting

- Supporting two views of each configuration screen. The Basic view (default) provides minimal prompts sufficient for configuring your server, shares, or users. The Advanced view gives you complete control over your service definitions.

Figure 8-17 shows the Samba Global Variables screen.

You should customize this screen to meet your local Microsoft network requirements. Many different kinds of configurations are possible, including on a Windows 9*x* network, in a workgroup with other Windows NT/2000/XP computers, and in

FIGURE 8-17

SWAT's Global
Variables screen,
Basic View

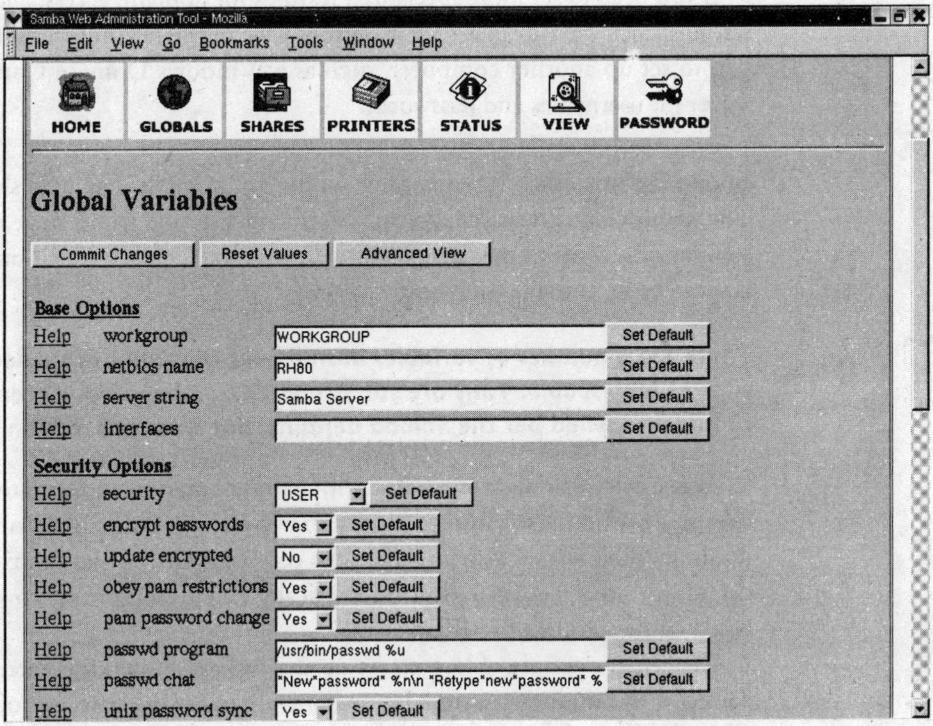

a domain with a mixed group of computers. Samba is easiest to set up for a Microsoft Workgroup, where the client computers are Windows NT/2000/XP computers. These are the only changes you need to make in this screen:

- **workgroup** Should match the name of the workgroup that you're using for other computers on your network.

- **netbios name** Will represent the name of your Linux computer on the Microsoft network.

- **server string** Represents the comment associated with your computer on a Microsoft network.

If you have a network where usernames are not required, set SHARE level security. In the Microsoft world, such networks generally include computers with Windows 9*x*/ ME operating system. Otherwise, you'll need to set some other form of security (USER, SERVER, or DOMAIN), depending on whether there is a central database or domain of usernames and passwords on your network.

If you need to set more specialized features for domain, access, and authentication settings, click the Advanced View button. One of the key Advanced features allows you to set up another computer, such as a Windows Domain Controller, as the server for usernames and passwords.

Share Definitions   The remainder of the smb.conf file is used for share definitions. The settings for each shared directory start with a section name, such as [tmp]. This section name contains the name that will be seen by Microsoft clients only if the service is set to be browseable (browseable = yes).

There are a number of variables in smb.conf that are not spelled correctly, such as browseable. They are still accepted Samba variables, and generally should be spelled per the Samba defaults, not standard written English.

Two special shares are associated with Samba: [homes] and [printers]. The default [homes] configuration automatically shares all user home directories as private, nonbrowseable shares with any user who connects with a valid Linux username. The default [printers] configuration automatically shares local printers over the network based on the printers' NetBIOS name.

Here is an example of how to set up sharing of Linux home directories. Done correctly, this limits access to a Linux home directory to the owner of that directory. Click the Shares button on SWAT. You should see the screen in Figure 8-18.

FIGURE 8-18
Setting up shares for user's home directories

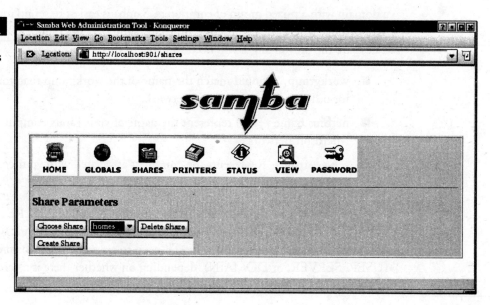

Now, click the unlabeled button drop-down between the Choose Share and the Delete Share buttons. Unless you've already reconfigured smb.conf, the standard option is the Homes share. Select Homes, and then click Choose Share to work with this share. You should see additional options as shown in Figure 8-19.

There is no default /homes directory. It's just a label. We don't need to supply a home directory, because Samba will read the user's account record in /etc/passwd and /etc/shadow to determine the directory to be shared. Scroll down through Samba's home share options. Notice that we do not allow access to unknown users (guest ok = no) and that we can limit the systems that can use this share (hosts allow = ?, and hosts deny = ?).

Note how Help links are available for most SWAT options.

Once you are satisfied with the setup for your homes share, click Commit Changes at the top of this Web page to activate your share.

Finally, make sure users are properly set up and enabled properly. Click the Password button in the top SWAT menu. You should see a screen similar to what is shown in Figure 8-20.

FIGURE 8-19

Detailed setup for user home directory shares

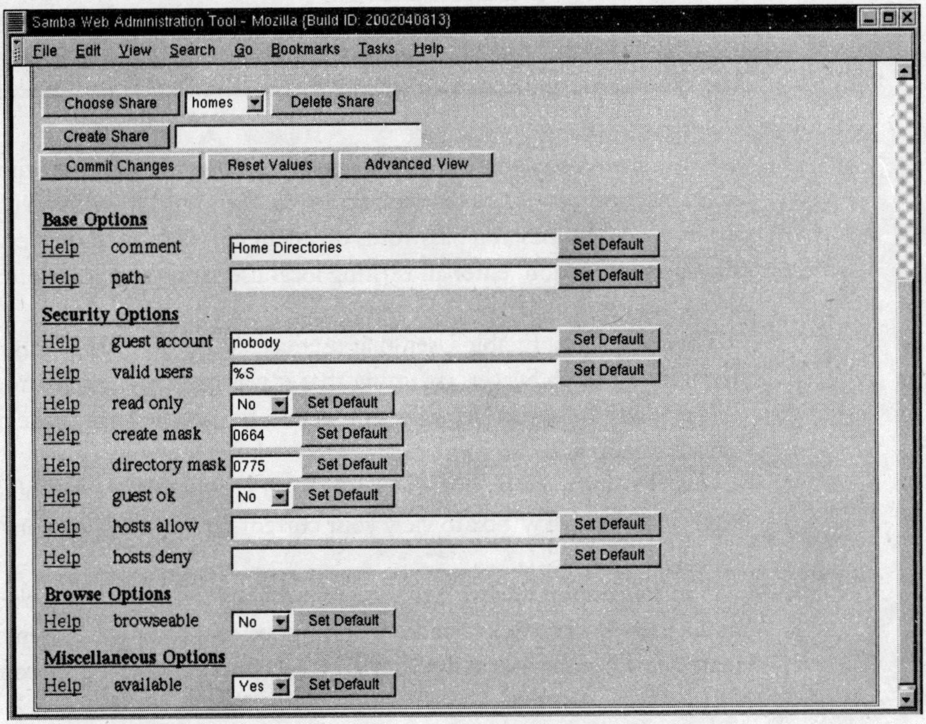

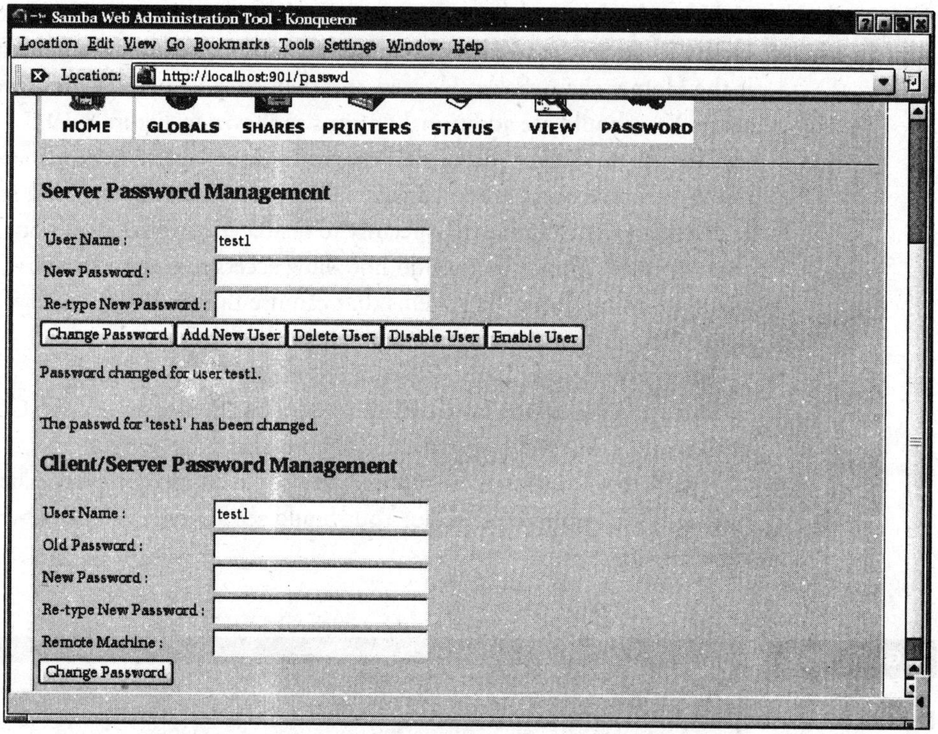

FIGURE 8-20

Setting up users
for Samba

This screen assumes that you're setting up users locally. As with NFS, the usernames and passwords that you set up on the local Linux Samba Server should match the usernames and passwords on client computers. In the Server Password Management section, enter an existing local username and password. Click Add New User.

Then when you Enable User, that user can access his or her home directory on your Linux Samba Server, assuming that it was properly shared. You can use the Client/Server Password Management section to actually change the password on the remote Windows computer.

Now, let's look at what SWAT did with our changes. At the top of the Samba Web page, click the VIEW box to view your current /etc/samba/smb.conf file. It should look like Figure 8-21.

If you're comfortable with the command line interface, the quicker way to set up Samba users is with the smbadduser and smbpasswd commands. Remember, you can create a new Samba user only from valid accounts on your Linux computer.

FIGURE 8-21

The /etc/samba/smb.conf file as reconfigured by SWAT

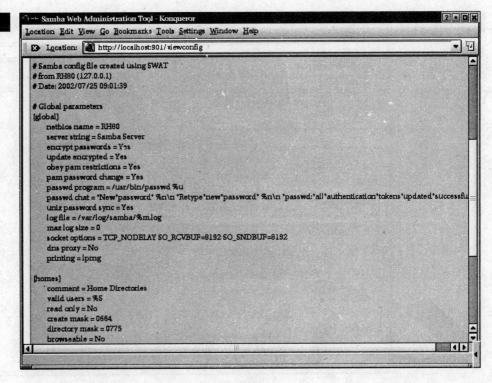

```
Samba Web Administration Tool - Konqueror
Location  Edit  View  Go  Bookmarks  Tools  Settings  Window  Help

Location:  http://localhost:901/viewconfig

# Samba config file created using SWAT
# from RH80 (127.0.0.1)
# Date: 2002/07/25 09:01:39

# Global parameters
[global]
        netbios name = RH80
        server string = Samba Server
        encrypt passwords = Yes
        update encrypted = Yes
        obey pam restrictions = Yes
        pam password change = Yes
        passwd program = /usr/bin/passwd %u
        passwd chat = *New*password* %n\n *Retype*new*password* %n\n *passwd:*all*authentication*tokens*updated*successful
        unix password sync = Yes
        log file = /var/log/samba/%m.log
        max log size = 0
        socket options = TCP_NODELAY SO_RCVBUF=8192 SO_SNDBUF=8192
        dns proxy = No
        printing = lprng

[homes]
        comment = Home Directories
        valid users = %S
        read only = No
        create mask = 0664
        directory mask = 0775
        browseable = No
```

In Figure 8-21, we can see that we have home directory shares as well as print sharing enabled, but nothing more. Also notice that all the comments (except for the header comments) are gone! For the sake of simplicity, we have left all server configurations set to the default. It also makes sense to change the Server String to something that uniquely identifies your Linux server.

Adding Linux to a Microsoft Windows NT/2000/XP network can be made easier by configuring the Samba service to look like another Windows host on the network. You can configure the Samba server to act as a WINS client of the WINS server, share files and printers just like all the other Windows hosts, and participate in the browser service.

Creating a Public Share

Now, let's create a public access share for use with the entire network. Click the Shares box to get to the correct Web page. Now, enter the name of our new share, **PublicShare**, in the input field beside the Create Share button, and then click that button. You should see the screen in Figure 8-22.

FIGURE 8-22

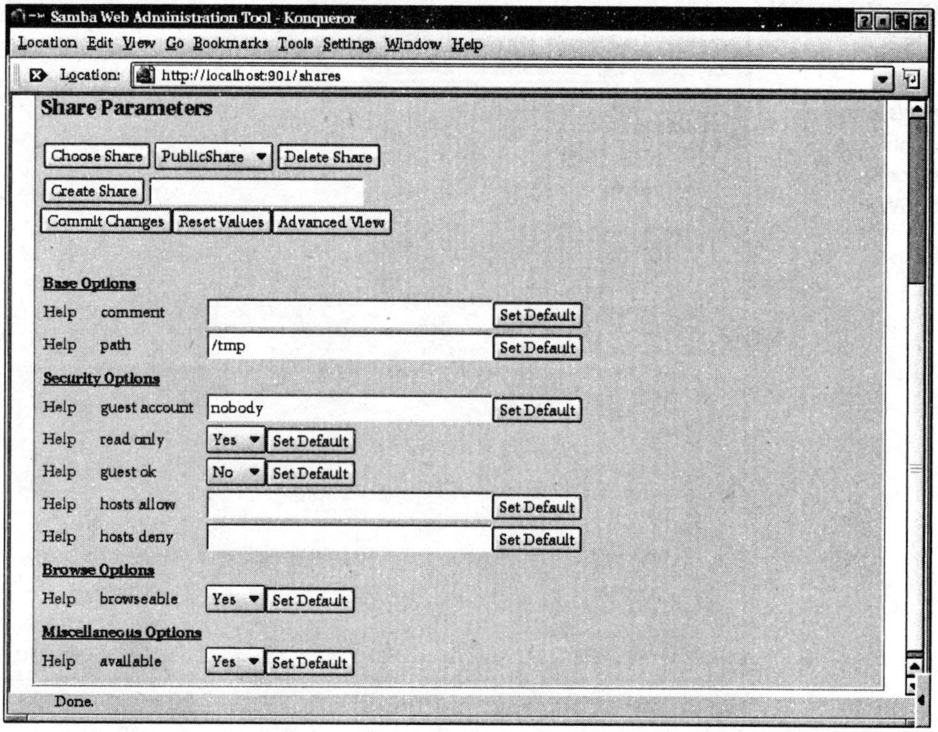

Creating a
public share

We want to set up the /home/PublicShare directory. It should be accessible to all
users with a Linux account on your computer. It will also deny access to guest users
and others. We wish to provide access to anyone in our domain (.myCompany.com),
and we wish to deny access to everyone in the suspect domain (which we'll call
evil.crackers.com). Finally, your shares should be browseable to valid users. An example
screen with these options set is presented in Figure 8-23.

Now, scroll back to the top of the page and select Commit Changes. Click the
VIEW box and examine the changes Samba has made to your /etc/samba/smb.conf
file. Finally, note that Samba will define the share attributes, but it will not make the
directories needed by the share. Let's do that now. Issue these commands:

```
[root@redhattest mj] # mkdir /home/PublicShare

[root@redhattest mj] # chmod 1777 /home/PublicShare
```

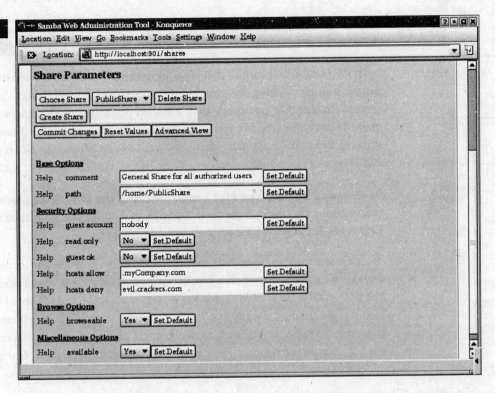

FIGURE 8-23

Defining a
public share

The digit '1' in front of the 777 directory permission string is the sticky bit.
By enabling the sticky bit, we are saying that anyone can do anything in the
directory (because of the 777 permission value) but only to files they make!
Otherwise, any user could delete or rename any file in our PublicShare,
regardless of the file's owner.

Client Configuration for Print Services

There is a simple option line in the /etc/samba/smb.conf file that shares all local
printer systems as if this were another Windows host. While it does not currently
support the NT/2000/XP style of downloading print drivers, the capability does
exist. One package designed to emulate this print driver sharing process is based
on the work of the Imprints project, at http://imprints.sourceforge.net.

As of this writing, the Imprints package is in beta and is therefore not included
in the current version of Red Hat Linux. However, it is reasonable to expect that
this or a similar package will be available for future versions of Red Hat Linux.

As printer management is a system administration function, you may need to know how to set up the Imprints package as soon as the RHCE 8.1 exam.

In /etc/samba/smb.conf, printer configurations start with the section heading named [printers]. Using the same share options used for directories, Samba can create a shared print service for each installed print queue. This can work for both major Linux print services, lpd (Line Print Daemon) and CUPS (Common UNIX Printing System). These print shares are available to Microsoft clients when users install network printers.

As discussed earlier, Red Hat has deprecated the Line Print Daemon. Yet it still remains the default for Red Hat 8.0. It is quite possible that the RHCE exam will focus on CUPS in the very near future.

There is a slight difference in configuration between a file service and a print service. File services are writable but not printable, whereas print services are printable but not writable. Printable shares allow printer shares to upload spool files to the Linux print queue (typically via /tmp). Once the print job is completed, the file is removed. Writable shares, such as the /home/PublicShare directory created earlier, permit users to upload their own files to the share for permanent storage.

Testing Changes to /etc/samba/smb.conf

After making any changes to /etc/samba/smb.conf, it is always a good idea to test your system before putting it into production. You can do a simple syntax check on the Samba configuration file with the **testparm** test utility as shown in Figure 8-24. This does not actually check to see if the service is running or functioning correctly, it checks only basic text syntax and groupings.

Enabling Samba Services

We can control Samba service daemons from within SWAT. Go to the STATUS box and click it. The Samba daemons, smbd and nmbd, may be stopped or running. Buttons should be available adjacent to the smbd and nmbd lines to Start, Stop, or Restart each daemon. One example of this is shown in Figure 8-25. Start or restart each daemon as appropriate. If you're restarting, this forces Samba to reread the /etc/samba/smb.conf configuration file. But remember, you may want to follow up with the /sbin/chkconfig command to make sure Samba is activated at the appropriate runlevels when you boot Linux.

FIGURE 8-24

Testing syntax
on smb.conf

```
[root@RH80 samba]# testparm | more
Load smb config files from /etc/samba/smb.conf
Processing section "[homes]"
Processing section "[printers]"
Processing section "[homemj]"
Processing section "[PublicShare]"
Loaded services file OK.
WARNING: You have some share names that are longer than 8 chars
These may give errors while browsing or may not be accessible
to some older clients
Press enter to see a dump of your service definitions
# Global parameters
[global]
        coding system =
        client code page = 850
        code page directory = /usr/share/samba/codepages
        workgroup = WORKGROUP
        netbios name = RH80
        netbios aliases =
        netbios scope =
        server string = Samba Server
        interfaces =
        bind interfaces only = No
        security = USER
        encrypt passwords = Yes
        update encrypted = Yes
        allow trusted domains = Yes
--More--
```

FIGURE 8-25

The Server Status
page allows you
to restart Samba.

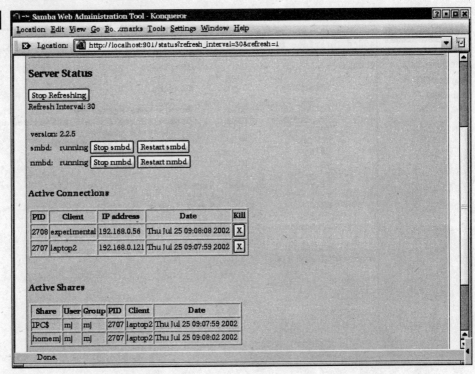

Another available option is to control Samba via the smb management script, /etc/rc.d/init.d/smb. As always, you can use the /sbin/service command with this script; for example, **/sbin/service smb restart** stops and then starts both the smbd and nmbd daemons.

Checking Samba File and Print Services

The last tool we'll discuss is **smbclient**. This can help you test connectivity to any SMB host on a Windows- or Samba-based Linux/Unix computer. It even provides a familiar (to most Linux and Unix users) FTP-like interface. You can use smbclient to connect to an SMB share with a valid username and password. Next, you get an SMB prompt, and then use FTP style commands to upload, download, and otherwise manipulate files remotely.

You can use smbclient to check the directories and printers that you're sharing from the local Samba server over the network. This should match what other Linux/Unix and Microsoft Windows users see of your system. For example, the smbclient command shown in Figure 8-26 checks the shares on the local computer. The command format is the same for any other computer on the network.

FIGURE 8-26	
Checking local shares with smbclient	

```
[root@RH80 samba]# smbclient -L \\RH80
added interface ip=192.168.0.222 bcast=192.168.0.255 nmask=255.255.255.0
Password:
Domain=[WORKGROUP] OS=[Unix] Server=[Samba 2.2.5]

        Sharename      Type      Comment
        ---------      ----      -------
        homemj         Disk      Mike's Home Directory
        PublicShare    Disk      General Share for all authorized users
        IPC$           IPC       IPC Service (Samba Server)
        ADMIN$         Disk      IPC Service (Samba Server)
        fdsaj          Printer
        mj             Disk      Home Directories

        Server                   Comment
        ---------                -------
        RH80                     Samba Server

        Workgroup                Master
        ---------                -------
        WORKGROUP
[root@RH80 samba]# []
```

There are two arguments you should use: -L to specify the name of the Samba server and -U to identify the username to connect as. If the command reaches the Samba server, you're then prompted for the appropriate password.

You can now connect via smbclient to your Samba server in order to use your PublicShare. This assumes, of course, that you remembered to create the /home/PublicShare directory earlier. As shown in Figure 8-27, the syntax is somewhat unusual. You actually use forward slashes (/) to connect to a specific share.

To connect to our share, we use smbclient //*server*/*sharename* -U *username* (note the forward slashes). If the share is a restricted access share, we are prompted for a password. Once we successfully connect, we are prompted by an smb>> prompt. Note in our session that some Unix commands work (pwd) and some do not (ls -l). The smbclient system is biased toward DOS- and FTP-style commands. To get a complete list of smbclient built-in commands, type a question mark and press ENTER.

There are both client and server portions to Samba services. You should be familiar with the basic steps of how to configure the server characteristics and the shared services.

FIGURE 8-27	
Attaching to a share with smbclient	

```
[root@RH80 root]# smbclient //RH80/mj -U mj
added interface ip=192.168.0.222 bcast=192.168.0.255 nmask=255.255.255.0
Password:
Domain=[WORKGROUP] OS=[Unix] Server=[Samba 2.2.5]
smb: \> ls f1*
  f1101.tif                    649842  Mon Jul  8 05:52:22 2002
  f1106.tif                   1062362  Mon Jul  8 06:03:59 2002
  f1107.tif                    649842  Mon Jul  8 06:06:07 2002

              45584 blocks of size 131072. 29454 blocks available
smb: \> 
```

Managing Samba Users

Users for Samba services are often set up in a list independent from users who have accounts on your Linux system. The Samba development team chose to do this because

- There is no reason to grant Samba access to all Unix users (e.g., root).

- You may wish to grant Samba access to users who do not have a Linux account.

- You may wish to manage user access via Windows NT/2000/XP, so Linux wouldn't necessarily even know about your Samba users.

- Samba user authentication may involve clear text passwords (for compatibility with Windows 95 and Windows 3.1). This could potentially compromise your Linux system.

To support these features, you can set up separate user accounts in /etc/samba/smbpasswd. In fact, that's what you did earlier in SWAT when you activated specific users.

As always, you can do the same things that you can do with a GUI tool like SWAT at the command line interface. In this case, two steps are required to make and enable a new Samba user:

1. Create a Samba user entry by name and add a password for the user. Samba users can be created only from the current users on your Linux system.

2. Enable Samba access for the new user.

Users can be managed by command line or via SWAT. If the username that you want does not yet exist, create it with the /usr/sbin/useradd command. Then you can set that user up as a Samba user with the smbpasswd command. Use the following command; you're prompted to enter a password. That password can be different from the regular login password.

```
[root@RH80 mj] # smbpasswd -a newUser
New SMB password:
Retype SMB password:
[root@RH80 mj] #
```

Next, to enable Samba access for this user, run the following command:

```
[ root@notebook / ] # smbpasswd -e newUser
Enabled user newUser
[ root@notebook / ] #
```

Changes made by smbpasswd are passed to the Samba server to be copied to the system with the username and password database for your network.

There are four basic authentication options: Share, User, Server, and Domain. The default is User; in this case, you'll want to make sure the Samba usernames and passwords that you create match those on individual Windows NT/2000/XP systems on your network.

If you use the Server authentication option, you can name another Samba server to carry the database of usernames and passwords.

If you use the Domain authentication option, you can name an NT/2000/XP Domain controller. You can set up a Samba server as a Domain controller as well, emulating the functionality of a Windows Domain controller.

Creating Local SMB Mounts

During the boot process, Linux reads the /etc/fstab configuration file, to determine what filesystems are to be mounted. These can be local filesystems such as /boot or /home, or remote filesystems that are connected through NFS and SMB.

You can update the /etc/fstab file with SMB entries. This can create a permanent connection to each SMB share on the network. One example entry is shown here. Remember, all entries in /etc/fstab have to be on one line, or Linux may not be able to read it.

```
//winxp1/downloads /home/mj/downloads smbfs
username=prime,password=abas43df 0 0
```

The SMB Filesystem   You can always use the **mount -t smbfs -o username =** *user // server/ sharename / mountpoint* command to make a temporary Samba connection. You're prompted for a password as required.

You can create a directory and then mount an SMB remote share service on it using the mount command. For Figure 8-28, let's assume we have a Microsoft system named laptop2 with a share called downloads. We want to connect and access the share named downloads.

In Figure 8-28, a directory (/mnt/smbshare) is created to act as the mount point for the SMB share. The root user can then connect to the share named downloads on the computer named laptop2, and then mount it on the newly created directory. You're prompted to enter a password. You can also see a list of all mounted directories with the **mount** command.

If your host connection is going to an NT/2000/XP workstation or Domain, a username and password are normally required. As you can see, the -o switch allows you to enter the username as part of the command.

FIGURE 8-28

Mounting an SMB
remote share

```
[root@RH80 root]# mkdir /mnt/smbshare
[root@RH80 root]# mount -o username=mjang //laptop2/downloads /mnt/smbshare/
Password:
[root@RH80 root]# \ls -l /mnt/smbshare/linux*
-rwxr-xr-x    1 root     root       30108170 02-25 18:40 /mnt/smbshare/linux-2.4.18.
tar.gz
-rwxr-xr-x    1 root     root       30108170 05-14 12:41 /mnt/smbshare/linux-2.4.18.
tar.gz.realdownload
[root@RH80 root]# mount
/dev/sda2 on / type ext3 (rw)
none on /proc type proc (rw)
usbdevfs on /proc/bus/usb type usbdevfs (rw)
/dev/sda1 on /boot type ext3 (rw)
none on /dev/pts type devpts (rw,gid=5,mode=620)
none on /dev/shm type tmpfs (rw)
//laptop2/downloads on /mnt/smbshare type smbfs (0)
[root@RH80 root]# umount /mnt/smbshare/
[root@RH80 root]# []
```

EXERCISE 8-5

Configuring Samba with Shares

In this exercise, you'll be configuring Samba to do something useful, sharing a
directory and any configured printers. For this purpose, you'll be using SWAT;
therefore, you'll need to be in a GUI such as GNOME or KDE.

1. Install the Samba RPMs as described earlier in this chapter.

2. If you want to use SWAT to configure SAMBA, make sure it's not disabled
   in /etc/xinetd.d/swat configuration file. Restart xinetd with the **/sbin/service
   xinetd restart** command to read the changes.

3. Open SWAT in the local computer. Open the Web browser of your choice
   and direct it to localhost:901.

4. If you have a WINS server configured, authorize Samba to participate as a
   WINS client. Use the IP of your WINS server.

5. Configure Samba to share as public, in read-only mode, the /home/ftp/pub
   directory tree.

6. Configure Samba to share all installed print queues to all users. Allow guest access to all public shares, create a guest account, associate it with an unused UID and GID 600. Set the password to be "anonymous."

7. Share all user home directories.

8. Create separate log files for each host that connects.

9. Make all print and file shares browseable, but not home directories.

The Red Hat Samba Configuration Tool

Red Hat has recently introduced its own graphical configuration tool for Apache, redhat-config-samba, which you can install from the RPM of the same name. Before using this tool, back up your current /etc/samba/smb.conf configuration file. As of this writing, work on this tool is not complete; any changes that you make with this tool may overwrite this file.

You will find that redhat-config-samba is a straightforward tool. You can configure general Samba settings such as NetBIOS name and workgroup through the Preferences | Basic Preferences command. The New button enables you to set up a new share. The Preferences | Modify Samba Users command is essentially a front end to the smbuseradd and smbpasswd commands.

As this tool is still fairly new, test it carefully before using it in a production environment. And definitely test it carefully before using it on the RHCE exam. At least for now, SWAT is the more reliable graphical configuration tool.

However, as long as you back up your current /etc/samba/smb.conf configuration file, testing redhat-config-samba can help further your understanding of Samba.

CERTIFICATION OBJECTIVE 8.04

Mail Services

If you have Linux installed on your computer, you can set up a powerful mail server. Perhaps the most common mail server on the Internet is sendmail, which may already be installed on your version of Red Hat Linux. Once it is installed and configured, you can set up sendmail as your own personal mail server (subject to the limitations of your ISP).

A number of alternatives to sendmail are not covered in this book; they include procmail, mail.local, and uucp.

When you install sendmail, you also get a huge and difficult-to-read configuration file. Do not be intimidated. There are only a few entries you are ever likely to have to change.

A mail server has three major components, as described in Table 8-3. You need all three of these components to have a fully functional mail system.

On your Linux computer, you can configure sendmail for various outbound services, such as forwarding, relaying, method of transport (such as TCP or UDP), lists of computers with other sendmail systems, optional aliases, and spooling directories.

E-mail systems are heavily dependent on name resolution. While you could handle name resolution through /etc/hosts on a small network, any mail system that requires Internet access needs access to a fully functional DNS server.

The sendmail program uses SMTP to send e-mail. But that is only one end of the mail system. You can also configure POP and or IMAP to receive e-mail.

SMTP

SMTP, the Simple Mail Transfer Protocol, has become one of the most important service protocols of the modern era. Much of the Internet-connected world lives and dies by e-mail and relies on SMTP to deliver it. SMTP is a *protocol*, a set of rules for transferring data used by various Mail Transfer Agents.

The sendmail daemon is configured from a set of files in /etc and a directory of configuration files in /usr/share/sendmail-cf. See Table 8-4 for a description of key sendmail configuration files and directories.

If you don't see some of these files or directories, you may not have both sendmail RPM packages installed: sendmail and sendmail-cf. Use the **rpm -q** *packagename* command to check if you have these packages installed, and install them as required.

| TABLE 8-3 | Required Components of a Mail System |

Abbreviation	Meaning	Examples
MTA	Mail transfer agent	sendmail, POP, IMAP
MUA	Mail user agent	mail, Mozilla, elm
MDA	Mail delivery agent	Procmail

TABLE 8-4	sendmail Files to Support SMTP

File	Description
/etc/sendmail.cf	Main configuration file
/etc/aliases	E-mail alias definitions for users and groups
/usr/share/sendmail-cf/cf	A directory of files that can help you configure and customize sendmail
/etc/mail	A directory of configuration files used by various mail programs

Configuring sendmail

When sendmail starts, it reads the /etc/sendmail.cf file. This is a long (1495-line) file that may seem difficult to decipher but includes a wealth of helpful comments. This file provides detailed rules (organized into rulesets) on how sendmail should process e-mail addresses, filter spam, talk to other mail servers, and more.

This file is extremely complex and uses cryptic syntax. Fortunately, most of the directives included in this file are standards that you don't need to change. Many are required by various Internet agreements relating to e-mail address, mail transfer agents, and more.

Red Hat tries to simplify this process with a smaller, 54-line file, /etc/mail/sendmail.mc, which contains only the most relevant configuration directives. It is composed entirely of macros that define key sendmail.cf settings. Once you've configured this file, you can use the m4 macro processor to generate a new, custom sendmail.cf file.

The following code illustrates the current default /etc/mail/sendmail.mc file.

```
=================================================================
divert(-1)
dnl This is the sendmail macro config file. If you make changes to this file,
dnl you need the sendmail-cf rpm installed and then have to generate a
dnl new /etc/mail/sendmail.cf by running the following command:
dnl
dnl         m4 /etc/mail/sendmail.mc > /etc/mail/sendmail.cf
dnl
include(`/usr/share/sendmail-cf/m4/cf.m4')
VERSIONID(`linux setup for Red Hat Linux')dnl
OSTYPE(`linux')
dnl Uncomment and edit the following line if your mail needs to be sent out
dnl through an external mail server:
dnl define(`SMART_HOST',`smtp.your.provider')
define(`confDEF_USER_ID',``8:12'')dnl
undefine(`UUCP_RELAY')dnl
```

```
undefine(`BITNET_RELAY')dnl
dnl define(`confAUTO_REBUILD')dnl
define(`confTO_CONNECT', `1m')dnl
define(`confTRY_NULL_MX_LIST',true)dnl
define(`confDONT_PROBE_INTERFACES',true)dnl
define(`PROCMAIL_MAILER_PATH',`/usr/bin/procmail')dnl
define(`ALIAS_FILE', `/etc/aliases')dnl
dnl define(`STATUS_FILE', `/etc/mail/statistics')dnl
define(`UUCP_MAILER_MAX', `2000000')dnl
define(`confUSERDB_SPEC', `/etc/mail/userdb.db')dnl
define(`confPRIVACY_FLAGS', `authwarnings,novrfy,noexpn,restrictqrun')dnl
define(`confAUTH_OPTIONS', `A')dnl
dnl TRUST_AUTH_MECH(`EXTERNAL DIGEST-MD5 CRAM-MD5 LOGIN PLAIN')dnl
dnl define(`confAUTH_MECHANISMS', `EXTERNAL GSSAPI DIGEST-MD5 CRAM-MD5
  LOGIN PLAIN')dnl
dnl define(`confCACERT_PATH',`/usr/share/ssl/certs')
dnl define(`confCACERT',`/usr/share/ssl/certs/ca-bundle.crt')
dnl define(`confSERVER_CERT',`/usr/share/ssl/certs/sendmail.pem')
dnl define(`confSERVER_KEY',`/usr/share/ssl/certs/sendmail.pem')
dnl define(`confTO_QUEUEWARN', `4h')dnl
dnl define(`confTO_QUEUERETURN', `5d')dnl
dnl define(`confQUEUE_LA', `12')dnl
dnl define(`confREFUSE_LA', `18')dnl
define(`confTO_IDENT', `0')dnl
dnl FEATURE(delay_checks)dnl
FEATURE(`no_default_msa',`dnl')dnl
FEATURE(`smrsh',`/usr/sbin/smrsh')dnl
FEATURE(`mailertable',`hash -o /etc/mail/mailertable.db')dnl
FEATURE(`virtusertable',`hash -o /etc/mail/virtusertable.db')dnl
FEATURE(redirect)dnl
FEATURE(always_add_domain)dnl
FEATURE(use_cw_file)dnl
FEATURE(use_ct_file)dnl
dnl The '-t' option will retry delivery if e.g. the user runs over his quota.
FEATURE(local_procmail,`',`procmail -t -Y -a $h -d $u')dnl
FEATURE(`access_db',`hash -T<TMPF> -o /etc/mail/access.db')dnl
FEATURE(`blacklist_recipients')dnl
EXPOSED_USER(`root')dnl
dnl This changes sendmail to only listen on the loopback device 127.0.0.1
dnl and not on any other network devices. Comment this out if you want
dnl to accept email over the network.
DAEMON_OPTIONS(`Port=smtp,Addr=127.0.0.1, Name=MTA')
dnl NOTE: binding both IPv4 and IPv6 daemon to the same port requires
dnl        a kernel patch
dnl DAEMON_OPTIONS(`port=smtp,Addr=::1, Name=MTA-v6, Family=inet6')
dnl We strongly recommend to comment this one out if you want to protect
```

```
dnl yourself from spam. However, the laptop and users on computers that do
dnl not have 24x7 DNS do need this.
FEATURE(`accept_unresolvable_domains')dnl
dnl FEATURE(`relay_based_on_MX')dnl
MAILER(smtp)dnl
MAILER(procmail)dnl
Cwlocalhost.localdomain
===================================================================
```

sendmail.mc Directives   The sendmail.mc file is made up of directives (macros) used to create content for sendmail.cf. These macros do the following:

- Add comments to aid in comprehension
- Define key variables and values
- Enable or disable features
- Create variables with specific settings

The most basic macro is **dnl**, which tells m4 to delete from this point through to the end of the line. It is used to comment out descriptive text or disable a feature that would otherwise be included.

The **include** directive instructs m4 to read the contents of the named file and insert it at the current location in the output. This is how additional configuration information (needed by sendmail but not relevant to mail configuration) is kept separately from settings we may wish to change.

The **undefine** directive deletes the named keyword. As shown in sendmail.mc, by undefining UUCP_RELAY and BITNET_RELAY, we disable mail relaying through these two older types of networks. These systems were common on international networks in the 1970s and 1980s.

The **define** directive sets files or enables features that we wish to use. In the preceding example, we set the path to our e-mail name user ALIAS_FILE as (/etc/aliases), identify where procmail lives (PROCMAIL_MAILER_PATH), and provide the path for the official database of e-mail users; in this case, in virtualusertable.db.

The **FEATURE** directive enables specific features. For example, we use **FEATURE** to set accept_unresolvable_domains. This allows us to accept mail where we can't figure out the domain of the user who sent the e-mail. Specifically, an unresolvable domain refers to a case where it isn't possible to find a domain name through a reverse IP address lookup. If you don't have reliable DNS access, you may need this feature, or else your sendmail configuration may refuse a lot of valid e-mail.

DAEMON_OPTIONS directly controls the SMTP daemon. In the default case, we do not accept any mail from outside our own system (note the loopback address on this line).

Configuring Your System for Internet Mail

You only need to make a couple of adjustments to get your system ready for use on the Internet. First, comment out the DAEMON_OPTIONS directive by adding dnl to the front of it. You're no longer limited to mailing users only on the local computer; mail processing is enabled on all network interfaces.

Next, assuming you have reliable DNS access, comment out the **FEATURE** directive that sets accept_unresolvable_domains. This blocks spammers who use just an IP address, or spammers who fake their domain name to hide themselves from sending us mail.

Back up the current sendmail.cf file. Then you can generate a new sendmail.cf file and restart sendmail services with the following commands:

```
[root@redhattest mj] # cp /etc/mail/sendmail.cf /home/mj
[root@redhattest mj] # m4 /etc/mail/sendmail.mc > /etc/mail/sendmail.cf
[root@redhattest mj] # /sbin/chkconfig sendmail --level 235 on
[root@redhattest mj] # /etc/rc.d/init.d/sendmail restart
```

Your sendmail (SMTP) service should now be up and running and ready to accept mail from any (valid) source.

Incorrect Mail Setup

When your name resolution is not working, sendmail doesn't know where to send your outbound e-mail. These messages are placed in a queue that tries to resend your e-mail at regular intervals. Other mail forwarders and relay hosts on the Internet provide the same functionality if a network segment is not working. As an administrator, you need to monitor this queue. If it gets overloaded, you may wish to reconfigure messages for that network to be sent at more irregular times. See the following code for an example of a problem message.

```
=================================================================
[root@redhattest mj] # mail
Mail version 8.1 6/6/93.  Type ? for help.
"/var/spool/mail/mj" 1 messages 1 unread
>>U  1 MAILER-DAEMON@linux6  Wed May 29 08:55  60/1914  "Warning: could not send"
&     # simply press <ENTER> key to see each message
Message 1:
From MAILER-DAEMON@localhost.localdomain  Tue May  28 03:55:39 2002
Date: Sun, 28 May 2002 03:55:39 -0500
```

```
From: Mail Delivery Subsystem <ER-EN@localhost.localdomain>
To: michael@mommabears.cob
MIME-Version: 1.0
Content-Type: multipart/report; report-type=delivery-status;
        boundary="DAA03153.938948139/localhost.localdomain"
Subject: Warning: could not send message for past 4 hours
Auto-Submitted: auto-generated (warning-timeout)
This is a MIME-encapsulated message
--DAA03153.938948139/localhost.localdomain
     *********************************************
     **       THIS IS A WARNING MESSAGE ONLY       **
     **   YOU DO NOT NEED TO RESEND YOUR MESSAGE   **
     *********************************************
The original message was received at Mon, 27 May 2002 22:53:31 -0500
from mj@localhost
---- The following addresses had transient non-fatal errors ----
michael@mommabears.cob

     ---- Transcript of session follows ----
michael@mommabears.cob... Deferred: Name server: mommabears.cob.: host
name lookup failure
Warning: message still undelivered after 4 hours
Will keep trying until message is 5 days old

--DAA03153.938948139/localhost.localdomain
... # internal message format removed from here
--DAA03153.938948139/localhost.localdomain-
& d     # delete current read buffer
& q     # quit mail
[root@redhattest mj] #
=================================================================
```

In the previous example, the destination name server (mommabears.cob) could not be resolved (it is mommabears.com). Consequently, sendmail notifies the sender (mj@localhost.localdomain) that the mail could not be delivered.

Command Line Mail

To test your mail system, you can use the built-in command line **mail** utility, a simple text-based interface. The system keeps each user's mail in a system directory. Once users read a message, they can reply, forward, or delete it. If they do not delete the message before quitting the mail utility, the system stores the message in the /var/mail directory, in a file named after the applicable username.

You can certainly use any of the other mail readers, such as **pine** and **elm**, or the e-mail managers associated with different GUI Web browsers to test your system. Other mail readers store messages in different directories. For example, pine would create and store messages for user mj in the /home/mj/mail directory.

To send mail to another user, you can use the **mail** command line utility. There are two basic methods for using **mail**. First, you can enter the subject and then the text of your message. When you're done, press CTRL-D and then enter another addressee in the cc: line, if desired. When you press ENTER, the message is sent and the **mail** utility stops and sends you back to the command line.

```
[mj@redhattest mj]# mail Michael
Subject: Test Message
Sent and received
Cc: mjang@geocities.com
[mj@redhattest mj]#
```

Alternatively, you can redirect a file as the text of an e-mail to another user. For example, the following command sends a copy of /etc/hosts to the root user, with the Subject name of "hosts file:"

```
[mj@redhattest mj]# mail root@localhost -s 'hosts file' < /etc/hosts
```

Reading Mail Messages   By default, the mail system doesn't open unless you actually have e-mail in your in box. Once it is open, you'll see a list of new and already read messages. To read a specific message, enter the number of the message and press ENTER. If you press ENTER with no argument, the mail utility assumes you want to read the next unread message. To delete a mail message, use the **d** command after reading the message, or use **d#** to delete the message numbered #.

Mail Group "Alias" Lists: Aliases   If you have a distribution list of people for the same e-mail, you can set it up in the /etc/aliases file. By default, it's set up to forward e-mail from pseudo-accounts such as system and apache to root. You can change it, for example, by adding a group list similar to the following:

```
groupname:  user01, user02, othergroupname
```

You can then run the **newaliases** command to compile this database. Then, all you need to do is name the group of users as addressees for your e-mail.

POP

The Post Office Protocol (POP) is one of the two major mail delivery protocols. It includes some basic commands that allow you or an e-mail client to send and retrieve messages. A mail service can be configured to be a central depository for incoming mail messages from any other MTA service. Client applications then download the mail messages off the POP server for processing at the local host. The ipop3d daemon service handles all requests.

You can enable the ipop3d service by editing the /etc/xinetd.d/ipop3 configuration file.

You can configure user accounts that are only designed to service POP user accounts, where users log in and receive mail only, and no interactive service is provided. Just set up the appropriate mail client in the login configuration sequence for a given user.

IMAP

The IMAP service is the other major mail delivery protocol. While POP downloads all e-mail to the client, an IMAP server maintains all mail messages on the server, as a database. IMAP is commonly used by businesses that service users who log in from different locations. It's also the most common mail delivery protocol for Web-based mail services.

Configured POP and IMAP with xinetd

Both POP3 and IMAP servers can be installed and configured from a package on one of the Red Hat Installation CDs. Both servers are part of the imap* RPM package. Install it as required. You can then enable it using the basic techniques described earlier for other xinetd super-server packages.

There is only one RPM for mail delivery protocols. Both POP and IMAP are part of the imap RPM.*

CERTIFICATION OBJECTIVE 8.05

Printing

There are two mutually exclusive options for Linux print services: lpd (line print daemon) and CUPS (Common UNIX Printing System). lpd, modeled after the BSD print service, uses /etc/printcap to define the printer queues, their characteristics, and their destinations. Red Hat includes some graphical tools to help you configure a printer through lpd. As discussed earlier, CUPS is eventually expected to take over as the default print daemon for Red Hat Linux. But for now, lpd is still the default.

CUPS provides a Web-based interface that can also help you detect printers over a network. CUPS and lpd are mutually exclusive, since you can't run both services simultaneously and still expect data to get to your printer.

Both systems include service scripts in the /etc/rc.d/init.d/ directory. You can enable and disable these services in the same way that you've enabled and disabled other scripts in previous chapters. Just add the start or stop switch after the desired script. For example, to stop lpd and start CUPS, run the following commands:

```
[root@redhattest mj]# /sbin/service lpd stop
[root@redhattest mj]# /sbin/service cups start
```

Configuring LPD Printers

The improved printconf-gui GUI is used to manage printers. It is a "front end" that can help you configure /etc/printcap. It can configure print queues to local ports or through remote systems:

- Local Unix ports
- Remote Unix lpd print services
- Windows Print Shares
- Novell NCP Print Queues
- HP JetDirect print servers

Be aware that previous versions of Red Hat used the printtool GUI printer manager, which was replaced by the printconf-gui utility. As of this writing, redhat-config-printers is also a front end for this utility. You should be able to connect to just about any type of printer available on your network. Figure 8-29 illustrates the main printconf-gui main screen.

After installation, you do not have any print queues defined. As an example, you can add an HP LaserJet 4L printer to your local parallel port. Click the New button. This should automatically start the Add a New Print Queue wizard as shown in Figure 8-30.

Click Next, and then as shown in Figure 8-31, you can select the type of Queue, as described earlier. Remember to enter a Queue Name as well, and then click Next.

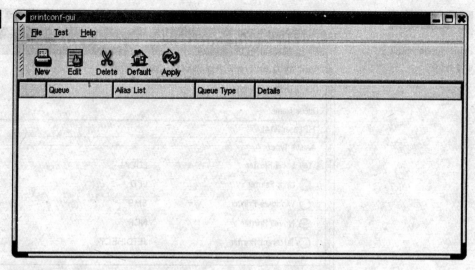

FIGURE 8-29

The Red Hat
printconf-gui
printer
configuration tool

If you selected a Local Printer, the next step is to select a printer port. The
normal default is the first printer port, /dev/lp0. This corresponds to LPT1: in
the Microsoft world.

Alternatively, if you selected a network printer, you'll need to enter the configuration
information for that printer, which normally includes the host name or IP address of
the print server, the name of the printer, and any required usernames and passwords

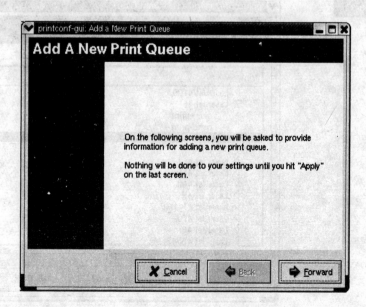

FIGURE 8-30

Adding a new
print queue

FIGURE 8-31

Print queue name
and type

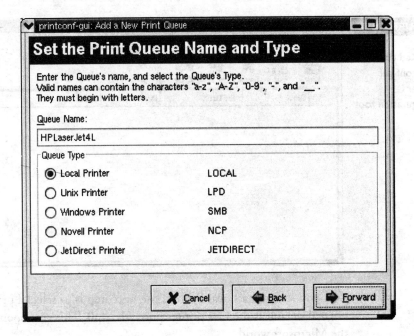

to authorize access to that network printer. Once you've identified the printer
location, click Next. Now you can select a print driver, as shown in Figure 8-32.

FIGURE 8-32

Selecting a
print driver

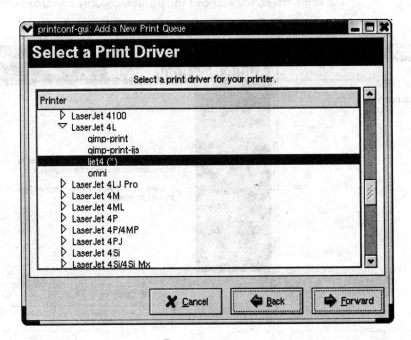

Select a driver and then click Next. Before printconf-gui creates a print queue, it documents what it's about to do. If you're satisfied with the configuration, click Finish. This returns you to the main printconf-gui menu shown in Figure 8-29. It should now include the name of your printer. To write these changes to the /etc/printcap configuration file, click the Apply button. The next step is to test your printer. In the printconf-gui menu, click Test and then select the default print sample of your choice.

One last step is advisable. Linux will use the printer with the alias **lp** as the default print queue. Since this is the only print queue we have, you should probably set it to be the default. Select Edit, and under the Name and Aliases tab in the Edit Queue dialogue box, click Add. Enter the name **lp** and click OK. Finally, close the Edit Queue dialogue by clicking OK. Notice that the lp alias is now present under the Aliases column of printconf-gui.

/etc/printcap

Now review the changes in /etc/printcap. The new /etc/printcap for a HPLaserJet 4L printer on a Samba server is shown in Figure 8-33.

The entry for your queue is made up of a number of colon-separated commands. As you can see, there is typically one command per line; the line continuation character (the backslash [\]) allows lpd to see this entry as if it were all one line. Table 8-5 lists the meaning of each of these commands.

| **FIGURE 8-33**<br><br>Revised<br>/etc/printcap | ```
█ /etc/printcap
#
# DO NOT EDIT! MANUAL CHANGES WILL BE LOST!
# This file is autogenerated by printconf-backend during lpd init.
#
# Hand edited changes can be put in /etc/printcap.local, and will be included.

HPLaserJet4L:\
        :ml=0:\
        :mx=0:\
        :sd=/var/spool/lpd/HPLaserJet4L:\
        :af=/var/spool/lpd/HPLaserJet4L/HPLaserJet4L.acct:\
        :sh:\
        :lp=|/usr/share/printconf/util/smbprint:\
        :lpd_bounce=true:\
        :if=/usr/share/printconf/util/mf_wrapper:

###########################################################################
## Everything below here is included verbatim from /etc/printcap.local   ##
###########################################################################
# printcap.local
#
# This file is included by printconf's generated printcap,
# and can be used to specify custom hand edited printers.
``` |

1,1   All
```

| TABLE 8-5 | /etc/printcap Command Descriptions |

Field	Description
HPLaserJet4L|lp	The name of the queue and alias. Since lp is the alias, this is the default printer.
ml=0	Minimum number of characters in this print job.
mx=0	Max number of pages per print job. A value of 0 means no limit.
sd	Spool directory.
af	Accounting filter. File that collects records of each print job.
sh	Suppress header, sometimes known as a separator page.
lp=	Points to the device where the print job is sent.
lpd_bounce=	If true, the job is filtered locally. If false, the job is sent to a remote print daemon.
if=	Input filter. Processes the file into a form readable by the printer.

Each of these directives is needed to print correctly. If you set up a printer and get gibberish, you probably need to change the input filter (that is, select a different print driver).

Access Control to Printing

By default, access to printing is open to all users. You have two ways to limit print access:

■ List computers that are allowed to print in /etc/hosts.lpd.

■ Add :rs: to /etc/printcap, which requires users with accounts on the print server.

The Line Print Daemon Commands

Three major commands are associated with the lpd service: lpr, lpq, and lprm. They are used to add print requests, list queued print requests, and remove print requests, respectively. One more command can help you administer one or more print queues: lpc.

lpc—Line Print Control   The root user can use lpc to control, start, and stop all local queues. To view all known queues, run the **/usr/sbin/lpc status** command. Some other lpc switches are useful, such as the following:

disable/enable [queue]	Blocks or allows jobs into one or all print queues
stop/start [queue]	Blocks or allows jobs from the print queue from the printer

So, if our HPLaserJet4L printer were out of ink, we could issue this command:

```
[root@redhattest mj] # /usr/sbin/lpc stop HPLaserJet4L
```

This stops current print jobs without closing the queue.

lpr—Line Print Request   Any user can use lpr to send print requests to any local print queue. You can lpr any files to a queue, or you can redirect any output via lpr. If you wanted to print to the queue named color, you'd use a command such as lpr -Pcolor *filename*. Note there is no space between the -P switch and the name of the queue.

lpq—Line Print Query   Note that our printer is no longer printing requests. Now, let's queue up a new job. Issue these commands:

```
[root@redhattest mj] # lpq
Printer: HPLaserJet4L@redhattest 'lp' (printing disabled)
 Queue: 1 printable job
 Server: no server active
 Rank   Owner/ID                Class Job Files          Size Time
 1      mj@redhattest+923         A   923 /etc/printcap  842 12:22:32
```

We can let the job go to the printer by restarting the queue with the following command:

```
[root@redhattest mj]# lpc start HPLaserJet4L
```

Alternatively, you can just delete all print jobs belonging to a specific user. For example, the following command deletes all print jobs belonging to user mj in the queue:

```
[root@redhattest mj]# lprm mj
```

CUPS: Common UNIX Printing System

An alternative to the Line Print Daemon is CUPS, the Common UNIX Printing System. It is based on the Internet Printing Protocol. CUPS works like a server that can also easily connect to remote printers. The connections are easy and can easily be made through a Web-based interface, similar to Samba's SWAT. CUPS works well with its Web-based interface because it is configured with an HTTP server configuration file.

TABLE 8-6	CUPS RPM packages

CUPS Package	Function
cups-*	Main CUPS daemon
cups-drivers-*	Printer drivers for CUPS (may include several RPMs)
cups-libs-*	Program libraries
cups-devel-*	CUPS development package

Before you can set up CUPS, you need to install the appropriate packages, as shown in Table 8-6.

Setting Up CUPS

As of this writing, both CUPS and lpd are installed on Red Hat Linux. However, only one of these systems can be active on your computer. As of this writing, lpd is active and CUPS is not by default. You can activate CUPS and deactivate lpd using the service commands described earlier in this chapter.

Using the CUPS Interface

The easiest way to use CUPS is through the Web-based interface. Open up the browser of your choice on the local Linux computer. Direct it to the http://localhost:631 address to get to the main CUPS configuration menu, as shown in Figure 8-34. There are seven options atop the Administration menu:

- **ESP** Brings you to the Easy Software Products home page at www.easysw.com. CUPS is officially one of their products, licensed under the Linux GPL.

- **Admin** Is a basic interface that allows you to set up Classes of printers, manage print jobs, and add or manage printers. You can also administer these features through the Classes, Jobs, or Printers options.

- **Classes** Enables you to set up groups of printers together.

- **Help** Provides extensive documentation.

- **Jobs** Enables you to view and manage active print jobs.

- **Printers** Enables you to manage existing printers and set up new printers.

- **Software** Enables you to review the current version and upgrade if appropriate.

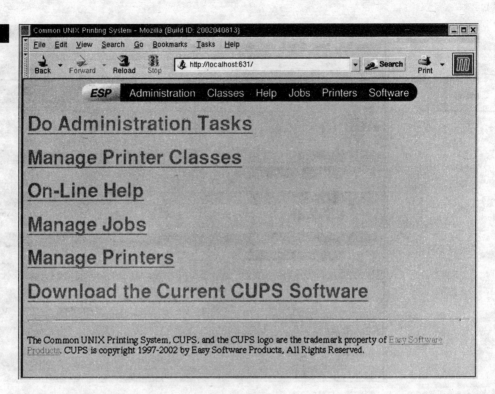

FIGURE 8-34

Main CUPS
Configuration
menu

You can manage Classes, Jobs, and Printers from the Administrative menu. You can read the Help section on your own. And software upgrades to CUPS are not covered in this book. So the heart to CUPS is in the Administrative menu. Click it to continue.

CUPS Administration

This brings you to the Admin setup page shown in Figure 8-35. There are three sections here. Classes enable you to configure a group of printers together. When you use a specific class, CUPS directs your print job to the first available printer in this class. Jobs help you manage the print jobs currently in the print queue. And Printers allow you to add new printers and manage existing printers.

Select Add Printer in the Admin menu. There are three basic fields as shown in Figure 8-36. The Name assigns a label to the print queue. If the Location is local, enter the appropriate device; the first printer port corresponds to /dev/lp0. You can enter whatever helps your users in the Description field. Click Continue.

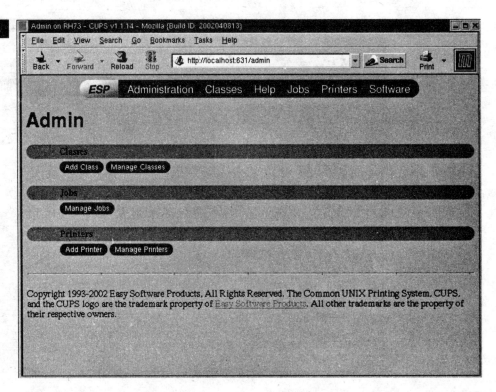

FIGURE 8-35

CUPS
Administration
menu

In the next screen, shown in Figure 8-37, you can select a device. Devices can be on local parallel or serial ports. They can also be on network ports such as those on a JetDirect Device or accessible through the Internet Printing Protocol. Select the device for your printer and then click Continue.

Selecting a driver is a two-stage process. First, you select the printer manufacturer and click Continue, then you can select the printer model. Finally you'll see a message that the printer with the name that you specified earlier "…has been added successfully."

Testing a CUPS Printer

Prudent administrators test their printers after they are configured. Click Printers atop the CUPS menu. You should see details of the printer that you just configured—and any others that you've configured previously. An example is shown in Figure 8-38. As you can see, you can test and reconfigure a number of printer functions. Click the Print Test Page button and see what happens.

FIGURE 8-36

Setting up a printer in CUPS

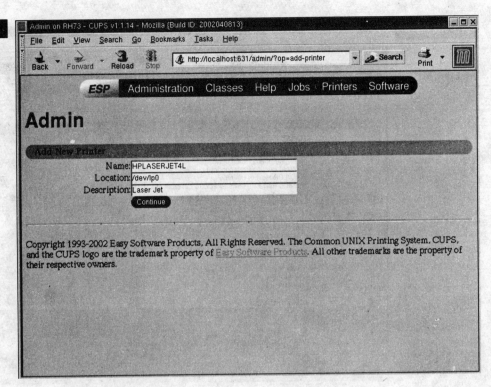

CERTIFICATION SUMMARY

A number of important network client services are associated with Red Hat Linux. Apache is the most important Web server on the Internet. FTP services enable you to let users transfer files to and from your server efficiently. Samba sets up interoperability between Microsoft Windows and Linux/Unix computers. Mail services enable you to set up e-mail send and receive functions on your network. And Red Hat Linux includes two print services that can enable you to set up printers locally or over the network.

Apache was developed from the NCSA Web server. Once the appropriate packages are installed, you have a structure and sample Web pages in the /var/www/home directory, based on the /etc/httpd/conf/httpd.conf configuration file. The httpd.conf file is organized in containers. You can create virtual hosts for multiple Web sites on your computer, even if you have only one IP address.

FIGURE 8-37

Setting a
print device

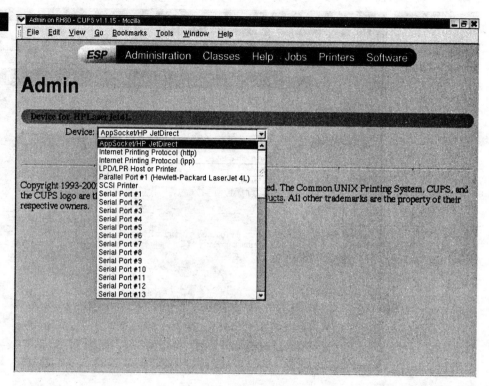

FTP has two parts: the client and the server. FTP clients are almost always available from the command line; graphical FTP clients such as GFTP can provide additional functionality. Two important FTP servers include anonftp and wu-ftpd; they provide anonymous and password-protected FTP services.

Samba allows a Linux computer to appear like any other Microsoft computer on a Microsoft Windows–based network. Samba is based on SMB, which allows Microsoft computers to communicate on a TCP/IP network. It includes two daemons, smbd and nmbd. The main Samba configuration file, /etc/samba/smb.conf, includes separate sections for global settings and share definitions. SWAT is a GUI tool that makes it easier to configure smb.conf. One useful device is to use SWAT to create a public share on a Linux computer that is readable and writable by all users. Changes to smb.conf can be easily tested with the testparm utility.

The sendmail program is a powerful mail server that can be installed with Red Hat Linux. It relies on SMTP to send e-mail over the Internet. While it includes

FIGURE 8-38

Managing a
configured
printer

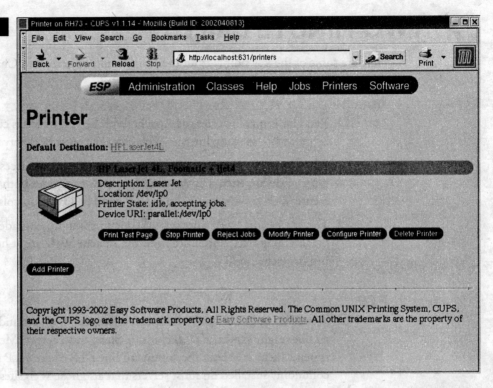

a difficult-to-read configuration file, /etc/sendmail.cf, it also includes an easier-to-configure Red Hat configuration script, /etc/mail/sendmail.mc. Red Hat Linux also provides a variety of e-mail clients, including mail, pine, elm, and the mail clients that come with the various Web browsers that are also available for Linux. These clients either use POP or IMAP protocols to receive e-mail.

Linux includes two mutually exclusive print services: lpd and CUPS. While the packages for both services are installed, you can activate only one print service at a time. With lpd, you can edit the /etc/printcap configuration file directly, or use Red Hat's graphical printconf-gui configuration tool. CUPS, on the other hand, includes a Web-based interface similar to SWAT that also enables you to configure local or network printers.

Because RHCE is a performance-based exam, it is important to practice all the skills discussed in this chapter. You may need to use these skills on the exam!

✓ TWO-MINUTE DRILL

Here are some of the key points from the certification objectives in Chapter 8.

Apache

❑ Red Hat Linux includes the Apache Web Server, which is currently used by over twice as many Internet Web sites as all other Web servers combined.

❑ Web services are an easy way to provide simple, secure access to many types of documents. The Apache Web Server provides both normal and secure Web services using the HTTP and HTTPS protocols.

❑ You can get the latest information, documentation, upgrades, options, patches, bug fixes, and more from the Apache Web site at http://httpd.apache.org/.

FTP

❑ The FTP, or File Transfer Protocol, service has been around a long time. As one might expect, FTP includes a client and a server. Most operating systems include at least the command line FTP client. FTP servers are commonly installed on most servers that also host Web sites.

❑ Two of the available FTP servers are anonftp and wu-ftpd. The anonftp package provides anonymous access, which does not require individual user accounts.

❑ Anonymous FTP server files are installed by default in /var/ftp, which looks like the root directory for connecting users.

❑ The wu-ftpd server allows you to manage users who connect. It also allows you to control transfer and command logs, set up automatic compression, classify users and their locations, limit users on a per-class (local, remote) basis, manage directory upload permissions, create restricted guest accounts, and more.

❑ The FTP service daemon is actually started through the xinetd super-server daemon. In most cases, including FTP, you need to make sure the service is not disabled in the appropriate configuration file in the /etc/xinetd.d directory.

Samba

❑ Samba allows Microsoft Windows computers to share files and printers across networks, using the Server Message Block (SMB) protocol on the TCP/IP protocol stack.

❑ Samba includes a client and a server. Variations on the **mount -t smbfs** command allow you to connect to a Microsoft Windows shared directory.

❑ The main Samba configuration file is /etc/samba/smb.conf. You can configure it in a text editor or use a tool such as SWAT.

❑ SWAT is a separately configured service through the xinetd super-server. Once it is configured and enabled, you can access SWAT by directing your browser to http://localhost:901.

❑ Samba allows you to configure your Linux computer as a member of a Microsoft Windows 9x–style Workgroup.

❑ Samba allows you to configure your Linux computer as a Microsoft Windows server. It can also provide Microsoft browsing, WINS, and Domain Controller services.

Mail Services

❑ Linux includes sendmail, which is a very powerful mail server, popular on the Internet.

❑ The main sendmail configuration file is /etc/mail/sendmail.cf. This is a large file that you could configure by hand with some difficulty.

❑ Alternatively, you can use the /etc/mail/sendmail.mc configuration file, along with the m4 macro processor, to make it easier to customize the sendmail.cf file that you need.

❑ Mail clients can work to POP or IMAP. Mail clients such as mail, pine, and elm are available at the command line. GUI Mail clients are also available, usually as part of a Web browser package.

Printing

❑ Two mutually exclusive print services are available for Linux: lpd and CUPS.

❑ lpd uses the /etc/printcap text file to define the printer queues, their characteristics, and their destinations.

❑ The printconf-gui program can be used to configure most popular printers in /etc/printcap.

❑ CUPS provides a Web-based interface similar to Samba's SWAT. Once it is enabled through the xinetd super-server, you can get to this interface in your browser by navigating to http://localhost:631.

SELF TEST

The following questions will help you measure your understanding of the material presented in this chapter. Read all the choices carefully, as there may be more than one correct answer. Choose all correct answers for each question.

Apache

1. What service would you use to provide human resource documents to selected users on the network?

   A. Samba

   B. Apache

   C. X Window

   D. FTP

2. The Human Resources department wants to restrict access to its Web site. What configuration features of Apache could you incorporate for this purpose?

   A. A virtual host

   B. Port 4001

   C. Allow from mycompany.com

   D. All of the above

3. The sales department wants to amalgamate its Web service with the HR department to save money. What is the easiest way to do this?

   A. A virtual host

   B. .htaccess

   C. DocumentRoot

   D. memory

4. The sales department wants to keep detailed and separate log files about page hits and error messages. Which options should it use?

   A. VirtualHost

   B. CustomLog

   C. DocumentRoot

   D. ErrorLog

5. When you view all system processes, you notice that over 35 HTTP daemons are running. You thought you configured 10. What has happened?

   A. It is spiraling out of control.

   B. Each virtual service can start additional daemons.

   C. There may be some FTP service requests.

   D. Apache is dynamically configuring for current load needs.

6. You're converting from IIS (The Microsoft Web Server) to Apache. You copy the Web site files directly, set up the virtual host. You try to find the home page in your browser, but it fails. Which of the following items is the most likely problem? Assume that you've used Apache before and have previously configured a working Virtual Host container.

   A. DocumentRoot

   B. Port Number

   C. index.htm

   D. Wrong browser settings

7. You're trying to access your Web site from home, late at night. Your modem connection is slow. You have a lot of graphical images on your Web site that you don't need. How can you get to your Web site without a graphical interface?

   A. SWAT

   B. lynx

   C. CUPS

   D. konqueror -text

8. The sales department wants to make test results, FAQs, and new product data sheets available to resellers for their own sales literature. How would you make the material available for quick downloads over an Internet connection?

   A. Samba

   B. Apache

   C. FTP

   D. Anonymous FTP

FTP

9. The Sales department wants to know if it can selectively give certain users access to specific directories. Which FTP options could be used to make their request a reality?

   A. .htaccess

   B. ftpaccess

   C. rpm

   D. hosts.allow

10. You notice no FTPD service running when you randomly check your system, but no complaints have been made. Why is there no daemon?

    A. It is started by xinetd as needed.

    B. It only runs at designated intervals during the day.

    C. Nobody uses it, and the system cleans house regularly.

    D. We ran out of memory.

11. The sales force complains occasionally that they are refused an FTP connection, even though customers never have a connection problem. What may be set too low?

    A. Access times

    B. Local login limit

    C. Limited number of daemons

    D. System memory

Samba

12. The rogue curriculum people have set up a Windows 2000 server to handle their file and print sharing services. This server uses WINS for name resolution and configures all user logins through the domain server. You want to make connections to some server-hidden shares and back up the shared files. What options would you configure in Samba?

    A. Browse Master

    B. WINS Server IP as Client

    C. 2000 Server for Authentication

    D. Connect to the special backup share service from Linux

13. Which is not a component of the Samba file-sharing service?

    A. /usr/bin/smbd

    B. /usr/bin/nmbd

    C. /usr/bin/smbclient

    D. /etc/samba/smb.conf

14. You made a couple of quick changes to your Samba configuration file and you need to test it quickly for syntax errors. Which utility should you run?

    A. smbmount

    B. smbclient

    C. smbfs

    D. testparm

15. You are asked to share the HR downloadable documents to Windows users who are not that familiar with FTP and want a shared drive connection. What can you use to force the Samba service to reread the configuration file immediately after you have made the configuration changes?

    A. testparm

    B. /etc/smb.conf

    C. /etc/rc.d/init.d/smb restart

    D. /etc/samba/restart

16. Windows users are complaining that they cannot see the HR document share in their Network Neighborhood diagram. What option is missing from smb.conf?

    A. Hidden = no

    B. Browseable = yes

    C. NetworkDisplay = on

    D. Viewable = no

Mail Services

17. Which of the following is the main configuration file for sendmail?

    A. /etc/mail/sendmail.mc

    B. /etc/sendmail.mc

C. /etc/mail/sendmail.cf

D. /etc/sendmail.cf

18. Some of the salespeople are no longer local, and they need to be able to get their mail from any Web-based server in the world. What option would you configure for this?

A. sendmail-Web interface

B. POP3 daemon

C. IMAP daemon

D. Apache Mail interface

Printing

19. You want to look at your current printer configuration in an X Window interface. Depending on your current print daemon, what utility might you use?

A. CUPS

B. /etc/printcap

C. printconf-gui

D. lprsetup

20. The HR and Sales departments want to restrict users who can print to their printers. What file can be used to restrict access to print services?

A. printconf-gui

B. /etc/printcap

C. /etc/lpraccess

D. /etc/hosts.lpd

LAB QUESTION

In our Lab, we will install and configure Samba services.

Part 1: Installing and Starting Samba

1. Ensure that all four components of the Samba service are correctly installed. What RPMs did you install and where are they located (which CDs)?

2. Use one of the three service management tools available to us to ensure that the Samba services are configured to start correctly when you boot Linux. What tool did you use?

3. Start Samba services now. You can use either the service management script located directly in /etc/rc.d/init.d, or you can use the "service" startup tool. How did you start your Samba service?

4. Verify that Samba services are now running. How did you do this?

Part 2: Configuring Samba's Global Settings

1. We'll use SWAT to configure our Samba service. Start SWAT now and log in as the SWAT administrator. What ID/password did you have to enter?

2. Configure the Samba global settings. We will provide Workgroup services to our users. Set the Workgroup name to something appropriate for your company.

3. Set the hosts allow string to your company's domain name (e.g., example.com)

4. Set the hosts deny string to evil.cracker.com.

5. Commit your changes.

Part 3: Configuring File Shares

1. Activate the File Share screen.

2. Select the predefined homes share.

3. Ensure that the homes share is available only to hosts on our example.com network.

4. Ensure that the share is writable to authenticated users but not available to guest users.

5. Commit your changes.

6. Create a new share called public.

7. Change the path to the public share to /home/public.

8. Configure the public share so anyone in our domain can access the share.

9. Disallow authenticated users.

10. Make the /home/public directory in a terminal window. Change the permissions to this directory to 1777.

11. Why do we set permissions to 1777?

12. Commit your changes.

Part 4: Setting Up Printer Shares

1. Our Linux server has many printers defined. We want to offer access to them to our desktop client users. Enable access to the generic printers share now.

2. Surprisingly, printers are not browseable by default. Change that now.

3. Again, restrict access to our print shares to members of our example.com domain.

4. Commit your changes.

Part 5: Verifying the smb.conf file

1. We want to verify our changes. Click on the View button at the top of the SWAT Web page.

2. Review the /etc/samba/smb.conf file. Look over each section including the [globals] section. Ensure that all updates are correct and reflect the requirements previously stated. Go back and make changes, if necessary. Commit all changes.

3. Start a terminal window. Run the syntax tester tool on our Samba configuration tool. What program did you use?

4. Again, go back and make revisions if the test program indicates problems with the smb.conf file.

Part 6: Starting the Samba Servers

1. Click the Status button at the top of the SWAT Web page.

2. Start the smbd server.

3. Start the nmbd server.

4. If possible, go to a Microsoft Windows computer on your network. Use a Microsoft browsing tool such as Network Neighborhood or My Network Places in Windows Explorer. See if you can connect to the Samba public share.

5. Go back to the SWAT window. Refresh the list of connected users. Can you see your connection on the screen?

6. Congratulations! You have just configured your Samba server to share files with your local workgroup.

Part 7: Persistency Check

It is important for your server (and critical to pass the RHCE exam) that any changes you make to your server should be persistent. This means that changes should be active when after you reboot Linux. Perform an orderly reboot of your server now and verify that Samba starts up at boot time.

1. How did you make your changes persistent?

2. What command did you use to perform an orderly shutdown?

SELF TEST ANSWERS

Apache

1.   ☑ **A, B, or D.** Samba can serve files to PC users, Apache can serve HTML documents, and FTP can serve any type of file to any type of client. You would need to select a method appropriate for your document type.

    ☒ **C** is incorrect because the X Window System is a series of graphics packages. While it can provide file access via various X client programs, it does not serve files directly.

2.   ☑ **C.** By restricting access to a site to clients on a particular network, we can limit access to our content. The allow directive is typically used inside a <Directory> container to limit access to specified hosts or networks.

    ☒ **A** is incorrect because Virtual Host directives are used to support multiple domain names on a single IP address. **B** is incorrect because the Port 4001 directive is used to have Apache listen on a nonstandard port. This hides the Web server, but not very well. Any port scanner (such as nmap or nessus) could easily find the hidden port. Once the port is found, a simple test could easily verify that a Web server is listening on that port. **D** is incorrect because **A** and **B** are incorrect.

3.   ☑ **A.** We would set up a virtual host on our server and then host the Sales department's site under that name.

    ☒ **B** is incorrect because the .htaccess directive is used for overriding default permissions. **C** is incorrect because the DocumentRoot directive is used to specify the location for HTML documents. **D** is incorrect because additional memory may not be required to host the Sales site on our existing server.

4.   ☑ **B and D.** CustomLog and ErrorLog. These directives specify where page hit logs (CustomLog) and error logs (ErrorLog) entries should be saved.

    ☒ **C** is incorrect because DocumentRoot is the directory with our Web site files. **A** is not correct because a VirtualHost is used to define additional Web sites on the local Apache server.

5.   ☑ **B.** Apache starts up to an additional MaxSpareServers per virtual host. It does this so it can limit the number of servers that can respond to an individual host name. Consequently, you may see many more httpd servers running than you would have guessed.

    ☒ **A** is incorrect. If you think you are spiraling out of control, it is probably just because you aren't used to seeing so many servers. Apache will strictly control the number of servers it starts for each virtual host. **C** is incorrect because FTP services are separate from http. Additional FTP daemons do not affect the number of HTTP daemons. Finally, **D** is incorrect because Apache does not dynamically configure itself beyond specified limits.

6. ☑ **C.** Assuming you copied over the content to the correct directory, Windows normally uses the index.htm as the default home page. In contrast, Apache uses index.html. However, you could set the DirectoryIndex directive to look for index.htm files. Case is also important. If the Windows home page file is INDEX.HTM, Apache may not be able to find this file.

☒ **A, B,** and **D** are incorrect. While it is possible an incorrect DocumentRoot or Port Number could cause Apache to fail, you've used Apache before successfully. A filename problem is still more likely. Also, browser settings do not typically prevent you from seeing basic HTML documents, especially home pages.

7. ☑ **B.** lynx is a fast text-based Web browser. By default, it does not download image files, ignores font requests, and renders your page in text mode. However, lynx can work with advanced HTML directives like forms.

☒ **A, C,** and **D** are incorrect. None of the other options would let you browse a site in text mode. konqueror has no such command option as -text.

8. ☑ **B, C,** or **D.** Each of these methods involves file transfers to remote networks.

☒ **A** is incorrect because Samba is typically configured to work only with known networks and/or local users. It is rarely used to share files over the Internet.

FTP

9. ☑ **B.** The /etc/ftpaccess file is used to customize WU-FTP's configuration, including access rights.

☒ **A** is incorrect because it is an Apache Web Server configuration file (.htaccess). **C** is wrong because the Red Hat Package Manager is used to install, query, test, and delete packages, not to limit access on FTP. **D** is incorrect because /etc/hosts.allow (like /etc/hosts.deny) is used by TCP wrappers to limit access to desired domains and networks, not users.

10. ☑ **A.** The FTP service is controlled by the xinetd super-server daemon. A new FTPD session is started for each incoming FTP request.

☒ While **B** is possible through the cron daemon, it is not the default behavior. **C** and **D** are incorrect because the system does not unconfigure a service just because it hasn't been used in a while. Memory use is not a common issue; FTP requires much less RAM memory than most other services, especially those related to the GUI.

11. ☑ **B.** There is a facility within WU-FTP to set user counts and session counts. This directive is called limit. That would limit logons from the local network, without setting a limit on customer access from outside networks.

☒ **A** could not be correct or it would apply to all users. **C** is incorrect because there is no inherent limit on the number of FTP daemons. **D** is incorrect because system memory does not discriminate between local and remote users.

Samba

12. ☑ **C.** To gain access to files on the Windows 2000 server, we would need an account that could be used to log into that server. Then we could use that account's permissions to gain access to the desired shares and back them up.

☒ **A** is incorrect because being a Browse Master does not give us inherent rights to access a local server's resources. It just gives us a record of browseable resources. **B** is incorrect because WINS is just a Microsoft naming service. **D** is incorrect because there is no such thing as a special backup share.

13. ☑ **C.** This is a tricky question. smbclient is a client program; it is not part of the service that provides Samba file shares.

☒ **A, B,** and **D** are all components that are either daemons (smbd and nmbd) that manage the service or are the server's configuration file (smb.conf).

14. ☑ **D.** testparm is the smb.conf configuration file syntax and semantics checker.

☒ **A** is wrong because mount -t smbfs is used to make remote SMB shares available to Linux. It wouldn't test your local configuration. **B** is wrong because smbclient is the Linux SMB client program for accessing Samba services on the network. **C** is incorrect because smbfs is the filesystem type used when a Samba share is mounted through the mount command or via /etc/fstab.

15. ☑ **C.** This is one way to tell Samba to restart itself (and thus reread its configuration file).

☒ **A** is incorrect because testparm is just a syntax checker for smb.conf. **B** is incorrect because smb.conf is just the Samba configuration file (albeit in the wrong location, it should be /etc/samba/smb.conf). Finally, **D** is incorrect because there is no such command.

16. ☑ **B.** A share must be marked as Browseable before it will show up in Network Neighborhood. Otherwise, the shares will be available but you won't be able to see them from a Microsoft Windows computer.

☒ **A, C,** and **D** are all invalid Samba directives.

Mail Services

17. ☑ **C.** The /etc/sendmail.cf file is the main configuration file for sendmail.

☒ **A, B, and D** are all incorrect. A and B are incorrect because the sendmail.mc file is just the Red Hat configuration template. It still must be processed by m4 before it can be used as the sendmail configuration file. D is incorrect because /etc/mail/sendmail.cf is in the wrong location.

18. ☑ **C.** The IMAP protocol allows users to access their e-mail through Web-based interfaces.

☒ **A, B, and D** are incorrect because there are no such services as the Apache Mail interface or sendmail-Web interface. And the POP3 daemon isn't used for Web-based e-mail interfaces.

Printing

19. ☑ **A and C.** CUPS provides a Web-based tool of the same name to configure printers for that daemon. printconf-gui is the X Window–based tool for configuring and managing printers through the line print daemon (lpd).

☒ **B** is wrong because /etc/printcap is the lpd printer definition and configuration file. But it is not a program. D is wrong because there is no such file as lprsetup.

20. ☑ **D.** The /etc/hosts.lpd identifies the systems that can use the local lpd print service.

☒ **A** is incorrect because printconf-gui is used for configuring printers, not printer access. B is incorrect because it doesn't contain system access information. C is incorrect because there is no such file as /etc/lpraccess.

LAB ANSWER

Our end-of-chapter lab is designed to be easy to follow. However, you'll need explicit Linux knowledge to complete some specific steps. Answers to these steps can be found in the following:

Part I

Step 1: Samba-Common and Samba-Client from the Red Hat installation CD. You'll also need to install the samba and samba-swat RPM packages, possibly from a different Red Hat installation CD. Use mount /dev/cdrom to mount the Red Hat CDs. Use rpm -Uvh to install the packages. All RPMs are located in the /mnt/cdrom/RedHat/RPMS directory.

Step 2: You could use either /usr/sbin/ntsysv or /sbin/chkconfig to configure the Samba service to run. ntsysv is the easiest and doesn't require graphics mode.

Step 3: Use the **/sbin/service smb start** command to begin Samba.

Step 4: One way to verify Samba is to look for the existence of the smbd and nmbd processes in the process table. Use **ps aux | grep mbd** to see if these processes are present. Another way is with the service command. Try **/sbin/service smb status**.

Part 2

Step 1: To configure Samba via SWAT, you need to log in with the root username and password.

Step 2: Many administrators stick with the default Microsoft Windows workgroup name of WORKGROUP. You can find it in the output from the smbclient -L //*clientname* command.

Step 3: You can set the hosts allow setting in SWAT under the Globals menu, in the Security Options.

Step 4: You can set the hosts deny setting in SWAT under the Globals menu, in the Security Options.

Step 5: In SWAT, after clicking the Commit Changes button, you should also restart smb in order to make sure Samba reads your new configuration file. Before committing the changes, you can test them with the testparm command.

Part 3

Step 1: Return to SWAT. Click Shares and select the predefined homes share.

Step 2: In the SWAT Shares menu, under security options, configure the *read only* and *guest ok* settings to no.

Step 3: Commit your changes. Restart or reload smb under the Status menu or with the appropriate /sbin/service command.

Step 4: Create a new directory, /home/public; configure that share in SWAT and call it public. Set the hosts allow setting in SWAT under the Shares menu, and list the domain associated with your network. Deny to all others.

Step 5: Set permissions for the public share, with the following commands:

```
# mkdir /home/public
# chmod 1777 /home/public
```

Step 6: The 777 aspect of permissions grants read, write, and execute/search permissions to all users (root, root's group and everyone else). The 1 at the beginning of the permission value sets the sticky bit. This bit, when set on directories, restricts users from deleting or renaming files they don't own.

Step 7: Commit your changes.

Part 4

Step 1: In SWAT, click the Printers menu. Select the generic printers from the list, then click Choose Printer. The process is similar to selecting the homes directory share.

Step 2: Make the printers share browseable by default, under Browse Options.

Step 3: Under Security Options, use the hosts allow and hosts deny settings as before.

Step 4: Commit your changes.

Part 5

Step 1: This is more of an exercise than a lab. The steps are generally self-explanatory; you can review the Samba configuration file, /etc/samba/smb.conf, through the View menu in SWAT.

Step 2: You can also use the Samba syntax checker, testparm, to make sure there are no glaring problems to your Samba configuration file.

Part 6

Step 1: Again, this is more of an exercise than a lab. The steps are generally self-explanatory; if your Samba configuration is successful, you should be able to review browseable shares from a Microsoft Windows computer on the same LAN.

Part 7

Step 1: To complete many Linux configuration changes, you need to make sure that the service will start automatically when you reboot your computer. In general, the key command is /sbin/chkconfig. In this case, the **/sbin/chkconfig --level 35 smb on** command sets up the smbd daemon to become active when you boot Linux into either runlevel 3 or runlevel 5.

Step 2: The command you should always use to perform an orderly shutdown is **shutdown -r now**.

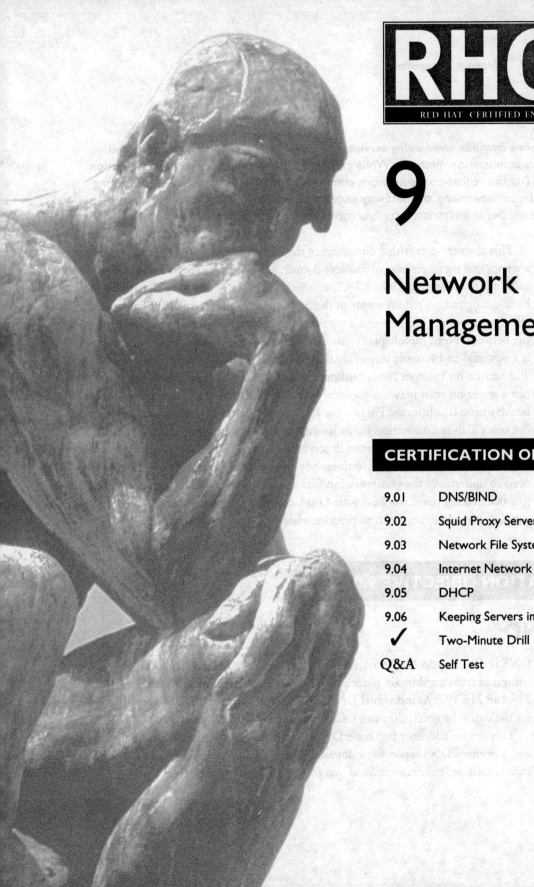

RED HAT CERTIFIED ENGINEER

9

Network Management

CERTIFICATION OBJECTIVES

More complex networking services in Red Hat Linux require more advanced administration methods. While graphical tools such as Network Configuration (via the redhat-config-network command) are available to assist in configuring all aspects of Linux networking, the best way to learn networking is by practicing with the key command line utilities and associated configuration files.

This chapter starts with a discussion of the Domain Name System (DNS). DNS is a service that translates human-readable domain names such as www.mommabears.com to IP addresses such as 199.93.70.2, and vice versa. It continues by describing the basic configuration requirements of the Squid proxy server, which can improve the effective response time between a user and the Internet while reducing the load on the network. Next, this chapter continues with the Network File System (NFS), which is a powerful and versatile way of sharing filesystems between servers and workstations. The section on Internet News outlines the old familiar Usenet system, and how to run a server on your network for local users. DHCP allows a Linux server to serve out dynamic IP addresses. Finally, the PPP section demonstrates how a Linux server can use a dial-up connection for individual or network Internet access.

As you learn about these network services, you're learning about the services that you might configure and/or troubleshoot on the RHCE exam. Take the time you need to understand the configuration files associated with each of these services, and practice making them work on your Linux computer. In some cases, two computers running Linux will be useful to practice what you learn in this chapter.

CERTIFICATION OBJECTIVE 9.01

DNS/BIND

DNS is the Domain Name System, which maintains a database that can help your computer translate domain names such as www.redhat.com to IP addresses such as 216.148.218.197. As individual DNS servers are not large enough to keep a database for the entire Internet, they can refer requests to other DNS servers.

This section addresses two basic DNS server configurations: a caching-only server, and a primary DNS server for a domain. The key configuration files to support such servers include /etc/nsswitch.conf, /etc/resolv.conf, and /etc/hosts.

e x a m

W a t c h

DNS operation assumes that the server that you do set up is not blocked by a firewall from making queries to other DNS servers.

DNS is based on the *named* daemon, which is built on the BIND (Berkeley Internet Name Domain) package developed through the Internet Software Consortium. More information is available from the BIND home page at www.isc.org/products/BIND.

The named daemon is included in most Red Hat Linux installations and is usually installed as /usr/sbin/named.

If you don't see a /usr/sbin/named file, you'll need to install the following BIND packages:

- **bind** includes the basic name server software, including /usr/sbin/named.

- **bind-utils** contains tools such as dig and host that allow you to ask a DNS server for more information about a specific Internet host.

- **bind-devel** adds the libraries required for BIND development.

- **redhat-config-bind** is a GUI configuration tool useful for adding host and reverse address lookup data.

Red Hat Linux is currently configured using BIND version 9. If you're still using BIND version 8, review the BIND home page for the latest security updates.

Don't edit any of these files directly if you're planning to use the GUI BIND configuration tool, redhat-config-bind. What you configure with this GUI tool overwrites whatever you might change in various BIND configuration files with a text editor.

o n t h e

J o b

redhat-config-bind is the successor to bindconf. As of this writing, the latest version of Red Hat Linux includes a link from bindconf to redhat-config-bind.

If you've used BIND in the past, note that the nslookup command is deprecated in the latest versions of Red Hat Linux; use the dig or host command instead.

A Caching-Only Name Server

When you request a Web page such as www.osborne.com, your network asks the configured DNS server for the associated IP address. This is usually known as a name query. If the DNS server is outside your network, this request can take time. If you have a caching-only name server, these queries are stored locally, which can save significant time while you or others on your network are browsing the same sites on the Internet.

When configuring a caching-only name server, the first step is to look at the /etc/named.conf configuration file. The default version is shown in Figure 9-1.

The "directory" line tells named where to look for files. All files named in the named.conf configuration file are in the /var/named directory. The /etc/named.conf file continues with a zone file for the local computer (localhost.zone) and a second zone file associated with the loopback address (named.local).

FIGURE 9-1

The /etc/
named.conf
caching-only
nameserver
configuration file

```
// generated by named-bootconf.pl
options {
        directory "/var/named";
        /*
         * If there is a firewall between you and nameservers you want
         * to talk to, you might need to uncomment the query-source
         * directive below.  Previous versions of BIND always asked
         * questions using port 53, but BIND 8.1 uses an unprivileged
         * port by default.
         */
        // query-source address * port 53;
};

//
// a caching only nameserver config
//
controls {
        inet 127.0.0.1 allow { localhost; } keys { rndckey; };
};
zone "." IN {
        type hint;
        file "named.ca";
};

zone "localhost" IN {
        type master;
        file "localhost.zone";
        allow-update { none; };
};

zone "0.0.127.in-addr.arpa" IN {
        type master;
        file "named.local";
        allow-update { none; };
};

include "/etc/rndc.key";
~
```

37,0-1   All

An excerpt from the /var/named/named.ca file is shown in Figure 9-2; it includes the root name servers for the Internet. This list changes from time to time and must be maintained. A shell script for maintaining this file can be found at the end of this section.

The default /var/named/localhost.zone file is shown in Figure 9-3. It incorporates a basic DNS entry for the local computer, which you can use as a template for other computers on your network.

FIGURE 9-2					

The named.ca file for root name servers

```
; formerly NS.INTERNIC.NET
;
.                              3600000  IN  NS  A.ROOT-SERVERS.NET.
A.ROOT-SERVERS.NET.            3600000      A   198.41.0.4
; formerly NS1.ISI.EDU
;
.                              3600000      NS  B.ROOT-SERVERS.NET.
B.ROOT-SERVERS.NET.            3600000      A   128.9.0.107
; formerly C.PSI.NET
;
.                              3600000      NS  C.ROOT-SERVERS.NET.
C.ROOT-SERVERS.NET.            3600000      A   192.33.4.12
; formerly TERP.UMD.EDU
;
.                              3600000      NS  D.ROOT-SERVERS.NET.
D.ROOT-SERVERS.NET.            3600000      A   128.8.10.90
; formerly NS.NASA.GOV
;
.                              3600000      NS  E.ROOT-SERVERS.NET.
E.ROOT-SERVERS.NET.            3600000      A   192.203.230.10
; formerly NS.ISC.ORG
;
.                              3600000      NS  F.ROOT-SERVERS.NET.
F.ROOT-SERVERS.NET.            3600000      A   192.5.5.241
; formerly NS.NIC.DDN.MIL
;
.                              3600000      NS  G.ROOT-SERVERS.NET.
G.ROOT-SERVERS.NET.            3600000      A   192.112.36.4
; formerly AOS.ARL.ARMY.MIL
;
.                              3600000      NS  H.ROOT-SERVERS.NET.
H.ROOT-SERVERS.NET.            3600000      A   128.63.2.53
; formerly NIC.NORDU.NET
;
.                              3600000      NS  I.ROOT-SERVERS.NET.
I.ROOT-SERVERS.NET.            3600000      A   192.36.148.17
; temporarily housed at NSI (InterNIC)
;
.                              3600000      NS  J.ROOT-SERVERS.NET.
J.ROOT-SERVERS.NET.            3600000      A   198.41.0.10
```

23,1   54%

FIGURE ? ?

The
localhost.zone
DNS zone file

```
$TTL    86400
$ORIGIN localhost.
@                   1D IN SOA       @ root (
                                    42              ; serial (d. adams)
                                    3H              ; refresh
                                    15M             ; retry
                                    1W              ; expiry
                                    1D )            ; minimum
[]
                    1D IN NS        @
                    1D IN A         127.0.0.1
~
~
~
~
~
~
~
~
~
~
~
"/var/named/localhost.zone" [readonly] 11L, 195C                9,0-1           All
```

Then, the /var/named/named.local provides a reverse-lookup record for your
computer, as localhost. As shown in Figure 9-4, the PTR record (on the last line in
the file) is 1, which associates the loopback address, 127.0.0.1, with your computer.

Next, look at your /etc/resolv.conf file. It should look something like Figure 9-5.
The "search" line specifies where DNS looks for a host name. If it does not find the
host, it proceeds to the following line, the "nameserver" line. This line specifies the
address of the local nameserver; in this case, the local server on the loopback address
of 127.0.0.1. You can add the IP addresses of as many nameservers as you have available,
in the same format.

Let's illustrate the lookup process. Assume your computer is looking for another
computer named bigshot. Based on the /etc/resolv.conf file shown in Figure 9-5, it
looks for *bigshot.subdomain.your-domain.com*, followed by *bigshot.your-domain.com*,
then finally bigshot.

If a client tries to look up ftp.redhat.com, ftp.redhat.com.*subdomain.your-domain.com*
is tried first, then ftp.redhat.com.*your-domain.com*, and finally ftp.redhat.com. The
number of domains in this line should be kept to a minimum; you don't want to waste
resources looking for www.redhat.com on your LAN. In any case, the search line should
not contain a TLD (top level domain, ".com" in this case). If there is a frequent need

FIGURE 9-4						
	`$TTL`	`86400`				
	`@`	`IN`	`SOA`	`localhost. root.localhost. (`		
The named.local				`1997022700`	`; Serial`	
pointer file				`28800`	`; Refresh`	
	`[]`			`14400`	`; Retry`	
				`3600000`	`; Expire`	
				`86400 )`	`; Minimum`	
		`IN`	`NS`	`localhost.`		
	`1`	`IN`	`PTR`	`localhost.`		

```
~
~
~
~
~
~
~
~
~
~
"/var/named/named.local" [readonly] 10L, 433C          5,1          All
```

to connect to hosts in another domain, that domain can be added to the search line directly as *other-domain.com*:

```
search subdomain.your-domain.com your-domain.com other-domain.com
```

Next, look at /etc/nsswitch.conf. This is a long file, specifying where to get different kinds of data types, from what file or database. Read the description and comments at the beginning of the file. Next, find the line starting with "hosts:". It should read something like:

```
hosts:        files nisplus dns
```

This line directs your computer to look first in the /etc/hosts file, followed by the NIS database of local computers, and then check DNS.

FIGURE 9-5	
	`search subdomain.your-domain.com your-domain.com`
	`nameserver 127.0.0.1`
Configuring	
/etc/resolv.conf	

Starting named

Make sure your computer is connected to an external network such as the Internet. Now you can start named with the **/sbin/service named start** command. View the syslog message file (usually called /var/log/messages) with the **tail -f /var/log/messages** command; you should see something like the listing in Figure 9-6.

If there are any error messages, named will display the file with the error. Stop the named service with the **/sbin/service named stop** command and check the applicable configuration files.

Now test the setup. Use the dig command to examine your work. For example, if you use dig to look up the address of www.redhat.com, you'll see something like the output shown in Figure 9-7.

The dig command asks your DNS server to look for the www.redhat.com server. It then contacts one of the nameserver computers listed in /etc/resolv.conf. If that doesn't work, it goes to one of the nameservers listed in the named.ca file and makes its requests from there. The request may be passed onto other DNS servers. Therefore, it can take some time before you see an answer.

Each time you reconfigure /etc/named.conf, restart named and try again.

FIGURE 9-6	`[root@RH80 root]# tail -f /var/log/messages`
	`Jul 24 10:37:16 RH80 named[1380]: using 1 CPU`
Start messages	`Jul 24 10:37:16 RH80 named: named startup succeeded`
for a DNS server	`Jul 24 10:37:17 RH80 named[1383]: loading configuration from '/etc/named.conf'`
	`Jul 24 10:37:17 RH80 named[1383]: no IPv6 interfaces found`
	`Jul 24 10:37:17 RH80 named[1383]: listening on IPv4 interface lo, 127.0.0.1#53`
	`Jul 24 10:37:17 RH80 named[1383]: listening on IPv4 interface eth0, 192.168.0.22`
	`2#53`
	`Jul 24 10:37:17 RH80 named[1383]: command channel listening on 127.0.0.1#953`
	`Jul 24 10:37:17 RH80 named[1383]: zone 0.0.127.in-addr.arpa/IN: loaded serial 19`
	`97022700`
	`Jul 24 10:37:17 RH80 named[1383]: zone localhost/IN: loaded serial 42`
	`Jul 24 10:37:17 RH80 named[1383]: running`

| FIGURE 9-7 | ```
[root@RH80 root]# dig www.redhat.com

; <<>> DiG 9.2.1 <<>> www.redhat.com
;; global options:  printcmd
;; Got answer:
;; ->>HEADER<<- opcode: QUERY, status: NOERROR, id: 31616
;; flags: qr aa rd ra; QUERY: 1, ANSWER: 2, AUTHORITY: 3, ADDITIONAL: 3

;; QUESTION SECTION:
;www.redhat.com.                         IN      A

;; ANSWER SECTION:
www.redhat.com.         600     IN      A       216.148.218.197
www.redhat.com.         600     IN      A       216.148.218.195

;; AUTHORITY SECTION:
redhat.com.             600     IN      NS      ns1.redhat.com.
redhat.com.             600     IN      NS      ns2.redhat.com.
redhat.com.             600     IN      NS      ns3.redhat.com.

;; ADDITIONAL SECTION:
ns1.redhat.com.         300     IN      A       66.187.233.210
ns2.redhat.com.         600     IN      A       66.77.185.41
ns3.redhat.com.         600     IN      A       63.240.14.66

;; Query time: 214 msec
;; SERVER: 207.217.126.81#53(207.217.126.81)
;; WHEN: Wed Jul 24 10:39:01 2002
;; MSG SIZE  rcvd: 166

[root@RH80 root]# []
``` |
|---|---|
| DNS query using dig | |

In fact, whenever a change is made in a DNS database, it takes some time before the change is noted (aka propagated) to other DNS servers on the Internet. Therefore, whenever you change something such as the IP address associated with a Web server, it's advisable to keep the old IP address available for that Web server until the new IP address has time to propagate.

A Simple Domain

Now you can define a simple domain for the computers on your network; call it your-domain.com. Note the lack of a period (.) at the end of the domain names in /etc/named.conf, in contrast with the other DNS configuration files.

Look at the zone "0.0.127.in-addr.arpa" IN line. This says that the zone 0.0.127.in-addr.arpa will be defined, that the localhost is the master server for it, associated data is stored in a file called named.local (see Figure 9-4), and no other DNS server is allowed to "update" or change the IP address associated with the localhost.
```

on the
job

Not all characters are allowed in host names. DNS can read only regular letters, numbers, and the dash (-) character. Unlike Linux, DNS does not distinguish between upper- and lowercase characters; for example, Mail.Your-Domain.Com is equivalent to mail.your-domain.com.

Now look at /var/named/named.local, back in Figure 9-4. This is a zone file that contains three resource records (RRs).

- SOA is short for Start of Authority. The @ is a special notation, which normally just sends you back to the current computer (localhost). It's actually based on reverse DNS lookups, which in this case refer to the 127.0.0.0 subnet.

- NS is the Name Server RR. The @ in the SOA line still applies; the name server is localhost.

- PTR refers to the host at address 1. As this is the 127.0.0.0 subnet, the full IP address is 127.0.0.1

The SOA record is the preamble to all zone files, and there should be exactly one in each zone file. It describes the zone where it comes from (a computer called localhost), who is responsible for its contents (root@localhost), what version of the zone file this is (serial: 42). The remaining fields—refresh, retry, expire, and minimum—are generic; but zone files should be customized for each network.

Time to start configuring your network. Insert a new zone section in named.conf:

```
zone "your-domain.com" {
    type master;
    file "your-domain.com.zone";
};
```

Note again that we do not use a period at the end of any address in /etc/named.conf. Now, populate the your-domain.com zone file with the listing in Figure 9-8.

Two things must be noted about the SOA record in /var/named/*your-domain.com.*zone file. The ns.your-domain.com record must be an actual computer with an A record. You're not allowed to use a CNAME (canonical name) for a computer in the SOA line. Next, hostmaster.your-domain.com should be read as hostmaster@your-domain.com— this should be an actual e-mail address for the DNS administrator. Any mail regarding the domain will be sent to the address listed here.

CNAME is a way to assign several names to each computer. For example, ftp and news are shown as aliases for www. In general, other computers, especially an

FIGURE 9-8

The
your-domain.com
.zone file

```
;
; Zone file for your-domain.com
;
; The full zone file
;
$TTL 3D
@      IN    SOA   ns.your-domain.com. hostmaster.your-domain.com.
                   200209101           ; serial, today's date + today's serial
[]                 8H                  ; refresh
                   2H                  ; retry
                   4W                  ; expiration
                   1D                  ; minimum
       NS    ns.your-domain.com.
       NS    abc.def.ghi.       ; some external DNS
       MX    10 mail.your-domain.com. ; Primary Email Server

localhost     A     127.0.0.1

RH80          A     192.168.0.129
RH80laptop    A     192.168.0.209
ns            A     192.168.0.129

www           A     192.168.1.231
ftp           CNAME www
news          CNAME www
                                                          9,1          All
```

MX (Mail Exchanger), CNAME, or SOA, should never refer to another CNAME. Also, a CNAME is not a legal host name for an e-mail address: for example, admin@ftp.your-domain.com won't work in terms of the file shown in Figure 9-8. Because of the confusion this can cause, many DNS administrators avoid using CNAME altogether.

The MX RR tells mail systems where to send mail that is addressed to someone@your-domain.com; in this case, to mail.your-domain.com. If you have more than one mail server, the number before the name of each MX computer signifies the priority. The MX with the lowest number (10) gets higher priority for mail. Save this file, and restart named with the **/sbin/service named restart** command. Examine the results with the **host -l your-domain.com** command.

This means that all records should be listed. The results ought to look very similar to the zone file itself.

The Reverse Zone

Now programs can convert the names in your-domain.com to real IP addresses. You're ready for the next step: a *reverse zone* file, which allows DNS to convert backward, from an IP address to a host name. Reverse zone lookups are used by many servers of different kinds (FTP, IRC, WWW, and others) to decide if they even want to talk to a computer asking for information. Therefore, for full access to all Internet services, you need a reverse zone. Start by adding another zone to named.conf:

```
zone "1.168.192.in-addr.arpa" IN {
        type master;
        file "your-domain.com.rr.zone";
        allow-update { none; };
};
```

This is similar to the 0.0.127.in-addr.arpa zone, and the contents of the your-domain.com.rr.zone file should resemble what is shown in Figure 9-9.

Once again, restart named and examine the output of **host -l your-domain.com**. If the results do not look similar to the actual zone file, look for error messages in /var/log/messages.

on the **Job**

Reverse zones are required to run several different services, such as sendmail and Apache. The reverse zone DNS database allows a server to verify if the name of a requesting computer matches its IP address, which can keep crackers from trying to "spoof" your system.

FIGURE 9-9
A reverse DNS zone file

```
$TTL    86400
@       IN      SOA     ns.your-domain.com. hostmaster.your-domain.com. (
                                200209101 ; Serial
                                28800     ; Refresh
                                14400     ; Retry
                                3600000   ; Expire
                                86400 )   ; Minimum
        IN      NS      ns.your-domain.com.
1       IN      PTR     linux.your-domain.com.
2       IN      PTR     laptop2.your-domain.com.
3       IN      PTR     experiment.your-domain.com.
4       IN      PTR     www.your-domain.com.
5       IN      PTR     ns.your-domain.com.
```

9,0-1   All

Common DNS Pitfalls

DNS is an Internet-wide database of domain names and IP addresses. If you want your DNS server to participate, make sure the information that goes into the database is up-to-date and properly formatted. Many network outages can be traced to poorly administered DNS servers. A few examples of common DNS errors are described in the following sections.

The Serial Number Wasn't Incremented

The single most common DNS error occurs when an administrator makes updates to a zone file, restarts DNS, and notices that no one else on the Internet knows about the updates. If another DNS server doesn't detect a new serial number on a zone file, it assumes the file is the same, and sticks with its cache. No data is taken from the update, and other DNS servers don't get the revised information.

When you update a zone file, update the serial number. It's best done with the current date in the format shown in the examples (four-digit year, two-digit month, and two-digit date, followed by a one-digit increment number). If you've updated the DNS more than once today, increment the last number as well.

The Reverse Zone Isn't Delegated

Not all network administrators have control over their DNS servers. Some administrators contract with an ISP for this service.

Now assume you're that ISP administrator. You'll need to assign this customer a range of IP addresses for their domain name. Then you'll need to assign the domain name and IP addresses to a specific DNS "zone of authority."

Next, you'll also need to set up the reverse zone. For example, if you assign the 192.168.1. network, you'll need to add NS records in the forward zone, and PTR records in the reverse zone.

From an end-user perspective, DNS might be considered the glue that holds the Internet together. Pay special attention to the nuances of the configuration files, so that network-wide problems are avoided.

Keep It Working

Assuming you're running your own DNS, you also need to keep the /var/named/named.ca file up to date. The easiest way to do this is by using *dig*, which is also known as the DNS Information Groper. If your DNS is working properly and is connected to the Internet, you can run commands such as **dig www.osborne.com.**

Let us analyze the dig command further. First, run dig with no arguments. You will get information from the local named.ca file. Then ask one of the listed root servers with a command such as **dig a.ROOT-SERVERS.NET.** The output should resemble a named.ca file. Save it to a file with a command such as **dig @a.root-servers.net.ns > named.ca.new**) and replace the old named.ca file. Remember to reload the named daemon after replacing the named.ca file.

Alternatively, the following script can be run automatically to update named.ca. The text of the base script is also available in the DNS-HOWTO available from the Linux Documentation Project at www.tldp.org. At the time of this writing, the base script in the HOWTO is still written to BIND 8; if you're using this file, change all of the "root.hints" filenames to "named.ca", and then replace the mail-alias "hostmaster" with a working e-mail address.

Once you're satisfied with the configuration, set up a crontab entry to run it once a month, and forget it.

```
#!/bin/sh
 #
 # Update the nameserver cache information file once per month.
 # This is run automatically by a cron entry.
 #
 # Original by Al Longyear
 # Updated for bind 8 by Nicolai Langfeldt
 # Miscellaneous error-conditions reported by David A. Ranch
 # Ping test suggested by Martin Foster
 #
 (
 echo "To: hostmaster <hostmaster>"
 echo "From: system <root>"
 echo "Subject: Automatic update of the named.ca file"
 echo

 PATH=/sbin:/usr/sbin:/bin:/usr/bin:
 export PATH
 cd /var/named
```

```
# Are we online?  Ping a server on the Internet
case 'ping -qnc 1 www.redhat.com' in
  *'100% packet loss'*)
        echo "The network is DOWN. named.ca NOT updated"
        echo
        exit 0
        ;;
esac

dig @A.ROOT-SERVERS.NET . ns > named.ca.new 2>>&1

case 'cat named.ca.new' in
  *Got answer*)
        # It worked
        ;;;
  *)
        echo "The named.ca file update has FAILED."
        echo "This is the dig output reported:"
        echo

        cat named.ca.new
        exit 0
        ;;
esac

echo "The named.ca file has been updated to contain the following
  information:"
echo
cat named.ca.new

chown root.root named.ca.new
chmod 444 named.ca.new
rm -f named.ca.old
mv named.ca named.ca.old
mv named.ca.new named.ca.hints
/etc/rc.d/init.d/named restart
echo
echo "The nameserver has been restarted to ensure that the update
  is complete."
echo "The previous named.ca file is now called
/var/named/named.ca.old."
) 2>>&1 | /usr/lib/sendmail -t
exit 0
```

EXERCISE 9-1

DNS/Bind

Following the example files shown previously, set up your own DNS server. Set it up to serve the domain called rhce.test.

1. Edit the /etc/named.conf file to reflect the configuration files that you plan to use. Name the zone file rhce.test.zone and set it to be a master domain.

2. Edit the file /var/named/rhce.test.zone and place the proper zone information in it. Start by adding in the header with the serial number and expiration information.

3. Add the SOA RR with a proper administrative e-mail address contact.

4. Add NS and MX RRs for the domain. Use the 192.168.*.* address range. If you're configuring an actual TCP/IP network with static IP addresses, feel free to use the assigned IP addresses on your network.

5. Add several hosts to the zone file. Use WWW, FTP, and mail for a few.

6. Save the zone file and then restart named with the **/sbin/service named restart** command.

7. Use dig to check the rhce.test domain.

CERTIFICATION OBJECTIVE 9.02

Squid Proxy Server

Squid is a high-performance HTTP and FTP caching proxy server. It can make your network connections more efficient. As it stores data from frequently used Web pages and files, it can often give your users the data they need without having to look to the Internet.

Extremely large studies have shown bandwidth reduction of 10–20 percent for all HTTP and FTP traffic, which is economically compelling for large installations. You can join the worldwide hierarchy of Harvest Cache sites; see http://www.ircache.net/ for more information.

Squid conforms to the Harvest Cache architecture and uses the Inter-Cache Protocol (ICP) for transfers between participating peer and parent/child cache servers. It can be used either as a traditional caching proxy or as a front-end accelerator for a traditional Web server. Squid accepts only HTTP requests but speaks FTP on the server side when FTP objects are requested.

Required Packages for Squid

To run Squid, you need the following files installed on your computer:

- **/etc/rc.d/init.d/squid**   Start/stop script
- **/etc/squid/**   Configuration directory
- **/usr/share/doc/squid-*version***   Documentation, mostly in HTML format
- **/usr/lib/squid/**   Support files and internationalized error messages
- **/usr/sbin/client**   Command line diagnostic client program
- **/usr/sbin/squid**   Main Squid daemon
- **/var/log/squid/**   Log directory
- **/var/spool/squid/**   Cache directory (Hundreds of MB and maybe more in many hashed directories)

Initializing Squid

When you start Squid for the first time, the **/etc/rc.d/init.d/squid start** script automatically runs **squid -z** to create the /var/spool/squid/ cache directories and then starts the Squid daemon. Squid runs as a caching proxy server on port 3128. You can then set up Web browsers on your LAN to point to your computer through port 3128 as the proxy server.

Configuration Options

Advanced configuration features are adjusted via the /etc/squid/squid.conf configuration file. The default configuration file allows you to tune and secure Squid in a number of ways. A key configuration section contains *cache_peer* lines, which specify parent and sibling Squid cache servers. If your Linux computer is part of a group of Squid servers in a harvest cache, these lines allow your Squid servers to check these other Squid servers before going to the Internet. Figure 9-10 illustrates an excerpt from the default squid.conf configuration file, which specifies one parent and two sibling cache hosts.

Squid first checks its own cache and then queries its siblings and parents for the desired object such as a Web page. If neither the cache host nor its siblings have the object, it asks one of its parents to fetch it from the source. If no parent servers are available, it fetches the object itself.

Squid can greatly improve the performance of a corporate intranet. If your company has many employees who surf the Net, a Squid server can reduce your network connection costs by decreasing the bandwidth you need for your Internet connection.

FIGURE 9-10

Squid can refer to parent and sibling Squid servers

```
# OPTIONS WHICH AFFECT THE NEIGHBOR SELECTION ALGORITHM
# ---------------------------------------------------------------------------
#
# TAG: cache_peer
#       To specify other caches in a hierarchy, use the format:
#
#               cache_peer hostname type http_port icp_port
#
#       For example,
#
#                                                   proxy  icp
#       #                                           port   port   options
#       #   hostname                    type        ----   ----   -------
#       #   --------------------        ------
#       cache_peer parent.foo.net       parent      3128   3130   [proxy-only]
#       cache_peer sib1.foo.net         sibling     3128   3130   [proxy-only]
#       cache_peer sib2.foo.net         sibling     3128   3130   [proxy-only]
#
#          type:   either 'parent', 'sibling', or 'multicast'.
#
#     proxy_port: The port number where the cache listens for proxy
#                 requests.
#
#       icp_port: Used for querying neighbor caches about
#                 objects.  To have a non-ICP neighbor
#                 specify '7' for the ICP port and make sure the
#                 neighbor machine has the UDP echo port
#                 enabled in its /etc/inetd.conf file.
#
#        options: proxy-only
#                 weight=n
#                 ttl=n
#                 no-query
#                 default
#                 round-robin
#                 multicast-responder
```

150,2-8   4%

EXERCISE 9-2

Configuring Squid to Act as a Proxy for Web and FTP Service

This exercise assumes you have a LAN. One of the computers on the LAN is also a server that is connected to the Internet. In this exercise, you'll install Squid on that server. Then you can configure Squid to act as a proxy for Web and FTP service for your LAN.

1. Open the Squid configuration file, /etc/squid/squid.conf. If you have enough computers on your LAN, configure one parent and one child cache site.

2. Start and stop the Squid service.

3. Configure a test client such as a Web browser to use your Squid service. Test your client by using both HTTP and FTP addresses in the browser address. Use it to retrieve files from various sites on the Internet, such as www.redhat.com and ftp.redhat.com.

CERTIFICATION OBJECTIVE 9.03

Network File System (NFS)

NFS is the standard for sharing files and printers on a directory with Linux and Unix computers. It was originally developed by Sun Microsystems in the mid-1980s. Linux has supported NFS (both as a client and a server) for years, and NFS continues to be popular in organizations with Unix- or Linux-based networks.

NFS Server Configuration and Operation

NFS servers are relatively easy to configure. All that is required is to export a filesystem, either generally or to a specific host, and then mount that filesystem remotely.

Required Packages

Two RPM packages are associated with NFS: portmap and nfs-utils. Use the **rpm -q** *packagename* command to check for these packages, which should provide a number of key files. The nfs-utils package includes:

- /etc/rc.d/init.d/nfs   (start/stop script for NFS)
- /etc/rc.d/init.d/nfslock   (start/stop script for lockd and statd)
- /usr/share/doc/nfs-utils-*version*   (documentation, mostly in HTML format)
- Server daemons in /usr/sbin: rpc.mountd, rpc.nfsd
- Server daemons in /sbin: rpc.lockd, rpc.statd
- Control programs in /usr/sbin: exportfs, nfsstat, nhfsstone, showmount
- Status files in /var/lib/nfs: etab, rmtab, statd/state, xtab

The portmap package includes the following key files:

- /etc/rc.d/init.d/portmap   (start/stop script)
- /usr/share/doc/portmap-*version*   (documentation)
- Server daemon in /sbin: portmap
- Control programs in /usr/sbin: pmap_dump, pmap_set

Starting and Stopping NFS

Once it is configured, you can set up NFS to start during the Linux boot process, or you can start it yourself with the **/sbin/service nfs start** command. NFS also depends on the portmap package, which helps secure NFS directories that are shared through /etc/exports. Because of this dependency, make sure to start the portmap before starting NFS, and don't stop it until after stopping NFS.

exam
ⓦatch

Remember that both the portmap and nfs daemons must be running before NFS can work.

The nfs service script starts the following processes:

- **rpc.mountd**   Handles mount requests
- **nfsd**   Starts an nfsd kernel process for each shared directory

■ **rpc.rquotad**   Reports disk quota statistics to clients

If any of these processes are not running, NFS won't work. Fortunately, it's easy to check for these processes. Just run the **rpcinfo -p** command.

The /etc/exports File

The /etc/exports file is the only major NFS configuration file. You can set it up to list the directories that are to be exported via the exportfs command. Each line in this file lists one directory that may be exported, the hosts it will be exported to, and the options that apply to this export. You can export a given directory only once. Take the following examples from an /etc/exports file:

```
/pub                    (ro,sync) someone.mylocaldomain.com(rw,sync)
/home                   *.mylocaldomain.com(rw,sync)
/opt/diskless-root      diskless.mylocaldomain.com(rw,no_root_squash,sync)
```

In the preceding example, /pub is exported to all users as read-only. It is also exported to one specific computer with read-write privileges. /home is exported, with read-write privileges, to any computer on the .mylocaldomain.com network. /opt/diskless-root is exported with full read-write privileges (even for root users) on the diskless.mylocaldomain.com computer.

All of these options include the sync flag. This requires all changes to be written to disk before a command such as a file copy is complete. This is a new change for Red Hat 8.0; in future releases, sync may become the default for all NFS shares.

Wildcards and Globbing

In Linux network configuration files, you can specify a group of computers with the right wildcard. This process in Linux is sometimes also known as *globbing*. What you do for a wildcard varies with the type of configuration file. The NFS /etc/exports file is somewhat conventional in this respect; for example, the *.mydomain.com entry specifies all computers within the mydomain.com domain. In contrast, /etc/hosts.deny is less conventional; .mydomain.com, with the leading dot, specifies all computers in that same domain.

Sometimes you can specify a group of computers with the right IP address line; for example, 192.168.0.0/255.255.255.0 specifies the 192.168.0.0 network of computers with IP addresses that range from 192.168.0.1 to 192.168.0.254. Some services allow the use of CIDR (Classless Inter-Domain Routing) notation; in that case, you can specify the same network with the 192.168.0.0/24 entry. For details, see the discussion for each applicable service in Chapters 7–11.

Activating the List of Exports

Changing /etc/exports is not enough. This file is simply the default set of exported directories. You need to activate them with the **/usr/sbin/exportfs -a** command. This file can be set up to run when Linux boots. Alternatively, you can run this command yourself to test your changes to /etc/exports. You can even use /usr/sbin/exportfs to export a directory directly, bypassing /etc/exports.

When you add a share to /etc/exports, the **/usr/sbin/exportfs -r** command adds the new directories. However, if you're modifying, moving, or deleting a share, it is safest to first temporarily unexport all filesystems with the **/usr/sbin/exportfs -ua** command before reexporting the shares with the **/usr/sbin/exportfs -a** command.

Once exports are active, they're easy to check. Just run the **/usr/sbin/showmount -e** command on the server. If you're looking for the export list for a remote NFS server, just add the name of the NFS server as an argument to this command. If this command doesn't work, you may have NFS messages blocked on the client or the server with a firewall.

NFS Client Configuration and Operation

Now you can mount a shared NFS directory from a client computer. The commands and configuration files are similar to those used for any local filesystem.

NFS and /etc/fstab

NFS clients can be configured to mount remote NFS filesystems, as well as local filesystems during the boot process, based on the configuration in /etc/fstab. For example, the following entry in a client /etc/fstab mounts the /homenfs share from the computer named nfsserv, on the local /nfs/home directory:

```
## Server Directory    Mount Point   Type  Mount Options      Dump Fsckorder
nfsserv:/homenfs        /nfs/home     nfs   soft,timeout=100   0    0
```

Alternatively, an automounter, such as autofs or amd, can be used to dynamically mount NFS filesystems as required by the client computer. The automounter can also unmount these remote filesystems after a period of inactivity.

Client-Side Helper Processes

When you start NFS as a client, it adds a few new system processes, including:

- **rpc.statd**   Tracks the status of servers, for use by rpc.lockd in recovering locks after a server crash

- **rpc.lockd**   Manages the client side of file locking

Diskless Clients

NFS supports diskless clients, which are computers without a hard drive. A diskless client may use a boot floppy or a boot PROM to get started. Then embedded commands can mount the appropriate root (/) directory, swap space, the /usr directory as read-only, and other shared directories such as /home in read/write mode. If your computer uses a boot PROM, you'll also need access to DHCP and TFTP servers for network and kernel information.

Quirks and Limitations of NFS

NFS does have its problems. An administrator who controls NFS mounts would be wise to take note of these limitations.

Statelessness

NFS is a "stateless" protocol. In other words, you don't need to log in separately to access a shared NFS directory. Instead, the NFS client normally contacts rpc.mountd on the server. The rpc.mounted daemon handles mount requests. It checks the request against currently exported filesystems. If the request is valid, rpc.mounted provides an *NFS file handle* (a "magic cookie"), which is then used for further client/server communication for this share.

The stateless protocol allows the NFS client to wait if the NFS server ever has to be rebooted. The software waits, and waits, and waits. This can cause the NFS client to hang as discussed later.

This can also lead to problems with insecure single-user clients. When a file is opened through a share, it may be "locked out" from other users. When an NFS server is rebooted, handling the locked file can be difficult. The security problems can be so severe that NFS communication is blocked even by the default Red Hat Linux firewall.

In theory, the recent change to NFS, setting up sync as the default for file transfers, should help address this problem. In theory, locked-out users should not lose any data that they've written with the appropriate commands.

Absolute and Relative Symbolic Links

If you have any symbolic links on an exported directory, be careful. The client interprets a symbolically linked file with respect to its own local filesystem. Unless the mount point and filesystem structures are identical, the linked file can point to an unexpected location, which may lead to unpredictable consequences.

You have a couple of ways to address this issue. You can take care to limit the use of symbolic links within an exported directory. Alternatively, NFS offers a server-side export option (*link_relative*) that converts absolute links to relative links; however, this can have nonintuitive results if the client mounts a subdirectory of the exported directory.

Root Squash

By default, NFS is set up to "root_squash," which prevents root users on an NFS client from gaining root access to a share on an NFS server. Specifically, the root user on a client (UID 0) is mapped to the *nobody* unprivileged account.

This behavior can be disabled via the no_root_squash server export option in /etc/exports.

NFS Hangs

Because NFS is stateless, clients normally wait for a server for up to several minutes. In some cases, an NFS client may wait indefinitely if a server goes down. During the wait, any process that looks for a file on the mounted NFS share will hang. Once this happens, it is generally difficult or impossible to unmount the offending filesystems. You can do several things to reduce the impact of this problem:

- Take great care to ensure the reliability of NFS servers and the network.

- Avoid mounting many different NFS servers at once. If several computers mount each other's NFS directories, this could cause problems throughout the network.

- Mount infrequently used NFS exports only when needed. NFS clients should unmount these clients after use.

- Set up NFS shares with the *sync* option, which should at least reduce the incidence of lost files.

- Don't configure a mission-critical computer as an NFS client, if at all possible.

- Keep NFS mounted directories out of the search path for users, especially that of *root*.

- Keep NFS mounted directories out of the root (/) directory; instead, segregate them to a less frequently used filesystem such as /nfs/home or /nfs/share.

Soft Mounting

Consider using the *soft* option when mounting NFS filesystems. When an NFS server fails, a soft-mounted NFS filesystem will fail rather than hang. However, this risks the failure of long-running processes due to temporary network outages.

In addition, you can use the *timeo* option to set a timeout interval, in tenths of a second. For example, the following command would mount /nfs/home with a timeout of 30 seconds:

```
mount -o soft,timeo=300 myserver:/home /nfs/home
```

Inverse DNS Pointers

An NFS server daemon checks mount requests. First, it looks at the current list of exports, based on /etc/exports. Then, it looks up the client's IP address to find its host name. This requires a reverse DNS lookup.

This host name is then finally checked against the list of exports. If NFS can't find a host name, rpc.mountd will deny access to that client. For security reasons, it also adds a "request from unknown host" entry in /var/log/messages.

File Locking

Multiple NFS clients can be set up to mount the same exported directory from the same server. It's quite possible that people on different computers end up trying to use the same shared file. This is addressed by the File Locking daemon service.

NFS has historically had serious problems making file locking work. If you have an application that depends on file locking over NFS, test it thoroughly before putting it into production.

Filesystem Nesting

It is impossible to export two directories in the same filesystem if one is inside the other. For example, /usr and /usr/local cannot both be exported unless /usr/local is mounted on a separate partition from /usr.

Performance Tips

You can do several things to keep NFS running in a stable and reliable manner. For example:

- Eight kernel NFS daemons, which is the default, is generally sufficient for good performance, even under fairly heavy loads. If your NFS server is busy, you may want to add additional NFS daemons through the /etc/rc.d/init.d/nfs script. Just keep in mind that the extra kernel processes consume valuable kernel resources.

- NFS write performance can be extremely slow, particularly with NFS v2 clients, as the client waits for each block of data to be written to disk.

- One solution is specialized hardware with nonvolatile RAM, which can store data to be written.

- In applications where data loss is not a big concern, the filesystem can be mounted by the client with the *async* option. Speed is increased because *async* NFS mounts do not write files to disk until other operations are complete. A loss of power or network connectivity can result in a loss of data.

- Host name lookups are performed frequently by the NFS server; you can start the Name Switch Cache Daemon (nscd) to speed lookup performance.

exam ***watch*** **NFS is a powerful file-sharing system. But there are risks associated with NFS. If an NFS server is down, it could affect your entire network. It's also not secure enough to use on the Internet. NFS is primarily used on secure LAN/WAN networks.**

NFS Security

NFS includes a number of serious security problems and should never be used in hostile environments (such as on a server directly exposed to the Internet), at least not without strong precautions.

Shortcomings and Risks

NFS is an easy-to-use yet powerful file-sharing system. However, it is not without its problems. The following are a few security issues to keep in mind:

- **Authentication**   NFS relies on the host to report user and group IDs. However, this can expose your files if root users on other computers access your NFS shares. In other words, any data that is accessible via NFS to *any user* can potentially be accessed by *any other* user. This may also hold true for users who can reboot their own computers.

- **Privacy**   Not even Secure NFS encrypts its network traffic.

- **portmap Infrastructure**   Both the NFS client and server depend on the RPC portmap daemon. The portmap daemon has historically had a number of serious security holes. For this reason, portmap is not recommended for use on computers that are directly connected to the Internet or other potentially hostile networks.

Security Tips

If NFS *must* be used in or near a hostile environment, you can do some things to reduce the security risks:

- Educate yourself in detail about NFS security. If you do not clearly understand the risks, you should restrict your NFS use to friendly, internal networks behind a good firewall.

- Export as little data as possible, and export filesystems as read-only if possible.

- Use root squash to prevent clients from having root access to exported filesystems.

- If an NFS client has a direct connection to the Internet, use separate network adapters for the Internet connection and the LAN. Use the right firewall commands (iptables or ipchains) to block the routing on the TCP and UDP ports associated with portmapper, mountd, and nfsd.

- Use a firewall system such as iptables or ipchains to deny access to the portmapper, mountd, and nfsd ports, except from explicitly trusted hosts or networks. The ports are

```
111    TCP/UDP    portmapper    (server and client)
745    UDP        mountd        (server)
747    TCP        mountd        (server)
2049   TCP/UDP    nfsd          (server)
```

Use a port scanner to verify that these ports are blocked for untrusted network(s).

on the

Job

As of this writing, Red Hat is creating a GUI tool for configuring NFS servers, redhat-config-nfs. As with other Linux GUI tools, it is a "front end" that automates the process of editing the applicable configuration files and activating the service.

exam

Watch

While some may find it easier to learn with a GUI tool, these tools are usually more time consuming and less flexible than direct action from the command line. As time is often short on the RHCE exam, I recommend that you learn how to configure and activate NFS and other services from the command line.

EXERCISE 9-3

NFS

This exercise requires two computers, one set up as an NFS server, the other as an NFS client. On the NFS server:

1. Set up a group named IT for the Information Technology group in /etc/group.

2. Create the /MIS directory. Assign ownership to the MIS group with the chgrp command.

3. Set the SGID bit on this directory to enforce group ownership.

4. Update /etc/exports file to allow read and write for your local network. Run the **exportfs -a** command to set it up under NFS.

5. Restart the NFS service.

On a client:

1. Create a directory for the server share called /mnt/MIS.

2. Mount the shared NFS directory on /mnt/MIS.

3. List all exported shares from the server and save this output as /mnt/MIS/thishost.shares.list.

4. Make this service a permanent connection in the /etc/fstab file. Assume that the connection might be troublesome and add the appropriate options, such as soft mounting.

5. Reboot the client computer. Check to see if the share is properly remounted.

6. Test the NFS connection. Stop the service on the server, and then try copying a file to the /mnt/MIS directory. While the attempt to copy will fail, it should not hang the client.

7. Restart the NFS server.

8. Edit /etc/fstab again. This time assume that NFS is reliable, and remove the special options that you added in step 4.

9. Reboot the client computer. Test the service with the new settings.

Now test what happens when you shut down the server. The mounted NFS directory on the client should hang when you try to access the service.

Restart the server service and see if your client service resumes.

CERTIFICATION OBJECTIVE 9.04

Internet Network News Daemon

News services such as USENET have their own special protocol and port in TCP/IP. Internet newsgroups use the Network News Transport Protocol (NNTP) on TCP port 119. NNTP is a high-performance, low-latency message transfer protocol. On the Internet, a collection of NNTP servers accepts posts and distributes them worldwide, moving billions of characters daily.

InterNetNews (INN)

The InterNetNews (INN) service is one of the news servers that can work with NNTP. Like bind, INN is maintained by the Internet Software Consortium at www.isc.org/products/INN. If necessary, you can install the inn*, inn-devel*, inews*, and cleanfeed* RPM packages from the appropriate Red Hat installation CDs. As of this writing, the current version of INN is version 2.3, which supports circular message buffers as well as filesystem-based spooling. There are alternate news servers that also use NNTP, including CNEWS and Cyclone.

Configuring INN

Red Hat Linux stores INN configuration files in /etc/news. The basic INN configuration requires that you edit inn.conf, incoming.conf, and newsfeeds. If you want INN to serve other users or computers, edit readers.conf as well. If you have any special messages or policies for your news clients, you can add them to motd.news.

You should set the organization directive in inn.conf:

```
organization: Your Organization Here
```

Your ISP typically supplies NNTP services. Add the appropriate contact information (e-mail and telephone number) as a peer definition in your incoming.conf file. This can be handy for others who are troubleshooting your site.

```
# A peer definition.
# Myisp.net (800) 555 1212 joenews@myisp.net
peer myisp {
        hostname: news.myisp.net
    }
```

You also need to enter a domain in the fromhost: line such as example.com or localhost.localdomain.

If you want your news server to post articles, you need an entry in the /etc/news/newsfeeds configuration file. This example uses nntpsend to transmit your outbound traffic. nntpsend is run hourly from /etc/cron.hourly/inn-cron-nntpsend:

```
# Myisp.net (800) 555 1212 joenews@myisp.net
news.myisp.net/uunet:!junk,!control*/!foo:Tm:innfeed!
```

The number of messages in a newsgroup can grow quickly. Make sure there is sufficient room in the main newsgroup directory, /var/spool/news. The innfeed.conf and cleanfeed.conf configuration files in this directory govern the flow and deletion policies for each message. If possible, mount /var as a separate filesystem; when you format it, allocate plenty of inodes with something like the **mkfs -i 1024 /dev/***xdy#* command.

If you find that newsgroup performance is an issue, you can set up buffers through the /etc/news/cycbuff.conf configuration file. Add a *storageapi: true* directive to /etc/news/inn.conf. Then you can set up cycbuff.conf with space for cyclic buffers.

Once you've set up the desired configuration, use the following steps to get INN going as a news server.

1. Run /usr/lib/news/bin/inncheck. If you have problems with your configuration files, you'll see messages to that effect. For example, you may need to correct the permissions on /var/lib/news/active from 644 to 664. Correct this or any other problems that inncheck may identify before starting the INN daemon, innd.

A modmailer or moderatormailer error from the /usr/lib/news/bin/inncheck command is not a problem for INN. As of this writing, INN still works despite this error.

2. Run /usr/lib/news/bin/makehistory to start the INN history database of message IDs.

3. Create an empty history database. Log in as the user named news. As root, run the **su - news** command. This gives ownership for all files you create to the owner named news. Once there, run the following commands:

```
# cd /var/lib/news
# touch history
# makedbz -i
# mv history.n.dir history.dir
# mv history.n.hash history.hash
# mv history.n.index history.index
# exit
```

4. Start INN with /etc/rc.d/init.d/innd start.

5. Stop INN with /usr/lib/news/bin/ctlinnd shutdown *"Insert your reason here."*

6. Check status with /usr/lib/news/bin/innstat.

If you have any errors during this process, read the next section.

Troubleshooting

Here are a few common errors with news servers and their solutions.

News Won't Start
If innd won't start at all, check the following:

■ Try the **/usr/lib/news/bin/inncheck** command. Address any messages that are returned.

- If innd starts manually, but not when you restart Linux, check whether the start settings are correct with the **/sbin/chkconfig --list | grep innd** command.
- Make sure the user and group ownership in /var/lib/news corresponds to the user and group named news.
- Check the news log files in the /var/log/news/ directory.

Readers Can't Read

The INN daemon is running, but no one can read any news articles. If you have this problem, check the following items:

- Check /etc/news/readers.conf and confirm that the desired user(s) and or computers are allowed.
- Confirm innd is running with the **ps ax | grep innd** command.
- Telnet to port 119 and see if the banner comes up.
- See /var/log/news/news.err.

Posters Can't Post

If posters can't post:

- Check /etc/news/readers.conf and confirm that the desired poster is allowed.
- Telnet to port 119 from the problem host. For example, on the computer with the news server, run the **telnet localhost nntp** command. If it works, you'll see the InterNetNews server banner.
- See /var/log/news/news.err, or other logs in the same directory.

News logs are stored in the /var/log/news directory. Read them when there is a problem, especially /var/log/news/news.err. News databases are in /var/lib/news and can get very large. Keep an eye on disk space for the partition with the /var directory with the df command.

When you run the **telnet** *newsserver* **nntp** command from another computer, the banner should come up immediately. While you don't have a command prompt, you can still type newsgroup client commands. For example, the **mode reader** command should switch you to the NNRP server. Type **help** for a list of commands, and **quit** to exit. Figure 9-11 shows an example of a newsgroup debugging session.

FIGURE 9-11

Connecting to
a news server
via Telnet

```
[root@RH80 news]# telnet localhost nntp
Trying 127.0.0.1...
Connected to localhost.
Escape character is '^]'.
200 localhost.localdomain InterNetNews server INN 2.3.3 ready
mode reader
200 localhost.localdomain InterNetNews NNRP server INN 2.3.3 ready (posting ok).
help
100 Legal commands
  authinfo user Name|pass Password|generic <prog> <args>
  article [MessageID|Number]
  body [MessageID|Number]
  date
  group newsgroup
  head [MessageID|Number]
  help
  ihave
  last
  list [active|active.times|newsgroups|distributions|distrib.pats|overview.fmt|s
ubscriptions|motd]
  listgroup newsgroup
  mode reader
  newgroups [YY]yymmdd hhmmss ["GMT"|"UTC"] [<distributions>]
  newnews newsgroups [YY]yymmdd hhmmss ["GMT"|"UTC"] [<distributions>]
  next
  post
  slave
  stat [MessageID|Number]
  xgtitle [group_pattern]
  xhdr header [range|MessageID]
  xover [range]
  xpat header range|MessageID pat [morepat...]
  xpath MessageID
Report problems to <news@localhost.localdomain>
.
quit
205 .
Connection closed by foreign host.
[root@RH80 news]# []
```

EXERCISE 9-4

INN

Based on the previous section, create a new news service for your company. Specify
a domain name such as mycorp.com if appropriate.

1. Open the /etc/news/inn.conf file in a text editor.

2. Enter your company name as the organization. Set the host name of the
   computer with the INN server to the fromhost variable.

3. Open the /etc/news/incoming.conf file in a text editor, and identify your ISP as the peer.

4. Use the **/usr/lib/news/bin/inncheck** command. If you see error messages other than modmailer, address them.

5. Use the **/sbin/service innd start** command to start the INN daemon. Check the status with the **/sbin/service innd status** command.

6. Use nntpsend to transmit your outbound traffic. Check the /etc/cron.hourly directory to make sure nntpsend is updated hourly.

7. Configure your banner in /etc/news/motd.news to indicate "only corporate data is allowed, all feeds are moderated."

8. Run the makehistory command to set up the appropriate history database.

9. Log in as the news user and create the necessary history files in the /var/lib/news directory.

10. Restart your news service. Check the status and ensure it is configured to start at runlevels 3 and 5.

11. Test the service by running telnet to access the NNTP port.

12. Once connected, change to mode reader.

13. Test the news server. Post a message. Log in as a different user and try to read the message. Try to reply to the message as well.

DHCP

There are two protocols that allow a client computer to get network configuration information from a server: DHCP (Dynamic Host Configuration Protocol) and bootp. DHCP works if you have a DHCP server on the local network. The bootp protocol is required if you're getting information from a DHCP server on another network.

DHCP servers can simplify and centralize network administration if you're administering more than a few computers on a network. They are especially convenient for networks with a significant number of mobile users. Since bootp is essentially just a way to access a DHCP server, this section will cover only the configuration of DHCP.

As with most network services, DHCP has a client and a server. These are based on the dhcp* and dhclient* RPM packages. Install them as required.

Red Hat seems to change the commands and packages related to the DHCP client frequently. The dhclient* package is new for Red Hat 8.0. Recent versions of Red Hat have used dhcpcd and pump as DHCP clients. If you are using a different version of Red Hat Linux, make sure you've installed the right packages and are using the right commands: examine the packages and applicable documentation carefully.

DHCP Server Configuration

First, make sure that multicast is running on the server's network interface with the **/sbin/ifconfig** command. The output should look something like what you see in Figure 9-12, and should include a MULTICAST setting for the network card that you want to configure.

FIGURE 9-12

Current network configuration

```
[root@RH80 root]# /sbin/ifconfig
eth0      Link encap:Ethernet  HWaddr 00:50:56:40:1E:65
          inet addr:192.168.0.222  Bcast:192.168.0.255  Mask:255.255.255.0
          UP BROADCAST RUNNING MULTICAST  MTU:1500  Metric:1
          RX packets:1420 errors:0 dropped:0 overruns:0 frame:0
          TX packets:220 errors:0 dropped:0 overruns:0 carrier:0
          collisions:0 txqueuelen:100
          RX bytes:179204 (175.0 Kb)  TX bytes:19365 (18.9 Kb)
          Interrupt:10 Base address:0x10a0

lo        Link encap:Local Loopback
          inet addr:127.0.0.1  Mask:255.0.0.0
          UP LOOPBACK RUNNING  MTU:16436  Metric:1
          RX packets:548 errors:0 dropped:0 overruns:0 frame:0
          TX packets:548 errors:0 dropped:0 overruns:0 carrier:0
          collisions:0 txqueuelen:0
          RX bytes:43667 (42.6 Kb)  TX bytes:43667 (42.6 Kb)

[root@RH80 root]# []
```

FIGURE 9-13

A sample
DHCP server
configuration file
(/etc/dhcpd.conf)

```
ddns-update-style interim;
ignore client-updates;

subnet 192.168.0.0 netmask 255.255.255.0 {

# --- default gateway
        option routers                  192.168.0.1;
        option subnet-mask              255.255.255.0;

        option nis-domain               "domain.org";
        option domain-name              "domain.org";
        option domain-name-servers      192.168.1.1;

        option time-offset              -18000; # Eastern Standard Time
#       option ntp-servers              192.168.1.1;
#       option netbios-name-servers     192.168.1.1;
# --- Selects point-to-point node (default is hybrid). Don't change this unless
# -- you understand Netbios very well
#       option netbios-node-type 2;

        range dynamic-bootp 192.168.0.128 192.168.0.255;
        default-lease-time 21600;
        max-lease-time 43200;

        # we want the nameserver to appear at a fixed address
        host ns {
                next-server marvin.redhat.com;
                hardware ethernet 12:34:56:78:AB:CD;
                fixed-address 207.175.42.254;
```

If you don't see MULTICAST associated with your network card, you'll have to recompile the kernel to add multicast support. For more information on this process, see Chapter 6.

Now configure the DHCP server daemon, dhcpd, by creating or editing /etc/dhcpd.conf. The standard DHCP configuration includes a random assignment of IP addresses from a specific range. This setup is illustrated in Figure 9-13, which is based on a sample dhcpd.conf.sample configuration file in the /usr/share/doc/dhcp* directory.

Let's break down this file in detail:

■ **ddns-update-style interim** Nearly conforms to the new Dynamic DNS standard, where the DNS database is updated when the DNS server renews its DHCP lease. It is "interim" because the standards for DDNS are not complete as of this writing.

- **ignore client-updates**   A good setting if you don't want to allow users on client computers to change their host names.

- **subnet 192.168.0.0 netmask 255.255.255.0**   Describes a network with an address of 192.168.0.0 and a subnet mask of 255.255.255.0. This allows you to assign addresses in the range 192.168.0.1–192.168.0.254 to different computers on this network.

- **option routers**   Lists the default router. You can add additional option routers lines if you have more than one connection to an outside network. This is required to give the computers on your network the default gateway, which is required for access to outside networks such as the Internet.

- **option subnet-mask**   Specifies the subnet mask for the network.

- **option nis-domain**   Notes the server that provides the NIS shared authorization database. If you don't have an NFS network, you can comment out this option.

- **option domain-name**   Adds the domain name for your network.

- **option domain-name-servers**   Notes the IP address for the DNS server for your network.

- **option time-offset**   Lists the difference from Greenwich Mean Time, also known as UTC, in seconds.

- **option ntp-servers**   Notes any ntp servers for keeping the time on the local computer in sync with UTC.

- **option netbios-name-servers**   Adds the location of any WINS servers for your network.

- **option netbios-node-type 2**   Peer-to-peer node searches, associated with WINS.

- **range dynamic-bootp 192.168.0.128 192.168.0.254**   Notes the assignable IP addresses to *remote* networks, using the bootp protocol. Remember the space between the IP addresses!

- **default-lease-time**   Specifies the lease time for IP address information, in seconds.

- **max-lease-time**   Specifies the maximum lease time for IP address information, in seconds.

- **next-server**   Notes the boot server for network computers. If you don't have any network computers, you can comment out this entire stanza.

You can also assign a specific IP address to a computer based on a client's Ethernet address. Just add an entry similar to the following to /etc/dhcpd.conf:

```
host dragonfire {
        hardware ethernet 08:00:12:23:4d:3f;
        fixed-address 192.168.0.201;
}
```

This will assign the IP address 192.168.1.201 to a client named dragonfire with the Ethernet hardware address 08:00:12:23:4d:3f.

To assign an IP address to a specific network card on a specific computer, you need the hardware address, which can be found via a /sbin/ifconfig command.

DHCP can be customized for individual computers. You can set up static IP addresses for servers. Once you're ready, start the dhcpd server with the following command:

/etc/rc.d/init.d/dhcpd start

By default, this starts a dhcpd server, which listens for requests on the eth0 network card. Alternatively, to have dhcpd listen on eth1, run the following command:

/etc/rc.d/init.d/dhcpd start eth1

You can watch the dhcpd server in action. Stop dhcpd, and restart it in the foreground with the following command:

/usr/sbin/dhcpd -d -f

Start another client, and then watch the console of the server. A number of DHCP communication messages are shown illustrating the process of leasing an IP address to a client.

Another easy way to get the MAC address for a given client is to watch the dhcpd server messages.

Once you've configured your dhcpd server to your satisfaction, remember to activate it at the appropriate runlevels. For example, the following command activates the dhcpd daemon when you boot Linux into runlevels 3 and 5:

```
[root@redhattest mj] /sbin/chkconfig --level 35 dhcpd on
```

DHCP and Microsoft Windows

In order for the dhcpd server to work correctly with picky DHCP clients such as Microsoft Windows 9*x*, the server needs to send data to the broadcast address: 255.255.255.255. Unfortunately, Linux insists on changing 255.255.255.255 into the local subnet broadcast address. This results in a DHCP protocol violation, and while Linux DHCP clients don't notice the problem, Microsoft DHCP clients do. Normally, such clients can't see DHCPOFFER messages and therefore don't know when to take an IP address offered from the DHCP server. If you're configuring a DHCP server for a network with Microsoft Windows computers, run the following command:

```
route add --host 255.255.255.255 dev eth0
```

where eth0 is the name of the NIC that connects the server to the network.

Client Configuration

You can set up DHCP as a client through the /sbin/dhclient command, or you can use the GUI redhat-config-network utility. Configuring a DHCP client at the command line is not difficult. Make sure that the /etc/sysconfig/network configuration file includes the following line:

```
NETWORKING=yes
```

Next, make sure that the /etc/sysconfig/network-scripts/ifcfg-eth0 script contains the following lines (if you're using a different network device, modify as required):

```
BOOTPROTO='dhcp'
ONBOOT='yes'
```

The next time you reboot, your network configuration should look for DHCP address information automatically from the DHCP server for your network.

There is a subtle difference in the Linux names for the DHCP client and server. The DHCP server daemon is dhcpd; the DHCP client daemon is dhclient.

Alternatively, you can use the Network Configuration tool from a GUI to configure DHCP. Start a GUI, open a terminal console, and run the redhat-config-network command. When the tool opens, select your network card and click Edit. You should see a window similar to what is shown in Figure 9-14. If you want DHCP, select the

FIGURE 9-14

Configuring a
network device
as a DHCP client

"Automatically obtain IP address settings with:" option. You'll then get to choose
between getting IP address information from a DHCP server on your local network,
using bootp to get IP address information from a remote network, or going through
a dialup connection, such as to an ISP. Once you've activated the changes, restart the
network daemon (**/sbin/service network restart**). Then your network card will look
for IP address information from a DHCP server.

DHCP Client Troubleshooting

If the DHCP client configuration instructions in this chapter are not working, there
may be a problem with the way the network is set up on your Linux computer. For
example:

- The NIC is not configured properly. See Chapter 4 for information on
  reconfiguring your network card.

- If the network works for a few minutes and then stops responding, check to
  see if *zebra,* the gateway daemon, is running.

- If the computer is still having problems finding a DHCP server, check your
  firewall. If port 67 or 68 is blocked, your computer won't be able to get a
  message to the server.

The new gateway daemon, starting with Red Hat 8.0, is zebra, which is part of the zebra RPM. gated is now obsolete.

EXERCISE 9-5

DHCP

To run this exercise, you'll need two different computers: a DHCP server and a DHCP client on the same LAN.

1. Open /etc/dhcpd.conf. Configure the server with an IP address range of 192.168.11.11–192.168.11.15 and with a network mask of 255.255.255.0.

2. Configure the client computer to use DHCP. Restart the network service on the client and record the IP address that it gets.

3. Add Gateway and DNS server options with IP addresses of 192.168.11.254 and 12.34.45.56, respectively. If you already have a gateway and a DNS server, substitute the appropriate IP addresses. Restart the DHCP service. Restart networking on the client to make it renew the lease on the IP address.

CERTIFICATION OBJECTIVE 9.06

Keeping Servers in Sync

A number of companies keep servers in different time zones around the world. This allows users to select the server closest to them, maximizing network performance. As a Linux administrator, it may be your responsibility to make sure that all of these servers are on the same time. You can set up time synchronization on a centralized server through the Network Time Protocol (NTP).

The Network Time Protocol

NTP works by synchronizing a computer to UTC, through a connection to a time server. Time is distributed through a hierarchy of NTP servers, through port 123. One point worth noting is that NTP will never run a system clock backward. If the clock on your computer is fast, NTP slows down the clock until it is in sync with UTC.

NTP Configuration

The configuration file for NTP is /etc/ntp.conf. In the latest version of Red Hat Linux, it is already preconfigured to use your computer as a time server. But synchronizing your computer with your computer may not help you. Open the /etc/ntp.conf file in a text editor. You'll find a server that is listed. The default is 127.127.1.0. As this is within the "loopback" subnet, this points right back at your computer. Alternatively, you can set it to one of the standard time servers described in the NTP home page at http://www.eecis.udel.edu/~ntp/ntp_spool/html/ntpd.htm.

Another way to synchronize your computer is to use dateconfig to set NTP. In a GUI, open up a command line console. Enter the dateconfig command. (dateconfig is now a front end to redhat-config-date.) You should see the Date/Time Properties dialog box shown in Figure 9-15.

When you select the Enable Network Time Protocol option and set a time server, ntpd is started and the name of the server is added to /etc/ntp.conf. If you want to set NTP to work after a reboot, you still need to set it up with /sbin/chkconfig.

FIGURE 9-15

The dateconfig tool

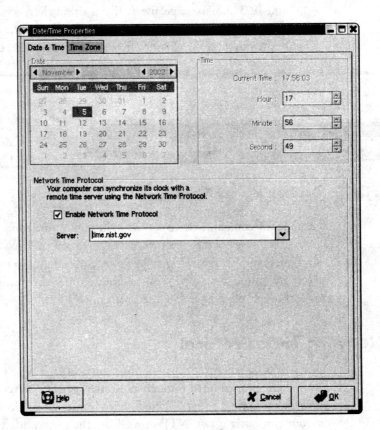

CERTIFICATION SUMMARY

Networking services are an integral part of Red Hat Linux. DNS, Squid, NFS, INN, and NTP are a few of the services that you can configure.

DNS provides a database of domain names and IP addresses that help Web browsers and more find sites on the Internet. It's a distributed database, where each administrator is responsible for his or her own zone of authority. The diagnostic tool for DNS is now dig. You can use nslookup, but it has been deprecated.

Squid is a proxy server that allows a network to filter its HTTP and FTP traffic through a cache. Requests are taken from the cache when possible. This reduces the load between the LAN and the Internet and makes network performance appear faster to your users.

NFS allows you to share filesystems between Linux and Unix computers. This is a powerful method of controlling data, and distributing I/O load, but there are many security concerns involved with its use. Care should be taken when setting up an NFS share on an unprotected network.

News services provide users with an open forum of information exchange with other users on the Internet. With INN, Internet news is easy to set up and maintain. But news messages can build up quickly. A watchful eye should be kept out for full disk volumes or a lack of inodes.

DHCP allows a network administrator to manage IP address assignments of the computers on a LAN from a centralized server. DHCP requires some specialized setup on both the client and the server; however, it is easy to maintain once it is configured.

NTP allows you to set up any computer to be synchronized to a central time standard, based on UTC.

TWO-MINUTE DRILL

Here are some of the key points from the certification objectives in Chapter 9.

DNS/BIND

❑ DNS, the Domain Name System, includes a database of computer names and IP addresses.

❑ DNS is based on the Berkeley Internet Name Domain (BIND), using the named daemon.

❑ Critical DNS configuration files include /etc/named.conf and the files in the /var/named directory.

❑ The SOA record, also known as the Start of Authority record, is the preamble to all zone files.

❑ CNAME is a way to assign an additional name to a computer.

❑ Caching-only nameservers store requests and their associated IP addresses on a computer.

❑ To set up a DNS server, you need a zone file with A resource records for each computer, and PTR resource records for reverse lookups.

❑ Every time you change DNS, remember to update the serial number in your zone file. Otherwise, other DNS servers don't realize that you've changed anything.

Squid Proxy Server

❑ Squid is a high-performance HTTP and FTP caching proxy server.

❑ Squid can refer requests to sibling and parent proxy servers. If the request still isn't available, a parent proxy server refers the request to the Internet.

❑ Once Squid is configured, you can set each computer on the LAN to browse Web pages to the Proxy Server on port 3128.

Network File System (NFS)

❏ NFS is the standard for sharing files and printers between Linux and Unix computers.

❏ Two key NFS packages are nfs* and portmap*. Remember to start the portmap daemon before starting NFS.

❏ Key NFS processes are rpc.mountd for mount requests, rpc.rquotad for quota requests and nfsd for each network share.

❏ NFS shares are configured in /etc/exports and activated by /sbin/exportfs -a.

❏ Clients can make permanent connections for NFS shares through /etc/fstab.

❏ If an NFS server fails, it can "hang" an NFS client. When possible, avoid using NFS on mission-critical computers.

❏ NFS and portmap have security problems. Limit their use when possible to secure internal networks protected by an appropriate firewall.

Internet Network News Daemon

❏ Red Hat stores INN configuration files in /etc/news.

❏ Configuring innd requires you to configure inn.conf, incoming.conf, and newsfeeds.

❏ Edit readers.conf if you want to allow readers on other computers.

❏ You can add banners and newsgroup policies to motd.news.

❏ You should set the organization directive in inn.conf.

❏ Your ISP typically supplies NNTP services. Put the appropriate e-mail and telephone number in your incoming.conf file.

❏ If you want to post articles, you need an entry in newsfeeds.

❏ Update nntpsend to transmit your outbound traffic and make sure it runs hourly from /etc/cron.hourly/inn-cron-nntpsend.

DHCP

❑ DHCP (Dynamic Host Configuration Protocol) allows a client computer to obtain network information (such as an IP number) from a server.

❑ The bootp protocol allows a client computer to access a DHCP server on a remote network.

❑ DHCP servers are configured through /etc/dhcpd.conf.

❑ Remember that the DHCP server daemon is dhcpd; the DHCP client daemon is dhclient.

Keeping Servers in Sync

❑ You can keep the time on a server in sync with UTC using the Network Time Protocol (NTP).

❑ The configuration file for NTP is /etc/ntp.conf.

❑ dateconfig, which is a front end to redhat-config-date, is a GUI utility that can help you configure /etc/ntp.conf.

SELF TEST

The following questions will help you measure your understanding of the material presented in this chapter. Read all the choices carefully, as there may be more than one correct answer. Choose all correct answers for each question.

DNS/Bind

1. Which program checks the DNS setup?

   A. dnscheck

   B. BIND

   C. dig

   D. resolve

2. You have added the addresses for several new servers into your primary DNS server. The zone files are formatted properly, and you've restarted named. You advertise the new servers, and your help desk immediately starts getting calls that no one outside your domain can see the new servers. What is the most likely cause?

   A. Your servers are not connected to the network.

   B. The serial number was not incremented in the zone file.

   C. Someone has changed the zone files without your knowledge.

   D. The users at the other end are having ISP problems.

3. Which is an example of a properly formatted MX record?

   A. MX 10.mail.domain.com.

   B. MX mail.domain.com.

   C. MX 10 mail.domain.com

   D. MX 10 mail.domain.com.

4. Which of the following resource records should not refer to a name specified by a CNAME RR?

   A. An Apache Server

   B. A proxy server

   C. A news server

   D. A mail server

Squid Proxy Server

5. Squid serves as a caching server for which Internet protocols?

    A. FTP

    B. News

    C. HTTP

    D. DNS

6. You have a series of Squid proxy servers connected together. Some are "parents" and others are "siblings" in a group. What happens if the system can't find a Web page in any of your proxy servers?

    A. The sibling sends a request to the Internet for the Web page.

    B. The parent sends a request to the Internet for the Web page.

    C. The original proxy server sends a request to the Internet for the Web page.

    D. Your browser gets a file not found message.

7. You work at a large company. Every day at about noon, the network slows to a crawl. The CEO just noticed he has trouble reading and sending e-mail at that time and wants answers. What should you do?

    A. Reconfigure your DNS servers to increase their local cache.

    B. Upgrade your network.

    C. Route all Web surfing through a Squid server.

    D. Route the CEO's mail over a different subnet.

Network File System (NFS)

8. In the /etc/exports file, if we want to export /data as read-only to all hosts and grant read and write permission to the host superv in domain.com, the proper entry is

    A. /data (rw,sync) superv.domain.com(ro,sync)

    B. /data (ro,sync) superv.domain.com(rw,sync)

    C. /data (ro,async) *.domain.com(rw,async)

    D. /data superv.domain.com(rw,async)

9. When Linux boots, what configuration file does Linux use to see what NFS shares to mount?

    A. /etc/exports

    B. /etc/nfs.conf

C. /etc/fstab

D. /nfs/conf

10. Your company has just suffered an external security breach. As a result, the security department has tightened the screws on all the servers, routers, and firewalls. Up until this point, all user data had been mounted over NFS, but now, nothing works. What happened?

A. The hackers erased the NFS data, and they got the backups, too.

B. The NFS ports are no longer allowed through the necessary firewalls.

C. The two problems are unrelated. Check your disk space.

D. The filesystem is no longer shared from the server.

11. You're experiencing problems with NFS clients for various reasons, including frequent downtime on the NFS server and network outages between NFS clients and servers. Which of the following steps can help address this problem?

A. Remove all firewalls on individual computers inside your network.

B. Avoid setting up mission-critical computers as NFS clients.

C. Always make sure the portmap daemon is active before starting NFS.

D. Configure NFS with "soft" mounts.

Internet News

12. Assume that the partition with /var fills up. What will restore the operation of your News service?

A. Remove /var/spool/news/articles/alt/binaries.

B. Remove /var/lib/news/history.pag.

C. Expire aging news articles.

D. Make more inodes.

13. A message pops up that News is out of space, but df -k shows plenty of room in the partition where /var is mounted. What's wrong?

A. You are out of inodes on the filesystem.

B. There be hackers afoot! Yaaar!

C. Invisible files on the filesystem.

D. df is broken.

14. No news traffic has come in, but innd is running. How could this be?

    A. Your ISP has dropped you.

    B. The TCP/IP link is down.

    C. The Internet has vanished and no one is posting.

    D. innd is overloaded.

DHCP/Bootp

15. DHCP has been installed and configured properly, and the network is responding. Which of the following commands would you use to get IP address information from a DHCP server?

    A. /sbin/dhcp

    B. /usr/sbin/dhcpd

    C. /sbin/dhclient

    D. /etc/rc.d/init.d/dhclient start

16. You add a new workstation to your dhcpd.conf file. You're in a hurry to finish, so you save and go to lunch. When you return, your phone mail is full of user complaints that they can't access the Internet, but the local network is fine. You surmise that you accidentally changed something in the dhcpd.conf file that you shouldn't have. What is the most likely cause?

    A. The absence of a "routers" line.

    B. The subnet mask was changed.

    C. The IP range was thrown off.

    D. The broadcast address was changed.

Keeping Servers in Sync

17. Which are proper keywords that can be used in an ntp.conf file?

    A. server

    B. client

    C. peer

    D. child

LAB QUESTION

Your network has over 500 hosts with users in three major groups wanting to share their files within their groups. There are also 30 Windows XP clients in the publishing department that cannot use the Linux OS for their proprietary software needs. Everything is time-critical, as the outputs are related to stock quotes and therefore need to be synchronized to the same clock. What should you do?

SELF TEST ANSWERS

DNS/Bind

1. ☑ **C.** dig checks the configuration of the nameserver against the resolv.conf file.

   ☒ **A, B,** and **D** are incorrect. Neither dsncheck nor resolve are valid utilities. BIND refers to the Berkeley Internet Naming Domain, the basis for the DNS software.

2. ☑ **B.** Make absolutely sure that the serial number at the top of the zone file is changed each time you revise a zone file. Otherwise, other DNS servers won't know that anything has changed in your domain, and won't update their databases.

   ☒ **A** might be correct if something strange happened to your server, but the original server name still works internally, so your service is still connected to the network. **C** and **D** are also not likely scenarios, as root access is needed locally to edit the DNS configuration files and your ISP may or may not be between your servers and all your clients.

3. ☑ **D.** Make sure the preference is defined, and the trailing "." is included at the end of the record.

   ☒ **A, B,** and **C** are incorrectly formatted.

4. ☑ **D.** By default, Mail Servers (MX) can't refer to CNAME resource records.

   ☒ **A, B,** and **C** are incorrect, as Web, proxy, and news servers commonly use CNAME RRs.

Squid Proxy Server

5. ☑ **A** and **C.** HTTP and FTP sessions are cached by Squid.

   ☒ **B** and **D** are incorrect. There is no need to cache News services. There is something called a DNS caching server, but this is part of the DNS (named) service, not Squid.

6. ☑ **B.** In a "Harvest Cache" grouping of Squid servers, one squid server first looks to sibling and parent servers for a requested Web page. If the request is not available in any of the caches, one of the parent servers requests the page from the Internet.

   ☒ **A, C,** and **D** are incorrect. The parent takes responsibility. While **D** could happen if a Web site is down, it is a less likely result.

7. ☑ **C.** The users are most likely surfing the Web on their lunch hour. All 500 of them just started browsing the Web site for the local newspaper. If you have a Squid server, all of these people can be served through a Squid cache, which saves room (bandwidth) on the Internet connection.

☒ **A** may help a little if all users are looking for the same Web pages every day, but Squid is a better solution. **B** is expensive. **D** is possible, if you put the CEO on a different subnet. But that can also be expensive.

Network File System (NFS)

8. ☑ **B.** Export the filesystem as a general read-only; then specify the computer with read/write permission.

☒ **A** provides read/write to all general hosts and gives the superv.domain.com computer read-only access. **C** provides read-only to all but allows all computers on the domain.com subnet to have read/write access. **D** gives read/write access only to the superv.domain.com computer. The *sync* and *async* options can both be appropriate under different circumstances.

9. ☑ **C.** /etc/fstab can be configured with all the necessary information for a computer to mount a shared NFS directory.

☒ **A** is the exported filesystems configuration file for nfs, /etc/exports. **B** and **D** are bogus files.

10. ☑ **B.** Ports 111, 745, 747, and 2049 must be open through firewalls to allow NFS to function. Since the security problems associated with NFS may have been to blame for the break-in, it is a good idea to restrict its use to isolated or protected subnets.

☒ **A**, **C**, and **D** are all possibilities you should check for, but the most likely culprit is **B**.

11. ☑ **A**, **B**, **C**, and **D** are all to some extent correct. Ideally, you should be able to set NFS on computers inside a "trusted" network, which means that you can remove firewalls on computers inside that network. If you avoid setting up mission-critical computers on NFS, you'll have fewer problems with NFS. The portmap daemon has to be running before NFS can work. To some extent, **D** is the best answer, because it can help an NFS client cope with downtime on an NFS server.

☒ None of the answers are incorrect.

Internet News

12. ☑ **C.** News articles should be deleted, or expired on a daily basis through /etc/cron.daily/inn-cron-expire. Look in this file. This runs the /usr/bin/news.daily delayrm command as the news user.

☒ **D** may help if the error log indicates you are out of inodes. You would need to either replace the current partition; use another bigger partition with more inodes; or back up this partition, reformat with more inodes, and then restore the data. **A** and **B** refer to nonexistent files.

13. ☑ **A.** You are out of inodes. Backup /var, and then reformat the partition. Run mkfs with a smaller -i (bytes-per-nodes) option or use cycbuffs. Confirm this diagnosis with **df -i**.

☒ **B** is always a possibility (but likely not the cause this time), and **C** is not possible. There are no invisible files, just hidden filenames. The df command may be broken, but that would not be related to running out of inodes, so **D** is also incorrect.

14. ☑ **D.** Use ctlinnd mode to confirm this. The reason can then be traced through the error logs.

☒ **A** and **B** are possible and lead to **C**, but you can always confirm that all three of these possibilities are not true with a ping of a remote host.

DHCP/Bootp

15. ☑ **C.** The /sbin/dhclient command looks for a DHCP server on the local network for IP addressing information.

☒ **A, B,** and **D** are not correct. There is no dhcp command, and there is no dhclient (DHCP client) script in the /etc/rc.d/init.d directory. The /usr/bin/dhcpd command starts the DHCP server, not the client.

16. ☑ **A.** The lack of a router declaration in /etc/dhcpd.conf would keep your hosts from getting the gateway address, which is required to access the Internet from an internal network.

☒ **B, C,** and **D** would probably cause a general network outage.

Keeping Servers in Sync

17. ☑ **A** and **C** are correct. In /etc/ntp.conf, a server and a peer are both alternate time servers.

☒ **B** and **D** are incorrect. Client and child are not relevant in the ntp.conf file.

LAB ANSWER

You need to configure a few services on your central host. NIS can be used to manage all the users so that all hosts use the same user IDs. Then configure a central server with Samba and NFS and sufficient disk space for the four groups, restricting each service to members of each group only. Use NTP to synchronize the NFS server to an Internet time server, if available, and then have all the other hosts synchronize their time to the NFS server host on an hourly basis.

10

Systems Administration and Security

A s a Red Hat Linux systems manager, you probably wear several hats, one of which is security manager. This is especially true if you work for a small company. Even if you work for a large organization that has a dedicated network or systems security staff, most of the administrators are probably responsible for other operating systems; you're probably responsible for security policies on your Linux systems.

You may spend very little time thinking about Linux security, or it may turn out to be a full-time job. For most Linux systems administrators, the amount of time spent on securing systems falls somewhere between these two extremes. The level of security you choose to configure depends on many factors, including the purpose of the system and the overall security policies of your company or organization, as well as the size and number of computers in the company.

For example, a Red Hat Linux system at home does not require as much security as a Red Hat Linux server that is being used to process credit card orders for a Web site.

Red Hat Linux comes with a large and varied assortment of tools for handling security. This includes tools for managing the security on individual Linux computers and tools for managing security for an entire network of systems, both Linux and otherwise. In this chapter, we look at some of the tools Red Hat Linux provides for managing security. We start out by looking at tools for controlling access to individual Linux host systems; then we look at tools for securing networks.

exam
ⓦatch

You'll need to know how to protect your computer and network. Sometimes this means you'll turn off, deactivate, or even uninstall a service. Other times, you'll set specific levels of security for different users. You can even regulate the type of traffic coming in, going out, and being transferred through your computer.

You have different ways to secure your system and network. The Network Information System (NIS) can provide a common database of authentication and configuration files for your network. The PAM (Pluggable Authentication Module) system lets you configure how users are allowed to log in or access different services. System logging often provides the clues that you need to solve a lot of problems. The Extended Internet Services Daemon governs a lot of services that do not have their own individual daemons. IP Aliases allow you to set up more than one IP address on a specific network card. With iptables, you can set up firewalls to accept or block many different kinds of network traffic. Network Address Translation allows you to protect computers inside your network by hiding their address information.

CERTIFICATION OBJECTIVE 10.01

Configuring NIS Clients

Generally, access to a Red Hat Linux system requires a valid username and password. One problem with a large network of Linux systems is that "normally," each user requires an account on every Linux computer.

The Network Information System (NIS) allows you to set up one centrally managed database of usernames and passwords for your Unix and Linux systems. With NIS, you can maintain one password database on an *NIS server* and configure the other systems on the network as *NIS clients*. When a user logs into an NIS client, that system first checks its local password file, usually /etc/passwd. If it can't find your username, it looks up the corresponding file on the NIS server.

NIS clients and NIS servers are organized in *NIS domains*. You can have multiple NIS domains on a single network, but clients and servers can belong to only one domain. If you are using NIS, you can find out the name of your NIS domain by using this command:

```
domainname
```

NIS domains are different from BIND domains. In fact, for security reasons, your NIS domain name should be different from your BIND domain name. If you are coming from the Microsoft Windows NT world, NIS domains are analogous to LAN manager domains.

NIS provides you with more than a shared authorization database. With NIS, you can provide shared access to any kind of information. By default, NIS under Red Hat Linux shares the following files:

- /etc/passwd
- /etc/group
- /etc/hosts
- /etc/rpc
- /etc/services
- /etc/protocols
- /etc/mail/*

You can configure NIS to share other files as well. This is easy to configure in the NIS configuration file, /var/yp/Makefile.

NIS services require at least one *NIS master server.* This is where the centralized NIS database files, known as *maps,* are stored. NIS changes require an update to the map on the master server. You can have only one NIS master server per NIS domain. (NIS maps are stored in the /var/yp/*DOMAIN* directory, where *DOMAIN* is the name of your NIS domain.)

For larger networks or redundancy, you may also want an *NIS slave server.* NIS slaves take copies of the NIS maps from the master server. NIS clients can then get their configuration files from either the master server or a slave server. You can have multiple NIS slave servers on a network.

NIS clients are systems that use information from an NIS server. NIS clients don't store any information that is contained in the NIS databases; whenever that information is needed, it is retrieved from a server.

You may notice that most NIS commands start with yp. This is a holdover from the previous name of NIS when it was known as the Yellow Pages service.

NIS Components on Red Hat Linux

The */usr/lib/yp* directory includes the utilities you need to configure and manage NIS services. The *ypinit* program can configure an NIS server. Table 10-1 lists the files needed to configure an NIS server.

Although NIS was designed to enable you to manage security by controlling who has access to the systems on your network, NIS is not a very secure product. Anyone who knows your NIS domain name and can connect to your network can read all the information stored in your NIS databases, such as /etc/passwd.

You can do a couple of things to help protect your NIS database. The */var/yp/securenets* file can control who can connect to your NIS server. This file is easy to configure. Only two lines are required for a LAN:

```
host 127.0.0.1
255.255.255.0  192.168.0.0
```

The first line allows access from the local computer. The second line may look a bit backward, but it allows access from all of the computers with IP addresses on the 192.168.0.0 network.

File	Description
/usr/lib/yp/ypinit	Shell script to build initial database maps on an NIS server in /var/yp; **ypinit -m** builds the databases for a master server.
/var/yp/Makefile	Configuration file. Edit this file to control which files are shared via NIS. Implement the changes from the /var/yp directory with the *make* command.
/usr/sbin/ypserv	NIS server daemon. Remember to use /sbin/chkconfig to make sure it will start when you boot Linux.
/usr/sbin/yppasswdd	NIS password update daemon. Allows users to change their NIS passwords with the yppasswd command. Remember to use /sbin/chkconfig to make sure it starts when you boot Linux.
/etc/ypserv.conf	The ypserv daemon configuration file.
/var/yp/securenets	Controls which systems can access NIS databases. See the ypserv man page for an example.

TABLE 10-1 NIS Configuration Files and Commands

Once you've configured an NIS server, it's easy to configure an NIS client. Just use *authconfig*. Figure 10-1 shows the authconfig screen used to configure NIS. This will configure your system to use the *ypbind* daemon, and add the appropriate entries in the /etc/yp.conf, /etc/nsswitch.conf, and /etc/pam.d/system-auth files. All you need is the name of the NIS domain, and the name of the computer where it's located.

The other command you need to know about when running an NIS client is *yppasswd*. All users can manage their NIS password with this command.

 on the job

One security risk to keep in mind if you use NIS is that anyone with access to the root account on any system that uses NIS can use the su - *username command (note the space on both sides of the dash) to switch to any account in your NIS database.*

The Name Service Switch File

The Name Service Switch file (*/etc/nsswitch.conf*) governs the search order. For example, when an NIS client looks for a computer host name, it might start with the following entry from /etc/nsswitch.conf:

```
hosts: files nisplus nis dns
```

FIGURE 10-1

Configuring an
NIS Client with
authconfig

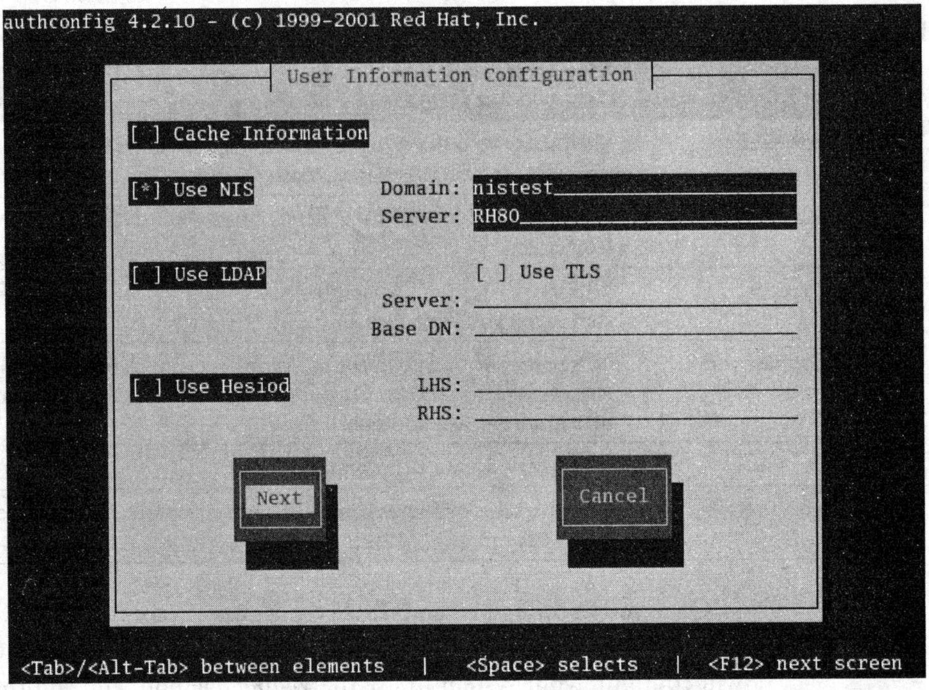

```
authconfig 4.2.10 - (c) 1999-2001 Red Hat, Inc.

                      ┌──── User Information Configuration ────┐

        [ ] Cache Information

        [*] Use NIS              Domain: nistest_____
                                 Server: RH80_____

        [ ] Use LDAP                     [ ] Use TLS
                                 Server: _____
                                 Base DN: _____

        [ ] Use Hesiod           LHS: _____
                                 RHS: _____


                  ┌──────────┐              ┌──────────┐
                  │   Next   │              │  Cancel  │
                  └──────────┘              └──────────┘


 <Tab>/<Alt-Tab> between elements  |  <Space> selects  |  <F12> next screen
```

This line tells your computer to search through name databases in the following order:

1. Start with the database of host names and IP addresses in */etc/hosts*.

2. Next, search for the host name in a map file based on NIS+ (NIS Version 3).

3. Next, search for the host name in a map file based on NIS (Version 2).

4. If none of these databases includes the desired host name, refer to the DNS server.

CERTIFICATION OBJECTIVE 10.02

Basic Host Security

A network is only as secure as the most open system in that network. Although no system can be 100 percent secure, you can follow certain basic host measures to enhance the security on any given system and, consequently, your network. When devising security measures, you have to plan for two types of security violations: user accidents and break-ins.

Accidents happen because users lack adequate training or are unwilling to follow procedures. If security is too burdensome, productivity may suffer, and your users will try to get around your rules. Password security falls into this category.

When a cracker breaks in to your system, some crackers may be looking for secrets such as credit card information. Others may just want to bring down your system. You can do several things to keep your network secure. Monitor Red Hat errata for the latest issues. With the up2date utility, you can keep your Red Hat system updated with the latest packages.

As you'll see later in this chapter, you can manage your computer's response to certain requests through the /etc/hosts.allow and /etc/hosts.deny files. You can set up protection within the kernel through firewalls based on iptables or ipchains. One simple way to promote security is to uninstall as many network access programs as possible.

Password Security

Good password security is important. Good passwords include a combination of letters and numbers that aren't easily guessed. Good password security requires users to change their password on a regular basis.

Password security also means disabling or deleting unused accounts. These accounts are a common way for a cracker to try to break into your system.

You can also check system log files for suspicious activity. Login records are kept in a database in /var/log/wtmp. While you can't read this file directly, you can use the utmpdump command to make this file readable. For example, the **utmpdump /var/log/wtmp** command lists recent login activity. Take a look at Figure 10-2. Note the login from IP address 172.132.4.8. If you don't have any users from a computer with that IP address, you have a reason for concern.

Security Updates

Another step you can take to keep your Red Hat Linux system secure is to install the latest errata releases from Red Hat. These contain patches or fixes for problems in applications or the operating system that could result in security violations. A list of the latest errata is available as of this writing at www.redhat.com/apps/support/errata.

FIGURE 10-2

Suspicious login
activity

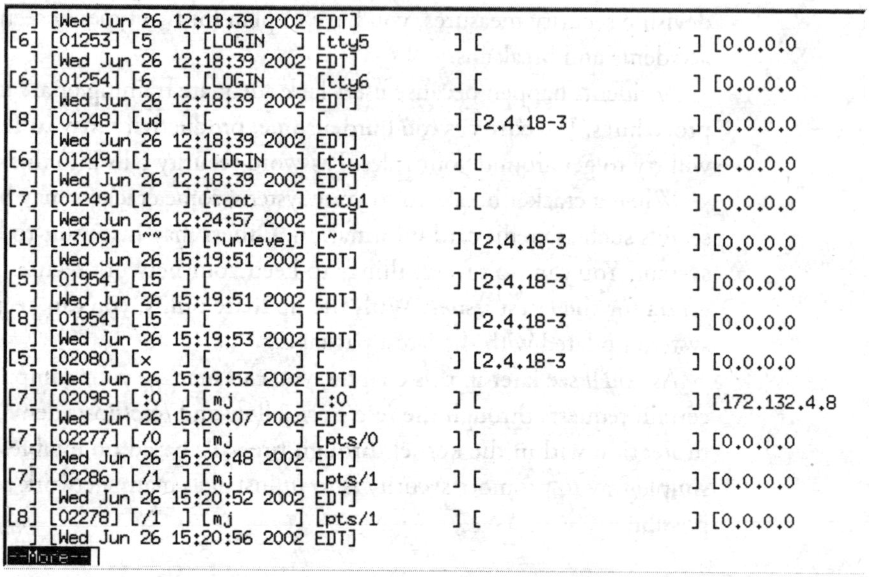

```
        ] [Wed Jun 26 12:18:39 2002 EDT]
[6] [01253] [5    ] [LOGIN   ] [tty5         ] [                    ] [0.0.0.0
        ] [Wed Jun 26 12:18:39 2002 EDT]
[6] [01254] [6    ] [LOGIN   ] [tty6         ] [                    ] [0.0.0.0
        ] [Wed Jun 26 12:18:39 2002 EDT]
[8] [01248] [ud   ] [         ] [            ] [2.4.18-3            ] [0.0.0.0
        ] [Wed Jun 26 12:18:39 2002 EDT]
[6] [01249] [1    ] [LOGIN   ] [tty1         ] [                    ] [0.0.0.0
        ] [Wed Jun 26 12:18:39 2002 EDT]
[7] [01249] [1    ] [root    ] [tty1         ] [                    ] [0.0.0.0
        ] [Wed Jun 26 12:24:57 2002 EDT]
[1] [13109] [~~   ] [runlevel] [~            ] [2.4.18-3            ] [0.0.0.0
        ] [Wed Jun 26 15:19:51 2002 EDT]
[5] [01954] [15   ] [         ] [            ] [2.4.18-3            ] [0.0.0.0
        ] [Wed Jun 26 15:19:51 2002 EDT]
[8] [01954] [15   ] [         ] [            ] [2.4.18-3            ] [0.0.0.0
        ] [Wed Jun 26 15:19:53 2002 EDT]
[5] [02080] [x    ] [         ] [            ] [2.4.18-3            ] [0.0.0.0
        ] [Wed Jun 26 15:19:53 2002 EDT]
[7] [02098] [:0   ] [mj      ] [:0           ] [                    ] [172.132.4.8
        ] [Wed Jun 26 15:20:07 2002 EDT]
[7] [02277] [/0   ] [mj      ] [pts/0        ] [                    ] [0.0.0.0
        ] [Wed Jun 26 15:20:48 2002 EDT]
[7] [02286] [/1   ] [mj      ] [pts/1        ] [                    ] [0.0.0.0
        ] [Wed Jun 26 15:20:52 2002 EDT]
[8] [02278] [/1   ] [mj      ] [pts/1        ] [                    ] [0.0.0.0
        ] [Wed Jun 26 15:20:56 2002 EDT]
--More--]
```

Red Hat provides a built-in service to check for updates called up2date that you can configure if your computer is directly connected to the Internet. Just run up2date from a command line in the X Window of your choice. If you haven't already done so, you'll need to register the settings on your computer. Then follow the prompts; up2date connects to rhn.redhat.com for updates. A sample result is shown in Figure 10-3, which suggests an update to three packages, including the kernel.

Delete Extra Services

One simple way to promote security on your system is to delete the packages associated with network services that you aren't going to use. For example, a cracker can't use Telnet to break into your system if the Telnet RPM is not installed. Any firewall or other configuration that you may add to the service still means that you are theoretically vulnerable to an attack through that service. If you're not going to use a network service, you may want to remove the associated RPM packages.

To review currently installed network services, check the /etc/xinetd.d, the /etc/rc.d/init.d directories.

FIGURE 10-3

up2date at work

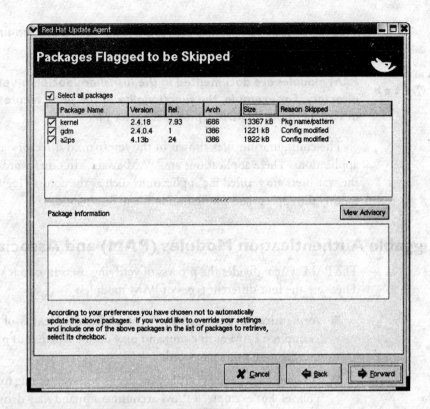

CERTIFICATION OBJECTIVE 10.03

The Pluggable Authentication Module (PAM) System

Red Hat Linux uses the Pluggable Authentication Modules (PAM) system to check for authorized users. PAM includes a group of dynamically loadable library modules that govern how individual applications verify their users. You can modify PAM configuration files to suit your needs.

PAM was developed to standardize the user authentication process. For example, the login program uses PAM to require usernames and passwords at login. Open th /etc/pam.d/login file. Take a look at the first line:

```
auth  required      /lib/security/pam_securetty.so
```

This line means that root users can log in only from secure terminals as defined in the /etc/securetty file.

PAM modules are documented in the /usr/share/doc/pam-versionnumber/txts directory. For example, the functionality of the pam_securetty.so module is described in the README.pam_securetty file.

The configuration files shown in the /etc/pam.d directory are named after applications. These applications are "PAM aware." In other words, you can change the way users are verified for applications such as the console login program. Just modify the appropriate configuration file in /etc/pam.d.

Pluggable Authentication Modules (PAM) and Associated Files

The PAM system divides the process of verifying users into four separate tasks. These are the four different types of PAM modules:

- **Authentication management**   Establishes the identity of a user. For example, a PAM **auth** command may decide whether to prompt for a username and or a password.

- **Account management**   Allows or denies access according to the account policies. For example, a PAM **account** command may deny access according to time, password expiration, or a specific list of restricted users.

- **Password management**   Manages other password policies. For example, a PAM **password** command may limit the number of times a user can try to log in before a console is reset.

- **Session management**   Applies settings for an application. For example, the PAM **session** command may set default settings for a login console.

The code shown in Figure 10-4 is an example PAM configuration file, /etc/pam.d/login. Every line in all PAM configuration files is written in the following format:

```
module_type  control_flag  module_path  [arguments]
```

The module_type, as described previously, is **auth**, **account**, **password**, or **session**. The control_flag determines what PAM does if the module succeeds or fails. The module_path specifies the location of the actual PAM module file. Finally, as with regular shell commands, you can specify arguments for each module.

FIGURE 10-4

The PAM login module

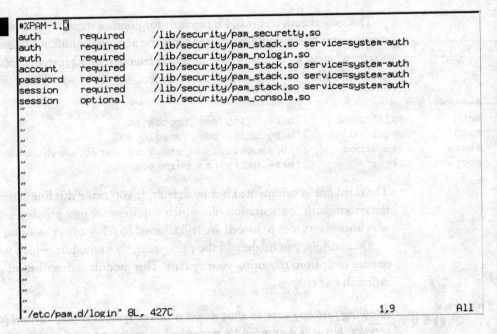

```
#%PAM-1.0
auth       required    /lib/security/pam_securetty.so
auth       required    /lib/security/pam_stack.so service=system-auth
auth       required    /lib/security/pam_nologin.so
account    required    /lib/security/pam_stack.so service=system-auth
password   required    /lib/security/pam_stack.so service=system-auth
session    required    /lib/security/pam_stack.so service=system-auth
session    optional    /lib/security/pam_console.so
~
~
~
~
~
~
~
~
~
~
~
~
~
"/etc/pam.d/login" 8L, 427C                                    1,9            All
```

The control_flag field requires additional explanation. It determines how the configuration file reacts when a module flags success or failure. There are four different control flags, each described in Table 10-2.

To demonstrate how control flags work, take a look at the /etc/pam.d/reboot configuration file. The first **auth** command checks the **pam_rootok.so** module. If the root user runs the reboot command, and the control_flag is *sufficient,* the other **auth** commands in this file are ignored. Linux runs the reboot command.

TABLE 10-2   PAM Control Flags

control_flag	Description
required	If the module works, the command proceeds. If it fails, go to the next command in the configuration file—but the command will still fail.
requisite	Stop the process if the module fails.
sufficient	If the module works, the login or other authentication proceeds. No other commands need be processed.
optional	PAM ignores module success or failure.

The second **auth** command is run only for nonroot users; it just governs the console parameters. The module associated with the **account** command (pam_permit.so) accepts all users, even those who've logged in remotely. In other words, this configuration file would allow any root user, local or remote, to reboot your Linux computer.

```
#%PAM-1.0
auth       sufficient    /lib/security/pam_rootok.so
auth       required      /lib/security/pam_console.so
#auth      required      /lib/security/pam_stack.so service=system-auth
account    required      /lib/security/pam_permit.so
```

The third line is commented out by default. If you make this line active, it refers to the system-auth configuration file, which requires root user privileges. Remote users who know your root password are still allowed to reboot your computer.

Alternatively, you might add the pam_securetty.so module, which would keep remote users from rebooting your system. This module is described in more detail earlier in this chapter.

Allowing just any user to shut down a server system is not normal for corporate servers, but it is a commonly accepted practice on workstations. In this way, users can shut down their own laptop or desktop without having to change to the root account.

PAM Configuration Example: /etc/pam.d/login

This section refers back to the /etc/pam.d/login configuration file shown in Figure 10-4. When a user opens a text console and logs in, Linux goes through this configuration file line by line. The first line in /etc/pam.d/login was already analyzed in the previous section. The next line brings the login program through the following service, system-auth, which also happens to be a PAM configuration file.

```
auth   required    /lib/security/pam_stack.so service=system-auth
```

Essentially, this calls the **auth** commands in the /etc/pam.d/system-auth configuration file shown in Figure 10-5. This sets up environment variables and allows different users to log in. The last **auth** line in /etc/pam.d/system-auth checks the /etc/nologin file. If this file exists, no regular users are allowed to log into your console.

FIGURE 10-5

The /etc/pam.d/
system-auth
configuration file

```
#%PAM-1.0
# This file is auto-generated.
# User changes will be destroyed the next time authconfig is run.
auth        required      /lib/security/pam_env.so
auth        sufficient    /lib/security/pam_unix.so likeauth nullok
auth        required      /lib/security/pam_deny.so

account     required      /lib/security/pam_unix.so

password    required      /lib/security/pam_cracklib.so retry=3 type=
password    sufficient    /lib/security/pam_unix.so nullok use_authtok md5 shadow
password    required      /lib/security/pam_deny.so

session     required      /lib/security/pam_limits.so
session     required      /lib/security/pam_unix.so
~
~
~
~
~
~
~
~
~
~
~
~
"system-auth" 15L, 643C                                          1,1         All
```

The **account** and **password** commands in /etc/pam.d/login also refer to
the /etc/pam.d/system-auth configuration file. The **account** command in
/etc/pam.d/system-auth refers to the pam_unix.so module, which sets up the
normal username and password prompts. There are two **password** commands
in /etc/pam.d/system-auth. The file shown in Figure 10-5 sets a maximum
of three retries and sets up the use of md5 and shadow passwords.

*The authconfig utility can modify the Linux password configuration through
the /etc/pam.d/system-auth configuration file.*

Finally, there are two **session** commands in the /etc/pam.d/login file. The first
command refers to the /etc/pam.d/system-auth configuration file, which can allow you
to set limits on individual users through /etc/security/limits.conf, and environment
variables through the pam_unix.so module. The second command manages file
permissions while users are logged onto your Linux computer.

EXERCISE 10-1

Configuring PAM

In this exercise, you can experiment with some of the PAM security features of Red Hat Linux.

1. Make a backup copy of /etc/securetty: cp /etc/securetty /etc/securetty.sav.

2. Edit /etc/securetty and remove the lines for tty3 through tty8. Save the changes and exit.

3. Use ALT-F3 (CTRL-ALT-F3 if you're running X Window) to switch to virtual console number 3. Try to log in as *root*. What happens?

4. Repeat this process as a regular user. What happens?

5. Use ALT-F2 to switch to virtual console number 2 and try to log in as root.

6. Restore your original /etc/securetty file: mv /etc/securetty.sav /etc/securetty.

exam
ⓦatch

Make sure you understand how Red Hat Linux handles user authorization through the /etc/pam.d configuration files. When you test these files, make sure you create a backup of everything in PAM before making any changes, because any errors that you make to a PAM configuration file can disable your system completely (it is that secure).

CERTIFICATION OBJECTIVE 10.04

System Logging

An important part of maintaining a secure system is keeping track of the activities that take place on the system. If you know what usually happens, such as understanding when users log into your system, you can use log files to spot unusual activity. Red Hat Linux comes with several utilities you can use to monitor activity on a system. These utilities can help you identify the culprit if there is a problem.

Red Hat Linux comes with two logging daemons. The kernel log daemon service, klogd, logs kernel messages and events. The syslog daemon, syslogd, logs all other process activity. You can use the log files that syslogd generates to track activities on your system. If you are managing multiple Red Hat Linux systems, you can configure the syslogd daemon on each system to log messages to a central host system.

Both daemons are typically active by default, and both can be activated by the /etc/rc.d/init.d/syslog script. Once these daemons start, syslog examines /etc/syslog.conf to find configured logging options.

System Log Configuration File

You can configure what syslogd records through the /etc/syslog.conf configuration file. As shown in Figure 10-6, it includes a set of rules for different facilities: auth, auth-priv, cron, daemon, kern, lpr, mail, mark, news, security, syslog, user, and uucp.

FIGURE 10-6

The /etc/ syslog.conf log configuration file

```
# Log all kernel messages to the console.
# Logging much else clutters up the screen.
#kern.*                                                 /dev/console

# Log anything (except mail) of level info or higher.
# Don't log private authentication messages!
*.info;mail.none;news.none;authpriv.none;cron.none      /var/log/messages

# The authpriv file has restricted access.
authpriv.*                                              /var/log/secure

# Log all the mail messages in one place.
mail.*                                                  /var/log/maillog


# Log cron stuff
cron.*                                                  /var/log/cron

# Everybody gets emergency messages
*.emerg                                                 *

# Save news errors of level crit and higher in a special file.
uucp,news.crit                                          /var/log/spooler

# Save boot messages also to boot.log
local7.*                                                /var/log/boot.log


#
# INN
#
news.=crit                                              /var/log/news/news.crit
news.=err                                               /var/log/news/news.err
news.notice                                             /var/log/news/news.notice
~
                                                        1,1              All
```

Each facility is associated with several different levels of logging, known as the priority. In ascending order, log priorities are: debug, info, notice, warn, err, crit, alert, emerg. The "none" priority logs all messages at all levels.

For each facility and priority, log information is sent to a specific log file. For example, take the following line from /etc/syslog.conf:

```
*.info;mail.none;news.none;authpriv.none;cron.none          /var/log/messages
```

This line sends log information from all of the given facilities to the /var/log/messages file. This includes:

- All facility messages of info level and higher
- All log messages related to mail, news, authpriv (authentication), and cron

You can use the asterisk as a wildcard in /etc/syslog.conf. For example, a line that starts with *.* tells the syslog daemon to log everything. A line that starts with auth.* means you want to log all messages from the auth facility.

By default, syslogd logs all messages of a given priority or higher. In other words, a **cron.err** line will include all log messages from the cron daemon at the *err, crit, alert,* and *emerg* levels.

Most messages from syslogd are written to files in the /var/log directory. You should scan these logs on a regular basis and look for patterns that could indicate a security breach.

Managing Logs

Logs can easily become very large and difficult to read. By default, the *logrotate* utility creates a new log file on a weekly basis. You can also configure /etc/logrotate.conf to compress, mail, and remove desired log files. By default, the cron daemon runs logrotate on a regular basis, using the configuration files located in the /etc/logrotate.d directory.

As you can see in Figure 10-7, this process works fairly well; five or more weeks of logs are kept for a number of log facilities.

The Red Hat Log Viewer

There is a new Red Hat GUI tool that can help you scan though applicable logs. It can be useful if you don't remember the locations of the key log files and don't

FIGURE 10-7

Typical log files
in /var/log

```
[mj@RH80 mj]$ ls /var/log/
boot.log      fax        maillog.1    rpmpkgs.1        spooler    wtmp
boot.log.1    gdm        maillog.2    rpmpkgs.2        spooler.1  wtmp.1
boot.log.2    httpd      maillog.3    rpmpkgs.3        spooler.2  xdm-errors
boot.log.3    ksyms.0    maillog.4    rpmpkgs.4        spooler.3  xferlog
boot.log.4    ksyms.1    messages     sa               spooler.4  xferlog.1
cron          ksyms.2    messages.1   samba            squid      xferlog.2
cron.1        ksyms.3    messages.2   scrollkeeper.log up2date    xferlog.3
cron.2        ksyms.4    messages.3   secure           up2date.1  xferlog.4
cron.3        ksyms.5    messages.4   secure.1         up2date.2  XFree86.0.log
cron.4        ksyms.6    news         secure.2         up2date.3
cups          lastlog    pgsql        secure.3         up2date.4
dmesg         maillog    rpmpkgs      secure.4         vbox
[mj@RH80 mj]$ []
```

remember to look through /etc/syslog.conf for those locations. In the Red Hat GUI, run the redhat-logviewer command to open up the tool shown in Figure 10-8.

As you can see, the Red Hat Log Viewer simply provides a front end. For example, you can review the information shown in Figure 10-8 simply by looking through the latest mail log files in the /var/log directory. And as of this writing, the regular text log files provide more complete information.

FIGURE 10-8

The Red Hat
Log Viewer

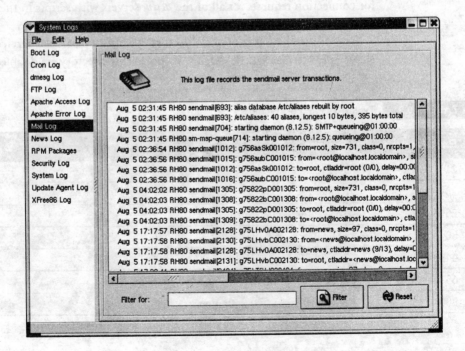

CERTIFICATION OBJECTIVE 10.05

The Extended Internet Services Daemon (xinetd)

Linux typically supports network communication between clients and servers. For example, you can use Telnet to connect to a remote system. The Telnet client on your computer makes a connection with a Telnet server daemon on the remote system.

To establish the connection on a TCP/IP network, a client application needs the IP address of the server, and the *port number* associated with the server daemon. All common TCP/IP applications have a standard port number; some examples are shown in Table 10-3.

If you don't specify the port number, TCP/IP assumes that you're using the default port for the specified service. Clients can't connect unless the corresponding server is running on the remote system. If you are managing a server, you may have a number of server daemons to start when Linux is booted.

The *xinetd* (which stands for *Extended Internet Services Daemon*) program can start a number of these server daemons simultaneously. The xinetd program listens for connection requests for all of the *active* servers with scripts in the /etc/xinetd.d directory.

Each file in the /etc/xinetd.d directory specifies a particular service you want to allow xinetd to manage. By default, scripts in this directory are disabled. The following

TABLE 10-3   Typical TCP/IP Port Numbers

Port Number	Service
21	FTP
23	Telnet
25	SMTP (outgoing mail)
80	HTTP
443	HTTPS (secure HTTP)
631	Internet Printing Protocol (CUPS configuration)
901	SWAT (Samba Configuration)

code shows a sample of the /etc/xinetd.d/ntalk configuration file, with this service disabled:

```
# default: off
# description: The ntalk server accepts ntalk connections, for chatting \
#       with users on different systems.
service ntalk
{
        disable        = yes
        socket_type                    = dgram
        wait                           = yes
        user                           = nobody
        group                          = tty
        server                         = /usr/sbin/in.ntalkd
}
```

This is a typical /etc/xinetd.d configuration file. The fields are described in Table 10-4. This is a versatile configuration file; other fields are described in the man pages for xinetd.conf. Read this man page; the only_from and no_access fields may be of particular interest.

CIDR notation is based upon "Classless Inter-Domain Routing." Under CIDR, you do not need to specify the full IPv4 subnet address; 192.168.0.0/255.255.255.0 is the same as 192.168.0.0/24. As of this writing, the RHCE exam does not require any detailed understanding of IPv6 addresses.

TABLE 10-4   Typical /etc/xinetd.d Configuration Parameters

Field	Description of Field Entry
disable	Yes by default, which disables the service
socket_type	Specifies the communication stream
wait	Yes for single-threaded applications, or No for multithreaded applications
user	Account under which the server should run
group	Group under which the server should run
server	The server program
only_from	Host name or IP address allowed to use the server. CIDR notation (e.g. 192.168.0.0/24) is okay
no_access	Host name or IP address not allowed to use the server. CIDR notation is okay

You have two ways to activate a service. You can edit the configuration file directly by changing the **disable** field from no to yes. Then make the xinetd daemon reread the configuration files with the **/sbin/service xinetd reload** command.

Alternatively, you can use the **/sbin/chkconfig** *servicename* **on** command, which automatically makes this change and makes xinetd reread the configuration file.

In some cases, it is possible to limit xinetd-based services by username. One prime example with an FTP server is the /etc/ftpaccess file, which allows you to restrict (or expand) user privileges by User ID number or username. As with other default Red Hat network configuration files, the default /etc/ftpaccess file is instructive. Try it out with your own users!

e x a m
ⓦ a t c h

Always remember to make sure that a service will be active after a reboot. The /sbin/chkconfig servicename on command is one way to do this for xinetd services. Otherwise, anything you configure may not work after your computer is rebooted.

EXERCISE 10-2

Configuring xinetd

In this exercise, we will enable the Telnet service using xinetd. Attempt to establish a Telnet session using the command **telnet localhost**. Telnet is disabled by default in Red Hat Linux, so your attempt should fail, unless you have already enabled Telnet.

1. Edit /etc/xinetd.d/telnet and change the value of **disable** from **yes to no.**

2. Tell xinetd to reread its configuration file using the command:

   ```
   kill -SIGUSR1 'cat /var/run/xinetd.pid'
   ```

3. Try the **telnet localhost** command again. It should work.

4. Use the /sbin/chkconfig command to disable Telnet. Do you have to restart or reload xinetd? What happens when you use /sbin/chkconfig to enable Telnet? Does it change the /etc/xinted.d/telnet configuration file?

tcp_wrappers and the libwrap Packages

The best way to prevent a cracker from using a service is to remove it completely from your Linux system. But what if you still need some Extended Internet Services (xinetd) packages?

You can achieve some measure of security by disabling or removing unused services in /etc/xinetd.conf. But you need to take other measures to protect yourself against attacks through enabled services. With xinetd, you have two approaches. You can set up fields in individual /etc/xinetd.d configuration files to block computers by host name or IP address. Alternatively, you can set this up for some or all xinetd services through the /etc/hosts.allow or /etc/hosts.deny file. This system is known as tcp_wrappers, which is enabled by default.

When xinetd receives a network request for a service, it passes the request on to tcp_wrappers. This system logs the request and then checks its access rules. If there are no limits on the particular host or IP address, tcp_wrappers passes control back to xinetd to start the needed service.

The key files are /etc/hosts.allow and /etc/hosts.deny. The philosophy is fairly straightforward; clients listed in *hosts.allow* are allowed access; clients listed in *hosts.deny* are denied access. When xinetd receives a request, the tcp_wrappers system takes the following steps:

1. It searches /etc/hosts.allow. If tcp_wrappers finds a match, it grants access.

2. It searches /etc/hosts.deny. If tcp_wrappers finds a match, it denies access.

3. If the host isn't found in either file, access is automatically granted to the client.

You use the same access control language in both /etc/hosts.allow and /etc/hosts.deny to tell tcp_wrappers which clients to allow or deny. The basic format of the lines in both files is this:

```
daemon_list : client_list
```

The simplest version of this format is:

```
ALL : ALL
```

This specifies all services managed by xinetd and makes the rule applicable to all hosts on all IP addresses. If you set this line in /etc/hosts.deny, all access is prohibited to all services. However, you can create finer filters. For example, the following line:

```
in.telnetd : 192.168.1.5
```

in /etc/hosts.allow allows the client with an IP address of 192.168.1.5 to connect to your system through Telnet. The same line in /etc/hosts.deny would prevent the computer with that IP address from using Telnet to connect to your system. You can specify clients a number of different ways, as shown in Table 10-5.

As you can see in Table 10-5, there are two different types of wildcards: *ALL* can be used to represent any client or service. The dot specifies all hosts with the specified domain name or IP network address.

You can set up multiple services and addresses with commas. Exceptions are easy to make with the *EXCEPT* operator. See the following excerpt from a /etc/hosts.allow file for an example:

```
#hosts.allow
ALL :.asafe.dom.com
in.ftpd : 192.168.25.0/255.255.255.0 EXCEPT 192.168.25.73
in.fingerd, in.rshd : 192.168.1.10
```

The first line in this file is simply a comment. The next line opens ALL xinetd services to all computers in the .asafe.dom.com domain. The following line opens FTP to any computer on the 192.168.25.0 network, except the one with an IP address of 192.168.25.73. Then, the finger and Remote Shell (rsh) services are opened to the computer with an IP address of 192.168.1.10.

The code that follows contains a hosts.deny file to see how lists can be built to control access.

```
#hosts.deny
ALL EXCEPT in.fingerd : .xyz.com
in.telnetd : ALL EXCEPT 192.168.1.10
ALL:ALL
```

TABLE 10-5 Address Fields in /etc/hosts.allow or /etc/hosts.deny

Client	Description
.example.com	Domain name. Since this domain name begins with a dot, it specifies all clients on the example.com domain.
172.16.	IP address. Since this address ends with a dot, it specifies all clients with an IP address of 172.16.$x.y$.
172.16.72.0/255.255.254.0	IP network address with subnet mask. CIDR notation not recognized.
ALL	Any client, any daemon.
user@linux1.example.com	Applies to the specific user on the given computer.

The first line in the hosts.deny file is a comment. The second line denies all services except finger to computers in the .xyz.com domain. The third line states that the only computer that is allowed to telnet to us has an IP address of 192.168.1.10. Finally, the last line is a blanket denial; all other computers are denied access to all services controlled by tcp_wrappers.

You can also use the **twist** command in /etc/hosts.allow or /etc/hosts.deny to access shell commands. For example, take the following line in a /etc/hosts.deny file:

```
in.telnetd : .crack.org : twist /bin/echo Sorry %c, access denied
```

This sends a customized error message for Telnet users on the crack.org domain. Different operators such as %c are described in Table 10-6. Some of these operators may be able to help you track the intruder.

EXERCISE 10-3

Configuring tcp_wrappers

In this exercise, we will use tcp_wrappers to control access to network resources. Since tcp_wrappers is enabled by default, you shouldn't have to make any modifications to /etc/xinetd.conf.

1. Verify that you can telnet to the system using the address localhost.

2. Edit /etc/hosts.deny and add the following line (don't forget to write the file):

   ```
   ALL : ALL
   ```

3. What happens when you try to telnet to the address localhost?

4. Edit /etc/hosts.allow and add the following line:

   ```
   in.telnetd : LOCAL
   ```

5. Now what happens when you try to telnet to the address localhost?

6. If you have other systems available to you, try restricting access to the Telnet service using some of the other tcp_wrappers rules.

7. Undo your changes when finished.

| TABLE 10-6 | tcp_wrappers Operators |

Field	Description	Field	Description
%a	Client address	%h	Client host name
%A	Host address	%H	Server host name
%c	Client information	%p	Process ID
%d	Process name	%s	Server information

CERTIFICATION OBJECTIVE 10.06

Firewall Policies

A firewall sits between your company's internal LAN and an outside network. A firewall can be configured to examine every network packet that passes into or out of your LAN. When configured with appropriate rules, it can filter out those packets that may pose a security risk to your system. To understand how *packet filtering* works, you have to understand a little bit about how information is sent across networks.

Before you send a message over a network, the message is broken down into smaller-sized units called *packets*. Administrative information, including the type of data, the source address, and destination address, is added to each packet. The packets are reassembled when they reach the destination computer. A firewall examines these administrative fields in each packet to determine whether to allow the packet to pass.

Red Hat Linux comes with everything you need to configure a system to be a firewall. Three basic Linux firewall commands are available: **ipfwadm**, **ipchains**, and **iptables**. The first command, ipfwadm, was associated with Linux kernel 2.0.x and is now generally obsolete. The ipchains command was developed for Linux kernel 2.2.x and is still in active use, even on Linux distributions based on Linux kernel 2.4.x.

The RHCE exam explicitly requires that you know how to use iptables, which was developed for Linux kernel 2.4.x. Therefore, this chapter focuses on iptables.

Configuring iptables

The philosophy behind iptables is based on "chains." These are sets of rules applied to each network packet. Each rule does two things: it specifies the conditions a packet must meet to match the rule, and it specifies the action if the packet matches.

Before you can set up iptables commands, you need to make sure that the appropriate modules are part of your Linux kernel. Check your current rules. Run the **/sbin/iptables -L** command to list the current chains. If you see error messages similar to the following:

```
iptables: Incompatible with this kernel
```

you'll need to upgrade your modules. Use the **/sbin/rmmod** *modulename* command to delete any ipchains-related modules. Then use the **/sbin/insmod ip_tables** command to add the iptables kernel module. Now you're ready to start configuring iptables rules. The iptables command uses the following basic format:

```
iptables -t tabletype <Action / Direction> <Packet Pattern> -j <What to do>
```

Now let us analyze this command, step by step. First there is the **-t** *tabletype* switch. There are two basic *tabletype* options for iptables:

- **filter**   This sets a rule for filtering packets.
- **nat**   This sets up Network Address Translation, which is discussed in the last section of this chapter.

The default is **filter**; if you don't specify a **-t** *tabletype*, iptables assumes that you're trying to affect a filtering rule. Next is the <Action / Direction>. There are four basic Actions that you can take with an iptables rule:

- **-A (--append)**   Appends a rule to the end of a chain.
- **-D (--delete)**   Deletes a rule from a chain. Specify the rule by the number or the Packet Pattern.
- **-L (--list)**   Lists the currently configured rules in the chain.
- **-F (--flush)**   Flushes all of the rules in the current iptables chain.

If you're appending to (-A) or deleting from (-D) a chain, you'll want to apply it to network data traveling in one of three directions:

- **INPUT**   All incoming packets are checked against the rules in this chain.

- **OUTPUT** All outgoing packets are checked against the rules in this chain.
- **FORWARD** All packets being sent to another computer are checked against the rules in this chain.

Next, you need to configure a <Packet Pattern>. Your firewall checks every packet against this pattern. The simplest pattern is by IP address:

- **-s *ip_address*** All packets are checked for a specific source IP address.
- **-d *ip_address*** All packets are checked for a specific destination IP address.

Packet Patterns can be more complex. In TCP/IP, packets are transported using the TCP, UDP, or ICMP protocol. You can specify the protocol with the **-p** switch, followed by the destination port (**--dport**). For example, the **-p tcp --dport 80** parameters prevent users outside your network from looking for an HTTP connection.

Once iptables matches a Packet Pattern, it needs to know what to do with that packet, which leads to the last part of the command, **-j <what to do>**. There are three basic options:

- **DROP** The packet is dropped. No message is sent to the requesting computer.
- **REJECT** The packet is dropped. An error message is sent to the requesting computer.
- **ACCEPT** The packet is allowed to proceed as specified with the -A action: INPUT, OUTPUT, or FORWARD.

We will look at some examples of how you can use iptables commands to configure a firewall. The first step is always to see what is currently configured, with the following command:

```
/sbin/iptables -L
```

If iptables is properly configured, it should return chain rules in three different categories: INPUT, FORWARD, and OUTPUT.

Let's look at some examples. The following command defines a rule that rejects all traffic from the 192.168.75.0 subnet, and it sends a "destination unreachable" error message back to any client that tried to connect:

```
/sbin/iptables -A INPUT -s 192.168.75.0/24 -j REJECT
```

This rule stops users from the computer with an IP address of 192.168.25.200 from "pinging" our system (remember that ping uses the ICMP protocol):

```
/sbin/iptables -A INPUT -s 192.168.25.200 -p icmp -j DROP
```

The following command guards against TCP SYN attacks from outside our network. Assume that our network IP address is 192.168.1.0. The exclamation point (!) means "everything but":

```
/sbin/iptables -A INPUT -s !192.168.190.0/24 -p tcp -j DROP
```

Then, if you wanted to delete the rule related to the ping command in this list, use the following command:

```
/sbin/iptables -D INPUT -s 192.168.25.200 -p icmp -j DROP
```

The default rule for INPUT, OUTPUT, and FORWARD is to ACCEPT all packets. One way to stop packet forwarding is to add the following rule:

```
/sbin/iptables -A FORWARD -j DROP
```

You can save your firewall configuration to a file using the following command:

```
/sbin/service iptables save
```

This saves your chains in the /etc/sysconfig/iptables configuration file. The iptables service script then reads this file, if it is active for the appropriate runlevel when you start Linux. You can configure iptables so that it is active for all network runlevels (2, 3, 4, and 5) with the chkconfig command, as follows:

```
# /sbin/chkconfig --level 2345 iptables on
# /sbin/chkconfig --list iptables
ipchains        0:off   1:off   2:on    3:on    4:on    5:on    6:off
```

exam
watch

Knowing how to secure a Red Hat Linux system against unauthorized access is critical. Be sure you understand the concepts and commands discussed in this chapter.

Network Address Translation

Network Address Translation (NAT) lets you hide the IP address of the computers on your network that make a connection to the Internet. NAT replaces the source address with the IP address of the firewall computer. That address information is cached.

When the firewall receives data such as a Web page, the process is reversed. As the packets pass through the firewall, the originating computer is identified in the cache. The header of each packet is modified accordingly before the packets are sent on their way.

This approach is useful for several reasons. Disguising your internal IP addresses makes it harder for someone to break into your network. NAT allows you to connect computers to the Internet without having to have an official IP address for each computer. This allows you to use the private IP addresses discussed in Chapter 1 on your internal LAN. In the Linux world, this process is known as IP masquerading.

IP Masquerading

Red Hat Linux supports a variation of NAT called *IP masquerading*. IP masquerading allows you to provide Internet access to multiple computers with a single officially assigned IP address. IP masquerading lets you map multiple internal IP addresses to a single valid external IP address.

Connecting multiple systems to the Internet using IP masquerading is a fairly straightforward process. Your firewall computer will need one network card to connect to your LAN, and a second network card for the Internet. This second network card can be a telephone modem, or it can be connected to a cable "modem" or DSL adapter. This configuration requires the following steps:

- Assign your official IP address to the network card that is directly connected to the Internet.

- Assign computers on your LAN one of the private IP addresses described in Chapter 1.

- Reserve one private IP address for the network card on your firewall that is connected to the LAN.

- Use iptables to set up IP masquerading.
- Enable IP forwarding on the firewall computer.
- Configure the computers on your LAN with the IP address of your firewall computer as their Internet gateway.

Let us take a careful look at when a message comes from a computer on a LAN, through a firewall, to the Internet. When a computer on your LAN wants a Web page on the Internet, it sends packets to the firewall. The firewall replaces the source IP address on each packet with the firewall's official IP address. It then assigns a new port number to the packet. The firewall caches the original source IP address and port number.

When a packet comes in from the Internet to the firewall, it should include a port number. If your firewall can match it with the port number assigned to a specific outgoing packet, the process is reversed. The firewall replaces the destination IP address and port number with the internal computer's private IP address and then forwards the packet back to original client on the LAN.

The next step in the process is to use iptables to enable masquerading. The following command assumes that eth1 represents the network card that is directly connected to the Internet, and that your LAN has a network address of 192.168.0.0/24:

```
/sbin/iptables -t nat -A POSTROUTING -s 192.168.0.0/24 -o eth1 -j MASQUERADE
```

The following command enables FTP access through your firewall:

```
/sbin/modprobe -a ip_conntrack_ftp ip_nat_ftp
```

Similar modules are available in your kernel directory, under /usr/src/linux-2-4/net/ipv4/netfilter. But there is one more thing. IP masquerading does not work unless you've enabled IP forwarding, as described in the next section.

IP Forwarding

IP forwarding is more commonly referred to as *routing*. Routing is critical to the operation of the Internet or any IP network. Routers connect and facilitate communication between multiple networks. When you set up a computer to find a site on an outside network, you need a gateway address. This corresponds to the IP address of your router on your LAN.

A router looks at the destination IP address of each packet. If the IP address is on one of its LANs, it routes the packet directly to the proper computer. Otherwise, it sends the packet to another gateway closer to its final destination. To use a Red Hat Linux system as a router, you must enable IP forwarding in the /etc/sysctl.conf configuration file by changing:

```
net.ipv4.ip_forward = 0
```

to

```
net.ipv4.ip_forward = 1
```

These settings take effect the next time you reboot your system. Until you reboot, you can enable forwarding directly in your kernel with the following command:

```
echo 1 > /proc/sys/net/ipv4/ip_forward
```

Now that you have seen some of the security capabilities of Red Hat Linux, refer to the following Scenario & Solution for some possible scenario questions and their answers.

SCENARIO & SOLUTION

You have installed an FTP server on your corporate network, and you want to restrict access to certain departments. Each department has its own subnet.	Use the /etc/hosts.deny file in the tcp_wrappers package to block FTP access (in.ftpd) to the unwanted subnets.
You have only one official IP address, but you need to provide Internet access to all of the systems on your LAN. Each computer on the LAN has its own private IP address.	Use iptables to implement IP masquerading. Make sure IP forwarding is active.
You have a LAN of Linux and Unix computers, and want to implement a single authentication database of usernames and passwords for the network.	Implement NFS file sharing on the network. Set up an NIS server. Set up the other computers on your LAN as NIS clients.
You want to modify the commands associated with halting and rebooting your computer so they're accessible only to the root user.	Set up the appropriate Pluggable Authentication Module configuration files in /etc/pam.d to use the system-auth module.

The Red Hat Firewall Configurator

You can automate the process of configuring a firewall. Run the redhat-config-securitylevel command. This brings up the Red Hat Firewall Configurator, as shown in Figure 10-9. If you've installed Red Hat Linux before, this menu should look familiar; the choices are identical to those shown during the standard Red Hat Linux installation process.

The choices here are similar to what you may find with the /usr/sbin/lokkit tool. Both tools are front ends to creating the appropriate iptables commands to control traffic coming in, going out, and moving through your computer.

Three basic security levels are available:

■ High security blocks all inbound request traffic except replies from DNS servers. In other words, you can still send messages out; DNS replies allow you to browse the Internet. However, other computers won't be able to connect to servers on your computer.

<table>
<tr><td>

FIGURE 10-9

The Red Hat
Firewall
Configurator

</td><td>

</td></tr>
</table>

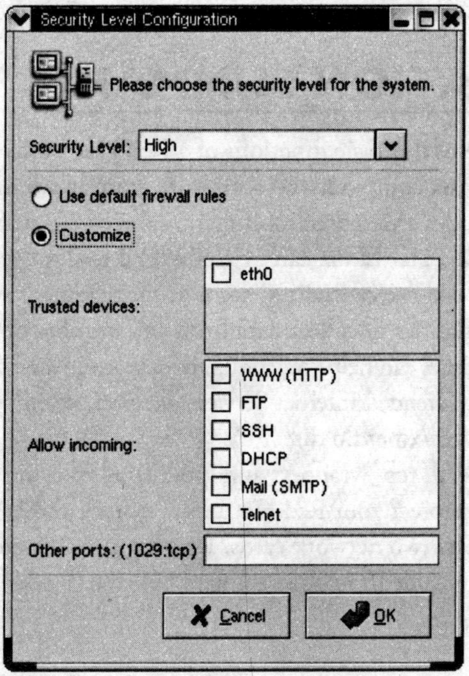

■ Medium security blocks requests to many servers on your computer. Specifically, it blocks traffic to TCP/IP ports below 1023, as well as the NFS server, the X Window display, and the X Font Server. It allows you to use special services on external networks such as RealAudio.

■ No security disables any rules that you've previously created using the Red Hat Firewall Configurator. It does not delete any rules that you've created directly with the iptables command.

For medium or high security, you can create exceptions to each rule, by selecting the Customize radio button. Firewalls are not applied to "Trusted Devices." If you allow incoming traffic, others can access the associated server on your computer. For example, if you select Allow Incoming WWW (HTTP), others can connect to a Web server on your computer.

The settings that you create are documented in /etc/sysconfig/iptables. But there may be more firewall rules. You may have added some firewall chains with an iptables command. You still need to apply the **/sbin/iptables** -L command to list current iptables firewall chains.

CERTIFICATION SUMMARY

One of the basic functions of a Red Hat Linux system administrator is protecting a Linux computer and a network from inside and outside attacks. Red Hat Linux includes a variety of tools that can help you establish a secure computing environment.

Red Hat Linux can be a powerful tool for securing networks from outside attack. You can use centralized account management with an NIS service. Log files can be configured to collect data from any number of services. Pluggable Authentication Modules can help you configure how individual services verify usernames and passwords. The Extended Internet Services daemon, xinetd, governs the services configured though the /etc/xinetd.d directory.

With tcp_wrappers and iptables at your disposal, you can create a firewall which can protect your Red Hat Linux system and LAN. Firewalls require a computer with at least two network cards. Routing must be enabled on that computer. The firewall can include IP masquerading to hide the IP addresses of the computers inside your LAN.

✓ TWO-MINUTE DRILL

The following are some of the key points from the certification objectives in Chapter 10.

Configuring NIS Client

❑ NIS allows you to configure one centrally managed username and password database with other Linux and Unix systems on your LAN.

❑ With NIS, you maintain one password database on an *NIS server* and configure the other systems on the network to be *NIS clients*.

❑ You can configure NIS to share other configuration files, including many of those in the /etc directory.

❑ To configure NIS, you need to configure at least one computer as an NIS server.

❑ The NIS server stores the centralized NIS database files, which are also known as *maps*.

❑ You can have only one NIS master server per NIS domain.

❑ The NIS maps are stored in the /var/yp/*DOMAIN*, where *DOMAIN* is the name of your NIS domain.

Basic Host Security

❑ Password security requires good passwords from your users.

❑ You can check for suspicious login activity with the **utmpdump /var/log/wtmp** command.

❑ Many security updates are available through Red Hat errata releases.

❑ You can update many packages with up2date.

❑ The best way to promote security is to delete the packages associated with services that you do not need.

The Pluggable Authentication Module (PAM) System

❑ Red Hat Linux uses the Pluggable Authentication Modules (PAM) system to check for authorized users.

❑ PAM modules are called by configuration files in the /etc/pam.d directory. These configuration files are usually named after the service or command that they control.

❑ There are four types of PAM modules: authentication, account, password, and session management.

❑ PAM configuration files include lines that list the module_type, the control_flag, the path to the actual module, followed by arguments such as system-auth.

❑ PAM modules are well documented in the /usr/share/doc/pam-*versionnumber*/txts directory.

System Logging

❑ Red Hat Linux includes two logging daemons: klogd for kernel messages and syslogd for all other process activity. Both are activated by the syslog service script.

❑ You can use log files generated by the syslogd daemon to track activities on your system.

❑ Most log files are stored in /var/log.

❑ You can configure what is logged through the syslog configuration file, */etc/syslog.conf.*

The Extended Internet Services Daemon (xinetd)

❑ xinetd is the Extended Internet Services Daemon, which acts as a "super-server" for a number of other network services, such as IMAP, POP, FTP, rsh, and Telnet.

❑ Individual services have their own management scripts in the /etc/xinetd.d directory.

❑ Most xinetd services are disabled by default.

❑ You can activate an xinetd service with the appropriate chkconfig command, or by directly editing its xinetd script.

❑ xinetd listens for connection requests from client applications.

❑ When xinetd receives a connection request, it starts the server associated with the TCP/IP port, then waits for other connection requests.

❑ Red Hat Linux comes with a package known as libwrap or tcp_wrappers. This package, which is enabled by default, allows you to limit access to various xinetd services.

❑ You configure the access rules for tcp_wrappers through the /etc/hosts.allow and /etc/hosts.deny configuration files.

❑ Clients listed in /etc/hosts.allow are allowed access; clients listed in /etc/hosts.deny are denied access.

❑ Services can also be configured in /etc/hosts.allow and /etc/hosts.deny. Remember to use the actual name of the daemon, such as in.telnetd.

Firewall Policies

❑ Firewalls can secure an internal network as a *packet filter* that controls the information that comes in, goes out, and is forwarded through the internal network.

❑ The current firewall configuration utility is iptables, which has replaced ipchains.

❑ The iptables utility retains a number of elements of ipchains. iptables directives are sets of rules, chained together, which are compared and then applied to each network packet.

❑ Each rule sets conditions required to match the rule, and then specifies the action taken if the packet matches the rule.

❑ Use the **/sbin/service iptables save** command to save any chains that you configure in the /etc/sysconfig/iptables configuration file.

Network Address Translation

❑ NAT modifies the header in packets coming from a LAN. The source address is replaced with the public address of the firewall computer, with a random port number. Both are stored in cache.

❑ Linux supports a variation of NAT called *IP masquerading*.

❑ IP masquerading allows you to provide Internet access to multiple computers with a single officially assigned IP address.

❑ With IP masquerading, messages for the network are sorted by the port number. The original source address is taken from the cache and added to the packet, so the message gets to the right computer.

❑ A firewall computer needs at least two network cards: one on the LAN, and the other on an external network such as the Internet.

❑ IP forwarding is more commonly known as *routing*.

❑ Routing is critical to the operation of the Internet or any IP network.

❑ A router checks the destination IP address of each packet. If the address is on a connected LAN, it sends the packet directly to that computer. If the address is outside the LAN, it sends the packet to another router closer to its final destination.

❑ To enable IP forwarding, edit /etc/sysctl.conf and change the line to net.ipv4.ip_forward to 1.

❑ To enable IP forwarding immediately, type the **echo 1 > /proc/sys/net/ipv4/ip_forward** command.

SELF TEST

The following questions will help you measure your understanding of the material presented in this chapter. Read all the choices carefully, as there may be more than one correct answer. Choose all correct answers for each question.

Configuring NIS Clients

1. You have a network with 50 Linux workstations and five Linux servers. Most of the workstations are in public areas, and your users need to be able to log in from any workstation on the network. How might you satisfy this requirement?

   A. Keep a master copy of /etc/passwd on one of the servers, and do a backup and restore of that copy to all the workstations every evening.

   B. Set one of the servers up to be an NIS server. Arrange another server to be an NIS slave server. Make the workstations NIS clients.

   C. Set the workstations up to be NIS clients.

   D. Create a common account on every workstation and give each person the password to this account.

2. How would you set up the workstations to be NIS clients?

   A. Edit /etc/passwd and add the line USE_NIS at the end of the file.

   B. Start the ypbind daemon.

   C. Add a line to start ypbind to /etc/xinetd.conf.

   D. Run authconfig and enable NIS.

3. A user on one of the NIS workstations calls you and tells you she is having trouble changing her password using the passwd command. What should you tell her?

   A. You'll change her password for her.

   B. Try picking a more secure password.

   C. Make sure the caps lock key isn't on.

   D. She must use yppasswd to change her NIS password.

Basic Host Security

4. Which of the following are *not* good basic host security measures?

   A. Jotting down the root password on your desk blotter.

   B. Checking system log files regularly for unusual activity.

   C. Hanging on to unused accounts in case their original users want to reactivate them.

   D. Providing users with adequate training so they know how to properly use the tools at their disposal.

5. Which of the following measures is the most effective way to prevent attacks through various network services?

   A. Disable a service in the appropriate /etc/xinetd.d configuration file.

   B. Block service requests with the appropriate commands in /etc/hosts.deny.

   C. Use a firewall to drop all requests to unneeded services.

   D. Uninstall unneeded network services.

The Pluggable Authentication Module (PAM) System

6. What are the four steps that PAM breaks the authentication process into?

   A. Authentication management, account management, session management, and password management

   B. Authentication management, account management, network management, and password management

   C. Authentication management, account logging, session management, and password management

   D. Authentication management, account management, session management, and firewall management

7. You are editing the PAM configuration file by adding a module. How would you indicate the authentication process should immediately terminate and succeed if the module succeeds?

   A. Make sure the module is either an auth module or a password module, since these must always succeed.

   B. Use the required control flag.

   C. Use the sufficient control flag.

   D. It doesn't matter; the authentication process always stops as soon as a module fails.

8. You experience a moment of forgetfulness and try to log in to the root account of your server via Telnet from your Internet connection at home. Why doesn't this work?

   A. You are using iptables to filter out Telnet access to the root account.

   B. You miskeyed your password.

   C. Login to the root account is never allowed from any terminal other than the console.

   D. The network terminal device you are trying to log in from is not listed in /etc/securettys; therefore, the root account will not be allowed to log in from that terminal.

System Logging

9. Assume you normally work from a user account called sysadm. How might you configure your Red Hat Linux System to notify you whenever there is a serious problem with the kernel?

   A. Edit /etc/syslog.conf and add an entry such as this:

   ```
   kern.err          root,sysadm
   ```

   B. Recompile the kernel to include error notification and specify sysadm as the user to be notified.

   C. Write a C program to monitor the /proc/err directory and send any messages that appear there to sysadm.

   D. Edit /etc/syslog.conf and add an entry such as this:

   ```
   *.*               root,sysadm
   ```

The Extended Internet Services Daemon (xinetd)

10. You would like to restrict access to your FTP site to clients in a particular subnet. How can you do this?

   A. Use iptables to filter out FTP requests for all but the given subnet.

   B. Disable the configuration for wu-ftpd in the /etc/xinetd.d directory.

   C. Edit /etc/ftp.conf and add a reject line for all networks other than the given subnet.

   D. Add the appropriate lines to /etc/hosts.allow and /etc/hosts.deny.

11. You are using the xinetd program to start services. How could you restrict Telnet access to clients on the 192.168.170.0 network?

   A. Edit /etc/xinetd.d/telnet and add this line

   ```
   DENY EXCEPT 192.168.170.0.
   ```

B. Edit /etc/hosts.allow and add this line:

```
in.telnetd : 192.168.170.0/255.255.255.0
```

C. Edit /etc/hosts.deny and add this line:

```
in.telnetd : 192.168.170.0/255.255.255.0
```

D. Edit /etc/hosts.deny and add this line:

```
in.telnetd : ALL EXCEPT 192.168.170.0/255.255.255.0
```

12. You work at a company with several divisions. Each division is part of the headquarters LAN, but each division has its own logical subnet and its own domain. You would like to set up an internal FTP server for just one division, and you do not want to allow access to users in other divisions. What configuration would work?

A. Set up a user's workstation in each division to be the FTP server and delegate the management of that server to the user of that workstation.

B. Use NIS and set up shared virtual FTP directories.

C. Edit the /etc/hosts.deny file to specify the in.ftpd service. Deny access to all, except for the one division.

D. Edit /etc/xinetd.d/wu-ftpd and set enable = yes.

13. Based on the configuration described in question 10, what would you do to restrict access from a specific user mj with a user ID of 500?

A. Edit the /etc/xinetd.d/wu-ftpd configuration file, and add **nouser=mj**.

B. Edit the /etc/hosts.deny file and add **in.ftpd : user=mj**.

C. Edit the /etc/ftphosts file and add the user ID for mj to the list.

D. Edit the /etc/ftpaccess file and add **deny uid %500**.

Firewall Policies

14. You have just recently connected your organization's network to the Internet, and you are a little worried because there is nothing other than your router standing between your network and the Internet. You have a spare 200 MHz PC lying around that just happens to have two Ethernet cards. You also have a mixture of systems on your network that includes Macintosh,. Windows 98, and Linux. What might you do to ease your mind?

A. Nothing, you're not advertising the systems on your LAN via DNS, so no one will ever find them.

B. Install Red Hat Linux on the 200 MHz PC and use iptables to set it up as a firewall.

C. Install Red Hat Linux on the 200 MHz PC and use tcp_wrappers to set it up as a firewall.

D. Install Linux on all systems on your network.

15. Consider the following command:

```
/sbin/iptables -A INPUT -s 192.168.77.77 -j REJECT
```

What effect will this have when the client with an IP of 192.168.77.77 tries to connect to your system?

A. No effect at all.

B. Access will be denied, and the client computer won't get any message on what happened.

C. Access will be denied, and the client application will get a message that the target destination is unreachable.

D. You will receive a notification message on the system console.

Network Address Translation

16. You are setting up a small office and would like to provide Internet access to a small number of users, but you don't want to pay for a dedicated IP address for each system on the network. How could Linux help with the problem?

A. Assign the official IP address to a Linux system and create accounts on that system for all of the office personnel.

B. Install Linux and configure it for IP forwarding.

C. Install a Linux router.

D. Use the Linux system to connect to the Internet; then use iptables to set up IP masquerading.

LAB QUESTION

Part 1

You want to set up a secure Web server on your corporate LAN that supports inbound requests from your LAN and the Internet, but you do not want any of these requests from the Internet to get into your intranet. What can you do?

Part 2

You want to set up Telnet service on your internal LAN, accessible only to one specific IP address. You want to block access from outside the LAN. Assume that your LAN's network address is 192.168.1.0, and the IP address of the computer that should get access is 192.168.1.33. For the purpose of this lab, feel free to substitute the IP address of a second Linux computer on your network. What do you do?

SELF TEST ANSWERS

Configuring NIS Clients

1. ☑   **B.** This is an ideal situation for NIS.
   ☒   **A** is incorrect because it is labor intensive and would lead to many password and database inconsistencies. **C** is incorrect because you need at least one NIS server. **D** is incorrect because this is obviously an insecure way to run a network.

2. ☑   **D.** Although you can configure NIS clients manually, the easier way is to use the authconfig utility.
   ☒   **A** is incorrect because this is invalid syntax. **B** is incorrect because you need to do more than start ypbind. **C** is incorrect because ypbind should be started from /etc/rc.d/init.d.

3. ☑   **D.** She must use the NIS yppasswd command to change her NIS password.
   ☒   **A, B,** and **C** are all incorrect because the user's account is an NIS account; therefore, the only valid choice is **D**.

Basic Host Security

4. ☑   **A** and **C** are both not recommended.
   ☒   **B** and **D**, on the other hand, are both good security practices.

5. ☑   **D.** The most effective way to prevent an attack through a network service is to make sure that it is not installed.
   ☒   **A, B,** and **C** are all incorrect. Since the service is still installed on the system, it is still at least theoretically possible to attack through that service.

The Pluggable Authentication Module (PAM) System

6. ☑   **A.** PAM breaks the authentication process into these four steps.
   ☒   **B, C,** and **D** are not the four steps that PAM breaks the authentication process into.

7. ☑   **C.** The *sufficient* flag is used to indicate the authentication process should end immediately if the module succeeds.
   ☒   **A** is incorrect because any PAM module can fail and the authorization process will continue. **B** is incorrect because failure would be delayed until any other modules of the same type have been checked. **D** is incorrect because the control flag determines when the authorization process terminates.

8. ☑ **D.** The root account is allowed to log in only from terminals listed in /etc/securettys.
   ☒ **A** is incorrect because this is not a typical firewall function. **B** is obviously incorrect. **C** is incorrect because answer **D** explains how access can be granted.

System Logging

9. ☑ **A.** Although **D** might seem like a good choice, this would also show you all messages from every facility. It would be very difficult to pick out just the kernel messages from everything else that would be coming to your screen.
   ☒ **B** and **C** are obviously incorrect because there is too much effort involved.

The Extended Internet Services Daemon (xinetd)

10. ☑ **D.** This is a good situation for tcp_wrappers, and its /etc/hosts.allow and /etc/hosts.deny configuration files.
    ☒ **A** is incorrect because iptables is better used to filter entire protocols. **B** is incorrect because this would disable FTP completely. **C** is incorrect because there is no ftp.conf file.

11. ☑ **D.** Although **B** would allow the requested access, since no other configuration has been done for tcp_wrappers, /etc/hosts.deny will be empty, so other clients will be allowed access by default. The best choice is to restrict all access to the telnet daemon and then make an exception for clients in the requested subnet.
    ☒ **A** is incorrect because the syntax is wrong. **C** is incorrect because it would result in Telnet access being denied to the 192.168.170.0 network.

12. ☑ **C.** The in.ftpd service is the actual name of the ftp daemon. It is easy to block access to other divisions (and the rest of the Internet) through the /etc/hosts.deny file.
    ☒ **A, B,** and **D** are all incorrect. It's a poor idea to delegate any service to a nonadministrative user. NIS does not configure FTP. There is no enable flag for xinetd configuration files.

13. ☑ **D.** The /etc/ftpaccess file allows you to block users by username or user ID.
    ☒ **A, B,** and **C** are all incorrect, as they are not viable options for the specified configuration files.

Firewall Policies

14. ☑ **B.** Your best choice would be to take the unused PC and turn it into a firewall using Linux and iptables. If you use a router to connect to the Internet, then your firewall system sits between your LAN and the router. This results in a two-node network consisting of the router and one of the network interfaces in your firewall that serves as a buffer zone between the

Internet and your LAN. You assume that any traffic on this side of the firewall is potentially unsafe.

☒   **A** is incorrect because this is a poor way to secure a network. **C** is incorrect because although you might also want to use tcp_wrappers as part of your security strategy, it is designed to secure individual computers, not an entire network. Although **D** might be a good option in general, it won't necessarily make your network more secure.

15.   ☑   **C.** Because of the REJECT target, the client will receive an error message. If the target was DENY, the client would not get any error message.

☒   **A, B,** and **D** do not describe what happens with this firewall when the client with an IP address of 192.168.77.77 tries to connect to your system.

Network Address Translation

16.   ☑   **D.** If you need to connect several systems to the Internet but have only one official IP address to use, IP masquerading is the perfect solution.

☒   **A** is incorrect unless your users want to telnet to a single system and use a command line interface. **B** and **C** are essentially the same answer and are both incorrect because a router will not help in this situation.

LAB ANSWER

Part 1

Scenario 1: Cost is not an object. This means you can build a DMZ, demilitarized zone, using two firewalls and a separate Web server, all running Linux. You should have the Web server dedicated only to the Web. You configure two more Linux hosts, each with two network cards, and essentially isolate the intranet behind one firewall. You then put the Web server in the middle, placing the second firewall between the Web server and the Internet. You configure the firewall on the intranet with IP masquerading to ensure anonymity for all your intranet hosts.

Scenario 2: You have one old computer available, and the Web server is a separate computer. Use your one computer as the firewall between you and the Internet and only forward HTTP packets to the Web server IP address directly; use NAT for all intranet requests going out to the Internet for HTTP and FTP. Disallow all other services.

Part 2

When you set up any xinetd service such as Telnet, there are several steps in the process. You'll need to modify the xinetd Telnet configuration file, and set up filtering in one of three ways: in the /etc/xinetd.d/telnet configuration file, through tcp_wrappers, or the appropriate firewall commands:

1. First, you want to enable Telnet. Make sure that the Telnet RPM is installed.

2. Activate Telnet. Use the **/sbin/chkconfig telnet on** command to revise the /etc/xinetd.d/telnet configuration script.

3. Edit the /etc/xinetd.d/telnet configuration file. Add the **only_from = 192.168.1.33** line.

4. Save the configuration file and reload the xinetd service script with the **/sbin/service xinetd reload** command. Try accessing Telnet from the local computer. What happens?

5. Try accessing Telnet from the computer with the IP address of 192.168.1.33. What happens? Try again from a different computer on your LAN.

6. Restore the previous /etc/xinetd.d/telnet configuration file. Don't forget to reload the xinetd service script with the **/sbin/service xinetd reload** command.

7. Edit /etc/hosts.deny. Add the **in.telnetd : ALL EXCEPT 192.168.1.33** line.

8. Try accessing Telnet from the computer with the IP address of 192.168.1.33. What happens? Try again from a different computer on your LAN.

9. Restore the previous /etc/hosts.deny file.

10. Save any iptables chains. Back up /etc/sysconfig/iptables, if that file currently exists to ~/bak.iptables.

11. Flush current firewall rules with the **/sbin/iptables -F** command.

12. Block the Telnet port, 23, for all IP addresses except 192.168.1.33 with the **/sbin/iptables -A INPUT -s ! 192.168.1.33 -p tcp --dport 23 -j DROP** command.

13. Try accessing the Telnet server from the computer with the IP address of 192.168.1.33. What happens? Try again from a different computer on your LAN.

14. Flush current firewall rules with the **/sbin/iptables -F** command.

15. Restore any previous firewall rules with the **/sbin/iptables-restore < ~/bak.iptables** command.

16. EXTRA CREDIT: Repeat these commands for other services and networks.

11

Operational Administration Recovery and Security

CERTIFICATION OBJECTIVES

T he themes of this chapter are *security* and *recovery*. These are two critical concepts for the RHCE exam. This continues the discussion of system security started in the last chapter, with a look at secure ways to run certain network services and a Red Hat Linux–specific way of specifying file security.

This chapter includes a description of setting up security with groups. You can set up special groups in Red Hat Linux. The users in these groups have access to a common directory.

Next, you'll learn about the part of the administrative process related to maintaining your temporary directories with the tmpwatch utility.

Also discussed is one of the most fundamental and important topics of concern to any systems administrator: what to do when a system will not boot. When the inevitable happens, knowing the right things to look for and having some tricks up your sleeve may possibly help you avoid a potential nightmare and a major loss of service for your users. Understanding these tools is fundamental to getting through the RHCE Debug exam.

CERTIFICATION OBJECTIVE 11.01

Services and Special Users

The programs that run on Linux are all processes. When Red Hat Linux starts on your computer, it first starts a special process known as *init*. The init process then starts other basic processes required for a working Linux system, including the shell, the basic user consoles, startup daemons, and more. Because it needs the authority, init runs as root.

Interestingly enough, most other services, especially network daemons, do not run under the root user ID. This is one important way Linux protects your network security.

Suppose you have configured a system to start several network services running under the root user ID. Even if you loaded the latest security patches, the risk is still high. If a cracker stumbles upon your system and is able to break in, he or she can quickly get root access through the service daemon.

To circumvent problems like this, Red Hat Linux normally configures services to run under their own user accounts. If a cracker does succeed in breaking into one daemon, the damage is limited because the service is running as a normal, unprivileged user. Alternatively, some services can be run through the *nobody* account. Figure 11-1 shows a typical /etc/passwd file. Notice that most common network services have their own user accounts.

EXERCISE 11-1

Verifying That Services Have Their Own Accounts

In this exercise, you will verify that certain system and network services run with their own accounts. You should try this exercise on a system that is configured to offer various network services.

At a shell prompt, issue the following command:

```
[root]# ps aux --headers | less
```

What account is the Web server (httpd) running under? What account is the xfs service running under?

FIGURE 11-1	
| Services have their own accounts in /etc/passwd. | ```
root:x:0:0:root:/root:/bin/bash
bin:x:1:1:bin:/bin:/sbin/nologin
daemon:x:2:2:daemon:/sbin:/sbin/nologin
adm:x:3:4:adm:/var/adm:/sbin/nologin
lp:x:4:7:lp:/var/spool/lpd:/sbin/nologin
sync:x:5:0:sync:/sbin:/bin/sync
shutdown:x:6:0:shutdown:/sbin:/sbin/shutdown
halt:x:7:0:halt:/sbin:/sbin/halt
mail:x:8:12:mail:/var/spool/mail:/sbin/nologin
news:x:9:13:news:/var/spool/news:
uucp:x:10:14:uucp:/var/spool/uucp:/sbin/nologin
operator:x:11:0:operator:/root:/sbin/nologin
games:x:12:100:games:/usr/games:/sbin/nologin
gopher:x:13:30:gopher:/var/gopher:/sbin/nologin
ftp:x:14:50:FTP User:/var/ftp:/sbin/nologin
nobody:x:99:99:Nobody:/:/sbin/nologin
vcsa:x:69:69:virtual console memory owner:/dev:/sbin/nologin
rpm:x:37:37::/var/lib/rpm:/bin/bash
nscd:x:28:28:NSCD Daemon:/:/bin/false
ntp:x:38:38::/etc/ntp:/sbin/nologin
apache:x:48:48:Apache:/var/www:/bin/false
radvd:x:75:75:radvd user:/:/bin/false
mailnull:x:47:47::/var/spool/mqueue:/sbin/nologin
smmsp:x:51:51:/var/spool/mqueue:/sbin/nologin
pcap:x:77:77::/var/arpwatch:/sbin/nologin
sshd:x:74:74:Privilege-separated SSH:/var/empty/sshd:/sbin/nologin
ident:x:98:98:pident user:/:/sbin/nologin
"/etc/passwd" [readonly] 37L, 1610C                    1,1            Top
``` |
```

CERTIFICATION OBJECTIVE 11.02

Red Hat User Private Group Scheme

One major difference between Red Hat Linux and other versions of Unix or Linux is how new users are assigned to groups. Traditionally, users are assigned to one or more groups such as *users* in /etc/group. For example, you might configure *accgrp* for the accounting department and *infosys* for the information systems department in your company.

If you have access to one of these other versions of Unix or Linux, check the third and fourth fields in /etc/passwd. Many users will have the same fourth field, which represents their *primary* group. Then, when you create a new user, each account receives a unique user ID but shares the same group ID with other users in the acct group. Users can still belong to other groups as well.

On the other hand, Red Hat Linux normally gives each user a unique user ID and group ID in /etc/passwd. This is known as the *user private group* scheme.

A Linux group allows its members to share files. Unfortunately, that also means everyone in the same primary group has access to the home directories of all other group members. Users may not always want to share the files in their home directories with others. For example, if you're setting up an ISP, your users pay for their privacy.

With Linux, you can set up a specific shared directory for a secondary group. The group ownership of a new directory can be reconfigured for all members of that group. All authorized users are added to the appropriate entry in /etc/group. When you set the group ID bit (SGID) on this directory, any file created in this directory inherits the group ID. Assuming you have set appropriate permissions, all group members can then access files in that the directory.

For example, suppose you have a group set up for the users in the accounting department called accgrp, and you would like to create a shared directory called accshared under /home:

```
# mkdir   /home/accshared
# chown   nobody:accgrp  /home/accshared
# chmod   2770  /home/accshared
```

Any user who is a member of the accgrp group can now create files in the /home/accshared directory. Any files generated will then be associated with the accgrp group ID, and all users listed on the accgrp line in the /etc/group file will have read, write, and execute access to the accshared directory.

```
[root]# grep accgrp /etc/group
accgrp:x:1212:stewardh,jamiec,davidw,debl,callend,vanessar
```

The permissions associated with the **chmod 2770 /home/accshared** command are important. Otherwise, users who are members of accgrp and belong to another primary group would have to remember to use the chgrp command on every file they put in /home/accshared. While clumsy, that command allows other users in that group to access the file.

But it isn't necessary. The solution to this particular problem is the *set group ID bit*, or the *SGID bit*. When the SGID bit is set for a directory, any files created in that directory automatically have their group ownership set to be that of the group owner of the directory. There are two ways to set the SGID bit for the /home/accshared directory:

```
chmod  g+s  /home/accshared
```

or alternatively:

```
chmod  2770 /home/accshared
```

Setting the SGID bit solves the problem of making sure all files created in a shared directory belong to the correct group—as long as the umask is set properly.

By default in Red Hat Linux, all regular users have a umask of 0002. If you are coming from a traditional Unix environment, you may be concerned. With the traditional user/group scheme, any member of that user's primary group will automatically have write access to any file that the user creates in his home directory.

This is the advantage behind the user private group scheme. Since every user account is the only member in its own private group, having the umask set to 002 does not affect file security.

EXERCISE 11-2

Controlling Group Ownership with the SGID Bit

In this exercise, you will create new files in a directory where the SGID bit is set.

1. Add users called *test1*, *test2*, and *test3*. Check the /etc/passwd and /etc/group files to verify that each user's private group was created:

```
# /usr/sbin/useradd test1; passwd test1
# /usr/sbin/useradd test2; passwd test2
# /usr/sbin/useradd test3; passwd test3
```

2. Edit the /etc/group file and add a group called *tg1*. Make the *test1* and *test2* accounts a member of this group. The line you add should look like this:

```
#  echo 'tg1::9999:test1,test2' >> /etc/group
```

Make sure the group ID you assign to group *tg1* is not already in use.

3. Create a shared director for the *tg1* group:

```
# mkdir  /home/testshared
```

4. Change the user and group ownership of the shared directory:

```
# chown  nobody.tg1  /home/testshared
```

5. Log in as *test1* and *test2* separately. Change the directory to the *testshared* directory and try to create a file. What happens?

```
[test1]$ date  >>test.txt
```

6. Now as the root user, set group write permissions on the *testshared* directory. Log in again as user test1, and then try to create a file. Check the ownership on the file:

```
# chmod 770 /home/testshared
[test1]$ date  >>test.txt
[test1]$ ls -l test.txt
```

7. From the *root* account, set the SGID bit on the directory.

```
[root]# chmod g+s  /home/testshared
```

8. Switch back to the *test1* account and create another file. Check the ownership on this file:

```
[test1]$ date >> testb.txt
[test1]$ ls  -l
```

9. Now log in as the test2 account. Go into the /home/testshared directory, create a different file, and use ls -l to check permissions and ownership again.

10. Switch to the test3 account and check whether you can or cannot create files in this directory, and whether you can or cannot view the files in this directory.

CERTIFICATION OBJECTIVE 11.03

tmpwatch

The tmpwatch command (/usr/sbin/tmpwatch) is used to remove files that have not been accessed in a specified number of hours. As its name implies, it is normally run on directories such as /tmp and /var/tmp. The tmpwatch command works recursively, so if you specify the top-level directory in a tree, tmpwatch will search through the entire directory tree looking for files to remove.

Here is an example, which uses tmpwatch to delete all files in the /tmp directory that haven't been accessed within a week (7×24 = 168 hours):

```
/usr/sbin/tmpwatch  168  /tmp
```

Although you can run the tmpwatch command from the command line, it is often more practical to set it up to be run by the cron daemon on a regular basis. By default, Red Hat Linux sets up tmpwatch to delete files in /tmp and /var/tmp every 10 and 30 days, respectively.

EXERCISE 11-3

Clearing an Imaginary /db Directory

In a bizarre twist of fate, a runaway process has just created 200 temporary files in /db that it did not remove. You could remove them manually, or you can let tmpwatch delete all the files that are more than one hour old. Note that this removes all files over an hour old, not just these imaginary files, so this should *not* be done on a production server directory. If you have /db, do *not* use it. If necessary, create a separate directory just for the purpose of this exercise.

```
[root]# cp /etc/* /db    # copying a large number of files to /db
[root]# ls /db | wc -w  # how may files need to be removed
```

Wait at least an hour.

```
[root]# /usr/sbin/tmpwatch 1 /db
[root]# ls /db            # files should be gone
```

Alternatively, you can copy or extract files from an older backup or tar archive to the /db directory, and have tmpwatch delete them. If they are all more than seven days old, then use 168 as the waiting period. You could even try various times to see which files are deleted.

CERTIFICATION OBJECTIVE 11.04

The Linux Rescue Process

At some point in your career as a Red Hat Linux systems administrator, maybe even on the RHCE exam, you're going to be faced with a system that will not boot. It will be up to you to determine the cause of the problem and implement a fix. Sometimes, the problem may be due to hardware failure: the system in question has a bad power supply or has experienced a hard disk crash.

Quite often, however, the failure of a system to boot can be traced back to the actions of a user: you, the system administrator! When you are editing certain system configuration files, typographical errors can render your system unbootable.

Any time you plan to make any substantial modifications to your system or change key configuration files, back them up first. Then, after making changes, you should actually reboot your system rather than assume that it will boot up the next time you need a reboot. It's much better to encounter problems while you can still remember exactly which changes you made. It is even better if you can go back to a working configuration file.

To prepare for boot failures, you should make sure you have a valid boot floppy for your system. But boot floppies can be lost. So it's also important to know how to use the Red Hat installation boot disk or CD to get to the **linux rescue** mode, first discussed in Chapter 3. Refer to that chapter for more information on creating a installation boot disk.

Know every detail that you can about linux rescue mode.

A mkbootdisk Boot Floppy

When you installed Red Hat Linux, the last screen may have asked whether you wanted a boot disk. If you answered No to this prompt, you can still create a valid boot floppy for your computer using the /sbin/mkbootdisk command. The /sbin/mkbootdisk command reads the selected kernel images in /boot and the default boot loader, GRUB or LILO, to create a LILO-style boot image on a floppy disk. For example, if your current kernel is version 2.4.24-2, use this command:

```
[root]#  mkbootdisk  2.4.24-2
```

You may be able to fix a few problems, such as accidentally deleting your master boot record, by booting from your boot disk. If the kernel can't locate the root filesystem, or if the root filesystem is damaged, the Linux kernel will issue a kernel panic and halt as shown in the following code:

```
Creating root device
Mounting root filesystem
kjournald starting. Commit interval 5 seconds
EXT3-fs: mounted filesystems with ordered data mode.
pivotroot: pivot_root (/sysroot,/sysroot/initrd) failed: 2)
Freeing unused kernel memory: 272k freed
Kernel panic: No init found. Try passing init= option to kernel
```

Although this may look very bad the first time you encounter it, often the problem can easily be fixed from rescue mode with a little bit of work. Other problems may also require the use of rescue mode.

Installation Disk Rescue Mode

As discussed in Chapter 3, you can start Linux in rescue mode from the Red Hat Linux installation CD or boot disk. When you type **linux rescue** at the installation boot prompt, a compact version of a root filesystem is installed. As this information has to fit on a 1.44MB floppy disk, it includes a minimal set of utilities that will allow you to mount a disk and either repair the problem with the disk or edit the broken files on the disk.

To boot into rescue mode, first boot your system either using your boot floppy or directly with the first binary CD in a bootable CD-ROM drive, as shown in Figure 11-2.

At the boot: prompt, type **linux rescue** and press ENTER. At first, it's as if rescue mode isn't working; you're taken through the first steps of Red Hat Linux installation,

FIGURE 11-2

Entering rescue
mode from an
installation disk

```
    -  To install or upgrade Red Hat Linux in graphical mode,
       press the <ENTER> key.

    -  To install or upgrade Red Hat Linux in text mode, type:
       linux text <ENTER>.

    -  Use the function keys listed below for more information.

[F1-Main] [F2-Options] [F3-General] [F4-Kernel] [F5-Rescue]
boot: linux rescue_
```

in text mode. You'll need to enter a language, a keyboard type, and the location of the Red Hat Linux installation files. If you started **linux rescue** from a bootnet.img floppy, you may also need the network location of the Red Hat Linux installation files. Once the files associated with linux rescue mode are loaded, you'll see the screen shown in Figure 11-3.

As you can see, you now have three choices:

- **Continue** will search through and mount the available filesystems.

- **Read-Only** performs the same tasks as Continue, except all filesystems that are found are mounted read-only.

- **Skip** does not try to look through the available filesystems. Instead, it proceeds directly to a root shell prompt.

Standard Linux Rescue Mode

When you select Continue in Figure 11-3, you're taken through the standard Linux rescue mode. The rescue files search for your root directory (/) filesystem. If found,

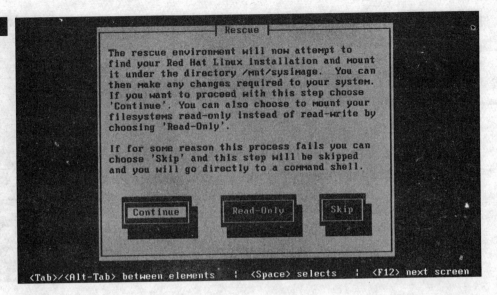

FIGURE 11-3

linux rescue
mode

your root directory (/) is mounted on /mnt/sysimage. All of your other regular filesystems are subdirectories of root; for example, your /etc directory will be found on /mnt/sysimage/etc.

Not all of your filesystems may mount properly. You may see error messages such as:

```
Error mounting filesystem on sdb1: Invalid argument
```

This suggests that at least the filesystem that you would normally mount on /dev/sdb1 isn't working for some reason. If the linux rescue system can mount your root directory (/), you'll see a message like Figure 11-4.

Click OK. You'll use the chroot command shortly. Now you can work on repairing any files or filesystems that might be damaged. First, check for unmounted filesystems. Run a df command and compare the output to the /mnt/sysimage/etc/fstab configuration file. If some filesystem is not mounted, it may be configured incorrectly in the fstab file. Alternatively, the label associated with a partition may not match the filesystem shown in fstab. For example, to find the label associated with /dev/sda1, run the following command:

```
# e2label /dev/sda1
```

which should return the name of a filesystem to be mounted on that partition such as /boot. An example of this is shown in Figure 11-5.

FIGURE 11-4

Linux rescue
mounted your
root directory.

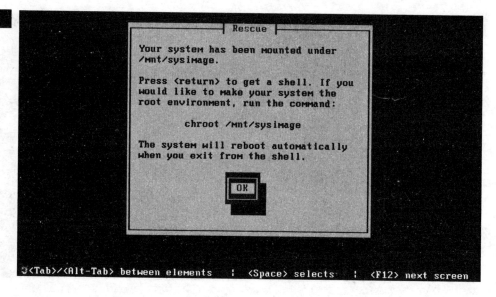

```
                          ┤ Rescue ├

        Your system has been mounted under
        /mnt/sysimage.

        Press <return> to get a shell. If you
        would like to make your system the
        root environment, run the command:

                chroot /mnt/sysimage

        The system will reboot automatically
        when you exit from the shell.

                        ┌────┐
                        │ OK │
                        └────┘
```

```
 <Tab>/<Alt-Tab> between elements  :  <Space> selects  :  <F12> next screen
```

Sometimes an unmounted filesystem just needs a little cleaning; remember, a command such as the following cleans the /dev/sdb1 partition.

```
# fsck /dev/sdb1
```

The fsck command works only on an unmounted filesystem.

Remember the message in Figure 11-4? All you need to do to restore the original filesystem structure is to run the following command:

```
# chroot /mnt/sysimage
```

When you use the rescue disk, your standard root directory (/) is actually mounted on the /mnt/sysimage directory. This command resets your standard root directory (/), so you don't have to go to the /mnt/sysimage subdirectory.

FIGURE 11-5

Finding labels,
filesystems, and
partitions

```
# df
Filesystem        1k-blocks     Used Available Use% Mounted on
rootfs                 2401      724      1540  32% /
/dev/root.old          2401      724      1540  32% /
/dev/ram              15491     8222      6469  56% /tmp/ramfs
/dev/sda2           3644800  1497608   1962044  43% /mnt/sysimage
/dev/sda1            101089     9514     86356  10% /mnt/sysimage/boot
# e2label /dev/sda1
/boot
# _
```

This command allows you to run any commands or utilities that may be sensitive to the PATH such as the **man** command. So if you need to look up some **man** documentation, run the **chroot /mnt/sysimage** command first. When you've made your changes, run the **sync** command three times and type the **exit** command. Linux should automatically stop, allowing you to reboot or restart your computer.

Normally it should not be necessary to run the sync command. However, running it several times does make sure that any pending data is actually written to your floppy and hard disks.

Read-Only Linux Rescue Mode

There is little difference between regular and read-only rescue mode. The linux rescue system attempts to do everything that it would under regular mode, except all partitions are mounted read-only.

This is appropriate if you have a large number of mounted filesystems; it can help you cull through what is and isn't working with less risk of overwriting key configuration files.

No Mount Linux Rescue Mode

A minimal root image from this rescue mode is loaded into a RAM disk created by the kernel. Once it is loaded, you are taken to a root shell prompt (#). At this point, you have access to a basic set of commands. You can mount filesystems, create directories, move files, and edit files using vi. You can apply the fdisk and fsck commands to various hard disks and partitions. A few other basic commands are also available.

The great difficulty in operating from the rescue environment is that you are working with a minimal version of the Linux operating system. Many of the commands you are used to having at your disposal are not available at this level. If your root partition has not been completely destroyed, you may be able to mount this partition to your temporary root directory in memory and access commands from there.

If you mount partitions from your hard drive in rescue mode and then make changes to files on those partitions, remember to use the sync command. Otherwise, the changes may not be written to disk before you reboot. Alternatively, a umount command applied to any partition performs the same task.

Single-User Mode

One other option to help rescue a damaged Linux system is *single-user mode*. This is appropriate if your system can find at least the root filesystem (/). Your system may not have problems finding its root partition and starting the boot process, but it may encounter problems such as damaged configuration files, or an inability to boot into one of the higher runlevels. In this case, you can try booting into single-user mode. If this is the case, you can still use the boot partition and root partition on your hard drive, but you want to tell Linux to perform a minimal boot process. Assuming that you're using GRUB, press P to enter the GRUB password if required. Press A to modify the kernel arguments. When you see a line similar to

```
grub append> ro root=LABEL=/
```

add one of the following commands (shown in bold) to the end of that line:

```
grub append> ro root=LABEL=/ single
grub append> ro root=LABEL=/ 1
grub append> ro root=LABEL=/ init=/bin/sh
```

Alternatively, if you're using LILO, the linux single command will do nicely. Any of these commands will boot Linux into a minimal runtime environment, and you will receive a bash shell prompt *(bash#).*

When you boot into single-user mode, no password is required to access the system. Running your system in single-user mode is somewhat similar to running a system booted into rescue mode. Many of the commands and utilities you normally use are unavailable. You may have to mount additional drives or partitions and specify the full pathname when running some commands. When you have corrected the problem, you can reboot the system or use the init or telinit commands to bring the system up to its normal runlevel, probably 3 or 5.

on the Job

In single-user mode, any user can change the root password. You do not want people rebooting your computer to go into single-user mode to change your root password. Therefore, it's important to keep your server in a secure location. Alternatively, you can password-protect GRUB to keep anyone with physical access to your computer from booting it in single-user mode.

What to Look for When Things Go Wrong

Although there are potentially many things that will cause a system not to boot, they can roughly be categorized as either hardware problems or software and configuration problems. The most common hardware-related problem you will probably encounter is a bad hard disk drive; like all mechanical devices with moving parts, these have a finite lifetime and will eventually fail. Fortunately, the RHCE exam does not require you to address hardware failures.

Software and configuration problems, however, can be a little more difficult. At first glance, they can look just like regular hardware problems.

In addition to knowing how to mount disk partitions, edit files, and manipulate files, you will need to know how to use several other commands in order to be able to fix problems from rescue mode or single-user mode. The most useful of these are the fdisk command and the fsck command. Unfortunately, when you boot into single-user mode, you can't get to the man pages. Therefore, if you don't have access to the man pages in another way, you need to know how these commands work at least at a rudimentary level.

fdisk

The Linux fdisk command has already been covered in Chapter 3. When you use fdisk, you can find the partitions you have available for mounting. For example, the **fdisk -l /dev/hda** command lists available partitions on the first IDE hard disk:

```
[root]# fdisk -l /dev/hda

Disk /dev/hda: 240 heads, 63 sectors, 559 cylinders
Units = cylinders of 15120 * 512 bytes

    Device    Boot    Start       End     Blocks   Id  System
/dev/hda1      *         1        41     309928+    6  FAT32
/dev/hda2               42       559    3916080     5  Extended
/dev/hda5               42        44      22648+   83  Linux
/dev/hda6               45        53      68000+   82  Linux swap
/dev/hda7               54       192    1050808+   83  Linux
```

Looking at the output from the fdisk command, it's easy to identify the only partitions configured with a Linux format, /dev/hda5 and /dev/hda7. Given the size of each partition, it is reasonable to conclude that /dev/hda5 is associated with /boot, and /dev/hda7 is associated with root (/).

For simple partitioning schemes, this is easy. It gets far more complicated when you have lots of partitions, as in this next example. You should always have some documentation available that clearly identifies your partition layout within your filesystem:

```
[root]# fdisk -1 /dev/hda
Disk /dev/hda: 255 heads, 63 sectors, 2495 cylinders
Units = cylinders of 16065 * 512 bytes

    Device   Boot   Start      End    Blocks    Id  System
/dev/hda1     *       1       255   2048256     c  Win95 FAT32 (LBA)
/dev/hda2            256       257     16065    83  Linux
/dev/hda3            258      2495  17976735     5  Extended
/dev/hda5            258       576   2562336    83  Linux
/dev/hda6            577       608    257008+   83  Linux
/dev/hda7            609       634    208813+   83  Linux
/dev/hda8            635       660    208813+   83  Linux
/dev/hda9            661       673    104391    83  Linux
/dev/hda10           674       686    104391    83  Linux
/dev/hda11           687       699    104391    83  Linux
/dev/hda12           700       712    104391    83  Linux
/dev/hda13           713       723     88326    82  Linux swap
/dev/hda14           724       978   2048256    83  Linux
/dev/hda15           979      1900   7405933+   83  Linux
/dev/hda16          1901      2495   4779306    83  Linux
```

In this example, it's easy to identify the Linux swap partition. Since /boot partitions are small and normally configured toward the front of a drive, it's reasonable to associate it with /dev/hda2.

e2label

Based on the previous example, you probably could use a little help to identify the filesystems associated with the other partitions. That's where the e2label command can help. When you set up a new filesystem, the associated partition is normally marked with a label. For example, the following command tells you that the /usr filesystem is normally mounted on /dev/hda5.

```
[root]# e2label
Usage: e2label device [newlabel]
[root]# e2label /dev/hda5
/usr
[root]#
```

dumpe2fs

You can get a lot more information on each partition with the dumpe2fs command. For example, take a look at the following output from a **/sbin/dumpe2fs /dev/sda1** command in Figure 11-6.

The dumpe2fs command not only does the job of e2label but also tells you about the format, whether it has a journal, and the block size. Proceed further down this list, and you'll find the locations for backup superblocks, which can help you use fsck or e2fsck command to check select the appropriate superblock for your Linux partition.

on the **Job**

fsck is a "front end" for e2fsck, which is used to check partitions formatted to the ext2 and ext3 filesystems.

FIGURE 11-6

dumpe2fs gives lots of information.

```
Filesystem volume name:   /boot
Last mounted on:          <not available>
Filesystem UUID:          35b95402-8ea4-11d6-87b1-8029935a99e0
Filesystem magic number:  0xEF53
Filesystem revision #:    1 (dynamic)
Filesystem features:      has_journal filetype needs_recovery sparse_super
Filesystem state:         clean
Errors behavior:          Continue
Filesystem OS type:       Linux
Inode count:              26104
Block count:              104391
Reserved block count:     5219
Free blocks:              91603
Free inodes:              26064
First block:              1
Block size:               1024
Fragment size:            1024
Blocks per group:         8192
Fragments per group:      8192
Inodes per group:         2008
Inode blocks per group:   251
Last mount time:          Thu Jul  4 01:41:18 2002
Last write time:          Thu Jul  4 01:41:18 2002
Mount count:              1
Maximum mount count:      -1
Last checked:             Thu Jul  4 01:41:01 2002
Check interval:           0 (<none>)
Reserved blocks uid:      0 (user root)
Reserved blocks gid:      0 (group root)
First inode:              11
Inode size:               128
Journal UUID:             <none>
Journal inode:            8
Journal device:           0x0000
:
```

Filesystem Check—fsck

You should also know how to use the fsck command. This command is a front end for most of the filesystem formats available in Linux, such as ext2, ext3, reiserfs, and more. This command is used to check the filesystem on a partition for consistency. In order to effectively use the fsck command, you need to understand something about how filesystems are laid out on disk partitions.

When you format a disk partition under Linux using the mkfs command, it sets aside a certain portion of the disk to use for storing *inodes,* which are data structures that contain the actual disk block addresses that point to file data on a disk. The mkfs command also stores information about the size of the filesystem, the filesystem label, and the number of inodes in a special location at the start of the partition called the *superblock.* If the superblock is corrupted or destroyed, the remaining information on the disk is unreadable. Because the superblock is so vital to the integrity of the data on a partition, the mkfs command makes duplicate copies of the superblock at fixed intervals on the partition, which you can find with the dumpe2fs command described earlier.

The fsck command checks for, and corrects problems with, filesystem consistency by looking for things such as disk blocks that are marked as free but are actually in use (and vice versa), inodes that don't have a corresponding directory entry, inodes with incorrect link counts, and a number of other problems. The fsck command will also fix a corrupted superblock. If fsck fails due to a corrupt superblock, you can use the fsck command with the -b option to specify an alternative superblock. For example, the command:

```
# fsck -b 8193 /dev/hda5
```

tells fsck to perform a consistency check on the filesystem on disk partition /dev/hda5, using the superblock located at disk block 8193.

Get to know the key commands and the associated options for checking disks and partitions: fdisk, e2label, dumpe2fs, and fsck. Practice using these commands to check your partitions—on a test computer! (Some of these commands can destroy data.)

Boot Loaders

There are two boot loaders, GRUB and LILO. While you may be more familiar with LILO, Red Hat Linux is adapting GRUB as the default boot loader. One of the benefits is that any changes that you make to the GRUB configuration file, /boot/grub/grub.conf, need not be written to your hard disk's Master Boot Record.

Alternatively, if you are using LILO, you need to run the /sbin/lilo command whenever you rebuild your Linux kernel or change the disk partition associated with the /boot directory. Otherwise, LILO may not be able to find your boot files. In this case, you will have to use linux rescue mode to fix the problem.

In either case, errors to the boot loader configuration file are a common problem that can keep Linux from booting properly.

Places to Look First

Two places where you are likely to make errors that result in a nonbootable system are in the bootloader and filesystem configuration files, /boot/grub/grub.conf and /etc/fstab. In each case, identifying the wrong partition as the root partition (/) can lead to a kernel panic. Other configuration errors in /boot/grub/grub.conf can also cause a kernel panic when you boot Linux. Whenever you make changes to these files, the only way to test them out is to reboot Linux.

As a Red Hat Linux administrator, you will be expected to know how to fix the operating system when key files are improperly configured. For this reason, a substantial portion of the exam is devoted to testing your troubleshooting and analysis skills.

Summary of the Linux Rescue Process

The easiest way to rescue a system is with a customized boot disk. If that is not available, you'll also need to know how to use the Linux rescue mode to rescue a system, using the following basic steps:

■ Boot using a Red Hat Linux installation floppy or CD.

■ Know the location of your installation files, from CD or over a network. You are taken to single-user mode.

■ At the rescue shell prompt, use **fdisk -l** *diskdevice* to identify your partitions.

■ If filesystem problems are suspected or indicated, run fsck on the afflicted partitions.

■ If the problem is with a configuration file:

  1. Create (a) temporary mount point(s), if necessary

  2. Mount the appropriate partition(s), if necessary.

  3. Use the vi editor to fix the problem in the broken file(s).

- Sync your changes to the drive.
- Unmount any mounted partitions.
- *Exit* and restart the system.

on the **job**

Whenever you're working in rescue mode or single-user mode, always remember to sync your drives before halting.

EXERCISE 11-4

Performing an Emergency Boot Procedure

To do this exercise, you should have a test system at your disposal. Do not try this exercise on any system on which you are not prepared to lose all of the data on the system.

In this exercise, you will "break" your system by purposely misconfiguring a file and then reboot into rescue mode to fix the problem. You will have to replace the partitions used in the commands for the /boot and root partitions with the actual partitions that are used for the /boot and root partitions on your system.

1. Make sure you have the Red Hat Linux distribution cd mounted:

   ```
   # mount  /dev/cdrom  /mnt/cdrom
   ```

2. Install the mkbootdisk RPM if required:

   ```
   # rpm  -ivh  /mnt/cdrom/RedHat/RPMS/mkbootdisk*
   ```

3. If you do not have a boot disk, make one. Insert a floppy into the disk drive and type the following:

   ```
   # /sbin/mkbootdisk `uname -r`
   ```

4. Edit the file /boot/grub/etc/grub.conf and make a copy of your boot stanza. Title this stanza badboot. Change the location of the root device to point to an invalid partition. For example, if your original grub.conf looks like this:

   ```
   default=0
   timeout=10
   splashimage=(hd0,0)/grub/splash.xpm.gz
   title Red Hat Linux (2.4.18-5.58)
           root=(hd0,0)
           kernel /vmlinuz-2.4.18-5.58 ro root=LABEL=/
           initrd /initrd-2.4.18-5.58.img
   ```

your new version should look like this:

```
default=0
timeout=10
splashimage=(hd0,0)/grub/splash.xpm.gz
title Red Hat Linux (2.4.18-5.58)
        root=(hd0,0)
        kernel /vmlinuz-2.4.18-5.58 ro root=LABEL=/
        initrd /initrd-2.4.18-5.58.img
title badboot
        root=(hd0,1)
        kernel /vmlinuz-2.4.18-5.58 ro root=LABEL=/
        initrd /initrd-2.4.18-5.58.img
```

5. Reboot your system. In the GRUB menu, select badboot. GRUB will return a File Not Found message.

6. Since you left a valid boot stanza, your system isn't really broken. To fix the problem, however, we're going to boot into rescue mode. Insert your Installation CD (or Installation boot disk and Installation CD), and reboot the system. At the prompt, type **linux rescue**.

7. Proceed through the first steps of the Red Hat Linux installation process.

8. When you see the Rescue menu, select Skip. None of your partitions will be mounted.

9. Although you know the source of the problem, once you boot into rescue mode, you should familiarize yourself with some of the repair utilities:

```
# fdisk  -l
   Device Boot    Start      End    Blocks  Id  System
/dev/hda1   *        1        3    22648+   83  Linux
/dev/hda2           54      559  3916080    83  Linux
/dev/hda3           45       53    68000+   82  Linux swap

fsck  -y  /dev/hda1  # your output will vary
e2fsck 1.27, 8-Mar-2002
/dev/hda1: clean, 23/5664 files, 3008/22648 blocks
```

10. Create (a) temporary mount point(s) for your /boot and root partitions, and mount those partitions (if they are not already mounted). If the output from **fdisk -l** is different for you, revise the mounted devices accordingly.

```
# mkdir  /tmpmnt
# mount  /dev/hda2  /tmpmnt
# mount  /dev/hda1  /tmpmnt/boot
```

11. Edit the bad stanza in grub.conf and fix the problems:

```
# vi /tmpmnt/boot/grub/grub.conf
```

12. Your new version should look like this:

```
title badboot
        root=(hd0,0)
        kernel /vmlinuz-2.4.18-5.58
        initrd /initrd-2.4.18-5.58.img
```

13. Save your changes to the grub.conf file.

14. Sync your changes and unmount any mounted partitions:

```
# sync
# sync
# sync
```

15. Remove any boot media from your disk drives. Type **exit** to unmount all drives and restart the system. You should now be able to boot from the badboot stanza.

CERTIFICATION OBJECTIVE 11.05

The Secure Shell Package

Red Hat Linux includes the OpenSSH Secure Shell package. The Secure Shell (ssh) and secure copy program (scp) are secure replacements for the rsh, telnet, and rcp programs. The secure daemon, sshd, listens for all inbound traffic on port 22. The SSH configuration files are located in the /etc/ssh directory.

The Secure Shell daemon works because it encrypts messages.

Basic Encrypted Communication

Basic encryption in computer networking normally requires a private key and a public key. You keep the private key and send the public key to others. When they want to send data to you though SSH, their messages are encrypted with the public key. Your computer can descramble the message with the private key.

Encryption keys are based on random numbers. The numbers are so large (typically 512 bits or more), the chance that someone will break into your system, at least with a PC, is quite small in the foreseeable future. Private and public encryption keys are based on a matched set of these random numbers.

Private Keys

Your private key (essentially a file with your special number) must be secure. When you enable an application, it can attach the key to your messages. Anything you send, say from your e-mail account, can then be digitally signed and encrypted. The public key is added to the end as part of your signature. Only the recipient will be able to decrypt the message.

Public Keys

Your public key value is just that, publicly available. A central authority such as Verisign, Globalsign, or Thawte provides public access to public keys they have created. If they generate a private key for you, they'll keep a secure copy on their system. You can just attach your public key to the e-mail, or the end users can publicly retrieve it from the Web site associated with the central authority.

The example shown in Figure 11-7 lists the directories and files associated with SSH usage as well as a public key that has been "added" to your "keyring."

This key is like a password used to encrypt your data. Imagine trying to remember the 1024-bit number expressed in hexadecimal value as shown in Figure 11-8! That is why the applications save this value for you, on a "public keyring." You can add as many public keys from other users, sites, and services as you wish.

FIGURE 11-7

A public key

```
[root@RH80 root]# ls .ssh/
id_dsa  id_dsa.pub identity  identity.pub
[root@RH80 root]# cat .ssh/id_dsa.pub
ssh-dss AAAAB3NzaC1kc3MAAACBAMEoM4z7ad8EwdyyUyH1ZHdhsnN+MzCO1h1EL5Nt7LZjL7nyvMLj
6guYR/O9QOYmfvXOiUyOjDROvXukR367fPkdmI3r1XpBBz6Dj21sfbOWtJExOtI10d80j41fRC4ZzPoh
rGMAy+bLVRDlThiSKIYOP/DDpcA2q86mtZUW9w7XAAAAFQD8jEridN4XTOokOYfMmOPIVxs4iQAAAIEA
uZuZUymr1FZWsdo+XCRg9xbjNBUP1WE+DN6k7HObNO2bx0zmgDGB+1qK4yEGqm8ZtyMoSUQajvLQjEAr
Bjnms+vo5/oPj/2LgQiKiIQCPx4/QVi1P520oU+2rVYGKcUs2cqx3+eowZfGqsZoCxr2CYe8P4VnqD5a
O/qcx10Goi4AAACBAJ4jd9eot+15hCgZ3J2Po03WtUq/eQi5CTuYu13mIDqLPw4KT2Wtx2rI9we8510K
yradQ3+P89T+y3O2U6YHEPnNqTRHfxDfpU+HCyhOc5bLLJNA+DqYSC/2Ed6TV3RuI5DfxgtOnBfWIQbA
z20RW5CkoiTeOhwUqkUUTt5415Xc root@RH80
[root@RH80 root]# █
```

FIGURE 11-8

A sample
1024-bit public
key certificate

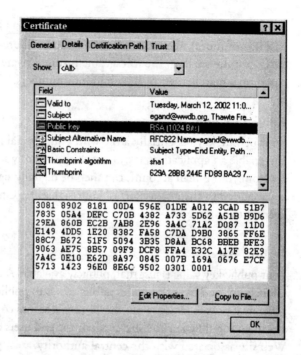

Your private key is similar, *but you must keep it private,* or this whole system fails. Keeping it private means no one should have access to your PC, or if they do, add a passphrase (password), as shown in Figure 11-9, in order to use this key.

FIGURE 11-9

Generating
encryption keys

```
[root@RH80 root]# ssh-keygen -t dsa
Generating public/private dsa key pair.
Enter file in which to save the key (/root/.ssh/id_dsa):
Enter passphrase (empty for no passphrase):
Enter same passphrase again:
Your identification has been saved in /root/.ssh/id_dsa.
Your public key has been saved in /root/.ssh/id_dsa.pub.
The key fingerprint is:
bd:93:34:d5:a5:0b:2f:52:67:0e:bc:d7:c9:f4:6d:d8 root@RH80
[root@RH80 root]# ssh-keygen -t rsa1
Generating public/private rsa1 key pair.
Enter file in which to save the key (/root/.ssh/identity):
Enter passphrase (empty for no passphrase):
Enter same passphrase again:
Your identification has been saved in /root/.ssh/identity.
Your public key has been saved in /root/.ssh/identity.pub.
The key fingerprint is:
3f:8f:ca:20:cc:9b:a8:6a:4f:b3:d9:49:34:71:4c:21 root@RH80
[root@RH80 root]# []
```

How to Generate Your Keys

There are a few SSH-oriented utilities you need to know about:

- **sshd** The daemon service; this must be running for inbound Secure Shell client requests.

- **ssh-agent** A program to hold private keys used for RSA authentication. The idea is that ssh-agent is started in the beginning of an X session or a login session, and all other windows or programs are started as clients to the ssh-agent program.

- **ssh-add** Adds RSA identities to the authentication agent, ssh-agent.

- **ssh** The Secure Shell command, ssh, is a secure way to log in to a remote machine, similar to Telnet or rlogin. To make this work, you need a private key on the server, and a public key on the client. Take the public key file, identity.pub or id_dsa.pub, created later in this section. Copy it to the client. Place it in the home directory of an authorized user, in the ~/.ssh/authorized_keys or ~/.ssh/authorized_keys2 file.

- **ssh-keygen** A utility that will create your keys for you. The **ssh-keygen -t** *keytype* command will create the keys you desire. The *keytype* can be dsa (Digital Secure Algorithm) or rsa1 (RSA Security). The commands work as shown in Figure 11-9.

All you need to do is transfer the public key, with the .pub extension, to an authorized user. It's important to add a passphrase to protect that digital signature. In the worst case, a cracker could use this file to effectively steal your identity.

Why Use SSH?

The Internet is a public network. If you're connected to the Internet, anyone in the world could conceivably access your computer through this public network. All that is needed is Internet access from an anonymous location. In other words, a skilled cracker may be able to capture your passwords from a computer in a public library.

In contrast, private networks are used for security applications. Merchants who dial into a central server to check authorized credit card numbers are connecting to a private network. Access to such private networks can be expensive.

Unix and the network that became the Internet started in an educational setting, where there is a premium on the free exchange of information. While the resulting openness of the Internet is good, it can present security challenges. The original Unix tools developed for networks were not designed with security in mind.

These tools include: telnet, ftp, and the "r" (remote) commands (rlogin, rcp, rsh). These utilities pass all information, including login names and passwords, across the network in clear text format. Anyone with a simple protocol analyzer such as Ethereal can find your password in this way. The Ethereal output shown in Figure 11-10 highlights one of the letters in a Telnet password on my private LAN (it's an "e"). The other Telnet packets contain the other letters and or numbers of the password.

on the **Job**

This does not in any way endorse the cracking of passwords. However, as a system administrator, you do need to know your vulnerabilities. If you can trace clear text passwords on your own network, others may be able to trace these passwords as well.

FIGURE 11-10

Deciphering clear text passwords can be easy.

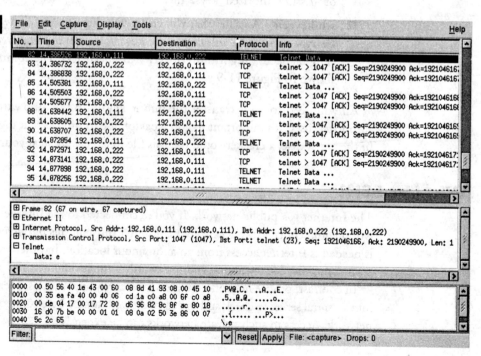

The Secure Shell utilities were an answer to this problem, using high encryption standards. The Secure Shell tools replaced their insecure brethren and provided full encryption of all data between the hosts that is very hard to break, even by the "brute force" method.

Brute Force Decryption

All computer data, including passwords, can be broken down into bits and bytes, in other words, 1s and 0s. If you can see the pattern of bits and bytes, you can decipher the password.

By convention, every character is associated with 7 of the 8 bits in a byte. Now assume you have 8 characters in a password. This makes for a 56-bit password. All you need to do to find the password is to compare it with every possible combination of bits and bytes. In other words, one of the values between 0 and 2^{56} (72,057,594,037,927,936) represents your password.

While this may seem like a large number, it is in fact trivial for a higher-end PC, which could decipher such a password in a matter of hours. This suggests that the older standard for secure HTTP Web pages, 40-bit encryption, is not very secure. On the other hand, the higher-level 128-bit-encrypted browsers are a lot more secure. It would take more than a few years for the latest PCs to break through such encryption.

By default, the ssh-keygen command creates encryption keys with 1024 bits. Breaking into such systems is beyond the capabilities of the latest PCs, using brute-force methods.

Lost Passphrase on Private Keys

Unfortunately, if you lose the passphrase on your private encryption key, there is no way to recover. You would need to start over, which means you would need to create a new set of keys and send your new public key to all concerned for them to replace your old public key.

PGP—Pretty Good Privacy

E-mail has become a standard fixture in everyday business; e-mail security is a significant issue. One of the current standards for managing e-mail security is known as PGP (Pretty Good Privacy), developed by Phil Zimmerman. Like SSH, PGP provides a private- and public-key system for e-mail clients. The public key is usually attached to the end of the data, as shown in the next example.

The Linux implementation of PGP is known as GPG, the Gnu Privacy Guard. GPG is an implementation of the OpenPGP standard. Both standards are now common ways people and companies protect their correspondence.

```
**************************************************************************
To:   Dreg (SD444466)
From: The SANS NewsBites service


************************

---BEGIN PGP SIGNED MESSAGE---
Hash: SHA1
... (text removed)

Please feel free to share this with interested parties via e-mail (not
on bulletin boards).  For a free subscription, (and for free posters)
e-mail sans@sans.org with the subject: Subscribe NewsBites


...

-----BEGIN PGP SIGNATURE-----
Version: GnuPG v1.0.4 (BSD/OS)
Comment: For info see http://www.gnupg.org

iD8DBQE63beV+LUG5KFpTkYRAu/WAJ0fUwoQFUOETTd+wAbe1L784S3PDwCfULr0
DXDk20qZotKDLMfjLz1Gty4=
=K1Av
-----END PGP SIGNATURE-----
```

Notice in the previous listing that the BSD/OS (Berkeley Software Distribution / Operating System) is also using GPG, which is also known as GnuPG.

Validating RPMs with GPG

If you download an RPM from the Internet and would like to verify that it is an official unadulterated Red Hat RPM, GPG can help. All you need is the Red Hat Linux public key. It's available from at least three different locations:

- Each Red Hat installation CD, in the main directory, in the RPM-GPG-KEY file
- On a standard Red Hat Linux installation, in /usr/share/rhn/RPM-GPG-KEY
- Online from www.redhat.com

First, you need to import the key. For example, if you want to import the key from the Red Hat installation CD, mounted on /mnt/cdrom, run the following command:

```
# rpm --import /mnt/cdrom/RPM-GPG-KEY
```

Now you should find the RPM-enabled key in the /var/lib/rpm/Pubkeys file. Next, you can verify the package's PGP-encrypted checksum using the **rpm -K packagename** command. For example, if you wanted to verify the setup package on a downloaded Installation CD, run the following command:

```
# rpm -K /mnt/cdrom/RedHat/RPMS/setup-*
```

 *Older versions of Red Hat Linux used the gpg --import keyfile **command to download the Red Hat public GPG key. This is no longer possible with the advent of RPM version 4.1.***

SCENARIO & SOLUTION

You come into work one morning and find that an extended power failure caused your Web server to shut down even though it was on a UPS. When you try to reboot the system, you get a "kernel panic" message on the console. What is the first thing you should try?	In this situation, the first thing you should try would be to see if you can boot the system from a boot floppy. If the boot floppy fails, then you will have to boot into rescue mode to repair whatever problem is causing the kernel panic.
One of your colleagues is newer at Linux. You've encouraged him to learn everything that he can about the critical files associated with starting Linux. Now his computer won't boot. What should you do?	Ask for a boot floppy. Ideally, you'll have one made with the mkbootdisk command. Otherwise, use a Red Hat installation floppy and go into linux rescue mode. Check several key files, including /etc/grub/grub.conf, /etc/fstab, and /etc/inittab.
You have a limited amount of space on your Linux server, and want to delete files that are more than a year old on users' home directories. You do perform regular backups and can restore older files upon request.	Configure tmpwatch in /etc/cron.daily to delete files in /home that haven't been accessed in more than 8760 hours (365 days × 24 hours/day).

CERTIFICATION SUMMARY

As you've seen in the past two chapters, there are many facets to system security. Making sure that network services run under nonprivileged accounts helps minimize the risks associated with outside attack.

By default, Red Hat Linux assigns unique user and group ID numbers to each new user. This is known as the User Private Group scheme. This scheme allows you to configure special groups for a specific set of users. The users in the group can be configured with read and write privileges in a dedicated directory, courtesy of the SGID bit.

The tmpwatch system is used to clear files from specified directories on a regular basis. The default Red Hat cron daemon configuration sets tmpwatch to clear /tmp and /var/temp. You can reconfigure it to meet your needs.

One of the most valuable skills you can have as a Red Hat Linux systems administrator is knowing how to rescue a system. Some configuration problems can prevent a system from booting. Others can keep you from logging in. Key tools to manage configuration problems include: a boot disk from the /sbin/mkbootdisk command, the linux rescue mode from a Red Hat installation floppy or CD, and single-user mode at the GRUB or LILO prompt. Linux rescue mode loads basic utilities and attempts to remount your directories on /mnt/sysimage. Key tools for managing problems include fdisk, fsck, e2label, and dumpe2fs.

Any network that is connected to an insecure network such as the Internet is vulnerable. Linux's OpenSSH package can help you set up encrypted communication between computers to help protect your passwords and much more. Encryption uses private and public keys. Whether you're using SSH or GPG, the default 1024-bit encryption scheme provides a "reasonable" level of security.

TWO-MINUTE DRILL

Here are some of the key points from the certification objectives in Chapter 11.

Services and Special Users

❑ When Red Hat Linux starts on your computer, it triggers a special process known as init. The init process then opens the other basic processes required for a working Linux system.

❑ Many services have their own user ID, as shown in /etc/passwd.

❑ Alternatively, some services can run under the nobody account.

❑ Service user IDs are not for real users.

Red Hat User Private Group Scheme

❑ Red Hat includes the user private group scheme where users get their own unique user and group ID numbers. The SGID scheme allows you to configure a shared directory for a specific group of users.

❑ Setting the SGID bit ensures that all files created in a shared directory belong to the correct group.

❑ Setting the SGID bit is easy; use chown to set nobody as the user owner, and the name of the group as the group owner. Then run chmod 2770 on the shared directory.

tmpwatch

❑ The tmpwatch command (/usr/sbin/tmpwatch) is used to remove files that have not been accessed in a specified number of hours.

❑ Current versions of Linux have a cron job that runs regularly to clean up the /tmp and /var/tmp directories.

❑ You can configure tmpwatch to clean other directories of your choice.

❑ You can use the tmpwatch command whenever necessary to clean up any directory with older files.

The Linux Rescue Process

❑ One common cause of boot failures is errors by system administrators. Boot disks aren't always available. Be prepared to use the linux rescue mode from a Red Hat installation floppy or CD.

❑ One good boot disk customized for your system can be created with the mkbootdisk command.

❑ When you use linux rescue mode, be able to access the Red Hat installation files.

❑ The linux rescue mode system may be able to mount your filesystems on /mnt/sysimage. It will provide a minimum set of commands such as fdisk and fsck, and utilities such as vi.

❑ If your filesytems are properly mounted, you can access documents such as man pages normally after a **chroot /mnt/sysimage** command.

❑ Linux may not be able to mount all of your filesystems.

❑ Some mount points fail because of bad labels. Check the label on a specific partition with the e2label command.

❑ The fsck command is used to check the filesystem on a partition for consistency.

❑ The dumpe2fs command can provide a lot of information about each partition, including the label, the journal, and the block size.

❑ One alternative to the linux rescue system is single-user mode.

❑ Common problem files that can prevent Linux from booting include /boot/grub/grub.conf and /etc/fstab.

The Secure Shell Package

❑ The OpenSSH utilities—sshd, ssh, ssh-keygen, ssh-add, and ssh-agent— provide secure remote services over any network connections.

❑ Encryption is based on private and public keys.

❑ You can keep your private key secure with a passphrase.

❑ Public keys are to be shared with others, so that they can communicate with you through ssh.

❑ As it is easy to decipher traffic, even passwords, from telnet, ftp, and the "r" commands, it is best to use ssh on any publicly accessible network.

❑ The Secure Shell commands include enough bits to prevent any practical brute-force decryption.

❑ PGP, Pretty Good Privacy, is the way much e-mail is encrypted today.

❑ The Linux implementation of PGP is GPG.

❑ You can validate the signature of any RPM using the gpg utility.

SELF TEST

The following questions will help you measure your understanding of the material presented in this chapter. Read all the choices carefully, as there may be more than one correct answer. Choose all correct answers for each question.

Services and Special Users

1. You are setting up a Red Hat Linux system and are adding several new services. What can you do to make sure your system is more secure from outside attack?

   A. Create individual accounts for each service.

   B. Pick a really secure password for the root account.

   C. Run the services under the nobody account.

   D. Make sure the system is stored in a secure room.

Red Hat User Private Group Scheme

2. You have created a shared directory, owned by a special group. You want to ensure that all members of that group have access to files created in that directory. What should you do?

   A. Assign directory ownership to root.

   B. Assign directory ownership to nobody.

   C. Make sure the directory is in each user's PATH.

   D. Set the SGID bit on the directory.

3. You've just issued the following command: **chown nobody.developgrp /home/developer**. How would you set the SGID bit on this directory?

   A. chmod 2775 /home/developer

   B. chgrp 2775 /home/developer

   C. chmod 775 /home/developer

   D. chmod g+s /home/developer

4. What command would allow full permissions for the user and the group that owns the file?

   A. Instruct all users to type **umask 002** *filename* whenever they create a file.

   B. Place the command umask 002 in /etc/profile.

C. Instruct all users to type **chmod 002** *filename* whenever they create a file.

D. Place the command umask in /etc/profile.

5. When you properly configure the SGID scheme on a special directory, there may be users who are not members of the directory-owning group. What can these users do?

A. Read the files in the directory.

B. Write new files to the directory.

C. Confirm the existence of the directory.

D. It depends on the permissions assigned to others for that directory.

tmpwatch

6. What would you use the tmpwatch command for?

A. To monitor the system for break-in attempts

B. To clean up unused user account directories

C. To scan system-wide temporary directories and clean up old temporary files

D. To monitor the /tmp directory for the appearance of certain files

The Linux Rescue Process

7. The junior system administrator at your site has just come to you to report a suspected bad hard drive on the system he was working on. Whenever he tries to boot the system, he gets a kernel panic with a message saying the root partition cannot be found. What is the most likely cause?

A. The hard drive has crashed.

B. The I/O bus is going bad.

C. Intermittent RAM problems are masquerading as disk problems.

D. The junior system administrator was modifying a system configuration file and has managed to configure the system so that it will not boot.

8. What emergency repair items should you always have on hand?

A. A custom boot floppy for your system

B. A Red Hat installation boot disk or CD

C. Documentation on the partition layouts for the disk drives on your system

D. Documentation on using the repair utilities

9. How would you obtain a boot disk if you don't have one?

   A. Order one from Red Hat.

   B. Run the mkrescuedisk utility.

   C. Place a floppy in the floppy drive, mount the latest Red Hat distribution CD, and issue the command **cp /mnt/cdrom/images/rescue.img /dev/fd0**.

   D. Place a floppy in the floppy drive, mount the latest Red Hat distribution CD, and issue the command **cat /mnt/cdrom/images/boot.img >>/dev/fd0**.

10. How can you boot a damaged Linux system in order to perform repairs?

    A. Boot from your system's custom boot floppy.

    B. Boot into linux rescue mode.

    C. Boot into single-user mode. At the end of the kernel command line in GRUB, add the word *single*.

    D. Boot into runlevel 4.

11. When you boot your Linux system, the boot process does not get much further past the GRUB menu. What should you do?

    A. Boot into rescue mode and run fsck.

    B. Boot into rescue mode and check /etc/fstab for errors.

    C. Boot into rescue mode and check /boot/grub/grub.conf for errors.

    D. Reinstall Linux.

12. You are a consultant and are helping a client who has managed to render his system unbootable. You have booted into rescue mode, but the client doesn't have any documentation on the partition layout on his disk drive. What can you do?

    A. Use the **fdisk -l /dev/devicename** command to display the partition table for the drive.

    B. Reinstall Linux.

    C. Use the fsck command and look for the superblock.

    D. Use the fdisk command in interactive mode.

13. You are trying to boot a system and keep receiving a message about a corrupted partition. You manage to boot into rescue mode. From this point, what might you do to fix the problem?

    A. Use fdisk and delete the partition; then add it back.

    B. Use the **fdisk -l** command.

    C. Run grub-install to rebuild the boot block.

    D. Run the command **fsck -b 8193**.

14. How would you check the name of the directory associated with a specific partition?

    A. Open up /etc/fstab.

    B. Run **fdisk -l** *partitionname*.

    C. Use the sync command to flush changes you make to disk.

    D. Run **e2label** *partitionname*.

15. Where are some likely places for configuration errors that can prevent your system from booting? (Choose all that apply.)

    A. /boot/grub/grub.conf

    B. /etc/fstab

    C. /etc/passwd

    D. /boot

The Secure Shell Package

16. The OpenSSH package allows you to set up a private key and a public key. What do you do with the public key?

    A. Keep it in a protected file on your home directory, accessible only to you and root.

    B. Send it to all of your friends so they can encrypt their e-mail to you.

    C. Send it with your private key to all of your friends so they can encrypt their e-mail to you.

    D. Use it to check the validity of your RPM packages.

17. When you set up a set of secure RSA keys for Secure Shell access, what should you do?

    A. Run **ssh-keygen -t dsa1**, and then enter a passphrase for your public key.

    B. Run **ssh-keygen -t rsa**, and then enter a passphrase for your private key.

    C. Run **ssh-keygen -t dsa1**, and then enter a passphrase for your private key.

    D. Run **ssh-keygen -t rsa1**, and then enter a passphrase for your private key.

18. What do you need to do before you can use a Red Hat GPG to verify the validity of the RPM packages that you've just downloaded?

    A. Mount a Red Hat installation CD-ROM and then run
       gpg --import /mnt/cdrom/RPM-GPG-KEY.

    B. Download the GPG key from the Red Hat Web site to /tmp/RPM-GPG-KEY, and then run
       rpm --import /tmp/RPM-GPG-KEY.

    C. Run **ssh-keygen -t rsa1**.

    D. Run **ssh-keygen -t dsa**.

LAB QUESTION

Part 1

For this exercise, use a test computer. Do not use a production computer. Do not use a computer where any data might be important to you. If something goes wrong, and you are unable to restore from a backup, you may need to reinstall Linux. This exercise assumes that you're using the default Red Hat Linux bootloader, GRUB.

Navigate to the /boot directory. Change the name of the initrd-*versionnumber*.img file. Make sure it's something easy to remember such as initrd-*versionnumber*.bak. Reboot Linux. As GRUB goes through the boot sequence, it will probably stop when it can't find your Initial RAM disk (initrd) file, similar to what is shown in Figure 11-11.

Now that your boot loader isn't working, what do you do? Can you try to start Linux in single-user mode?

Part 2

Your company bought another competitor on the opposite coast recently, just as the new corporate application was being deployed everywhere, so you sent the app to them, too. They use a Unix host for this application on their network. You need to be able to connect to this host for maintenance purposes on the new system-wide application you deployed. Both networks have Internet access.

FIGURE 11-11

Example of GRUB failing to find a file

```
Booting 'Red Hat Linux (2.4.18-5.58)'

root (hd0,0)
 Filesystem type is ext2fs, partition type 0x83
kernel /vmlinuz-2.4.18-5.58 ro root=LABEL=/
   [Linux-bzImage, setup=0x1400, size=0x10f410]
initrd /initrd-2.4.18-5.58.img

Error 15: File not found

Press any key to continue..._
```

SELF TEST ANSWERS

Services and Special Users

1. ☑ **A and C.** You should run network services under their own accounts or the nobody account. If a cracker does find a security hole, the damage will be limited to that service.

   ☒ **B and D** are incorrect. B is a good idea, but most outside crackers get root account privileges through security holes they find in programs or services. D is always a good idea but does nothing to protect your system from attacks from the outside, i.e., over a network.

Red Hat User Private Group Scheme

2. ☑ **D.** When you enable the SGID bit on a directory, ownership for all files that are created in that directory is assigned to the group.

   ☒ **A, B, and C** are incorrect. A is not correct, since you do not want to let other users join the root group. B is not correct, as members of the nobody group do not have many useful privileges. C is not correct, since the PATH variable is where the system looks for binary commands, and it is unrelated to the SGID bit.

3. ☑ **A and D.** Both commands will set the SGID bit. Answer D is sometimes more appropriate, as it does not affect the permissions for the owner or others.

   ☒ **B** is incorrect, as chgrp does not modify SGID bits, and **C** is incorrect because it does not include the proper value for the SGID bit (2*xxx*).

4. ☑ **B.** Placing the command umask 002 will set the default umask for all users.

   ☒ **A, C, and D** are incorrect. Typing the umask command without any arguments displays the current umask setting for your process (**D**). The umask command does not change file permissions; chmod does that (**A**). The **chmod 002** *filename* command would set the file to write for all other users; the owner and the group owner of the file would not be able to do anything to it (**C**).

5. ☑ **D.** Users who are not members of the group that owns the special directory are "others." The owner of the special directory is nobody; the permissions that you assign for others determine what these outsiders can do.

   ☒ **A, B, and C** are incorrect. Since you do not know what the permissions are for others, it is not possible to know which of these answers are actually true.

tmpwatch

6. ☑ **C.** The tmpwatch command is usually run periodically by the cron daemon. It recursively searches through temporary directories and remove files that have not been accessed for a fixed amount of time.

☒ **A, B,** and **D** are incorrect. While tmpwatch does not monitor break-in attempts, you may be able to do this by creating /var/log/btmp using the system logging service (**A**). While it is a good idea to clean up unused account directories (**B**), you may not want to delete directories of people who are just on vacation. The tmpwatch utility (**D**) does not monitor any directory for the appearance of specific files.

The Linux Rescue Process

7. ☑ **D.** In a situation like this, the cause is most likely human error.

☒ **A, B,** and **C** are incorrect. If you have a kernel panic, then you know that your PC has checked its hardware and run through its initial BIOS checks. Therefore, you know that the hard disk is not bad (**A**), the I/O bus still works (**B**), and RAM was detected (**C**).

8. ☑ **A, B, C,** and **D** are all good to have on hand if you need to rescue your Linux system.

☒ There are no incorrect answers.

9. ☑ **D** is the correct way to make a boot disk from the first Red Hat installation CD.

☒ **A, B,** and **C** are incorrect. At least as of this writing, (**A**) you can't order a boot disk from Red Hat. There is no mkrescuedisk utility (**B**). The copy command, cp, is not the correct way to transfer the image to a floppy (**C**); only the dd or cat *imagefile* >> /dev/fd0 commands will work.

10. ☑ **A, B,** and **C** are correct procedures to boot a damaged Linux system in order to perform repairs.

☒ **D** is incorrect. By default, Red Hat Linux does not use runlevel 4.

11. ☑ **C** and possibly **A.** GRUB is telling you that it got part of the way through the boot process but couldn't continue because of errors in grub.conf or because of possible disk errors. If you suspect disk problems, you might run fsck on the /boot partition. If your disk isn't having problems, then you should examine grub.conf for errors.

☒ **B** and **D** are incorrect. The boot process has not gotten far enough at this point for /etc/fstab to have anything to do with the problem (**B**). Reinstallation (**D**) is a last resort, and it isn't allowed on the RHCE Debug exam.

12. ☑ **A** is a good starting point, which will allow you to determine what partitions are available. Alternatively, **D** will give you some clues as to partition sizes. In addition, you could then try the e2label command; if you're fortunate, you'll see the labels associated with actual mounted partitions such as /boot or /home. One other approach is to just mount each partition, look at the file contents, and deduce what filesystem it represents.

☒ **B and C** are incorrect. The fsck might tell you the name of the partition (**C**), but you may end up waiting a long time. Reinstallation is a last resort (**B**), and it isn't allowed on the RHCE Debug exam.

13. ☑ **D.** Try running the fsck command with an alternative superblock, such as 8193, 16385, etc. You can use the dumpe2fs command to help determine the appropriate superblock size.

☒ **A** might fix the problem but would have the unfortunate side effect of deleting all the data on the partition. **B** would just list the partitions, and **C** does not do anything to your existing partitions.

14. ☑ **D.** Assuming everything was properly configured, the **e2label** *partitionname* command returns the name of the directory associated with a specific partition.

☒ **A, B, and C** are incorrect. The /etc/fstab file may contain only the labels and may not include the actual device name of the partition (**A**). The **fdisk -l** *partitionname* command does not identify the directories to be mounted on a partition (**B**). The sync command is unrelated to the name of a partition (**C**).

15. ☑ **A, B, and D.** Any typo in /boot/grub/grub.conf or /etc/fstab can make a good system unbootable. Any time you make changes that affect the files in /boot, you should make sure grub.conf reflects these changes.

☒ **C** is incorrect. The /etc/passwd file contains user authentication information and does not affect how Linux boots on your computer.

The Secure Shell Package

16. ☑ **B.** The public key is what you distribute to others to allow them to communicate securely with you.

☒ **A, B, and D** are incorrect. Others need the public key to communicate securely with you (**A**). You want to protect your private key (**C**). And only a special public key is used to check the validity of genuine Red Hat Linux RPM packages (**D**).

17. ☑ **D.** RSA keys are configured by the **ssh-keygen -t rsa1** command. A passphrase can be used to protect your private key.

☒ **A, B, and D** are incorrect. As of this writing, there are no dsa1 key options for ssh-keygen; even if there are, it would work with Digital Signature Algorithm keys (**A, C**). The rsa option is currently obsolete (**D**).

18. ☑ **B.** As of RPM version 4.1, you need to use the **rpm --import** *publickey* command to import the appropriate GPG key.

☒ **A, C,** and **D** are incorrect. The gpg command no longer works for this purpose. The ssh-keygen command does not influence how **rpm -K** *packagename* checks the validity of a specific RPM package.

LAB ANSWER

Part 1

As you practice learning about Linux for the RHCE exam, it's important to know how GRUB works. By default, it requires an initial RAM disk file, initrd-*versionnumber*.img. If GRUB can't find this file, it'll give you the error shown in Figure 11-11. Since your computer does not boot, you'll need to boot with a rescue disk before you can fix the initrd file. Remember to make sure that the filename matches the name shown in /boot/grub/grub.conf *exactly*.

You can repeat this process with the vmlinuz file, or the root directive in grub.conf. Make sure to have backups of key files so you can restore your original configuration. When you repeat this process, what happens after you select a kernel from the GRUB menu? Do you see a different error? Is it associated with a different file?

Understanding these answers can help you learn to use GRUB messages to better diagnose specific problems with Linux.

Part 2

If you need access now, and both systems are connected to the Internet, you can set up SSH for secure communications. If the other network does not already have it installed, have them download it from the Internet, install it, and then create an account for you.

The basic steps which are outlined here may vary with the version of Unix used on the other network.

Get the OpenSSH utility source from the Net and put it into a specific directory. Since RPMs are not yet made for Unix, you'll need to unpack a "tarball." You can then unpackage the files in the tarball and use the files in the resulting directory to compile and configure a Secure Shell server. Once it is configured, set up private and public keys.

If you don't need immediate access, you could, alternatively, configure a computer with Linux and a Secure Shell Server. Send the computer to the administrator of the remote Unix network. Have them add it to their network, and you can check the problem from your site securely. The application is running on the Linux computer that you sent.

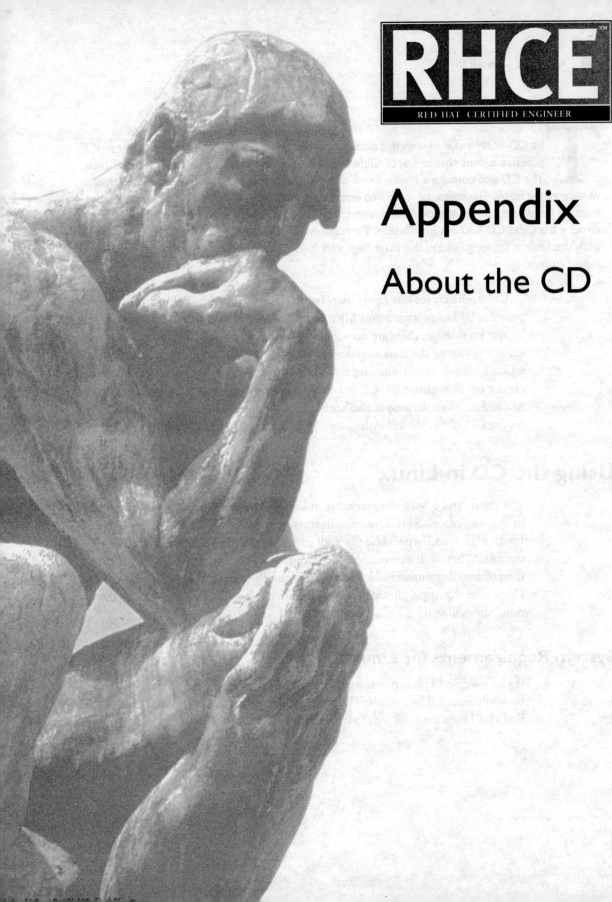

RHCE
RED HAT CERTIFIED ENGINEER

Appendix

About the CD

The CD-ROM included with this book comes with two complete pencil-and-paper RHCE practice exams that are accessible in Linux with the Web browser of your choice. The CD also contains a MasterExam multiple-choice exam simulation and the electronic version of the book. The software is easy to install on any Windows 98/NT/2000 computer and must be installed to access the exam simulation. You may, however, browse the electronic book directly from the CD without installation. To register for a second bonus MasterExam, simply click the Online Training link on the Main Page and follow the directions to the free online registration.

Unfortunately for our Linux users (which is all of you), the MasterExam software provided by LearnKey requires Microsoft Windows. We apologize for this limitation. To our knowledge, there are no vendors currently providing Linux-based practice exam software or the associated source code for Linux, and thus, we cannot provide a Linux version of this software for you. Fortunately, it is used only for the multiple-choice portion of the RHCE exam. The multiple-choice questions used in the MasterExam simulation are also are available in the pencil-and-paper HTML files on the CD accessible in Linux.

Using the CD in Linux

The exams and e-book are accessible in Linux. The exams are available on the CD in the mnt/cdrom/RHCE/exams directory. The e-book is accessible through the Linux PDF reader, xpdf. Use the xpdf command from an X Window terminal console. When xpdf opens, click o, the xpdf open command, and navigate to the mnt/cdrom/Programs/eBook directory to open the e-book chapter of your choice. Please note that these directories assume that you've mounted your CD on the mnt/cdrom directory.

System Requirements for Linux

If you have Red Hat Linux installed, you'll need the xpdf-* RPM package. It is normally installed by default. The standard graphical hardware requirements for Red Hat Linux are sufficient to use the files on the CD.

Installing and Running MasterExam in Microsoft Windows

We understand that as an RHCE candidate, you may be using Linux as your only operating system. As there is no version of the LearnKey software available for Linux, we have no choice but to provide a Microsoft Windows version of this software. Fortunately, this is only required to simulate the test environment for the multiple-choice version of the RHCE exam.

If you've taken other multiple-choice computer certification exams before, you'll find the LearnKey software to be quite familiar, but be careful. The look and feel of the multiple-choice portion of the RHCE exam is quite different.

If you have Microsoft Windows installed, and if your computer CD-ROM drive is configured to autorun, the CD-ROM will automatically start up upon inserting the disk. From the opening screen, you may install MasterExam or MasterSim by pressing the MasterExam or MasterSim buttons. This will begin the installation process and create a program group named "LearnKey." To run MasterExam or MasterSim, use Start | Programs | LearnKey.

System Requirements

If you have Microsoft Windows installed, the LearnKey software requires Windows 98 or higher and Internet Explorer 5.0 or above and 20MB of hard disk space for full installation. The electronic book requires Adobe Acrobat Reader. To access Online Training from LearnKey, you must have RealPlayer Basic 8 or Real1 Plugin, which will be automatically installed when and if you decide to purchase and launch additional online training.

MasterExam

The Microsoft Windows MasterExam software provides you with a simulation of the multiple-choice portion of the RHCE exam. The look and feel provided by the MasterExam software is different from what you'll actually see on the exam. And it does not provide any information with respect to the other two parts of the RHCE exam.

You have the option of taking an open book exam, including hints, references, and answers; a closed book exam; or the timed MasterExam simulation. When you launch MasterExam, a digital clock display will appear in the upper left-hand corner of your screen. The clock will continue to count down to zero unless you choose to end the exam before the time expires.

Electronic Book

The entire contents of the Study Guide are provided in PDF. Adobe's Acrobat Reader has been included on the CD.

Help

A help file is provided through the help button on the main page in the lower left-hand corner. An individual help feature is also available through MasterExam.

Removing Installation(s)

MasterExam is installed to your hard drive. For *best* results, to remove programs use Start | Programs | LearnKey | Uninstall to remove MasterExam.

If you want to remove Real Player, use the Add/Remove Programs Icon from your Control Panel. You may also remove the LearnKey training program from this location.

Technical Support

For questions regarding the technical content of the electronic book or MasterExam, please visit www.osborne.com or e-mail customer.service@mcgraw-hill.com. For customers outside the 50 United States, e-mail international_cs@mcgraw-hill.com.

LearnKey Technical Support

For technical problems with the software (installation, operation, removing installations), and for questions regarding LearnKey Online Training, please visit www.learnkey.com or e-mail techsupport@learnkey.com.

Glossary

Address Resolution Protocol (ARP)   A protocol that maps an IP address to the hardware address on a network card.

Aliasing support   Aliasing support allows you to assign multiple IP addresses to one network card.

Apache Web server   The Apache Web server provides both normal and secure Web services. Apache is controlled by the httpd daemon.

APM (Advanced Power Management)   The APM BIOS primarily monitors and controls the system battery, controlled by the apmd daemon.

arp (Address Resolution Protocol) command   The arp command is used to view or modify the kernel's ARP table. Using arp, you can detect problems such as duplicate addresses on the network. Alternatively, you can use arp to add the required entries from your LAN.

Authentication   The way Linux checks the login rights of a user. Linux users are normally authenticated through use of a user name and password, checked against /etc/passwd and related files.

BIND (Berkeley Internet Name Domain)   BIND is the Unix/Linux software that is used to set up a Domain Name System (DNS) service. The associated daemon is named.

BIOS (Basic Input/Output System)   The BIOS is a set of programs that handle the hardware startup sequence on a PC.

BOOTP   A TCP/IP protocol for transmitting IP address information from a DHCP server to a remote network.

Caching-only name server   A caching-only name server performs many of the functions of a DNS server for a LAN. It stores the IP address associated with recent name searches, and it can serve the same answer to other computers on your LAN. Caching-only name servers can be set up through */etc/named.conf.*

CGI (Common Gateway Interface)   CGI programs allow Web servers to dynamically interact with users.

Chains   Chains are iptables (or ipchains) commands that are linked together. These are linked rules that are applied to each network packet that passes through a Linux firewall computer. Each iptables rule has two functions: it looks for characteristics of a packet, and it specifies the action to take if a packet matches the characteristics specified in the rule.

chkconfig   The chkconfig command manages runlevel information for specified services. With chkconfig, you can activate or deactivate services. When allowed, you can customize this for specific runlevels.

Client   A client is a computer that accesses information or resources on another computer known as a server.

CNAME (Canonical name)   The CNAME is a way to assign several different names to a computer in a DNS database. For example, you can set up www as an alias for a computer that happens to include your Web server. CNAME records cannot be assigned to a mail server (MX) or an SOA (Start of Authority) record.

Custom installation   The Red Hat Linux Custom Installation option gives you the most flexibility to select packages.

Daemon   A process such as the Web service (httpd) or X fonts (xfs) that runs in the background and executes as required.

DHCP (Dynamic Host Configuration Protocol)   DHCP clients lease IP addresses for a fixed period of time from a DHCP server on a local network. The BOOTP protocol allows DHCP clients to get IP address information from a remote DHCP server. The DHCP server daemon is dhcpd; the DHCP client daemon is dhclient. (It was called dhcpcd or pump in previous incarnations of Red Hat Linux.)

Disk Druid The Red Hat Linux hard disk management program. While the functionality is similar to fdisk, it is easier to use. However, Disk Druid is available only during the Linux installation process.

Display manager A Linux display manager includes a dialog box for your username and password. Three major display managers are used in Red Hat Linux: gdm (GNOME), kdm (KDE), and xdm.

DNS (Domain Name System) This service is a database of domain names such as www.redhat.com and IP addresses such 206.132.41.202. If the domain name is not in the local DNS database, the service can be configured to look to other, more authoritative DNS servers. Since it uses bind software, the associated daemon is called "named."

edquota The edquota command edits the quota.user or quota.group file for a specific user. By default, it uses the vi editor.

Environment The environment specifies default user settings such as login prompts, terminals, the PATH, mail directories, and more.

/etc/exports The /etc/exports file defines the filesystems to be shared by NFS. These shares are announced via the **exportfs -a** command. As of Red Hat Linux 8.0, you need to specify the sync or async option for each share.

/etc/inittab The inittab configuration file sets the default runlevel and starts other key processes such as gettys.

/etc/X11/prefdm The /etc/X11/prefdm configuration file specifies the preferred display manager. Normally, this is either xdm (X display manager), kdm (KDE display manager), or gdm (GNOME display manager).

Extended partition An extended partition is a container on a hard disk. It replaces one of the four primary partitions that you can make on a hard disk. You can then configure as many as 11 SCSI or 12 IDE logical partitions within the extended partition.

fdisk   A standard disk partition utility, which allows you to modify the physical and logical disk partition layout.

fips   The First Interactive Partition Splitter, fips, allows you to split existing partitions.

Firewall   A hardware or software system that prevents unauthorized access over a network. Normally used to protect a private LAN from attacks through the Internet.

fsck   The fsck command checks the filesystem on a Linux partition for consistency.

FTP (File Transfer Protocol)   A TCP/IP protocol designed to optimize file transfer between computers. Linux allows you to select between a number of different text and graphical FTP clients. There are also several major FTP servers, such as anonftp and wu-ftpd.

Gateway   A gateway is a route from a computer to another network. A default gateway address is the IP address of a computer that is used to connect a LAN to a larger network such as the Internet.

getty   A getty is a terminal program, which includes prompts for a login and a password. Virtual console gettys are configured through the mingetty program via /etc/inittab.

GNOME (GNU Network Object Model Environment)   GNOME is the default desktop for Red Hat Linux.

GPG (Gnu Privacy Guard)   GPG is an implementation of the OpenPGP standard included with Red Hat Linux.

Home directory   The home directory is the default login directory for Linux users. Normally, this is /home/*username*, where *username* is the user's login name.

HTTP (Hypertext Transfer Protocol)   The protocol used by the World Wide Web and supported by servers such as Apache. The associated daemon is httpd.

ICMP (Internet Control Message Protocol)   A protocol for sending error/control messages. Associated with the ping utility.

ifconfig   The ifconfig command is used to configure and display network devices.

IMAP (Internet Message Access Protocol)   The Internet Message Access Protocol (IMAP) is for e-mail. It allows users to keep their e-mail on a central server. The currently active version of this protocol is IMAP4.

init   The init process is the first Linux process called by the kernel. This process starts other processes that compose a working Linux system, including the shell.

kbdconfig   The kbdconfig utility allows you to configure Linux to work with your keyboard. The configuration is saved to the /etc/sysconfig/keyboard file.

KDE   A GUI for Linux and Unix computers. Also known as the K Desktop Environment.

Kernel   The kernel is the heart of any operating system. It loads device drivers. You can recompile a Linux kernel for additional drivers, for faster loading, and to minimize the required memory.

Kernel module   Kernel modules are pluggable drivers that can be loaded and unloaded into the kernel as needed. Some loaded kernel modules are shown with the /sbin/lsmod command.

Kickstart   Kickstart is the Red Hat automated installation system. It allows you to supply the answers required during the installation setup process. When properly configured, a kickstart floppy can allow you to start your computer and install Red Hat Linux automatically from a local CD or a network source.

Laptop-class installation   A Red Hat Linux laptop-class installation is similar to a workstation-class installation, with a few changes to accommodate the laptop environment.

LDP (Linux Documentation Project)   The LDP is a global effort to produce reliable documentation for all aspects of the Linux operating system. Its work is available online at www.tldp.org.

Logical partition   Logical partitions can be configured within the space allocated for an extended partition. IDE hard disks can have up to 12 logical partitions; SCSI hard disks are limited to 11 logical partitions.

logrotate utility   The logrotate utility allows you maintain log files. By default, Red Hat Linux uses the cron daemon to rotate, compress, and remove various log files. You can configure it to your needs, even mailing key log files to specific administrators.

lpc   You can use the lpc command to control, start, and stop all local print queues.

lpq   You can use the lpq command to view print jobs still in progress.

lpr   You can use the lpr command to send print requests.

lprm   You can use the lprm command to remove print jobs from the queue.

Masquerading   Masquerading enables you to provide Internet access to all of the computers on a LAN with a single public IP address. Masquerading lets you map multiple internal IP addresses to a single valid external IP address.

MBR (Master Boot Record)   The first sector of a bootable disk. Once the BIOS cycle is complete, it looks for a program on the MBR, which then loads a program such as GRUB that can start an operating system.

mkbootdisk   The mkbootdisk utility can create a bootdisk, customized for your system.

Modular kernel   A modular kernel can load or unload driver modules as needed.

Monolithic kernel   A monolithic kernel incorporates all driver devices directly into the main kernel.

mouseconfig   The mouseconfig utility allows you to configure your mouse. The settings are documented in the /etc/sysconfig/mouse file.

NAT (Network Address Translation)   NAT is a feature associated with firewall utilities such as iptables and ipchains that allows you to connect computers inside your LAN to the Internet while disguising their true IP addresses. NAT works by modifying the header information in IP packets as they pass through the gateway. The process is reversed for return messages.

netstat   The netstat command can display connectivity information for your network cards. For example, the **netstat -r** command is used to display the routing tables as stored in your kernel.

NFS (Network File System)   NFS is a file-sharing protocol originally developed by Sun; it is the networked filesystem most commonly used for networks of Linux and Unix computers. By default, Red Hat Linux uses NFS version 2 servers and version 3 clients.

NIC (Network Interface Card)   A NIC connects your computer to a network. A NIC can be anything from a Gigabit Ethernet adapter to a telephone modem.

NIS (Network Information System)   NIS allows you to share one centrally managed authorization database for the Linux and Unix systems on your network. For example, NIS can maintain one password database on a NIS server; other computers on the network can be configured as NIS clients. Normally, a NIS client checks its own authorization file (/etc/passwd) first, then it will look up the authorization information on the NIS server.

NNTP (Network News Transfer Protocol)   The Network News Transfer Protocol is used to distribute newsgroup messages.

ntsysv   The ntsysv utility takes the functionality of chkconfig and sets it up in an easy-to-use screen interface. You can specify the runlevel; for example, the **ntsysv --level 5** command can help you configure the services at runlevel 5.

PAP (Password Authentication Protocol)   The protocol used when logging onto a network. In PAP, the username and password information is transmitted in clear text.

PAM (Pluggable Authentication Module)   PAM separates the authentication process from individual applications. PAM consists of a set of dynamically loadable library modules that configure how an application verifies its users before allowing access.

POP (Post Office Protocol)   A protocol for receiving e-mail. POP messages are downloaded directly into e-mail clients such as pine or Mozilla.

PGP (Pretty Good Privacy)   A technique for encrypting messages, often used for e-mail. It includes a secure private- and public-key system similar to RSA.

Primary partition   Hard disks can have a maximum of four primary partitions. One primary partition can be reallocated as an extended partition.

Private key   Encryption standards such as PGP, GPG, or RSA are based on public/private key pairs. When you create a public/private key pair, you can send the public key to others. When you send a message encrypted with the private key, others can decrypt it with the public key. The converse is also true; they can send messages encrypted with the public key, which your computer can then read with the help of the private key.

/proc   /proc is the Linux *virtual* filesystem. *Virtual* means that it doesn't occupy real disk space. /proc files are used to provide information on kernel configuration and device status.

Public key   See private key.

RAID (Redundant Array of Independent Disks)   RAID can be set up in Linux using either hardware or software. You can use Anaconda, the Red Hat Linux installation utility, to set up software RAID 0, 1, or 5 arrays. Also known as Redundant Array of Inexpensive Disks.

RAID 0   A RAID 0 array requires two or more partitions. Reads and writes to the hard disks are done in parallel, increasing performance, filling up all hard drives equally. As there is no redundancy in RAID 0, a failure of any one of the drives will result in total data loss. RAID 0 is also called striping without parity.

RAID 1   A RAID 1 array requires two or more partitions. RAID 1 is also known as mirroring, because the same information is written to both partitions. If one disk is damaged, all data will still be intact and accessible from the other disk.

RAID 4   A RAID 4 array requires three or more partitions. As with RAID 0, reads and writes are done in parallel to all partitions. One partition is dedicated to maintaining the parity information for all the data on the RAID system. If one partition fails, the parity information can be used to reconstruct the data. While reliability is improved, parity information is updated with every write operation. This makes the parity disk a bottleneck on the system. While RAID 4 is not explicitly supported by Red Hat Linux, it is allowed in the current Linux kernel.

RAID 5   A RAID 5 array requires three or more partitions. Parity information is striped across all partitions. If one disk fails, the data can be rebuilt. It can be written onto a spare disk.

redhat-config-xfree86   The X configuration utility that has recently replaced Xconfigurator. If you use this command in a text console, it starts a minimal X Window where you can configure your video card and monitor.

Red Hat Hardware Compatibility List   The Red Hat Hardware Compatibility List (HCL) specifies all hardware that has been tested on systems running Red Hat Linux. Red Hat will provide installation support for any hardware that is listed as "support" on their HCL.

Red Hat Package Manager (RPM)   The Red Hat Package Manager system sets up software in discrete packages. The RPM includes instructions for adding, removing, and upgrading those files. When you upgrade an RPM, it should automatically back up configuration files as needed.

Refresh rate   This is the rate at which the image you see on your screen is redrawn. The refresh rate is expressed in Hertz (Hz). A refresh rate of 60 Hz means that an image is redrawn 60 times in one second. Computer monitors have both vertical and horizontal refresh rates. Some monitors, known as multisync monitors, support multiple vertical and horizontal refresh rates.

Reverse (inverse) zone   A DNS reverse (inverse) zone is required by some servers, such as ftpd and httpd, to verify the validity of an IP address. If the reverse zone host name does not match the IP address, the server might not respond.

Router   A computer that transfers messages between LANs. Computers that are connected to multiple networks often serve as routers.

RPM query mode   You can check if a package is installed with the **rpm -q** *packagename* command. Alternatively, if you need to locate a file on a package, install the rpmdb-redhat RPM, then use the **--redhatprovides** switch. For example, to find the package associated with /etc/passwd, run the **rpm --redhatprovides /etc/passwd** command.

runlevel   A mode for Linux: standard Red Hat Linux runlevels include single-user mode, full multiuser mode, and X11.

Samba   The Linux and Unix implementation of the Server Message Block protocol. Allows computers that run Linux and Unix to communicate with computers that are running Microsoft Windows operating systems.

sendmail   A standard e-mail server application. Most Internet e-mail uses sendmail.

Server   A computer that controls centralized resources such as files and printers. Servers can share these resources with client computers on a network.

Server installation   The Red Hat server installation option preconfigures a server-class installation. By default, it includes a number of standard server applications and daemons.

Single-user mode   Single-user mode sets up Linux for just the root user. If your Linux system is having problems such as not being able to find the root partition, single-user mode may afford you sufficient access to fix the problem.

SMB (Server Message Block)   The SMB is a protocol used by Microsoft Windows and IBM's OS/2 operating systems for file and printer sharing.

SMTP (Simple Mail Transfer Protocol)   A TCP/IP protocol for sending mail. sendmail uses SMTP.

SOA (Start of Authority)   In a DNS database, the SOA record is the preamble to all zone files. It describes the zone, the DNS server computer (such as ns.*your-domain*.com), the responsible administrator (such as hostmaster@your-domain.com), the serial number associated with this file, and other information related to caching and secondary DNS servers.

Soft limit   Associated with user quotas. Specifies the maximum amount of space a user can have on a partition. Soft limits can be configured with grace periods.

Spec file   Spec files are associated with SRPMs. You can modify an SRPM spec file to change the way a RPM package is built.

Squid   Squid is a high-performance HTTP and FTP caching proxy server.

SRPM (Source RPM)   SRPMs include the source code required to build a binary RPM package. SRPMs are installed with the -i option, which installs SRPM files within the /usr/src/redhat directory. You can then use the rpmbuild command, from the rpm-build-* package, to create a binary RPM.

startx   The startx command triggers the X Window interface manually from a command line prompt.

switchdesk   A utility that allows you to switch default GUI desktop environments.

TCP/IP   See Transmission Control Protocol/Internet Protocol

telnet   A terminal emulation program that allows you to connect to remote computers. The Linux telnet server is controlled by the /etc/xinetd.d/telnet configuration file.

timeconfig   The timeconfig utility allows you to set your time zone. Changes are saved to the /etc/sysconfig/clock file.

tmpwatch   The tmpwatch command removes files that have not been accessed in a specified number of hours. By default, Red Hat Linux configures the crond daemon to periodically delete such files from the /tmp and /var/tmp directories.

Transmission Control Protocol/Internet Protocol (TCP/IP)   TCP/IP is a suite of communications protocols for internetwork communication. It is primarily used as the communication system for the Internet.

UPS (Uninterruptible Power Supply)   The UPS is a battery that can supply continuous power to a computer system if the power fails.

Window manager   The window manager is a special type of X client. It controls how other X clients appear on your display.

X client   An X client is an application that uses the X server services to display output.

X Display   The X Display is a console and a virtual window. By default, there are six virtual consoles configured with Linux; the X Display is associated with virtual console number seven.

xinetd daemon   The xinetd "super-server" daemon governs connections to servers in the /etc/xinetd.d directory such as ftp and telnet.

X server　The X server is the component of the X Window system that runs on your desktop. The X server is responsible for drawing images on your screen, getting input from your keyboard and mouse, and controlling access to your display.

xterm　xterm is an X client application that creates a terminal window in your GUI.

X Window System　The GUI for Linux is also known as X Window. Unlike other applications, the X Window System is a layered application. Thus, you can have a fully functioning Linux system without the X Window interface.

INDEX

D

E

F

G

K

L

X

Z

OTHER CERTIFICATION TITLES

Linux

RHCE Red Hat Certified Engineer Linux Study Guide, 3rd Edition (RH302)
Author: Michael Jang • Pages: 736 • Price: Rs. 399/- w/CD

RHCE Linux Exam Cram, 2nd Edition (RH 302)
Author: Kara J.Pritchard• Pages: 408 • Price: Rs. 199/-

Red Hat Linux 7.3 Bible
Author: Christopher Negus •Pages: 1096 • Price: Rs 499/- w/3CDs.

Red Hat Linux 7.3 Secrets
Author: Naba Barkakati • Pages: 1080 • Price: Rs 499/- w/2CDs.

Installing and Administering Linux, 2nd Edition
Author: Linda & Al McKinnon • Pages: 540 • Price: Rs 329/-

Linux/Unix Programming Toolset (releasing soon)
Author: Andreas Zeller • Pages: 352 • Price: Rs. 279/-

Linux Programming : A Beginner's Guide
Author: Richard Peterson • Pages: 448 • Price: Rs. 249/-

Red Hat Linux 7.x in 2 1/2 Days
Author: Nana Barkakati & Kurt Wall • Pages: 363 • Price:.Rs. 169/-

Red Hat Linux 7.3 For Dummies
Author: Jon 'maddog' Hall & Paul Sery • Pages: 408 • Price: Rs.329/- w/2CDs

Linux Database Bible
Author: Michele Petrovsky, Stephen Wysham • Pages: 736 • Price: 329/-

Linux Programming with KYLIX (KYLIX Power Solutions)
Authors: Don Taylor, Jim Mischel & Tim Gentry •Pages: 348• Price: Rs. 249/-

Linux in Easy Steps
Author: David Nash • Pages: 192 • Price: Rs. 79/-

Red Hat Press

Red Hat Linux Security and Optimization
Author: Mohammed J. Kabir • Pages: 708 • Price: Rs. 399/- w/CD

Red Hat Linux Networking and System Administration
Author: Terry Collings • Pages: 868 • Price: Rs. 449/- w/CD

Red Hat Linux Internet Server (releasing soon)
Author: Paul Sery & Jay Beale • Pages: 504 • Price: Rs. 399/- w/CD

The Official Red Hat Linux Administrators Guide (releasing soon)
Author: Red Hat, Inc. • Pages: 600 • Price: Rs. 399/-

MCSE

MCSE/MCSA Windows 2000 Server Certification Passport Exam (70-215)
Author: Dan Newland & Rog Scrimger.• Pages: 444• Price: Rs. 249/- w/CD

MCSE/MCSA Windows XP Professional Certification Passport (70-270)
Author: Brain Culp.• Pages: 460 • Price: Rs. 249/- w/CD

MCSE Windows 2000 Elective Pack w/3CDs (Contains 3 books on spl.price)
Price: Rs. 999/- w/3CDs

MCSE Windows 2000 Directory Services Design Exam Study Guide (70-219)
Author: J. Peter Bruzzese, et.al • Pages: 732 • Price: Rs. 399/- w/CD

MCSE Windows 2000 Network Design Exam Study Guide Exam (70-221)
Author: Anoop Jalan, Alexander, et.al • Pages: 756 • Price: Rs. 399/- w/CD

MCSE Windows 2000 Security Design Exam Study Guide Exam (70-220)
By Author: Richard A. McMohan, et.al • Pages: 648 • Price: Rs. 399/- w/CD

MCSE Windows 2000 Network Exam Study Guide Exam.(70-216)
Author: Tammy Smith et.al • Pages: 620 • Price: Rs. 399/- w/CD

MCSE Windows 2000 Directory Services Exam Study Guide Exam (70-217)
Author: David V. Watts,Will Willis, et.al • Pages: 688 • Price: Rs. 399/- w/CD

MCSE Exchange 2000 Adminstration Exam Study Guide Exam (70-224)
Author: Phillip G. Schein, et.al .• Pages: 928 • Price: Rs. 399/- w/CD

MCSE Windows 2000 Migrating from NT 4 Exam Study Guide Exam (70-222)
Author: Glen Bergen & Graham Leach.• Pages: 780 • Price: Rs. 399/- w/CD

MCSE Windows XP Professional Exam Study Guide Exam (70-240)
Author: Michael Stewart & Neall Alcott . • Pages: 748 • Price: Rs. 399/- w/CD

MCSE Windows 2000 Professional Exam Study Guide Exam (70-210)
Author: Michael D. Stewart, et.al..• Pages: 632 • Price: Rs. 399/- w/CD

MCSE Windows 2000 4-in-1 Study System (70-210, 70-215, 70-216, 70-217)
Author: Alan R. Carter.• Pages: 1512 • Price: Rs.799/- w/2CDs

MCSE Windows 2000 Accelerated Exam Study Guide Exam (70-240)
Author: Lance Cockcroft, et.al. • Pages: 892 • Price: Rs. 399/- w/CD

MCSE Windows 2000 Server Exam Study Guide Exam (70-215)
Author: David Johnson & Dawn Rader.• Pages: 784 • Price: Rs. 399/- w/CD

MCSE SQL 2000 Administration Exam Cram (70-228)
Author: Kalani Kirk Hausman.• Pages: 424 • Price: Rs. 199/-

MCSE Exchange 2000 Administration Exam Cram (70-224)
Author: David Watts, Will Willis,et.al.• Pages: 455 • Price: Rs. 229/-

MCSE Windows 2000 Network Exam Cram (70-216)
Author: Hank Carbeck, et.al • Pages: 352 • Price: Rs. 199/-

MCSE Windows 2000 Directory Services Exam Cram (70-217)
Author: Will Willis• Pages: 468 • Price: Rs. 199/-

MCSE Windows 2000 Professional Exam Cram (70-210) (Best Seller)
Author: Dan Balter & Dan Holme • Pages: 400 • Price: Rs. 199/-

MCSE Windows 2000 Core 4 Exam Cram Pack (70-210, 70-215, 70-216, 70-217) (Best Seller)
Author: CIP Author Team • Pages: 1600 • Price: Rs. 699/-w/CD

MCSA

MCSA Managing a Windows 2000 Network Environment Certification Passport (70-218)
Author: Walter Glenn • Pages: 448 • Price: Rs. 249/- w/CD

MCSE/MCSA Windows 2000 Server Certification Passport Exam (70-215)
Author: Dan Newland & Rog Scrimger • Pages: 444 • Price: Rs. 249/- w/CD

MCSE/MCSA Windows XP Professional Certification Passport Exam (70-270)
Author: Brain Culp • Pages: 460 • Price: Rs. 249/- w/CD

Three-in-one MCSA Windows 2000 Certification Exam Study Guide (70-210,70-215,70-218)
Author: Damir Bersinic• Pages: 990 • Price: Rs. 549/- w/CD

MCAD/MCSD

All-in-One MCAD/MCSD Visual C# .NET Certification Exam Study Guide (Exam 70-315, 70-316, 70-320)
Author: Kenneth S. Lind, Marj Rempel • Pages: 928 • Price: Rs. 499/- w/CD

MCDBA

MCDBA SQL Server 2000 Exam Study Guide 2-in-1 (70-228, 70-229)
Author: Dave Parkovich• Pages: 612 • Price: Rs. 449/- w/CD

CCNA

CCNA 2.0 Certification Passport (640-607)
Author: Louis R. Russi & Ron Anthony • Pages: 428 • Price: Rs. 249/- w/CD

All-in-One CCNA 2.0 Exam Study Guide (640-607) (Best seller)
Author: Robert E. Larsen • Pages: 1128 • Price: Rs. 499/- w/CD

CCNA Routing & Switching 2.0 Exam Study Guide (640-507)
Author: Mark A. Poplar & Jason Waters • Pages: 760 • Price: Rs. 399/- w/CD

CCNA 2.0 Exam Cram (3rd Edition) (640-507)
Author: Sheldon Barry • Pages: 360 • Price: Rs. 199/-

CISSP

Advanced CISSP Prep Guide: Exam Q&A
Author: Ronald L. Krutz, Russell Dean Vines • Pages: 344 • Price: Rs. 449/- w/CD

All-in-One CISSP Certification Exam Study Guide (Best Seller)
Author: Shon Harris • Pages: 996 • Price: Rs. 499/- w/CD

CISSP Exam Cram
Author: Mandy Andress • Pages: 289 • Price: Rs. 199/-

CISSP Certification Passport (Releasing soon)
Author: Shon Harris • Pages: 432 • Price: Rs. 299/- w/CD

A+

A+ Certification Passport
Author: Mike Meyers & Tracey Rosebleth • Pages: 540• Price: Rs. 299/- w/CD

Your Road Map to Certification Success

Comprehensive and Interactive that teaches the Technology or Application with an Exam Perspective

ISBN: 81-7722-282-1
Price: Rs. 299/-w/CD
Pages: 540

ISBN: 81-7722-273-2
Price: Rs. 249/-w/CD
Pages:460

ISBN: 81-7722-278-3
Price: Rs. 249/-w/CD
Pages:448

ISBN: 81-7722-269-4
Price: Rs. 249/-w/CD
Pages:444

ISBN: 81-265-0144-8
Price: Rs. 799/-w/2CDs
Pages: 1512

ISBN: 81-7722-265-1
Price: Rs. 449/-w/CD
Pages:612

ISBN: 81-7722-266-X
Price: Rs. 499/-w/CD
Pages: 1128

ISBN: 81-7722-251-1
Price: Rs. 499/-w/CD
Pages:996

For more information visit our website: **www.wileydreamtech.com**